M000204783

ARTHUR J MARDER was a meticulous researcher, teacher and writer who, born in 1910, was to become perhaps the most distinguished historian of the modern Royal Navy. He held a number of teaching posts in American universities and was to receive countless honours, as well as publish some fifteen major works on British naval history. He died in 1980.

BARRY GOUGH, the distinguished Canadian maritime and naval historian, is the author of *Historical Dreadnoughts: Arthur Marder, Stephen Roskill and the Battles for Naval History*, recently published by Seaforth Publishing.

ADMIRAL OF THE FLEET LORD FISHER
First Sea Lord, Oct. 1914–May 1915

From the bust by Jacob Epstein, by permission of the trustees of the Imperial War Museum

FROM THE
DREADNOUGHT
TO
SCAPA FLOW

The Royal Navy in the Fisher Era 1904–1919

VOLUME II
THE WAR YEARS: TO THE EVE OF JUTLAND 1914–1916

ARTHUR J MARDER
INTRODUCTION BY BARRY GOUGH

Naval Institute Press

Annapolis

Seaforth
PUBLISHING

For
ROBERT NORTH
and the ideals he exemplifies

THE MAPS
Large-scale versions of the maps located at the back
can be downloaded from the book's page
on the publishers' websites.

Copyright © Arthur J Marder 1965
Introduction copyright @ Barry Gough 2013

First published in Great Britain in 2013 by
Seaforth Publishing,
Pen & Sword Books Ltd,
47 Church Street,
Barnsley S70 2AS

www.seaforthpublishing.com

Published and distributed in the
United States of America and Canada by the
Naval Institute Press,
291 Wood Road, Annapolis,
Maryland 21402-5034

www.nip.org

British Library Cataloguing in Publication Data
A catalogue record for this book is available from the British Library

Library of Congress Control Number: 2013937405

(UK) ISBN 978 1 84832 163 2
(US) ISBN 978 1 59114 260 7

All rights reserved. No part of this publication may be reproduced or transmitted in any form
or by any means, electronic or mechanical, including photocopying, recording, or any
information storage and retrieval system, without prior permission in writing of both the
copyright owner and the above publisher.

Printed and bound by CPI Group (UK) Ltd, Croydon, CRO 4YY

Introduction

THE OUTBREAK OF the First World War, and the many disappointing events involving the Royal Navy in the first twenty-two months of the war at sea, constitute the essence of this second volume here reprinted. From the vaunted expectations of how such a well-trained, well-commanded naval force with its powerful traditions and pride, dating to the age of Nelson and before, would acquit itself, only disappointment ensued: the Navy faced many setbacks that placed the Admiralty and the political head of the Admiralty, the First Lord, Winston S Churchill, under the greatest pressure. So much was this an internal question of high command, that the First Sea Lord, Prince Louis of Battenberg, was removed from his post (largely on grounds of inefficiency and lack of initiative, not on account of his German birth), and Admiral of the Fleet Lord Fisher (who had retired from office in 1910) was brought back in with the greatest of hopes for carrying through to completion a naval triumph over Imperial Germany and its allies. But this was not to be. At the end of the day, Fisher resigned from his post taking Churchill with him, forcing the reconstitution of the Liberal Government and bringing in the Unionists. The Dardanelles campaign, which forms the central story here, was the ruin of statesmen, admirals, generals and many others, to say nothing of the thousands lost on land and sea from shellfire, mines, torpedoes and disease.

But the opening salvoes of the historian's treatment of these years leading up to the eve of Jutland (31 May/1 June 1916) are mainly confined to the appalling set of circumstances that allowed the German battlecruiser *Goeben* and the light cruiser *Breslau* to escape via Messina and find their way through the Dardanelles to Constantinople. Many books have been written about this episode and not one of them shies away from the consequences and disadvantages faced by the Allies in consequence of this escape, and the inability of the British fleet in the Mediterranean to bring the German ships to account. Many another episode crowds the pages of Marder's Volume II, including but not limited to the following:

Coronel and the Falklands, the German invasion prospect, the early submarine peril and the insecurity of the Grand Fleet's base at Scapa Flow, the Scarborough tip-and-run raid and the genesis of Room 40, the Zeppelin peril, and the Dogger Bank action, and, along with the latter, Vice Admiral Sir David Beatty's first difficulties at sea. Marder continues with discussion of the difficulties of blockade, both close and distant, and he discusses Churchill's Baltic project and his differences with Fisher about this.

Throughout these early months and indeed years the public, press and Parliament grew restless at the inactivity of the Fleet and the lack of victory. The deplorable loss of the three *Cressy* class armoured cruisers off the coast of Holland to a single U-boat is indicative of the difficulties of waging war in narrow seas where anti-submarine measures are almost non-existent. Marder goes into the details in depth. There were other errors of judgment. The threat of the U-boat had been underestimated. Admiral Sir Lewis Bayly, blithely exercising his squadron off of Start Point, suffers the torpedoing of the battleship *Formidable*, and, lacking the confidence of Their Lordships, is moved from the Channel Command. In microcosm, this episode typifies British ill-preparedness (and perhaps bad luck) that characterised the lengthening and sorry months leading up to the Dardanelles campaign. Marder gave only scant attention to the sinking of the Cunard Line's *Lusitania*, unarmed and unescorted, by *U-20* without warning. Any culpability in this matter that might be placed on the shoulders of the Admiralty was not Marder's concern. But he gave an excellent evaluation of the German High Seas Fleet, its leaders and its capabilities. He had the advantage of having access to the massive Tambach archives, that is, naval documents captured by the US Army in 1945 before their intended destruction by the Germans. He used these sources to recreate the German dispositions at the outset of the war and the naval strategy being developed to command the North Sea. As to Admiral Sir John Jellicoe, commanding the Grand Fleet, and Vice Admiral Sir David Beatty, commanding the Battle Cruiser Squadron, the two are portrayed as working happily in harness and agreement. Other admirals and captains are noted in regards to abilities and spirit, giving the reader an appreciation of the faces in the crowd, so to speak – the human dimension of commanders trying to deal with unfolding events, many of them of a nature quite unimagined. Such is the course of war and wars generally.

The opening words of this book gave warning that it would take Marder not one but four volumes. Volume III due on the fiftieth anniversary of the Battle of Jutland was eagerly expected. However, no explanation had been given in Volume II for the delay that had occurred in the production of that equally anticipated instalment. What was the cause of this? Once again we are reminded that Marder had fought valiantly to get access to Admiralty papers kept under lock and key, and he had been favoured by his supporters in the Navy not then serving in the Admiralty or on its Board. The Preface dutifully repeats what had been said in Volume I: it regrets the impossibility of giving the precise source of materials quoted in footnotes.

Given the circumstances Marder kept his tangle with Admiralty censors from public scrutiny. There was much talk at the time in informed circles that perhaps some persons in higher authority had delayed the appearance of the book. They were right. Marder could not say so at the time. But pressed as he was to reveal the reason he was later to write by way of explanation that the Admiralty Board (part of the Ministry of Defence from 1 April 1964) had found fault with his appreciation of the Court Martial of Captain (later Rear Admiral Sir) Ernest Troubridge. This officer was tried for giving up his pursuit of the fleeing enemy ships. The Admiralty was incensed, for Marder should never have seen the documents in the first place, let alone quoted from them. Paraphrasing could be allowed but the author was not to indicate its source. When Marder had been permitted access to the papers in question no restrictions had been placed on him. He was shocked, for he had written the chapter in good faith. The book was ready to be printed; there would be costly delays and resetting expenses; and, most important, as Marder argued, any sanitizing of the account would have robbed the chapter of much of its historical value. Marder had been corresponding informally with the Head of Naval Historical Branch demanding the necessary clearance. Eventually the Admiralty caved in, and Marder was eventually informed that he could now make inclusion in his text of quotations from the court martial proceedings. The reason given was that inasmuch as Marder had seen these papers before the institution of the rule by which they were to remain closed for 100 years it had been decided that the quotations and footnote references to the court martial proceedings could be retained in the text in the form as given by Marder. In future, Marder was directed to send any further manuscripts submitted for scrutiny to the Ministry of Defence, marked for the attention of the Head of the Defence Secretariat. One senses here that the Ministry of Defence was taking the matter out of Admiralty Board hands and putting these issues on a more general footing. It was Marder's estimation that certain higher placed persons upon whose assistance he called intervened to put a stop to the forces of darkness and overruled the lower echelon bureaucrats. Troubridge got off easily, for the Board at the time feared a deplorable controversy might ensue; he was never again employed afloat but rose to the rank of Admiral in 1919.

If the *Goeben* episode, the story of which was told in full here for the first time, gave Volume II its scholarly brilliance, Marder's account of the unhappy Dardanelles affair from beginning to end gave a chance to write about the war behind the war. The decision to undertake it, the faltering progress of it and Gallipoli, and the resignation of Fisher and the resulting exit of Churchill from the Admiralty offered Marder a chance to tell an epic from his unique vantage point. An admirer of Churchill's offensive spirit, and equally partial to Fisher's enthusiasms, Marder wrote of the inception of the campaign, then analysed the faltering process of it. The Admiralty papers made available to him proved most rewarding. The Cabinet Office objected to his treatment and opposed his quoting from, and citing in footnotes, the unpublished proceedings of the Dardanelles Commission of 1916–17. The commission had tried to get at the root of the disaster. Marder was told he should never have seen the thousand loosely printed pages of testimony, and was obliged to reference the unpublished proceedings as if they were part of the already-published report of the Commission. To Marder this had been a form of guerrilla war, but eventually the problem passed, and the text was released for printing and binding.

The first part of the book may be said to deal with the period dominated by Churchill and Fisher, until May 1915. The second belongs to the Balfour–Jackson regime at the Admiralty, the quiet time, from then until the eve of Jutland. If the second part is half the length of the first in terms of pages and of chapters this is because Marder had decided on the relative importance of the periods. In his view, those formidable titans at the Admiralty had been succeeded by men quite unable to fill such large shoes. Because Marder was interested in policy and policy-formation his account is a series of selected episodes, each of which he uses to analyse how the personalities acted in regards to the circumstances presented. He demonstrated an interest in decision-making at various levels of authority, therefore offering to the reader the interplay of character and circumstance. The issues are considered; there is occasional edification. Most of the time, we see the agonies faced by those who were ill-equipped to make decisions, decisions forced upon them by the demands of the hour. Marder always believed that any fool could be wise after the event, as Homer had said. He was aware that hindsight was dangerous, and by bringing compassion tinged with awe into the equation Marder displayed a strong humanist perspective that set him apart from what he most disliked: the 'drum and bugle' school of military history.

The dimensions of the larger story, the depth of analysis of battles and campaigns, and the freshness of new sources ably used, particularly in regards to the escape of the *Goeben*, gave readers every indication that subsequent volumes, which would bring the whole to a conclusion, would be equally fascinating. They were not to be disappointed. But all the same, Marder, fighting against time and pressed by many obligations at home and university, still had to bring into final state his rendering of the two biggest challenges the Royal Navy had to face: first, the perils of Jutland and the surrounding controversy and, second, the thorny problem of instituting convoys as a countermeasure to the expanded U-boat peril. Everything Marder had described in Volumes I and II indicated that he would bring new insight based on new evidence gathered from near and far. Readers were not disappointed, and in his final grand instalment of the series, Volume V, he drew the strands together, identified lessons learned, attacked the paucity of strategic thought, deplored the lack of initiative of certain admirals, and much more including technical deficiencies and poor communications in the heat of battle. Naval history had not been written this way before, particularly that of the Royal Navy. It needs to be said, in closing, that it was British admirals, captains and other officers who found his history to be most revealing, and they sent the author many letters of congratulations for a job well done.

BARRY GOUGH,
Victoria, BC, Canada

Preface

I must begin with an apology. I had, in all innocence, hoped that I could tell the story of the Royal Navy during the war and down through the scuttling of the High Seas Fleet in the single volume promised. This has proved impossible. Indeed, this study has grown into a tetralogy, with Volume iii, *Jutland and After*, to appear shortly after the present volume.

I have not attempted, as regards detail, to rival the official combat narrative in *Naval Operations* by Sir Julian Corbett and Sir Henry Newbolt. These five stout volumes cover the details of the war at sea more than adequately, indeed to the point where one often finds oneself in need of a machete to hack one's way through the jungle of facts. Rather have I, in the first place, preferred to single out the more important engagements and themes, and to summarize and analyse them with the use of a considerable body of fresh material. (Jutland, the exception, will receive detailed treatment.) This has meant virtually ignoring a myriad of minor engagements in all the theatres of war and some of the most wonderful pages in the history of the Navy, for example, the exploits of the submarines in the Baltic. And so, for instance, those who want to know why the Germans in 1915 began to call the Baltic 'Horton's Sea' will not find the answer here. Nor do I pay too much attention to the R.N.A.S., since aviation played a very modest role in the war at sea. (The growing recognition of its potential is another matter, and this will be treated at some length in the final volume.)

In the second place, I am far more interested than Corbett and Newbolt were in the story of the formulation of naval policy at the top level. The 'war behind the war' could well be the caption for this facet of the war volumes.

Then again, theirs is a kindly, on the whole uncritical, narrative. Writing as they did so close to the end of the war—all the wartime Prime Ministers, First Lords of the Admiralty, and leading Admirals were living—they were careful not to give unnecessary offence. This explains their extremely circumspect use of Admiralty materials which reflect unfavourably on this or that person. They were, moreover, forced by various official and unofficial pressures to modify such strong opinions as they did express in preliminary drafts on controversial matters like the introduction of the convoy system in 1917. And they did not have access to the personal papers of the history-makers of 1914–18, to say nothing of the plethora of biographies, autobiographies, and monographs, and a number of Naval Staff monographs and volumes in the German Official History, that have been published since their labours ceased. The present account does not suffer from these limitations, although I must acknowledge the tremendous help that *Naval Operations* has been. It remains the indispensable source to all students of the naval history of the First World War.

As with the previous volume, I have been most fortunate in having had the manuscript read constructively by a number of officers whose qualifications for the task are by no means ordinary, and who, in addition, patiently answered a never-ending flow of queries. Reading the manuscript in its entirety were: Admiral Sir William James, who served in the Grand Fleet until May 1917, as a commander in the battle cruiser *Queen Mary*, then as Flag-Commander to Vice-Admiral Sir Doveton Sturdee, Commanding the 4th Battle Squadron, after which he took charge, under the D.N.I., of the Secret Intelligence Department at the Admiralty, the famous 'Room 40'; Admiral the Hon. Sir Reginald Plunkett-Ernle-Erle-Drax, who was Beatty's Flag-Commander (in effect, his staff officer for operations), 1913–16; Vice-Admiral Sir Peter Gretton, late Deputy Chief of Naval Staff and Fifth Sea Lord; the Official Naval Historian, Captain S. W. Roskill; Lieutenant-Commander P. K. Kemp, Head of the Historical Section and Librarian of the Admiralty; Commander M. G. Saunders, of the Historical Section; and Captain John Creswell, onetime Director of the Tactical School, who, as a young officer in the war, served in the Grand Fleet, the Dover Patrol, and the Mediterranean. Captain Creswell also loaned me his splendid Naval Staff College lectures of 1932 on the *Goeben* episode, the Scarborough Raid, and the Heligoland Bight and Dogger Bank actions, and gave most valuable help in the compilation of the maps. Admiral Sir Lionel Preston, who commanded the Grand Fleet Minesweeping Flotilla, 1914–16, and then became Director of the Minesweeping Division at the Admiralty, read the mining and minesweeping material in Chapters IV and XIV; Rear-Admiral W. S. Chalmers, Beatty's official biographer and a member of his operational staff from August 1915 until after the war, read Chapters XVI and XVII; and Lieutenant-Commander D. W. Waters, a keen student of commerce warfare, read the trade defence material in Chapters VI and XIV. Although the assistance so graciously extended to me was, literally, invaluable, I must absolve all these gentlemen from any responsibility for such errors as remain.

I am also grateful to these institutions and individuals: the American Philosophical Society and the University of Hawaii, for their continued generous financial support; Admiral of the Fleet Lord Chatfield, Beatty's Flag-Captain, for setting me right on a number of points; Admiral H. W. W. Hope, the War Staff liaison officer with Room 40, 1914–16, for providing data on the functioning of Room 40; Vice-Admiral Harold Hickling, for allowing me to see the Coronel and Falklands chapters (he was then a lieutenant in the *Glasgow*) of his forthcoming book, *Sailor at Sea*; Rear-Admiral S. P. Start, the Chief Engineer in the *Canopus* in the autumn of 1914, for important background material on the Battle of Coronel; Rear-Admiral H. E. Dannreuther, Gunnery-Lieutenant of the *Invincible* in the Falklands action, for similar material on that battle; Rear-Admiral E. G. Irving, Hydrographer of the Navy, for clarifying some points and advising on maps; Mr. N. Atherton and Miss G. M. P. Savage, of the Hydrographic Department, for helping with the preparation of the maps; the late Commander F. Barley, of the Historical Section, for some useful information on minesweeping; Admiral of the Fleet Earl Mountbatten of Burma, the second Earl Jellicoe, Admiral Sir Charles Madden, second Baronet, Mrs. Sheila Elton, Secretary of the Beaverbrook Foundations, Vice-Admiral K. G. B. Dewar, Professor Robin Higham, of Kansas State University, Mr. Ulrich Mammitzsch, of the University of Hawaii, Lieutenant H. C. Beaumont and Messrs. H. F. Langley and Walter Pfeiffer, of the Historical Section, and Commander W. B. Rowbotham, formerly of the Historical Section, for various kindnesses; Mrs. Violet Borges, assisted by Mrs. Judith Tokunaga, for their superb secretarial work; Dr. Carl Stroven, Librarian of the University of Hawaii, and his magnificent staff, for their willing and efficient service; and Mr. D. W. King, the War Office Librarian, his staff, and the staffs of the Admiralty Library (in particular, Mr. A. P. Young), the British Museum, the Public Record Office (especially Mr. Peter Fellows), the National Maritime Museum Library, the

University of California (Los Angeles), and the Library of Congress, for replying to many queries with thoroughness and dispatch. It is a pleasure once more to acknowledge the gracious co-operation and kindnesses extended to me by the Publisher and his staff at Amen House. I must also pay tribute to the three University of Hawaii janitors of imperishable memory for services above and beyond the call of duty which, to their surprise and mine, proved a boon to the project.

I wish to thank the following publishers for their kind permission to quote from the copyright material indicated: the executors of the estate of Mr. C. P. Scott, from J. L. Hammond, *C. P. Scott of the Manchester Guardian*; Constable & Co., Ltd., from Major-General Sir C. E. Callwell, *Experiences of a Dug-Out, 1914–1918*, and R. H. Gibson and Maurice Prendergast, *The German Submarine War, 1914–1918*; Eyre & Spottiswoode, Ltd., from *The Naval Memoirs of Admiral of the Fleet Sir Roger Keyes*; Her Majesty's Stationery Office, from Brigadier-General C. F. Aspinall-Oglander, *History of the Great War. Military Operations. Gallipoli*, and from *Dardanelles Commission. First Report* and *Final Report*; Hodder & Stoughton, Ltd. and Messrs. A. P. Watt & Son, Ltd. (and, for the first title, the executors of the estate of Admiral Sir Reginald Bacon), from Admiral Sir Reginald Bacon, *The Life of Lord Fisher of Kilverstone*, Rear-Admiral W. S. Chalmers, *The Life and Letters of David, Earl Beatty*, and Taffrail (Captain Taprell Dorling), *Swept Channels*; Hutchinson & Co., Ltd., from Admiral Sir Reginald Bacon, *From 1900 Onward*, Admiral Sir William Goodenough, *A Rough Record*, and J. A. Spender and Cyril Asquith, *Life of Herbert Henry Asquith, Lord Oxford and Asquith*; The University of Michigan Press, from Marion C. Siney, *The Allied Blockade of Germany, 1914–1916*; Frederick Muller, Ltd., from Admiral Sir Reginald Bacon and F. E. McMurtrie, *Modern Naval Strategy*; Odhams Press, Ltd. and Charles Scribner's Sons, from Winston Churchill, *The World Crisis* and *Great Comtemporaries*; Oxford University Press, from Franklyn A. Johnson, *Defence by Committee: the British Committee of Imperial Defence, 1885–1959*; the Royal United Service Institution, from Admiral Sir T. H. Binney, 'Gallipoli and Normandy', in the February 1945 *Journal of the Royal United Service Institution*. Unpublished Crown copyright material in the Public Record Office is published by permission of the Controller of Her Majesty's Stationery Office.

In conclusion, a few explanatory notes may be helpful. All times, except where otherwise noted, are Greenwich Mean Time, which was one hour slow on German time. . . . The bibliography promised for Volume ii will be appended to the last volume. The larger meanings and lessons of the war at sea are reserved for a concluding chapter of 'reflections' in the same volume. . . . I have made good use once more of the many pertinent articles in the *Naval Review*, but without quoting this restricted journal, in accordance with its policy. . . . The unpublished primary source material referred to in footnotes may need this clarification (it has, unfortunately, not been possible to indicate the precise source of some of the documents cited in footnotes):

Admiralty MSS.: the Admiralty records (Public Record Office).
Asquith MSS.: the wartime papers of the Liberal Prime Minister of 1908–16 (the Bodleian).
Balfour MSS.: the papers of the First Lord of 1915–16, A. J. Balfour (British Museum).
Beatty MSS.: the Admiral's papers (Earl Beatty).
Crease MSS.: the papers of Captain Thomas E. Crease, Fisher's Naval Assistant (Commander T. C. Crease).
Duff MSS.: the Grand Fleet diary, 1914–16, of Admiral Sir Alexander Duff, then Rear-Admiral, 4th Battle Squadron (Lady Duff). (The other Duff papers, not used in this volume, are at the National Maritime Museum, Greenwich.)
Esher MSS.: the papers of the second Viscount Esher (Viscount Esher).
German Ministry of Marine MSS.: the records of the Imperial German Navy (Historical Section, Admiralty; since returned to the Militärgeschichtliches Forschungsamt in Freiburg i.B.).*
Graham Greene MSS.: the papers of the Secretary of the Admiralty of 1911–17 (National Maritime Museum).
Hamilton MSS.: 1915–16 diary and correspondence of the Second Sea Lord of 1913–17, Admiral Sir Frederick Hamilton (National Maritime Museum).

*Since the publication of Volume i, I have found confirmation from the Levetzow Papers in the German records (apparently notes for an article by Rear-Admiral Magnus von Levetzow, 22 Apr. 1932) that German naval circles took Fisher's 'Copenhagening' talk (i. 112–14) seriously. The High Seas Fleet, when it passed through the English Channel overnight early in August 1908, en route home from a cruise to the Canaries, was in full combat readiness!

Jackson MSS.: correspondence of Admiral of the Fleet Sir Henry Jackson when First Sea Lord, 1915–16 (Historical Section, Admiralty).

Jellicoe MSS.: the Admiral's papers (British Museum).

Keyes MSS.: the papers of Admiral of the Fleet Lord Keyes (the Dowager Lady Keyes).

Kilverstone MSS.: Lord Fisher's papers (Lord Fisher).

Lennoxlove MSS.: Lord Fisher's papers (the Duke of Hamilton).

Lloyd George MSS.: War-time Cabinet papers (Lord Beaverbrook).

McKenna MSS.: the papers of Reginald McKenna, the First Lord of 1908–11 (Mr. David McKenna).

Noel MSS.: the papers of Admiral of the Fleet Sir Gerard Noel (National Maritime Museum).

Oliver MSS.: post-war recollections of Admiral of the Fleet Sir Henry Oliver, Chief of the Admiralty War Staff, 1914–17 (Vice-Admiral R. D. Oliver).

Richmond MSS.: the diary and correspondence of Admiral Sir Herbert Richmond (National Maritime Museum).

Sturdee MSS.: the papers of Admiral of the Fleet Sir Doveton Sturdee (Commander W. D. M. Staveley).

Tyrwhitt MSS.: the papers of Admiral of the Fleet Sir Reginald Tyrwhitt (Lady Tyrwhitt).

Windsor MSS.: the Royal Archives (Windsor Castle).

To all the individuals and institutions named above I owe heartfelt gratitude.

*   *   *

ABBREVIATIONS USED IN THE TEXT
(whether official or in common Service usage)

A.D.O.D.	:	Assistant Director of Operations, Admiralty War Staff
B.C.F.	:	Battle Cruiser Fleet
B.C.S.	:	Battle Cruiser Squadron
B.E.F.	:	British Expeditionary Force
B.S.	:	Battle Squadron
C.I.D.	:	Committee of Imperial Defence
C.I.G.S.	:	Chief of the Imperial General Staff

C.O.S.	:	Usually Chief of the Admiralty War Staff (1912–1917), but also Chief of Staff to a Flag Officer Commanding
C.S.	:	Cruiser Squadron
D.M O.	:	Director of Military Operations, War Office
D.N.C.	:	Director of Naval Construction, Admiralty
D.N.I.	:	Director óf Naval Intelligence, Admiralty*
D.N.O.	:	Director of Naval Ordnance, Admiralty
D.O.D.	:	Director of Operations (Division), Admiralty War Staff
G.F.	:	Grand Fleet
H.S.F.	:	High Seas Fleet
L.C.S.	:	Light Cruiser Squadron
N.I.D.	:	Naval Intelligence Division, Admiralty†
R.F.C.	:	Royal Flying Corps‡
R.N.A.S.	:	Royal Naval Air Service‡
S.M.	:	Submarine
S.N.O.	:	Senior Naval Officer
T.B.D.	:	Destroyer
U-boats	:	German submarines, of course§
W/T	:	wireless telegraphy

Irvine, California   ARTHUR J. MARDER
 Trafalgar Day, 1964

*The title of pre-War Staff days (–1912), revived in 1918. Strictly speaking, I should use 'D.I.D.' (Director of the Intelligence Division of the War Staff), which was the official title, 1912–18.

†'I.D.' (Intelligence Division of the War Staff), 1912–18; but I will use N.I.D. throughout.

‡Incorporated in the Royal Air Force (R.A.F.) on 1 April 1918.

§It is a useful term, as it avoids confusion between the British and German submarines. As used in this work, no evil connotations are intended!

Contents

Page

CHAPTER XI. THE MAY CRISIS (May 1915)

PART II.

THE BALFOUR–JACKSON PERIOD:
THE FIRST YEAR (May 1915–May 1916)

CHAPTER XII. THE NEW BOARD OF ADMIRALTY

CONTENTS

CHAPTER XV. UNREST IN THE COUNTRY AND THE FLEET
(December 1915–March 1916)

CONTENTS

List of Illustrations

(The highest rank and title attained by June 1916 are the ones given.)

Admiral of the Fleet Lord Fisher, First Sea Lord,
October 1914–May 1915 *Frontispiece*
(*From the bust by Jacob Epstein, by permission of the trustees of the Imperial War Museum*)

Facing page

List of Maps and Charts
at end of book

PART I

The Churchill–Fisher Period,
August 1914 – May 1915

I

Of Ships and Men

(AUGUST 1914)

The battleships of Britain served the North Sea as double-barred doors serve a house. So long as Admiral Jellicoe and the Dover Patrol held firm, the German Fleet in all its tremendous strength was literally locked out of the world. The Hohenzollern dreadnoughts could not place themselves upon a single trade route, could not touch the outer hem of a single oversea Dominion, could not interfere with the imports on which the British Isles depended, could not stem the swelling stream of warriors who came from every land and clime to save the cause of civilization.

GEOFFREY CALLENDER, *The Naval Side of British History*.

I. THE SETTING

(*Map* 1)

IN ANY war with Germany, Great Britain started with the crucial geographical advantage of stretching like a gigantic breakwater across the approaches to Germany. To be able to interfere with British colonies or the main lines of British commerce, German ships must break out of the North Sea into the Atlantic. This meant passing either through the 20-mile broad Straits of Dover, and beyond it the English Channel, whose breadth for a distance of 200 miles does not exceed 60 miles; or passing through the restricted and stormy waters, about 200 miles in width, between the Orkneys–Shetlands and Norway. If the Dover Straits could be closed to the Germans, all their vessels would be forced to adopt the northern route, and in the most favourable circumstances could hope to reach a point at which injury could be inflicted upon British commerce or colonies only after consuming a large quantity of coal. Even when ships of war had made this passage of about 1,100 miles (to a point 20 miles west of Cape Clear), they could carry on warlike operations only if able to coal at sea from captures, a very difficult and uncertain process. The same geographical advantage favoured Britain's ability to intercept

3

German trade across the Atlantic, which was of the greatest importance to Germany, and any overseas expeditions beyond the North Sea.

It was, therefore, perfectly clear that Britain's principal strategical aims at sea, offensive and defensive, could be met by keeping the two holes to the north and south blocked. It would be impossible to prevent individual raiders slipping through, but the bulk of the enemy's forces, including his capital ships, were sealed in the North Sea so long as they did not successfully challenge the British command of that sea. The Grand Fleet (Churchill called it the 'crown jewels'), at Scapa Flow in the Orkneys, blocked the northern passage with the assistance of what became the famous Northern Patrol (10th Cruiser Squadron), a line of ships patrolling east and north from the Shetlands. A secondary cordon in the north was soon formed by one or two Grand Fleet cruiser squadrons, and later a battle squadron, based on Cromarty. The Grand Fleet could move south if a powerful German force tried to attack the cross-Channel communications or to convoy an invading army.

The Grand Fleet was thus constituted at the outbreak of war: the 1st, 2nd, 3rd, and 4th Battle Squadrons and the 1st Battle Cruiser Squadron (the last-named was moved to Cromarty Firth late in October and to the Firth of Forth at the end of December) —in all, twenty-one dreadnoughts, eight pre-dreadnoughts (the 'King Edwards' of the 3rd Battle Squadron), and four battle cruisers. (Three other battle cruisers were in the Mediterranean, one in the Pacific, and one at Queenstown.) Attached to the Grand Fleet were the eight armoured cruisers of the 2nd and 3rd Cruiser Squadrons and the four light cruisers of the 1st Light Cruiser Squadron, nine other cruisers, and forty-two destroyers. (Later in the war, armoured cruisers became simply 'cruisers'.) This was the Grand Fleet proper or the 'main fleet'. Opposing it was the German High Seas Fleet, which in August 1914 had thirteen dreadnoughts, sixteen pre-dreadnoughts, five battle cruisers (counting the *Blücher*), fifteen light cruisers, two cruisers, and eighty-eight destroyers.[1] The greater portion of the German Fleet was in the Jade River; only the older pre-dreadnoughts and

---

[1] For qualitative comparisons of *matériel*, see below, pp. 437–40, also *From the Dreadnought to Scapa Flow*, i. 413–20, and for a table of British and German dreadnoughts and battle cruisers in August 1914, *ibid.*, pp. 439–42.

cruisers were in the Baltic. Further west a light force (two or three cruisers) was based on the Ems River; and smaller patrol craft were based on Sylt and Heligoland.

The Channel Fleet was the other main British force in Home waters. Based on Portland, it held the Straits of Dover, sealing the only outlet to the south. As reconstructed on 7 August 1914, it was composed of the 5th, 7th, and 8th Battle Squadrons—nineteen of the older pre-dreadnoughts. At the southern end of the North Sea, between East Anglia and the Dutch coast, was a strong force of light cruisers and modern destroyers, based on Harwich. The functions of the Harwich Force, organically part of the Grand Fleet, were to patrol the waters between 52°N. and 54°N., assist in the sweeps of the Grand Fleet, and join the Channel Fleet if it moved north. Acting as an East Coast defence force were Patrol Flotillas, based on Dover, the Humber, the Tyne, and the Forth, under an Admiral of Patrols (G. A. Ballard), who was responsible to the C.-in-C., Grand Fleet. The Grand Fleet guaranteed defence against an invasion in sufficient force to conquer the country, but could not guarantee preventing a landing in considerable force on the East Coast which might have done much harm in smashing up the shipbuilding industry, not to mention causing a panic, if the Germans were prepared to accept the fact that their troops would never get home again. This threat was taken quite seriously, and it was to discount it that the Patrol Flotillas were formed in 1912. The hope was that by attacking the transports they could prevent most of the soldiers from landing. The 6th Patrol Flotilla, or 'Dover Patrol', for which the Admiral of Patrols (title changed to Rear-Admiral Commanding East Coast of England in the autumn of 1915) was responsible to the Admiralty direct, had the special duty of denying the Straits of Dover to the enemy. It was detached from Ballard's command on 11 October 1914 and given to Admiral Hood. At the dockyard ports—the Nore, Portsmouth, Devonport, Pembroke, and Queenstown—were the Local Defence Flotillas under the command of the respective S.N.O.s. Their main duties were to support the shore defences of the dockyard ports against naval raids and to serve as night patrols off the ports. The vessels allotted to the Patrol and Local Defence Flotillas (with the latter getting the left-overs) were the older destroyers, the torpedo boats (an obsolescent type of craft which had not been included in building programmes since

1907–8), and the older submarines ('A', 'B', and 'C' classes), which were fit for coastal work only. The newer submarines ('D' and 'E' classes), under a Commodore (S), were based on Harwich and earmarked for offensive operations. Finally, the 12th Cruiser Squadron patrolled at the western end of the English Channel. The Channel Fleet and forces west of Dover were under direct Admiralty control. This, then, was the disposition of the British Fleet in Home waters as the war got under way.

Thanks to a pair of 'portcullises' formed by the Royal Navy in the North Sea, the following dividends of sea command promised to be realized: the safe crossing to France of the troop transports; the reasonable security of Britain's seaborne supplies; the safety of the United Kingdom and the Empire from invasion; and the exertion of economic pressure upon Germany through cutting off German trade from the oceans. One object only required more than a defensive attitude, the annihilation of the High Seas Fleet, and this was necessary only if that fleet threatened to interfere with the collection of the above-mentioned dividends.

2. ADMIRALS AND CAPTAINS

Who were the men on whom the destinies of the nation, and of the Allied cause, depended? To understand the character, ability, and outlook of the senior officers of the 1914–18 war it is necessary to look back at their earlier life in the Navy. It was during their Service life that the steam-*cum*-sail Victorian Navy, showing the flag and policing the seas and with no thought of fighting a maritime war, was transformed into a tremendous fighting machine of dreadnoughts, battle cruisers, light cruisers, destroyers, and submarines. In their younger days their aim, as first lieutenants of small ships and commanders of big ships, was to be first at seamanship drills and to have the whitest decks and the best display of polished brightwork in the Fleet. Many of them spent part of their pay on gratings and on extra brass fittings and enamel paint to beautify their ships. Promotion to commander and captain often went to the men who succeeded best in this aim, and it was quite a good test, as the most successful men were evidently good organizers and men who could get hard work from those under them.

But since commissions prior to 1904 were long, and ships spent years away from civilization, quite out of touch with cultured people, the officers had few opportunities to develop intellectually. There was probably no body of men with their outlook so strictly limited to their job. It was said that the only papers in the ward-room were the *Sporting Times* and one or two illustrated magazines. When the naval renaissance began in 1904, and most of the ships on foreign stations were withdrawn, and the building and training of a fleet to meet the challenge from Germany got under way, and service in Home waters took the place of service in out-of-the-way corners of the world, this narrow outlook did to some extent change to a broader one. Officers were now, when on leave or in Home ports, in the company of informed people who talked of world affairs, political affairs, the arts, etc. This wholesome influence was, unfortunately, largely neutralized by the drive for battle efficiency. With the great concentration on gunnery and the tor-pedo, and with the development of the submarine, the destroyer, and wireless communications, inevitably the officers became wholly absorbed in technical matters. This made for too narrow an outlook for high command. We cannot blame them; there was an immense amount to be done, and done quickly. But the upshot was that very few officers found the time to think about war and strategy. A War College (the 'War Course') had existed since 1900, but it touched only the upper fringe of the Service and was more concerned with teaching flag officers and captains how to handle fleets than to make war plans. There was no Staff College, concerned with strategy and tactics, until 1912. The majority of admirals, moreover, held that these matters were solely the concern of flag officers. The idea that junior officers should interest them-selves in such things was one they would not countenance. Furthermore, initiative was somewhat damped by a century of peace and the regrettable peacetime routine of 'Follow senior officers' motions' and when in doubt 'Request instructions'.

There were, consequently, many admirals in 1914 who were good seamen, devoted to the Service, and who could be relied on to handle their squadrons in battle with courage and skill, but who lacked the imagination and a sound knowledge of the 'more sublime' facets of their profession for the top appointments at sea or ashore. It is fair to say that such defects or failings as British admirals possessed were equally or more conspicuous in nearly all other navies.

Before seeing who were the senior officers holding the most important appointments in Home waters when the guns began to fire in anger, let us note the holders of the key posts at the Admiralty. One of the most flamboyant personalities in His Majesty's Government was the First Lord of the Admiralty, Winston Churchill. His intellectual gifts were acknowledged on all sides to be considerable. He had, as Asquith once put it, 'a pictorial mind brimming with ideas'. This talent was fortified by extraordinary powers of argument. The D.N.I., Captain W. R. Hall, has recorded that Admiralty officials were repeatedly hypnotized into accepting opinions diametrically opposed to their own.[2] Despite his possession of many of the qualities of real greatness, he had a bad press on account of alleged flaws in character—undependability and vanity, to mention two. In the Navy he was *persona non grata* to many of the senior officers because he tried to do too much. 'No one department, hardly one war, was enough for him in that sublime and meteoric moment,' declared the first Earl of Birkenhead. His dynamic energy and imagination could not resist the temptation in 1914–15 (any more than when he was First Lord again, in 1939–40) to intervene in the day-to-day conduct of naval operations and to plaster his professional advisers with bold schemes and ideas on every branch of the war at sea—technical, strategic, and tactical.

The Secretary was William Graham Greene—wise, imperturbable, a tireless worker, and a tower of strength to all department heads. He enjoyed the complete confidence of three successive First Lords.

Naval Secretary to the First Lord was Rear-Admiral Sir Horace Hood, an officer of exceptional merit, possessing all the 'aces'[3]

---

[2] See Admiral Sir William James, *The Eyes of the Navy* (London, 1955), pp. 81–2, for a wonderful story of how Hall was himself once hypnotized by the First Lord. On Churchill as a pre-war First Lord, see *From the Dreadnought to Scapa Flow*, i. 252–327, *passim*.

[3] The three aces, as defined by Admiral Sir William James, are the attributes of Nelson, 'the perfect Admiral': 1. A gift for leadership, for drawing loyal, wholehearted service from officers and men. This was the most important ace; it transcended everything else. The finest leadership included the other aces. 2. Fertile imagination and a creative brain, as in the ability to plan battles. 3. Eagerness to make full use of the brains and ideas of juniors and to take them into one's confidence. The third attribute was particularly rare in the Navy of 1914–18. Some of the admirals, who had viewed with apprehension the increasing need for staff officers, but who had perforce to make some use of their knowledge, were loath to admit that they really helped them. Few admirals apart from Jellicoe, Beatty, Tyrwhitt, Hood, and Duff had all three

and, in Admiral Richmond's judgment, 'an intense sense of duty and moral courage of the highest order'. He would undoubtedly have gone to the very top if he had not fallen at Jutland. His shyness and child-like simplicity of manner did not stand him in good stead at the Admiralty. He was unable to hold Churchill's impetuosity in check, and it was undoubtedly with relief that he went to sea in October 1914 as head of the new Dover command.

The First Sea Lord was the brilliant Admiral Prince Louis of Battenberg. He entered the war with a reputation second to no admiral on the active list, having won fame as a handler of a squadron and then of a fleet.[4] The Second Sea Lord, Vice-Admiral Sir Frederick Hamilton, was a rather lazy officer of no great distinction. He owed some of his success to his Court entrée through his sister, who was married to Vice-Admiral Sir Colin Keppel, in command of H.M. yachts before the war. 'Freddy' Hamilton's greatest asset was his popularity throughout the Fleet. Rear-Admiral Sir Frederick Tudor, the Third Sea Lord, was a fairly competent officer, the best of the Junior Sea Lords. The Fourth Sea Lord, Commodore Cecil F. Lambert, with a face 'like a sea-boot or a scrubbed hammock', was a good seaman who was out of his element. Saturnine and unpleasant to juniors, he spent four unhappy years on the Board before he went to sea. He took over the command of the 2nd Light Cruiser Squadron at the end of 1916 and quickly proved his efficiency.

Vice-Admiral Sir Doveton Sturdee became Chief of the War Staff in August 1914 because he had a reputation for being a student of history and war. Beresford, whose chief of staff he had once been, described him in 1909 as 'one of the most brilliant, if not the most brilliant, officer of my acquaintance'. He was, nevertheless, not a success as C.O.S. His trouble was that he thought he was the only man who knew anything about war. It was, in any case, he believed, not a subject for junior officers. He

---

aces, and few captains, apart from W. W. Fisher and Chatfield. There was a fourth Nelsonian attribute that was particularly important in war: offensive spirit. As regards this ace, we know which of the senior officers had it—Jellicoe (with reservations perhaps), Beatty, Tyrwhitt, Keyes, Cowan, Chatfield, Arbuthnot, and one or two others. But we do not know whether all those senior officers who never had the opportunity of showing it were also imbued with it. In other words, we can say that certain senior officers held this ace, but cannot say that the others did *not* have it. Therefore, in assessing the qualities of all other senior officers I do not include this ace.

[4] See further, *From the Dreadnought to Scapa Flow*, i. 406–7.

lacked the gift of leadership and never used the brains of his subordinates. The D.O.D. under him was Rear-Admiral Arthur Leveson, a stocky, broad-shouldered figure who walked with such a pronounced nautical roll that his youngest daughter refused to walk with him because it made her feel seasick! Leveson had a good brain, plenty of ability, and a powerful personality. But he was a 'driver', even a bully, and not a leader—the sort of man who shouted down opposition. Actually, his bullying manner was in part a pose. Beneath his ferocious exterior there was a kind heart. Unfortunately, only those near him appreciated this, with the result that few were keen to serve under the domineering 'Levi', whether at the Admiralty or at sea.

The Commander-in-Chief of the Grand Fleet, Admiral Sir John Jellicoe, was unimpressive in appearance and short in stature (about 5 ft. 6 in.). But his personality was such that he possessed the unreserved confidence and trust of the fleet. 'He was a man of wonderful understanding of the human heart. He was kindly and thoughtful to every one of every kind, in every rank, with whom he was brought into contact, and he had in full measure that gift of inspiring with affection all who worked with him, and for him, and with that, and an absolutely concomitant part of it, a flawless sincerity and complete selflessness. He was loved by every officer and man who served with him.'[5] One of his ablest captains, Fisher, wrote (1916) of 'our beloved Commander-in-Chief, the finest character that ever was'.[6] His professional capability was also held in the highest regard by nearly all of his contemporaries. Jellicoe, and Beatty as well, had an exceptional attribute, one which very few leaders in war have the opportunity of revealing. Admiral James calls it an 'eye for battle'. 'Jellicoe went to the compass and in a minute made up his mind on the deployment at Jutland. Beatty after a few minutes thought decided to go into the Heligoland Bight on 28 August 1914. It is more applicable to land battle. Montgomery several times saw in a flash what to do to gain victory.'

But no man is perfect. Jellicoe's kindness of heart and loyalty to old friends tended to blind him to the war-revealed limitations and failings of his brother officers—Burney, for example—or to stand by them even when he was aware of their serious deficiencies.

[5] The Prime Minister, Stanley Baldwin, in the House of Commons, 12 Dec. 1935.
[6] Admiral Sir William James, *Admiral Sir William Fisher* (London, 1943), p. 68.

as in the case of Warrender. (Beatty's magnanimity, and his desire to do nothing that would weaken fleet morale, had the same result as Jellicoe's kindness and loyalty.) A more serious weakness in Jellicoe was his inability to delegate authority, which, explains one of his biographers, stemmed 'from his immense capacity for work and his exceptional knowledge of technicalities; he was liable to use up an undue amount of time and energy by attending to details which might sometimes have been left to subordinates'.[7] Admiral Duff spelled it out: 'Had a discussion with the V.A. [Vice-Admiral Gamble, commanding the 4th B.S.]. I agree with him that the Fleet is very badly run. The Staff in the *Iron Duke* is far too large, which prevents decentralisation, and takes all initiative and authority out of the hands of the Vice Admirals' (i.e., the battle-squadron commanders).[8]

Sir David Beatty, Vice-Admiral Commanding the Battle Cruiser Squadron, was dashing and handsome, a well-known figure in hunting circles and London society. He was regarded as a 'beau sabreur' who had twice been promoted for service in colonial wars, and only those who knew him intimately before the war knew that he was thinking a great deal about the conduct of war. The idea that he was just a gallant fighter and no more was soon dispelled when war broke out. First the officers of the battle cruisers, then the officers of the Grand Fleet, knew that their Admiral was a master of his trade, even if he had scraped through his Courses with third-class Certificates. Not deeply involved in weapon development (he had never specialized in any particular branch of his profession), he always had a wider horizon. He was, as Admiral James puts it, 'a big man who thought big and was able to take the big view of all naval affairs'. Admiral Sir William Goodenough, who served under Beatty throughout the war, has best succeeded in spotting the sources of Beatty's greatness as a naval commander.

I have often been asked what it was that made him so pre-eminent. It was not great brains. . . . I don't know that it was great professional knowledge, certainly not expert knowledge of gun or torpedo. It was his spirit, combined with comprehension of really big issues. The gift of distinguishing between essentials and not wasting time on non-essentials. . . . The spirit of resolute, at times it would seem almost

[7] Captain Edward Altham, *Jellicoe* (London, 1938), p. 179.
[8] Diary, 8 Jan. 1915; Duff MSS.

careless, advance (I don't mean without taking care, I mean without care of consequence) was foremost in his mind on every occasion.[9]

To these outstanding leadership traits we should add Beatty's independence of character and great self-reliance and self-confidence, his approachability—his biographer has noted how 'on many occasions he would send for young officers who had ideas or "brain-waves", which he would not hesitate to adopt if in his opinion they had practical value'[10]—and his cheerful and colourful personality. Those from his family downwards who lived their lives with him, or under his command, loved him or admired him.

Beatty was a sartorial individualist—the only one in the Fleet. His six- (instead of the usual eight-) buttoned monkey-jacket was *sui generis*. His famous cap, tilted at a sharp angle over his eyes, captured the popular fancy. To the man in the street it embodied the spirit of the Navy. One peculiarity was his addiction to fortune tellers, whose predictions he liked to hear. There was one in particular, a Madame Dubois in Edinburgh ('Josephine' in his correspondence), whom Beatty's admirals and captains would consult on his behalf and inform him of her prognostications! A firm believer in the value of hard exercise, he would, when he could get ashore to his home at Aberdour (near Rosyth), play tennis as long as he could find anybody who would stand up to him. On one occasion he played sixty-five singles games with scarcely a pause!

Jellicoe's Chief of Staff was his brother-in-law, Rear-Admiral Charles E. Madden, a simple, reserved, very sound and knowledgeable officer, pre-eminent as a tactician, and somewhat lacking only in imagination.

The 1st Battle Squadron was commanded by Vice-Admiral Sir Lewis Bayly. 'Luigi' Bayly was a 'character'—a hard, tough, independent man, a stern disciplinarian, and a most redoubtable autocrat. He certainly did not suffer fools or weaklings gladly. He 'had a gentle and pleasing habit of flicking all and sundry with signals that always removed the skin, and frequently the flesh'. 'He attributed his success,' another officer claimed, 'to working a minimum of eleven hours a day on six days a week, never smoking

[9] Goodenough, *A Rough Record* (London, 1943), p. 91.
[10] Rear-Admiral W. S. Chalmers, *The Life and Letters of David, Earl Beatty* (London, 1954), p. 204.

before 10 p.m., walking at least twenty miles on Sunday, playing tennis for an hour at 6:30 a.m. on fine mornings and running round Greenwich Park at 5:30 p.m.' Bayly was a keen student of naval history, and he had a reputation of being a great tactician (he had, for instance, conceived the use of a smoke screen for tactical purposes).

Vice-Admiral Sir George Warrender, commanding the 2nd Battle Squadron, had the reputation of being a very able man. His war experience lessened that reputation. He excelled in no one respect.

The 3rd and 4th Battle Squadrons were commanded by Vice-Admirals Edward E. Bradford and Sir Douglas Gamble, respectively. They were much the same type—good seamen who lacked the gift of magnetic leadership and had never revealed any creative powers or willingness to use the brains of their subordinates.

The cruiser-squadron commanders with the Grand Fleet were Rear-Admiral the Hon. Somerset A. Gough-Calthorpe (2nd C.S.), Rear-Admiral William C. Pakenham (3rd C.S.), and William E. Goodenough (1st L.C.S.). The aristocratic Gough-Calthorpe was conscientious and hard-working, a good all-round officer who held no aces. Pakenham held the first and third aces. Old 'Paks' was an urbane, picturesque, rather old-worldly figure who did such strange things as play tennis at Rosyth in a boiled shirt and always go to bed fully dressed so as to be ready for any emergency. He was quite a character, extremely anxious, for example, that the Age of Chivalry should last for ever. When an ordinary seaman explained that he had broken his leave and missed the boat because, on waking up, he had found that the girl in bed with him had on his flannel and he did not like to wake her, the Admiral decreed, 'Dismiss the case. Thank God the Age of Chivalry is not past!' 'Barge' Goodenough, though more talkative than most of his kind, was a very attractive character, full of enthusiasm, and with a salty air about him. He had one clearly marked ace: a great gift for leadership. He also possessed the firmest of grips on the essentials of his business as a cruiser admiral.

Rear-Admiral William L. Grant, a mediocrity (in the sense of a man of middling ability, commanded the 6th Cruiser Squadron, which was intended for the Grand Fleet but was soon scattered in all directions for commerce protection. His appointment made no sense. Witness this Beatty outburst: 'A man called Grant, who hasn't been to sea for 4 years, knows nothing of cruiser work, has been appointed to command the 6th Cruiser Squadron, as he happens to be one place senior to me on the List. He is the Senior Cruiser Admiral afloat. It was done out of pure good nature to give him a job . . . All Bertie Hood's fault. It is maddening. The C. in C. is upset . . .'[11]

Vice-Admiral Sir Cecil Burney, commanding the Channel Fleet, and from December 1914, Second-in-Command of the Grand Fleet, held no aces. He was a man of powerful physique, though in chronically poor health, and with little imagination, though reputed to be a fine seaman.

The other flag officers holding the most important commands in Home waters at the outbreak of the war were Keyes, Tyrwhitt, De Chair, Wemyss, and Colville.

Roger Keyes, in charge of the Submarine Service, as Commodore (S), was a very warm-hearted and attractive man whom everybody loved, a born leader, full of dash, an officer of the Nelson tradition who believed that the Navy should not wait for opportunities but should create them. His was the old maxim that attack was the best defence. He was as full of fire and as buoyant and eager for battle when he was a retired admiral of the fleet as when, a young lieutenant in China in 1900, he was charging forts and squeezing through a hole in the legation wall with a white ensign wrapped around him to be the first to announce that the army had arrived. On the other hand, Keyes was aggressive and fearless to the point where it endangered sound judgment. Admiral James is certain that his consuming passion was to win the V.C. An exceptionally fine leader without intellectual capacity would be a fair résumé of the man, but he caught the public eye as few other naval officers have.

The heaviest and most dangerous services were demanded of the Harwich Force; no other unit experienced so many sea-days and suffered such great losses. And yet for no other force was there so much enthusiasm. The explanation is simple: Reginald Yorke Tyrwhitt, who was completely successful in his command of the Harwich Force. The Commodore was a magnificent man of more than middle height, with a sharp-featured, bronzed face, a strong nose above a determined chin, and bright eyes shielded by bushy

[11] Beatty to Lady Beatty, 1 Aug. 1914; Beatty MSS.

black eyebrows. He was simple in his habits, little attracted by ceremonial display, and was without conceit or propensity for intrigue. Although reserved, in the tradition of the 'Silent Service', his great charm and kindness, to say nothing of his professional skill, earned him the profound trust and affection of all who served under him. He was a hard taskmaster, which prompted this remark by one of his officers: 'A very good fellow, but God bless you when he bites!' His greatest professional assets were his ability to act on his own initiative and his intense desire to engage the enemy. 'I am sick to death of sitting in harbour,' he wrote to his wife in December 1914, 'and nearly wept with disgust at being stopped today.' Lord Fisher considered him the personification of pugnacity. Not terribly interested in strategy, he was wrapped up in ships, *matériel* generally, and tactics. Noteworthy was his pioneer work in sea-air co-operation, in which he showed real vision and enterprise. The efficiency of his flotillas was proverbial—'la belle force d'Harwich', Admiral Castex called it.

Rear-Admiral Dudley de Chair, in command of the 10th Cruiser Squadron, was a charming man, though hardly an inspiring leader or strong character. Jellicoe's opinion of him was a bit generous: 'A very first-rate sea officer, suited to any command afloat.'[12] His only clear ace was the third.

Rear-Admiral Rosslyn E. Wemyss commanded the 12th Cruiser Squadron, which with the French 2nd Cruiser Squadron formed the combined Western Patrol, guarding the passage of the B.E.F. (In September his ships were detached to escort the Canadian convoy.) 'Rosy' Wemyss was a fine leader who took his subordinates into his confidence but had no opportunity of proving if he had creative brains for evolving new tactics and planning battle. He merits fuller treatment in a later volume, as befits a First Sea Lord.

Vice-Admiral the Hon. Sir Stanley Colville was Admiral of the Orkneys and Shetlands, a new command established early in September 1914. He was responsible, under the C.-in-C., for the naval defence of the islands and for the naval establishments in them. Colville was a very able man and a charming personality. He had, so to speak, just missed the sea war because he had completed two years in command of a battle squadron shortly before the war.

[12] Jellicoe to Sir Henry Jackson, 23 July 1915; Jackson MSS.

Of the fifty or so captains in the Grand Fleet who commanded battleships, battle cruisers, or cruisers, mediocrities clearly predominated. This is not surprising. The captains of the war owed their promotions mainly to their performance as commanders of big ships, and many of them who got results—smart ships, good at drills, etc.—had few qualities for higher command. Moreover, in the pre-war decade, when the Navy was expanding so fast, the half-yearly promotions to commander and captain were very numerous, and, inevitably, the quality was not of the standard when promotions were few and far between.

The very-good-to-outstanding Grand Fleet captains at the start of the war were seven in number. Michael Culme-Seymour (*Centurion*, 2nd B.S.) was a clever, able man who probably would have reached the top if he had not died as a vice-admiral. E. S. Alexander-Sinclair (*Téméraire*, 4th B.S.) was a first-class sea officer who rose to command a Grand Fleet cruiser squadron. He was, however, not gifted with much brain and was never expected to serve on the Board or reach the highest posts.

W. W. Fisher (*St. Vincent*, 1st B.S.) represented, with Chatfield (see below), the cream of the Grand Fleet captains. Known as 'the Tall Agrippa', because he was a large man of imposing appearance, Fisher was perhaps the most brilliant wartime captain and the outstanding admiral in the inter-war period. He was a man of personal charm, exuberant vitality, mental and physical, of keen intellect and fine character, with a taste for the classics and the arts, particularly music, and an interest in social questions and in people. 'This universality of his interest, coupled with his unquestioned grasp of his profession and technical duties, was one of the secrets of his success. It enabled him to see every problem in the round, and not merely from the professional angle, and in its proper setting and background.' But for his death when C.-in-C., Portsmouth, he would probably have succeeded Chatfield and become, no doubt, one of the great First Sea Lords in British naval history.

The remaining four Captains—de B. Brock, Halsey, W. R. Hall, and Chatfield—were battle-cruiser captains under Beatty. The unworldly, retiring Osmond de B. Brock (*Princess Royal*) was far more studious and intellectual than most of his contemporaries and had wide interests. He was a great reader and thinker, and had sound judgment, an analytical brain, and great tact. He lacked one ace: despite his charm of manner, he was very impersonal, and so not a leader. He could never remember the names of the staff officers, who were to him so many cogs in the machine.

Lionel Halsey (*New Zealand*) was one of the most popular officers of his day—a delightful, outgoing, frank person, a fine leader, a very zealous and competent officer, who was to join Jellicoe's staff as Captain of the Fleet (June 1915) and later to become Fourth Sea Lord, then Third Sea Lord, before the war was over. He might have gone to the very top after the war, but for his retirement to take up a Court appointment.

W. R. Hall—'Blinker' Hall because he blinked incessantly, accompanying this with a pronounced facial twitch—was a little man with a prematurely bald head, large hooked nose, and piercing eyes. Full of charm, he was at the same time a man of dynamic energy, force of character, and imagination who exuded vitality and confidence. He was an exceptional sea captain as commander of the *Queen Mary* in 1913–14. Uncertain health forced him to give up his command after three months of war.[13] Fortunately for the country, the post of D.N.I. fell vacant. It was one that gave full play to his gifts and in which he won world-wide fame.

The dedicated Ernle Chatfield, the best all-rounder of his day, was destined for the highest posts from the time he was a commander. He was Beatty's Flag-Captain throughout the war, commanded the *Lion* in all the major actions in Home waters with great ability, became Controller after the war, C.-in-C., Atlantic and Mediterranean Fleets (successively), First Sea Lord, and Minister for Co-ordination of Defence. The foundation of his successful career, writes an officer who knew him well, was 'a character of flawless integrity and a high sense of honour . . . He has an even, steady outlook on life, a good understanding of human nature . . . Above all he was blessed with a strong, well-balanced intelligence, without any trace of that canker of genius

---

[13] His successor was a catastrophe. Beatty was angry that the appointment had been made by Hood without consulting him—he would have stopped him. 'When I was Naval Secretary [1912–13] I never appointed a Captain to a ship without first communicating with Admiral Com^dg. That was in peace, and in war it is infinitely more important to have the right man.' 'The new captain of the Q.M. is not quite the type of man required for a battle cruiser. Too slow in the brain, ponderous, and I fear the ship will deteriorate in consequence.' Beatty to Lady Beatty, 13 Dec., 26 Nov. 1914; Beatty MSS. There were, alas, other such 'Blimps' in the Navy, too many, indeed, for comfort.

which has wrecked the advancement of many a better brain and which is so peculiarly disastrous in the naval profession. Chatfield's feet were always firmly planted on the ground, his mind well in control of his actions. He made no excursions into cloud cuckoo land.' On the bridge he made up his mind instantly, and when dealing with administrative matters he very quickly arrived at a decision. He was rather austere, and if he lacked anything, it was a sense of humour. Although the two men were in many characteristics poles apart, Beatty thought the world of Chatfield and always wanted him close by, whether on the bridges of the *Lion* and *Queen Elizabeth* or, after the war, at the Admiralty.

With reservations, we might include Frederic C. Dreyer (*Orion*, 2nd B.S.) and Walter Cowan (*Zealandia*, 3rd B.S.) among the elect. Dreyer was a very large man of commanding figure with lots of drive and determination. But he lacked the gift of leadership. He was rough on subordinates, did not welcome suggestions or other displays of initiative by them, tried to do everything himself, and rather too meticulously organized everything he did. On the other hand, he had great brain power and ability, though mainly in a technical direction. He was a pioneer in the development of long-range gunnery. 'These two are unique in brain power amongst [the] young captains' was Jellicoe's opinion of Dreyer and Roger Backhouse (of whom more in another volume).[14] Dreyer became Jellicoe's Flag-Captain in October 1915.

Cowan was, like Keyes, not of the scientific or academic type of naval officer, but was like him essentially a man of action and of unusual gallantry. Ever eager to follow the sound of the guns, he was 'a good man to be with on a death or glory enterprise'. One of his officers wrote of him: 'I think the only person on board who thoroughly enjoyed the War was Captain Walter Cowan. He was a thoroughbred fire-eater and neither his anxiety to get at the enemy nor his energy ever waned for a second.'[15] Too hot-tempered, he had trouble in every ship he commanded. 'His unusual display of medal ribbons saved him from being relegated to the unemployed list on more than one occasion,' a contemporary has observed.

Taken as a whole, the flag and captains' lists at the outbreak of

[14] Jellicoe to Jackson, 6 Oct. 1915; Jackson MSS.
[15] Vice-Admiral Humphrey H. Smith, *A Yellow Admiral Remembers* (London, 1932), p. 272.

the war contained relatively few officers of exceptional ability. Despite this paucity of outstanding talent at the top, the officers of the Royal Navy had two great advantages over their German opposites. They had had considerably longer and more thorough sea training. Admiral Sir Percy Scott was hardly exaggerating when he wrote: 'The German sailors were made in Kiel Harbour. This harbour is like the Serpentine—and a sailor cannot be trained on the Serpentine, and that is what was the matter with the German Navy.'[16] Even more decisive than the high standard of British seamanship and sea experience were the relative numerical strength of the two navies and the confidence of the British officers in their superiority, which was founded on the proud old traditions of the Royal Navy and belief in the superiority of their *matériel*. The German Navy, by contrast, entered the war with a clearly marked inferiority complex.[17]

[16] Scott, *Fifty Years in the Royal Navy* (London, 1919), p. 290.

[17] See further, *From the Dreadnought to Scapa Flow*, i. 411–13, 435–6, and Admiral von Ingenohl's opinion of the Royal Navy in the German Official History, by Captain Otto Groos and (for Vol. vi) Admiral Walther Gladisch, *Der Krieg zur See, 1914–1918. Der Krieg in der Nordsee* (Berlin, 1920–37, 6 vols.), i. 50. (Hereafter cited by main title only.)

II

The Mediterranean: A Tragedy of Errors

(AUGUST 1914)

(*Map 2*)

Of all the orders to an officer, those directing him or permitting him to attack an enemy under all circumstances and at all costs are the most agreeable. Such orders are easy and simple, and whatever the issue, he must receive the applause of those who know little and the approval of those who know much. The more superior the enemy force, the greater the honour of victory, the greater the honour of death. But the order to *avoid* being brought to action by an enemy is of all orders the most trying for an officer to receive.

REAR-ADMIRAL E. T. TROUBRIDGE at his Court Martial,

9 November 1914.

Much as there was in these crowded opening days to excuse the failure, it must always tell as a shadow in our naval history.

SIR JULIAN CORBETT, *Naval Operations*.

I. THE ESCAPE OF THE *GOEBEN*

WHILE the Grand Fleet was momentarily expecting a major action in the North Sea, the naval war in the Mediterranean got off on the wrong foot with a performance that jarred the confidence of the country in the Navy.

In the Adriatic at the end of July were (in addition to six Austrian battleships, three of them dreadnoughts, and a few light cruisers and destroyers) the German battle cruiser *Goeben* and her consort, the light cruiser *Breslau*. The *Goeben* was a fine ship, considerably larger and more heavily armoured than any British ship in the Mediterranean, and with a nominal full speed of 27 knots, making her the fastest of the capital ships in that sea. She had, however, been hurried out to the Mediterranean from the builder's yard, even before she had completed her trials, and grave boiler defects had developed. Even with repairs at Pola after

Sarajevo, she was able during the first war days to achieve a sustained speed of no more than 18 knots. The Admiralty knew nothing of her true speed or of her scheduled replacement by the battle cruiser *Moltke* in October. Although the *Goeben* only mounted 11-inch guns as opposed to the 12-inch of the British battle cruisers, she carried ten of them and could fire a broadside of eight guns, and, for limited arcs of training, ten guns, to the British ships' six or eight. Moreover, the German 11-inch gun was not greatly inferior to the British 12-inch, and she also had a secondary armament of 5·9s. In short, the *Goeben* was distinctly superior to any individual British battle cruiser in the Mediterranean. The *Breslau* (27 knots, 12 4·1-in.) was superior to the British light cruisers in speed, but inferior in gun-power. The squadron had been commanded since October 1913 by the alert, energetic, imaginative Rear-Admiral Wilhelm Souchon.

Souchon's potential opponent was Admiral Sir Archibald Berkeley Milne ('Arky Barky' to the Service), C.-in-C., Mediterranean. He was an officer of inferior calibre, utterly lacking in vigour and imagination, whose appointment to the Mediterranean command in 1912 had largely been due to Court influence. (He had commanded the royal yacht and been a friend of Queen Alexandra.) Milne had an overwhelming *matériel* advantage over Souchon. His fleet, which had been concentrated at Malta by 30 July, consisted of the 2nd Battle Cruiser Squadron and the 1st Cruiser Squadron. The former had the battle cruisers *Inflexible* (flag of the C.-in-C.), *Indefatigable*, and *Indomitable*, each with eight 12-inch guns. They had a trial speed of just over 25 knots, but being coal-burners were unlikely to keep up more than 23 for long spells even when in good condition. There were other conditions that would have a limiting effect on their speed over long periods: the *Indomitable* was due for a refit, and all three were badly under-manned as regards stokers, their engine-rooms being based on a peace establishment. The 1st Cruiser Squadron comprised four good armoured cruisers with 9·2- and 7·5- or 6-inch guns. The total British broadside was 23,980 lbs. (battle cruisers, 15,300, armoured cruisers, 8,680), as against the *Goeben's* 6,680, or 6,870 with the *Breslau's* included. Milne also had under his command four light cruisers (6-inch guns) and sixteen destroyers. Rear-Admiral Ernest Troubridge, the Second-in-Command (his flag in the cruiser *Defence*), was a magnificent figure of a man and a born leader, although he had not a creative brain or much interest in weapon development.

The naval situation in the Mediterranean was obscure. Would Austria-Hungary enter the war, which seemed imminent, against France and England? Would Italy join her Triple Alliance Allies? Until Austrian and Italian intentions were clear, the Admiralty intended to have the entrance to the Adriatic watched. What was the *Goeben's* objective? The last was, immediately, the crucial question, as the primary concern of the Admiralty was the safe transit of the French Algerian Corps to Marseilles. Souchon was expected to attack its communication lines, then escape through the Straits of Gibraltar or return to the Adriatic and join the Austrian Fleet. Accordingly, on 30 July, six days before Anglo-German hostilities began, the Admiralty informed Milne of the possibility of war and that his 'first task should be to aid the French in the transportation of their African army by covering [meaning here *shadowing*], and, if possible, bringing to action individual fast German ships, particularly *Goeben*, who may interfere with that transportation.... Do not at this stage be brought to action against superior forces, except in combination with the French as part of a general battle.'[1]

The more one studies the melancholy *Goeben* episode, the more one is disposed to accept Admiral K. G. B. Dewar's singling out of this telegram as 'the principal factor in this almost incredible train of errors emanating from Whitehall'. At the very least, one must agree with the Official Naval Historian, Sir Julian Corbett, who attributes to the telegram 'very regrettable consequences'. The expression 'superior forces' was not defined, and this was to create serious difficulties for Troubridge on 7 August in his chase of the *Goeben*. More disastrous still, the practical consequence of the telegram was to focus Milne's attention almost exclusively on the protection of the French transports. This was a natural and entirely legitimate interpretation of his instructions, although we know this is not what the Admiralty intended. Unfortunately, despite all subsequent Admiralty telegrams pointing to gaining

---

[1] The British telegrams and signals are in Naval Staff Monograph No. 21 (1923), *The Mediterranean, 1914-1915*, pp. 259-70, 343-64. The Naval Staff Monographs (Historical) on the war, as well as the other Naval Staff Monographs and the Technical History series, are in the Admiralty Library and, with exceptions, are no longer restricted. This is true of most of the other Naval Staff publications on the war. The time used throughout this section is local, that is, Central European, time.

contact with the *Goeben* as his real object, Milne stuck to his original interpretation of the telegram.

Admiralty strategy throughout the entire affair was vitiated by the fact that it never contemplated the possibility that the *Goeben* might proceed to the Dardanelles, although the Turkish political situation definitely pointed in the direction of a German–Turkish understanding or even alliance. Enver Pasha, the War Minister, was known to be intriguing with the German Ambassador, and the Army was mobilizing under the direction of the head of the German military mission. Only the other contingencies, the *Goeben* making for the Adriatic or the Straits of Gibraltar, were provided for.

The *Goeben* and *Breslau* arrived at Messina, on the north-east coast of Sicily, on 2 August. After a bombardment of Bône and Philippeville (Algeria) on the morning of 4 August, to hamper the transport of French troops from North Africa, they returned to Messina early on the morning of the 5th. They were shadowed on their way back from just after 10.30 a.m. by the *Indomitable* and *Indefatigable*, later reinforced by the light cruiser *Dublin*. At about 4 p.m. the enemy ships increased speed and began to draw away. By 4.36 they were out of sight of the battle cruisers, and by 9 p.m., of the *Dublin*. The German Official History states that, 'to preserve *Goeben's* reputation as the fastest ship in the Mediterranean' (this was considered vital for the success of the planned breakthrough to the Dardanelles), Souchon had, through certain extraordinary measures, managed to increase her speed to 24 knots for a short period. Her mean speed from noon until 8 p.m. was 22·5 knots.[2] As regards the British ships, the *Indomitable* probably never reached 23 knots, and it is doubtful if the *Indefatigable* reached 24. *Dublin* logged a steady 25, but this does not agree with her reported positions. As a result of this 'escape' (Great Britain and Germany, remember, were not yet at war), the speeds of the *Goeben* and *Breslau* seem to have been exaggerated in the reports. This was to have a considerable effect on all subsequent British movements, for it strengthened Milne's idea of *Goeben's* superiority in speed.

The British ultimatum to Germany of 4 August having expired, the two countries found themselves at war at 11 p.m. that night (midnight, 4/5 August, Central European time). This was the

[2] Rear-Admiral Hermann Lorey, *Der Krieg zur See, 1914–1918. Der Krieg in den türkischen Gewässern* (Berlin, 1928–38, 2 vols.), i. 6–7.

situation on 5 August. The German cruisers were at Messina, but about to leave. Early on 4 August, Souchon had received a W/T message from Berlin telling him that an alliance had been concluded with Turkey (2 August), and that he was to proceed to Constantinople. Besides, the Italians had informed him (evening of the 5th) of Italy's neutrality and warned him that his ships would be interned if they stayed over 24 hours. Thanks to circumstantial evidence, Milne suspected the enemy squadron was in Messina. (At 5 a.m. on the 6th he received definite news that it was there.) His logical course would have been to concentrate superior forces at both ends of the Straits of Messina : two battle cruisers at the northern entrance and the remaining battle cruiser and the 1st Cruiser Squadron at the southern entrance. Such a disposition would have forced Souchon to fight or to submit to internment. This golden opportunity was thrown away. Milne had Troubridge, with the 1st Cruiser Squadron and a destroyer flotilla, watching the mouth of the Adriatic on the east side of Otranto Straits below Corfu. The light cruiser *Gloucester* (Captain Howard Kelly), watching off the southern entrance to the Straits of Messina, was hardly a sufficient force to stop the *Goeben* if she ventured to the east, although the three submarines at Malta could have been rushed to help the *Gloucester.*

Milne's attention was focused to the west. He had sent the *Indomitable* to Bizerta (Tunisia) to coal (5.30 p.m., 5 August), and with the other two battle cruisers and supporting forces he had then proceeded to patrol off Pantelleria Island, midway between Sicily and Tunisia. This was in line with his 'primary objective', which was to cover the French transport lines by preventing the *Goeben* from steaming westward. Had not the order (3 August) to send two battle cruisers to Gibraltar (the Admiralty had the notion that the enemy ships were en route to the Atlantic to harry the trade routes) showed that that was also in the mind of the Admiralty? Milne afterwards claimed that his dispositions had been made with the full knowledge and apparent approval of the Admiralty, since after reporting his intended dispositions late on 4 August, the only reply he received (afternoon of 5 August) was that he should continue watching the Adriatic 'for double purpose of preventing Austrians emerging unobserved and preventing Germans entering'.

Milne's dispositions were probably influenced by an Admiralty telegram of 4 August (received at 5.48 p.m.), which gave effect to the Cabinet decision that Italy must not be antagonized. (Throughout, the Government discounted the friendly feelings of the Italian Government and Navy.) The telegram read: 'The Italian Government have declared neutrality. You are to respect this neutrality rigidly and should not allow any of H.M. ships to come within 6 miles of the Italian coast.' This unfortunate order, accepted without protest, manacled Milne's strategy. As he wrote afterwards, it 'absolutely debarred me from either following the *Goeben* into the Straits of Messina *or* catching her if she emerged from them'. The first alternative was ruled out by the fact that the Straits have a minimum width of two miles; the second, by the fact that, as contended by the C.-in-C., the *Goeben*, with her superior speed, could have escaped within the six-mile limit from any ships stationed outside that limit.

On 6 August, at 5 p.m., the *Goeben* slipped out of Messina, followed by the *Breslau* twenty minutes later. Luckily for Souchon, Milne and the battle cruisers were well to the westward, and Troubridge and the armoured cruisers to the north-east. Only the *Gloucester* was close to Messina, and at 6.10 p.m. she reported to the Rear-Admiral that the enemy ships were outside the Straits and steering to the east. Souchon feinted up the Adriatic, then suddenly altered course at 10.45 p.m. and steered southeastward for Cape Matapan at the southern end of Greece. The *Gloucester* would not be shaken off. At 10.46 p.m., she signalled that the enemy ships were altering course to the southward. Only Troubridge, with the 1st Cruiser Squadron and its eight destroyers (shortly to be reinforced by the light cruiser *Dublin* and two destroyers), stood between Souchon and his objective.[3]

[3] The German Official History (*Der Krieg in den türkischen Gewässern*, i. 25–6) is critical of the British for not using their destroyers offensively under the favourable conditions that presented themselves during the night. The facts are that Troubridge would not send his destroyers on to attack the *Goeben* because they were short of coal and incapable of much high-speed steaming. (These slow, 27-knot coal-burners of the 'Beagle' class, with only two torpedo tubes, were much inferior to the Grand Fleet destroyers, particularly the 'M' class and later.) The two with the *Dublin* (Captain John Kelly) were intended to attack. (The *Dublin* had left Malta at 2 p.m. on the 6th to join the Rear-Admiral. At 8.30 p.m. she received orders from the C.-in-C. to obtain from the *Gloucester Goeben's* course and speed and to sink her during the night 'if possible'. Troubridge confirmed that the *Dublin* was to attack 'during the dark hours' [received at 10.08 p.m.]). *Dublin* found herself early on the morning of the 7th in a good position for intercepting the *Goeben*. 'Dammit, we must get her,' Kelly remarked. He was set to attack at 3.30 a.m., when he expected to sight the enemy in

The sounding of the tocsin found Troubridge patrolling off the island of Cephalonia, south of Corfu, an excellent position had the *Goeben* made for Pola, the main Austrian base, as he expected. He immediately steamed north with the intention of engaging Souchon near Corfu. Thinking *Goeben's* alteration of course to the southward was a feint, he did not turn south to intercept her until just after midnight (6/7 August).

At about 2.45 a.m. Troubridge's Flag-Captain, Fawcet Wray, a gunnery expert, went to the Admiral and asked him, 'Are you going to fight, Sir? because, if so, the squadron ought to know.' Troubridge replied, 'Yes. I know it is wrong, but I cannot have the name of the whole Mediterranean Squadron stink.'[4] This, Troubridge explained to the Court Martial, was 'a desperate decision', contrary to his orders not to engage a 'superior force', but he made it, and he stuck to it for about an hour.

At about 3.30 a.m. Wray went back to Troubridge in the chart-house and told him that he did not like the prospect. 'Neither do I; but why?' asked Troubridge, who seemed very worried. 'I do not see what you can do, Sir. There are two courses open to the *Goeben*; one was directly on sight of you to circle round you at a radius of the visibility at the time, and another course was for her to circle round you at some range outside 16,000 yards which her guns would carry and which your guns will not. It seems to me it is likely to be the suicide of your squadron.' Troubridge balked. 'I cannot turn away now, think of my pride.' Wray countered, 'Has your pride got anything to do with this, Sir; it is your country's welfare which is at stake.' At 3.55 a.m., after consulting the Navigator as to the possibility of closing in to the range of the squadron's guns, and receiving a negative answer, the Admiral decided to turn away. At 4.05 he signalled the C.-in-C. that, as he could only meet *Goeben* outside the range of his guns, and inside the range of hers, he had abandoned the chase. The squadron was then off Zante (one of the Ionian Islands, north-west of the Peloponnesus), 67 miles from the *Goeben*. Wray was relieved.

---

the moonlight on his port bow. But something went wrong and his force never found the *Goeben*. Captain Creswell thinks it 'probable that *Goeben* passed to the northward, i.e. to starboard of the *Dublin*, while all hands were looking out to port [on her expected bearing]'. Creswell's Naval Staff College lectures (1932), 'Mediterranean, 1914' (Lecture III).

[4] Wray's testimony, *Proceedings of the Troubridge Court Martial* (hereafter cited as *Troubridge Court Martial*), p. 42; Admiralty MSS.

'Admiral, that is the bravest thing you have ever done in your life.' Troubridge was in tears—it had been an extraordinarily difficult decision.[5] It had gradually

forced itself more and more upon my mind that though my decision [to fight] might be natural, might be heroic, it was certainly wrong and certainly in the teeth of my orders. The result was that after a mental struggle between my natural desire to fight and my sense of duty in view of my orders I came to the conclusion that I was not justified in allowing her [*Goeben*] to bring me to battle under the conditions in which we should sight one another. It was at this psychological moment, or rather just as I was reaching this conclusion in my own mind, that my Flag Captain came back to me . . .[6]

There was one overriding consideration present in Troubridge's mind. 'The real question,' he submitted, was: 'Had the *Goeben* a substantial superiority of effective range? By "effective range" I mean a range at which she could get in her initial hits and keep on hitting. . . . My own conviction, and that of my Flag Captain, a most distinguished gunnery expert, at the time was that the *Goeben* greatly outranged us.'[7] In his testimony, Wray put the extreme effective range of the *Goeben* at 24,000 yards, versus 16,000 for the British armoured cruisers. Troubridge, in his reports of 16 and 26 August, put the normal opening range at 16,000 yards and 8,000 yards, respectively. (Commander Wilfred French, an

[5] Wray's testimony; *ibid.* Wray's advice was partly based on the fact that the battle cruisers were not within easy reach. The main consideration, though, was the fact that the range of the *Goeben's* guns was substantially greater than the maximum range of the guns of the 1st Cruiser Squadron. For the advice he had tendered the Admiral, Wray was afterwards virtually ostracized by the Service. The First Lord refused to hear his explanation, and the Admiralty would not offer him any employment until February 1915. Troubridge himself told Wray (28 January 1915) that, had it not been for him, he would have fought the *Goeben*. To 'clear his honour and reputation' (the Troubridge Court Martial had not allowed him to make any statement to clear his honour) Wray prepared a deposition in 1917. In it he maintained that his approval of Troubridge's decision 'did *not* mean his decision to abandon the chase, but his decision to abandon the idea of lying across her [*Goeben's*] bows in the open sea', which had been the Admiral's intention, as expressed in a signal of 2.45 a.m. to the squadron. ['I am endeavouring to cross the bows of the *Goeben* by 6 a.m. and intend to engage her if possible'.] 'When,' continues Wray, 'the Rear-Admiral gave orders to alter course from South to S.30°E., I thought that he was merely hauling off to gain time while he asked the Commander-in-Chief for instructions, and also to reconsider the problem. I frankly admit I was astounded when he announced his intention to the Squadron of abandoning the chase.' Wray's deposition, 3 Aug. 1917; document in the possession of Captain S. W. Roskill.

[6] Troubridge's testimony; *Troubridge Court Martial*, p. 75.

[7] *Ibid.*, p. 78.

Admiralty gunnery expert who testified at the Court Martial, put the effective ranges down as 17,000 to 18,000 versus 12,000 to 13,000.) 'For this reason,' Troubridge explained, 'I designed to meet her [*Goeben*] at night, or at dawn, or in narrow waters, or, in fact, under any conditions under which I could engage her within my own range and counteract the tactical advantages of speed and range . . .'[8]

When the C.-in-C., some hours later, asked him why he had abandoned the chase, this is what Troubridge had signalled:

> With the visibility at the time [at daylight] I could have been sighted 20 to 25 miles away. I could never have got near her unless the *Goeben* wished to bring me to action, which she could have done under circumstances most advantageous to her. I could never have brought her to action. I had hoped to engage her at 3.30 in the morning in dim light. . . . In view of the immense importance of victory or defeat at each ['? such'] early stage of the war, I would consider it a great imprudence to place the squadron in such a position as to be picked off at leisure and sunk, while unable to effectively reply. The decision is not the easiest of the two to make, I am well aware.[9]

In other words, he realized that it would be broad daylight before he could hope to engage the *Goeben*. Before leaving Malta, he had made it clear to his officers that his armoured cruisers would not engage with battle cruisers in open sea in daylight. His reasoning all along was that, with a speed seven knots above that of the Cruiser Squadron, and favoured by the high visibility of a clear Mediterranean day, the *Goeben* could choose the range at which her 11-inch guns would outrange the 9·2-inch guns of the British cruisers, which would be sunk at the *Goeben's* leisure one by one.

Also, Troubridge felt that if he took on the *Goeben* in daylight, he would be disobeying the Admiralty's instructions of 30 July (which the C.-in-C. had included in the Rear-Admiral's sailing orders on 2 August, when Troubridge left Malta) not to engage 'superior forces'. 'Superior forces' had not been defined, although

---

[8] *Ibid.* In all the Court of Inquiry, Court Martial, and Board discussions about relative forces, there is a strange lack of reference to armour protection, which would seem to have been as crucial a factor as the effective ranges. The *Goeben* was immeasurably superior in belt and deck armour to the British cruisers, and it is possible, therefore, to argue that Troubridge's 9·2-inch and 7·5-inch shell would have broken up on the *Goeben* without doing serious damage, whereas her 11-inch might well have blown up his ships. However, not even Troubridge made any use of this argument.

[9] Milne's testimony; *ibid.*, pp. 16–17. All other orders and telegrams exchanged by Milne and Troubridge cited below are quoted from the *Troubridge Court Martial.*

it is clear from the sentence, 'the speed of your Squadrons is sufficient to enable you to choose your moment', that the Admiralty was referring to the Austrian Fleet, and certainly not to the *Goeben*, which the same telegram singled out as *the* vessel that had to be brought to action. The idea was that the Mediterranean Fleet should not be drawn into a general action with the *Austrian* battleships prematurely, that is, before the mobilization of the French Fleet gave the Allies a definite superiority. This was, unfortunately, never spelled out by the Admiralty, nor by Milne in his signal to Troubridge on the evening of 4 August, which repeated the Admiralty injunction not to get involved in a serious engagement with a superior force. Although he testified at the Court Martial that he understood 'superior forces' to mean the Austrians, the C.-in-C. must have suffered from the same misunderstanding as did Troubridge, because, when notified by the latter on 3 August that the *Goeben* represented a 'superior force', he promised to reinforce the 1st Cruiser Squadron with two battle cruisers.

A basic difficulty was Troubridge's unquestioning assumption that the *Goeben* could steam at her reputed speed (actually, her speed seems not to have exceeded 17 to 18 knots), and that she had ample coal and no anxiety about expending a large amount of irreplaceable ammunition in a long-range action.

Although not much was made of it during the Court Martial, a consideration that influenced Troubridge was Milne's signal of 4 August, which had instructed him to 'remain watching entrance of Adriatic'. (This was in accordance with the Admiralty order of 2 August to the C.-in-C.: 'Approach to Adriatic must be watched by cruisers and destroyers.') But this was before the *Goeben*'s escape to the east. The only function Troubridge now had at the entrance to the Adriatic was to keep an eye out for the Austrians. It is difficult to see what his armoured cruisers could have accomplished against the Austrian Fleet, dreadnoughts and all, had it elected to come out.

To resume the narrative, the *Gloucester* clung tenaciously to the enemy, in spite of inferior speed and vastly inferior power, and Milne's order 'to drop astern to avoid capture'. Her coal bunkers nearly empty, and having received at 1.47 p.m. an order from the C.-in-C. not to go further east than Cape Matapan, she had to break off the chase at Cape Matapan (4.40 p.m., 7 August) and turn about to rejoin Troubridge. Touch with the enemy ships had been completely lost. One last opportunity remained to bring them to action, since Souchon was forced to pause in his headlong flight. He coaled frantically at the Aegean island of Denusa, where he had arrived in the late afternoon of 9 August. He left at 5.45 a.m. the next day and cruised about rather aimlessly, not sure he would be allowed by the Turks to enter the Dardanelles. Meanwhile, after stopping at Malta to replenish the coal of the *Inflexible* and *Indefatigable*—he has been criticized by Corbett and others for not having sent the *Indomitable* on alone[10]—Milne took up the chase with the three battle cruisers and a light cruiser (12.30 a.m., 8 August), shaping a course for Cape Matapan.

'Then fortune played another trick.' When halfway to Cape Matapan, at 2.30 p.m., 8 August, the C.-in-C. received an Admiralty telegram, 'Commence hostilities at once against Austria.' This was a horrible blunder. War was not declared until four days later. The signal, prepared for that contingency, had been dispatched without authority by an Admiralty clerk who had spied it lying on an official's desk and considered it urgent. Milne broke off the chase and steamed northward to join Troubridge at the entrance to the Adriatic, in implementation of long-standing and explicit orders of what he should do if Austria entered the war. Four hours later he was informed that the signal was a false alarm, but that the Austrian situation was 'critical'. This warning only strengthened Milne's resolve to effect a concentration with Troubridge. The report of his position the next day (12.30 p.m., 9 August) shocked the Admiralty, which immediately signalled Milne, 'Not at war with Austria. Continue chase of

[10] But see Milne's reasons, not entirely convincing, among them that boiler defects in the *Indomitable* necessitated her spending twelve hours at Malta for repairs, in his *The Flight of the 'Goeben' and the 'Breslau'* (London, 1921), pp. 110–12. Captain Creswell, after examining the fuel situation in the three battle cruisers on arrival at Malta, concluded: 'All three, even *Indefatigable*, could therefore have steamed at high speed, say 22 knots, to the Eastern limits of the Mediterranean and returned to Malta without difficulty. If he followed up hard he would only be a few hours astern. But throughout this period he seems to have been obsessed by *Goeben*'s superior speed as displayed on 4th August [when she had got away from *Indomitable* and *Indefatigable*] and considered that mere chasing was out of the question. . . . It would no doubt be unfair to suggest that he should have taken into account the possibility of the boiler failures in *Goeben* which did in fact occur. But the fact remains that you will never catch a ship if you don't chase her, and that it is only by making the utmost use of every second of time available that one can hope to bring an unwilling enemy to action.' Creswell's lecture, 'Mediterranean, 1914' (Lecture III).

Goeben . . .' The chase was resumed after this loss of a precious 24 hours.

Milne's force entered the Aegean in the early morning of 10 August and was about 40 miles north of Denusa at noon, 11 August, on the track steered by the *Goeben* the day before when she had left Denusa. About that time Milne was startled by news from the Admiralty that the *Goeben* had entered the Dardanelles the night before at 8.30 p.m. Until the bitter end he believed that the Germans did not intend to stay in the eastern Mediterranean, let alone go up the Straits, but would return to the Adriatic. On reaching Constantinople, the *Goeben* and the *Breslau* were nominally sold to the Turks and renamed, although the German crews remained on board and Souchon continued as their commander. Milne stationed two of his battle cruisers and the *Gloucester* at Besika Bay to keep a watch on the Dardanelles. He returned home on 18 August.

2. RESPONSIBILITIES

Milne's explanation of his conduct in the entire episode apparently satisfied the Admiralty. The official announcement to the press, published on 30 August, included their Lordships' approval 'in all respects' of 'the conduct and dispositions' of the C.-in-C. in regard to the German ships, and added that the measures taken by him were successful, in that 'they prevented the Germans from carrying out their primary role of preventing French troops crossing from Africa'. Having been publicly vindicated, Milne confidently expected to relieve Sir Richard Poore after the expiration of his Nore Command, as had been officially announced on 22 July. On 19 November, however, Churchill informed Milne that he would not be appointed (Callaghan eventually got the appointment), as 'circumstances have been entirely altered by the War'.

The revised position of the Admiralty can be explained in part by the belated realization of the disastrous consequences of the escape of the *Goeben*, and in part by the fact that Fisher had become First Sea Lord on 30 October. He believed Milne to be incompetent for high command, and had told Churchill so in the strongest terms at the time of Milne's appointment. Fisher also had a violent personal prejudice against Milne, 'a serpent of the lowest type'. This dated from the Beresford Inquiry of 1909, when Milne 'was Beresford's chief witness, but when the sneak saw the case was going against him, he declined to give evidence!'[11] Fisher was also one for seeing heads roll whenever anything went wrong. 'Personally I should have shot Sir Berkeley Milne for the *Goeben* (like Admiral Byng, *"pour encourager les autres"*, as Voltaire said! . . .).'[12] 'Sir Berkeley Goeben' became Fisher's sobriquet for Milne! His specific charge against Milne's conduct of the operation was that he 'had no excuse whatever for not surrounding Messina with all his entire force right round the harbour mouth—CLOSE UP! *as if international law mattered a d—n*!! and the Italians would have loved him for ever!'[13] 'Surely,' Fisher pleaded with Churchill's Private Secretary, 'he is going to be superseded at once! Surely he is not going to be allowed to hoist his flag at the Nore after such utterly effete incapacity! The Nore should be kept for Jellicoe when he comes back with one arm!!'[14]

For being to the westward of Sicily with his main force when the *Goeben* made her dash to the east, Milne, in his published *apologia*,[15] pleaded 'unquestioning obedience' to Admiralty orders and the fact that the Admiralty had not found fault with his dispositions then or afterwards. His case was, technically, sound, as he had carried out his instructions to the letter in a situation full of ambiguities and imponderables. That he use his discretion in the interpretation of instructions or submit any doubts, let alone protests, about their wisdom to the Admiralty was utterly unthinkable to him.

The aftermath makes unpleasant reading. Briefly, Milne languished on half-pay, until the end of the war hounding the Admiralty for an appointment or at least a fresh Admiralty announcement approving his actions in the Mediterranean. It was 'essential to his reputation'. In placing the Admiral on the retired list in February 1919, the Admiralty publicly exonerated him from blame for the escape of the *Goeben*, and stated that his failure to

[11] Fisher to Pamela McKenna, 6 Mar. 1911; Arthur J. Marder, *Fear God and Dread Nought: the Correspondence of Admiral of the Fleet Lord Fisher of Kilverstone* (London, 1952–9, 3 vols.), ii. 360. (Hereafter cited by title only.)

[12] Fisher to Commander T. E. Crease, 18 Aug. 1914; *ibid.*, iii. 52.

[13] *Ibid.*, p. 53.

[14] Fisher to Edward Marsh, 12 Aug. 1914; Christopher Hassall, *Edward Marsh, Patron of the Arts: a Biography* (London, 1959), p. 292.

[15] *The Flight of the 'Goeben' and the 'Breslau'*, pp. 87–91, and his article, 'Mr. Churchill's Animadversions', *National Review*, Aug. 1923.

take up the Nore Command or to receive further employment had been 'solely owing to the exigencies of the Services'. Milne was appeased for a time, but the publication in 1921 of the first volume of Corbett's naval history of the war sent him scurrying once more for his martyr's crown.

Now, what of Troubridge? His report to the Admiralty (16 August), stressing the fact that he could never have brought the *Goeben* to action in daylight, impressed nobody, least of all the First Sea Lord. 'Not one of the excuses which Ad. Troubridge gives can be accepted for one moment.' He had 22 9·2-inch guns, 14 7·5-inch, and 20 6-inch; the *Goeben*, 10 11-inch and 12 6-inch [5·9-inch]. 'The effective gun range of 11 in. and 9·2 in. does not differ greatly. The German single target was much larger than each of the four separate British targets opposed to the enemy. Superior speed (which undoubtedly existed) in a single ship can be nullified by proper tactical dispositions of four units. The escape of the *Goeben* must ever remain a shameful episode in the War.'[16] Battenberg proposed, and Churchill concurred, that Troubridge be recalled at once and that a court of inquiry examine his conduct. On 9 September Troubridge was ordered to return to England.

The Court of Inquiry, consisting of Admirals Sir George Callaghan and Sir Hedworth Meux, was held at Portsmouth on 22 September. It confined itself entirely to the question as to whether Troubridge should have endeavoured to engage the *Goeben*. The Court in its finding (23 September) would not admit the superiority of the *Goeben* to Troubridge's force, on which the Admiral's whole case rested. The weight of broadside from the four armoured cruisers was at least equal to the *Goeben*'s and would have been greater, per minute, in view of the greater rapidity of fire of the 9·2-inch over the 11-inch guns. The Court considered Troubridge's failure to endeavour to engage 'deplorable and contrary to the tradition of the British Navy', particularly because 'although the *Goeben* might through superior speed have declined action, yet if she had accepted battle the four cruisers, possibly assisted by *Gloucester* and *Dublin* (with long-range torpedoes), and her two Torpedoboat Destroyers *Beagle* and *Bulldog*, had a very fair chance of at least delaying *Goeben* by materially damaging her'.[17]

[16] Battenberg's minute; Admiralty MSS.
[17] Finding of the Court of Inquiry; *ibid.*

In accordance with this judgment a Court Martial tried Troubridge on board H.M.S. *Bulwark*, at Portland, 5–9 November. The Court was comprised of nine flag officers and senior captains, with Admiral Sir George Egerton, C.-in-C., Plymouth, as President. It was an extraordinary occasion, only two flag officers having been tried in the preceding forty years. Feeling in the Navy was running strongly against the accused, to the point where pressure was put on the Prosecutor, Rear-Admiral Sydney Fremantle, to try him on the charge of cowardice. This was quite impossible to prove, as Troubridge's entire career was a refutation of that ridiculous charge. The official charge, under the third section of the Naval Discipline Act, was that Troubridge did 'from negligence or through other default, forbear to pursue the chase of His Imperial German Majesty's ship *Goeben*, being an enemy then flying'.

The prosecution made these main points: (1) Troubridge had definite orders, twice reiterated by the C.-in-C. in the early morning of 3 August, that *Goeben* was to be his 'objective', which could only mean he was to attack her, given the opportunity; (2) *Goeben* was not a superior force. Milne, called as a witness, asserted that Troubridge should have continued the chase. Despite the disparity of speed, his squadron could have engaged the *Goeben* successfully, though at the loss of perhaps two cruisers. The range of her guns was not much greater than the guns of the 1st Cruiser Squadron (which Troubridge would not accept), and it would have been difficult for the *Goeben* to engage more than two ships at once. At no time during their many conversations at Malta (31 July–2 August) had Troubridge indicated that he would not engage the 1st Cruiser Squadron or that he considered the *Goeben* too strong. He did say he would lose some ships. But Troubridge claimed that at Malta on 2 August he had told the C.-in-C., 'You know, Sir, that I consider a battle cruiser a superior force to a cruiser squadron, unless they can get within their range of her.' Milne had replied, according to Troubridge: 'That question won't arise as you will have the *Indomitable* and *Indefatigable* with you.' Troubridge testified that he expected that either the C.-in-C. would himself use the battle cruisers to shadow the *Goeben* and bring her to action, or if she steamed into the waters of the Cruiser Squadron, that he would return the two battle cruisers (*Indomitable*, *Indefatigable*) to the Rear-Admiral's command (they had been detached on 3 August to search for the *Goeben* to the west-ward) or himself effect a junction with the Cruiser Squadron.[18]

The Court, impressed with the merits of Troubridge's case, and possibly influenced by the brilliant defence conducted by Leslie Scott, the distinguished K.C., acquitted the Rear-Admiral. The crucial paragraphs in its finding (9 November) read:

That, in view of the instructions received from the Admiralty by the Commander-in-Chief and repeated by him in his sailing orders to the accused, and also the signal made on the 4th August, viz., 'First Cruiser Squadron and *Gloucester* are not to get seriously engaged with superior force,' the Court are of opinion that, under the particular circumstances of weather, time, and position, the accused was justified in considering the *Goeben* was a superior force to the First Cruiser Squadron at the time they would have met, viz., 6 a.m. on the 7th August, in full daylight in the open sea.

That, although it might have been possible to bring the *Goeben* to action off Cape Malea, or in the Cervi Channel, the Court considers that, in view of the accused's orders to keep a close watch on the Adriatic, he was justified in abandoning the chase at the time he did, as he had no news or prospect of any force being sent to his assistance.

The Court therefore finds that the charge against the accused is not proved, and fully and honourably acquits him of the same.[19]

The Board, stung by the implied criticism of their instructions, were critical of the Court's judgment. In the opinion of Tudor, the Third Sea Lord, Troubridge's instructions, that his squadron and the *Gloucester* were 'not to get seriously engaged with superior force', taken in conjunction with the fact that he was twice informed *Goeben* was his objective, 'must, or should have, conveyed to him that his Squadron was not considered an inferior force, and that he was expected to attack her.' Tudor also used the theoretical argument that, although Troubridge's squadron stood a chance of being mauled during an engagement with the *Goeben*, it could not have been destroyed, or nearly destroyed, before the *Goeben* had expended all her 11-inch ammunition. The same point was made by Admiral of the Fleet Sir Arthur Wilson, the one-time First

[18] *Troubridge Court Martial*, p. 76. Troubridge had, on the afternoon of 2 August, before leaving Malta, sent for the officers of his command and 'made it quite plain that he would regard *Goeben*, if he hadn't the assistance of the battle cruisers, as a "superior force", on account of the marked superiority of the *Goeben* over the armoured cruisers and the greater range of the *Goeben*'s guns.' Statement of the Prosecutor, accepted by Wray; *ibid.*, p. 43.

[19] *Ibid.*, p. 91.

Sea Lord (1910–11), who was acting as a sort of general consultant to the Board, and, in retrospect, by Churchill in *The World Crisis*. The basis of Tudor's reasoning was that the percentage of the *Goeben*'s hits would have been very small because of the long ranges and the appreciable time given to Troubridge to alter position and range between her salvoes. Hamilton, the Second Sea Lord, emphasized that Troubridge had been distinctly told the *Goeben* was his objective. If he considered the order incompatible with the former order to hold the entrance to the Adriatic, he should have pointed this out to the C.-in-C.[20]

Fearing the 'deplorable controversy' that would result if, in the face of the Court Martial's verdict, Troubridge were put on half-pay and deprived of further employment, the Board did what they considered the next best thing. They gave Troubridge various appointments and promoted him vice-admiral in 1916 and admiral in 1919; but they never again employed him afloat—a terrible tragedy for this very proud man who was a descendant of Nelson's Troubridge.

I am inclined to agree with Admiral Fremantle, who believed that 'Troubridge should have maintained his original, and instinctive, decision to bring her [*Goeben*] to action at daylight, and hoped for the best. . . . Troubridge might well have expected to lose one or two of his ships, but he might also have expected to do the *Goeben* such damage as would make it possible for Milne with the battle cruisers to come up and finish her off. If the *Goeben* elected to use her superior speed to evade the Third [First] Cruiser Squadron by steaming round them, at any rate some time would have been gained.'[21] But if Troubridge was guilty, it was of erroneous judgment, no more, and even that with extenuating circumstances.

[20] Minutes of the Sea Lords and A. K. Wilson on the *Goeben* Court Martial, 4–11 Dec. 1914; Admiralty MSS.

[21] Admiral Sir Sydney Fremantle, *My Naval Career, 1880–1928* (London, 1949), p. 174. Captain Creswell (and others, no doubt) is not impressed with the Fremantle argument. 'That was the traditional argument of the British Navy—Nelson's "By the time the enemy has beat our [weaker] fleet soundly, they will do us no harm this year." And no doubt it was Cradock's honourable argument at Coronel. But it didn't work. The technical changes had been too drastic. Not only would most of our ships have been knocked out, but even if they got within range of the *Goeben*, our 9·2 shells would have bounced off her armour without doing any crippling damage.' Letter to the author, 20 Feb. 1962. Nevertheless, I am not entirely convinced by Captain Creswell's argument.

Whatever the degree of Troubridge's guilt, one can only sym-
pathize with his sentiment, that 'whichever course an officer's
honest judgment dictates, whether it subsequently prove right or
prove wrong, the Admiralty who ask of him to take so great a risk
to his reputation must in their turn take upon them the responsibility of his resulting action. No doubt they will.'[22] The Admiralty
did nothing of the kind. Nor would they even admit any errors on
their part, which is perhaps only natural and normal for a government department. Their Lordships were open to criticism on
various related counts, an understanding of which will go a long
way towards explaining the errors of omission and commission in
the war at sea.

(1) There was little appreciation of the true functions of a War
Staff. Rear-Admiral H. G. Thursfield, who served in the Operations Division in the first months of the war, has made this acid
comment on the role of the Staff:

Neither the Chief of the War Staff [Sturdee] nor the Director of
Operations Division [Leveson] seemed to have any particular idea of
what the War Staff was supposed to be doing, or how they should
make use of it; they had been brought up in the tradition that the
conduct of the operations of the fleet was a matter for the admiral
alone, and that he needed no assistance in assimilating the whole
situation in all its ramifications, and in reaching a decision, probably
instantaneously, upon what should be done and what orders should be
issued in order to get it done. Consequently the dozen or so commanders
—of whom I was one—were set to the task of recording the movements
of ships, or, rather of those ships which were not engaged on anything
of great importance at the moment; for, if they were, it was considered
so secret that it was not even allowed to be marked up on the chart in
the War Room.

As deadly to the proper functioning of the Staff was the First
Lord's impassioned temperament, which was not inclined to submit to the curbings of a staff (the same could later be said of
Fisher), and the quality of the personnel. 'With the exception of
the six from the War College, it may be doubted whether any of
the officers who were summoned hastily to recruit the War Staff
had ever made a special study of any aspect of naval war.'[23]

(2) There was excessive centralization of authority at the top.

[22] *Troubridge Court Martial*, p. 71.
[23] Naval Staff Monograph, *The Naval Staff of the Admiralty* (1929), p. 59.

An Admiralty 'War Staff Group' (or 'Admiralty War Group') emerged at the outbreak of war, consisting of the First Lord, the First Sea Lord, the Second Sea Lord, the Chief of the War Staff, and the Secretary. It met every morning under the First Lord's chairmanship, examined the whole situation, and embodied its decisions in minutes and telegrams which were sent to all departments and authorities concerned. Especially after Fisher became First Sea Lord the War Staff Group became, in Churchill's words, 'the supreme and isolated centre of naval war direction'. It settled everything connected with the conduct of operations, not troubling to consult with the Junior Sea Lords. It was unwilling to delegate much authority to commanding officers, and even tried to run the movements of the Grand Fleet by wireless, much to Jellicoe's disgust.

From the start of the war the Admiralty governed the movements of the Grand Fleet by dispatching appropriate wireless instructions to the C.-in-C.

It is possible to say that one reason for the control exercised by the Admiralty was that the most accurate intelligence of enemy movements was to be found in Whitehall. As the war progressed the Grand Fleet became more and more dependent on Admiralty intelligence. For example, [in] the Scarborough Raid, December 16, 1914, the ordering out of the B.C.F., L.C.S. and one B.S. came from the Admiralty. Similarly at the Battle of the Dogger Bank, January 24, 1915, all the preliminary signals were sent out by the Admiralty. The Lowestoft Raid, Jutland, and the operations of August 19, 1916, also furnish further examples of Admiralty control. . . .

Sweeps off the Norwegian coast and movements to intercept raiders, the sphere in which the C.-in-C. exercised control, may be regarded as belonging rather to the sphere of tactics than of strategy.

Farther south, the movements of the Harwich Force, which worked independently of the Grand Fleet and Battle Cruiser Fleet, were also directly controlled by Admiralty order. . . . All minelaying operations were under Admiralty control with a few exceptions. . . . All convoys were organised and controlled by the Convoy Section of the Admiralty. Anti-submarine operations were also planned and controlled in Whitehall. In fact in 1917 and 1918 most anti-submarine operations and all convoy movements were under Admiralty control.

Operations abroad were controlled in the same way. Admiral Cradock's operations were distinctly dependent on Admiralty instructions, and in the case of the *Goeben* and *Breslau* the original plan of war was changed by the Admiralty's telegraphed instructions to Admiral Milne to send the *Invincible* [*Indefatigable*] and *Indomitable* to Gibraltar.[24]

In the case of the *Goeben*, the Admiralty should have instructed the commander on the spot as to his object, fed him all the information available, and for the rest should have allowed, and indeed encouraged, him to act on his own initiative according to circumstances. He should not have been sent so many direct instructions, for example, as to whether to engage. (My account does not bring out the full extent of the direction of the operation by the Admiralty.) Inevitably, there were misunderstandings with two authorities trying to conduct the same operation. This is not to exonerate Milne of lack of command initiative. An interesting minute by the Third Sea Lord with a different incident in mind illuminates the Admiralty outlook on the whole problem of divided command. '. . . we have to remember that whilst cables and more especially W/T have put into the hands of the Admiralty very great power and very great advantages in directing the movements and operations of Fleets and units, this power involves certain disadvantages, in that it must to a certain extent weaken the sense of responsibility of the Officers in command, *and the Admiralty must therefore be prepared to accept more detailed responsibility than in former days.*'[25]

(3) Churchill says that the War Staff Group 'arrived at a united action on every matter of consequence'. Actually, as the Chief of Staff (Sturdee) informed Jellicoe, there was 'very little *united* decision'. The First Lord had too inflated a conception of his functions. 'I accepted,' he writes, 'full responsibility for bringing

[24] Historical Section, Admiralty, paper, 'Admiralty Control of Naval Operations', July 1932; Admiralty MSS. The basic reason for the Admiralty control of the Grand Fleet was that the only intelligence of German movements and intentions was derived from the brilliant and laborious work of Room 40. (See below, pp. 132–4.) It was vitally important to keep this one source of intelligence completely secret from the enemy, and the resulting centralization appeared to the Admiralty to be fully justified. The Admiralty paraphrased any messages before sending them on to Jellicoe, sent on only what he had to have, and arranged his dispositions. In retrospect, it appears that there were occasions when they could, with advantage, have told the C.-in-C. (and the Battle Cruiser Admiral) all that was known about the German intentions and left it to him to make his own dispositions. The Admiralty were in land line communication with the C.-in-C. and Battle Cruiser Admiral when they were in harbour, and there would have been no risk of leakage if the information was given to them by personal message.

[25] The italics are mine. Rear-Admiral Tudor's minute on the report of the Court of Inquiry into the loss of the three 'Cressys', 7 Dec. 1914; Admiralty MSS.

about successful results, and in that spirit I exercised a close general supervision over everything that was done or proposed. Further, I claimed and exercised an unlimited power of suggestion and initiative over the whole field, subject only to the approval and agreement of the First Sea Lord on all operative orders.'[26] Churchill's large idea of his office—'his business everything and his intent everywhere'—worked badly, and it tended to diminish the authority of the First Sea Lord and the Chief of the War Staff, and to cramp their freedom of action.

(4) Divided objectives and loose instructions is another count against the Admiralty. Milne had to concern himself with the *Goeben*, the Austrian Fleet, and the French transports. The emphasis in his orders was on watching the *Goeben* and, after the declaration of war, on bringing her to action. But the ambiguous language of many of the Admiralty operational telegrams, which were drafted hurriedly, and often by the First Lord, confused Milne. He could never be sure he was getting his priorities straight or that he was correctly interpreting his instructions.

(5) Delays in communications from Whitehall more than once prevented vital operational signals and intelligence from reaching the C.-in-C. in good time. This was the result of an overburdened War Registry at the Admiralty, itself the product of the Admiralty policy of deciding all kinds of petty matters which should have been left to the people on the spot. Admiral Dewar cites these examples of the type of message which delayed vitally important signals at that time. From a cruiser in the Atlantic: 'Permission is requested to issue an extra ration of lime juice.' To a cruiser in the North Sea: 'Has Herbert Brown, A.B., been discharged to hospital and did he take his kit with him?'

The responsibilities for the escape of the *Goeben* must be shared by Troubridge and the Admiralty equally, with Milne in third place. Only the pertinacious and gallant Howard Kelly came out of the affair with honour and glory. The tragedy is that a change in any one of a number of circumstances would have ended the story of the *Goeben* early. The 'ifs' will explain, but they cannot excuse. Instead of a smashing success which was easily within the

[26] Winston S. Churchill, *The World Crisis* (6 vols., London, 1923–31), i. 240. (Hereafter cited by title only, and note that the pagination of the American edition is different.) I wish I could remember who it was that said of this history of the war (with all its self-justification and errors of fact an indispensable source), 'Winston has written an enormous book about himself and called it *The World Crisis*'!

British grasp and which would have been of inestimable psychological, political, and strategic value at the beginning of the war, a bitter disappointment was the result. The escape of the *Goeben* was a blow to British naval prestige and naval morale. 'To think that it is to the Navy to provide the first and only instance of failure,' moaned Beatty. 'God, it makes me sick.'[27]

The Admiralty had at first looked upon the escape almost as a success. Only later was it fully realized what an unmitigated disaster it had been. The arrival of the German ships at Constantinople was probably the decisive factor in bringing Turkey into the war on the side of the Central Powers (5 November). This eventually led to the costly and unsuccessful Dardanelles and Mesopotamian campaigns, which were a decisive factor in isolating Russia from her Allies and knocking her out of the war. It is interesting to speculate on the different course the war might have taken if the *Goeben* had been sufficiently damaged not to make Constantinople. Another consequence of the *Goeben* episode was the shock of the country, to say nothing of the Admiralty, on realizing that the Navy was not commanding the seas with the thoroughness all Englishmen had been brought up to expect. This led to the levelling of the first charge of 'bungling in high places', meaning the First Lord, that was nearly to topple him in October.

The miserable performance in the Mediterranean was scarcely relieved by the naval show in the North Sea, the main theatre of operations.

[27] Beatty to Lady Beatty, 11 Oct. 1914; Beatty MSS.

III

Home Waters: Frustrations and Disappointments

(AUGUST 1914–SEPTEMBER 1914)

No one, who is not steeped in professional dogma, believes that the naval forces of the Allies can force a decision, or do more than render the lives of the Allied peoples secure and that of the enemy impossible. We shall remain immune from attack. The French will be free to receive supplies from oversea. The Germans will become a beleaguered garrison. These achievements are those of modern sea command. But a battle of Actium is unlikely.

VISCOUNT ESHER, Journals, 14 August 1914.

We get back to coal with a feeling of thank God I've got in again, and yet when we go out again that same day or the next, we are filled with hope that perhaps this time the opportunity will come, and think of nothing else, and it never comes. Surely this is the hardest and the most cruelly trying kind of warfare.

BEATTY to Lady Beatty, 7 November 1914.

I. THE GRAND FLEET AND THE HIGH SEAS FLEET

ON 1 August the High Seas Fleet was concentrated in the mouth of the Jade ready for war. There it remained. Except for a submarine flotilla reconnaissance sweep, the dispatch of a minelayer and a commerce raider, and patrolling the Heligoland Bight, the entire German Fleet lay idle in the first days of the war. On 12 August it was decided that the stay of the Fleet in the mouth of the Jade would be indefinite. No attempt was made to seek out the Grand Fleet or to stop the British Expeditionary Force. Since the Emperor had decided that the ships (the battle fleet, above all) must not be risked in offensive actions, the orders sent to the C.-in-C., Admiral von Ingenohl, from the beginning stressed the importance of preserving the Fleet. This decision was made over the strong objections of the Secretary of the Navy, Admiral von Tirpitz.[1] That did not matter too much, since Tirpitz, the creator of the German Fleet, was restricted by the nature of his office to administrative matters. The whole conduct of the naval war, on the German side, was in the hands of the Naval Staff (*Admiralstab*), which was directly responsible to the Emperor.

What is the explanation of German naval strategy? For one thing, the Emperor and the Chancellor, Bethmann Hollweg, saw in an intact fleet a valuable bargaining asset at the peace table. The control of higher naval strategy by the Army General Staff was another reason for holding back the High Seas Fleet. For the generals the chief function of the Fleet was to protect the Army's flank and rear against possible English or Russian landings on the coasts of the North Sea or Baltic Sea, respectively. The influence of the High Command was also decisive in keeping the Navy tied to a leash during the transit of the B.E.F. The generals were confident they could wipe it out on land, so why risk ships to effect that object at sea?

Also, the German Naval Command believed that a general engagement would be a disaster on account of the marked British superiority in capital ships. As it happens, the prospects of German success were greatest in the first months, particularly between November 1914 and February 1915. At one time, towards the end of October 1914, the Grand Fleet was without eight of its capital ships: a mine had sunk the *Audacious*; the *Ajax* and *Iron Duke* had developed leaky condenser tubes; the *Orion* was having turbine trouble; the *Conqueror* was refitting; the requisitioned Turkish ships, *Erin* and *Agincourt*, were not ready for action, having been too recently commissioned; the battle cruiser *New Zealand* was in dry dock. Had the High Seas Fleet chosen this moment to challenge the Grand Fleet, the Germans would have pitted their entire fleet of fifteen dreadnoughts and five battle cruisers (including the *Blücher*) against Jellicoe's seventeen and five, respectively, a dangerously small margin of superiority. The Grand Fleet

---

[1] In Tirpitz's opinion, 'it was simply nonsense to pack the fleet in cotton wool'. He never tired of preaching the 'power of audacity', stressing the quality of German *matériel* and personnel. He thought that a policy of 'continual activity' and 'minor successes' by the High Seas Fleet might force the Grand Fleet to seek out the German Fleet in its own waters, where the latter would have its best chance of success. Tirpitz, *My Memoirs* (London, 1919, 2 vols.), ii. 307-8, 366. 'Prestige tactics' was the contemptuous term used by the Chief of the Naval Cabinet, Admiral von Müller.

was weakened to the critical point with the detachment (5 November) of the battle cruisers *Invincible* and *Inflexible* to hunt down von Spee's squadron in the South Atlantic, and of the battle cruiser *Princess Royal* (12 November) for service in the western Atlantic. To be sure, the new battle cruiser *Tiger* joined Beatty's flag on 6 November, and the new dreadnoughts *Benbow* and *Emperor of India* joined Jellicoe soon after. But these ships were raw and would not be fit to lie in the line for some weeks. That the Germans were not aware of the favourable situation late in October must be attributed mainly to their weak naval intelligence service, since ships in dry dock or refitting (five of the eight capital ships mentioned above) are not easily hidden. From early in 1915 the Grand Fleet steadily pulled away from the High Seas Fleet in number of capital ships.

There was another reason why the German battle fleet did not challenge the British command of the North Sea. (This factor applied only to the first weeks of the war.) The Ministry of Marine and naval officers of all ranks, unaware of the change from a close to a distant blockade strategy in 1912, confidently expected the Royal Navy would immediately institute a close blockade of the Heligoland Bight, although they reckoned that the British would ultimately shift to a distant blockade. Thus, in the German naval manœuvres of 1913 the 'British Fleet' stormed into the Bight. 'There was only one opinion among us,' Admiral Scheer has recorded, 'from the Commander-in-Chief down to the latest recruit, about the attitude of the English Fleet. We were convinced that it would seek out and attack our Fleet the minute it showed itself and wherever it was. This could be accepted as certain from all the lessons of English naval history . . .'[2] One of the last reports from the Naval Attaché in London confirmed the expectations of a swift battle.

In discussing the last ship movements of the English Fleet the English press emphasized, in an article which was obviously inspired and which was meant to pacify, that the task of the English Fleet is defensive 'and *the defence of the English Fleet begins at the coast of the enemy.*' . . . The English Government seems to think it essential that such a war should come to an end *as fast as possible.* . . . The German Navy has to be

[2] Admiral Reinhard Scheer, *Germany's High Sea Fleet in the World War* (London, 1920), p. 11.

prepared for an *immediate attack* by the English Fleet *at the moment* of the outbreak of war between Germany and France.[3]

A close British blockade, with the acceptance of the chance of a major battle in waters close to the German bases, would give the German Fleet excellent opportunities to weaken the Royal Navy by mines and torpedoes to the point at which a fleet action could offer reasonable hopes of success.

Nothing of the kind developed, for the simple reason that British naval strategy called for a blockade of the North Sea instead of one of the Bight. The failure of the Grand Fleet to appear in the Bight on 28 August and offer battle (see below) upset the whole strategy of the German Navy. It was pretty certain now that Jellicoe was not coming over. The mission of the German Navy, as it evolved thereafter, was to secure the western and central Baltic (especially the vital ore traffic from Sweden), protect the North Sea frontier, and, in continuation of the original policy, though under less favourable conditions, to whittle down the British Fleet through an aggressive mining and submarine policy as a prelude to engaging the Grand Fleet under favourable conditions when an equalization of forces had been attained.

Many post-war writers, both German and British, have been very critical of the German passivity at sea, particularly in the early days. A vigorous thrust in the direction of the Channel would probably have indefinitely delayed the passage of the Army with possibly decisive results on the campaign in France. The same strategy would have drawn the Grand Fleet to the southern part of the North Sea and given the Germans opportunities to equalize forces.

The general passivity of the German Fleet continued. 'It was,' recalls Admiral James, 'a matter of the greatest surprise to all of us in the Grand Fleet that there were not more "tip and run" sorties from Wilhelmshaven. Repeated excursions might have seriously weakened us.'[4] If the Emperor had given the Admirals more freedom and listened to Tirpitz, and if the Admirals had taken full advantage of the unique scouting force at their command, the war might have taken a different course. The British had nothing

---

[3] Captain Erich von Müller to Tirpitz, 30 July 1914; German Ministry of Marine MSS. The italics (underlining in the original) were by Admiral von Pohl, the Chief of the Naval Staff.

[4] Admiral James's letter to the author, 12 Jan. 1962.

with which to destroy Zeppelins at sea. Their only success was on 4 May 1916, when *L-7* was brought down by the light cruisers *Galatea* and *Phaeton*, assisted by the submarine *E-31*, ten miles south of Horns Reef. (R.A.F. fighter aircraft from the carrier *Furious* got two more at Tondern (shed) on 19 July 1918.) 'If we saw them sailing about overhead,' says Admiral James, 'we could do nothing but swear at them.' The German naval authorities sadly mismanaged this scouting force. True, these craft were of no use in misty weather, but on fine days they were incomparable for scouting, as they could see everything that was afloat in the North Sea. Given good visibility, the German Fleet or units of it could put to sea in the hope of meeting weaker British forces without the slightest fear of running into stronger forces—if the Zeppelins were on patrol. Had the Germans used the Zeppelins for what they were intended—naval scouts—the war might have taken an interesting turn. Surprising to the Royal Navy was the way the Germans sacrificed this priceless advantage by making bombing attacks on coastal towns that cost them many of their Zeppelins with very little to show for the losses. R.F.C. (R.A.F. from 1 April 1918) fighter aircraft destroyed six over England, anti-aircraft gunfire disposed of four more over England, and six were lost directly or indirectly (not attributable to British action) as a result of raids on England.

The position of the German Fleet was a sorry one. '. . . a finely prepared weapon rusted in the hands of men who seem to have made their calculations in the negative terms of what would happen if they were beaten, rather than in the positive terms of what injury it could inflict upon the fighting forces, both naval and military, of the enemy.'[5] The psychological consequences of the passive role were disastrous. The German Fleet was disheartened, and the inferiority complex with which the officers and men entered the war was strengthened. Jellicoe considered it 'highly probable' that the gradual weakening of morale was ultimately responsible for the mutinies in the High Seas Fleet during 1917 and 1918 and the collapse of the Fleet in November 1918.[6]

In the belief that Germany's best hope was to strike almost

[5] Admiral Sir Herbert Richmond, *National Policy and Naval Strength, and Other Essays* (London, 1928), p. 73.
[6] Jellicoe, *The Grand Fleet, 1914-16* (London, 1919), p. 39. (The pagination of the American edition is different.)

immediately, before Britain could begin collecting the dividends of sea command, it was taken for granted in England that the High Seas Fleet would quickly sally forth and offer battle, and that the war at sea would therefore be short and sharp. Retired Admiral Sir Reginald Custance, one of the brainier officers of his time, asked his opinion on 1 August (just after the mobilization order had gone out) as to the probable duration of hostilities, replied, 'Oh, these things are generally over in a few months !'[7] A decisive battle in the early stages of a war had been a prominent feature in all the imaginary war stories before 1914. But the roots of the general expectation go deeper and constitute an indictment of the way naval history had been taught and written in Great Britain.

For a century preceding the Great War the British public had been fed on the strong meat of the naval victories in the war of the French Revolution and the Napoleonic Wars. The strategy of those wars had not been dwelt on; the real causes of our victory, to wit, our incessant blockade of the enemy's commerce, was never stressed; but the glorious nature of the results achieved in battle had been thoroughly exploited. Any minor reverses that we had experienced had been glossed over. The result was that in the minds of the people a fixed idea was created that battles were the main features of a war.[8]

The expectation of battle was not confined to the man in the street. The Admiralty and the flag officers at sea anticipated a battle as a result of one of the three probable objectives of German naval strategy: to break out of the North Sea in order to attack British trade; to raid or invade the East Coast of England; or to break through the Dover Straits and attack the Channel communications.

The Grand Fleet ships were readied for instant action, which, among other things, involved the removal of 'superfluous' wood-work, anything detachable or portable that was inflammable, including pianos, chairs, and even most of the ship's boats. In some ships 'this frenzy to strip the ships reached masochistic proportions'. A week later, a decisive action no longer seeming imminent, 'a violent reaction set in as ships began to demand sofas, settees, and the necessary refurnishings'.[9]

[7] Lady Victoria Wester Wemyss, *The Life and Letters of Lord Wester Wemyss* (London, 1935), p. 157.

[8] Admiral Sir Reginald Bacon and Francis E. McMurtrie, *Modern Naval Strategy* (London, 1940), p. 182.

[9] Commander Stephen King-Hall, *My Naval Life* (London, 1952), pp. 99–100.

The B.E.F. was safely in France by 19 August. No attempt had been made to attack it in transit, nor did any of the other enemy offensive possibilities materialize. There was perplexity at White-hall when it became clear, after a few weeks, that the Germans were not anxious to join issue in the North Sea in the historic manner. In a fit of annoyance, ,the First Lord bombastically asserted, in a speech at Liverpool (21 September), that if the German Navy did not come out to fight, 'it would be dug out like rats from a hole'. There was a sixteenth-century ring about the statement, which might have been made by an Elizabethan sea-dog. Unhappily for Churchill, the digging-out operation was hardly feasible, the 'hole' being heavily defended by shore guns, mines, destroyers, and submarines. The King complained to the Prime Minister that the First Lord's reference to 'rats in a hole' was both unfortunate, seeing that 'the rats came out of their own accord and to our cost' [the sinking of the 'Cressys', 22 September], and 'hardly dignified for a Cabinet Minister'.[10] The Fleet was no happier. Admiral Bayly informed the Second Sea Lord 'how very annoyed and angry the senior officers (and possibly juniors) in the First [Grand] Fleet are . . . we all pride ourselves on keeping from any bombast, and remaining quiet and ready . . . we feel that we have been dragged down to the level of boasting and breathing bombastic defiance, and we hate it'.[11]

In the Fleet there was growing impatience when the big battle did not come off. Beatty feared 'the rascals will never come out but will only send out minelayers and submarines. . . . It really is very disappointing and looks as if we sh⁴ go through the War without ever coming to grips with them. Such a thought is more than I can bear.' A few days later he pleaded with Keyes, 'Oh, my dear Roger, can't you make the beggars be a little more enterprising with their battle cruisers? If they don't do something soon, I shall blow up.'[12] The Vice-Admiral Commanding the 3rd Battle Squadron had to 'tell my people it was 16 months before Lord Howe got his opportunity at the French Fleet in 1794, so they must

[10] Lord Stamfordham (the King's Private Secretary) to Maurice Bonham Carter (Asquith's Private Secretary), 22 Sept. 1914; Asquith MSS.
[11] Bayly to Hamilton, 2 Oct. 1914; Hamilton MSS. Churchill came to regret the expression. Heckled on it in the House, 7 March 1916, he admitted that 'digging them out' was 'a very foolish phrase, and I regret that it slipped out'.
[12] Beatty to Lady Beatty, 12 Sept. 1914, Beatty MSS; Beatty to Keyes, 18 Sept. 1914, Keyes MSS.

make up their minds for a long watch and wait before they can expect to see their foes out on the ocean'.[13]

Many Englishmen experienced a sense of profound disappointment as week succeeded week and no great naval battle was recorded in the North Sea or in the Mediterranean, while in the outer seas a relatively small number of swift enemy cruisers evaded action. Some newspapers taunted the Germans with pusillanimity. Impatient or simple-minded Englishmen were more and more asking, 'What is the Fleet doing?' They did not understand the silence that had descended upon the sea, nor why 'nothing was done' to eliminate once and for all the inconvenient German Navy. There was nothing new in this. During the wars of the sailing era their ancestors were always asking fretfully what the Fleet was doing and why it was not attacking the French or Spanish Fleet. As time passed and there was no battle, they began to grumble and to think that the admirals were lacking in initiative and playing for safety. Even Nelson at one period came under this ill-informed criticism. The general public never would realize that the object in maritime war is to sever the enemy's sea communications and safeguard one's own communications, that the vessels which attack and defend trade routes operate under the protection of the main fleets, and that it is only when the severing of communications (blockade) threatens the ability to continue to wage war that the trial of strength between the main fleets occurs. Some of the sailing-ship admirals, Hawke, Nelson, etc., had to wait and watch for years before their chance came. Britain's naval commanders of the past at least had the inestimable advantage of not living in a democratic age. They had to exercise patience, but they did not have to persuade their countrymen, too, to be patient. In the twentieth century, however, public opinion could not be ignored.

Nearly all the responsible newspapers and periodicals worked hard to allay public impatience. They reminded the country of British naval history with its many and prolonged periods of watchful waiting. They also pointed out that, as no enemy battle squadron had put to sea, there had been no possibility of a general naval action. The enemy could not be forced to fight against his will. The principle tack was the claim that the country was enjoying 'all the advantages of a new Trafalgar'. 'The Fleet has never

[13] Bradford to Adm. of the Fleet (ret.) Sir Gerard Noel, 15 Oct. 1914; Noel MSS.

49

been inactive,' lectured *The Times* (25 August). 'Although unseen and unheard, the Fleet is exerting continual and progressively stringent pressure upon the vitals of the foe.' The press mirrored the attitude of the Admiralty, where despite the initial perplexity over German inactivity, it was appreciated that so long as Germany tied up her Fleet to her coast, its power for controlling the sea was nullified.

The ever restless First Lord was an exception. Late in October the D.O.D., Captain Richmond, who had the First Lord to dinner, found him in

low spirits . . . oppressed with the impossibility of *doing* anything. The attitude of waiting, threatened all the time by submarines, unable to strike back at their Fleet . . . and the inability of the Staff to make any suggestions seem to bother him. I have not seen him so despondent before. . . . I urged mining their coast, but he won't have it. I suggested a raid . . . upon these confounded intelligence fishing craft. [Fishing vessels under neutral colours were alleged to be working as intelligencers for the Germans in the North Sea, using wireless or pigeons.] He liked that. . . . He wanted to send battleships—old ones—up the Elbe, but for what purpose except to be sunk I did not understand . . .[14]

2. HELIGOLAND BIGHT AND THE 'CRESSYS'

More successful than the educational campaign of the press in brightening for a time the prevailing gloom was the Heligoland Bight action on 28 August. Its initiator was Keyes, who was eager for action. 'When are we going to make war? [he asked the D.O.D.] and make the Germans realize that whenever they come out—destroyers, cruisers, battleships, or all three—they will be fallen on and attacked?'[15] With assistance from Tyrwhitt (the two got along famously) he hatched an operation which was accepted with amendments on 24 August. It called for intercepting the German destroyer day patrols off Heligoland, which served as a defence against submarines and minelaying. The plan involved the use of two light cruisers and two destroyer flotillas of

[14] Diary, 24 Oct. 1914; Arthur J. Marder, *Portrait of an Admiral: the Life and Papers of Sir Herbert Richmond* (London, 1952), p. 121. (Hereafter cited by title only.) Tyrwhitt, who had just returned from an Admiralty conference, remarked on Churchill's having been 'very much on the warpath and was seeing very red. He is determined to get them out of harbour somehow.' Tyrwhitt to his wife, 12 Nov. 1914; Tyrwhitt MSS.
[15] Keyes to Leveson, 21 Aug. 1914; Keyes MSS.

Tyrwhitt's Harwich Force, with three of Keyes's submarines luring the enemy destroyers away from Heligoland, and five others attacking any enemy ships which might come out in support. Rear-Admiral Sir Archibald Moore, commanding two battle cruisers at the Humber, was to support Tyrwhitt to the north-westward. It was not until the afternoon of the 26th that Jellicoe learned that a sweep had been ordered. He considered the force too weak in case German heavy ships came out to support their light forces, and at once suggested co-operating with the whole of the Grand Fleet. In a further signal that day he showed quite clearly that he was uneasy about the way in which the affair was being organized, and made some suggestions with regard to it. The Admiralty replied that the co-operation of the battle fleet was not required, but that the battle cruisers 'can support if convenient'. At the last moment, on the morning of the 27th, Jellicoe sent Beatty's three battle cruisers (1st B.C.S.) and Goodenough's 1st Light Cruiser Squadron to support the operation, and *then* informed the Admiralty.[16] Moore's two ships were to join Beatty. A message (1.10 p.m., 27 August) informed Tyrwhitt and Keyes that the 1st Battle Squadron and the Light Cruiser Squadron were taking part, but by a serious error in staff work this vital information never reached them. It was sent to Harwich, where no attempt was made to forward it by W/T, and it lay there awaiting their return. No one troubled to ascertain whether the message had been received by them. The consequences could easily have been disastrous, for Tyrwhitt, and later Keyes, at first mistook their Grand Fleet supports for enemy ships.

Of the confused action itself, I will note the essentials only. The plan went awry, and Tyrwhitt and Keyes soon found themselves (forenoon, 28 August) in the presence of superior German forces when the German Fleet Command sent out all available light cruisers to cover the retirement of their destroyer flotilla. Tyrwhitt, entangled with a 'hornet's nest' of enemy light cruisers (six had converged on him by about 12.30), fought gallantly but was in serious trouble. Beatty with the five battle cruisers was 40 miles north of Heligoland. Sensing the critical situation that was

---

[16] Jellicoe, 'A Reply to Criticism', Jellicoe MSS; Jellicoe, *The Grand Fleet*, p. 109. The British telegrams and signals on the operation are in Naval Staff Monograph No. 11 (1921), *The Battle of Heligoland Bight, August 28th, 1914*, in Naval Staff Monographs, iii. 149–53. The German signals are in *Der Krieg in der Nordsee*, i. 272–89.

developing, at 11.29 a.m. he sent Goodenough in to support Tyrwhitt. At about this time Beatty received signals from Tyrwhitt indicating that he was hotly engaged only 25 miles west of Heligoland and in distress. There was a good chance, as Beatty sized up the situation, that the enemy had sent a powerful force to sea and that Goodenough's force would not be sufficient to save Tyrwhitt. The Admiral was placed in a position of great difficulty. He knew things were not going well. Yet, if he moved into the Bight, he would face the serious risk of running into mines and meeting hostile submarines, to say nothing of British submarines and the possibility of surprise by German capital ships, aided by the low visibility. He seemed to hesitate. 'What do you think we should do?' he asked his Flag-Captain. 'I ought to go forward and support Tyrwhitt, but if I lose one of these valuable ships the country will not forgive me.' Chatfield, 'unburdened with responsibility, and eager for excitement', replied, 'Surely we must go.'[17] The Admiral needed little encouragement. Reckoning that prompt intervention and the high speed of his squadron discounted the dangers, he promptly (11.35 a.m.) turned to E.S.E. and sailed full speed far into the Bight, arriving on the scene (12.37 p.m.) at the exactly right moment. 'I really was beginning to feel a bit blue,' Tyrwhitt wrote after the battle, 'as the new [light] cruiser [*Strassburg*] was firing heavy stuff at us.' Beatty finished off two cruisers, scattered the Germans, then ordered a general retirement (1.10 p.m.), after all contact with the enemy had been lost.

Jellicoe commended the Vice-Admiral for taking 'the only action which was possible . . . and his action is fully justified by the results'. Churchill agreed. 'It was a fine feat of arms— vindicated by success.'[18] It may have been lucky for the attackers (or was it due to forethought in planning?) that the tide was too low over the bar at the entrance to the Jade. This made it impossible for the High Seas Fleet, at Wilhelmshaven, to move

[17] Admiral of the Fleet Lord Chatfield, *The Navy and Defence* (London, 1942), p. 124.
[18] Jellicoe to Admiralty, 31 Aug. 1914, and Admiralty minutes; Admiralty MSS. Beatty afterwards noted: 'The end justified the means, but if I had lost a Battle Cruiser I should have been hanged, drawn and quartered. Yet it was necessary to run the risk to save two of our Light Cruisers and a large force of Destroyers which otherwise would most certainly have been lost.' Beatty to Balfour, 21 June 1916; Beatty MSS.

before noon. On the other hand, Admiral Ingenohl, the German C.-in-C., at no time gave any indication of wishing to commit his battle fleet. About an hour after the British retirement he half-heartedly sent the battle cruisers out. They proceeded a short distance to the westward, and, finding nothing, returned to harbour.

The operation was hardly a masterpiece of planning. There was an utter lack of co-ordination, and apart from the failure to notify Tyrwhitt and Keyes of the change in plan, which had exposed Goodenough's squadron in particular to great danger, the plan itself was so loose that three British squadrons were operating practically independently in the same waters. Jellicoe's main recommendations, after he had studied Beatty's and Goodenough's reports of the battle, were: (1) that it was 'essential that in any future combined operations full information should be given to all officers commanding units of southern forces as to the ships which are taking part in these operations'; and (2) that commanding officers, when signalling their positions or asking for assistance, give their course and speed, something both Keyes and Tyrwhitt had neglected to do. The Admiralty concurred in the C.-in-C.'s proposals.[19]

The German Official Naval History says it was a fatal error for their Naval Command to have assumed that the British light forces would have attacked so far from their bases without the support of heavy ships. The Germans had fought well against what, in the later stages of the action, had been far superior forces, but they had lost three light cruisers (three others were battered) and a destroyer, with over 1,200 officers and men killed, wounded, and taken prisoner. The British lost no ships, and only the light cruiser *Arethusa* and three destroyers had suffered any serious damage. Casualties were 35 killed and about 40 wounded.

There were far larger consequences of the action. The bold, deep penetration of German home waters confirmed the German Fleet in its exaggerated respect for the Royal Navy. The Emperor was more determined than ever to restrict his Fleet to a defensive strategy and not risk important units. It was not to fight an action outside the Bight or in the Skagerrak, and not even in the Bight against superior forces for fear of submarine attack. The Emperor did approve of occasional sorties by the battle cruisers, as

[19] Admiralty MSS.

well as the continuation of the energetic prosecution of the war by the submarines, destroyers, and minelayers.

On the British side, the Heligoland Bight action was hailed as a glorious victory. It cheered the country, the Navy, and the Army at a most opportune time; the German advance in France was then at its crest. 'We had a great reception all the way from the Nore to Chatham,' Tyrwhitt reported after his ship, the light cruiser *Arethusa*, had limped into Sheerness under tow. 'Every ship and everybody cheered like mad. Winston met us at Sheerness and came up to Chatham with us and fairly slobbered over me. Offered me any ship I liked and all the rest of it. . . . everybody quite mad with delight at the success of our first naval venture.'[20]

Yes, they had won the first important action of the war at sea. The *Daily Express* banner headline exulted: 'We've Gone to Heligoland and Back. Please God, We'll Go Again!' One writer likened the exploit to Drake's expedition. As he had singed the King of Spain's beard, so Beatty & Co. had now singed the Kaiser's moustache. It was left for the *New Statesman* (5 September) to put the action in its true perspective. The battle was of 'immense moral, if of slight material, importance in its effect upon the two fleets'. Or as Chatfield summed up the battle years later, 'It was no great naval feat, but carried out under the nose of the German Commander-in-Chief it actually meant a good deal both to Germany and to England. We had shown our sea ascendancy, our will to seek every opportunity of engaging the enemy even at his very front door.'[21]

On 10 September Tyrwhitt's force had 'another go at what the sailors call "biting the Bight" ', the Admiralty idea being to tempt to sea some at least of the enemy's heavy ships. The Grand Fleet came down within a hundred miles of Heligoland, in case the High Seas Fleet, or a portion of it, put to sea. The Harwich Flotillas penetrated deeply into the Bight, to within twelve miles of Heligoland, but to everyone's intense disappointment they sighted no enemy vessels and returned empty-handed. Later in September Keyes and Tyrwhitt tried to arrange another 28 August type of operation. It was by now too difficult, minefields having replaced advance patrol lines. The Bight was so thickly mined that they 'could not go messing about there any more', wrote Tyrwhitt.

[20] Tyrwhitt to his wife, n.d. (*ca.* 6 Sept. 1914); Tyrwhitt MSS.
[21] Chatfield, *The Navy and Defence*, p. 126.

He tried to console himself (2 October) with the thought that 'We, the Navy, are not doing much, but if the Germans won't come out, what can we do?'

Less than a month later a deplorable incident in the North Sea, the first real shock to the Navy, practically nullified the moral advantages gained by the success in the Bight. The date was 22 September, and the plaçe was the Broad Fourteens, off the Dutch coast. The old armoured cruisers *Cressy, Hogue,* and *Aboukir,* three of the four crocks in the 7th Cruiser Squadron ('Bacchante' class), nicknamed the 'live-bait squadron' by the Grand Fleet, were steering a steady course at a speed of under 10 knots. This was inexcusably risky, even if Admiral Christian, commander of the squadron (but not with it on the 22nd), afterwards attempted to justify the low speed by the necessity to conserve coal. 'The maintenance of a three-quarter speed of thirteen or fourteen knots would have entailed an expenditure of coal which would have resulted in continual withdrawal of vessels from the patrol.'[22]

The squadron had received no special warning about submarines, but it was fully aware of the possibility of attack, hence, in the judgment of the Court of Inquiry, the Senior Officer (Captain John E. Drummond) 'should have zigzagged his course as much as possible'. Perhaps he was over-confident of the immunity of his ships. After all, no warship of any great value had been sunk by submarines in the first seven weeks of war. Suddenly, the *Aboukir,* his own ship, was struck by a torpedo from a solitary German submarine and sank in 25 minutes. Drummond was rash in ordering the other two cruisers to close the *Aboukir* when hit, since he did not know whether it was by mine or torpedo. For this he was criticized by the Court. The Captains of the *Hogue* and *Cressy* chivalrously stopped their ships after closing and lowered their boats to rescue the survivors. This was an 'error of judgment' (Court of Inquiry), since it offered two sitting ducks for the torpedoes of the U-boat commander, and down went the pair. The First Sea Lord made allowances for the two Captains, who 'were placed in a cruel position, once they found themselves in waters swarming with drowning men'.[23] All told, 62 officers and

[22] Christian's letter in *The Times,* 23 Feb. 1923.
[23] Battenberg's minute on the findings of the Court of Inquiry, 24 Oct. 1914; Admiralty MSS.

1,397 men of the 2,200 on board the three cruisers were lost. These are the bare facts. What is the story behind the story?

The 'Southern Force', under Rear-Admiral Arthur H. Christian, included his flagship *Euryalus* (a 'Bacchante' class cruiser), the Harwich Flotillas (1st and 3rd Destroyer Flotillas and ten submarines of the 8th Flotilla), and the 7th Cruiser Squadron (*Bacchante, Cressy, Aboukir, Hogue*). The 7th Cruiser Squadron, at the Nore, under Rear-Admiral Henry H. Campbell, had among its objectives the support of the Harwich Flotillas in their task of keeping the area south of the 54th parallel free of enemy minelayers and torpedo craft. The Flotillas had two patrol areas, the Broad Fourteens and off the Dogger Bank, with the five supporting cruisers usualiy divided between the two areas. (The *Euryalus* took her turn on patrol owing to the shortage of cruisers.) On 17 September bad weather forced both flotillas to return to their bases. This left Admiral Campbell patrolling the Dogger Bank with three of the five 'Bacchantes', one (*Euryalus*) having been detached to coal and another (*Bacchante*) sent in for repairs.

That same day, at a conference in Jellicoe's flagship, the *Iron Duke*, attended by Churchill and Sturdee, the Chief of the War Staff, Keyes and Tyrwhitt had pointed out the danger of exposing these cruisers to such an advanced position.[24] The First Lord was impressed, and on his return to London the next day he strongly recommended to the First Sea Lord that 'the "Bacchantes" ought not to continue on this beat. The risk to such ships is not justified by any services they can render. The narrow seas, being the nearest point to the enemy, should be kept by a small number of good modern ships. The "Bacchantes" should go to the western entrance of the Channel and set Bethell's battleships [7th B.S., which had taken over the Western Patrol from Wemyss *pro tem.*]—and later Wemyss' cruisers—free for convoy and other duties.'[25] Note that this minute did not deal with the submarine menace. Battenberg agreed. He had never been convinced of the merits of the plan that had the 'Bacchantes' 'peddling up and down' in the North Sea. But on 19 September Sturdee persuaded him to approve a telegram which ordered the cruisers to concentrate in the south.

[24] Keyes had warned Leveson on 21 August against keeping the cruisers where they were. 'For Heaven's sake,' he had told the D.O.D., 'take those 'Bacchantes" away!... I don't say those cruisers will be attacked, but the Germans must know they are about, and if they send out a suitable force, God help them...' Keyes MSS.

[25] Churchill's minute of 18 Sept. 1914; *The World Crisis*, i. 324.

'The Dogger Bank patrol need not be continued. Weather too bad for destroyers to go to sea. Arrange for cruisers to watch Broad Fourteens.'[26] Churchill claims that he never saw 'this routine message'. It put the hapless three cruisers in a very dangerous area, wedged in between the Dutch coast and a German minefield and without destroyer protection. After the tragedy that followed, Battenberg observed, 'I should not have given in to them.'[27]

The main reason for the importance attached by the Admiralty to the Broad Fourteens seems to have been the desire to ensure early notice of any raid on the Channel to attack the British transports. Another reason was the guarantee to the Belgians at the beginning of the war to keep the Scheldt open. The Admiralty had information that steamers were loading with cement and sand in Hamburg, possibly for the purpose of blocking it. A third reason was the desire to intercept minelayers en route to the English coast. These considerations notwithstanding, there was no good reason for keeping the cruisers practically at Germany's doorstep, without any precautions and in an area full of fishing vessels, which could report every movement of the three cruisers.

Also, if it was deemed important to keep the cruisers on patrol, why did not the destroyers rejoin immediately the weather moderated on the night of 21–22 September? The error seems to have been due to a division of responsibility. Obviously, the proper person to order the destroyers to rejoin was the officer commanding the cruisers at the time, Captain Drummond. Being on the spot, he was in the best position to know the weather conditions. The Admiralty, it appears, expected him to take the initiative. Drummond, unfortunately, was not clear as to his powers in this respect, and he understood that the destroyers would be ordered out by somebody else. A destroyer flotilla was actually on its way at dawn on the 22nd, but it had started too late. The *Aboukir* was hit at 6.30 a.m., and within an hour all three cruisers were at the bottom.

The report of the Court of Inquiry flatly stated that the War

---

[26] *Ibid.*

[27] Admiral Mark Kerr, *Prince Louis of Battenberg, Admiral of the Fleet* (London, 1934), p. 248. When Keyes (possibly at the *Iron Duke* meeting) remonstrated with Sturdee for keeping the cruisers on that patrol, the C.O.S. replied, with superb conceit: 'My dear fellow, you don't know your history. We've always maintained a squadron on the Broad Fourteens.' Admiral Sir William James's letter to the author, 14 Apr. 1962. (He got the story from Keyes.)

Staff telegram of 19 September was 'undoubtedly' responsible for what happened. In the opinion of the Court, 'a cruiser patrol established in a limited area at so short a distance from an enemy's submarine base was certain to be attacked by submarines, and the withdrawal of the destroyers increased the chance of a successful attack, while diminishing those of saving life; but while placing this opinion on record the Court is not in a position to judge of or comment upon the expediency of making the cruisers take the risk they ran'. The Third and Fourth Sea Lords and Sir Arthur Wilson concurred in the criticism of the Admiralty. (The Sea Lords, remember, other than the First Sea Lord, had little to do with operational decisions.) The First Sea Lord took umbrage at the principal finding of the inquiry; the Court naturally was ignorant of all the reasons that had dictated the establishment of a patrol in the Broad Fourteens.[28]

Battenberg did not think a court martial for Drummond was 'necessary or expedient' in view of all the circumstances, but he was to be kept on half-pay for the present and denied important commands at sea for the future. There remained the problem of the two Admirals, Campbell and Christian, who had been in harbour with the knowledge and sanction of the Admiralty when the disaster occurred. No explanation was given to the Court as to why Campbell had not shifted his flag when his flagship, the *Bacchante*, had to remain in harbour for repairs. (Campbell's evidence at the inquiry was extraordinary. He stated that he did not know the object for which the patrol had been formed, had received no instructions, and apparently had issued none himself.) In the case of Christian, the weather had been too bad for him to shift his flag to one of the other cruisers when the *Euryalus* left the patrol to return to harbour for coaling and the repair of her wireless (20 September). He had accordingly turned over the patrol to Drummond of the *Aboukir*. The Court was not satisfied with the reasons given for the absence of the Admirals. Battenberg exonerated them; the Second Sea Lord and A. K. Wilson believed their absence was immaterial to the issue. Only the Third Sea Lord took the view that the absence of an admiral at the time of the disaster had 'a material effect because the whole attention

---

[28] *Report of the Court of Enquiry into the Loss of the Three Bacchante Class Cruisers*, 5 Oct. 1914, and minutes: Wilson, n.d., Lambert, 4 Dec., Tudor, 9 Dec., Battenberg, 24 Oct. 1914; Admiralty MSS.

of the Captain, Senior Officer, unprovided with a Flag Officer's staff and organisation, would naturally be taken up with his own sinking ship; whereas, the Admiral if present would have taken the more detached view, and have considered the safety of the Squadron as a whole, and perhaps have prevented the procedure which led to the loss of the other two cruisers'.[29] Campbell and Christian were placed on half-pay, though not for long. Both officers held important commands until 1917.

The Emperor was reported to be 'in seventh heaven' over the sinking of the 'Cressys'. In Britain the press and the Admiralty assured the country that the loss was no more than a regrettable incident, it made no appreciable diminution in the Navy's great margin of strength, and consequently there was no need to feel nervous. Criticism of the Admiralty there was, none the less, with the brunt of it falling on Churchill. It was charged that he had abrogated to himself the disposition of the ships against the advice of the Sea Lords. Few knew that the disposition in this case was primarily the work of the First Sea Lord and the Chief of Staff.

The loss of the three cuisers called attention to the U-boat danger, and this brings us to the story of the Grand Fleet, its trials and tribulations.

[29] Tudor's minute on the report of the Court, 7 Dec. 1914; Admiralty MSS.

IV

The Triple Menace

(AUGUST 1914–NOVEMBER 1914)

It is suicidal to forego our advantageous position in the big ships by risking them in waters infested with submarines. The result might quite easily be such a weakening of our battle fleet and battle cruiser strength as seriously to jeopardise the future of the country by giving over to the Germans the command of the open seas.

JELLICOE to Churchill, 30 September 1914.

[In view of the submarine danger] no big ship of the Fighting Fleet should go into the North Sea! WHEN the German Big Fleet comes out, THEN our Big Fleet will come out! WHEN the German battle cruisers come out, THEN our battle cruisers will also come out . . .

FISHER to Churchill, 26 December 1914.

I. THE INVASION PROBLEM

AMONG the many documents of Section A of the Naval Staff, which was responsible for operational planning on the part of the German Navy, one finds no indication that an invasion of England by Germany was either planned or discussed at any time during the war. Indeed, just the opposite was the case. Thus, in September 1916 there was a fear on the part of the German Naval Staff and the Army General Staff that the British would land on Jutland and, with or without Danish support, proceed against Schleswig-Holstein.[1] In Britain, however, the possibility of a German attempt to land on the East Coast occasioned some concern from the beginning of the war. This was especially the case in the first two weeks, when it was reasoned at the Admiralty that the enemy might well try to delay the departure, or interrupt the transport, of the B.E.F. by a raid or raids on the East Coast. On 12 August the Admiralty wired Jellicoe this appreciation of the position: 'We cannot wholly exclude the chance of an attempt at a landing during this week on

[1] Documents of the *Admiralstab*; German Ministry of Marine MSS.

a large-scale supported by High Sea Fleet. . . . extraordinary silence and inertia of enemy may be prelude to serious enterprises.'[2]

Battenberg and Churchill were so confident of the Navy's ability to protect the country against invasion or a serious raid that the First Lord was able on 5 August to waive the requirement in the conclusions of the ‚C.I.D. Sub-Committee on Oversea Attack (May 1914)[3] that two regular divisions should be held back in Britain as a safeguard against invasion. All six divisions could leave England at once. Kitchener, who was appointed Secretary of State for War that day, held back two divisions, and it was not until 8 September that the 6th and last remaining infantry division was sent to France. The Secretary of the C.I.D. attempted to dispel the uneasiness created by this situation. He reviewed the invasion question and concluded that while 'raids were by no means improbable now or later on in the war' (one of the objects might be to entice the Navy on to their minefields), an invasion was 'very improbable'. Germany's military preoccupation on two fronts made it impossible for her to raise sufficient troops.[4]

At the beginning of October, when the new 7th Division was dispatched for the relief of Antwerp, with Admiralty concurrence, there were only four regular battalions and the partially trained Territorial force in the country. This decision practically to denude the country of regular troops impelled the Prime Minister to ask the C.I.D. to review the whole defence problem in the light of the experience of the first two months of the war. The discussion on 7 October resulted in agreement on one major point only: the Germans would not attempt a raid or invasion for the present, since they had no troops to spare.

At this meeting Kitchener revealed his apprehensiveness that a deadlock in the land war in the not distant future would liberate troops for an invasion in force (150,000–200,000 men). Germany, he was certain, had ample shipping for such a venture, which would be attempted under cover of a fleet action and be aided by Zeppelins. He hoped to have enough trained troops available by

---

[2] *The World Crisis*, i. 258–9.

[3] See *From the Dreadnought to Scapa Flow*, i. 357.

[4] C.I.D. paper No. 74-A (by Hankey), 'Attack on the British Isles from Oversea', 18 Sept. 1914; Asquith MSS.

the middle of January to end the danger of invasion. As regards raids, Churchill was prepared to accept responsibility for preventing more than 70,000 men landing (this had been the Admiralty position for years and had been accepted by the C.I.D. in 1908 and 1914),[5] if Kitchener would guarantee the defeat of anything up to that number. That is, he was prepared to accept responsibility for preventing an invasion, if the War Office would guarantee the defeat of a raid. This Kitchener would not do. There were few troops left at home, and to withdraw men from the Continent at that moment would be 'most inadvisable'.[6] This left unsolved the problem posed by raids.

* * *

The meeting of 7 October was one of the last held by the C.I.D. during the war. (It was revived in 1922.) It was summoned in the first months of the war to consider special problems, like home defence and joint operations. On 25 November its work was taken over by the War Council (only the Historical Section of the C.I.D. was kept active), which closely resembled its predecessor and, like it, was a special committee of the Cabinet, with the inclusion of the First Sea Lord and Chief of the Imperial General Staff, to aid the Cabinet in the higher direction of naval and military operations. Maurice Hankey (Lieutenant-Colonel, Royal Marines, who, in Fisher's opinion, had 'the genius of Napoleon and the thoroughness of Cromwell') was the Secretary, and Balfour attended as the unofficial representative of the Conservative Party. A. K. Wilson was added on 7 January 1915.

There were two essential differences between the two bodies. The War Council had much larger executive authority; it was not a purely advisory body as was the C.I.D. It often carried out its decisions without bothering to get Cabinet sanction. The second major difference was a most unfortunate one in its consequences. 'The position and prestige of the Chief of the Imperial General Staff, the First Sea Lord and their expert advisers *vis-à-vis* the cabinet ministers in the wartime councils were greatly reduced ... In the C.I.D. these professional leaders had been genuine members and tended to speak frankly and fully before the civilians. ... This was now changed . . . The military members were brought into

---

[5] See *From the Dreadnought to Scapa Flow*, i. 350, 356–7.
[6] Minutes of the 129th meeting of the C.I.D.; Asquith MSS.

the war councils in a secondary status, as advisers to their departmental chiefs rather than as the supreme professional experts of the armed forces and advisers to the government as a whole.'[7]

*   *   *

An invasion scare swept Whitehall in November, infecting both the generals and the admirals. The War Office was apprehensive, seeing in the lull on the Western Front the German chance to detach a quarter of a million crack troops for an invasion. Churchill was of the same mind. 'From 1st Nov. begins the maximum danger period for this country, ending during January when new armies and territorials acquire real military value. During this period, very likely deadlock on land enabling Germany to economize troops for an invasion. If ever to be attempted, this is the time. I am confident of our ability to inflict military punishment if it is tried, but no precaution must be neglected.'[8] Battenberg was in agreement. Fisher, when he returned to power a few days later, seriously expected an imminent invasion. 17 November was the date he chose: the tides and moon then would be favourable for night-time landings. Kitchener predicted an attempt on 17 or 20 November. Jellicoe believed the most favourable time for an invasion or raid was about the 20th.

Naval preparations early in November included bringing the 3rd Battle Squadron down to Portland to join the Channel Fleet. (On 18 November the squadron rejoined the Grand Fleet, but with Rosyth as its new base, after Jellicoe's strong plea for its immediate return.) Arrangements were made for mines to be exploded and block ships to be sunk in the mouths of undefended harbours. Military precautions included the deployment of some 300,000 half-trained troops along the East Coast. The Admiralty sent Jellicoe 'most secret' orders on 12 November covering the contingency of invasion or raid. If the Germans moved, they would move with their whole Fleet. To cover the landings and to seek a naval battle on favourable terms, the High Seas Fleet would position itself between the main landing, the Grand Fleet, and its own base. The enemy would doubtless

[7] Franklyn A. Johnson, *Defence by Committee : the British Committee of Imperial Defence, 1885–1959* (London, 1960), pp. 151–2.
[8] Churchill to Battenberg and Sturdee, 23 Oct. 1914; Admiralty MSS.

protect himself by minefields, and, as you have so clearly foreseen, will endeavour to draw you on to these and to his submarines before engaging.[9] He will count on your being hurried by panic in England, and by eagerness to bring him to battle. . . . You will concern yourself exclusively with the destruction of the High Sea Fleet, taking your own time, choosing your own method, and not troubling yourself at all with what is going on in England. . . . The Channel Fleet and the Flotillas deal first with the invaders and their escort, and thereafter at the earliest moment come under your command for the main battle if it has not been already fought.[10]

Nothing happened, and by 21 November Fisher was no longer expecting an invasion attempt. He exulted in the 'splendid "dress rehearsal" that the scare had provided'.

More real and persistent dangers, so far as the Admiralty and the Fleet were concerned, were the German mines and submarines.

2. THE SUBMARINE PERIL

While impatiently waiting for the new Trafalgar, the Grand Fleet worked hard to make itself battle-ready. Gunnery and torpedo practice were held mornings except Sundays inside the Flow, and at regular intervals a battle squadron went outside, to the west of the Pentland Firth, for heavy-gun firing.[11] The dreadnoughts and the battle cruisers were at sea frequently, training or making sweeps as far south as the 54th parallel in search of the enemy. In the first three months alone the Grand Fleet steamed

[9] See below, pp. 75–6.

[10] Admiralty to Jellicoe, 12 Nov. 1914 (signed by Fisher and Churchill); Jellicoe MSS. The C.-in-C. would not guarantee the Grand Fleet's ability to stop the landing of a large force, since enemy submarines made it impossible to keep watching cruisers near the German coast. The fleet, therefore, could not learn in time of the departure of the raiding force. He did suggest various steps such as defensive mining, blocking ships at various rivers and harbours from Harwich to the Firth of Forth, the use of large quantities of petrol for creating surface fires on the water, and preparation for the rapid demolition of jetties by explosives. These measures would free the Navy for its 'proper role', the destruction of the enemy's fleet. Jellicoe to Admiralty, 14 Nov. 1914; Admiralty MSS.

[11] Main armaments were exercised in the Flow, but with sub-calibre. This consisted of fixing a 3-lb. or 6-lb. gun inside the bore of any 12-inch or bigger gun, so that the sub-calibre could be fired at a target only by moving the turrets and exercising the whole of the main armament control. The battle cruisers could do very little gunnery in the Forth, and the submarine menace was too great to permit any beyond. They carried out sub-calibre practice behind the anti-submarine defences of the Forth; such full-calibre practice as they could manage was done outside Cromarty, though, perhaps two or three times a year, a squadron went to Scapa for the purpose.

some 15,000 miles. One object of the early sweeps was to have the Fleet in a better position to pounce on any large-scale movement to interfere with the transit of the B.E.F. Southward sweeps were forbidden, once the B.E.F. had been transported to France. Another purpose of the sweeps was to keep morale up, since inaction was obviously not very good for morale. A third and main reason was the insecurity of the base in the early stages of the war.

The fleet spent much time in Scapa Flow, since to keep it constantly at sea would have meant excessive wear and tear on ships and personnel and too great an expenditure of fuel. Life could be pleasant at Scapa. To maintain the health and good spirits of the officers and men, Jellicoe encouraged all kinds of recreation. An 18-hole golf course, constructed by the fleet on Flotta Island, near its anchorage, was well patronized by the officers, often including the C.-in-C. (he had the right of way) in the afternoon. Football was also popular in the fleet—a number of fields were made for the men—and regattas, theatricals, cinemas, lantern lectures, concerts, boxing, shooting, fishing, walking, boating picnics, and even educational classes had their devotees.

This happy state of affairs did not last. Scapa Flow became 'really beastly' in the winter. Darkness set in as early as 3.30 or 4 p.m., and it would often blow hard for days (the winter gales reached a hundred miles per hour). Heavy seas damaged ships, immobilized the destroyers, and made it impossible to lower boats. Far worse than the discomforts imposed by nature was the insecurity of the fleet's principal war anchorage. There was an absence of anti-submarine defences (mines, nets, booms) when war came; nor were there any other defences, whether guns, searchlights, or fortifications. The Firth of Forth (Rosyth) and Cromarty Firth (Invergordon), too, lacked anti-submarine defences. Churchill's post-war explanation is that such defences would have involved 'enormous expense' in the last years of peace, at a time when the Cabinet was carefully scrutinizing every penny of naval expenditure; and no recommendations for the provision of defensive obstructions were made by the War Staff or the Sea Lords, probably because 'they did not think the danger had yet assumed a sufficiently practical form to justify such extraordinary measures'.[12] The fact is that there was small understanding of the

[12] *The World Crisis*, i. 383.

potentialities of the submarines. Because British submarines had never been able to keep the sea for periods sufficient to enable them to carry out operations so far afield as Scapa Flow is from Heligoland, the pre-war Admiralty had judged Scapa Flow, some 450 miles from the German bases, to be beyond enemy submarine range. It was not until after the war started that the U-boat's radius of action became known to the Navy, although when the first reports came in of German submarines in the vicinity of Scapa, it was believed that they must be operating from Norwegian territorial waters or the Danish Faeroe Islands.

The danger of submarines materialized as soon as the U-boat commanders found they could get as far as the Orkneys; this was in the first week of the war. Jellicoe did all he could to make the anchorage submarine-proof, although he hoped that the fierce tidal streams of the Pentland Firth would afford a measure of security. He immediately sank a few old merchant ships to block the lesser entrances to the Flow on the eastern side. Batteries were placed on either side of the southern and main entrance, Hoxa Sound, puny 12- and 3-pounder guns collected from the Grand Fleet battleships. Despite the C.-in-C.'s energy and improvisations, the measures for the safety of the anchorage were far from complete. Jellicoe's anxiety when the fleet was at anchor in Scapa Flow was so great that he preferred to keep the fleet at sea. Fortunately for the British, the Germans were not aware of the true situation. As the commander of their 3rd Battle Squadron revealed after the war, they 'gave the English credit of supposing they had protected their bases the same as we had'.[13]

Reports of submarines made the battle fleet jumpy when lying at anchor. 'The sighting of a submarine in Scapa produced the same sort of excitement as would a cobra in a drawing-room.' On 1 September occurred the 'First Battle of Scapa', as it was named by Grand Fleet wags. When a cruiser sighted a 'periscope', the ships put out their torpedo nets and raised steam at full speed, the small craft ran hither and yon searching for the intruder, guns were fired, etc. The innocent cause of the excitement is now thought to have been a seal, mistaken for the periscope of a submarine in the bad light. Jellicoe could take no chances, and the fleet was promptly hustled out to sea until 5 September, cruising

[13] Vice-Admiral Paul Behncke, in a review of Jellicoe's *The Grand Fleet, 1914–16*, *The Times*, 26 Apr. 1919.

between the north-east coast of Scotland and Norway. The 3rd Battle Squadron returned to Scapa, but the dreadnought battle fleet proceeded to the war anchorage of Loch Ewe on the north-west coast of Scotland, out of submarine range. It did not return to Scapa until 24 September, although it moved into the North Sea to support the destroyer sweep to the Bight on 10 September. Had the Germans known of Jellicoe's absence from the North Sea, the High Seas Fleet could have cut the cross-Channel communications with little risk, as he could not have reached the southern part of the North Sea in time.

The battle cruisers were not to be outdone by the battle fleet. One afternoon in October they steamed into the main anchorage of Cromarty Firth, off Invergordon, which was protected with guns but not anti-submarine nets. One of them sighted a ripple that had been made in shoal water by the bow-wave of a passing destroyer. Mistaking the ripple for the wake that follows a submarine periscope, which it closely resembled, she opened fire on the 'U-boat' with her 4-inch guns and was joined by at least one other ship. The bombardment damaged some roofs and chimneys in the village of Jemimaville and slightly wounded an infant in its cot. The ship's doctor treated the little girl, and the Flag-Lieutenant pacified, and indeed delighted, the parents with the news that two or three U-boats had been sunk without a single survivor! Admiral Sir Reginald Drax, who tells the story, concludes: 'Up to the time of going to press no Bar has yet been issued for the Battle of Jemimaville, but for those who were present it remains a treasured memory of the lighter side of the war.'

Particularly after the loss of the three 'Cressys' on 22 September had called dramatic attention to the submarine danger, Jellicoe feared that submarines might come into the Flow any night and send his fleet to the bottom. He pressed strongly for harbour defences. 'I *long* for a submarine defence at Scapa; it would give such a feeling of confidence. I can't sleep half so well inside as when outside, mainly because I feel we are risking such a mass of valuable ships in a place where, if a submarine did get in, she practically has the British Dreadnought Fleet at her mercy up to the number of her torpedoes.'[14] But the work progressed slowly.

The 'Second Battle of Scapa', on 16 October, followed sightings

[14] Jellicoe to Churchill, 30 Sept. 1914; Jellicoe MSS.

of periscopes and even of a torpedo. Again there was much milling and churning of ships in the waters of the Flow, and again Jellicoe withdrew his dreadnoughts, this time to Lough Swilly on the north coast of Ireland, more than 300 miles away. The Fleet was back at Scapa by 9 November. The situation remained tense. When Admiral Sir Percy Scott said goodnight to Jellicoe after an interview at Scapa, 13 November, the C.-in-C.'s terse reply was, 'I wonder.' Scott, looking back, could not imagine why the fleet was not destroyed. 'Either the German submarines lacked pluck, or possibly as the Commander-in-Chief of the Grand Fleet suggests in his book, the German mind could not believe that we would be such fools as to place our Fleet in a position where it was open to submarine or destroyer attack. . . . If the Germans had had half a dozen men of the stamp of our submarine commanders, we should now be a German colony.'[15] We hear of a battle-cruiser captain who seriously considered accepting an Admiralty post because he thought that the day of the capital ship was over and that the submarine reigned supreme on the seas!

Churchill felt that the C.-in-C. was unduly anxious about possible submarine attack on the fleet at Scapa. 'But Scapa,' he says, 'was believed to be protected by its currents from submarine attack.'[16] There are no currents at Scapa. It is true that the approaches to Hoxa Sound, the only wide and deep entrance, are through some eight miles of the turbulent tidal streams of the Pentland Firth, which would have made navigation by a submerged submarine very difficult. But as Jellicoe pointed out, 'It was recognised in the Fleet that a submarine could approach the entrance to Scapa Flow in spite of the Pentland Firth currents, by proceeding on the surface at night, or submerged with periscope showing by day . . .'[17] Once at the entrance of the Sound, it would have been plain sailing, and the exploit of *U-18* on 23 November (see below) showed that the difficulties of approach were not insuperable. There was, therefore, full justification for Jellicoe's belief in the possibility of attack, and his feelings were shared by all the flag officers.

One of them, Beatty, found the thought of the Grand Fleet 'gradually being pushed out of the North Sea' by the submarine

[15] Scott, *Fifty Years in the Royal Navy*, pp. 289–90.
[16] *The World Crisis*, i. 381.
[17] Jellicoe, 'A Reply to Criticism'.

and mine threats so intolerably humiliating that he took the unusual course of writing direct to the First Lord. 'No *seaman* can dispute that these three bases [Scapa Flow, Cromarty, Rosyth] could have been made *absolutely* safe from submarine attack during the two and a half months that the war has been in progress. . . . it is only Divine Providence that has saved us from an appalling disaster.'[18] And an officer in Beatty's flagship, H.M.S. *Lion*, wrote privately that, as a result of 'the incessant menace' from the U-boats, 'there are signs that the morale of officers and men (i.e. their cheerfulness, confidence, and optimism) is beginning to fail. They may be quite unreasonable, but they argue thus: In 2½ months it was expected that our bases would be made impregnable against all forms of torpedo attack. It has not been done. As a result we are hunted about the sea and have nowhere we can rest.'[19]

The fleet was heartened on 23 November by the successful attack of a patrol trawler on a German submarine which had succeeded in penetrating right into Hoxa Sound. The submarine was rammed, and though managing to crawl away to the eastward, she had finally to scuttle herself near the Pentland Skerries. This was one of the last submarine alarms, real or imaginary, until the last days of the war, since Scapa Flow was now gradually developed until, by the middle of 1915, it could be regarded as a safely protected harbour for the Grand Fleet. Sunken old merchant ships obstructed some of the channels, and booms were laid to bar entrance through other channels. Defensive minefields were laid in the principal entrances to the Flow. Seaplanes, nets, 4- and 6-inch guns, searchlights, and, later, hydrophones were installed. The battle fleet at last had a sense of security when at its base.

The submarine danger to the Grand Fleet when at sea remained, and it increasingly occupied the thoughts of the C.-in-C. He believed that they should not risk heavy ships until that threat had been 'minimized'. Among his suggestions for scotching the menace was the use of the battle fleet at latitude 60° to 61° (with the cruisers about 120 miles to the southward) to reinforce the Northern Patrol. This would enable him, besides the more

[18] Beatty to Churchill, 17 Oct. 1914; *The World Crisis*, i. 389–91. The last sentence is from a copy of the letter in the Beatty MSS.

[19] Commander the Hon. R. A. R. Plunkett (now Admiral the Hon. Sir Reginald Drax) to Richmond, 21 Oct. 1914; Richmond MSS.

effectively strangling German trade, to detach with safety his flotillas for submarine-hunting, since northern waters were free from the submarine danger. 'Only we must give up the idea— whilst so employed—of southerly Battle Fleet movements. The Battle and Light Cruisers could do so occasionally when I get a few more of the latter.' Churchill showed no interest in Jellicoe's proposal. For one thing, the battle fleet, cruising at sea for long periods, would attract submarines to the area. The C.-in-C. did not press the matter.[20]

3. THE MINE THREAT

Mines posed as great a danger to the Fleet, real and psychological, as did the torpedoes of the submarine. The Navy was unprepared for large-scale, indiscriminate mining warfare, despite the successful use of mines by both sides in the Russo-Japanese War. Mines simply were not taken seriously before the war. They were regarded (as were submarines) as 'the weapon of the weak' and as 'rather expensive luxuries'. 'In fact,' writes the Official Historian of British mining in the war, 'we despised the mine, we considered it was a weapon no chivalrous nation should use and acted accordingly.'[21] Complacency and a sense of security were bred by the Hague Convention of 1907, which permitted the laying of mines only in an enemy's territorial waters (that is, within three miles of the coast), and by the forceful disavowal of the use of mines, on grounds of humanity, by the chief German delegate at the Hague Conference. Then again, minelaying from submarines was unknown; surface minelayers could be dealt with by the coastal patrols, it was thought.

This is not to say that the Admiralty were taken completely by surprise in August 1914. They had since about 1908 suspected that the enemy would scatter mines off the British coasts, and

[20] Jellicoe to Churchill, 30 Sept. 1914, Jellicoe MSS.; *The World Crisis*, i. 384–7. The jitteriness of the C.-in-C., however justifiable, was communicated to the fleet. When Jellicoe was once, for a short time, unwell, the Rear-Admiral of the 4th Battle Squadron found Burney a more restful C.-in-C. 'By that, I mean he is not subject to such excursions and alarms as J.R.J. With J., the faintest rumour of a submarine sets the whole Fleet in motion. Burney, on the other hand, uses his judgment, and by taking legitimate responsibility thereby saves the expenditure of much useless energy. This seems greatly to his credit, as most *locum tenens* would err in the opposite direction.' Diary, 5 Feb. 1915; Duff MSS.

[21] Captain Lockhart Leith, *The History of British Minefields, 1914–1918*, p. 15, an undated Naval Staff monograph (early post-war).

beginning in 1909–10 they had made preparations against this form of warfare. In August 1914 there was a Trawler Reserve of 82 Admiralty-chartered ships trained in minesweeping, manned by ordinary fishing crews and officered mainly by mercantile officers enrolled in the Royal Naval Reserve. (The idea of using trawlers for minesweeping goes back to a suggestion by Lord Charles Beresford in 1907.) On the other hand, the Admiralty had not realized that the mine would be used indiscriminately and become a serious menace to both warships and merchant ships. This will explain why (apart from a few trawlers keeping the base clear) the total minesweeping force allotted to the protection of the Grand Fleet in the first months of the war consisted of only six minesweepers.

These fleet sweepers were somewhat ancient torpedo gunboats, which were the only type of minesweeping craft with sufficient speed to accompany the fleet. At the end of 1914 the six were augmented by six cross-Channel passenger boats. This only lasted a couple of months, when, having more or less learned their trade, they were ordered to the Dardanelles. The Grand Fleet Mine-sweeper Flotilla went on, terribly overworked until Jellicoe's 'herbaceous border', as it was known, began to bloom. I refer to the sloops, all named after flowers, that began to join the Grand Fleet in the latter part of 1915. Let it be said here that Captain Lionel Preston, who commanded the Grand Fleet Minesweeping Flotilla through 1916, was absolutely first class. He brought the minesweeping to a high degree of efficiency.

The 'A' sweep was the standard searching and clearance sweep throughout the war. This consisted of a single wire, regulated for depth by water 'kites', towed between two trawlers steaming abreast. Eventually as many as six, or even eight, sweepers abreast were used, linked by the sweep wires.

The Germans began the war with a large stock of efficient mines and the intention to use them against British warships and merchant shipping, as well as to defend their harbours and home waters. Except within 30 miles of Norway, the North Sea is very shallow and therefore particularly suitable for moored contact-type mines. In the very first day of the war a German minelayer planted a field of 180 mines about 30 miles off the seaside resort of Southwold on the Suffolk coast. She was quickly sunk by destroyers, but the new light cruiser *Amphion* struck one of these mines on 6 August and sank with the loss of 151 lives. (Tyrwhitt wrote privately that her commander, Captain Cecil H. Fox, was sent for by the King and congratulated on being the first Captain to lose his ship in the war!)

The Germans continued to lay mines in the open sea, in defiance of the Hague Convention. Tyrwhitt was appalled by the enemy's 'indiscriminate' and 'distinctly barbaric' mining. 'It will be months before the North Sea is safe for yachting . . .!'[22] The Germans met the formal British protest with the specious excuse that the Convention was not binding, since not all the belligerents had ratified it. (Russia was the sole exception.) Since it became risky for the Germans to use surface minelayers, beginning in June 1915 most mines were laid by special minelaying submarines. New minefields were constantly being found, forcing British ships to move with the greatest circumspection.

The vigorous German mining policy prompted the angry A.D.O.D., Richmond, to call the North Sea 'the German Ocean'. (The Victorians knew it as the 'North Sea' or 'German Ocean', so Richmond was not coining the name. But he was obviously using it in a sense not very flattering to the Navy.) In the first five months of the war the Royal Navy lost through mines, besides the *Amphion* and the dreadnought *Audacious*, the gunboat *Speedy*, a submarine, and eight trawlers and two drifters (lost while engaged in minesweeping), to which we should add 13 merchantmen (35,000 tons) and 17 fishing vessels. Altogether, the Germans laid over 43,000 mines during the war, about 25,000 of them in the North Sea and around the British Isles. They accounted for 214 British minesweepers, 46 warships (including five battleships and three cruisers), 225 auxiliaries, 259 merchant ships of 673,000 tons (84 more of 432,000 tons were damaged), and 63 fishing vessels.[23]

To cope with this danger, scores of trawlers and drifters were quickly added to the minesweeping service, minesweeping flotillas were established at the principal ports, and in mid-September a flag officer, Rear-Admiral E. F. B. Charlton, was appointed as Admiral of Minesweepers with the function of supervising and co-ordinating the work of the minesweepers on the East Coast.

[22] Tyrwhitt to Beauchamp Tyrwhitt, 9 Aug. 1914; Tyrwhitt MSS. The yachting remark should be read against the background of the general expectation of a short war at sea.

[23] Taffrail, *Swept Channels* (London, 1935), p. 335.

It was an organization quite distinct from the armed trawlers, yachts, drifters, and motor boats that was known as the Auxiliary Patrol.[24]

At the end of the war the British Minesweeping Service consisted of 726 ships of every description—mainly fishing trawlers, drifters, and regular naval vessels. The magnitude of the task is indicated in the statement of Admiral Bacon, Commanding the Dover Patrol, 1915–17, that the minesweepers in his area alone swept a distance equal to twelve times the circumference of the globe. 'Our minesweepers were at it eternally,' writes 'Taffrail'.

In September 1914 the Admiral of Minesweepers experimented unsuccessfully with the spotting of mines by seaplane. The waters of the North Sea, he reported, were too thick with mud and sand to spot mines from the air under general weather conditions. Seaplanes from the seaplane carrier *Campania* had no more luck in the summer of 1915. In the clear water of the Mediterranean, however, aerial reconnaissance of minefields, as developed in 1917–18, was a great aid to minesweeping. Kite balloons and aircraft were both used here.

But the sweepers, adequate enough for maintaining swept channels and clearing enemy minefields in coastal waters, were not fast enough to accompany the Fleet and protect it from mines while at sea. It was not until the invention of the paravane by Lieutenant C. Dennistoun Burney (the original idea was Commander Cecil V. Usborne's), an ingenious, sure, and not too costly device for cutting mine moorings, that ships had effective protection against mines.[25] Burney submitted his first plans in October 1914; the first set of paravanes was fitted to a destroyer for trials in May 1915. By August satisfactory performance had been achieved, and it was decided that all capital ships and

[24] See below, p. 357. In September 1915 the greater part of the minesweeping trawlers were absorbed in the Auxiliary Patrol and employed as patrol vessels generally, though held available for sweeping when required. The first months of the war altered the Navy's outlook on minesweepers. Whereas in pre-war days they were considered 'no better than lavatory attendants' (as Admiral Preston recalls), they were now almost fêted, as each fleet sweeper when in harbour was allowed to berth alongside a battleship and use its canteen and hear its band.

[25] The principle was that a ship never hit a mine with her stem, but was endangered by the fact that the bow wave washed the mine aside and it swung in again on its mooring, like an inverted pendulum, and hit the ship on the beam or quarter. The paravane (one on each side of the bow) prevented this by cutting the mine mooring on the return swing. The mine would then rise to the surface where it could be destroyed by gunfire.

cruisers should be equipped as soon as paravanes could be provided and ships' stems modified for towing them. The latter could only be done as ships came in for dry-docking, and so it was 1917 before the whole Fleet was equipped. At first paravanes were looked upon as a nuisance. Thus, when streaming them, if anything got foul in the cutter, either the speed of the squadron had to be reduced until it was cleared, with a consequent bad effect on the formation of a squadron; or the ship concerned had to make up a lot of ground when it had cleared the mess, utilizing additional fuel it could ill spare. But after the battle cruisers went through mines off the Firth of Forth early in 1918, cutting several with their paravanes, their was no question about their effectiveness. Paravanes had a major effect on strategy towards the end of the war, for they gave sufficient confidence to allow ships to operate freely in waters where there were no *known* minefields.[26]

Mines, no less than submarines, jeopardized the capital-ship superiority of the Grand Fleet. As early as the end of the second week of the war, Jellicoe was expressing deep concern over the underwater weapons.

You will have received my proposals for the next sweep into the North Sea. There is, of course, an element of considerable risk in traversing the North Sea with the Battle Fleet. It does not appear that mines are laid yet, but at any moment they may be, and even with mine-sweepers ahead, which can only be done at 10 knots speed, there is no certainty they will be discovered before a ship hits one. An objection to having the mine-sweepers ahead is that the slow speed this entails on the Battle Fleet makes it an easier prey to submarines.[27]

The first Grand Fleet Battle Orders, dated the same day, contained this admonition: 'When engaging the enemy's battlefleet it must

[26] Paravanes were actually used in the war for three distinct purposes: (a) as an explosive 'high-speed anti-submarine sweep' for use against submerged submarines; (b) as a 'high-speed mine sweep' for cutting channels through minefields at high speed, but not for clearing a minefield; (c) in the form of protector gear to protect individual ships from damage by moored mines. For (a) and (b), paravanes were fitted only to destroyers. For (c), they were fitted to larger warships and merchant ships. In the case of the merchant ships, from October 1916 a simpler and cheaper design of mine-cutting paravane was used—the 'M' type, or 'Otter'. But the paravane system when applied to merchant ships was under suspicion for a rather long time (David Bone, in his *Merchantmen-at-Arms*, speaks of 'the insistence with which they dive for a snug and immovable berth under our bilge keels'), and there were some failures with resultant losses.

[27] Jellicoe to Battenberg, 18 Aug. 1914; Jellicoe MSS.

be borne in mind that all German destroyers carry mines, and that it is therefore dangerous to cross a locality that has been occupied by those vessels.'[28] This warning was to have an important bearing on the outcome of the Dogger Bank action in January 1915.

The altered conditions produced by mines and submarines profoundly influenced Jellicoe's battle tactics. The presence of submarines in the North Sea from the start of the war, as far north as the Orkneys, forced the Grand Fleet to go to sea with a destroyer screen. One result was to reduce the effective fuel endurance of the fleet to that of destroyers (no more than 1,800 miles), although the battleships could steam 5,000 miles. This was nothing new, however. It had been foreseen and provided for before the war. What was new was summarized by Jellicoe in his historic letter to the Admiralty of 30 October 1914.

He expected the Germans to make the fullest use of submarines and minelayers in a fleet action. Since they could count on having their full complement of minelayers and submarines with the fleet only if the battle were fought in the southern part of the North Sea, it would be his object to fight in the northern part of that sea. This had the further advantage of being closer to his own bases. As for the actual battle tactics, Jellicoe foresaw that the German submarines would be used in one of two ways. First, with the cruisers (or possibly with the destroyers), the submarines being led by them to a position favourable for attacking the British battle fleet as it deployed. The Grand Fleet cruisers, if present in sufficient number and operating well in advance of the battle fleet, could defeat this move by 'forcing the enemy's cruisers to action at a speed which would interfere with submarine tactics'. Destroyers, acting with the cruisers, would deal with the U-boats. Second, the German submarines could be used with the battle fleet, being 'kept in a position in the rear, or to the flank, of the enemy's battlefleet, which would move in the direction required to draw our own Fleet into contact with the submarines'. This move, declared Jellicoe in the most pregnant passages,

can be countered by judicious handling of our battlefleet, but may and probably will, involve a refusal to comply with the enemy's tactics by moving in the invited direction. If, for instance, the enemy battlefleet were to turn away from an advancing Fleet, I should assume that

---

[28] Admiralty MSS. Throughout the war the only German torpedo craft that carried mines (four mines each) were the torpedo boats *A-1* to *A-25*.

the intention was to lead us over mines and submarines, and should decline to be so drawn.

I desire particularly to draw the attention of their Lordships to this point, since it may be deemed a refusal of battle [this letter, be it noted, was written on the eve of the Troubridge Court Martial], and, indeed, might possibly result in failure to bring the enemy to action as soon as is expected and hoped.

Such a result would be absolutely repugnant to the feelings of all British Naval Officers and men, but with new and untried methods of warfare new tactics must be devised to meet them. I feel that such tactics, if not understood, may bring odium upon me, but so long as I have the confidence of their Lordships I intend to pursue what is, in my considered opinion, the proper course to defeat and annihilate the enemy's battlefleet, without regard to uninstructed opinion or criticism.

The situation is a difficult one. It is quite within the bounds of possibility that half our battlefleet might be disabled by under-water attack before the guns opened fire at all, if a false move is made, and I feel that I must constantly bear in mind the great probability of such attack and be prepared tactically to prevent its success.

The safeguard against submarines will consist in moving the battle-fleet at very high speed to a flank before deployment takes place or the gun action commences. This will take us off the ground on which the enemy desires to fight, but it may, of course, result in his refusal to follow me. If the battlefleets remain within sight of one another, though not near the original area, the limited submerged radius of action and speed of the submarines will prevent the submarines from following without coming to the surface, and I should feel that after an interval of high speed manœuvring I could safely close.[29]

The new Board (Fisher had just become First Sea Lord) approved the C.-in-C.'s views (7 November) and assured him of their 'full confidence' in his contemplated battle tactics. Jellicoe sent the original of the Admiralty reply to his bankers for custody. The C.-in-C.'s letter had fateful consequences on his subsequent strategy and tactics. They were controlled by the fear that the mine and torpedo might, by chance or through a trap, suddenly alter the balance of naval strength. This fear was one of the two considerations that made Jellicoe so cautious. The other was his firm belief that maintenance of command of the sea, the principal

[29] Admiralty MSS.; reproduced in Admiral Sir Frederic C. Dreyer, *The Sea Heritage: a Study of Maritime Warfare* (London, 1955), pp. 82–4. (It was first published in Command Paper 1068 (1920), *Battle of Jutland. Official Despatches, with Appendices*, pp. 601–3.)

object of the Grand Fleet, could be achieved without the absolute necessity of defeating the High Seas Fleet, however desirable that might be. As Churchill afterwards epitomized the issue, 'Jellicoe was the only man on either side who could lose the war in an afternoon.'

4. *MATÉRIEL* FIASCOS

Threatened by mine and torpedo, the Royal Navy was in the frustrating position of being unable to retaliate effectively with the same weapons. Since the pre-war Admiralty had been a lukewarm believer in the value of the mine, early British wartime minelaying was, not surprisingly, a fiasco. There were but seven minelayers (old, 17-knot, 3,400-ton cruisers with a very small coal supply which had been fitted as minelayers with a laying capacity of a hundred mines each) at the start of the war and a relatively small stock of mines (some 4,000, and only about 9,000 as late as 1 February 1915). These mines, with their 5-cwt. sinkers, may have been perfect in the mud in Fareham Creek, but they did not hold in the North Sea on sand or shingle. One, for example, was found to have dragged 18 miles in three weeks. For this reason the hundreds of mines laid east of Dover Straits at the outbreak of war, to shield the Channel passage of the B.E.F. against large ships, were, as Admiral Oliver puts it, 'an infernal nuisance'. In June 1915 we find Jellicoe bitterly complaining that 'as fast as our mines have been laid, they have drifted away, owing to our idiotic habit of using too small mooring rope'. This was not all.

British mines were more dangerous to the Navy than to the enemy. They had the nasty habit of blowing off the sterns of the minelayers. If, as often happened, the mines broke adrift, the safety apparatus did not always work. The mines commonly failed to explode when struck by a ship, and if they did explode, frequently did little damage. Many German warships carried a British mine mounted on a stand as a souvenir! Fisher's bitter comment in his *Memoirs* is rather ironic in view of the neglect of mining warfare during his years at Whitehall. 'Our mines were squibs; the enemy's ship always steamed away and got into harbour, while ours always went down plump.' British mines remained inefficient and unreliable as late as 1917. In April 1917 only 1,500 mines of the stock of 20,000 were fit for laying, and it was not until the following September that an efficient type of mine, the 'H.II', became available in quantity—copied 'nut for nut and bolt for bolt' from a captured German mine of a type in use since the start of the war! During the remainder of the war, the Admiralty, by then a convert to mines, had ample stocks of efficient types, which were used to attack German submarines, harass enemy coastal traffic, and protect certain waters. All told, British minelayers deposited about 131,000 mines during the war, and there were 60,000 in hand when the war ended. By that time there were about 100 minelayers of all types in commission, the largest carrying 400 mines, the whole with a laying capacity of 5,000 mines.

H.M.S. *Vernon*, the Torpedo School at Portsmouth, was as badly adrift over torpedoes as over mines. The torpedoes had not been sufficiently tested with war-heads on, and the war-heads were too heavy. The result was that when a submarine got a beam shot at a German dreadnought at about 400 yards range (17 December 1914, see below, p. 141), the torpedo ran to the bottom. When the torpedoes did hit, they often produced little effect. Thus, Fisher was infuriated when a British submarine scored a fair hit on an enemy 'barrier breaker' but did not sink her. 'Our torpedoes seem to be filled with sawdust!!! The mine-breaker steamed off gaily to Wilhelmshaven! and reported herself as not much damaged! There's a heavy reckoning coming for everyone connected with the *Vernon* during the last four years . . . I hope to get a good many officers disgraced for it all.'[30] Fisher's extreme irritation with the *Vernon* extended to the inadequate wireless with which it fitted the submarines. Whereas in the spring of 1915 the German submarines were able to send 250 miles (Intelligence knew the range from the intercepts), British submarine wireless could send a mere 50 miles.

Although Fisher ranted and raved about sacking the 'principal culprits' in the *Vernon* and other *matériel* departments (he preferred that they be shot or hanged), he was unsuccessful in weeding out many of the inefficient officers. Thus, Charlton, who had been Assistant Director of Torpedoes, 1911–14, and was now Admiral of Minesweeping ('quite unfit for so immense a job', and he 'ought to have been blown from a gun', thought Fisher), and Captain Philip W. Dumas, the Assistant Director of Torpedoes, two particular *bêtes noires* of Fisher, stayed on until December 1915 and

[30] Fisher to Jellicoe, 16 Apr. 1915; *Fear God and Dread Nought*, iii. 197.

early 1917, respectively. 'Everyone,' he justly complained, 'is far too careful about susceptibilities and interfering with other people's business, forgetting that the fate of the Empire is at stake in this War and that NOTHING should interfere with efficiency.'[31]

The course of the war was to reveal other *matériel* failures even more serious: the shell and the lack of flash tightness in the turrets.

But we are getting ahead of our story. In the autumn of 1914 the Cabinet, the Fleet (including the C.-in-C.), and many officers at the Admiralty (Richmond, for one) urged an aggressive policy of mining in the North Sea, particularly in the Heligoland Bight. They were opposed by the Chief of the War Staff and by the First Lord, who were willing only (beginning in October) to introduce controlled anti-submarine mining for the permanent defence of Scapa Flow and various other harbours, and to mine certain proclaimed areas off the English and Scottish coasts, notably the Straits of Dover (the latter was completed in February 1915). The general view at the Admiralty was that large-scale mining would impede British submarine and fleet operations in those waters. Sturdee rejected all offensive mining proposals with the argument that they wanted the Germans to come out and fight. His successor, Oliver, also had serious reservations about a vigorous mining policy.

A long discussion took place in the Cabinet on 12–13 October on the expediency of further mining the North Sea, whether of the mouths of the Scheldt and Rhine, or, as strongly favoured by Kitchener, at the entrance of the Bight of Heligoland. Since Churchill and his naval advisers were unanimously opposed to it, no decision was reached. In the teeth of demands for a strong mining policy, Churchill circulated a strong paper in the Cabinet summarizing his views. He rejected 'ambush mining', or the scattering about of mines in patches or short lines around enemy ports, or at the approaches to British ports or landing places, on the chance of enemy ships running into them. 'The chance is not great. The seas are very large, the area mined, even if on a great scale, very small.' And since the position of even one's own minefields could not be accurately known (mines had the tendency to drag with their moorings in tide and sea), every patch of mines laid hampered the movements of the Royal Navy. 'You instinctively try to avoid the waters you have yourself fouled.'

[31] Fisher to Jellicoe, 29 Apr. 1915; *ibid.*, p. 207.

79

The 'general failure' of German ambush mining strengthened these opinions. Only two British warships had been sunk by mines in the first month and a half. Churchill's conclusion was that ambush mines 'should be very sparingly used, used chiefly in sight of land, and that not very much is to be expected from them'. Ambush mines did have a tactical use. 'To lay mines in the course of an enemy before or during a battle or across his homeward path if he has put to sea, may be operations of the greatest consequence and value.' As regards 'blockade mining', it would accomplish nothing 'unless superior force is maintained in the neighbourhood of the minefield to prevent the mines being removed. . . . It would not be possible to keep such a watch now without exposing the vessels so engaged to almost certain destruction from the enemy's submarines.' (It was an objective of the German policy of mining the British coasts to provoke the British into a close blockade.) Neither ambush mines nor blockade mines could stop enemy submarines from putting to sea.[32]

Kitchener was shocked by the paper. The weak mining policy, in his opinion, increased the chances of a successful German invasion. Churchill's mining views underwent no change. 'We have never laid one we have not afterwards regretted,' he lectured Jellicoe early in the new year. 'It is a delusion to suppose that mines will stop submarines unless strung together in a regular net. . . . Mine in haste and sweep at leisure! It would be folly to mine while the good information lasts.'[33]

Fisher, a convert to mining, had all the zeal of a convert. The 'pusillanimous' mining policy enraged him. Once back at his old post, he tirelessly advocated the sowing of the North Sea with mines on such a scale as to automatically establish a complete blockade of Germany. He summed up his position in a strong memorandum of 31 December 1914: 'Minelaying appears desirable from three points of view: To place the German Fleet under the same handicaps as our own ships are subject to in the North Sea ['If our main Fleets wish to proceed to a point on the East Coast, they can only do so by making a wide detour, or by hugging the coast along a mine-swept channel.']; to give

[32] Churchill's Cabinet Paper, 'Notes on Mining', 18 Oct. 1914; Asquith MSS., reproduced with slight changes in *The World Crisis*, i. 519–21.

[33] Churchill to Jellicoe, 18 Jan. 1915; Jellicoe MSS. He never regretted his views on mining. See *The World Crisis*, i. 519. The 'good information' reference is to the work of Room 40. See below, pp. 132-4.

protection to our East Coast trade [which had already been seriously affected by German minelaying] by hampering the enemy's movements [that is, of minelayers]; and to serve as a blockade of the German ports.'[34] The last *desideratum*, a favourite of Jellicoe's, meant that, a close blockade of the German bases by surface ships being impossible on account of the submarine danger, only an extensive mining policy in enemy waters would give the Navy adequate warning of the exit of German forces. The latter would, in clearing a channel, give the British the warning signal they were coming out.

In January 1915 the first British minefield was laid in the Heligoland Bight, off the Amrum Bank. Two others were laid in the Bight early in May 1915, and this was the extent of offensive mining while Churchill was at the Admiralty. His opposition, and that of the Foreign Office, which was always afraid of the reactions of the neutrals, dished an aggressive mining policy until 1917.

Returning to the autumn of 1914, we find that Admiralty mining policy enraged the many mining enthusiasts among the naval writers and officers, who wanted to see the enemy mined into his ports. It was one more count in the indictment against the First Lord.

[34] Fisher's memorandum, 'Mine Laying', 31 Dec. 1914; Lennoxlove MSS.

V

The Revolution at Whitehall

(OCTOBER 1914)

He [Fisher] was far more right than wrong, and his drive and life-force made the Admiralty quiver like one of his great ships at its highest speed.

CHURCHILL, *The World Crisis*.

I. TWO SCAPEGOATS: CHURCHILL AND BATTENBERG

THE NAVY was, by October, in the mood for a shake-up at Whitehall. The slow progress of anti-submarine defences at the principal East Coast bases angered the officers of the Grand Fleet, from Jellicoe down, as did the weak mining policy. Many officers, afloat and at the Admiralty, were disgusted with the defensive strategy. 'We are only playing at war,' moaned Beatty. 'We are as nervous as cats, afraid of losing lives, losing ships, and running risks. We are ruled by Panic Law, and until we risk something, shall never gain anything.'[1] Richmond was unhappy for the same reason. 'If we harried the Germans more, they would be less free to harry us.'[2] Lieutenant-Commander Ramsay's opinion was probably typical of the junior officers.'I don't like the feeling of waiting to see what the enemy will do first . . . we should have a plan ready which will force the Germans to fight under conditions we desire . . .'[3] As for the Government, the falling off of confidence in the Navy had reached the point where the Prime Minister believed the Germans 'are so much better than we are on the sea'.[4]

[1] Beatty to Lady Beatty, 8 Oct. 1914; Chalmers, *Beatty*, p. 161, which includes this extract as part of a letter of 2 November.

[2] Diary, 21 Oct. 1914; *Portrait of an Admiral*, p. 121.

[3] Diary, n.d. (autumn, 1914); Rear-Admiral W. S. Chalmers, *Full Cycle: the Biography of Admiral Sir Bertram Home Ramsay* (London, 1959), pp. 21–2.

[4] Asquith to Mrs. Edwin Montagu, 4 Nov. 1914; Robert Blake, *The Unknown Prime Minister: the Life and Times of Andrew Bonar Law, 1858–1923* (London, 1955), p. 232. The same day the Prime Minister reported to the King on the Cabinet meeting that day: 'The Cabinet were of opinion that this [*Coronel*] incident, like the escape of the *Goeben*, the loss of the *Cressy*, and her two sister-cruisers, and that of the *Hermes* last week is not creditable to the officers of the Navy.' Asquith MSS.

Churchill was held to blame, for the most part unfairly, for the series of shocks administered to the nation's absolute confidence in the supremacy of the Navy: the *Goeben*, the 'Cressys', the 'inactivity' of the Fleet, and the merchant-ship sinking sprees on which the armed merchant ship *Kaiser Wilhelm der Grosse* and the cruisers *Emden* and *Karlsruhe* were engaged, and which suggested to many Englishmen that their trade overseas was at Germany's mercy. It was being said on many sides that the First Lord was a brilliant but erratic amateur whose indomitable energy and invincible cocksureness led him to interfere in technical and strategic matters beyond his province and competence, even to taking the conduct of naval operations out of the hands of his professional advisers. The feeling at sea was not very different, as witness Beatty: 'Winston I hear does practically everything and some more besides.' 'If he would either leave matters entirely alone at the Admiralty, which w^d be the best thing to do, or give it his entire and complete attention, we might get forward, but this flying about and putting his fingers to pies which do not concern him is bound to lead to disaster.' 'If we only had a Kitchener at the Admiralty we could have done so much and the present state of chaos in naval affairs would never have existed. It is inconceivable the mistakes and blunders we have made and are making.'[5] Antwerp was pretty nearly the last straw for the critics.

Churchill had left London on the evening of 2 October for a week-end visit to Dunkirk. At 11 p.m., when 20 miles out, en route to Dover, the train was suddenly reversed and returned to London. Churchill was rushed to Kitchener's home. There he heard from his distressed colleagues that the Belgian Government intended to evacuate Antwerp, under siege since 28 September, the next day. The city would probably fall in a few days, and this would pose an immediate threat to the Channel ports and cross-Channel communications. Early in the morning of 3 October the British Government decided to send aid to the defence in the shape of the Royal Marine Brigade. With Kitchener's blessings, the First Lord returned to Victoria Station and set out for Antwerp to keep the Government abreast of developments. He arrived there in mid-afternoon. The Germans, realizing how much Churchill's presence had strengthened the Belgian Government's will to resist, put 20,000 marks and the Iron Cross on his head. Feeling it was his

[5] Beatty to Lady Beatty, 19 Aug., 19, 20 Oct. 1914; Beatty MSS.

'duty to see the matter through', he proposed his resignation to the Prime Minister (4 October), with Runciman (President of the Board of Trade) to succeed him, so that he could take command in the field of the British forces engaged in Antwerp. Churchill's telegram, read to the Cabinet by Asquith on the 5th, provoked 'roars of incredulous laughter'. Only Kitchener saw nothing amusing in this gesture of the ex-Lieutenant of Hussars. He offered to make Churchill a lieutenant-general if the Prime Minister would release him from the Government. Churchill, I am certain, would have been superb as a field commander. He never got the chance. Asquith telegraphed 'a most decided negative', saying he could not be spared from the Admiralty and ordering him peremptorily to return, which he did on 7 October.

The Royal Marine Brigade had arrived in Antwerp on 4 October, and, at Churchill's express request (3 October), the 1st and 2nd Naval Brigades (raw naval reservists), on 5 October. These three infantry brigades made up the Royal Naval Division. With the Belgian troops they delayed but could not prevent the capitulation of Antwerp on 10 October to overwhelming force. Casualties were heavy: 20,000 Belgians, 1,500 British of the Naval Division interned in the Netherlands and a thousand missing. Churchill's post-war justification for throwing everything into the defence of Antwerp was that 'Antwerp was not only the sole stronghold of the Belgian nation: it was also the true left flank of the Allied front in the west. It guarded the whole line of the Channel ports. It threatened the flanks and rear of the German armies in France. It was the gateway from which a British army might emerge at any moment upon their sensitive and even vital communications. No German advance to the sea-coast, upon Ostend, upon Dunkirk, upon Calais and Boulogne, seemed possible while Antwerp was unconquered.'[6] It is Churchill's claim that the British naval detachment had prolonged the city's defence for several crucial days (seven, to be exact, as the Belgians would have begun to evacuate Antwerp on 3 October but for the promise of the Naval Division), and had given the Allies time to secure Dunkirk and Calais.[7] However that may be, at the time the country and the Navy regarded the Antwerp expedition as a fiasco and blamed Churchill, although it was Kitchener who had

[6] *The World Crisis*, i. 332.
[7] *Ibid.*, pp. 378–9.

initiated it. The Navy particularly chastised the First Lord for using untrained men in the Royal Naval Division and for the internment of so many of the Division. Richmond's thoughts on Antwerp probably reflected naval opinion generally. 'I don't mind his tuppenny untrained rabble going, but I do strongly object to 2000 invaluable marines being sent to be locked up in the fortress & become prisoners of war if the place is taken. They are our last reserve. No Board of Admiralty with two-pennyworth of knowledge & backbone would have allowed marines to be used in such a way. . . . It is a tragedy that the Navy should be in such lunatic hands at this time.'[8] Beatty fumed that Churchill had made 'such a darned fool of himself over the Antwerp débâcle. The man must have been mad to have thought he could relieve [Antwerp] . . . by putting 8000 half-trained troops into it.'[9] Churchill's critics ascribed the 'failure' to the vanity and mock-heroism of the First Lord, a charge with more than a shred of truth.[10]

By late October Churchill's position had become very shaky. He inspired such a profound mistrust among his Cabinet colleagues (to say nothing of the Opposition), mainly on account of his flamboyance, excessive self-confidence, and vaulting ambition to get to the top, that few of them were prepared to lift a finger to keep him in office. The country was in the mood for a sacrifice to assuage its deep disappointment over the Navy's alleged lacklustre performance. It got its burnt offering—but it was not Churchill.

In 1909, Lord Knollys, King Edward's Private Secretary, had predicted that Prince Louis, although 'even more English than you or I', would find himself the object of public hostility if things went wrong in time of war.[11] Prince Louis himself had realized that his position would be very difficult and possibly untenable if war came. This came to pass. He became the victim of a mean and foolish clamour against him because of his German birth. (It did not help him that his wife's brother-in-law was Prince Henry, the Emperor's brother and High Admiral of the German Navy.) All the reputable newspapers were on his side, decrying the cruel prejudice and expressing confidence that he was performing his

[8] Diary, 4 Oct. 1914; *Portrait of an Admiral*, pp. 111–12.
[9] Beatty to Lady Beatty, 18 Oct. 1914; Beatty MSS.
[10] See the undated entry in Asquith's diary for October, in the Earl of Oxford and Asquith, *Memories and Reflections* (London, 1928, 2 vols.), ii. 54–5.
[11] Knollys to Esher, 22 Oct. 1909; Esher MSS.

duties ably. It was only the sensational organs of the press, led by such (erstwhile) scum as the weekly *John Bull*, that raised the German cry. As the latter declaimed on 24 October: 'Blood is said to be thicker than water; and we doubt whether all the water in the North Sea could obliterate the blood-ties between the Battenbergs and the Hohenzollerns when it comes to a question of a life and death struggle between Germany and ourselves.'

The whole charge was perfectly ridiculous and the outcry absurd. The Royal Navy has had few more devoted and more high-minded officers than Prince Louis. His brother, Prince Henry of Battenberg, had already given his life for his adopted country, a nephew, Prince Maurice of Battenberg, was killed in the retreat from Mons, and his (Prince Louis's) two sons were serving in the Royal Navy. The King noted in his diary, when Battenberg resigned, 'There is no more loyal man in the country.'

The fact remains that the man-in-the-street—the less enlightened representatives of that amorphous group—was suspicious of Prince Louis and prepared to believe the rumours that circulated in September that he was locked up in the Tower. Both Prince Louis and his Naval Assistant, Rear-Admiral Beamish, received many anonymous letters. The press, too, received many letters, very few of which were published. Thus, the *Globe*, although it had no doubt whatsoever about Prince Louis's honour and loyalty, reported (26 October): 'We receive day by day a constantly growing stream of correspondence, in which the wisdom of having an officer who is of German birth as the professional head of the Navy is assailed in varying terms. We would gladly dismiss all these letters from our mind, but we cannot. They are too numerous, too insistent, and too obviously the expression of a widespread feeling.'

Prince Louis's biographer puts the onus for the campaign against him on 'a few Senior Officers, mostly retired, who had always been jealous of Prince Louis' on account of his ability, the high regard and affection of his subordinates, and the complete confidence placed in him by the Admiralty and senior officers.[12] This squares with Prince Louis's sentiments. His correspondence with Lord Fisher has more than one reference to the attitude of his brother officers towards him. Here is one example: 'Whilst I was in I heard by chance what the reasons were which [Admirals]

[12] Kerr, *Prince Louis of Battenberg*, p. 246.

PLATE I

THE RT. HON. WINSTON CHURCHILL, First Lord of the
Admiralty, Oct. 1911–May 1915, and his successor, May 1915–Dec.
1916, THE RT. HON. ARTHUR JAMES BALFOUR

[Photograph: Radio Times Hulton Picture Library

PLATE II

ADMIRAL SIR HENRY JACKSON
First Sea Lord, May 1915–Dec. 1916

[Drawing by Francis Dodd · Imperial War Museum

ADMIRAL PRINCE LOUIS OF BATTENBERG
First Sea Lord, Dec. 1912–Oct. 1914

[Photograph · Radio Times Hulton Picture Library

Beresford and Lambton and all that tribe gave out *urbi et orbi* against my going Second [Sea] Lord—or any other Lord and fleet command presumably—viz. that I was a d—d German, who had no business in the British Navy and that the Service for that reason did not trust me. I know the latter to be a foul lie . . . It was, however, such a blow to me that I seriously contemplated resigning my command there and then.'[13]

The Admiral had had enough by late October. Churchill 'up to the end stood by me and first the Prime Minister too, but the pressure from without became at last too strong—at least the Cabinet did not feel themselves to be strong enough to protect one of their principal servants.· The moment this was made clear to me I walked out of the building and gave those in charge to understand that they would neither see nor hear from me until Peace was signed.'[14] Prince Louis sent his resignation to the First Lord on 28 October. It was prompted by the 'painful conclusion that at this juncture my birth and parentage have the effect of impairing in some respects my usefulness on the Board of Admiralty.'[15] Churchill accepted the resignation the next day and paid tribute to his work. Although a number of prominent people expressed their sincere regrets to him (Jellicoe was one) or wrote to *The Times* to express their sense of shame, the resignation was regarded even by many of Prince Louis's supporters as the proper thing to have done, since his position had been weakened, and national confidence was a vital asset in war.

The campaign of innuendo and defamation in the popular press by itself could not have brought matters to a head. The politicians were not that cowardly, disloyal, and unjust. Prince Louis was openly accused of weakness in not keeping a proper check on Churchill and allowing him to run the whole show. For instance, Vice-Admiral Sir Stanley Colville could write to the Second Sea Lord that the talk about Prince Louis being a spy was ' "rot", but from all one has heard and knows it is pretty well self-evident he had become a nonentity and a simple tool in W.C.'s hand'. This, too, was Fisher's opinion. 'Battenberg was a cypher and Winston's facile dupe!'[16]

[13] Battenberg to Fisher, 24 July 1906; Lennoxlove MSS.
[14] Battenberg to Jellicoe, 23 Nov. 1914; Jellicoe MSS.
[15] *The World Crisis*, i. 400–1.
[16] Colville to Hamilton, 10 Nov. 1914, Hamilton MSS; Fisher to Jellicoe, 20 Dec. 1914, *Fear God and Dread Nought*, iii. 100.

There was a closely related factor, probably the decisive one, namely, that Prince Louis was believed to be lacking in vigour and imagination as a result of poor health. Fisher singled out as one of the country's 'damnable war difficulties: Our directing Sea Lord played out.'[17] George Lambert, the Civil Lord of the Admiralty at that time, informed me (1950) that Prince Louis's resignation was 'due solely to his inefficiency', and he told how members of the Board were shocked to see the First Sea Lord in his office in the morning leisurely reading *The Times*. Lord Esher furnishes contemporary confirmation. 'It has been felt for some time that the Board of Admiralty required renovating; the personal attacks upon Prince Louis, grossly unfair as they are, have brought the matter to a head. . . . More driving power was required, and they will supply it.'[18] The 'they' were Sir Arthur Wilson and Lord Fisher, the 'septuagenarian sea-dogs', as Asquith called them.

It is significant that Prince Louis wrote few minutes and memoranda in the first three months of the war. It was Churchill who wrote the important minute of 18 September, four days before the 'Cressys' were sunk: 'These cruisers ought not to continue on this beat', etc. It was Churchill who wrote the important minutes in the weeks preceding the Battle of Coronel. Indeed, according to Balfour's Private Secretary, Prince Louis's nickname was 'quite concur'.[19] There is little hint in the unpublished papers or in published works of what Prince Louis was doing or thinking.

The initiative for Battenberg's resignation definitely came from the Cabinet, which, Admiral Oliver says, 'wanted him removed, and Mr. Churchill asked him to resign, and I had to take him the letter. He took it very well, and I felt very sorry for him.'[20] Further evidence that Battenberg was *asked* to resign is Fisher's statement to the Dardanelles Commission that he had been nominated on 20 October, 'but there was a struggle to get me there which resulted in my not arriving till the 30th October'.[21] Finally, we know that Churchill saw the King on 27 October, the

[17] Fisher to Pamela McKenna, 3 Oct. 1914; *ibid.*, p. 60.

[18] Journals, 4 Nov. 1914; M. V. Brett and Oliver, Viscount Esher (eds.), *Journals and Letters of Reginald, Viscount Esher* (London, 1934–8, 4 vols.), iii. 193–4. (Hereafter cited as *Esher.*)

[19] Kenneth Young, *Arthur James Balfour* (London, 1963), p. 351.

[20] Oliver MSS.

[21] *Dardanelles Commission.* See below, p. 201, note 2.

day before the Admiral's resignation, and suggested that Fisher replace Prince Louis.[22]

2. FISHER'S RESTORATION

Churchill decided, with Asquith's full support, to recall Fisher, having convinced himself through close study (he had been seeing him constantly) that the Admiral retained his vigour and mental alertness. Churchill wanted him despite the fears of his Naval Secretary, Rear-Admiral Henry F. Oliver, that the dynamic and intolerant Fisher might not work in double harness with a strong First Lord of his type (Churchill was confident he could manage him), and despite the serious misgivings of King George, who did all he could to prevent the appointment.

The King, on 27 October, suggested Admiral Sir Hedworth Meux. Churchill declared that he could never work with him. The King then brought up Sir Henry Jackson's name. Churchill conceded his scientific and intellectual attainments but did not think he would do . Nor would he accept Sturdee. The King appealed to the Prime Minister the next day (through Stamford-ham) to prevent the appointment. Asquith backed Churchill up. None of the King's nominees would do, he maintained. Meux would not inspire the confidence of the Navy, Jackson lacked personality, Sturdee was more suited to command a fleet than to be in an office. Besides, if Fisher were not brought back, Churchill would resign. Stamfordham saw a ray of hope. He pointed out that Churchill had intimated to the King on the previous day that he would not be sorry to leave the Admiralty: the work was uncongenial and, moreover, he wanted to see action as a soldier

[22] Lord Stamfordham's memorandum, 27–30 Oct. 1914; Windsor MSS. To wind up the sad story of Prince Louis (or the Marquess of Milford Haven as he became in 1917) on a happier note: he was invited to preside over the Royal Navy Club dinner given in London on 21 July 1921. Hundreds of members, an exceptionally large turnout, came up specially to attend this dinner as a gesture to the Admiral. When his health was proposed and he stood up to answer the toast, the cheering is said to have been the greatest ever heard in the Navy Club (founded in 1765) and continued for over five minutes. Older members agree that there has never been anything like this incident in the history of the Club. This moving occasion was followed on 10 August by Lord Milford Haven's special promotion ('to right a great wrong', said the First Lord, Lord Lee of Fareham) to the rank of Admiral of the Fleet on the retired list, to date 4 August, the seventh anniversary of the outbreak of the war. There was only one precedent for such an honour. A month later, on 11 September 1921, the Admiral died.

in France. 'The Prime Minister scouted the idea and said Mr. Churchill has a most intimate knowledge of the Navy and his services in his present position could not be dispensed with or replaced.' Stamfordham threw out A. K. Wilson's name with no more success.

The King saw the Prime Minister on the afternoon of the 29th. 'The King declared that he eliminated all personal feelings: his one wish was that what was done should be in the best interests of the Navy. The Service did not trust Lord Fisher and H.M. feared his return to the Admiralty would be detrimental to the Navy. He could not however oppose his ministers in this selection but felt it his duty to record his protest. The Prime Minister rejoined, "perhaps a less severe term, 'misgivings', might be used by your Majesty."' Later in the day the King signed the appointment and wrote to the Prime Minister, for the record, that he had approved the appointment 'with some reluctance and misgivings. I readily acknowledge his great ability and administrative power but at the same time I cannot help feeling that his presence at the Admiralty will not inspire the Navy with that confidence which ought to exist especially when we are engaged in so momentous a war. I hope that my fears prove to be groundless.'[23]

Though in his seventy-fourth year, Fisher was quite fit for the job. The King had to confess, when he received the Admiral at Buckingham Palace on 30 October (he had not seen him for six years): 'He seems as young as ever.' Lord Riddell, after meeting him at a luncheon party, noted: 'He is a wonderful old boy—full of life and energy. At lunch he got up and showed us how he taught a Polish countess dancing in the presence of King Edward. He waltzed round the room in great style.'[24] Major-General Callwell, Director of Military Operations at the War Office, who saw Fisher on official business early in 1915, found him younger than he had seemed during his Mediterranean command (1899–1902).

He covered the ground at such a pace that I was speedily toiling breathless and dishevelled far in the rear. . . . to have a hotch-potch of Shakespeare, internal combustion engines, chemical devices for smoke screens, principles of the utilization of sea power, Holy Writ, and

[23] The source for this paragraph and the preceding one is Stamfordham's memorandum (cited in the preceding footnote).

[24] Diary, 3 Feb. 1915; *Lord Riddell's War Diary, 1914–1918* (London, 1933), p. 58.

details of ship construction dolloped out on one's plate, and to have to bolt it then and there, imposes a strain on the internal economy that is greater than this will stand. After an interview with the First Sea Lord you suffered from that giddy, bewildered, exhausted sort of feeling that no doubt has you in thrall when you have been run over by a motor bus without suffering actual physical injury.[25]

The appointment was greeted with 'Hosannas' in the country and in the Navy. (Only the *Morning Post* among the major newspapers did not rejoice.) It was expected that Fisher would keep Churchill in his place and at the same time restore public confidence in the Navy, particularly through a more aggressive strategy. Thus, it was Beatty's appraisal that Fisher was

the best they could have done, but I wish he was ten years younger. He still has fine zeal, energy, and determination, coupled with low cunning, which is eminently desirable just now. He also has courage and will take any responsibility. He will recognize that his position is absolutely secure and will rule the Admiralty and Winston with a heavy hand. He has patriotism, and is a firm believer in the good qualities of the Navy, that it can do anything and will go anywhere, and please God we shall change our present method for a strong offensive policy.[26]

Admiral Wemyss was among the relatively few doubting Thomases. He found the news of Fisher's appointment 'horrible', fearing that Fisher would soon be busy with 'internal intrigue', and he predicted a falling out between him and Churchill. 'They will be as thick as thieves at first until they differ on some subject, probably as to who is to be No. 1, when they will begin to intrigue against each other.'[27] Beatty, too, on second thought, was not at all sure the two would work together in harmony for long.

Various other appointments made at about this time promised to instil more life into the Admiralty. Sir Arthur Wilson turned down Churchill's offer to be C.O.S. He would accept no official position, since he did not relish having to side with Fisher or Churchill against the other. But he was willing to come back in an entirely unofficial (and unpaid) capacity. He gave advice when asked and worked on a wide range of special tasks. He and Churchill's new and very competent and knowledgeable Naval

[25] Major-General Sir C. E. Callwell, *Experiences of a Dug-Out, 1914–1918* (London, 1920), pp. 121–2.
[26] Beatty to Lady Beatty, 2 Nov. 1914; Chalmers, *Beatty*, pp. 160–1.
[27] Letter of 31 Oct. 1914; Wester Wemyss, *Wester Wemyss*, p. 186.

Secretary, Commodore Charles de Bartolomé (who looked like Napoleon and even had some of his mannerisms), were added to the War Staff Group, and the Second Sea Lord was dropped. Admiral Sir Henry Jackson was now often called in, although not a regular member.

Rear-Admiral Henry F. Oliver, who had been Naval Secretary to the First Lord since 14 October, and, previously, D.N.I.,[28] replaced Sturdee as C.O.S., with the rank of Acting Vice-Admiral (5 November). He was unruffled and untiring (he regularly worked 14 hours a day, Sundays included, and never took leave), a down-to-earth sort of individual, not a great leader, not an inspiring person, but full of good common sense and a big man in many ways. The Navy regarded him as a great seaman and a very wise old bird. His well-known aversion to saying anything it was not absolutely necessary to say, coupled with a notably impassive countenance, no doubt explain his nickname, 'Dummy'. He had the distinction of being the worst-dressed officer in the Royal Navy! Oliver held all the strings in his hands—indeed, too much so.[29]

The War Staff had slumbered under Sturdee. For example, he had done nothing to kill the deep-rooted practice among flag officers of sending cruisers to patrol on fixed beats, even after the loss of the 'Cressys' and the *Hawke*. 'Sturdee takes any suggestions as personal insults to his own intelligence,' complained the A.D.O.D. Oliver has made the same complaint. Sturdee was 'a pompous man who would never listen to anyone else's opinion. I could not stick him.' Beatty, who had nothing against Sturdee personally, was no kinder: 'Sturdee has been one of the curses to the Navy [as C.O.S.] . . . He was principally responsible for all our disasters afloat, and Fisher showed his acumen by turning him

[28] 'Blinker' Hall had succeeded Oliver as D.N.I. He had exceptional gifts for intelligence work, including a natural aptitude for exploiting all possible sources of intelligence and ensuring that the useful was sifted from the mass of unreliable intelligence, and 'a flair for linking together items of information which, at first sight did not appear to be inter-related'.

[29] Oliver was 'so busy allocating craft for convoys of troops across the Channel, of store-ships to the Fleet, or of convoys to vessels carrying turrets & gun about . . . that he has no time for strategical schemes. He is doing the work of a Quartermaster-General, a Chief of Staff & a Director of Operations & Defence, all rolled into one. It is impossible for work to be done properly in such a way. The principle of decentralising & trusting subordinates has yet gained no ground; so seniors are worked to death & juniors find no use for their brains.' Richmond's diary, 14 Feb. 1915; *Portrait of an Admiral*, p. 142.

out. All I regret is that he gave him employment at all.'[30] Fisher held him responsible for a good deal of 'criminal folly', as in his alleged misuse of ships. He had worn out destroyers by employing them freely in the escorting of contraband vessels. Fisher relieved them of this duty by putting a small armed guard on each ship.

Able or not, Sturdee had to go, for Fisher and he were utterly antipathetic. Sturdee's membership in the Beresford camp was the decisive consideration. For this reason alone Fisher could never have worked with him.

At the first opportunity, Fisher also got rid of Leveson, the D.O.D., who relieved Arbuthnot in mid-January 1915 as Rear-Admiral in the 2nd Battle Squadron. Here again the motivation was both professional and personal. Leveson had been 'Willy' May's Flag-Captain, and Fisher and May (now Admiral of the Fleet, retired) were scarcely good friends. Leveson's successor at the Admiralty, Captain Thomas Jackson, was a real disaster, as we shall see in the next volume.

Fisher returned to Whitehall as the saviour of the country, the elect of the nation, to take over the management of the weapon he had forged for the safety of Great Britain and the Empire. At once he threw himself into the task of prosecuting the naval war with forcefulness and imagination, although he would not, as always, be bothered with routine business and details. 'Everything began to move. Inertia disappeared. The huge machine creaked and groaned; but it began to turn out work at an increased rate. He was known, feared, loved, and obeyed . . .'[31] He worked beautifully with Churchill at first, the pair of titans giving the Navy its most powerful leadership since the days of St. Vincent and Barham.

In the first three months of the war only twelve additional submarines and twelve additional destroyers had been ordered, besides the acceleration of ships building which could be completed in 1915. Sensing that the war would be of long duration, Fisher spent much of his energy on the task of constructing a vast armada of ships of every type. 'Lord Fisher hurled himself into this business with explosive energy. He summoned around him all

[30] Richmond's Diary, 9 Oct. 1914; *ibid.*, p. 113; Oliver MSS.; Beatty to Lady Beatty, 16 Nov. 1914, Beatty MSS.

[31] Admiral Sir R. H. Bacon, *The Life of Lord Fisher of Kilverstone* (London, 1929, 2 vols.), ii. 161–2.

the naval constructors and shipbuilding firms in Britain, and in four or five glorious days, every minute of which was pure delight to him, he presented me with schemes for a far greater construction of submarines, destroyers and small craft than I or any of my advisers had ever deemed possible.'[32] Fisher meant to have his ships quickly. On 3 November he arranged a meeting of all the principal Admiralty officials, to which Keyes was invited.

He opened the meeting by telling us his intentions as to future submarine construction, and turning to the Superintendent of Contracts, he said that he would make his wife a widow and his house a dunghill, if he brought paper work or red tape into the business; he wanted submarines, not contracts. He meant to have them built in eight months; if he did not get them in eight months he would commit *hara-kiri*. Addison, in an aside which I think Lord Fisher must have heard, remarked, 'Now we know exactly how long he has to live!' I laughed, and I suppose looked incredulous. It seemed absurd; we had not been able to wring submarines out of Vickers and Chatham Dockyard under two and a half years. He fixed me with a ferocious glare, and said, 'If anyone thwarts me, he had better commit *hara-kiri* too.'[33]

Some 600 ships were arranged for that day, of all shapes and sizes, including 37 monitors and 200 motor barges. Many of these vessels were invaluable at the Dardanelles, in Mesopotamia, and against the U-boats. 'This tremendous new Navy, for it was nothing less,' Churchill wrote afterwards, 'was a providential aid to the Admiralty when more than two years later the real German submarine attack began. Its creation on such a scale is one of the greatest services which the nation has owed to the genius and energy of Lord Fisher.'[34]

At the commencement of the war, two dreadnoughts of the 1914–15 programme (slightly modified 'Royal Sovereigns'), the *Repulse* and the *Renown*, had barely been started. (The two sister ships in the programme were never begun.) Construction was not pressed forward in view of the long time it would take to complete them. On 19 December, following the dramatic vindication of the battle cruiser at the Falklands, Fisher had the Director of Naval

---

[32] *The World Crisis*, i. 456–7.
[33] *The Naval Memoirs of Admiral of the Fleet Sir Roger Keyes* (London, 1934–5, 2 vols.), i. 130.
[34] *The World Crisis*, i. 459.

Construction radically redesign the *Repulse* and *Renown* as very fast battle cruisers. The new design (ready on 29 December) called for a displacement of 26,500 tons, a speed of 32 knots, and a primary armament of six 15-inch guns. The design 'was conceived as a direct result of the Falkland Islands Battle and also on account of the experience gained during the action fought on the 28th August 1914, which showed the immense value of very high speed with long-range powerful gunfire and large radius of action, which qualities, in association, enable a ship to run down those of the enemy under any circumstances, with the power of enforcing or declining action, as may be considered desirable. Features of such magnitude could only be obtained if the armour protection were comparatively light, unless very great size of ship were accepted.'[35] The protection was, accordingly, similar to the early 'Invincible' and 'Indefatigable' classes, a 6-inch armour belt and 7-inch barbettes. The particular argument Fisher used for the speed was that none of the British dreadnoughts had the speed to catch a 28-knot ship, which the new German battle cruiser *Lützow* was believed to be.

Churchill refused to attempt to obtain Cabinet sanction for the proposal. New battle cruisers would retard more urgent construction. Besides, he prophesied, the war would have been decided before they were finished. The wily Fisher, a master in the use of stratagem, asked Jellicoe (23 December) to write him 'a casual sort of letter which I can show to the Cabinet (*not as if you were responding to my request; not an official memorandum*)' in support of more battle cruisers.[36] Jellicoe was happy to oblige. The co-operation of the Third Sea Lord was also enlisted, and, as a final argument, Fisher may have threatened to resign. Churchill gave in, Cabinet approval was secured, and the two keels were laid down on 25 January 1915, Fisher's birthday. He insisted they be completed within fifteen months. 'We must "scrap" everyone who gets in the way.' The two ships took somewhat longer. The *Repulse* was completed in August 1916 and the *Renown* in September 1916, setting a modern record in the design and construction of capital ships.

No sooner had Fisher won his fight than he instructed the

[35] D.N.C. Department, Admiralty, *Records of Warship Construction during the War* (31 Dec. 1918, 2 vols.); Admiralty Library.
[36] *Fear God and Dread Nought*, iii. 107.

D.N.C. to design three other large armoured ships. Since Cabinet sanction was not likely for any more capital ships, while additional light cruisers had already been sanctioned, Fisher decided to build the new ships on the lines of very large light cruisers (they were officially 'large light cruisers'), 18,600 tons (the *Furious* was 19,100 tons), capable of 32 knots, and mounting a few guns of the heaviest calibre, but with thin light-cruiser protection. They were approved at the end of January, laid down between late March and early June, and completed in January (*Courageous*, *Glorious*) and July (*Furious*) of 1917. By May 1915 Fisher had conceived another batch of battle cruisers of immense speed (35 knots), very light draught of water, and *20-inch guns*! He left the Admiralty before his plan could mature.

The *Dreadnought* design was a brilliant conception—Fisher wisely saw that in battle the big gun would outrange and defeat a larger number of small guns—but he overdid the idea when he built the wartime battle cruisers. They were the fastest capital ships ever built. (Beatty called the *Repulse* and the *Renown* the 'Gallopers'.) But whereas all previous British battle cruisers had a primary armament of eight 12-inch or 13·5-inch guns, the *Repulse* and *Renown* carried six 15-inch guns, the *Courageous* and *Glorious*, four 15-inch guns, and the *Furious*, one 18-inch gun. (The *Furious* was designed for two 18-inch guns; in the end only one was mounted, the other being commandeered by General Haig in 1917 as the ship was being completed. She was converted into an aircraft carrier in 1917.) Especially the three ships with four guns or less had not sufficient rate of fire to produce a hitting pattern against a fast-moving target. Experience has shown that, to obtain good results, at least six, and preferably eight, primary guns are needed for salvo firing by director. Another criticism was that all five were 'light in the bone', that is, with very light protective armour. After Jutland the *Renown* and *Repulse* got additional deck armour over the magazines, but the side armour remained far too thin. At the same time the plating over the magazines was strengthened in the *Courageous* and *Glorious*. These deficiencies in armament and protection explain the unpopularity of the five ships when completed. They were regarded in the Grand Fleet as 'white elephants'. The *Furious*, *Courageous*, and *Glorious* were dubbed the 'Spurious', 'Outrageous', and 'Uproarious', respectively.

'None the less,' writes Churchill, 'their parent loved them dearly and always rallied with the utmost vehemence when any slur was cast upon their qualities.' These battle cruisers were admirably suited for the two purposes Fisher had in mind when he designed them—to overtake and annihilate the raiding, fast light cruisers of the enemy, and, chiefly, for use in a bold amphibious invasion of the German Baltic coast. These vessels had a special asset for the latter operation in their unprecedented light draught, which would enable them to operate in the shallow waters of the Baltic. The *Courageous* and *Glorious* were given a mean draught of 21 ft. 6 in., and the *Furious*, 21 ft., or over five feet less than any British dreadnought or battle cruiser. The *Renown* and *Repulse* were also given a comparatively light draught: 25 ft. 6 in. mean. By way of contrast, the 'Queen Elizabeths', the latest dreadnought class, drew 28 ft. 9 in. of water (30 ft. $1\frac{1}{2}$ in. after post-Jutland additions to protection). Long before the ships were completed, however, the light-cruiser threat to British trade routes had been overcome, and Fisher's famous Baltic Scheme had received an indecent interment.

Not so well known is the vital part Fisher played in the development of small non-rigid airships, the so-called S.S. (submarine scout) airships, or 'blimps' as they were later called, to combat the submarine menace.[37] On his second day in office he called a meeting at the Admiralty 'of all interested in the air'. A few weeks later he had his first airship. It was due to his policy in office and encouragement out of office that two years later, when the U-boat peril was most critical, there were airships and airship stations around the coasts which could protect the convoys when they reached the narrow waters, where lay the greatest dangers.

The original purpose of the S.S. airships was to give the Fleet extra protection against submarines when at sea. Fisher was as alarmed as Jellicoe over the possibilities of the underwater craft. The 'holocaust' of the three 'Cressys' (22 September), the loss of the cruiser *Hawke* (torpedoed off Peterhead on 15 October by *U-9*

[37] Airships were commonly divided into three classes. Non-rigids had no framework but maintained their shape simply by gas and air pressure. The semi-rigid had an exterior keel or spar, but lost its shape when the gas was allowed to escape. The rigid airship (the Zeppelins belonged to this category) had a framework which was covered with fabric and retained its shape even after the gasbags were withdrawn completely from the interior. I owe this neat distinction among the airship types to Professor Robin Higham.

with a loss of nearly 500 lives), the torpedoing of the seaplane carrier *Hermes* (off Calais, 31 October, by *U-27*), and the near loss of the cruiser *Antrim* off Skudesnaes (she was missed by a torpedo on 9 October by only a few yards) had made a deep impression on him. '*More men lost* [in the four cruisers] *than by Lord Nelson in all his battles put together!*' This immense number of officers and men were irreplaceable. It was of course even more vital to keep the capital-ship superiority of the Grand Fleet, in line with 'the one pervading governing condition of the present war at sea, which is to keep a big preponderance of sea force ever ready to cope with the Big German Fleet at its "SELECTED" moment and our "AVERAGE" moment (to use classic words!)'.[38] He made two proposals in the same letter (and in one to Jellicoe that day) to minimize losses through the U-boats. One was to have armed trawlers, supervised by armed wireless yachts, do the patrol work of cruisers in the North Sea. Only these ships should be in the North Sea. He went so far as to advocate, late in December, that the Grand Fleet stay in harbour. He hoped that Jellicoe would stop his 'insane cruises' in the North Sea, or they would 'have the *Cressy, Aboukir, Hogue, Hawke, Hermes* all over again, and the Admiralty will deservedly be kicked out of office for allowing such utter murder by prowling German submarines, who are not going to be kept off by these Chinese methods of frightening them with a big ship.'[39] Jellicoe disregarded the First Sea Lord's injunctions because he knew that his fleet would rapidly decline in efficiency and morale if not taken to sea periodically. Fisher did not press the point.

The torpedoing of the pre-dreadnought *Formidable* underscored the cogency of Fisher's appeal. Vice-Admiral Sir Lewis Bayly was C.-in-C., Channel Fleet, having succeeded Burney in December. Essentially a 'big ship' man, he had a slight contempt for the submarine. He just would not believe in submarines, and this proved to be his undoing.

Late in December 1914 Bayly received permission to take the 5th Battle Squadron from the Nore to Portland for exercises and firing. Believing there was no submarine danger (no U-boats had been reported in the Channel all the month), he refused the destroyer escort the Admiralty wished to send him. The C.O.S.

---

[38] Fisher to Churchill, 26 Dec. 1914; *Fear God and Dread Nought*, iii. 113.
[39] Fisher to Jellicoe, 28 Dec. 1914; *ibid.*, p. 115.

sent him six destroyers from Harwich anyway to accompany him during daylight as far as Folkestone (30 December), that is, through the Straits of Dover, and to leave him after dark. On arriving off Portland harbour at daybreak on the 31st, instead of taking his squadron in, Bayly practised tactics most of the day between Portland and Start Point. That night he steamed down the Channel with a view to resuming the exercises the next day. The last thing he expected was submarines in the western part of the Channel. The squadron was proceeding in a single line on a straight course (no zigzagging) at 10 knots in bright moonlight. At 2.30 a.m., 1 January, when the squadron was near Start Point, a submarine torpedoed the *Formidable*, the rear ship. She went down two-and-a-half hours later with the loss of 35 officers and 512 men of her complement of 780.

Bayly's explanations to the Admiralty (2, 13 January) stressed the deduction he had drawn from the failure to continue the destroyer escort beyond Folkestone and from the fact that 'Not a single enemy submarine had been reported in the Channel since I hoisted my Flag in this command ... and I had not the slightest idea that the Channel was "infested" with submarines.'[40] The Admiralty refused to overlook the Admiral's disregard of ordinary precautions against enemy submarines. Fisher, in particular, was angry at Bayly's handling of the squadron, 'for it must have been patent to every officer and man in his squadron that to steam at slow speed in close order on a moonlight night on a steady course in the vicinity of the Start Light[41] was to make his Squadron an easy target to the hostile submarines which all the precautions taken by the Admiralty to escort his Squadron from Sheerness must have convinced him was a very present danger'.[42] The Admiralty concluded from the evidence before them that Bayly's handling of the squadron 'was marked by a want of prudence and good seamanship in the avoidance of unnecessary risks inexplicable in an officer holding high and responsible command'.[43]

An Admiralty telegram of 16 January informed Bayly that he had 'lost Their Lordships' confidence', and directed him to haul

[40] Bayly to Admiralty, 13 Jan. 1915; Admiralty MSS.
[41] This Light was ' "the one light" the German submarines always make for [in] their run up Channel'. Fisher to Jellicoe, 5 Jan. 1915; *Fear God and Dread Nought*, iii. 125.
[42] Fisher to Oliver and Churchill, 6 Jan. 1915; *ibid.*, p. 126.
[43] Admiralty to Bayly, 11 Jan. 1915; Admiralty MSS.

down his flag the next day. His request for a court martial to clear his name was refused (10 February, and again in the spring of 1919, when he tried to reopen the case). Shortly before, he had been appointed to the Presidency of the Royal Naval College at Greenwich, replacing Admiral Bethell, who had taken over the Channel Fleet command. This was letting Bayly off quite easy, and was due to Churchill. The First Lord was 'grieved' about Bayly, who 'outraged every principle of prudence and good seamanship without the slightest military object'. But Churchill did 'his best for him—not for his own sake but because to terrorize Admirals for losing ships is to make sure of losing wars'.[44]

The loss of the *Formidable* prompted Fisher to send another alarmist letter to the C.-in-C. 'But I don't wish to fetter your discretion, but as sure as fate you'll lose another "Audacious" if you do send ships out! Tirpitz is going to mine more and more and submarine more and more. We can't touch their submarines. We know that two of them have gone 19 knots on the surface and they carry a 13 pr., so can fire at our submarines and kill them, and our best destroyers were beaten back by the "Formidable" gale in which the German submarine kept company with our ships . . .'[45]

Fisher's strategic ideas were by no means entirely defensive. A discussion of his offensive strategic policies may profitably be left for a later chapter, while we resume the narrative of the war at sea.

[44] Churchill to Jellicoe, 11 Jan. 1915; Jellicoe MSS.
[45] Fisher to Jellicoe, 4 Jan. 1915; *Fear God and Dread Nought*, iii. 120. He changed his tune by the spring of 1915. The German C.-in-C. 'may make a mistake so it's prudent for you to come out and once in the open ocean you are more free than bottled up in Scapa!' Fisher to Jellicoe, 23 Apr. 1915; Jellicoe MSS.

VI

Action in the Far Seas

(OCTOBER 1914–DECEMBER 1914)

... never was a nobler act, unsuccessful though it was, than that which he
[Cradock] performed. ... he and his gallant comrades lie far from the pleasant
homes of England. Yet they have their reward, and we ... are surely right in
saying that theirs is an immortal place in the great roll of naval heroes.

> BALFOUR at the unveiling of the Cradock
> memorial in York Minster, 16 June 1916.

... with the Battle of the Falkland Islands the clearance of the oceans was
complete, and soon, except in the land-locked Baltic and Black Seas and in
the defended area of the Heligoland Bight, the German flag had ceased to
fly on any vessel in any quarter of the world.

> CHURCHILL, *The World Crisis.*

I. DEFEAT AT CORONEL

(*Map* 3)

ON FISHER'S third day in office there occurred what
Churchill has called 'the saddest naval action of the war',
the Battle of Coronel. It was the outcome of faulty distribu-
tions against the German *guerre de course*. During the first six
months, before Germany had time to build up her submarine
flotillas, her war against commerce was mainly the work of five
detached light cruisers and five armed merchant ships, of which
nine were in foreign waters when hostilities began. Despite the
abolition of privateering by the Declaration of Paris (1856), and
the restrictions of the Hague Peace Conference of 1907, the armed
merchant cruiser had emerged as just as deadly an agent of trade
warfare. The most successful of the enemy raiders were the light
cruisers *Emden* (detached from the China Squadron), which in
three months sank or captured seventeen British merchant
ships of 68,000 tons in the North Pacific and the Indian Ocean,
and *Karlsruhe*, which in the same period accounted for fifteen

British merchant ships of 68,000 tons in the North and South Atlantic.[1]

In Britain's past wars mercantile convoy (the escorting of merchant ships by warships, usually in groups known as convoys or fleets) had been the principal measure of trade defence, and to the extent that the systematic movement of the mercantile and military convoys had governed the composition, disposition, and activities of the main forces. The Admiralty were now strongly opposed to the convoy of merchant ships, although they insisted upon it for naval and military transports, supply ships, and warships.

A second measure adopted in the old days was the cruising or patrol system. Patrol was now the principal trade defence measure used, but it differed fundamentally and totally from that operated in former times. Then the patrols had been disposed and operated as an integral part of the convoy system. Their prime business had been to reinforce the escorts of convoys traversing waters where the probability of enemy attack was high; their activities had thus been systematic and, since the movements of convoys were known, rationally organized and operated. But the patrols now instituted were organized, disposed, and operated on the basis of 'protecting' (as it was termed) immense 'sea areas' and intangible 'sea routes', *and not ships*, from attack. Indeed, these patrols had no specific knowledge of the movements of ships through their area or along the routes, and no idea of the numbers or performance of the ships involved. The activities of the patrols were thus inherently unsystematic. Cruisers, singly or in squadrons, patrolled up and down the terminal or focal areas of trade, which were the obvious hunting grounds of commerce destroyers. The 5th and 9th Cruiser Squadrons, for instance, between them attempted to cover the trade routes between Ushant and the Cape Verdes. Every obsolete and obsolescent ship that could get to sea was commissioned, also twenty-four liners were armed as auxiliary cruisers. Before the U-boats emerged as the principal commerce destroyers, the patrol system was reasonably successful, except on foreign stations—*that*

---

[1] All shipping losses will be given in gross tonnage, that is, in terms of the total measurement capacity of a vessel, reckoned at 100 cubic feet to the ton. The figures cited are from an invaluable little book published by the Director of Statistics, Admiralty, on 23 December 1918: *Statistical Review of the War against Merchant Shipping*. (There is a copy in the Admiralty Library.) The figures and tables of losses in the official work, by C. Ernest Fayle, *Seaborne Trade* (London, 1920–4, 3 vols.), are from this source, as are those in Command Paper 199 (1919), *Merchant Shipping (Losses)*.

PLATE III

ADMIRAL SIR JOHN JELLICOE
Commander-in-Chief, Grand Fleet, Aug. 1914–Nov. 1916

[Photograph: Radio Times Hulton Picture Library

PLATE IV

VICE-ADMIRAL SIR DAVID BEATTY
Commanding Battle Cruiser Squadron (afterwards Fleet),
Mar. 1913–Nov. 1916

[*Photograph : Imperial War Museum*

is, where enemy raiders were active. Because of troop convoy needs
these stations were thinly held by cruisers. But even if the cruiser
squadrons had not been halved by convoy, it would have made
little difference to the improbability of cruisers picking up a raider.
The ocean spaces covered by a patrolling cruiser force were simply
too vast, even allowing for the fact that the cruisers were concerned with the much more limited areas traversed by the trade
routes. The area of the China Station, for example, was over
sixteen million square nautical miles. In the first months of the
war some nineteen warships were stationed there. The combined
stations of the 5th and 9th Cruiser Squadrons (ten warships)
covered over five million square nautical miles.

The defensive arming of merchant ships was another principle
of commerce protection carried over from the past. Armament
had been provided for thirty-nine ships before the war—scarcely
a drop in the bucket, as ocean-going ships then numbered close
to 4,000. The principle was extended after the commencement of
the U-boat campaign in February 1915, though as late as April
1916 the number was still very small—about 1,100.

A fourth fundamental principle was to capture the enemy's
overseas bases, where possible. Since the German bases from
which a widespread attack on trade and seaborne expeditions
could have been developed soon fell, it seemed to be only a matter
of time before the surface raiders were disposed of. Coal and water
difficulties could not be overcome indefinitely.

The above measures or principles were, of course, in addition
to the trade protection afforded by the main forces in Home
waters and in the Mediterranean. They were disposed so as to
impose a distant blockade on the enemy's main forces and prevent
their egress on to the high seas.

During August shipping movements in the outer oceans almost
ceased through fear of the few enemy cruisers at large. Then the
State War Risks Insurance Scheme, which had been announced
at the outbreak of war, began to take effect and shipping revived,
although at a reduced level as compared to 1913. 'To this one
measure, above all else, was due the uninterrupted flow of seaborne trade through all the vicissitudes of the war.'[2]

Taking the long view has never been a *forte* of public opinion
in time of war. The country became restive and anxious as the

[2] Fayle, *Seaborne Trade*, i. 45.

captures by the raiders were made known. Losses in terms of total British tonnage were infinitesimal; but why had not one of the cruisers at large been brought to book? The Admiralty gave as one reason the fact that the cruisers in the outer seas had other and onerous duties to perform in the safe convoy of troop transports from Australia, India, and Canada. The chief reason, however, is that the sea is very large and afforded ample opportunities, with its many archipelagoes, for the game of hide-and-seek.

The most dangerous threat to British shipping lanes and bases in the outer seas was posed by the German China Squadron, based on Tsingtao and commanded by the aggressive Vice-Admiral Count von Spee. The start of the war found it at Ponape, in the Caroline Islands, on a training cruise. When Japan entered the war, 23 August, it was plain that Spee would not return to Far Eastern waters, nor remain for long anywhere in the Pacific. Superior British or Japanese forces would have blown his squadron to bits. He decided to operate off the west coast of South America and use the ports of friendly Chile for coaling. There were twin magnets in that area: important British trade routes and an inferior cruiser force consisting of the armoured cruisers *Good Hope* and *Monmouth*, the light cruiser *Glasgow*, and the armed merchant cruiser *Otranto*. (The last-named was known as 'the floating haystack' or 'sardine tin'.) By the end of October, when it appeared off Chile, Spee's reinforced squadron numbered five ships: the powerful armoured cruisers *Scharnhorst* and *Gneisenau*, and the light cruisers *Leipzig*, *Nürnberg*, and *Dresden*.

Through an intercepted message from the *Scharnhorst* the Admiralty were able, on 5 October, to inform Rear-Admiral Sir Christopher Cradock, in command of the South American station, that Spee was definitely making for South America with the *Scharnhorst*, *Gneisenau*, and possibly a light cruiser. 'You must be prepared to have to meet them in company . . . *Canopus* [en route] should accompany *Glasgow*, *Monmouth*, and *Otranto*, the ships to search and protect trade in combination.'[3] The Admiralty did nothing to strengthen Cradock beyond sending him the old battle-ship *Canopus*.

[3] The quotations from Cradock's and the Admiralty's telegrams are from a Cabinet paper of November 1914, 'Admiralty Telegrams Relating to the Concentration of H.M. Ships under Rear-Admiral Sir Christopher Cradock . . . 14th September to 4th November 1914'; Lennoxlove MSS. Most of these telegrams have been printed in *The World Crisis*, i. 409–20, in a somewhat different wording.

Cradock's whole squadron, even if combined, was decidedly inferior to the German squadron which was inexorably moving towards South America. Cradock's intelligence was that Spee would have *three* light cruisers, not one. He telegraphed this to the Admiralty on 8 October, adding: 'Have ordered *Canopus* to Falkland Islands, where I intend to concentrate and avoid division of forces.' A second telegram that day recommended that two forces, *individually strong enough to defeat the German squadron,* operate, one on each coast. This was to meet the contingency of Spee slipping past Cradock and proceeding into the Atlantic, where he might raise havoc with British trade and coaling bases in the South Atlantic and possibly reach the West Indies. The Admiralty concurred (14 October) in his proposed concentration 'for combined operation' and in his suggestion for a division of forces. Rear-Admiral A. P. Stoddart was to command an east coast concentration of four cruisers (including the powerful armoured cruiser *Defence*, which was ordered out from the Mediterranean) and two armed merchant cruisers. The vague expression 'combined operation' probably meant that Cradock's squadron would join Stoddart's in case Spee evaded the former.

Churchill's minute (12 October) on Cradock's first telegram, which was approved by Battenberg, made it clear that the idea of attacking German trade on the west coast had to be given up in favour of meeting Spee's ships. 'They, and not the trade, are our quarry for the moment, we must not miss them.' (The German merchant ships on the west coast were not trading ships, but supply ships to Spee's squadron.) Churchill appreciated that Cradock's concentrated squadron (that is, with the *Canopus*, which was about to join him) was not fast enough to force an engagement. He assumed all along, nevertheless, that Cradock would come to no harm *so long as he had Canopus with him. Canopus* would serve as 'a citadel around which all our cruisers in those waters could find absolute security';[4] the *Scharnhorst* and *Gneisenau* would not dare come within the range of her four 12-inch guns. He therefore expected Cradock would make use of her, slow though she was. Without her he would not stand a chance. The Admiralty were, in any case, unable to spare any more modern capital ship, as the British superiority in dreadnoughts and battle cruisers was at this time razor-thin.

[4] *Ibid.,* p. 414.

Churchill overstated the case for the obsolete *Canopus*. Up to 1914, this 15-year-old vessel had been at Pembroke for at least two years with only a care and maintenance party and the storekeeping officers, and was due to be scrapped in 1915. Officially, she could do 17 knots, which was the speed she managed in a three-hour, full-power trial in July 1914. Churchill credited her with an actual speed of 15½ knots, which was not far off the mark, we shall see. Jellicoe qualified this: 'She could steam 15½ knots for 3–4 days if she did not break down.'[5] The 'Canopus' class (launched 1897–9) were lightly armoured even for pre-dreadnoughts, their scale of protection being inferior to that of their immediate predecessors ('Majestics', 1894–6) or successors ('Formidables', 1898–9). For that reason contemporary naval constructors regarded the 'Canopus' class as second-class battle-ships. (Excepting for her heavy gun turrets, the *Canopus* was slightly inferior in protection to the *Scharnhorst* and *Gneisenau*.) She might therefore have not stood punishment from the German 8·2s any better than the *Good Hope* did. Of course, her 12-inch would have damaged the German armoured cruisers—if they had hit. There was some doubt about their ability to do that. The four 12-inch guns, of an obsolete mark, had a maximum range of 14,000 yards, or little more than the 13,500 yards of the 8·2-inch guns of the two German armoured cruisers.[6] More to the point, the *Canopus* was manned by an untrained crew, composed largely of reservists. The ship's gunnery efficiency must have been very low, as her Chief Engineer at the time has testified. 'Our fighting value was very small—our two turrets were in charge of Royal Naval Reserve Lieutenants who had never been in a turret before, and the only rounds we had fired until the 8th December [the Falklands action] were 2 six-pounders to stop a merchant vessel.'[7] This was the vessel described by Churchill as a 'citadel'.

Cradock especially mistrusted the speed of the *Canopus*. He voiced his doubts in a telegram of 18 October, the day she arrived at the Falklands and it was seen that her engines needed overhauling. 'I fear that strategically the speed of my squadron cannot

[5] Jellicoe's marginal comment on his copy of *The World Crisis* (in the possession of the Dowager Countess Jellicoe), i. 417. (Hereafter cited as Jellicoe Marginalia.)

[6] The source for the *Canopus* figure is Whale Island (Gunnery School) records; for the *Scharnhorst* and *Gneisenau*, Erich Gröner, *Die Deutschen Kriegsschiffe, 1815–1936* (Munich, 1937), p. 41.

[7] Rear-Admiral S. P. Start's letter to the author, 5 Nov. 1962.

exceed 12 knots owing to *Canopus*, but shall trust circumstances will enable me to force an action.'[8] 'These last words,' Corbett observes, 'shows that his order to "search and protect trade" led him to believe that he was expected to seek out the enemy and bring him to action as best he could.'[9] One can only speculate on exactly what the Admiral had in mind, since his 12-knot squadron (or even 16½-knot squadron, had he known the true speed of the *Canopus*) could not possibly 'force an action' on a 21-knot squadron which did not choose to fight. If Spee did elect to fight, the speed of his squadron would give him a great manœuvring advantage.

Cradock's misgivings did not at first disturb Churchill in view of the Admiral's declared intention to keep the *Canopus* with his cruisers. Then, on 27 October, there arrived a telegram from Cradock (of 26 October) which threw the First Lord 'into perplexity'. The Admiral (who had on 22 October left the Falklands to make a sweep round the Horn) now considered it 'impracticable, on account of *Canopus*' slow speed, to find and destroy enemy's squadron. Consequently have ordered *Defence* [which had just arrived at Pernambuco] to join me after calling at Montevideo for orders. *Canopus* will be employed on necessary convoying of colliers.' Churchill's fear that Cradock was courting

---

[8] Four days later the Captain of the *Canopus*, Heathcoat Grant, confirmed for Cradock the *Canopus*'s limitation: a report from his Engineer-Commander stated that the ship's faulty condensers did not permit her to exceed 12 knots. Grant afterwards learned that his principal technical adviser, no doubt because he was ill mentally (he was placed on the sick list on 31 October and soon after invalided out of the Service), made false reports on the state of the machinery (evidently on the ship's arrival at the Falklands), and that she was actually capable of 16½ knots. She did, in fact, attain this speed when she escorted the colliers northward, and managed 14–15 knots in the 48 hours following the battle. (The Chief Engineer was ignorant of the fictitious reports. He states that at no time from August 1914 to when she was paid off in April 1916 did the main machinery or boilers give any cause for anxiety. Admiral Start's letter to the author, 23 Oct. 1962.) Cradock had already left the Falklands on the sweep that was to lead to the Coronel action. 'But Cradock could only be informed by wireless that the *Canopus* could still achieve a speed near to that for which she had been designed; and Grant did not consider this justified since he did not believe the admiral would delay his northward progress so that the battleship could catch up with his faster cruisers.' Captain Geoffrey Bennett, *Coronel and the Falklands* (London, 1962), pp. 20, 24. It is unlikely, given Cradock's temperament and intentions, that Grant's correction of his misinformation would have made any difference, had it reached him.

[9] Sir Julian S. Corbett and (for Vols. iv and v) Sir Henry Newbolt, *History of the Great War. Naval Operations* (London, 1920–31, 5 vols., rev. eds. of i. and iii., 1938, 1940), i. 319.

trouble was mitigated by a poor War Staff appreciation of the 28th, which was summed up for him in a minute by Oliver, his Naval Secretary, on the 29th. 'The situation on the West Coast seems safe,' because a Japanese battleship (*Idzumo*) and cruiser (*Hizen*) and a British light cruiser (*Newcastle*) were moving across the northern Pacific and would shortly be on the west coast of South America. This squadron would 'force' the German ships south on Cradock's squadron. The *Hizen*, as it happens, was at Honolulu and did not leave until 10 November. And why should Spee have necessarily run into the *Idzumo* and *Newcastle* in the vast expanses of the Pacific? Supposing he did, why should he be forced south, and if forced south, why was it certain he would meet Cradock?

Meanwhile, on 28 October, the Admiralty had denied Cradock the reinforcement of the *Defence*, as it would have weakened Stoddart's squadron, which she was about to join. This still left 'sufficient force' on both coasts to deal with any enemy cruisers that appeared on the trade routes there. There was no comment on Cradock's proposed use of the *Canopus*.

Churchill says the telegram of 28 October did not reach Cradock; Corbett only says it 'perhaps never reached him—in any case it was too late to affect his movements'; and a note in the collection of pre-Coronel telegrams for the Cabinet states, 'It is not certain that this message reached *Good Hope*.' But Paymaster Commander Lloyd Hirst, who fought at Coronel in the *Glasgow*, which received the Admiralty message, is 'practically certain' that Cradock got the telegram just before the battle. 'Tired of protesting his inferiority, the receipt of this telegram would be sufficient spur to Cradock to hoist, as he did half an hour later, his signal, "Spread twenty miles apart and look for the enemy." ' If this telegram was received, 'then the Admiralty, by failing to comment on the employment of *Canopus* and by again calling his squadron "sufficient force", gave Admiral Cradock full justification for complying with his unrevoked instruction to search for and engage the enemy'.[10] He had not waited for the *Defence*, even if he could have had her, but had steamed up the Chilean coast with his vastly inferior squadron, the *Canopus* trailing 250 miles astern guarding the colliers. How inferior his squadron was can be judged from this table:

[10] Hirst, *Coronel and After* (London, 1934), pp. 97, 131.

THE TWO SQUADRONS[11]

GERMAN

	Class	Com-pleted	Tonnage	Speed (knots)	Guns	Weight of broadside (lbs.)
Scharnhorst	Armoured cruiser	1907	11,420	23·8	8–8·2″; 6–5·9″	1,957
Gneisenau	Armoured cruiser	1907	11,420	23·8	8–8·2″; 6–5·9″	1,957
Nürnberg	Light cruiser	1908	3,400	23·0	10–4·1″	176
Leipzig	Light cruiser	1906	3,200	23·3	10–4·1″	176
Dresden	Light cruiser	1909	3,592	24·5	10–4·1″	176
					TOTAL	4,442

BRITISH

	Class	Com-pleted	Tonnage	Speed (knots)	Guns	Weight of broadside (lbs.)
Good Hope	Armoured cruiser	1902	14,100	23·0	2–9·2″; 16–6″	1,560
Monmouth	Armoured cruiser	1903	9,800	22·4	14–6″	900
Glasgow	Light cruiser	1911	4,800	25·3	2–6″; 10–4″	325
Otranto (never intended to engage a regular warship)	Armed merchant cruiser	—	—	17·0	4–4·7″	90
					TOTAL	2,875

The *Scharnhorst* and *Gneisenau* were crack ships, newer and more powerful than the British cruisers. They had been in active commission over two years, were manned by long-service ratings, the pick of the German Navy, and were renowned for their gunnery. The British squadron was manned mostly by reservists, and its two

[11] The various published accounts of the battle do not agree on the speeds and weights of broadsides. I have chosen to use the German figures in the German Official History, by Captain E. Raeder and Vice-Admiral Eberhard von Mantey, *Der Krieg zur See, 1914–1918. Der Kreuzerkrieg in den ausländischen Gewässern* (Berlin, 1922–37, 3 vols.), i. 204–5. The German speed figures are the mean speed on trial of the fastest ship of the class. The British broadside figures are from official sources as published in *Brassey's Naval Annual* and *Jane's Fighting Ships*, and the speed figures (trial speeds) are from Corbett, *Naval Operations*, i. 350. Note that the *practical* total broadside of the *Good Hope* was 1,160 lbs. and of the *Monmouth*, 600 lbs., as the main-deck guns could not be fought in bad weather, as at Coronel. (See below.)

strongest units, the *Good Hope* and the *Monmouth*, having been mobilized on the outbreak of the war and hurriedly dispatched to their stations, had had no opportunity to fire their guns since commissioning. We should also note that the German cruisers were better protected on the water line and gun casemates, especially in comparison with the *Monmouth*, and that the armour-piercing shell of the 6-inch guns of the *Good Hope* and *Monmouth* were obsolescent, as were the fuses of the 4-inch and 6-inch common lyddite throughout the squadron.[12]

The perplexing question is, Why was Cradock so anxious to find and attack a force he knew was so superior to his own in speed, armour, armament, gunnery, and all-round efficiency? We can never know, as there were no survivors of Coronel among those who could tell us. One could attribute Cradock's action simply to impetuosity, a trait for which this gallant and skilled seaman had a Service reputation. 'He had no clear plan or doctrine in his head,' the Captain of the *Glasgow* has written, 'but was always inclined to act on the impulse of the moment. . . . Cradock was constitutionally incapable of refusing or ever postponing action, if there was the smallest chance of success.'[13] And, closely related, it would have been foreign to his nature to have avoided battle, no matter what the odds against him were. Beatty, for one, thought this was the explanation. 'The Germans had a concentrated force of two big cruisers and three small ones against his force, so I fear he saw red and did not wait for his proper reinforcement the *Canopus*.'[14] Churchill was afraid that Cradock had 'let himself be caught or has engaged recklessly with only *Monmouth* and *Good Hope* . . .'[15] This was the version adopted by the Cabinet. 'The mishap is the more regrettable as it would seem that the Admiral was acting in disobedience to his instructions, which were expressly to the effect that he must concentrate his whole squadron, including the *Canopus* and *Defence*, and run no risk of being caught in a condition of inferiority.'[16]

[12] Naval Staff Monograph No. 27 (1922), *Battles of Coronel and the Falkland Islands*, as slightly abridged in Naval Staff Monographs, Vol. ix, *The Atlantic Ocean, 1914–1915* (1923), p. 227. *Ibid.*, pp. 301–15, has the British signals made during both battles.

[13] Admiral John Luce's remarks on Coronel and the Falklands, 8 Oct. 1929, a paper in the possession of Vice-Admiral Harold Hickling.

[14] Beatty to Lady Beatty, 5 Nov. 1914; Chalmers, *Beatty*, p. 180.

[15] Churchill to Jellicoe, 5 Nov. 1914; Lennoxlove MSS.

[16] Asquith's report to the King of the Cabinet meeting of 4 Nov. 1914; Asquith MSS.

A more heroic (or charitable) explanation is offered by Lloyd Hirst, Bacon, Churchill, Corbett (indirectly), and Balfour (when First Lord). It is that Cradock, realizing he was going to certain doom, reckoned that he could at least badly damage some or all of Spee's ships far from any repairing yard, and force them to use up a large part of their impossible-to-replenish ammunition, so that they could be dealt with by a superior force.

There is yet another interpretation, one which I believe is closest to the truth. The Navigating Officer of the *Glasgow* shortly after the battle interpreted Cradock's behaviour thus: 'The *Defence* was refused him and he was as good as told he was skulking at Stanley. What else was there for him to do except go and be sunk? He was a very brave man and they were practically calling him a coward. If we hadn't attacked that night, we might never have seen them again, and then the Admiralty would have blamed him for not fighting.'[17] This is not a far-fetched explanation. When searching for Spee, Cradock wrote to an officer of high rank, alluding to the fact that Troubridge was to be tried by court martial for not having engaged the *Goeben*. 'I will take care I do not suffer the fate of poor Troubridge.'[18]

According to one story, Cradock knew he was going to his doom. Luce had it from the Governor of the Falklands, Sir William Allardyce, that (in Luce's words) 'Cradock thought his chances were small and that he had been let down by the Admiralty, especially when his request that *Defence* should join him had been vetoed'.[19] The Gunnery Officer of the *Glasgow* stated it as a fact that, just before Cradock left the Falklands for his ill-fated sweep, he went ashore at Port Stanley, 'buried all his medals and decorations in the Governor's garden and gave the Governor a large sealed packet to be sent home to the Admiralty as soon as his death was officially confirmed'.[20] Admiral Sir Francis Bridgeman, the onetime First Sea Lord (1911–12), made the same

[17] Lieutenant-Commander P. B. Portman to Miss Ella Haggard, 10 Nov. 1914; Admiralty MSS.

[18] Admiral Sir Ernest Troubridge, 'Rough Account of *Goeben* and *Breslau*', included in some undated (probably post-war) jottings in an old manuscript journal; quoted in a letter from the Admiral's grandson, Lieutenant-Commander Peter Troubridge, to the author, 11 Aug. 1960. The Admiral got the story from Cradock's correspondent, who may have been Admiral Sir Hedworth Meux. See note 21, below.

[19] Luce's remarks on Coronel and the Falklands, cited above.

[20] Lieutenant-Commander Charles Backhouse to Lieutenant-Commander Charles Woolcombe, H.M.S. *Excellent*, 12 Nov. 1914; H.M.S. *Excellent* Library.

statement in 1923 (*Morning Post* letter, 20 April 1923) on the authority of a 'brother officer' of Cradock (Admiral Meux?), who stated this in a letter after the battle. Allardyce categorically denied the first part of this story. He saw Cradock constantly during the period he was in port (9–22 October). 'Our respective positions at the time gave us much in common, and we freely exchanged confidences. I have therefore no hesitation in saying that the allegation that Cradock buried his decorations in my garden is absolutely untrue . . .'[21]

The new Board was aghast over the prospect. They reversed the decision with regard to the *Defence* on 3 November and ordered her to join Cradock on the west coast 'with all possible despatch'. (She was then at Montevideo.) A telegram to Cradock at about the same time made it clear that he was not expected to seek battle without first concentrating his whole squadron, including the *Canopus*. He was to use the *Glasgow* to find and keep touch with the enemy.

It was all too late. On 31 October, Spee, then 50 miles off Valparaiso, heard that the *Glasgow* had anchored at Coronel the evening before—190 miles to the south. (*Glasgow* had been detached to pick up any Admiralty messages via Montevideo.) He steamed at full speed to Coronel to gobble her up. Cradock, in the meantime (6 a.m., 30 October), had begun a sweep northward, following a report from the *Glasgow* that she had intercepted ciphered wireless messages, very probably German. (They were from the *Leipzig*.) The *Glasgow* rejoined the squadron at midday, 1 November. At 4.20 p.m. that day, Cradock sighted smoke to the

[21] Allardyce to Bridgeman, 19 Aug. 1924; letter in possession of the late Lady Allardyce. (Commander W. M. Phipps Hornby's information, 'admittedly verbal and at second hand', is that when Cradock sailed from Bermuda for his new command, he left his sword and decorations in the care of his old friend, Rear-Admiral R. S. Phipps Hornby, who was taking over the North American and West Indies command. Letter of Feb. 1963.) The Governor did receive a letter from Cradock to be forwarded to the Admiralty should he not survive. This he opened in order to make two copies in case the Germans captured the Islands. Lady Allardyce to the author, 2 June 1960. I have been unable to trace the original in the Admiralty records, and Lady Allardyce appears to have lost the copy among her husband's papers. Cradock also wrote the Governor at about this time, asking him to forward an enclosed letter to Admiral Meux '*only* in case of my "disappearance" . . . I mean to say, if* my squadron disappears and me *too*—COMPLETELY. I have no intention after 40 years at sea of being an unheard victim. . . . Somehow I think we shall say how d'ye do to these Teuton gentlemen; I am generally pretty lucky and we don't want any more disappointments.' Cited in Keith Middlemas, *Command the Far Seas* (London, 1961), pp. 160–1.* 'After' in the original source, Allardyce's 'Falkland Island Notes'; in possession of his family.

north, and, 20 minutes later, the enemy squadron. Although he had ample sea-room and could have at once altered to the south and (in all probability) escaped, this possibility could not have crossed his mind. He turned towards the enemy without hesitation. Both Admirals were surprised, each expecting that he was closing in on a solitary cruiser. The site was some 50 miles west of Coronel. 'It is not without emotion that one contemplates the feelings of so fine an officer when suddenly he found himself face to face with the hopeless situation in which, against all his protests and better judgment, he clearly believed himself to have been forced. A cloud that can never be lifted has fallen on one of the most tragic moments in our Naval history. All we can ever know is the silver lining. For whatever he thought and felt, Admiral Cradock did not flinch.'[22]

It was an absolutely hopeless business from the start—'the most rotten show imaginable', wrote one survivor. The battle was decided in the first hour. Having formed his squadron in single line ahead, at a little after six Cradock tried to close the enemy and force an action before sunset. This would have put the Germans in a very disadvantageous position, with the British ships between them and the glare of the sun. Spee used his superior speed to turn away and keep the range at about 18,000 yards. He patiently held his fire until the sun set, at 7 p.m., and then opened up at a range of 12,300 yards. By 7.35 this was reduced to 5,500 yards, as Cradock closed to the effective range of his 6-inch guns. Spee benefited from the silhouetting of Cradock's squadron against the sun's afterglow, whereas his own ships were 'smudged into low black shapes scarcely discernible against the background of gathering night clouds' and the dark background of the coast. The action took the form of a heavy pounding between two squadrons on parallel courses, with the Germans doing most of the pounding. Cradock suffered from his heavy dependence on 6-inch (seventeen on the combined broadsides of the *Good Hope* and *Monmouth*)—all his guns except the *Good Hope*'s two 9·2s—as against Spee's twelve 8·2s. And whereas the heavy sea on

[22] Corbett, *Naval Operations*, i. 346–7. The times given in the account that follows (and in the story of the Falklands action) are Chilean Zone time, that is, five hours slow on Greenwich Mean Time. The words on the Cradock monument in York Minster, from 1 Maccabees ix. 10, could hardly be more appropriate: 'God forbid that I should do this thing,/To flee away from them;/If our time be come, let us die manfully for our brethren,/And let us not stain our honour.'

Cradock's engaged bow seriously interfered with the firing of the seven main-deck 6-inch of the *Good Hope* and *Monmouth*, the Germans were able to fight, in addition to their 8·2s, all six (main-deck) 5·9s—though not very effectively, as the 'gun-crews could not see well in the rolling and pitching'.

The *Scharnhorst* concentrated on the *Good Hope*, the *Gneisenau* on the *Monmouth*. Within five minutes Spee had obtained decisive hits on the well-defined armoured cruisers. Towards 8 p.m., after taking at least thirty-five direct hits from the *Scharnhorst*, the *Good Hope* was blown to pieces by an exploding magazine amidships. To Spee she looked 'like a splendid firework display against the dark sky'. The *Monmouth* limped out of the battle line at about 7.30, fires raging within her hull. When the *Nürnberg* closed her, just before 9, she was listing so badly that she could not fire her port guns. But her flag was still flying and there was no thought of surrender even when the *Nürnberg* opened unmolested target practice on her at point-blank range (1,000 to 600 yards). The *Monmouth* went down a little after 9, and that was the end of the battle. The *Otranto* and the *Glasgow* had already escaped in the darkness. 'Individually and collectively,' an officer in the *Glasgow* remembers, 'we were humiliated to the very depths of our beings. We hardly spoke to one another for the first twenty four hours. We felt so bitterly ashamed of ourselves for we had let down the King. We had let down the Admiralty, we had let down England.'[23]

Superior force, skilful tactics, and extraordinary gunnery had won a tremendous tactical success for the Germans. Two second-rate British cruisers and all their crews had been wiped out—about 1,600 men, including the Admiral. The German squadron had received but six hits and had two men wounded. The over-joyed Emperor awarded three hundred Iron Crosses to the officers and men, which, alas, they were destined never to receive. The strategic gains, for the moment anyway, were not great. There was a temporary suspension of the nitrate, copper, and tin shipments from Chile and Peru. Spee had paid a price for the victory which weakened him critically in his return match with the Royal Navy a month later. His squadron had consumed 42 per cent of its 8·2-inch ammunition, and the nearest source of replenishment was Germany.

[23] Vice-Admiral Harold Hickling in his *Sailor at Sea*.

'Poor Kit! poor Kit Cradock!' sighed Rear-Admiral Sir Robert Arbuthnot on hearing the news. 'He always hoped he would be killed in battle or break his neck in the hunting-field.'[24] 'Poor old Kit Cradock has gone, poor old chap,' was Beatty's reaction. 'He had a glorious death, but if only it had been in victory instead of defeat . . . His death and the loss of the ships and the gallant lives in them can be laid to [the] door of the incompetency of the Admiralty. They have as much idea of strategy as the Board school boy, and have broken over and over again the first principles.'[25] Beatty's harsh indictment had some substance, although, as indicated, Cradock may have invited his fate by his impetuosity.

In the first place, that the *Good Hope* ('Drake' class) and *Monmouth* ('County' class) could not fight their main-deck 6-inch guns in a heavy sea was well known in the Navy. (Jellicoe, Fisher, and others had protested strongly against the placing of the 6-inch low down in the 'Drake' and 'County' class cruisers, as well as with the 6-inch guns of the dreadnoughts of the 'Iron Duke' class.) It is, therefore, surprising that, in sending them to an area notorious for bad weather, the War Staff had not discounted their combat value.

Secondly, it is a cardinal rule of war that if you try to guard everything, you are bound to be weak everywhere. Cradock had suggested two squadrons (8 October), *each* strong enough to defeat Spee. The Admiralty, after accepting the suggestion for two squadrons, had divided the available force into two weak squadrons, under Cradock and Stoddart, each inferior in fighting power to the enemy.

At the bottom of the disaster was this disregard of the principle of a single concentration. Although they had known for weeks that Spee's powerful squadron was crossing the Pacific, the Admiralty had failed to recognize the emergency nature of the situation. They had therefore made insufficient provision for eradicating the German squadron at all costs. 'Can you imagine anyone in his senses sending such a mixed and totally unsuitable mob down for the job?' was the rhetorical query of the *Glasgow's* Gunnery Officer after the action. The same criticism of the Admiralty was heard in the Grand Fleet. Sending Cradock the *Canopus* was not enough.

---

[24] Dreyer, *The Sea Heritage*, p. 90.
[25] Beatty to Lady Beatty, 10 Nov. 1914; Beatty MSS. Chalmers, *Beatty*, p. 161, reproduces part of this text but gives the date as 2 November.

Richmond, who had wanted to send out *Defence* and one or two other armoured cruisers of that class (14,600 tons, four 9·2-inch, ten 7·5-inch), held Sturdee 'primarily responsible' for the failure 'to get a real concentration of strength'.[26] Sturdee, if he sinned, did so in the best company, since even so intelligent an officer as the former C.O.S., Admiral Sir Henry Jackson (then serving as President of a C.I.D. sub-committee on overseas attack) believed that the *Canopus* and *Good Hope* could handle Spee's squadron. The Admiralty overrated the value of the *Canopus*. The first Admiralty statement published after the battle (5 November) declared that the *Canopus* 'had been specially sent to strengthen Admiral Cradock's squadron, and would have given him a decided superiority . . .' The second announcement (7 November) asserted that 'in the absence of the *Canopus* the enemy's preponderance of forces was considerable'.

Churchill's defence of the division is at first sight plausible.

It would, of course, have been much simpler to have concentrated the squadrons of Admiral Cradock and Admiral Stoddart in the Straits of Magellan and awaited events. But until we knew for certain that the German cruisers were coming to South America, there was a great disadvantage in denuding the main trade route from Rio of all protection. Suppose we had done this and Admiral von Spee had remained, as he could easily have done, for many weeks at Easter Island, or anywhere else in the Pacific, the whole of the Plate trade would then, for all we knew, have been at the mercy of the *Karlsruhe* or of any other German commerce destroyer. At least six different courses were open to von Spee, and we had, while our resources were at the fullest strain, to meet every one of them.[27]

The flaw in the argument is that the Admiralty were certain as early as 5 October that Spee was steaming towards South America. Once there, he would have three alternatives. (1) He could disrupt trade on the west coast; (2) he could proceed through the Straits of Magellan to attack the east coast trade or interfere with the campaign in German South West Africa; or (3) he could go northward with a view to breaking into the West Indies. The third alternative was amply provided for in the Japanese and British forces moving across the northern Pacific. Alternatives one and two could best be met by a concentration of force under Cradock.

[26] Diary, 4 Nov. 1914; *Portrait of an Admiral*, p. 125. But see below, pp. 128–9.
[27] *The World Crisis*, i. 423–4.

A temporary abandonment of trade protection on the east coast would be a calculated risk, and, whatever happened, a modest price to pay for a chance to annihilate Spee.

A third criticism levelled against the Admiralty is the fuzziness in the wording of the War Staff telegrams to Cradock. They 'lacked something in precision and completeness', as Corbett puts the matter. Churchill admits that the wording of the telegrams could have been more precise, but that 'on the main point nothing could have been more emphatic, nor, indeed, should any emphasis have been needed. It ought not to be necessary to tell an experienced Admiral to keep concentrated and not to be brought to action in circumstances of great disadvantage by superior forces. Still, even this was done, and in telegram after telegram the importance of not being separated from the *Canopus*, especially sent him for his protection, was emphasized.'[28] Then why did the Admiralty in its telegram of 28 October fail to comment on Cradock's decision to detach the *Canopus* for subsidiary duties? This is a crucial point if, as the evidence indicates, Cradock received the telegram.

The Admiralty got the news of Coronel on the morning of 4 November, mainly from German sources, and the details of the battle, from the *Glasgow*, on 6 November. The Admiralty announcements (5, 7 November) produced a painful impression on public opinion. Some newspapers were critical of Cradock. Why had he given battle with a hopelessly inferior force? Why was *Canopus* absent? Others shrugged their shoulders. Vigorous war could not be made without taking risks, etc. The principal reaction, however, was that there had been bungling at Whitehall. The Admiralty arrangements were at fault and Cradock was placed in a dangerous position when he was allowed to look for a powerful squadron with a very inferior force. The headlines of the half-penny press were about the 'fearful odds'.

However explained, Coronel was a blow to British naval prestige. It was a small affair from the point of view of *matériel*, and the losses were an infinitesimal diminution of British naval strength. But they were the first losses for a hundred years inflicted on a British squadron in a fair fight, and their imponderable effect began at once to weigh in the balance of neutral opinion. Coronel, moreover, put the British command of the Atlantic in some

[28] *Ibid.*, p. 424.

jeopardy. The account was not balanced by the ending of the careers of the *Karlsruhe* and *Emden* on 4 and 9 November, respectively. The *Emden* was reduced to a wreck by the Australian light cruiser *Sydney* off the Cocos Islands in the Indian Ocean and was finally beached on a reef. The *Karlsruhe* met her end in the Caribbean Sea, destroyed by an internal explosion, although it was not until late in March 1915 that the Admiralty knew of her loss.

In contrast to the gloom in England was the great enthusiasm in Germany over the 'severe blow to the tradition of English superiority at sea. This news filled us in the Fleet with pride and confidence . . .'[29]

Spee had a premonition of what lay ahead. As he returned to his ship, after being fêted by the Germans living in Valparaiso, he was offered a bouquet of roses by an admirer. They had better be kept for his funeral, he sadly observed. The German squadron headed south on 5 November, destination, Germany, in response to the advice of the Admiralty Staff and to the hard fact that 8-inch shell was running low. At Coronel the *Scharnhorst* had fired 422 8-inch shell, and had only 350 left; the *Gneisenau*, 244 and 528, respectively. Spee was determined to do as much damage as possible as he tried to break through and return home. For a starter, he planned to destroy the wireless station at Port Stanley, East Falkland Island. There is evidence that he expected to find and gobble up a weak British cruiser squadron coaling there.

2. VICTORY AT THE FALKLANDS

(*Map* 4)

Within an hour of the receipt of news of Coronel, Fisher and Churchill were hard at work on schemes to retrieve the situation. As the Admiralty viewed the situation, Spee had at least four alternatives. He might (1) interrupt the vital food supply routes on the east coast of South America running from Rio de Janeiro to London; (2) proceed north and then through the Panama Canal (the general right of innocent passage was recognized for warships as well as for merchant ships), smash the West Indies squadron, and release the armed German liners in New York harbour; (3) cross the South Atlantic and interfere with the

[29] Scheer, *Germany's High Sea Fleet*, p. 66.

PLATE V

2. COMMODORE R. Y. TYRWHITT
Commanding Harwich Force,
Dec. 1913–May 1919
[Photograph: Imperial War Museum

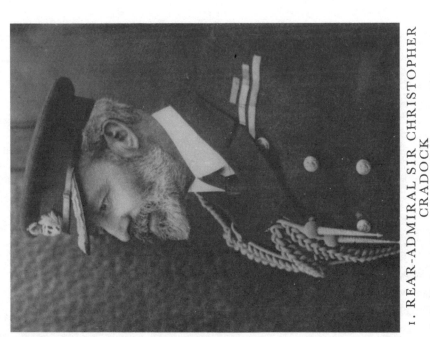

1. REAR-ADMIRAL SIR CHRISTOPHER
CRADOCK
C.-in-C., South-East Coast of America, Sept.–Nov. 1914
[Photograph: Radio Times Hulton Picture Library

PLATE VI

1. VICE-ADMIRAL SIR DOVETON STURDEE

C.-in-C., South Atlantic and Pacific, Nov. 1914–
Jan. 1915, Commanding 4th Battle Squadron,
Feb. 1915–Feb. 1918

2. COMMODORE ROGER B. KEYES

In charge of the Submarine Service, Aug. 1912–Feb. 1915,
Chief of Staff, Eastern Mediterranean Squadron, Feb. 1915–
June 1916, with Lt.-Col. Sykes at Kephalos in 1915

[Photograph: Imperial War Museum

campaign that Generals Smuts and Botha were about to resume against German South West Africa; (4) go to Duala, German Cameroons, which had been captured by an Anglo-French expedition as a base for the conquest of the colony, and destroy the Allied ships. All the alternatives had to be allowed for. To guard against contingency (2), the *Princess Royal* was pulled out of the Battle Cruiser Squadron. Cruiser reinforcements were dispatched to meet (3) and (4).

The first contingency was the one requiring the greatest concentration. Churchill wanted to reinforce Stoddart with the *Defence* and the battle cruiser *Invincible*. He found Fisher in 'a bolder mood'. With the instinct of a Nelson, Fisher wanted to dispatch a force that would annihilate Spee, not merely beat him. With Churchill's full support, on 4 November, within six hours of receiving the first reports of Coronel, he ordered Jellicoe to detach the sister ships *Invincible* and *Inflexible* from the 2nd Battle Cruiser Squadron at Invergordon, and hustle them off to Devonport, there to prepare for overseas service. It took both strategical genius and courage to detach three capital ships (including the *Princess Royal*) in view of the Grand Fleet's small margin and the indeterminate length of time they would be absent. Beatty was left with four battle cruisers against the five in the High Seas Fleet. The battle cruisers arrived at Devonport on 8 November. The next day the dockyard officials, having examined the *Invincible*, which needed repairs, stated that she would be ready to leave on the 13th. The irate First Sea Lord saw that time was of the essence. Besides, the 13th was a Friday. 'What a day to choose!' He shot back a stinger to the yard (9 November): the two ships *must* sail on the 11th, and if necessary, dockyard workmen were to be taken aboard to finish the job. The Admiral Superintendent protested in person. Fisher was inflexible, and he had the First Lord's backing. The ships sailed on the date ordered (the *Invincible* with a number of skilled workmen aboard!), which enabled them to reach the Falklands 21 hours before Spee. With another master stroke, Fisher had the *Canopus*, which was useless for fighting in the line, ground herself on the mud banks in the inner harbour of Port Stanley and take on the role of a fort.

With the two battle cruisers as they sped south was Sturdee, who had just been relieved as C.O.S. Fisher blamed him for the dispositions leading to Coronel. 'Never such utter rot as perpetrated by Sturdee in his world-wide dispersal of weak units! Strong nowhere, weak everywhere!'[30] On returning to the Admiralty, he had offered Sturdee the China command, to be extended to include the Indian and Pacific Oceans. Sturdee was not interested, since his headquarters would be ashore; he would leave the Admiralty only for a sea command. This awkward impasse was resolved when the first news of Coronel arrived. Fisher (on Churchill's prompting, says Captain Bennett) gave the 'pedantic ass' a chance to redeem himself by proposing (4 November) that he go out as C.-in-C., South Atlantic and South Pacific. This vast station was very appealing, and Sturdee accepted at once. He was to proceed south post-haste with the battle cruisers, add Stoddart's force and other ships, and move on to the coaling base at the Falklands. From this key position he was to hunt down and destroy the German squadron. The British squadron reached the Falklands on the morning of 7 December and anchored in Port Stanley and Port William. According to Sturdee's instructions, he was to leave the next day and round the Horn, as the intelligence available pointed to the Germans being in Chilean waters.

He could scarcely have arrived at a better time, but this was due to unforeseen circumstances. A day's delay had been caused by two minor incidents on the way south. A false alarm that the armed merchant cruiser *Kronprinz Wilhelm* was working in the South Atlantic caused Sturdee to make a sweep for her that cost him about twelve hours. He lost another twelve hours when the *Invincible* had to stop to clear the target towing wire which had fouled one of her propellers during gunnery exercises. This day was made good in unusual circumstances. On 26 November the two battle cruisers had arrived at Abrolhos Rocks (about 400 miles north of Rio de Janeiro and 70 miles off the Brazilian coast), where the *Glasgow* and the rest of the squadron were awaiting them. The Admiral announced his intention of sailing for the Falklands on the 29th, after he had completed with stores. (The store ship was due about then.) On the 27th, Luce, the Captain of the *Glasgow*, persuaded Sturdee to sail a day early on the ground that Spee would not remain long on the west coast, but would probably move on the Falklands, whose Governor was alarmed over the

[30] Fisher to Beatty, 19 Nov. 1914; *Fear God and Dread Nought*, iii. 77. But see the note at the end of this chapter.

possibility of a German landing. By losing a day, then gaining a day, the squadron arrived at the right moment. Had it been a day or so earlier or later, it would probably have missed Spee.

The squadron was in the midst of coaling, preparatory to sailing that afternoon, when, at 7.50 a.m., 8 December, a look-out spotted two unidentified warships approaching from the south. They were the *Gneisenau* and *Nürnberg*, which had been sent on in, five miles ahead of the main squadron, to scout. Sturdee was surprised, one story has it, in the act of shaving. Here were the enemy ships steaming towards him, and his own not ready for battle! By not having his squadron concentrated Spee missed a heaven-sent opportunity to stand off the entrance to the harbour and subject each ship as it emerged to a hail of shell. Again, what saved Sturdee's skin (apart from his refusal to become rattled) were two salvoes at about 9.15 from the 12-inch guns of the much maligned *Canopus*, the second of which fell within a hundred yards of the *Gneisenau*. The salvoes caused the German vessels to veer away to the south-east for some precious minutes, giving Sturdee's ships time to leave their anchorages. Then, at 9.40, the German captains got the shock of their lives. They saw tripod masts, which could only mean the presence of battle cruisers, the last thing they expected to see in the South Atlantic. It seems that everybody in South America but Spee was in on the poorly kept secret of the dispatch of the battle cruisers. Therein lies a story.

The Admiralty signal ordering the *Invincible* and *Inflexible* to proceed with all dispatch to Plymouth indicated that tropical uniform would be required, which made it fairly obvious that the ships were bound for South America. At the same time the utmost secrecy was to be observed. Soon after the ships arrived at Devonport it became generally known, not only in the dockyard but in the town itself, that they were off to the south seas. Their mission was obvious. Devonport had a plentiful supply of enemy agents; but their means of getting intelligence through to Germany had been so disorganized that, although it took 26 days to get from Devonport to the Falklands, information reached Germany too late to warn Spee. The Germans had good cable communication with Chile at the time, but the wireless message of warning sent to Spee never reached him, as he was then south of the Horn and out of wireless touch. Consequently, the first indication that Spee had of the presence of the two battle cruisers was seeing the tops of their tripod masts over the sand hills of Port Stanley.[31]

The two scouts turned away and scampered off to rejoin Spee. All Sturdee's ships but one had steam up by now. By 10 they were tumbling out of harbour in hot pursuit of the enemy, who were about 15 miles away and fleeing at top speed. At 10.20 Sturdee hoisted the exciting signal, 'General chase'. Everything favoured him: a calm sea, a clear sky, excellent visibility ('the visibility of the fresh and calm atmosphere surpassed anything which the experience of sailors regarded as possible,' recalled the Captain of the *Gneisenau*), plenty of sea-room, eight hours of daylight, and a crushing superiority—two battle cruisers (each with a broadside of 5,100 lbs. as against the 1,957 lbs. each of the *Scharnhorst* and *Gneisenau*), four armoured cruisers (*Defence, Carnarvon, Kent, Cornwall*), two light cruisers (*Glasgow, Bristol*), and an armed merchant cruiser (*Macedonia*).

The action developed into a stern chase to the south-east. At 12.47 p.m., with his squadron within range (16,000 yards) of the rearmost enemy ship, the *Leipzig*, Sturdee made the signal 'Engage the enemy.' Spee must have known that the combination of the rapidly shortening range and the 12-inch guns of the battle cruisers gave him no chance. He signalled his three light cruisers (about 1.20 p.m.) to try to save themselves while the two armoured cruisers occupied the attention of the battle cruisers. The *Leipzig, Nürnberg,* and *Dresden* scattered and made for the South American coast at full speed, chased by three of Sturdee's cruisers. The *Kent* overhauled the *Nürnberg*, and, after a fierce duel at about 3,300 yards, destroyed her (7.27 p.m.). The *Glasgow* and *Cornwall* disposed of the *Leipzig* (8.35 p.m.), and the *Bristol* and *Macedonia* sank two of the three German colliers. The third collier and the *Dresden* got away; the former was interned in Argentina in January, and the latter was eventually tracked down by the *Glasgow* and sunk at Juan Fernandez Island in March.

The main action between the battle cruisers and the armoured cruisers began at about 1.20 p.m. at 14,000 yards. Each Admiral jockeyed for a range favourable to his tactics. Sturdee tried to open up to beyond the maximum range of Spee's 8·2-inch guns (13,500 yards), but within the range of his own 12-inch guns (16,400

---

[31] Rear-Admiral H. E. Dannreuther's letter to the author, 5 Nov. 1962. He was then a lieutenant-commander and the Gunnery Officer of the *Invincible*.

yards). Spee tried to close to ranges (about 12,000 yards) at which he could use his 5·9 armament as well as his big guns. This would have given him an advantage, as the early British battle cruisers (and dreadnoughts) mounted no secondary armament. He was successful in reducing the range (at about 3) to 11,000 yards (according to the German Official History; Sturdee's dispatch says it fell by 3.15 to 10,000 yards), and then giving Sturdee a hammering. Sturdee used his superior speed to open the range to 14,000 yards, mainly to clear the battle cruisers' funnel smoke that was raising hob with his gunnery efficiency. By this time, however (3.15), his 12-inch had scored damaging hits and the end was in sight. By 3.30 the *Scharnhorst* was listing heavily and on fire fore and aft. She ignored Sturdee's signal to her to surrender and soon after plunged to the bottom (4.17). There were no survivors. The *Gneisenau*, fighting on alone, was subjected to leisurely target practice at shortening ranges from the two battle cruisers and the *Carnarvon*. At the end Sturdee was pounding her at 3,000 to 4,000 yards. The situation was hopeless. The *Gneisenau* had received at least fifty direct 12-inch hits. Her foremast had been shot away, her upper deck was a shambles, she was burning furiously and listing badly. Her Captain rejected a call to surrender, managed occasionally to fire her one undamaged gun, and hastened her sinking by opening the valves and exploding charges in the sides. At about 6 o'clock, as the gallant ship was settling, the Captain called for three cheers for the Kaiser. Ship was then abandoned. Suddenly she heeled over and sank. Nearly 200 of a complement of 850 were rescued. The Germans had fought most courageously against impossible odds and had displayed an amazing spirit to the bitter end of a hopeless fight.

The Falklands had been fought out in the old style, the last such action between surface ships by gunfire alone in the war. Thereafter, torpedoes, mines, submarines, and, to some extent, aircraft introduced complications unknown to Sturdee and Spee.

Cradock had been splendidly revenged and at slight cost. Sturdee's squadron had suffered no important damage and very few casualties, whereas four of the enemy's warships had been sunk and over 2,200 of their officers and seamen had been lost. The country and the Service were jubilant over the prompt retribution for Coronel. Declared Beatty, 'It has done us all a tremendous amount of good getting the news, and I hope will put a stop to a lot of the unpleasant remarks one can detect in a certain portion of the Press that the British Navy *has* been an expensive luxury and is not doing its job.'[32] Congratulations were heaped upon the First Sea Lord. Nothing in his later years gave Fisher greater satisfaction than the Falklands. His pride was heightened by the vindication of the battle-cruiser type. The action was 'the only "substantial victory" of ours in the War (and, as Nelson wished, it was not a Victory—it was Annihilation!). . . . And the above accomplished under the sole direction of a Septuagenarian First Sea Lord, who was thought mad for denuding the Grand Fleet of our fastest Battle Cruisers to send them 14,000 miles on a supposed wild goose chase. . . . And how I was execrated for inventing the Battle Cruisers!'[33] It was the nearest thing in the whole war to the smashing victories of Nelson's day, though, of course, the latter were achieved over equal (on paper) or superior fleets. After the war, Corbett told Luce that in his opinion the two really successful operations in the whole war were the Falklands action and Allenby's campaign in Palestine.

For his signal service, Sturdee was awarded a baronetcy in the New Year's honours, 1916. He was the first officer to receive this traditional honour for a successful action at sea since Captain Hoste's creation for his defeat of a Franco-Venetian squadron off Lissa in 1811. His brother officers showered him with warm congratulatory letters after the battle. 'You have made a grand name for yourself in history and you have done your country the most notable service' (Warrender), 'the greatest sea victory the British Navy has known since Trafalgar' (Webb), etc. Britain's Allies were jubilant. The French squadron in the East Indies, for example, signalled 'all sorts of nice things' to the British C.-in-C. on the station. Neutral countries were properly impressed.

Sturdee had his detractors. To Richmond it was 'an irony that Sturdee, the man who more than anyone else is responsible for the loss of Cradock's squadron, should be the person who profits principally by it, & should be made a national hero! . . . the enemy come in sight . . . running into his arms & saving him the trouble of searching for them. He puts to sea with his Squadron of greatly superior force . . . & has only to steer after them and sink them, which he not unnaturally does. If he didn't, he would

---

[32] Beatty to Lady Beatty, 10 Dec. 1914; Beatty MSS.
[33] Fisher to a friend, 22 Aug. 1917; Fisher, *Records* (London, 1919), pp. 231–2.

indeed be a duffer. Yet for this simple piece of service he is acclaimed as a marvellous strategist & tactician! So are reputations made!'[34]

Fisher was so angry with Sturdee that he deleted many names from his list of recommendations for honours. And when the Admiral passed through London early in February to take over the command of the 4th Battle Squadron from Gamble, Fisher and Churchill gave him a cool five-minute interview, during which 'neither evinced the slightest interest in the engagement'. Indeed, apart from an Admiralty telegram of 10 December which read 'Our thanks are due to yourself and to Officers and men for the brilliant victory you have reported', Sturdee received no Admiralty acknowledgement of the action, not even a private letter from the First Lord or the First Sea Lord.[35]

There were two particular reasons for Fisher's lack of graciousness. He was incensed over Sturdee's 'criminal ineptitude' in allowing the *Dresden* to escape. He had swept a limited area for a day, then had abandoned the search, partly on account of thick weather. On 13 December an Admiralty message informed him that the *Dresden* was at Punta Arenas, in the Magellan Straits, intending to coal, and ordered him to destroy her before she could be interned by the Chilean Government. The *Dresden* escaped again before Sturdee's cruisers could arrive at Punta Arenas. Fisher felt that Sturdee should have sent a ship to Punta Arenas directly after the action to cable the result to the Admiralty and to get information from H.M. Consul stationed there. In three rather rude telegrams early in January he was asked to explain this. The by now highly irritated C.-in-C. justified his action in a sharp dispatch: a report of the action from a ship sent to Punta Arenas could not have reached the Admiralty sooner than the report passed by W/T through the Falkland Islands station to Montevideo and thence direct to the Admiralty; under the 24-hour rule the ship would have had to leave before the *Dresden* arrived; he, the C.-in-C., had more information on her movements than he could have obtained at Punta Arenas; etc. Sturdee concluded: 'Their Lordships selected me as Commander-in-Chief to destroy the two hostile Armoured Cruisers and I endeavoured to the best

---

[34] Diary, 13 Dec. 1914; *Portrait of an Admiral*, pp. 130–1.

[35] Sturdee's memorandum, 'Admiralty Recognition of the Action off the Falkland Islands . . .,' 21 July 1915; Sturdee MSS.

of my ability to carry out their orders. I submit that my being called upon in three separate telegrams to give reasons for my subsequent action was unexpected.' The Admiralty took umbrage over this paragraph. It was 'improper and such observations must not be repeated. Their Lordships await your written report and despatches before coming to any conclusion.'[36] They never did anything when they received them. Sturdee's explanation had been perfectly credible.

Fisher even proposed, in a fit of pique (11 December), that Sturdee stay in the South Atlantic until he had finished off the *Dresden*. Churchill vetoed this; the battle cruisers could not be spared, and for Sturdee to transfer his flag to a cruiser would not befit his rank and position. Besides, the First Lord would do nothing to tarnish a victory that promised to dissipate the distrust of the Admiralty. The incident led to strained relations between Churchill and Fisher for several days.

Fisher was also annoyed over the time Sturdee had taken to dispose of Spee and by the consequent heavy expenditure of shell. The battle cruisers had between them fired 1,174 rounds. This was not remarkable, considering Sturdee's frequent changes of course, the continual enemy zigzagging, and especially the long ranges at which most of the action was fought. To have risked damage to the battle cruisers by closing the range made no sense to Sturdee, who was alert to the importance of restoring them to the Grand Fleet ready for action. And why should he have taken chances with all the trump cards in his hand? Nevertheless, Sturdee is not entirely blameless for the bad shooting of his ships, since it was partly due to his so handling the battle cruisers that their immense funnel smoke seriously hampered the firing. The Admiralty made much of the excessive smoke factor, and this had a serious result, as Captain Macintyre has brought out. 'The need for improved fire-control and intensive target practice was indicated, but was veiled by the failure being ascribed to the interference by funnel smoke.'[37]

The Falklands will never be cited in naval literature as an example of a tactical masterpiece. Strategically, however, its consequences were profound. The sweeping victory wiped out the defeat of Coronel, raised the morale of the nation and of the Navy,

[36] *Ibid.*
[37] Captain Donald Macintyre, *The Thunder of the Guns* (London, 1959), p. 187.

and removed a grave menace to British oceanic trade and overseas operations. Except for the fugitive *Dresden* and two armed merchant cruisers, German surface raiders had been eliminated from the face of all the oceans, and British commerce and troop transports were sailing with comparative immunity. The *Dresden* was destroyed in March 1915, and the following month saw the end of the first phase of the *guerre de course* with the internment at Newport News of the *Kronprinz Wilhelm*, the last of the armed liners.

The German commerce warfare, whether through surface raider, minelayer, or submarine, netted, through January 1915, 75 British merchant ships of 273,000 tons, of which the surface raiders accounted for some 215,000. (In the remaining years of the war surface craft were to sink little more than this again —227,000 tons—making a total destruction by this means of only 442,000 tons compared with over six and a half million tons sunk by submarine.) The 273,000 tons were a mere flea-bite to British trade, as they represented no more than 2 per cent of the steam tonnage flying the British flag at the outbreak of hostilities (12,439,800), or a little over 3 per cent if we include 82 ships of 182,000 tons detained in German or Turkish ports. The lost bottoms were quickly replaced, whereas the German loss of 287 steamers (sunk, captured, or detained in British or Allied ports) of 795,000 tons through January 1915 (mostly at the beginning of the war) were not replaced. Even if the enemy's building resources were not limited, there was no point in replacing the sunken tonnage. German overseas trade had ceased after 4 August except for the Baltic. The pre-war conclusion of the Admiralty about the threat of surface raiders' attacks on merchant shipping—that losses were inevitable, but that these could be kept within reasonable limits and would not be decisive—seemed to have been vindicated. 'None of those gloomy prophecies, which had formed the staple of so many debates and articles, that our merchant ships would be hunted from the seas by German raiders, that scores of additional British cruisers would be required for commerce protection, that British merchant ships once safe in harbour would not venture to sea, materialized; and they might be relegated to the limbo of exploded alarms.'[38] This was true enough—until the U-boats took over the brunt of the *guerre de course* in 1915.

Finally, after the Falklands the Admiralty were able to recall

[38] *The World Crisis*, i. 246.

many ships to Home waters, so nearly completing what Churchill, late in December 1914, described as the first of the three phases of the naval war: 'the clearance of the seas and the recall of foreign squadrons'.[39] For the first time in the war the Navy had, says Churchill, 'immense surpluses of ships of certain classes, trained men and naval supplies of all kinds'. This made possible adventures like the Dardanelles campaign.

There was a peculiar rhythm in the naval history of the first five months. The *Goeben* affair had been offset by the Heligoland Bight action, whose moral effect was nullified by the loss of the three 'Cressys'. The cycle was repeated in a new threesome: Coronel—the Falklands—the 'tip-and-run' raid on the East Coast.

A NOTE ON STURDEE

To give Sturdee his due, as C.O.S. he had urged the dispatch of a 'similar' battle-cruiser force to the South Atlantic, directly he knew Spee was crossing the Pacific, but he had been overruled. Commodore G. von Schoultz (the Russian Naval Attaché with the Grand Fleet), *With the British Battle Fleet: War Recollections of a Russian Naval Officer* (London, 1925), p. 73, on the authority of Sturdee, whom he visited in March 1916; Slade to Sturdee, 11 Dec. 1914, reminding Sturdee of his recommendation, Sturdee MSS.; and Sturdee's own statement in an unpublished, undated paper, 'My Service Connections with Lord Fisher' (*ibid.*), in which he says, without citing dates, 'Then they decided to send two Battle Cruisers out to reinforce our ships on the S.E. Coast of America. Previously I had tried to do the same, but after getting the *Defence* and a battle cruiser [which are not exactly 'the same'] from the Dardanelles to Gibraltar, had been blocked, and the battle cruiser had been ordered back.' Though one or two points are not clear, the facts seem to support Sturdee's claim. The *Indomitable* (the only battle cruiser that Sturdee could have meant) and the *Defence* were dispatched from the Dardanelles, though at widely separated dates—19 August and 10 September, respectively. The *Indomitable* was at Gibraltar, 26 August–8 September, presumably waiting until the Admiralty knew where Spee was heading. It was not until 7 September that the War Staff began to think that he was going to South America. But the next day *Indomitable* was sent to Port Said to pick up a troop convoy. The *Defence* got no farther than Malta (14 September), en route to Gibraltar, where she was to fill up with coal preparatory to joining Cradock. She was recalled to the Dardanelles as flagship on 20 September and did not leave the Mediterranean for the south-east coast of America until 15 October. It was probably Churchill's fear of weakening the naval position in the Mediterranean, with Turkey's attitude so uncertain, that blocked Sturdee. My version is in disagreement with two recent accounts. Middlemas (*Command the Far Seas*, pp. 157, 177) dates the origin of the proposal in mid-October (this is much too late), and gives Battenberg the credit for originating it, then working out the details with Sturdee, and for this I can find no evidence. Bennett (*Coronel and the Falklands*, p. 79) has Sturdee *and* Battenberg (on Earl Mountbatten of Burma's recollection of what his father had told him) soon after 7 September recommending the detachment of battle cruisers *from the Grand Fleet* to deal with Spee, Churchill refusing to overrule Jellicoe's strong protests, and,

---

[39] The two remaining phases were the closing of the Elbe and the domination of the Baltic, which last would be 'decisive'. Churchill to Asquith, 29 Dec. 1914; *ibid.*, ii. 45.

as a weak compromise, the *Defence* being sent to the South Atlantic. The evidence points to Sturdee as the sole originator, though no doubt he talked the plan over with the First Sea Lord and obtained his support. They *may* have discussed whether such a reinforcement should come from the Grand Fleet *or* from the Mediterranean.

Sturdee's proposal was not generally known outside the War Staff. Thus, Beatty could write after the Falklands: 'Truly the ways of Providence are strange, as Sturdee is the one man who was really responsible for the disaster to poor Kit, in that he sent a weak squadron on a hopeless quest. The victory ought to have been Kit's if they had only done what they ought, and sent the *Invincible* and *Inflexible* out to him long ago.' Beatty to Lady Beatty, 10 Dec. 1914; Beatty MSS. The reason that had not happened before was, as Beatty himself appreciated, 'We are as much obsessed with the North Sea as the French are with Alsace and Lorraine.' Beatty to Lady Beatty, 6 Nov. 1914; *ibid.*

VII

Alarums and Missed Opportunities

(DECEMBER 1914–JANUARY 1915)

> The time has passed when anyone—however ignorant and foolish—asked 'what is the Fleet doing?' . . . The British Navy has not dashed under the German shore guns, or danced among the enemy's mine-fields; yet it has undisputed command not of one, but of every sea . . .
>
> (London) *Daily Telegraph*, 16 February 1915.

> For some time I have been receiving letters which express a profound dissatisfaction with the Admiralty and our Admirals. Of late these letters have increased in number and intensity, and it is abundantly clear that an ever-increasing section of the public is coming to regard Winston Churchill as a 'gasbag', Lord Fisher as a 'noodle', and Admiral Jellicoe as an 'incompetent'. The only satisfactory feature of this state of affairs is that it is characteristically British—it happened regularly in the old wars. With the possible exception of the Trafalgar campaign, there was never a war in which the great British public was not firmly convinced of the incompetence of all those primarily responsible for its naval operations.
>
> FRED. T. JANE in *Land and Water*, 30 January 1915.

I. THE SCARBOROUGH TIP-AND-RUN RAID

(*Map* 5)

ON 3 November four German battle cruisers bombarded Yarmouth on the Norfolk coast. The Admiralty braced itself for some 'tremendous event', for which the raid was meant to serve as a diversion. Nothing happened because the enemy had no ulterior motive. It was actually a mine-laying operation, with the coastal bombardment as a side-show. Fisher played a hunch. He had the idea that the Germans would move again soon, knowing that important capital units of the Fleet were absent from Home waters. In late November–early December he alerted the Navy to the probability of a 'big naval operation' in the form of a 'flying raid' or 'insult bombardment' against the

East Coast. His instinct was correct, except for the date. He expected the Germans to move on 8 December, with the waning moon and the 'dawning' tide (high water at dawn, apparently) in their favour, or at Christmas, 'because of the hope of the Germans of our being happy at that season'.

It was still the German policy to postpone trial by battle until such time as they could reduce the British battle fleet by mines and submarines to approximate equality with their own. So far, however, the policy of attrition had had scant success. A submarine had sunk the three 'Cressys' and the *Hawke*. But submarines had done no material damage to the battle fleet, and though their effect on British strategy had been considerable, this was not what the Germans were aiming at. Mining had been more successful, for the *Audacious* had been sunk in a field laid by an auxiliary cruiser off the north of Ireland. But the principal mining operations in the North Sea had achieved very little. Fields had been laid off the Suffolk coast and off the Humber and Tyne, although the Admiralty did not consider that these would unduly hamper the movements of British forces, and no attempt was made to clear them. These areas were notified as dangerous areas, and all minesweeping effort was directed to keeping a clear passage along the coast inshore of these areas and sweeping a few channels to seaward between them. Under these circumstances, it is not surprising that the German Fleet Command were becoming disheartened, and that High Seas Fleet morale was deteriorating through the inaction of the ships. Something had to be done to lay the Grand Fleet open to mine and submarine attack.

Admiral von Ingenohl decided to take advantage of the absence of the *Invincible* and *Inflexible* to stage a battle-cruiser raid on the East Coast: a bombardment of Scarborough and Hartlepool at daylight on the 16th, while the *Kolberg*, one of the light cruisers of the 2nd Scouting Group, laid mines off Filey. The remaining three ships of the Scouting Group and two flotillas of destroyers were attached to the striking force for reconnaissance and screening duties. The battle fleet was to act in support and was to be in a position about half way across the North Sea at daylight. This was in disobedience of the Emperor's order to avoid actions that might result in heavy loss. The raid, it was hoped, would lure a part of the Grand Fleet down from the north and over the freshly laid minefield. The 1st Scouting Group (five battle cruisers under

Hipper) sailed at 3 a.m. on 15 December, and the battle fleet followed about twelve hours later.

The Admiralty were fortunate in having advance information on enemy fleet movements.[1] When the German light cruiser *Magdeburg* ran ashore in the Gulf of Finland on 26 August and was sunk by the Russians, the latter recovered from the person of a drowned signalman copies of the German Navy's cipher signal books and squared charts of the North Sea and Heligoland Bight by which the position of their own and enemy forces was indicated.[2] These 'sea-stained priceless documents' (Churchill) were handed over to the Admiralty in late October, and a special intelligence branch was set up on 8 November to decode the intercepted (in the sense of being heard) German naval wireless messages in cipher picked up by British listening stations.

The famous and mysterious 'Room 40' did a remarkable job in providing the Operations Division of the War Staff with information on German naval movements, despite the enemy's constant alteration of codes and keys. The Germans knew the British were intercepting and reading their signals, but were never aware of how good they were at it. The Royal Navy knew that the German Room 40 was very efficient, but they used as little wireless as possible (the Germans were free with their signals), so that the Germans never had anything approaching the material the British Room 40 had to work on.

The organization was a very secret affair. The mere mention of its name was forbidden (its intercepts were always known as 'Japanese Telegrams'), and entry to it (up to 1917) was severely restricted. Except for Operations Staff officers and a few seniors like the First Lord, First Sea Lord, Second Sea Lord, and the C.O.S., the hundreds of officers and officials in the Admiralty knew nothing at all about Room 40. Even the officers afloat (apart from Jellicoe, Beatty, Tyrwhitt, and a few officers on their

---

[1] For most of what follows on Room 40 I am indebted to several memoranda of 1961–2 from Admiral Sir William James, as well as to his *The Eyes of the Navy*, and to letters from Admiral H. W. W. Hope of 29 Jan. and 9 Feb. 1963, and an unpublished paper, 'Jutland' (16 Feb. 1958), by W. F. Clarke, Lieutenant, R.N.V.R., who joined Room 40 early in 1916; Captain Roskill has a copy. Also valuable in this connexion was the Naval Staff Monograph, *The Naval Staff of the Admiralty*.

[2] As regards the charts, this is the version in *The World Crisis*, i. 462, and *The Naval Staff of the Admiralty*, p. 63. Clarke has the recovery of the charts occurring some time later, when an English trawler in the North Sea found in its nets copies of the charts which had been jettisoned by a German destroyer sunk on 17 October.

staffs) had no idea how the Admiralty obtained information about the German Fleet. The Navy and the press ascribed to luck, or to the work of spies, contacts with the enemy brought about by Room 40 intelligence.

It became obvious very quickly that, since the little band of civilian cryptographers in Room 40 knew nothing about naval matters and naval terminology, it would be wise to add to the party a naval officer, who could make sense of their translations of the signals. Captain Hall, the D.N.I., suggested Commander Hope, of the War Staff, who joined Room 40 in November 1914. Lieutenant Clarke describes him as 'a wonderful character, mild and unassuming but an inspired chief who though he knew no German always drew the right conclusion from the messages decoded; he was universally loved by all of us who served under him'. Hope's job was to sift and 'vet' the intercepts and try to draw a picture from them as to what was happening on the other side of the North Sea. The deciphered messages, with an occasional comment by Hope, were put into red envelopes and taken by messenger direct to the Operations Room, where they were opened by the C.O.S. or the D.O.D., or in their absence by the Duty Captain.

The brilliant head of Room 40 until 1917 was the onetime Director of Naval Education, Sir Alfred Ewing. This 'short, thick-set man with keen blue eyes, overshadowed by ill-kept shaggy eyebrows and with a disarmingly quiet Scottish voice [who] might well resemble a benign physician or guileless dominie' [schoolmaster], was afterwards dubbed by the popular press the 'Sherlock Holmes of Whitehall', etc. He had a very good knowledge of German, an expert knowledge of radio-telegraphy, and a first-class brain.

Room 40 was a private organization at this time, standing apart from the War Staff and with its relations to it not clearly defined. It was not attached to the Intelligence Division of the Staff until July 1917. But Hall had access to it and used to come in and see the intercepts. He worked closely with Room 40 from the beginning, supplying much of its material, for example. It needed Hall's drive and imagination to make full use of a 'weapon' which exercised such immense influence on all operations and which, in Admiral James's opinion, was Britain's 'principal war-winning weapon'. In the spring of 1915 Hall was responsible for a project that enabled Room 40 to obtain by cross-bearings the position of every German ship that sent out a signal. Acting on a suggestion from Captain Round, of the Marconi Company, who had been impressed with the Western Front experiments with W/T directional apparatus, Hall soon dotted the East Coast with radio direction-finder stations. The directional wireless of these D/F stations enabled the Admiralty to locate the position of enemy warships which used their wireless. This was especially valuable in locating with fair accuracy the German C.-in-C.'s position as he communicated with his flotillas and squadrons by wireless.

Room 40 achieved its first great success on the evening of 14 December, when it pieced together from German naval messages a plan for an offensive operation by all five of the battle cruisers, *Seydlitz, Moltke, Von der Tann, Derfflinger*, and *Blücher*, with light cruisers and destroyers, directed against the British coast. (The Admiralty always classified the *Blücher*, which, strictly speaking, was an armoured cruiser, though a powerful one, as a battle cruiser.) N.I.D. also knew that this task force would leave the Jade early the next morning, the 15th, and would return on the evening of the 16th. Since they did not believe the German battle fleet was involved in the operation, the Admiralty ordered south only a detachment of the Grand Fleet, although Jellicoe wanted the whole of the Grand Fleet in the operation. The deduction was that the German squadron would be off the British coast at dawn on the 16th, its objective a raid on Harwich or the Humber. The Admiralty took immediate steps to intercept the enemy ships before they could get home.

Detailed by the Admiralty to spring the trap were Beatty's four battle cruisers (Cromarty), the 3rd Cruiser Squadron under Pakenham (Rosyth), Goodenough's 1st Light Cruiser Squadron (Scapa), the 4th Destroyer Flotilla (Scapa), attached to the 2nd Battle Squadron (rough weather prevented the use of more destroyers), and the 2nd Battle Squadron (six dreadnoughts), the fastest and most powerful of the Grand Fleet battle squadrons, under Vice-Admiral Warrender. The latter, who was in command of the whole force, was perhaps not the wisest choice. He had been trained in fleet work for three years and was well thought of in the Navy. His battle squadron was most efficient in gunnery and in all matters of *matériel*. His mind, on the other hand, did not turn to strategic matters, and his deafness made him slow to grasp things.

PLATE VII

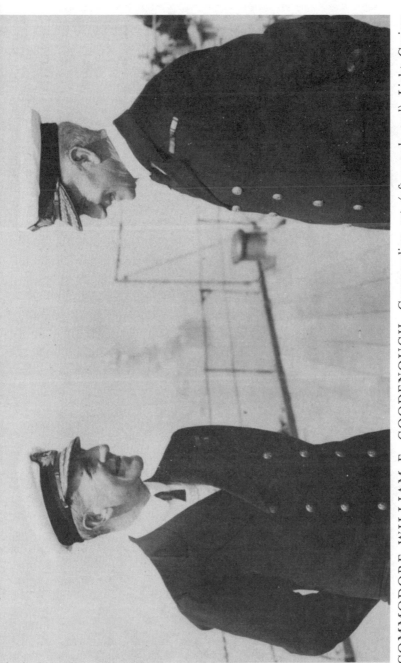

COMMODORE WILLIAM E. GOODENOUGH, Commanding 1st (afterwards 2nd) Light Cruiser Squadron, July 1913–Dec. 1916, and ACTING VICE-ADMIRAL SIR JOHN DE ROBECK, C.-in-C. Eastern Mediterranean Squadron, Mar. 1915–June 1916.

[Photograph: Imperial War Museum

PLATE VIII

CAPTAIN (afterwards REAR-ADMIRAL)
REGINALD W. HALL

Director of Naval Intelligence, Oct. 1914–Jan. 1919

[Drawing by Francis Dodd : Imperial War Museum

ACTING VICE-ADMIRAL
SIR HENRY OLIVER

Chief of Admiralty War Staff, Nov. 1914–May 1917

[Drawing by Francis Dodd : Imperial War Museum

The plan was for Warrender to be off the south-east corner of the Dogger Bank, in the centre of the North Sea, before dawn on the 16th. (The selected rendezvous was practically on a line joining Heligoland and Flamborough Head—180 miles from the former and 110 miles from the latter.) Keyes and his eight submarines were to be off Terschelling at the same time, positioned to pounce on the enemy if he planned a southerly raid. Finally, Tyrwhitt and his light cruisers and destroyers were to be off Yarmouth, awaiting further orders. The rendezvous position for Warrender's combined force was, as events turned out, the best that could have been chosen. Corbett and Churchill give the impression in their books that it was the Admiralty which placed the ships in the correct position for interception. As a matter of fact, it was Jellicoe who selected the rendezvous and issued the order, and who therefore must receive the credit for the opening moves of Warrender's force.[3]

The various squadrons, having joined up, steamed towards the rendezvous, which they were supposed to reach at 7.30 a.m., just before dawn, 16 December. At 5.15 a.m., when still pitch dark, Warrender's destroyers, which had got separated from the main body, ran into the German destroyer *V-155*. This was the beginning of a confused, intermittent close-range action between British destroyers and German cruisers and destroyers that continued for nearly two hours, with the enemy ships falling back. Without the British forces knowing it, they had bumped into the advance screen of the High Seas Fleet. Ingenohl had brought most of his battle fleet, fourteen dreadnoughts and eight pre-dreadnoughts, screened by two armoured cruisers, seven light cruisers, and fifty-four destroyers, into the North Sea to support Hipper's battle cruisers, which were then nearing the English coast.

The German fleet had just reached the rendezvous, on the eastern edge of the Dogger Bank, when *V-155*'s reports began to come in. At this moment (approximately 5.30 a.m.) the port-wing cruiser of Ingenohl's advance screen, the *Prinz Heinrich*, was less

[3] Jellicoe, 'A Reply to Criticism', commenting on *The World Crisis*, i. 464 (where he also makes the point that, had the dispositions been left to him, he would 'unquestionably have taken the whole Fleet to sea'); and see Jellicoe to Fisher, 18 Dec. 1914, and Fisher to Jellicoe, *ca.* 21 Dec. 1914, *Fear God and Dread Nought*, iii. 95, 101. The British telegrams and signals are in Naval Staff Monograph No. 28 (1925), *Home Waters—Part III. From November 1914 to the End of January 1915*, in Naval Staff Monographs, xii. 248–67. The German signals are in *Der Krieg in der Nordsee*, iii. 250–61.

than ten miles from the 2nd Battle Squadron. (The battle cruisers were four miles on Warrender's port bow.) 'Here at last,' as the Naval Staff Monograph sums up the situation, 'were the conditions for which the Germans had been striving since the outbreak of war. A few miles away on the port bow of the High Sea Fleet, isolated, and several hours' steaming from home, was the most powerful homogeneous battle squadron of the Grand Fleet, the destruction of which would at one blow have completed the process of attrition and placed the British and German fleets on a precisely even footing as regards numerical strength.'[4] But quickly concluding that he was in the presence of the Grand Fleet, fearful of a torpedo attack in the dark (though dawn was approaching) from what he imagined was the destroyer screen of the Grand Fleet, and bearing in mind the view of the Higher Command that he should not risk his heavy ships, Ingenohl signalled the fleet (5.30) to turn to port on a southeasterly course. Interference from the British destroyers delayed the order for the turn, and it was not until about 5.42 that it was carried out. For 40 minutes the two fleets were steaming on almost parallel courses. At 6.20 Ingenohl signalled a further turn to port (a turn by squadrons to E.S.E.$\frac{1}{2}$E.) and made off for home at high speed, rapidly pulling away from the British. Hipper was left to fend for himself, although Ingenohl did not think him to be in danger, since his appearance off the English coast would be a surprise.

Warrender, not suspecting from the sketchy reports of his destroyers that the enemy's battle fleet was in the vicinity, continued on his course and reached the rendezvous at 7.17 a.m. At about 8.05 Beatty received a delayed destroyer report, 'Am keeping in touch with large cruiser *Roon* and five destroyers steering East', which Warrender had received a quarter of an hour earlier. He at once turned to the eastward in pursuit, and away went the battle cruisers and light cruisers at full speed to cut off the enemy, with the 2nd Battle Squadron and 3rd Cruiser Squadron steering a similar course at 18 knots. Beatty had no idea that he was chasing the whole High Seas Fleet![5]

Beatty broke off the chase at 8.54 a.m., after intercepting three

[4] *Home Waters. From November 1914 to the End of January 1915*, p. 101.
[5] The Admiralty approved Beatty's action. 'When the *Roon* was sighted, the Vice-Admiral could hardly avoid following her, although it was taking his ships away from the coast, as there was no certainty at that time that any attack on the coast would be made.' Admiralty to Jellicoe, 6 Jan. 1915; Admiralty MSS.

signals in quick succession: one from the light cruiser *Patrol* reporting that she was heavily engaged with two battle cruisers (no position was given), a second from the destroyer *Shark* that she was being chased to the westward by light cruisers, and the third, from Scarborough to the Admiralty, that that place was being shelled. On receiving confirmation of the bombardment from the Admiralty, at 9.03 he altered course to W.N.W. for Scarborough. Some minutes later, Warrender, when he finally got the Admiralty signal, turned to follow the battle cruisers. This was the situation at 9.35: the British main force was in two groups steering similar courses for the East Coast, with the 2nd Battle Squadron and 3rd Cruiser Squadron about ten miles to the east-south-eastward of the Battle Cruiser Squadron and Light Cruiser Squadron, and with the whole force in visual touch. The weather was fine and clear, and the sea smooth. The enemy was located and appeared to be within the grasp of superior British forces.

The German battle cruisers (which had at 12.15 a.m. on the 16th crossed the course of the British ships, about an hour ahead of Beatty's squadron) had, between approximately 8 and 9.15 a.m., operating in two groups, shelled the towns of Scarborough, Hartlepool, and Whitby. Meanwhile, the *Kolberg* had laid her hundred mines off Filey. Article I of Convention No. 9 signed at the Hague Conference in 1907 read: 'The bombardment by naval forces of undefended ports, towns, villages, dwellings, or buildings is forbidden.' Hartlepool was a defended port (it boasted a battery of 6-inch guns) and a flotilla station, but Scarborough and Whitby were not defended towns and had no military character. British trust in the Hague Convention, coupled with the low visibility on the coast, had given Hipper a chance to get in close and to launch his attack before his presence was suspected. Unscathed and their mission accomplished, the battle cruisers turned about and shaped course for home shortly after 9.30 a.m. They were ignorant of the presence of any strong British forces on the line of retreat, nor were they aware that the main body of the High Seas Fleet was returning to harbour.

We left Warrender and Beatty steaming for Scarborough, although there was no information whether the enemy ships had left the coast. At 10.11 Warrender received an important signal from Jellicoe at Scapa. As noted above, the Germans had laid two minefields off the Tyne and Humber earlier in the war. The

C.-in-C., on learning of the bombardment, deduced that the enemy would probably retire through a 20-mile wide gap they had left off Whitby between the minefields. (It was the route Hipper took.) This he signalled to Warrender and Beatty. To guard against the Germans escaping to the northward inside the minefields, at 9.52 Jellicoe ordered the 3rd Battle Squadron down from the Forth to a position outside the northern minefield.

Warrender altered course so as to steer straight for the southern edge of the gap (10.25), proceeding south of the Dogger Bank Patch. (The south-west Patch of the Dogger Bank was a bad bit of ground with a least depth of seven fathoms and several wrecks scattered over it.) He signalled to Beatty to steer for the gap, keeping south of the Patch. Beatty, already too far to the northward to pass south of the Dogger Bank, was forced to go round the Patch northabout. He was sufficiently clear of it by 11 to alter to W.N.W. And so it came about that a navigational obstruction had created a gap between the two groups of the British forces. Separated by the Patch, they had lost sight of each other shortly after 10.30. Thereafter there was considerable uncertainty as to their relative positions, since ships in making reports at this stage of the war did not use the later system of reference positions based on the flagship's reckoning.

The Navy had an excellent opportunity to cut off the raiding force. Four battle cruisers and six dreadnoughts stood between Hipper and his bases. 'We went on tenterhooks to breakfast,' Churchill remembers. 'To have this tremendous prize—the German battle-cruiser squadron whose loss would fatally mutilate the whole German Navy and could never be repaired—actually within our claws, and to have the event all turn upon a veil of mist was a racking ordeal. . . . subject to moderate visibility we hoped that a collision would take place about noon.'[6] What the First Lord dreaded came to pass. Good visibility and a calm sea prevailed most of the morning. At about 11 the two forces were about a hundred miles apart, steaming right at each other. Then the weather suddenly turned foul after 11, high seas and driving rain squalls reducing the visibility to as little as a mile; it never exceeded 4,000 yards. And then, while everyone was wringing their hands at the frightfully bad luck, worse luck followed.

At 11.25 the most southerly ship of Beatty's light-cruiser screen,

[6] *The World Crisis*, i. 467–8.

Goodenough's flagship, the *Southampton*, sighted an enemy light-cruiser and destroyer force. It was part of the raiding force, acting as a far advanced look-out for the battle cruisers. The *Southampton*, supported by the light cruiser *Birmingham*, engaged. At 11.30 Goodenough signalled to his squadron to close. The *Nottingham* and *Falmouth* started to move southward to join in the fight. Beatty wanted to keep part of the light-cruiser screen ahead of him at a time when he had good reason to believe he was fast approaching Hipper's big ships. (Actually, Hipper was about 50 miles to the westward.) Besides, he considered the *Southampton* did not need their assistance, as only one enemy light cruiser was reported, and Goodenough had the support of the *Birmingham*. He accordingly signalled by searchlight to the *Nottingham* (11.50): 'Light cruisers —resume your position for look-out. Take station ahead five miles.' The signal was intended only for the two light cruisers not yet engaged, the *Nottingham* and the *Falmouth*. The *Nottingham* naturally interpreted the signal as meant for all the light cruisers and therefore passed it on to Goodenough, as did the *Birmingham*, which had also seen the signal. The unfortunate effect was to cause Goodenough reluctantly to order the *Southampton* and *Birmingham* to break off the contact and resume their places in the screen. Alerted to the presence ahead of an enemy force, Hipper altered course from east to south-east at 11.50 to support his light forces. But for the signalling error which had caused Goodenough to break off his engagement, he would in all probability have so continued and a battle-cruiser action would have resulted. The last thing Beatty had intended was to break off the action of the *Southampton* and *Birmingham*, and he was shocked and angered to learn (12.15 p.m.) that the light cruisers had lost contact. He wrote after the operation:

I do not understand how the Commodore could have thought that the signals made to *Nottingham* and *Falmouth* applied to him, observing that *Lion* was in visual touch with *Southampton* and in fact nearer to him than the *Nottingham*, the apparent source of his information. Even though the wrong call sign was used in addressing *Nottingham*, I consider that the situation in which the Commodore was placed should have made him doubt the intention of my order. I say this more especially as I had in personal interviews previously impressed on him that he might always use the freest discretion; and that if he, on the spot, considered any of my orders unsuitable to the existing situation, he should never hesitate to vary them and report to me. This indeed is an elementary duty of Cruiser Officers.[7]

The whole episode may be charitably written off, as Beatty's biographer has, as a 'regrettable misunderstanding . . . caused by a technical error in signalling'.[8] But the disagreeable fact is that this was the first of four serious errors made by Lieutenant-Commander Ralph Seymour, Beatty's Flag-Lieutenant. The second was at the Dogger Bank (see below, pp. 162–3), where, admittedly, the conditions were extremely difficult, and the third and fourth, at Jutland. He seemed unable on these crucial occasions to translate Beatty's intentions into action without ambiguity. Beatty at the time regarded the Scarborough and Dogger Bank mistakes as accidental and did not hold Seymour to account. This was thoroughly in keeping with his kind nature, which restrained him from blaming, let alone sacking, anyone for letting him down badly. It is probably also a reflection of his credo not to do anything to weaken the morale of the force he commanded. This, too, will explain his ambivalent attitude towards Goodenough (see below). Years afterwards, however, the Admiral told a friend, 'He [Seymour] lost three battles for me!'[9]

This stroke of luck for the Germans saved Hipper just as Warrender had been saved from certain doom by a similar bit of luck when Ingenohl had turned away. Lady Luck waved her magic wand over Hipper again. British dispositions still promised to bring the two forces together. Contact was recovered at 12.15

[7] Beatty to Jellicoe, 19 Dec. 1914; Admiralty MSS.

[8] Chalmers, *Beatty*, p. 171.

[9] In manœuvring a fleet in an action, it appears to have been the general practice for an admiral to say what he wanted to do, and to leave it to the signal officer, an expert in these matters, to put his intention into a suitable flag or wireless signal. Now, as regards Seymour, he was not a properly qualified signal officer, having only done a short course. Those were the days when the flag-lieutenant also carried out the duties of signal officer, and it is probable that Beatty selected him before war came more as a congenial flag-lieutenant than a signal officer. He was fond of the cheerful and extremely loyal Seymour and often referred to him as 'my little round Flag-Lieutenant'. An officer who served in the *Lion* points out that 'Seymour was perhaps a trifle stolid and unimaginative (common with the English), that is, he would await orders to send a signal and very seldom suggested making one that might clear up a complex situation. Many other officers in the same position I expect would have done no better.' Seymour was no fool, however. He benefited by his mistakes, and through experience he reached a reasonable standard of efficiency. Despite protests from fully qualified signal officers, Beatty took him with him as flag-lieutenant when he became C.-in-C., Grand Fleet, for the reason that Seymour had more experience of battle conditions than any other signal officer.

p.m., when Warrender, who was 15 miles south-east of Beatty, sighted and was sighted by the German light forces, still 40 miles ahead of their Admiral. So warned, Hipper escaped Warrender's clutches under cover of rain squalls and the miserable visibility by hauling well to the northward to make a wide detour (12.45). Rounding the Dogger Bank, he legged it for Heligoland.

Beatty missed one glorious chance to get at Hipper. When he received the news from Warrender (12.25) that he had sighted enemy light forces, he deduced that this was the same force Goodenough had engaged at 11.30, and that it was a look-out ahead of the battle cruisers. He had been steaming towards the middle of the minefield gap, but he now (12.30) turned around and proceeded to the east, acting on the sound strategical principle of putting himself between the enemy and his bases. It seems a pity that Beatty had been deflected from his westerly course by Warrender's signal. Had he stood on, it is almost certain that he would have sighted the German battle cruisers ahead of him at about 1 p.m. But his luck was out and there was no contact. Between 1.15 and 1.30 Beatty and Warrender turned north when it became clear that Hipper had not tried to get away through the southern outlet from the gap and must have escaped to the north. Nothing happened. Beatty turned to the east at 1.55 in a fresh attempt to get between Hipper and his base. Contact was never re-established and Warrender ordered the chase abandoned at 3.45.

The Navy had one last chance to get at the Germans. At 3.35 p.m. on the 16th Keyes received an Admiralty order to take his submarines from the Terschelling area into the Bight and try to intercept the High Seas Fleet. Since his submarines were submerged, Keyes was able to round up but four, and these he instructed to arrive at their new stations by 3 a.m. and to attack if the enemy ships came within range. Only one of the four got a chance—Lieutenant-Commander M. E. Nasmith in *E-11*, when he found himself on the morning of the 17th within range of the German battle squadrons. At 8.10, at a range of only 400 yards, he fired a torpedo at the leading ship, the dreadnought *Posen*, which, because the submarine was rolling heavily, ran too deep and passed under its target.

Not anticipating any luck with the submarines, the Admiralty had in desperation ordered Keyes with his two destroyers into the

Bight for a last-ditch torpedo attack. Churchill has described the tense scene when the War Staff Group reached this decision on the evening of the 16th. 'It seemed indeed a forlorn hope to send these two frail destroyers, with their brave Commodore and faithful crews, far from home, close to the enemy's coast, utterly unsupported, into the jaws of this powerful German force with its protecting vessels and flotillas. There was a long silence. We all knew Keyes well. Then some one said, "It is sending him to his death." Some one else said, "He would be the last man to wish us to consider that." There was another long pause.'[10] The First Lord never expected to see the gallant Keyes again. Keyes, however, did not get the Admiralty signal until 1.20 a.m., when he was nearly home, 200 miles from Heligoland. It was too late to get him on the scene in time. He was heartbroken, especially as he had been strongly tempted the preceding afternoon to move into the Bight on his own initiative. 'Thus ended,' in Churchill's epitaph, 'this heart-shaking game of Blind Man's Buff.'

Corbett's conclusion is poignant. 'In all the war there is perhaps no action which gives deeper cause for reflection on the conduct of operations at sea. . . . Two of the most efficient and powerful British squadrons, with an adequate force of scouting vessels, knowing approximately what to expect, and operating in an area strictly limited by the possibilities of the situation, had failed to bring to action an enemy who was operating in close conformity with our appreciations and with whose advanced screen contact had been established.'[11]

There was a feeling of bitter disappointment and exasperation in both the Fleet and the country. Beatty cursed the bad luck that had prevented Hipper's destruction. 'If we had got them Wednesday, as we ought to have done, we should have finished the war from a naval point of view.'[12] A strong letter to the C.-in-C. laid the principal blame at Goodenough's door. The same letter also reveals a number of interesting facets in Beatty's outlook.

There never was a more bitterly disappointing day as the 18th [16th]. We were within an ace of bringing about the complete destruction of the Enemy Cruiser Force—and failed. . . . There is no doubt whatever that his [Goodenough's] failure to keep touch with and

[10] *The World Crisis*, i. 470.
[11] *Naval Operations*, ii. 43.
[12] Beatty to Lady Beatty, 20 Dec. 1914; Chalmers, *Beatty*, p. 175.

report the presence of the Enemy Cruisers was entirely responsible for the failure . . . But the point is how can the question be dealt with to produce the best results for the future? That is the only point of view. He has been supplied with a copy of my narrative to V.A. 2 B.S. [Warrender], but not with a copy of my covering letter to you. For this reason, if he is to retain command of his Squad^n and they work with me, I do not wish to add, to his already lost confidence feeling, or destroy the harmony that exists between us. Without confidence and without harmonious working together which is all important in our work we shall never succeed. He naturally is very much distressed, and I think realizes the situation acutely, but the issues are too important for us to be allowed to indulge in the luxury of mistakes. We cannot afford to make any. And I am of the opinion that when men fail under the Test of War to carry out the most elementary duties of their work they should not be given opportunities of making others, which will have more disastrous results. If you take this view I would earnestly submit that an officer should be appointed in his place who we KNOW ABSOLUTELY would not fail; and I do not think there is anyone in the Service better fitted for the duty than Halsey of the *New Zealand*. He knows Cruiser work and Battle Cruiser work, and the relation of one with the other. If I had only had the L.C. Squad^n in peace I would have guaranteed those mistakes w^d not have occurred, although time after time I have impressed upon Goodenough the necessity of always using his own initiative and discretion—that my orders are expressions of intentions and that they are *not* to be obeyed too literally. The Man on the Spot is the only one who can judge certain situations. On the other hand if you think it undesirable to make any change or take any steps in that direction I would earnestly petition you not to destroy further his confidence in himself and if you could send me a wireless as to what you purpose I could set about restoring that confidence, and harmony in our relations with each other which has received a rude shock. . . . Truly the past has been the blackest week of my life . . .[13]

Fisher was sick over the German escape 'when they were all [at 12.45 p.m.] actually in our grasp!' The thick weather had saved the enemy *in the very jaws of death!* But human error there was, too—'all concerned made a hash of it'—and heads must roll. Before proceeding, it is important to establish the fact that Fisher's head-hunting was always primarily motivated by far higher considerations than feelings of rage and frustration over failures. As he once put it to the C.-in-C.,

[13] Beatty to Jellicoe, 20 Dec. 1914; Jellicoe MSS.

I suppose you have a very high opinion of Warrender and Bradford or you would not cling to them. I have no reason for making this remark beyond that they both seem somewhat stupid! . . . I can't stand a fool however amiable, and I don't believe that in war that it is anything short of criminal to keep the wrong men in any appointment high or low. 'Changing horses while crossing the stream' is an overdone saying! It's all rot (*and much worse*) having regard to anyone's feelings when the safety of our Empire is at stake. OLD WOMEN MUST GO![14]

The old warrior was howling in the wilderness. Neither Churchill, nor Jellicoe nor Beatty found these ideas appealing. After Scarborough, Fisher recommended sacking Warrender—he had not shown up at all favourably in the action, as Jellicoe admitted—and putting in Sir Robert Arbuthnot, then Rear-Admiral, 2nd Battle Squadron. He also wanted to get rid of Keyes, whom he held responsible for 'making a mess of the Submarines in the last 3 years'. In particular he was furious with him for the Navy not having more submarines.[15] Churchill, though as distressed as Fisher, was at his statesmanlike best. He would not hear of officers being 'got rid of for a single failure, unless there are other reasons for thinking they are incompetent. Men often learn by mistakes, and the anxieties of war are such that leaders must know that they will be supported, and not be worrying about their own positions and feeling themselves in personal jeopardy.'[16] There were no censures and no heads were chopped. All the same, Fisher made it impossible for Keyes to stay with the submarines much longer.

Jellicoe was '*intensely* unhappy' about the escape of the German ships. 'We had the opportunity of our lives.' After examining the reports of the flag officers engaged in the operation, he cited the thick weather at the critical time as the principal cause. Nobody will quarrel with that judgment, made as it was a quarter of a century before radar. Jellicoe also made the criticism that the Admiralty took too much time in passing Hipper's positions (learned through intercepted signals) on to Warrender. Messages took one to two hours and were received too late to be of much use to the Admirals.[17]

The C.-in-C. 'couldn't understand Goodenough's action at all. So totally unlike all he had previously done since the war began.'

[14] Undated letter (*ca.* 3 Apr. 1915); Jellicoe MSS.
[15] But see Keyes, *Naval Memoirs*, i. 20–1, 53–5, 129–34, 167.
[16] Churchill to Fisher, 23 Dec. 1914; *Fear God and Dread Nought*, iii. 109.
[17] Jellicoe to Fisher, 18 Dec. 1914; *ibid.*, p. 97.

He would not have been averse to the Commodore's relief by
Halsey.[18] It was Churchill, apparently, who saved Goodenough.
In his report to the Admiralty, Jellicoe thought it

quite conceivable that the enemy's escape was facilitated by the action
of [Goodenough] . . . in not keeping touch with the light cruisers
engaged by him between 11.25 and 11.50 a.m., and by his not fully
informing [Beatty] . . . of the number of enemy vessels sighted by him.
At 11.20 a.m., he sighted a light cruiser and destroyers, and at 11.40
a.m. three more light cruisers. *These vessels he did not report.* . . . The
Commodore gives as his reason for abandoning the chase of the enemy
the signal made by [Beatty] . . . to him to resume his station. This
signal was intended by the V.A. for the *Nottingham* and *Falmouth*
only . . . It was a most unfortunate error. Had the Commodore
disobeyed the signal, it is possible that the action between the light
cruisers might have resulted in bringing the battle cruisers to action.
The Commodore had reported the presence of the first light cruiser
and destroyers and knew that the V.A. was aware of their being in
sight; there is therefore every justification for his action in obeying the
signal from this point of view, but he had *not* reported the sighting of
the three other cruisers and in my opinion, he should certainly have
disobeyed the signal on this account, and kept touch with them until
he had informed the V.A.[19]

The same report criticized Warrender for not taking action on
receipt of the early destroyer reports of the presence of an enemy
force, and for not making the presence of the enemy known. 'This
omission had no effect on the actual escape of the enemy's force
from his own, but in my opinion he should most certainly have
warned the coast patrols at once and reported to the Admiralty
and to myself. The warning to the coast patrols, had it been given,
would have allowed more time for the heavy ships in the Tyne and
Humber, and at Rosyth, to have gone to sea, and would also have
given the submarines a far better opportunity.'

A week later, having digested the reports of the flag and senior
officers, the C.-in-C. reached this main conclusion for their
'information and guidance':

[18] Jellicoe to Fisher, 1 Jan. 1915; Lennoxlove MSS. In retrospect, Jellicoe took a
different view. A post-war note on the envelope of Beatty's letter of 20 Dec. 1914
reads: 'Beatty very severe on Goodenough but forgets that it was his own badly
worded signal to the Cruisers that led to the Germans being lost out of touch [*sic*].'
[19] Jellicoe to Admiralty, 23 Dec. 1914; Admiralty MSS.

Should the officer commanding a squadron, or the captain of a single vessel, when in actual touch with the enemy, receive an order from a senior officer which it is evident may have been given in ignorance of the conditions of the moment, and which, if obeyed, would cause touch with the enemy to be lost, such officers must exercise great discretion as to representing the real facts before obeying the order. It must be realised that a signal made under such conditions is in the nature of an *instruction*.[20]

The Admiralty's observations on Jellicoe's reports accepted the C.-in-C.'s criticisms of Goodenough and were even more critical than Jellicoe of Warrender.

When the Commodore, 1st Light-Cruiser Squadron received the signal to resume previous station, he was actually engaged with the enemy's light-cruisers. Before breaking off this action, he should have reported the fact to the Vice-Admiral Commanding, 1st Battle-Cruiser Squadron. The error in passing the signal to him would immediately have been discovered and he would have been told that it did not apply to him and that he should continue to attack the enemy. To break off an action, which has been begun, against an equal force is a most serious step: and an Officer so engaged should, in the absence of previous special instructions, make sure that his superior knows that he is fighting before relinquishing the action.[21]

It had been a day of 'confusion and lost opportunities' in which both sides had been lucky and unlucky, and both had good reason to be bitterly disappointed. Although the Germans made much in public of the bombardments, they realized that their policy

[20] Jellicoe's memorandum of 30 Dec. 1914 for the flag officers and commodores of the Grand Fleet; *ibid*. In British naval parlance there is a clear distinction between 'orders' and 'instructions'. Orders are to be carried out literally. Instructions are statements of how the admiral wants the job to be done in normal circumstances, but give discretion to the officer concerned to modify them if the circumstances are unforeseen.

[21] Admiralty to Jellicoe, with a copy to Warrender, Goodenough, *et al.*, 6 Jan. 1915; *ibid*. There were lesser strictures against Beatty, especially that, after the enemy's light cruisers had escaped from the battle squadron, he should have spread his ships in as long a line as possible north and south, so as to intercept the battle cruisers. Jellicoe sprang to Beatty's defence (14 January) with the submission that the 'invariable' and 'correct' rule was to keep the battle cruisers concentrated in any but the clearest weather. Beatty, too, maintained (26 February) that to have spread his battle cruisers 'would have been against all the experience gained and principles evolved during the past two years, which have received the entire approval of two successive C.-in-C.'s. The one principle by which I have been hitherto guided is that Battle Cruisers should be concentrated, more especially when the Enemy Force is equal if not superior to ours, and the visibility is low (as was the case on this occasion).' He had the last word on this matter. The documents quoted are with the Admiralty MSS.

of attrition had not proved more successful than before. There was great chagrin in the Imperial Navy over the priceless opportunity Ingenohl had thrown away to reduce the numbers of the Grand Fleet to a parity. 'On December 16th,' Tirpitz wrote a few weeks later, 'Ingenohl had the fate of Germany in the palm of his hand. I boil with inward emotion whenever I think of it.'[22] It can be argued, as Churchill has, that Warrender and Beatty could have, and would have, refused battle with the High Seas Fleet. They would have learned from their screen of what they were coming up against and would have taken advantage of their superior speed. The shock was as great in Britain. Reported Fisher, 'Had you heard the Prime Minister last night (at our secret War Council) talking of Beatty missing the German Battle Cruisers yesterday you would have thought England's last hour had arrived!'[23]

The startling news that a German squadron had bombarded the East Coast with impunity aroused the country as never before in the war. The Admiralty had, after all, led the public to believe that the German Fleet would not dare to venture beyond the Bight. The query used by the coroner at the Scarborough inquest was picked up and repeated everywhere: 'Where was the Navy?' A shoal of indignant letters in the press criticized the Admiralty dispositions and demanded measures, such as submarines and guns mounted on shore, which would render demonstrations against the East Coast too perilous to be attempted again. The major organs of the press, with an exception or two, stood by the Admiralty, pointing out that the raid had no military importance, asking the nation to trust the Navy without question, and stating the obvious fact that it was impossible to prevent descents upon

[22] Letter of 9 Jan. 1915; Tirpitz, *My Memoirs*, ii. 496. Opinion in the High Seas Fleet was just as furious. The Captain of the battle cruiser *Moltke* maintained that the C.-in-C. had turned back 'because he was afraid of 11 British destroyers which could easily have been eliminated. . . . Under the present leadership we will accomplish nothing.' Magnus von Levetzow to Admiral von Holtzendorff (the onetime C.-in-C., then unemployed), 15 Jan. 1915; Levetzow Papers, German Ministry of Marine MSS. The German Official History (*Krieg in der Nordsee*, iii. 73) severely criticizes Ingenohl for turning back on mere conjecture instead of using his light forces to determine the strength of the British Fleet. '. . . he decided on a measure which not only seriously jeopardised his advance forces off the English coast but also . . . deprived the German Fleet of a signal and certain victory.' The Official History, however, approvingly quotes Corbett's statement (*Naval Operations*, ii. 46): 'It was over two centuries since anything like it had occurred upon our shores, and not since De Ruyter's raid on Sheerness [1667] had a foreign enemy killed British troops on English soil.'
[23] Fisher to Jellicoe, 17 Dec. 1914; Jellicoe MSS.

unprotected points of a long coastline. 'The best police force,' remarked *The Observer* (20 December), 'may firmly preserve general order, but cannot prevent some cases of murder, arson and burglary'.

The Admiralty frankly admitted there was no absolute security against occasional raids. The German naval command may have hoped through the raid to stir up English opinion to demanding that the Grand Fleet be parcelled out into small squadrons spread along the coast in a defensive posture. Fisher, indeed, had evidence from a 'reliable source', an Italian officer in Berlin, that it was the German idea 'that these raids will greatly demoralize us and cause us to risk our ships and to divide them up . . .'[24] This German hope, if such it was, was quickly scotched. The Admiralty made it known at once that in no circumstances would they 'modify the general naval policy which is being pursued'. One did not have to be a Mahan or a Corbett to appreciate that the first condition of naval strategy was a foot-free Fleet, one not tied down in small and scattered units to the protection of portions of the coast, but massed, stationed, and prepared where it would be most needed on 'the Day'.

The Admiralty did make one strategic change under the influence, in part, of the public anger. Beatty had for many weeks been urging that his battle cruisers be moved from Cromarty to Rosyth or the Humber, positions much nearer to the enemy's bases. This would improve the chances of intercepting a German raid on the East Coast. After Hipper's raid, the Admiralty agreed with Beatty and gave him permission on 20 December to move the battle cruisers, also Goodenough's 1st Light Cruiser Squadron, to Rosyth as their permanent base.[25] The transfer was made on 21 December. (They joined the 3rd Battle Squadron and the 3rd Cruiser Squadron at Rosyth.) They were to remain integral parts of the Grand Fleet.

Part of the national anger was turned against the enemy. For shelling undefended towns and causing civilian casualties of

[24] Fisher's 'VERY SECRET' memorandum, 19 Dec. 1914, for Wilson, Oliver, and Bartolomé; *Fear God and Dread Nought*, iii. 106n.

[25] Strictly speaking, Rosyth, which is situated about 32 miles above May Island in the Firth of Forth, was only a naval dockyard, with the normal facilities for docking and refitting. The anchorage for the battle cruisers until 1918 was in the River Forth between Rosyth and the Forth Bridge, about two miles eastward. But, following common practice, I use 'Firth of Forth', 'the Forth', and 'Rosyth' interchangeably.

122 killed and 443 wounded the raiding squadron was branded with such epithets as the 'assassin squadron' and the 'Scarborough bandits', and its tactics as 'butcher and bolt' and 'murder and scuttle'. Churchill wrote publicly to the Mayor of Scarborough of 'the stigma of the baby-killers of Scarborough', which would forever brand the officers and men of the German Navy. Once again the Navy was angry at the First Lord's 'bombastic' public statements. Expressions like 'rats out of a hole' and 'German baby-killers' were 'so un-English', asserted one senior Admiral, 'and does no good, and so undignified for the head of the Navy.'[26] The Fleet was, however, just as aroused as the First Lord and the country, and in a mood to teach the enemy a lesson. Bayly, then C.-in-C., Channel Fleet, officially requested permission (which was denied) to carry out a retaliatory raid as an 'unexpected New Year's Gift' to the Germans. 'For the annoyance of the enemy, the prestige of the Navy, and to show that we are not afraid to do to Germany's fortified ports what she does to our watering places, we must insult her coast and make an offensive movement.'[27]

2. OTHER ALARUMS: ZEPPELINS AND BATTLE FLEETS

In one of the Zeppelin raids on Rosyth (2 April 1916), bombs dropped at Leith caused the products of a whisky distillery to fill the gutters. Many of the citizens were soon lying on their backs, unconscious. Such light moments in the wartime annals of the Zeppelin were rare. The Zeppelin posed a threat to Great Britain —a deadly threat in Fisher's opinion. On 3 September 1914, with nearly all the R.F.C. planes having gone to France, Churchill had accepted the responsibility of the Admiralty, specifically, of the R.N.A.S., for home air defence. (This naval commitment was relinquished to the R.F.C. in February 1916.) This was a bit presumptuous, since the Admiralty was as lacking in the means to do the job as was the War Office. Anti-aircraft guns and search-lights were conspicuous by their absence. The First Lord was not alarmed. He rated the Zeppelin as a poor weapon, an 'enormous bladder of combustible and explosive gas [which] would prove to

---

[26] Colville to Hamilton, 5 Jan. 1915; Hamilton MSS.

[27] Bayly to Churchill, 25 Dec. 1914; Admiralty MSS. The actual objective of the raid would have been a naval bombardment of Borkum, or Sylt as a second choice. This would also be 'the best possible form of target practice', that is, firing at a target which fired back. Bayly to Admiralty, 24 Dec. 1914; *ibid.*

be easily destructible. I was sure the fighting aeroplane, rising lightly laden from its own base, armed with incendiary bullets, would harry, rout and burn these gaseous monsters.'[28] The experience of the war vindicated Churchill's theory that aeroplanes, which he likened to hornets, would master the Zeppelin. Initially, however, the Zeppelin was no laughing matter. 'Aeroplane engines were not powerful enough to reach the great heights needed for the attack of Zeppelins in the short time available. Night flying had only just been born; the location of aircraft by sound was unknown; the network of telephones and observation points was non-existent.'[29] Until guns and searchlights were produced in quantity and an organization developed, the Admiralty could only try to reduce the enemy's airship strength by daring, though sporadic, offensives against the Zeppelin sheds by R.N.A.S. aircraft. These raids, in the first year of the war, destroyed two Zeppelins in their sheds and another in the air (over Bruges). The R.N.A.S. accounted for four others during the last three years of the war, all in the air.

Fisher was maddened by the Zeppelin raids and reconnaissances. The Zeppelins would 'massacre' London, and the Admiralty and all the Government buildings were an inviting target for a bombing attack, as were the ports, arsenals, and dockyards. The Chief of the Admiralty Air Department, Commodore Murray F. Sueter, reported at the very end of 1914 that there were up to twenty German airships which could reach London under cover of darkness. Each was capable of carrying a ton of high explosives. One ton of explosive bombs dropped in one place would wreck all the Admiralty buildings, and there was little that could be done about it. Disaster was in the offing, Fisher earnestly believed, unless something drastic were done at once. At the end of December he proposed in all seriousness that they should take a large number of hostages from the Germans in England and declare their intention of executing one for every Englishman killed by Zeppelin bombs.

Churchill, too, expected a large-scale Zeppelin attack on London in the near future, and he admitted that they had not the means to prevent such an attack if launched in favourable weather conditions. At first (1 January) he agreed to put a modified form

[28] *The World Crisis*, i. 313.
[29] *Ibid.*, p. 314.

of Fisher's proposal before the Cabinet—that the German Government be notified that H.M. Government reserved to itself full liberty to execute enemy males of military age up to the number of British civilians killed or wounded by aerial bombardment on points without military significance. The memorandum was never circulated in this form to the Cabinet, because Churchill had second thoughts on the subject. Executions would not influence German strategy and would only stain England's reputation. The amended version, as printed on 2 January and circulated on 4 January, abandoned the concept of reprisal through execution. The Government would inform Berlin that it reserved 'full liberty to regard these persons as hostages, in a similar manner to those regularly taken by the Germans in France and Belgium'.[30] This was not good enough for Fisher, for whom the only defence was 'reprisals to be officially announced beforehand to the German Government'. He submitted his resignation, 'because the Admiralty under present arrangements will be responsible for the massacre coming suddenly upon, and unprepared for by, the Public'.[31] He withdrew it at the Prime Minister's request.

Fisher seems to have offered his resignation a second time over the alleged 'air apathy' in Whitehall. The date was directly after the War Council of 7 January, which had refused to take any action on his report that the Admiralty had reliable information of a Zeppelin attack on an East Coast town in the near future, to be followed by one on London. The first materialized. During the night of 19–20 January the Zeppelins penetrated inland for the first time. Two of them dropped bombs on King's Lynn, Yarmouth, and Sheringham. Material damage and loss of life were low; 4 people were killed, 17 injured. (The infuriated Alexandra the Queen Mother implored Fisher to provide 'a lot of *rockets* with spikes or hooks on to defend our Norfolk coast'!)

If Fisher was irked with Churchill over the German airship problem (as well as his mining policy), Churchill was equally vexed with Jellicoe over quantitative fleet comparisons. Churchill and Fisher were confident of the superiority of the Grand Fleet in the line of battle over the High Seas Fleet. Jellicoe and Beatty felt differently. Throughout November Beatty protested his battle-cruiser inferiority to the Germans, owing to the detachment

[30] Admiralty MSS.
[31] Fisher to Churchill, 4 Jan. 1915; *Fear God and Dread Nought*, iii. 143.

of the *Princess Royal* and the fact that the newly commissioned *Tiger* was as yet unfit to take her place. He always understood that his duty would be to sail instantly and engage the German battle cruiser squadron if it put to sea. He now doubted his ability to 'annihilate' his squadron's 'opposite number'. Jellicoe, when Beatty sought guidance, could only advise him that his duty would be 'to bring the enemy's Battle Cruisers to action to the best of our ability and regardless of their superiority'.[32] The First Lord tried to comfort Beatty with the assurance that the Navy was, 'ship for ship', far ahead of the German Navy. 'Steer mid-way between Troubridge and Cradock and all will be well, Cradock preferred.'[33] He hoped to be able to strengthen Beatty's Squadron in the near future by returning the 'Straying Cat' (the *Princess Royal*, which rejoined Beatty on 2 January) and adding 'a still more formidable feline', the *Queen Elizabeth* (actually a very fast super-dreadnought). 'But for the present we must just put a bold face on it. The *Derfflinger* is new as well as the *Tiger* . . . You must all get the sixty-per-cent standard out of your minds.[34] No one has any grounds for complaint at fighting on even terms. But we shall do our best to reinforce you. Everything in this War has shown that we are their match, man for man and gun for gun.'[35] The 'all' meant Jellicoe even more than Beatty.

The C.-in-C., who was perhaps inclined by temperament to be pessimistic, viewed with increasing consternation the temporary or permanent loss of his capital ships through enemy action, accidents, the development of defects, and detachments dictated by high strategy, particularly since the Germans could strike with their full force at their selected moment. 'One must hope that the Germans have similar troubles, but that blessed "selected moment" is always against us.'[36] Also, he saw the necessity for a considerable margin of strength in the Grand Fleet in the 'probability' that the High Seas Fleet, when it did emerge, would try to draw the Grand Fleet over a minefield and over submarines before it could get into action with the High Seas Fleet.

Early in November Jellicoe initiated a lengthy correspondence

---

[32] Jellicoe to Beatty, 14 Nov. 1914; Beatty MSS.

[33] Churchill to Beatty, 22 Nov. 1914; *ibid.*

[34] A 60 per cent superiority over Germany in dreadnoughts and battle cruisers had been the official standard from 1909 to the outbreak of war.

[35] Churchill to Beatty, 30 Nov. 1914; *ibid.*

[36] Jellicoe to Fisher, 6 Jan. 1915; Lennoxlove MSS.

with the Admiralty on the theme of the strength of his battle line as compared with the German Fleet. The C.-in-C. became more importunate when the situation deteriorated further at the turn of the year. Ships were always docking. In addition now, the *Audacious* was sunk, the *Conqueror* and the *Monarch* were for some time under repair (badly damaged in a collision on 27 December), the *Orion*, *Ajax*, *King George V*, and *Iron Duke* were suffering from faulty condensers (the *Orion* also had turbine trouble), necessitating whole or partial re-tubing, the *Superb* had a stripped turbine, the *Emperor of India* and *Benbow* were not yet efficient, being newly joined, the *Inflexible* was in the Mediterranean, and the *Invincible* at Gibraltar. The C.-in-C. confided his uneasiness to the First Sea Lord, who was much more sympathetic to his problems than was the First Lord. 'It is astonishing how quickly our supposed superiority in dreadnoughts and Battle Fleets vanishes. To-day I have 19 battleships (dreadnoughts) plus 7 "King Edwards" to meet 16 German dreadnoughts and 8 "Deutschlands" plus twelve [pre-dreadnoughts of the] 4th and 5th Squadrons, which is what would come out if they meant business.'[37] Including battle cruisers and allowing for five capital ships absent for repairs or refitting, the Grand Fleet, he telegraphed the Admiralty, comprised twenty-five capital ships and seven pre-dreadnoughts, as compared with twenty and twenty, respectively, for Germany. 'The preponderance is very slight and more than counterbalanced by inferiority in number of destroyers and probable losses from mines and submarines.' He asked to have the *Invincible* and *Inflexible* brought home.[38]

In correspondence with Jellicoe, Churchill masked his annoyance over the C.-in-C.'s reasoning and fears, although he expressed himself freely to Fisher. His irritation spilled over into print after the war. The C.-in-C.

drew severe comparisons between the German Fleet and his own. He was a master of this kind of argument. From his own side he deducted any ship which had any defect, however temporary, however small —even defects which would not have prevented her from taking her place in the line in an emergency. [Jellicoe: 'Untrue.'] He sometimes also deducted two or three of the most powerful battleships in the world which had newly joined his command because they were

[37] Jellicoe to Fisher, 17 Jan. 1915; *Fear God and Dread Nought*, iii. 129–30.
[38] Jellicoe's telegram of 18 Jan. 1915; *ibid.*, p. 134n.

not trained up to the full level of efficiency of the others, and these were absolutely blotted out as if they were of no value whatever. [Jellicoe: 'So they were. A ship with an untrained crew is valueless in battle. The *Good Hope* was a sad example.'] He next proceeded to deal with the enemy. He always credited them with several ships more than we now know they had, or were then thought likely to have.[39]

Jellicoe's terse overall comment was that the First Lord did not understand 'the obvious fact that ships away refitting were lost to me for the time, and that a ship's company which had not yet been trained to fight their guns at long range under the complicated conditions of modern fleet action was in no way fit to take a place in the line of battle'.[40]

Jellicoe also made urgent representations that he was weak in cruisers and destroyers. The Grand Fleet cruisers were used mainly on blockade duty, with at least one squadron always away. The C.-in-C. could therefore never count on all his cruisers being with the battle fleet should there be a sudden call to meet the High Seas Fleet. He was still more anxious about the destroyers. The Germans could count on 88 accompanying the High Seas Fleet to sea. (53 actually went to sea at the time of the Scarborough raid.) Until the spring of 1915 the number of destroyers forming a part of the Grand Fleet averaged 42 to 44, of which number about six were generally refitting at any one time. The number immediately available was, he believed, 'totally inadequate' as a submarine screen and made him pessimistic about his ability to annihilate the High Seas Fleet if the opportunity arose. Indeed, at one time he asserted that

the only course left for me is to adopt the objectionable and difficult one of turning the Battle Fleet away when the attack takes place. This will lead to confusion even if the turn is successfully accomplished. Gunfire is deranged, or (if the turn is a large one) is altogether stopped, a position of tactical advantage possibly lost, and a good line of Battle thrown into temporary derangement. The menace of so large a number of torpedo boat destroyers attacking cannot however possibly be disregarded without the certainty of heavy losses in the Battle Line, and— failing an adequate destroyer force to counter the attack—I feel that I shall be forced to carry out this manœuvre.[41]

The Admiralty appreciated the C.-in-C.'s difficult position,

[39] *The World Crisis*, i. 443, with Jellicoe's marginalia in the brackets.
[40] Jellicoe, 'A Reply to Criticism'.
[41] Jellicoe to Admiralty, 4 Dec. 1914; Admiralty MSS.

especially as regards destroyers, even if they thought he tended to exaggerate the German destroyer total and to underestimate his own numbers. They were unable to send him any substantial reinforcements because of the great needs they had to meet elsewhere. Fisher deemed the Grand Fleet strength in capital ships and cruisers sufficient. He was, however, so concerned about the C.-in-C.'s depression at this time, 'because such a state of mind is infectious and may easily spread through the Grand Fleet', that he urged Churchill (20 January) to meet the C.-in-C.'s wishes if it could be done without prejudicing other requirements. Churchill did not think the Grand Fleet needed strengthening in view of the reinforcements it had received. Jellicoe had five more dreadnoughts than at the start of the war, for a total of 27 capital ships to a German maximum of 21. 'On his line of battle his broadside is much more than double that of the enemy.' The First Lord was, nevertheless, impressed with Fisher's minute, and the two agreed (21 January) to send the C.-in-C. a destroyer flotilla and a new light cruiser squadron. The *Inflexible* and *Invincible* would be sent to him in the near future; in an emergency the battle cruiser *Australia*, at Plymouth, would be sent to Scapa Flow; the two 'Lord Nelsons' and six 'Formidables' (5th Battle Squadron: Channel Fleet) were to be transferred from Portland to Rosyth, which would set the 3rd Battle Squadron, at Rosyth, free to rejoin the C.-in-C. at Scapa Flow. This transfer did not take place, as the 5th Battle Squadron was removed to the Dardanelles in February and March.

Both Jellicoe and Churchill had right on their side. The issues at stake were great. The defeat of the Grand Fleet, which had to contain and counter the High Seas Fleet, would have led to the downfall of the nation and the empire. Jellicoe was only behaving as any C.-in-C. would have under the circumstances in demanding that he have a reasonable margin of superiority. Fisher, indeed, privately admitted that, were he in Jellicoe's position, he would be acting no differently. On the other hand, Jellicoe tended to be unreasonable. The slightest thing wanted from him—for the Harwich or Dover forces, for example—was attacked as 'interference' with the Grand Fleet. Here is a concrete case in point. When the Naval Division was getting ready to leave for the Dardanelles, woefully short of machine-guns, Oliver telegraphed to the C.-in-C. for each large ship in the Grand Fleet to relinquish one Maxim and ammunition. 'I knew the G.F. would not kill many Huns with Maxims . . . Next day a private letter [from Jellicoe] suggested to Fisher that I was weakening the G.F. in principle. However, I got my way.'[42]

Churchill was himself unreasonable in querying why Jellicoe had to send so many of his ships away for refit and repairs at the same time, as if the C.-in-C. could help it, and in complaining that he ran the ships down by having them out too often! Nor does he seem to have given enough weight to the fact that the Germans could choose their moment when all their ships were ready for battle, but that Jellicoe had to send his ships in turn to refit and was never at full strength. On the other hand, the First Lord had to keep his sights constantly on the total strategic picture.

The situation improved progressively during 1915. The completion of the re-tubing of the defective condensers, the repair of the damaged battleships, and new construction steadily widened the Grand Fleet margin of superiority. On 1 April 1915, for example, Jellicoe had 32 dreadnoughts and battle cruisers to the German 21. Before the statistics could show substantial improvement, Jellicoe's apprehensions were put to a test of sorts.

3. THE DOGGER BANK ACTION

(*Map* 6)

The Emperor's reaction to various pressures for a more energetic offensive was to confirm (10 January) that the preservation of the Fleet was still his guiding policy. But he did grant Ingenohl the privilege of making more frequent sallies into the North Sea on his own initiative with the purpose of cutting off advanced British forces or of attacking the British Fleet with superior strength. The greater initiative now allowed Ingenohl produced a major naval action in the North Sea.

On 19 January Beatty made a reconnaissance in force west of the Bight that was spotted by a German aeroplane. This sweep and the continuation of British scouting operations in the Dogger Bank area caused Ingenohl to send Hipper towards the Dogger Bank to discover what enemy forces were in the area and to surprise and destroy any scouting forces he met. Hipper's force consisted of the battle cruisers *Seydlitz* (flag), *Moltke*, *Derfflinger*, and *Blücher*, supported by four light cruisers and eighteen destroyers.

[42] Oliver MSS.

It left the Jade at 5.45 p.m. on 23 January and was to return the next evening. Hipper had no idea that Ingenohl's orders to him had been intercepted and decoded at the Admiralty. The exact object of the operation could not be determined at Whitehall. All the Admiralty could be sure of was that there would be a reconnaissance in force at least as far as the Dogger Bank. Wilson and Oliver marched into the First Lord's room towards noon on the 23rd. 'First Lord,' announced Wilson, 'those fellows are coming out again.' He, Oliver, and Churchill concocted a clever plan to intercept the would-be interceptors with superior force. They fixed a rendezvous for the 24th at 7 a.m. at a position about 30 miles north of the Dogger Bank and about 180 miles west of Heligoland. This was the very spot where Oliver and Wilson had, with uncanny accuracy, reckoned Hipper would be at that time. Fisher, laid up with a cold, played no part in these decisions beyond approving them.

In the late afternoon of 23 January, minutes after Hipper left the Jade, Goodenough's 1st Light Cruiser Squadron and Beatty's battle cruisers left Rosyth. Since 15 January Beatty's ships had been organized in two squadrons. The 1st Battle Cruiser Squadron, under Beatty's direct control, had the *Lion* (flag), *Tiger*, and *Princess Royal*. (The *Queen Mary* was in dock.) The newly formed 2nd Battle Cruiser Squadron, under the Second-in-Command, Rear-Admiral Sir Archibald Moore, consisted of the *New Zealand* (flag) and the *Indomitable*. Tyrwhitt with three light cruisers and thirty-five destroyers was to join Beatty at the rendezvous at 7 a.m. on the 24th. Beatty commanded the entire force. To protect the East Coast and to lend distant support to Beatty, the 3rd Cruiser Squadron and the seven available pre-dreadnoughts of the 3rd Battle Squadron put to sea from Rosyth for a position that would enable them to cut off Hipper if he came north. Finally, the Grand Fleet left Scapa Flow at 9 p.m. on the 23rd for a sweep in the southern part of the North Sea, although it was evident that it could not reach the scene of the hoped-for action until the next afternoon. Jellicoe afterwards expressed his disappointment that he had not been directed to raise steam immediately the Admiralty knew Hipper was coming out, that is, in the late morning, instead of in the early afternoon. Had that happened, he says, the battle fleet could have been clear of Scapa by 5 p.m. and at the rendezvous by 9.30 a.m. Churchill states in *The World Crisis* that the reason Jellicoe was not hustled down in close support of Beatty was that a raid on the East Coast was clearly to be expected. How this conclusion was arrived at I cannot understand any more than Jellicoe could,[43] since there was nothing in the intercepted German orders which pointed to a raid on the coast. 'The truth is that the Admiralty, relying on the intercepted signal, thought that the battle cruisers and Harwich Force could do the job. The same mistake as was made in the case of the December raid, when they would not allow me to take out the whole Grand Fleet.'[44] As matters developed, Jellicoe was 140 miles from the battle cruisers during the action.

The trap was ready to be sprung. Everything favoured the British and a major victory seemed within reach. '. . . only one thought could reign—battle at dawn! Battle for the first time in history between mighty super-Dreadnought ships! And there was added a thrilling sense of a Beast of Prey moving stealthily forward hour by hour towards the Trap.'[45] Such were the thoughts of the First Lord during the afternoon and evening of the 23rd.

Beatty could reach the rendezvous in time only by passing over a reportedly mine-infested area. He missed them all, luckily. 'The truth is,' Jellicoe acidly commented afterwards, 'that Sir A. Wilson [who seems to have been mainly responsible for determining the position] has not realized the effect that mines and submarines have on present day warfare'.[46] Beatty and Goodenough reached the intercepting position just after 7 a.m. It was still dark, but dawn was about to break. At 7.10 Tyrwhitt was encountered right ahead. The sea was calm, there was plenty of sea-room between Hipper and Germany, and the visibility was perfect. 'The day was so clear,' Goodenough remembered, 'that only the shape of the earth prevented one from seeing everything on it.'

At about 7.20, gun flashes were sighted to the south-south-east.[47] These came from an action between the *Aurora*, leading a later division of the Harwich force, and the port-wing ship of Hipper's screen of light cruisers. Soon, steering towards the firing, first

[43] Jellicoe, 'A Reply to Criticism'.

[44] Jellicoe Marginalia, *The World Crisis*, ii. 130.

[45] *The World Crisis*, ii. 131.

[46] Jellicoe to McKenna, 23 May 1915; *Fear God and Dread Nought*, iii. 152n.

[47] The British telegrams and signals in the action are in Naval Staff Monograph No. 12 (1921), *The Action of Dogger Bank, January 24th, 1915*, in Naval Staff Monographs, iii. 219-22. The German signals are in *Der Krieg in der Nordsee*, iii. 282-9.

Goodenough's light cruisers and then the battle cruisers sighted the German ships, now seen to include battle cruisers. Beatty then shaped course to the south-east and increased speed, hoping to engage the enemy from to leeward (wind east by north), so as to clear the range of smoke, and eventually to get between the enemy and his base. Hipper, meanwhile, supposing from intercepted wireless call-signs that he was in the presence of the 2nd Battle Squadron, not the battle cruisers, was standing to the south-eastward under easy steam until the situation cleared.

The British force worked up to full speed (27 or 27½ knots—the speeds given in the dispatches, of up to 28½ knots, are without doubt exaggerated), though at the cost of letting the slower *New Zealand* and *Indomitable* drop back. The Germans were steadily overhauled, and at about 8.40, Hipper, whose view had been much hampered by smoke, became at last aware that his opponents were battle cruisers. He therefore increased to about 23 knots, which was the most the *Blücher* could do.

Soon after 9 the leading British ships opened fire as they drew within 20,000 yards of the *Blücher*, the rearmost ship. This was the first time the battle cruisers had fired at such a range. (The 16,000 yards in the battle cruisers' experimental firing in the spring of 1914 had been the maximum range until now.) Smoke still hampered the Germans, but a quarter of an hour later they, too, were firing. They were ordered to fire ship for ship, but because of the smoke they fired at whatever they could see, and this resulted in the *Lion* becoming the principal target. Towards 9.30 the *New Zealand* drew within range of the *Blücher* and opened fire on her. Only the *Indomitable* was a considerable distance astern and out of range. The relative positions were as follows:

Indomitable	
New Zealand	*Blücher*
Princess Royal	*Derfflinger*
Tiger	*Moltke*
Lion (Beatty)	*Seydlitz* (Hipper)

A misunderstanding now arose that had an unhappy consequence. When the range was down to about 17,500 yards, which brought all the German battle cruisers within effective range, Beatty signalled (9.35): 'Engage the corresponding ships in the enemy's line.' He intended that his ships should fire on their opposite numbers from right to left: The *Lion* on the *Seydlitz*, the *Tiger* on the *Moltke*, the *Princess Royal* on the *Derfflinger*, and the *New Zealand* on the *Blücher*. The Captain of the *Tiger*, Henry B. Pelly ('a little bit of the nervous excited type', in Beatty's opinion), erroneously thought the *Indomitable* was in action with her opposite, the *Blücher*. He concluded that the *New Zealand* was to fire on the *Derfflinger*, and the *Princess Royal* on the *Moltke*, permitting the *Tiger* and the *Lion* to concentrate on disabling the enemy flagship, the *Seydlitz*. The upshot was that the unmolested *Moltke* was able to make excellent target practice on the *Lion*. It did not improve matters that the *Tiger* apparently mistook the *Lion's* salvoes for her own, and thought she was making hits when actually her shots were falling more than 3,000 yards over the *Seydlitz*.

Meanwhile, Hipper's three big battle cruisers had got the range of the *Lion* and were hitting her often, despite Beatty's zigzagging. At 10.01 she was hit by an 11-inch shell from the *Seydlitz* that knocked out two of her dynamos, and at 10.18 by two 12-inch shells simultaneously, from the *Derfflinger*, one of which drove in the waterline armour and allowed sea water to get into the port feed tank. It was this hit, the only serious one, that eventually crippled her, for half an hour later the port engine had to be stopped. Though his flagship was dropping back, the Admiral was still in control, and at 10.47 he signalled: 'Close the enemy as rapidly as possible consistent with keeping all guns bearing.' A minute later he ordered the *Indomitable*, which had finally come into action, to complete the destruction of the moribund *Blücher*, by this time a listing, burning wreck, though still fighting.

An unfortunate event in the next minutes suddenly altered the entire complexion of the battle. At 10.54, by which time the *Lion's* last dynamo had failed and she had already dropped back two miles behind her uninjured consorts, 'submarines were reported on the starboard bow [Beatty wrote in his dispatch] and I personally observed the wash of a periscope 2 points on our starboard bow'. He therefore ordered a turn of eight points to port together (to N. by E.), heading across the enemy's wake almost at right angles.[48] The main significance of the turn was that it put the

[48] The times for the various signals in the climacteric phase of the action, between 10.54 and approximately 11.15, are in such a state of confusion that I have omitted them. There is little correspondence between the times as logged and as given in Beatty's dispatches. Evidently the *Lion's* signal log went a bit haywire in the crisis, which was not surprising in the circumstances.

British ships astern of the Germans when they were heading for home.

Beatty's action was the first of its kind in the war. Was the order to alter to port necessary? On the face of it, no. We know today that there were no enemy submarines within 60 miles. N.I.D. later suggested that the 'periscope' Beatty saw was probably a German destroyer's torpedo surfacing after its run. (According to the German track chart, one of the destroyer V-5's torpedoes, fired at 10.44, should have finished its run at just about this time and place.) Beatty obviously thought he was doing the wise thing, as he feared (or, more strictly, we are justified in believing that he feared) that he was running into a submarine trap—a concentration of submarines—on his starboard bow. Otherwise we must convict him of the stupidity of ordering his squadron to alter course to avoid a submarine which he believed he had seen, but which could not possibly have endangered his other ships. (The *Lion* was two miles astern of her consorts, and a submarine in the position reported could not have endangered the rest of the squadron.)

Bacon and McMurtrie are critical of Beatty's turn-away. 'Had he turned and steered straight for the supposed periscope and done nothing more except to warn the flotilla commodore to send one or more destroyers to search for the submarine, then our battle cruisers would have continued the chase, we should have sunk at least two of the enemy battle cruisers and probably more. . . . From the position of the *Lion* in relation to the other ships, and the bearing and possible distance of the submarine from the *Lion*, it was impossible for the submarine to have attacked the battle cruisers.'[49] Jellicoe made the same criticism, also years after the event: 'The best course was to turn *direct at the submarine*, not 8 points away. . . . I should say that Beatty himself broke off the action by his unfortunate signal to alter course to port.'[50] Both criticisms ignore the fact that it was not the submarine Beatty thought he saw, but other submarines of a supposed concentration that he wanted to avoid, a danger that had been so emphatically expressed by Jellicoe in his letter of 30 October 1914 to the Admiralty about being drawn over mines or submarines. Beatty was not immune to the submarine jitters which were not unnaturally prevalent in those

[49] *Modern Naval Strategy*, p. 71.
[50] Jellicoe Marginalia, *The World Crisis*, ii. 138.

days and which were enhanced by the woeful ignorance of most big-ship officers about what submarines could do and how they did it. As Captain Creswell observes, 'Only a badly handled submarine would have allowed its periscope to be sighted before it was quite close to its target—and a well-handled one would never be seen at all. The idea that a shoal of submarines could be sighted, the impression one gets from the reports, is fantastic.'[51]

In its train the reported sighting of submarines posed another problem. It was supposed by Beatty that the German destroyers carried mines, and he was determined to avoid steaming in their wakes. But he had now turned in that direction, and he assumed that the enemy would see this as the best moment to lay their mines. The spot where they then were must be avoided, but once clear beyond the German wakes his ships could haul round to starboard and engage the enemy on their starboard bow. Further consideration showed that the squadron need not stand quite so much to the northward to clear the danger spot. Almost immediately after hauling down the signal to alter course to port, therefore, he hoisted: 'Course N.E.'

Meanwhile, Hipper, who was not equipped for minelaying, had determined on an attempt to relieve pressure on the *Blücher* by sending in his eighteen destroyers to attack with torpedoes. To this end he turned to starboard, but, by coincidence, this was the moment when the British turned to port, thus throwing the German destroyers into the worst possible position for attacking. He therefore cancelled his orders and set course for home, abandoning the *Blücher* to her fate.

As the *Lion* began rapidly to drop astern, Beatty did his best to make clear his intentions that the battle cruisers were to press on after the *Derfflinger*, *Seydlitz*, and *Moltke*, leaving the crippled and lagging *Blücher* to be disposed of by the *Indomitable* and the light cruisers. With only two pairs of signal halyards left in the *Lion*, and with no electricity for signal searchlights or wireless, Beatty now hoisted 'Attack the rear of the enemy.'[52] The signal for

[51] Captain Creswell's letter to the author, 13 Mar. 1964.

[52] The hoisting of a signal merely warns all ships of the admiral's intention. Hauling down the signal is the executive order to execute it. Captain Creswell 'wonders why Beatty ever made "attack the *rear* of the enemy", when he presumably hoped that the *Tiger*, *Princess Royal*, and *New Zealand* would knock out the lot, the *Seydlitz* having been heavily damaged and the *Derfflinger* believed to be on fire. I have never heard any explanation of this. Perhaps he meant that he was now committed to crossing the

'Course N.E.' was still flying and, lucklessly, these two signals were hauled down together and were read, justifiably, by his ships as *one signal*, not two as intended: 'Attack the rear of the enemy, bearing N.E.' This was the bearing of the *Blücher*, and away swept this strong force to engage one severely battered ship, leaving the three big German battle cruisers to steam away unmolested. The *Lion* was now crawling away to the northward with a list of 10 degrees, and Beatty's final signal, 'Keep nearer the enemy', hoisted immediately after the previous ones had been hauled down, could no longer be read.[53] Not only that, his spirited leadership had now been lost and Moore had assumed command of the squadron, although no formal transfer was made. The consequences were tragic.

Had the final signal been seen and read, it might have prevented the misunderstanding which led Moore away on the wrong scent. There are other circumstances which explain the Rear-Admiral's faulty conclusions. Unaware that Beatty believed he had sighted submarines, Moore supposed that the squadron's 8-point turn to port was meant to ensure the destruction of the *Blücher*. He was doubly certain when he saw the *Blücher* bearing north-east from the British squadron, the direction apparently indicated in Beatty's signal. And so all thoughts of destroying the main force passed out of his mind.

Beatty was horrified when he saw what was happening. In a despairing attempt to undo the damage, he shifted his flag to a destroyer (at about 11.50). As she shoved off from the *Lion*, he stood on the destroyer's fo'c'sle acknowledging the cheers of the *Lion's* ship's company. He reached the squadron just as the *Blücher* was about to go down. She had put on a great show for three hours against the concentrated British fire, suffering at least 70 hits, yet continuing to fire until towards the very end. She suddenly rolled over and went down at 12.10. Corbett's tribute

---

wake of the German squadron and what he intended was: attack the enemy while crossing astern of them.' Lord Chatfield confirms that this supposition is correct in a letter to the author, 2 May 1962.

[53] Before this signal was hoisted, Beatty's Flag-Commander suggested to him, 'What we need now is Nelson's signal, "Engage the enemy more closely".' 'Yes, certainly,' Beatty replied. 'Hoist it.' Referring to the signal book, the Flag-Lieutenant found that it had been removed from the books. There was a miserable modern substitute, 'Keep nearer the enemy.' This, with its attendant compass signal, was duly hoisted. Admiral Sir Reginald Drax's letter to the author, 7 Feb. 1962.

was richly deserved: 'As an example of discipline, courage and fighting spirit her last hours have seldom been surpassed.'

Beatty transferred his flag to the *Princess Royal* (12.20) and ordered the pursuit to be resumed. At 12.45 he turned the squadron around and headed for home. Further pursuit would be pointless as well as dangerous, he realized. It was, as his Flag-Lieutenant put it, like 'trying to win the Derby after falling at Tattenham Corner'. Hipper had too long a lead, at least 12 miles, and he was only about 80 miles from Heligoland. It would take two hours, Beatty reckoned, to catch up with the Germans, and by then they would be too close to Heligoland and the German battle fleet, which was reported to be coming out.

The action had been a blessing in disguise for the Germans. A 13·5-inch shell from the *Lion* at 9.50 had struck the *Seydlitz* through the quarter deck and partially penetrated the 9-inch barbette armour of the after turret, igniting waiting charges in the working chamber. Flames spread to the magazine handing room (ammunition chamber) and then to the handing room of the adjacent, superimposed, turret, when the door to it was opened by men trying to escape. Flames roared up through this turret to a height of 200 feet above the ship. Both turrets were then out of action, 159 men having been killed. Explosion of the after magazines and the probable loss of the ship were prevented by the prompt and heroic action of the executive officer in flooding both magazines. After the battle the Naval Command promptly introduced adequate anti-flash arrangements into the capital ships. The British, unfortunately, required the heavy tuition costs paid at Jutland to learn the lesson of the Dogger Bank—the need to prevent a flash in a turret gunhouse penetrating to the magazine. The magazines were open to the handing rooms and the charges in the hoists were unprotected.

The Germans had good reason to be proud of the gallant fight put up by Hipper's inferior force and of the efficiency of their gunnery. The German Official History records that the only hits made on the German ships, excluding the *Blücher*, which came under fire at comparatively short range, were one on the *Derfflinger* and two on the *Seydlitz*. One of these, as noted, penetrated 9-inch armour and almost knocked the *Seydlitz* out. The other two hits did minor damage, though the one on the *Derfflinger* caused a fire visible from the British squadron. On the other hand, the *Lion*

and the *Tiger* were hit about 22 times (16 and 6, respectively).
Whereas the Germans could justifiably be proud of their
gunnery, there was nothing to show that their shells were better
than the British. Indeed, Beatty's judgment was that 'their guns
are good, calibration too close, gunlaying excellent, but the
projectile no good, and I am sure we can stand a lot of it'.[54]
The Fleet was told: 'The German heavy shell used in this action
were mainly A.P. [armour piercing] . . . For armour penetration
the shell seem very good, but in general destructive and incendiary
effect they are not equal to our lyddite, which have proved so
effective in every action of the war. Only one small fire was caused
in our ships by German shell, whilst three out of the four German ships [all but the *Moltke*] were heavily on fire at various
times.'[55]

There was profound depression in the German Naval Command, alleviated only by the gallant manner in which their ships
had fought, and a half-believed report that they had sunk the
Tiger. There was no doubt that German gunnery and German
shells had proved themselves efficient. Yet the dominant feeling
was that a thoroughly inept operation had met with the fate it
deserved. Tactically, the Germans had made the mistake of adding
the slow *Blücher* to the squadron. (Ironically, she had made
Hipper's escape possible.) Hipper strongly recommended that
in the future his battle cruisers not be handicapped in that
fashion. This seems a bit ironical on his part, as the *Blücher* was
unique.

The Dogger Bank action cost Admiral Ingenohl his command
(2 February). He had taken full responsibility for holding back
the support of the battle fleet. Moreover, the relative strength of
the two Fleets was more unfavourable to Germany than before the
raids which had commenced in November.

The new C.-in-C. was the outgoing Chief of the Naval Staff,
formerly an outstanding squadron commander, Admiral von Pohl.

[54] Beatty to Jellicoe, n.d. (soon after the battle); Jellicoe MSS.
[55] Gunnery Division, Naval Staff, *Grand Fleet Gunnery and Torpedo Memoranda on
Naval Actions, 1914–1918* (1922), p. 12. These memoranda were issued to the Fleet at
the time with a view to disseminating the lessons learned from the various major
actions. 'Armour penetration' in the quotation needs some qualification. The German
guns nearly blew up the *Lion* by penetrating her 5-inch waterline armour abreast the
after turret; but no German shells succeeded in penetrating the British 9-inch main-
belt armour amidships. They did press back the *Lion's* 9-inch plates and cause serious
leaks, but did not actually burst inside.

He was described by the last pre-war British Naval Attaché in Berlin as: 'Short and square built, but slim. Has the reputation of being a good seaman. Gives impression of ability, quickness of decision and force of character. . . . a very taciturn fellow who looks as if he had lost ½ a crown and found 6d. He won't enthuse people at all [but]. . . . a man of some character, and with a good knowledge of his profession. He does not look very healthy. . . . Ingenohl was a more cheerful personality. Pohl has the greater experience.'[56] On the whole, Pohl was an improvement on Ingenohl, particularly as regards tactical know-how. But he lacked real genius and the professional esteem of his brother officers, he was not a strong leader (his arrogance made him unpopular with the officers), and, under the Emperor's goading to be more cautious than Ingenohl, his strategy turned out to be a continuation of his predecessor's. Over a year was to pass before German capital ships dared show themselves in the North Sea again. In the interval submarine warfare emerged as the leading weapon of the High Seas Fleet.

Technically, the Dogger Bank was a British victory. The enemy had fled the field of battle, the *Blücher* had been sunk and the *Seydlitz* badly damaged (Beatty incorrectly reported the *Derfflinger*, too, as having suffered serious damage), over 1,000 German seamen had been lost (killed or taken prisoner). British casualties were less than 50 (killed and wounded); the *Lion*'s injuries were not vital, although she had to be towed to Rosyth by the *Indomitable* and it was four months before she was ready; the *Tiger* had received the only other hits on the battle cruisers, none of them serious; one destroyer was damaged. There was cause for satisfaction in the effectiveness of the organization for deciphering the enemy's wireless signals, in the outstanding engineering performance of the new battle cruisers, which had, so they thought, surpassed their designed speeds, and in the ability of the battle cruisers to absorb punishment.

The press, which was not in possession of all the facts, was elated over the results of the 'rout'. The Navy had avenged the Scarborough raid. 'It will be some time before they go baby-killing again,' vouchsafed the *Globe*. The action had also disproved the enemy's taunts that the old spirit of the Royal Navy was dead.

[56] Captain Hugh Watson to Jellicoe, 28 Feb. 1915; Beatty MSS.

Declared the *Pall Mall Gazette*, 'After yesterday's action, it will not be easy for the loud-mouthed boasters of Berlin to keep up the pretence that the British Fleet is hiding itself in terror.'

The fact is that what might have been an annihilating victory had dwindled to a mere 'successful action', or, in Ralph Seymour's words, 'an indecisive fight in our favour'. Fisher and Jellicoe had their doubts about the brilliance of the victory. The former was unable to discern in either the 16 December or the 24 January action 'any manifestation of any Nelsonic instinct. . . . There was no foresight or sagacity required on these two occasions as the rendezvous was given in both cases and the enemy appeared exactly on the spot named by the Admiralty. *It was South Africa both times!*'[57] Beatty wrote privately, 'The disappointment of that day is more than I can bear to think of, everybody thinks it was a great success, when in reality it was a terrible failure. I had made up my mind that we were going to get four, the lot, and *four* we ought to have got.'[58]

The Navy lost the chance of annihilating victory because the signal to attack the rear of the enemy had been misinterpreted and the action broken off. The memory of what might have been lingered. Many years after the war, Keyes wrote: 'I think the spectacle of Moore & Co. yapping round the poor tortured *Blücher*, with beaten ships in sight still to be sunk, is one of the most distressing episodes in the War.'[59] The Board of Admiralty took no action against Moore, partly because Beatty's exceptional tolerance and generosity to those who had failed him would not permit him to so much as hint in his official reports at any criticism of his Second-in-Command. And there was the morale factor. 'I am all against changes, it is upsetting and inclined to destroy confidence.'[60] He forwarded Moore's reports without comment and took full responsibility for the German escape. But 'frankly between you and I,' he admitted to Jellicoe, 'he is not of the right sort of temperament for a B.C.S. . . . Moore had a chance which most fellows w^d have given [the] eyes in their head for, and did nothing. . . . It is inconceivable that anybody should have thought it necessary for 4 B.C.'s 3 of them untouched to have turned on the

[57] Fisher to Jellicoe, 7 Feb. 1915; Jellicoe MSS.
[58] Beatty to Keyes, 10 Feb. 1915; Keyes, *Naval Memoirs*, i. 163.
[59] Keyes to Beatty, 17 June 1933; Keyes MSS.
[60] Beatty to Jellicoe, 8 Feb. 1915; Jellicoe MSS.

Blücher which was obviously a defeated ship and couldn't steam while 3 others also badly hammered sh^d have been allowed to escape.'[61] Let it be noted here that most of Beatty's officers thought that Moore was a very poor selection as Second-in-Command. We know today that he was the Admiralty's, not Beatty's, choice. At that war period the Admiralty did these posts; later in the war they permitted the C.-in-C. to select his own flag officers in the Grand Fleet.

Fisher lamented Moore's wooden tactics and cried out that his conduct in giving up the chase had been 'despicable!' 'No signals (often unintentionally ambiguous in the heat of action) can ever justify the abandonment of a certain victory such as offered itself here when the *Derfflinger* and *Seydlitz*, as reported by Commodore Tyrwhitt, "were blazing at the end of the action," and besides being thus heavily on fire were both of them very severely damaged.' Again, 'The Admiralty require to know WHY the *Derfflinger* and the *Seydlitz*, both heavily on fire and in a badly damaged condition, were allowed to escape, when as Admiral Moore states in this letter gun range with the leading ships of the Enemy could have been maintained by *Tiger* and *Princess Royal* at all events.'[62] Admiral Chalmers makes the same point. Moore 'had a unique opportunity to use his own initiative and continue the pursuit in spite of his interpretation of Beatty's signal. Had he done so he would have acted in accordance with the real intentions of his chief, and would in all probability have annihilated the whole German squadron. . . . All signals made by Beatty, prior to the tragic moment when he could no longer lead his squadron, had made it clear beyond doubt that Hipper's main force was the objective. To anyone who knew Beatty there could have been no other.'[63] Jellicoe, too, could only deduce from the reports that 'If as has since been stated two of the enemy battle-cruisers were very seriously damaged *and the fact was apparent at the time*, there is no doubt whatever that the Rear-Admiral should have continued the action.'[64]

[61] *Ibid.*

[62] Fisher's minutes of 5, 11 Feb. 1915, on reports of Tyrwhitt and Moore, respectively, of 29 Jan.; Admiralty MSS.

[63] Chalmers, *Beatty*, p. 192.

[64] Jellicoe to Admiralty, 3 Mar. 1915; Admiralty MSS. Captain Creswell's judgment is very much to the point and highlights one of the principal failings in the Navy of that era: 'One cannot help feeling that by present-day standards he [Moore] failed to display as much initiative as should be expected. The fault lay perhaps not with him personally, but with the doctrine of the Service at the time—a doctrine in which rigid

Fisher reserved his heaviest fire for Pelly. It was 'inexcusable that Captain Pelly should have left a ship of the enemy unfired at [*Moltke*] and so permitting her to fire unmolested at the *Lion*'.[65] What infuriated the old Admiral even more was that the 'poltroon', Pelly, 'was a long way ahead, he ought to have gone on, had he the slightest Nelsonic temperament in him, regardless of signals! Like Nelson at Copenhagen and St. Vincent! In war the first principle is to disobey orders. *Any fool can obey orders!*'[66] Beatty felt the same way. 'Pelly did very badly 1st in not carrying out the orders to engage his opposite number which had disastrous results and 2nd in running amuck after *Lion* fell out and not attacking Enemy's rear. He rode the P.R. [*Princess Royal*] right out and she had to put her helm over to clear him.' But he would not recommend any action against Pelly. He 'had done very well up to then, he had difficulties to contend with and I don't think he is likely to do the same again . . .'[67] Nor could Jellicoe find any excuse for Pelly's failure to comply with Beatty's signal to engage opposite numbers. 'Special emphasis is laid in Grand Fleet Orders on the fact that no ship of the enemy should be left unfired at, and a consideration of this rule should have led to the *Tiger* engaging No. 2 in the line. The concentration rules cannot be taken to apply to a chase of four ships by five when firing at extreme range.'[68]

Beatty himself came in for little criticism, apart from Fisher's complaint that he kept his ships full of coal and oil—enough to go 3,000 miles. To Fisher this made no sense in the restricted area of the North Sea, where 500 miles at top speed was all that Beatty could go in any action. This 'damnable dead weight of unnecessary

obedience far outweighed any other qualities or requirements. Immediate obedience to signals is of course essential; but not blind, uncritical obedience.' Creswell's Naval Staff College lecture, 'The Dogger Bank Action, 24th January, 1915' (1932).

[65] Minute on Jellicoe's memorandum to Beatty of 3 Mar.; Admiralty MSS.

[66] Fisher to Beatty, 31 Jan. 1915; *Fear God and Dread Nought*, iii. 150–1.

[67] Beatty to Jellicoe, 8 Feb. 1915; Jellicoe MSS.

[68] Jellicoe to Beatty, 3 Mar. 1915, with the same conclusion made in his letter of the same day to the Admiralty; Admiralty MSS. Pelly's explanations had made much of the Grand Fleet Battle Order that one of the chief objects to be kept in view was 'to disable the enemy's leading ships in order to throw his line into confusion, and that in a fleet action with fleets deployed on similar courses, the Commander of the leading division is to concentrate his four leading ships in pairs on the two ships of the enemy's van. . . . Captains are to reckon on it when selecting their target.' Pelly to Jellicoe, 26 Feb. 1915; *ibid.*

fuel' had robbed the battle cruisers of two knots on 24 January, with which 'you might have finished them off before the big fiasco!'[69] Beatty, however, kept the full confidence of the Admiralty and of the Fleet. Fisher hailed his conduct as 'glorious! *"Beatty beatus!"* ' When Churchill visited the *Lion* on 3 February, he 'heard from his Captains and his Admirals the expression of their respectful but intense enthusiasm for their leader. Well do I remember how, as I was leaving the ship, the usually imperturbable Admiral Pakenham caught me by the sleeve, "First Lord, I wish to speak to you in private," and the intense conviction in his voice as he said, "Nelson has come again." '[70]

The gunnery was not very successful, even when allowance is made for the German funnel smoke throughout the action and the dense smoke screens set up by their destroyers (the first time smoke screens were used in battle), which made spotting difficult, and for the fact that the heavy ships were firing at such long ranges for the first time. The *Tiger*, the one British battle cruiser equipped with the director system of central fire control, did not register a single hit. Part of the difficulty lay in her being a new ship. Commissioned on 3 October, she had joined the Grand Fleet on 6 November after nine days of shooting in Bantry Bay. She had not had sufficient opportunity for training during her ten days in the stormy waters of Scapa Flow. She had then joined the Battle Cruiser Squadron, but received only intermittent training in the winter months. When the *Tiger* went into action at the Dogger Bank, she had never before fired her big guns at a moving target! First-class gunnery efficiency in the battle would, in view of these conditions, have been a miracle. Her main difficulty lay in the fact that she had a very mixed ship's company, with a large number of recovered deserters. It had been an uphill task, as Beatty realized, for her Captain to pull them together in wartime. 'The same efficiency could not be expected from the *Tiger* as from the other ships. . . . It is not the time to complain but to do the best one can

---

[69] Fisher to Beatty, 9 Feb. 1915; *Fear God and Dread Nought*, iii. p. 157.

[70] *The World Crisis*, ii. 89. Beatty's showing in the battle, coupled with Churchill's waning enthusiasm for Jellicoe, put a bee in the First Lord's bonnet. 'How I wish I could have guided events a little better and a little longer,' he wrote to Beatty on 11 November 1924. 'Jutland would have had a different ring if the plans already formed in my mind after the Dogger Bank for securing you the chief command had grown to their natural fruition.' Beatty MSS.

with the material available. I assume the ship's company would have been better if it had been possible to make it so.'[71]

Jellicoe felt little satisfaction with the results of the action because they indicated a superiority in accuracy of fire of the enemy battle cruisers, 'thus confirming my suspicion that the gunnery of our Battle Cruiser Squadron was in great need of improvement, a fact which I very frequently urged upon Sir David Beatty'.[72] The distraught Fisher rated the *Tiger's* gunnery as 'villainously bad', and he sought a scapegoat in her Gunnery Lieutenant, whom he had relieved.

'The victory of the Dogger Bank brought for the time being abruptly to an end the adverse movement against my administration of the Admiralty, which had begun to gather. Congratulations flowed in from every side, and we enjoyed once again an adequate measure of prestige.'[73] Perhaps because the victory would have been spoiled if doubts were cast on its being a brilliant success, Churchill would not give in to Fisher's desire for an inquiry into the conduct of the battle or the disciplining of any officer, although the Admiralty concurred in Jellicoe's conclusions on Moore and Pelly (7 March). Thus, the First Lord saw no advantage in pursuing the Pelly matter—his leaving *Moltke* undisturbed—further. 'The future and the present claim all our attention.'[74] Churchill was, nevertheless, sufficiently incensed at Moore to meet Fisher half way. They found another appointment for him in February—the Command of the 9th Cruiser Squadron in the Canary Islands area. He was relieved by Pakenham. As for Pelly, he was still Captain of the *Tiger* when Jutland rolled around, despite the continued poor shooting of the ship![75]

One result of the Dogger Bank was that arrangements were

---

[71] Beatty to Hamilton, 17 Feb. 1915; Hamilton MSS. All the same, the firing of the *Tiger* had been so poor that Beatty held an inquiry into the ship's fighting efficiency. The result was, he admitted, 'bad'. He was afraid that Pelly had not given 'that assistance and guidance to his Gunnery Lieut' which is so essential'. The latter would, however, never make a good control officer. Beatty to Jellicoe, 5 Mar. 1915; Jellicoe MSS.

[72] Jellicoe, 'A Reply to Criticism'.

[73] *The World Crisis*, ii. 146.

[74] Minute of 7 Mar. 1915 on Jellicoe's memorandum of 3 Mar. to Beatty and the Admiralty; Admiralty MSS.

[75] On 7 May 1916 the C.-in-C. wrote to Beatty, 'I am sending you the results of the recent firings. The *Tiger's* was as usual unsatisfactory, so much so that I addressed a letter to the R.A. 1st B.C.S. . . . I heard from Bartolomé [the Naval Secretary] who said that "Pelly might perhaps go as Commodore R.N. Barracks" [Portsmouth]. . . .

made for the better distribution of fire. Jellicoe reworded the Grand Fleet Battle Orders as to concentration of fire so as to prevent in future such mistakes as Pelly's. The battle cruisers did not learn their lesson, as Jutland was to prove. The Admiralty speeded up the installation of the director (master-sight) system in all the battle cruisers. Heligoland Bight, the Scarborough Raid, and now the Dogger Bank had all emphasized the need for director firing. At night or in thick weather it was only by some form of central control high up and above the smoke, and not dependent on gunlayers and trainers seeing the target, that any gunnery efficiency was possible. 'We were all praying,' Admiral James recollects, 'that director firing would be given highest priority, as we really could not hope to do any good against German ships in thick weather—and if they had directors, it would be better if we did not meet them.'[76] Also, certain improvements were made in the signalling arrangements, such as provision for an auxiliary W/T set and addenda to the signal book. The failure to destroy Hipper's battle cruisers had been partly due to Beatty's difficulty in signalling the exact nature of the situation. The signal book did not contain the necessary hoists. This was now remedied by the following additions (27 February 1915):

Engage enemy more closely.
Admiral unable to make signals by W/T.
C.-in-C. transfers the command (may be used if C.-in-C. or his flagship is disabled temporarily or otherwise).
Flag officer making the signal is disabled.
C.-in-C. has resumed the command.[77]

Another result of the battle was to convince Churchill and Fisher that the strategic stations of the Grand Fleet were too remote. Fisher had always wanted the battle cruisers at the Humber, the nearest spot to Heligoland. This was strategically possible only if the battle fleet moved south. The First Lord was more interested in the battle-fleet facet of the problem. He was impressed with the fact that Jellicoe had not been able to come into action on the 24th

---

This I think would provide the necessary solution without causing heartburnings, discussion, etc.' Beatty MSS. Bartolomé's solution was adopted in June 1916.

[76] Admiral James's letter to the author, 12 Feb. 1962. On the significance and introduction of director firing, see *From the Dreadnought to Scapa Flow*, i. 414–15.

[77] Naval Staff Monograph No. 29 (1925), *Home Waters—Part IV. From February to July 1915*, p. 4.

because he had been too far off to the north, although, as indicated above, that need not have been the case. Churchill and Fisher now proposed that Jellicoe move the battle fleet from Scapa Flow down to Rosyth—the inner line of anti-submarine defences had been completed and the outer line was almost completed—and that Beatty vacate Rosyth for the Humber, where the submarine defence had been finished. These moves would bring the battle fleet into a much closer supporting position to the battle cruisers and would put both in a better position to intercept enemy raiders or the High Seas Fleet itself. As Fisher on a later occasion admonished the C.-in-C.: '*The fundamental fact* is that you never can be in time so long as you are at Scapa Flow and therefore there will NEVER be a battle with the German High Sea Fleet unless von Pohl goes north especially to fight you *and that he never will!*'[78]

Jellicoe had never cared for the move to Rosyth because of the thick fogs there, the 'haunting fear' of Beatty being mined in, and his desire to have the battle cruisers in closer relation with the main fleet. Beatty had had a change of heart about Rosyth, fearing he would be mined in at the Forth. Jellicoe now, with Beatty's strong support, countered the Admiralty scheme by asking that the battle cruisers be returned to Cromarty and that the battle fleet stay at Scapa. These bases were far less fogbound and vulnerable to submarine attack and minelaying than were Rosyth and the Humber. Moreover, there were difficulties in taking out a large number of ships from the anchorage above the Forth bridge, especially on an ebb tide at night. It would actually be quicker to get the battle fleet south from Scapa Flow under most conditions than from Rosyth. Scapa was also a first-rate base, as ships could carry out a large amount of gunnery and torpedo practice inside the Flow and therefore clear of the submarine menace. These considerations, the two Admirals felt, outweighed any strategic advantages of moving southward. Beatty, furthermore, could not understand the object of moving the battle fleet to Rosyth.

They say better strategically. I can understand that argument applied to Battle Cruisers which might have the opportunity of intercepting raids, etc. But our B. Fleet does not exist for that; but to crush the Enemy Fleet. And I cannot see that you are any more likely to catch the Enemy Battle Fleet from Rosyth than you are from Scapa. In fact unless he makes up his mind to fight you, I do not see how you are

[78] Fisher to Jellicoe, 23 Apr. 1915; Jellicoe MSS.

going to make him. Any more than I could make their B.C.'s turn round and fight the other day. And his Fleet will be surrounded by scouts, etc. which will provide ample warning if he doesn't mean business. I told the 1st Lord all this and he seemed to concur.[79]

Churchill and Fisher reluctantly dropped the matter (3 March) in the face of this firm united front. The battle fleet remained at Scapa, and the battle cruisers at Rosyth. The latter were constituted a separate fleet, the Battle Cruiser Fleet, in February, though remaining an organic part of the Grand Fleet.

There is one last important point which arises in connexion with the Dogger Bank action. The German Official History remarks, 'Again and again the fear of German mines, submarines, and torpedo boats [destroyers] deterred them [the British] from taking a firm grip.' There is no denying this. The fear of mine-dropping by the German destroyers prevented Beatty from closing the range as fast as he could have done. The fear of supposed submarines caused the 8-point turn. And again the fear of mine-dropping dictated the next course ordered (N.E.) and so added to the obscurity of the Admiral's intentions. 'We now know,' observes Captain Creswell, 'that these fears were not fully justified. But merely to be wise after the event is of no value. The question is how can we avoid such mistakes in the future.' He suggests that there are two ways to reduce the fear of novel forms of attack. One is 'to remember that new weapons are nearly always credited with greater power than they actually possess. The fear of the unknown is a very real fear and everything possible must be done to counteract it.' The other way is 'by building ships in which we have real confidence. If we have ships that we know to be reasonably immune from subsidiary attacks, they will not be deflected from their main object by the fear of such attacks. There is no doubt that in the early part of the war there was a widespread, and not unjustified, feeling that our ships were remarkably tender as regards underwater explosions.'[80]

* * *

Although the probability of a fleet action seemed more remote than ever, on the whole the country was satisfied with the naval situation at the end of the first six months. Thus, the *National*

[79] Beatty to Jellicoe, 8 Feb. 1915; *ibid.*
[80] Creswell's Naval Staff College lecture, 'The Dogger Bank Action'.

Review (February) saw in the restriction of 'the second Navy in the world to the mud-banks of the Elbe . . . as supreme an exhibition of superior sea-power as the world has witnessed'. This feeling was not unanimous (see the second introductory quotation to this chapter), and it certainly was not the mood of the Fleet. A substantial band of restless and active spirits, particularly among officers afloat, preached that a more vigorous and imaginative use of the Fleet would be more likely to lead to a decision than the 'passive role' so long accepted by the Navy. Churchill and Fisher were overt sympathizers. There was no agreement on the new strategy to be followed, except that it should be of an amphibious nature. An appreciation prepared by Lord Esher for the C.I.D. is a fair representation of this school of thought. After a reminder of the traditional English antipathy to continental wars, he recommended a reversion to Pitt's 'system of strategy' and making use of England's amphibious power.

When the army of Sir John French was committed to war on the Continent there was no irrevocable breach of this great principle, but, as time went on, and reinforcement after reinforcement was sent to France, absorbing all the available military reserves of the country, its amphibious power was gradually sapped, and has, at the present time, been practically destroyed. . . . It is as true to-day as it then was [Seven Years' War], that our military power, used amphibiously in combination with the Fleet, can produce results all out of proportion to the numerical strength of our Army. . . . the moment has come.[81]

Yes, the moment had come just as Esher was writing this paper.

[81] 'The War after Six Months', 29 Jan. 1915; Asquith MSS.

VIII

The Search for a Naval Offensive

(AUGUST 1914–JANUARY 1915)

We have the game in our hands if we sit tight, but this Churchill cannot see. He must see something tangible and can't understand that naval warfare acts in a wholly different way from war on shore. That Fleet in the north dominates the position. It's no business of ours to go trying to pluck occasional, small indifferent fruits in the south.

CAPTAIN HERBERT W. RICHMOND (Assistant Director of Operations), 12 August 1914.

Sir Arthur Wilson is obsessed with the idea of an attack on Heligoland, Lord Fisher's one idea is a Baltic campaign, Mr. Churchill thinks only of the Dardanelles. None of the three can see any good in either of the others' schemes. Of a truth none of the schemes were really thought out.

ACTING VICE-ADMIRAL HENRY F. OLIVER (Chief of the Admiralty War Staff) to Jellicoe, January 1915.

I. CHURCHILL AND CLOSE BLOCKADE

FROM the very beginning of hostilities Churchill was bitten with the idea that the Fleet should 'do something'. Although he had been a prime originator of the distant blockade policy, he failed to appreciate the real power the Grand Fleet was exercising and the fact that it might go through the war without fighting a battle and yet have been the dominating factor all the time. That did not mean that the fleet would refuse a battle. It welcomed it—only the enemy must come and fight *where the Grand Fleet wanted*. This was the point of view of the Staff and, with reservations, of the Sea Lords, but it was not Churchill's idea of naval warfare. All sorts of amphibious operations were continually presenting themselves to his fertile brain as he sought to use sea power in the traditional way. Unfortunately, these schemes often soared very easily over the real difficulties of a problem.

Uppermost in his mind in the first months of the war was a Baltic offensive that owed much to Fisher's thinking. It was 'to secure the eventual command of the Baltic that British naval operations must tend,' the First Lord informed the C.-in-C. on 8 October. This, he believed, would be possible under one of three alternative conditions: (1) the defeat of the German Fleet; (2) the breaking of the Kiel Canal; (3) an effective blockade of the Bight.

On 19 August he had, with the Prime Minister's approval, written to the C.-in-C. of the Russian Army, the Grand Duke Nicholas, that the naval command of the Baltic could be established through (1) or (2). The first, which depended on the High Seas Fleet's movements, could happen at any time; the second, 'a difficult enterprise', might be attempted at 'the right moment' by air or/and destroyer attack on the Brunsbüttel lock-gates. Success in either would make it 'feasible' to send a British fleet through the Belts into the Baltic. The fleet 'could carry, convoy, and land' the Russian troops for any of these operations: '(1) To turn the flank and rear of German armies holding the Dantzig–Thorn line, or which were elsewhere resisting the main Russian attack. (2) To attack Berlin from the North—only 90 miles in the direct line [this is pure Fisher]. (3) To attack Kiel and the Canal in force and to drive the German Fleet to sea.'[1] The Russians thought (24 August) 'the suggested landing operation, under favourable circumstances, would be quite feasible and fully expedient. We therefore gratefully accept in principle the First Lord's offer, but we add that we could avail ourselves thereof only should the general military situation lend itself to its application.'[2]

On a visit to the Grand Fleet at Loch Ewe on 17 September the First Lord and the C.O.S. discussed the Baltic project with the C.-in-C. and the flag officers. Bayly liked the idea. He would (1) send destroyers to arrive at the mouth of the Elbe at the earliest daylight and blow up the gates of the Brunsbüttel locks. At the same time, (2), destroyers, cruisers, and submarines would attack Kiel harbour and sink the ships there. Keyes thought an attack on Kiel feasible with submarines alone. Tyrwhitt saw many practical difficulties. As regards (1), there were navigational difficulties, and there were two gates to each lock—they would have to smash the outer gate to get at the inner. Concerning (2), there were difficulties posed by mines and submarines.[3] 'The general opinion,

---

[1] *The World Crisis*, ii. 38.
[2] *Ibid.*, p. 39.
[3] Jellicoe's memorandum of 17 Sept. 1914; Admiralty MSS.

based largely on the danger from minefields, was that it was not at this time advisable to risk any reduction in our naval forces by eccentric movements such as an attack on Kiel by light cruisers and destroyers . . . The despatch of submarines, however, to operate off Kiel and to attack the High Sea Fleet, portions of which were heard of constantly in the Baltic at this date, was on a different footing.'[4]

Since the first of Churchill's alternatives for establishing the naval command of the Baltic depended on a reluctant enemy, and the second had formidable difficulties (one favoured approach was to threaten Kiel by an invasion of Schleswig-Holstein from the sea), the third possibility was the one that came to the fore. This involved storming and holding one or more of the German islands from which a close blockade of the Heligoland Bight could be instituted by submarines, destroyers, and aircraft. Churchill assumed that the close and continuous support of the Grand Fleet would not be necessary. Close blockade was, actually, the old war plan which had been abandoned in 1912–14 in favour of the distant blockade. Churchill emphasized the probable extra advantage of this strategy: the capture and retention of a German island would be 'intolerable' to the enemy, and would probably force out his fleet for a 'supreme battle'.

The First Lord's thinking had pre-war roots. On 31 January 1913 the Admiralty, at Churchill's direction, had asked Rear-Admiral Bayly, then unemployed, to investigate and report on the question of seizing and holding a base on the 'Dutch, German, Danish, or Scandinavian Coasts for operations of Flotillas on the outbreak of war with Germany, the other countries named being either unfriendly neutrals or enemies'.[5] Colonel Aston, of the Royal Marines, and Captain Arthur Leveson were associated with him. On 30 June 1913 he presented a plan for seizing and holding Borkum by an expeditionary force. Warships were to run past the forts at night, each with a transport lashed to her off side, and aided by a smoke screen to obscure the shore electric lights, automatic gas buoys to show the way, and minesweepers working in the channels ahead of the ships; 10,000 troops would be landed on two

---

[4] Naval Staff Monograph No. 25 (1922), *The Baltic, 1914*, in Naval Staff Monographs, vii. 70. In the middle of October two submarines entered the Baltic, where they created a great nuisance value for themselves.

[5] 'Papers dealing with Borkum, Heligoland, etc., 1913–1914'; Admiralty MSS.

sides of the island, covered by the ships' guns and smoke screens, with 2,000 men to be held in reserve in the transports. A second report proposed the capture of Sylt in roughly the same way. Exclusive of transports and auxiliaries, Bayly asked for 10 large ships, 24 destroyers, and 12,000 troops to take either Borkum or Sylt. A third report dealt with Esbjerg in Denmark. There being no fortifications or troops there, and no evidence that the Danes proposed to defend it, Bayly saw no great difficulty in taking this place. Heligoland was the subject of another report, and, finally, Bayly recommended a scheme alongside which Heligoland would have been child's play. To destroy the floating docks, wharves, and shipping at Hamburg, and especially the locks at the entrance of the Kiel Canal (at Brunsbüttel), he proposed a raid up the Elbe River by a force of six fast destroyers, each equipped with six torpedoes and explosives. The serious navigational difficulties and the strong fortifications at Cuxhaven made the operation very hazardous, 'and therefore the raid must trust to surprise, without any intention at the back of the raiders' minds of returning . . .'

The D.O.D. evaluated the various projects as 'in the nature of a gamble at best', based as they were, admittedly, on a very imperfect knowledge of the strength of the enemy defences that would be met in war.

Gambles in war are justifiable if an adequate advantage may be forthcoming, but here that does not appear to be the case. The sole object of the proposed expeditions is to obtain an advanced flotilla base. If the attack is successful the islands would pass into our hands, but it is extremely doubtful even then as to whether the anchorages they enclose would answer our purpose. Destroyers and colliers lying inside Sylt would be within range of German siege artillery on the mainland. Inside Borkum they would be constantly harassed by small torpedo craft arriving by canal at Emden. In neither anchorage would they enjoy any rest. Moreover, they would be undefended against attack from the sea except by such a moveable armament as we could put and keep on the islands, since it is not to be supposed that the enemy would leave their heavy armaments in working condition for our use if they anticipated the success of our attack. We do not consider an undefended harbour a proper flotilla base on our own coast. Still less, therefore, would these practically undefended anchorages on the coast of the Continent within 3 hours steaming of the main German bases answer requirements.[6]

[6] Captain George A. Ballard to Jackson (C.O.S.), 10 July 1913; *ibid.*

Bayly's reports gathered dust until the eve of war, when Churchill sent copies to the Prime Minister. To ensure that any military and naval action be co-ordinated, he added the urgent recommendation that the War Office and Admiralty, through two representatives from each, study and report as swiftly as possible on each project. The experts were not to concern themselves either with 'questions of violation of neutrality' or 'whether the troops could be better employed elsewhere'. Higher authorities would settle these policy matters later. The First Lord set up this priority for the reports, to be furnished one by one: Ameland or Born Deep (Holland; the latter is a three-mile by one-half mile inlet on the Dutch island of Ameland situated between the Texel and Borkum); Ekersund (south-west coast of Norway); Laeso Channel (Denmark); Kungsbacka Fiord (south-west coast of Sweden); Esbjerg; Sylt; Borkum; Heligoland. The last four were 'less urgent' on account of the probable unavailability of the troops required.[7] Two marine officers were detailed from the Admiralty with Leveson as a consultant.

Jackson, the C.O.S., did not think much of these projects. Born Deep, for example, could be taken easily enough, and it would enable one flotilla at a time (sixteen destroyers, six submarines, and miscellaneous ships) to obtain shelter 140 miles nearer the Bight than Yarmouth. On the other hand, Holland, whose 'local defence vessels are by no means to be despised', would certainly declare war. Protecting Born Deep 'would tie a portion of our Fleet to its neighbourhood, within 60 miles of Borkum and the Texel, where it would be subject to attack from both sides, and it would tie up a stronger force to protect it than it would assist for operations at a distance. . . . its occupation would be a source of great anxiety, not commensurate with the slight gain in distance for our Flotillas if working off Heligoland.' Jackson was no more excited about the seizure of the other bases on the First Lord's list. 'The disadvantages of occupying an advanced but undefended base is the necessity of protecting it from an attack from seaward. This may definitely tie up a larger naval force in its vicinity as it will eventually shelter when defended, and adequate defences against cruiser attack take a considerable time to erect even under peace conditions.' From a naval point of view the seizure of Borkum made the most sense, as it was the most valuable of these

[7] Churchill to Asquith, 31 July 1914; *ibid.*

bases. The cost would be excessive, though; 12,000 troops and a huge naval force would be required, 'and most naval officers consider the advantages to be gained . . . are not worth the cost of the ships and men which must certainly take place in the operation. . . . It is considered that a decisive action between our Fleets, resulting in our favour, is necessary before direct attack on German territory is possible.'[8]

There does not appear to have been much, if any, consultation between the Services, as the First Lord had proposed. But a General Staff Officer, Major Wake, was detached by the Director of Military Operations to examine the matter. He was not carried away. The anchorage at Ameland was exposed to long-range fire from the mainland; holding Ekersund, Kungsbacka Fiord, and Laeso Channel, if Norway, Sweden, and Denmark, respectively, decided to employ force to protect their neutrality, would require sufficient forces to deal with their field armies; Laeso Island was so surrounded by shoals that it would be useful only as a temporary anchorage when seeking a lee in heavy weather; as regards Esbjerg, Sylt, Borkum, and Heligoland, they were fortified, troops would be needed, and this was probably out of the question at present. Information on vital points being lacking for all these places, extremely great risks would be involved in such expeditions. 'The question for consideration is whether the advantages to be gained are commensurate with the risks incurred. In the particular places examined this does not appear to be the case . . .'[9]

Churchill was never one to be discouraged easily. No matter what the experts thought, he knew better. He was at first especially partial to Ameland. He formally proposed to his professional advisers that the Navy capture and hold the island and establish in Born Deep an advanced flotilla base for 'a close observation and control of the Southern approaches to the Elbe'. He listed other advantages, among them that the operation might cause the enemy to send out their main fleet, that British aircraft would have a base from which they could report all naval activity in the Bight and later bomb the Kiel Canal, and 'above all to maintain in

[8] Jackson's memorandum, 'Born Deep (Ameland Gat) as a temporary advanced base for a Flotilla', 1 Aug. 1914, and an undated, untitled memorandum of the same period on the question of occupying a German base or a base in neutral territory; *ibid.*

[9] Major Sir Hereward Wake, 'Report on the Proposal to Occupy Certain Places as Temporary Naval Bases for Offensive Action against Germany', 11 Aug. 1914; *ibid.*

full vigour the spirit of enterprise and attack which, when excluded from warlike operations, means that you are only waiting wondering where you will be hit'. He included an outline of a plan to seize Ameland: 3,000 marines in two transports, four destroyer flotillas, nine cruisers, eighteen submarines, and auxiliary vessels, with the Channel Fleet 'in reserve support'.[10]

Churchill was very disappointed at the reception his plan received. Thus, Richmond, the A.D.O.D., was convinced of the 'strategical and tactical futility' of such an operation. It would be a 'gross error' to alienate Holland: it would antagonize the Cape Dutch and lead to a Japanese attack on the Dutch East Indies, which would not sit well with the Australians. Strategically, it would accomplish nothing, and anyway the harbour was not large enough to hold a substantial force.[11] The First Lord was forced to drop this harum-scarum project.

2. WILSON AND HELIGOLAND

For a while Heligoland held the stage. The island, about 18 miles from the entrance to the Elbe, Weser, and Jade, was 1,800 yards long, 650 yards wide, and surrounded by cliffs except at the south end. Churchill in 1913 called it 'an almost impregnable fortress'. Bayly had, at the First Lord's direction, studied the feasibility of taking the island and had concluded (June 1913) that the cost would be prohibitive.

This did not lessen A. K. Wilson's certainty that Heligoland could be taken and held without excessive cost. The Navy would enjoy these advantages: the island would form a base for aircraft which could keep a close watch on ship movements in the Elbe and Jade; it would give early warning to the submarines when the enemy's ships were coming out; and it could be used as a submarine and destroyer base for a more efficient watch over the mouths of the rivers than was possible when the craft had to return to England for supplies. Wilson was the prime mover of the project, and he 'always stuck like wax to the subject at issue'. During the first two months of the war he made strenuous efforts to persuade the Admiralty to bombard Heligoland and to capture it. When the matter was referred to Jellicoe semi-officially early in

[10] Churchill to Jackson and Battenberg, 9 Aug. 1914; Admiralty MSS.
[11] Diary, 9 Aug. 1914; *Portrait of an Admiral*, p. 96.

September, the C.-in-C. bluntly declared it was an impossible undertaking.

Undaunted, Wilson formally submitted his operational plans to the First Lord. He was confident of success with a fleet of pre-dreadnoughts and a landing party of marines. He emphasized the advantages that the fire of warships now had against that of forts in view of the immense improvements of recent years in range-finding, sighting, and fire control. Warship fire was at least as accurate as fire from forts, it was capable of 'enormously greater' concentration on a given point, and the range-finding of ships would not be affected as much as the forts by the dust and smoke caused by bursting shells. Wilson conceded that ships were more vulnerable and were exposed to the risk of destruction by mines and, especially in an attack on Heligoland, by submarines. But the advantages to be derived from the possession of the island made it well worth while to run the risk, while taking all possible precautionary measures. The best defence against recapture of the island would be to make it difficult and dangerous for the German Fleet to leave its bases. This would be accomplished by blocking the rivers with mines and watching the entrances with submarines. Under these conditions, submarines and a small garrison equipped with a dozen machine guns to cover the landing places, and a few 4-inch or 6-inch guns to beat off destroyers or light cruisers, would be sufficient.[12]

Churchill, though not an advocate of the Heligoland plan, was willing, with Battenberg's concurrence, to put it before Jellicoe and the flag officers of the Grand Fleet at the Loch Ewe meeting on 17 September. All the officers, with the single exception of Arbuthnot (Second-in-Command, 2nd B.S.), emphatically rejected the scheme as utterly impracticable, if not downright absurd. The reasons given were 'the unanswerable ones' (Jellicoe) that ships were at a very serious disadvantage against forts, particularly the very strong ones on Heligoland. A fort had the range quite easily, since it could comparatively easily spot the fall of its projectiles on the water, whereas a ship could hardly do so on land. There was the difficulty of getting at the guns on Heligoland, which were buried out of sight or sunk in deep trenches. Also, the risk of losing ships from submarines and the gunfire of the forts was too great. Even if they succeeded in taking the island,

[12] Wilson's memorandum of 10 Sept. 1914 for Churchill; Admiralty MSS.

the Germans could recapture it with ease, lying as it did within 30 miles of the main North Sea base of the High Seas Fleet.[13] The whole Admiralty War Staff, including Sturdee when C.O.S. and his successor, Oliver, were in agreement with the senior officers at sea.

When Wilson was brought back to the Admiralty and made a member of the War Staff Group, he again pressed the project and pushed for its execution by the Channel Fleet. Its C.-in-C., Burney, rejected it as decisively as had the other flag officers. It was 'unsound strategy', risking as it did a number of capital ships to mines, submarines, and gunfire, when it was absolutely essential for the Grand Fleet to be ready to annihilate the High Seas Fleet when it came out. 'The scheme if carried out would result in a national disaster.'[14]

The Heligoland project was now dead, leaving two consequences of the utmost importance. At the time of the inception of the Dardanelles scheme, in January 1915, Churchill, thoroughly aware of Grand Fleet sentiment on the issue of ships v. forts, made no attempt to consult the C.-in-C. In the second place, Wilson's Heligoland ideas helped to wreck his chances of succeeding Fisher in the crisis of May 1915. 'We one and all doubted Sir A.'s sanity. . . . Anyone who could put forward the proposition as he put it forward is capable of *anything*.'[15] One wonders, indeed, how a man of Wilson's attainments could have advanced such a proposal.

3. CHURCHILL AND BORKUM

The return of Fisher to the Admiralty gave Churchill a powerful ally in his search for a naval offensive. Fisher saw that the 'defensive attitude' of the Fleet was bad for its morale and, more clearly than anyone, that it was fighting that would decide the issue. 'It's all quite haphazard, any initiative. When the Germans kick our bottoms, then we move, but d—d slow at that!' 'DO SOMETHING!!!!! *We are waiting to be kicked!!!*'[16] Churchill agreed. The desire to retaliate for the enemy raids strengthened the eagerness for a naval offensive.

[13] Jellicoe's memorandum on the meeting, 17 Sept. 1914, Admiralty MSS.; Jellicoe, 'A Reply to Criticism'.

[14] Burney to Churchill, 8 Nov. 1914; Lennoxlove MSS.

[15] Jellicoe to McKenna, 23 May 1915; McKenna MSS.

[16] Undated Fisher note (Jan. 1915?), Fisher to Churchill, 21 Dec. 1914; *Fear God and Dread Nought*, iii. 44, 104.

The deadlock in the land fighting on the Continent played into the hands of the Admiralty. A fresh theatre had to be found for the new British armies. Hankey would use them in 'conquests beyond the seas . . . [which] combined with economic pressure is the natural weapon of the Power that possesses command of the sea'.[17] What he had in mind was an amphibious operation directed at Turkey, in conjunction with the Balkan states, to drive the Turks out of Europe. Balfour came out for an oversea base for the torpedo craft as 'the most effective way of crippling the movements of the enemy's Fleet and parrying any attempt at invasion', provided that a defensible base could be found and enough troops were available for its capture.[18] Lloyd George sent a memorandum to the Prime Minister on New Year's Day urging an attack on Austria in the spring, based on Salonika, to open up communications with Serbia and neutralize Bulgaria. Churchill, too, asked at the end of the year how they could best use their growing military strength. 'Are there not other alternatives than sending our armies to chew barbed wire in Flanders?' And he proceeded once again to outline the advantages that would flow from naval command of the Baltic, for which the essential preliminary was the blocking of the Heligoland debouche.[19]

A second memorandum to the Prime Minister two days later went into the details. It pointed to May 1915 as the date for securing the naval command of the Baltic and developing the war on two new fronts: the Kiel Canal and Berlin. He cited these as the required measures, and in this sequence: (1) British capture of Borkum as an oversea base as soon as possible (three first-class infantry brigades would be required), to be followed by very intensive mining of the channels and rivers of the German coast, with forces based on Borkum preventing the removal of the mines. With the German Fleet virtually excluded from the North Sea by the blocking of the Bight, (2) Schleswig-Holstein could be invaded in force and an advance made on the Kiel Canal. (To Fisher and Jellicoe on 4 January he suggested the invasion of Oldenburg as an alternative to Schleswig-Holstein.) Cutting the Canal would paralyse the German Navy, but it was not indispensable. (3) Once

[17] Untitled memorandum for the Prime Minister, 28 Dec. 1914; Asquith MSS.
[18] Memorandum of 3 Dec. 1914 to Hankey, who sent it on to Churchill the same day. 'Papers dealing with Borkum, Heligoland, etc., 1913–1914'.
[19] Churchill to Asquith, 29 Dec. 1914; *The World Crisis*, ii. 44–5.

the Army had established itself in Schleswig-Holstein, Denmark would be invited to join the Allies. Churchill apparently felt that the promise of naval and military protection and of the post-war restoration of her lost provinces would secure Denmark's accession. When this happened, British troops would occupy Fyn (Funen) Island, which would secure the Great Belt. (4) 'A British fleet, strong enough to fight a decisive battle, shd. then enter the Baltic and establish control of that sea, thus cutting Germany off from all northern supplies.' (5) It would then be possible to land Russian troops at various points on the Baltic coast within a hundred miles of Berlin, and, by threatening the whole coast, to immobilize large German forces.

'This plan of war,' the First Lord enthused, 'combines all conceivable forms of pressure on the Enemy.' 'The first and indispensable measure' was the capture of Borkum. Apart from its place in the general plan, its occupation would guard against surprise, raid, or invasion, and enable the Navy to keep overwhelming flotillas of submarines and destroyers in German waters, which would probably force a decisive naval action.[20]

The spotlight had, then, shifted to Borkum towards the end of the year. The island, four miles long by three miles wide, was situated at the entrance to the Ems River, 120 miles from Wilhelmshaven. Strategically and geographically, it had been regarded by the Admiralty since 1907 as the best advanced base for the flotillas and inshore squadrons blockading the German river mouths. It had deep water on two sides, was not too close to the mainland, and was far enough from Wilhelmshaven so that it might be taken before a relieving force could arrive. It was known that the island was heavily defended by batteries, minefields, and a strong garrison, and could be commanded by fire from the mainland.

The 'storming and seizure' of Borkum had been Churchill's favourite plan all along, even if it had had a low priority in the first months of the war. Prince Louis had liked it, in principle anyway, as did Wilson and, on his return to the Admiralty, Fisher. Bayly stubbornly pushed the scheme. It had from the beginning

---

[20] Asquith MSS. The Prime Minister found in the plan 'a good deal of food for thought. I am profoundly dissatisfied with the immediate prospect—an enormous waste of life and money day after day with no appreciable progress . . .' Diary, 29 Dec. 1914; Asquith, *Memories and Reflections*, ii. 52.

been understood that he would command the Channel Fleet, which was to be the nucleus of the bombarding fleet, and this was doubtless the reason for his assuming the command early in December 1914. It was the general belief at the Admiralty that the seizure of Borkum would quickly lead to a decisive clash between the two main fleets. In November Churchill and Fisher directed the War Staff to review Bayly's Borkum projects and to prepare plans for the operation in 1915. At the turn of the year Churchill was urging that a regular division of infantry be assigned to the operation, and that it be carried out 'at the earliest moment'. The idea had progressed to the point where on 7 January 1915 the War Council agreed in principle to the operation if and when circumstances made it desirable.

In December and early January the First Lord was also pushing for an operation against Sylt, a German island 20 miles long and in many places only a half-mile wide, situated just off the north Schleswig coast. Oliver has wryly commented that 'Churchill would often look in on his way to bed to tell me how he would capture Borkum or Sylt. If I did not interrupt or ask questions he could capture Borkum in twenty minutes.'[21] On 2 December Churchill proposed an attack on the northern end of Sylt. He made it look easy. Naval fire from a bombarding force of four pre-dreadnoughts, three monitors, and twenty destroyers (covered by the Grand Fleet) would overwhelm the enemy's guns, following which 5,000 men would be landed from four transports under naval protection. The island could be defended 'without any large or valuable naval force being required'.[22] Bartolomé, the Naval Secretary, slightly dampened the First Lord's ardour by singling out some of the very real difficulties, among them that even if the heavy guns of the battleships silenced the guns on the island, the landing of troops would be extremely hazardous. The Germans had no doubt made every defensive preparation, since the capture of Sylt had been discussed in England rather openly for some years. 'Boats would be unable to land in the face of the opposition provided by well-protected troops assisted by an armoured train, and such a train is in existence, the line being well protected.'[23]

---

[21] Admiral Sir William James, *A Great Seaman: the Life of Admiral of the Fleet Sir Henry F. Oliver* (London, 1956), p. 144, quoting from the Oliver MSS.

[22] 'Papers Dealing with Borkum, Heligoland, etc., 1913–1914'.

[23] n.d.; *ibid.*

The First Lord would not let go of the idea. Discounting the technical objections of his advisers, he addressed a minute to the War Staff Group on 3 January 1915 which began: 'All preparations should be made for the capture of Sylt.' The plans should be aimed at two dates, 1 March and 15 April, and all 'necessary appliances' should be ordered at once. Among the 'points relied upon' were these: (1) Gunfire of the bombarding squadron and monitors would, 'firing from several directions with cross and aerial spotting', subdue the fire of the batteries enough to allow (2) the transports to approach covered by darkness and smoke, and sheltered by older cruisers, and to land 8,000–12,000 'good infantry' during the night after the bombardment. (3) The High Seas Fleet would be 'cooped up behind Heligoland' by forty submarines operating during the day and sixty destroyers at night, with the Grand Fleet supporting the flotillas at about the 56th parallel. (4) Minefields laid the night before the bombardment, indicator nets, and destroyers towing charges would furnish protection from submarines to the bombarding ships and the transports. 'A resolve to have the island at all costs, coupled with exact and careful preparations, should certainly, with our great resources, be successful within three days of fire being opened.'[24] Note Churchill's confidence in the ability of battleship guns to silence forts.

The Borkum project—and with it Sylt—faded into the background after the middle of January and was practically dead by the end of the month. One reason was the loss of the *Formidable*, which clouded Bayly's reputation for some months and removed his fervid advocacy of the scheme at the crucial period. Another, effect as much as cause, was the transfer of the Channel Fleet, which was to have been the squadron used, to the Dardanelles in February and March. Most important was Churchill's failure to win much support among the sailors, among whom there was a growing awareness that the capture of Borkum by a bold *coup de main* in the face of the formidable defences would be a desperate venture. How desperate was brought out in memoranda by the C.O.S. and the A.D.O.D. Borkum, if captured, Oliver pointed out, could be more easily held than any other German island owing to its distance from the mainland: 22,000 yards or 11 miles; 12-inch or 14-inch naval guns could range this distance, but it

[24] *Ibid.*

would take some time to mount them. Borkum would, however, be very difficult to capture. It had a well-dispersed and considerable heavy armament; the soil was sand, meaning that you had to hit the gun itself to disable it, since shells bursting in sand had very little effect; the off-lying shoals would keep ships off between 12,000 and 14,000 yards; the approaches to the island were protected by mines; Juist Island, 10,000 yards from Borkum, would probably have to be taken also, as guns mounted there could shell Borkum. The C.O.S. was also very dubious about the operation because they did not have the troops to hold the island even if it were captured.[25]

Richmond, who was asked to prepare the plans, wrote one of his incisive, clearly reasoned memoranda condemning the Borkum scheme as impracticable. A long-range bombardment could not be depended upon in consequence of the prevailing haze; there was a ranging problem: the island being flat and featureless, there were no marks upon which to fix the ship; navigation of deep-draught ships in the vicinity of the island would be difficult on account of the extensive sandbanks surrounding the island.

The batteries are not visible from the sea in the clearest weather conditions, and aeroplane spotting is as yet untested in connection with moving ships. . . .

Until the batteries covering the approaches where you want the transports to go are destroyed, you have not got command of the sea. All ideas of rushing past them by smoke screens are impracticable, as you cannot tell off the wind to blow how you want it to blow. Also, until you have made the navigation safe as regards both mines and sandbanks, you cannot bring the transports in. You cannot remove the mines except by sweeping, and you cannot sweep till the batteries are destroyed. Whichever way you work at it, it comes back to that in every case—the batteries must be destroyed as a first measure, and no troops ought to be put upon the water until all the guns have been put out of action and the channels swept and buoyed.[26]

---

[25] Oliver's memorandum, 15 Dec. 1914; 'Papers Dealing with Borkum, Heligoland, etc., 1913–1914'.

[26] 'Attack upon Danzic' (the code name for Borkum), 19 Jan. 1915; *Portrait of an Admiral*, pp. 138–9. Privately, Richmond was much franker about the operation. 'It is *quite mad*. The reasons for capturing it are NIL, the possibilities about the same. . . . It remains with the Army, who I hope will refuse to throw away 12,000 troops in this manner for the self-glorification of an ignorant & impulsive man. . . . to risk troops in waters full of submarines, depending on such precarious defences as we now possess as against them, is pure foolery.' Diary, 4 Jan. 1915; *ibid.*, pp. 134–5.

Jellicoe's opinion of the capture of Borkum had been on record since July 1914, when he was still Second Sea Lord (Churchill had asked for his opinion in May). Basically, his objection was that the island as a naval base would be rendered untenable by intensive long-range bombardment and aerial attack from the German mainland. Therefore, it could be of no use to the Navy as an advanced base for small craft unless the Grand Fleet sailed into the Bight, which would risk heavy damage in the German mine-fields. Also, submarine minelaying, which could be carried out with great ease by night, would force them to keep at Borkum a much larger force of destroyers and other small craft than they could possibly spare.[27] Jellicoe could never understand 'how an attack on Borkum could possibly assist fleet operations in the Baltic or lead to the German Fleet being driven altogether from the North Sea . . . To suggest that we could mine them in their harbours *as the result of the capture of Borkum* is ludicrous, as is the idea that the capture of Borkum, even if it could be held, would have assisted us in a military attack on Schleswig-Holstein.'[28]

Jackson, if his attitude at this time can be judged from a paper of a few months later, envisaged considerable losses in an offensive against Borkum or other German islands that could be justified only if it was sure to bring out the High Seas Fleet and result in its defeat.[29]

Fisher's attitude was crucial. Up to a point he saw eye to eye with Churchill. He agreed with the First Lord (4 January) that Borkum offered 'great possibilities'.

But although the First Sea Lord's strategic conceptions were centred in the entry of the Baltic [Churchill complained], and although he was in principle favourable to the seizure of Borkum as a preliminary, I did not find in him that practical, constructive and devising energy which in other periods of his career and at this period on other subjects he had so abundantly shown. . . . He spoke a great deal about Borkum, its importance and its difficulties; but he did not give that strong

[27] Jellicoe, 'A Reply to Criticism'. Jellicoe had no more use for an offensive against Sylt, and for pretty much the same reasons as in the case of Borkum. Both could be commanded by long-range gunfire from the mainland. He was, however, prepared to consider a bombardment of either island, preferably Sylt, as a 'trap' to bring the Germans out over mines and submarines. Jellicoe to Fisher, 6 Jan. 1915; Lennoxlove MSS.

[28] Admiral Sir Reginald Bacon, *The Life of John Rushworth, Earl Jellicoe* (London, 1936), pp. 188–9, quoting Jellicoe's post-war autobiographical notes (Jellicoe MSS.).

[29] Jackson's minute of 31 Mar. 1915, requested by Fisher on an unspecified paper; 'Papers Dealing with Borkum, Heligoland, etc., 1913–1914'.

professional impulsion to the staffs necessary to secure the exploration of the plan.[30]

This lament makes it clear that Churchill viewed Fisher as the chief spoiler of his plan. Exactly what was the First Sea Lord's position?

4. FISHER AND THE BALTIC

Churchill and Fisher both believed the ultimate object of the Navy was to obtain access to the Baltic, and turn the German flank in the west by landing a large military force for the occupation of Schleswig-Holstein (which admittedly meant the infringement of Danish neutrality or active Danish co-operation), and landing a Russian army on the unprotected German coast in Pomerania. Where the two men differed was that Fisher had come to feel that Baltic operations could be launched without the intervening steps the First Lord regarded as essential, namely, the seizure of Borkum and the blockade of the Bight. 'I am wholly with you about the Baltic,' declared Churchill. 'But you must close up this side first. You must take an island and block them in, à la Wilson; or you must break the [Kiel] Canal or the locks, or you must cripple this Fleet in a general action. No scattering of mines will be any substitute for these alternatives.'[31] Elsewhere Churchill brought out the great difference in these terms: 'Again and again, orally and in writing, I confronted him with the issue "Before you can enter the Baltic you must first block up the Elbe. How are you going to do this? Are you ready to take the islands and fight the fleet action necessary to block the Elbe? Can you divide the fleet and enter the Baltic with a part while the Germans are free to sally out with their whole strength from either end of the Kiel Canal?" . . . he never would face this pretty obvious question.'[32]

Fisher never submitted his Baltic Scheme to Jellicoe for his remarks (the first time the C.-in-C. heard of it was in a letter from Fisher in 1916) or to the War Staff for the working up of a detailed plan of operations. (No detailed plans were ever worked out for any of the projects that were in the air at that time.) Nor did he ever ask for the opinion of the War Office. The fact is that the operation was never really threshed out. Why, we do not know,

[30] *The World Crisis*, ii. 41. As late as March, however, Churchill was hopeful that the attack on Borkum would take place on or about 15 May.
[31] Churchill to Fisher, 22 Dec. 1914; *Fear God and Dread Nought*, iii. 107.
[32] Churchill, *Great Contemporaries* (rev. ed., London, 1938), p. 339.

unless Churchill is correct in his conviction that Fisher 'never seriously intended to dare the prolonged and awful hazards of the Baltic operation . . .'[33] This does not tally with Fisher's description of the project to the Dardanelles Commission in 1916 as 'the real focus of all my purposes at the Admiralty', nor with the nature of his building programme or his sending the Baltic paper to Asquith (see below, pp. 195–6).

This much is certain. Fisher, strongly influenced by Corbett's teachings, had long been an ardent believer in Britain's traditional strategy of amphibious operations—the strategy of exploiting the mobility given by sea power. He had for years before the war urged that the B.E.F. be used, not as the War Office planned to and actually did use it, as an appendix to the French left wing ('simply criminal folly', he called it on 28 August 1914), but landed at some point on German soil, on the flank of the German advance. After returning as First Sea Lord, he fought to put British troops in Belgium—Ostend and Zeebrugge must not be left in German hands—and to threaten the German Army in France. He also played with the idea of a landing on the Frisian coast of Holland or the coast of Schleswig-Holstein. '. . . 750,000 men landed in Holland, combined with intense activity of the British Fleet against, say, Cuxhaven, would finish the War by forcing out the German High Sea Fleet and getting in rear of the German Armies! The First Lord has twice put before the War Council the Dutch Project and no one "gainsaid" it! Is it going to be done? Great preparations are involved. The frost so deadly to Holland is over in May. Cannot a definite decision be reached?'[34]

Fisher's complementary and even more beloved project was the Baltic Scheme proper: the landing of Russian troops on Germany's Pomeranian coast, at a point some 90 miles from Berlin. The only record he has left of the Baltic Project is a four-page paper under the same title, which was first printed in November 1914. He apparently got the idea of it from the naval historian Julian Corbett, who saw an analogy between the Seven Years' War (1756–63) and the World War. Fisher's paper was indeed prepared in close collaboration with Corbett. It only attempted to make out a general case for the scheme.[35]

[33] *Ibid.*
[34] Fisher to Churchill, 18 Jan. 1915; *Fear God and Dread Nought*, iii. 132–3.
[35] The text is in Fisher's *Records*, pp. 217–22.

What Fisher was proposing was a revival of the 'fatal stroke of 1761' (when a Russian army landed on the Pomeranian coast) through the occupation of the Baltic *'in such strength as to enable an adequate Russian army to land in the spring on the coast of Pomerania within striking distance of Berlin or so as to threaten the German communications eastward'*. The operation would require the whole battle fleet. This would leave the North Sea open to a counterstroke by the German Fleet, which would force a withdrawal from the Baltic. To prevent this, that is, to deny the North Sea to the High Seas Fleet, Fisher proposed to sow that sea with mines *'on such a scale* ['thousands and thousands', he says elsewhere] *that naval operations in it would become impossible'*, even if this meant offending the neutrals.

Corbett saw the mining proposal as the one 'unfortunately rather obvious objection' to the whole scheme which he could not answer. 'If it is possible for us to make the North Sea untenable with mines, is it not even more possible for the Germans to play the same game in the Baltic?'[36] There is no record of the Admiral's reaction. He may have felt that the last paragraph of his Baltic paper (see below) met this objection. The principal objection that Fisher saw to his scheme was the danger to the communications of the fleet once in the Baltic. 'This appears serious in view of the difficulty of securing an advanced base so long as the Scandinavian Powers remain neutral; but possibly it may be overcome by restricting our mining to a certain latitude.'

His conclusion was: 'The risks, of course, must be serious; but unless we are fairly sure that the passive pressure of our fleet is really bringing Germany to a state of exhaustion, *risks must be taken to use our Command of the Sea with greater energy . . .*' The marginal addendum on one print reads: 'Risks must be taken! Rashness in war is Prudence! Prudence in war is criminal!'

Fisher's building programme was designed, in part, with the requirements of the Baltic Scheme in view. This will explain the unprecedented light draught of the large light cruisers *Courageous*, *Glorious*, and *Furious*, the shallow-draught monitors, and the mine-layers, minesweepers, and landing craft in the programme. The *Renown* and *Repulse* were also intended to be employed in connexion with the project. And in the spring of 1915 a number of the fastest Atlantic liners were fitted as minelayers and a 'prodigious'

[36] Corbett to Fisher, 19 Dec. 1914; *Fear God and Dread Nought*, iii. 46.

number of mines ordered. The landing craft—motor-driven lighters of a special type—were designed to land large bodies of troops rapidly on an enemy's coast. Each lighter would carry about 500 men, and what Fisher had in mind was having enough to land 50,000 troops on a beach at one time. The vessels were quickly built. Although never used as originally intended, these self-propelled lighters were, ironically, extremely useful in the later stages of the Dardanelles campaign, especially in the landing at Suvla and during the final evacuations.

The many post-war critics of the Baltic Scheme have made these points:

(1) The Baltic plan was, like the Borkum plan, based on the idea of a combined or amphibious operation. But, as Captain A. C. Dewar has remarked, the exponents of that doctrine failed to grasp the fundamental distinction lying between an operation against enemy territory overseas, cut off from reinforcements and far distant from his dockyards and industrial centres (such as the Japanese attack on Tsingtao and the British expedition to the Cameroons), and an operation against the very coasts of a powerful enemy, where he could operate with his whole naval strength unimpaired and with the whole industrial strength of the nation at his back.

(2) Captain Dewar again: 'Any attempt to land and maintain a large force in the Baltic or Bight must have involved the blocking or blockade of Kiel and Wilhelmshaven. How on earth or sea this was to be effected neither Lord Fisher nor anyone else has ever ventured to explain.' Of course, Churchill had a solution—to capture a German island and use it for a close blockade. This, we have seen, did not appeal to the impatient Fisher.

(3) One technical objection is that Britain had nothing like the number of mines called for, and that whatever mines were laid, the Germans would soon sweep exits through them. (These defects appear to have been the ones that Admiralty critics aware of the Scheme pointed to at the time.)

(4) The principal and vital naval criticism has been that the lines of communication necessarily led through the Great Belt, 30 miles long and 6 miles wide, which had already been made impassable by mines; and Germany's greatest naval base, Kiel, was but 30 miles away. 'To place the Fleet and a host of transports beyond the narrow and easily mined channels of the Belts would

have been madness.' Oliver had no faith in the scheme because of a related argument. 'How the fleet would pass the Great Belt in single line ahead with the German battle fleet deployed and crossing the T did not interest him, or how the fleet could be supplied in the Baltic.'[37]

There has, indeed, been near unanimity among both Fisher's congenital critics and his supporters that the Baltic Scheme was a hare-brained one that offered no chance of success, and that it would have led to a first-class disaster, had it been attempted before the destruction or crippling of the High Seas Fleet—even if the Russian troops needed had been available. Among senior officers only Admiral Bacon has had a good word for the feasibility of the plan:

It is impossible to say, now, whether the scheme would have survived the detailed and critical examination essential before such an operation could be justifiably undertaken; but it is unjust to dismiss the project offhand as impracticable, and with a shrug of the shoulders to say that it was madness on Lord Fisher's part to propose it. Scientific and thorough preparation would certainly have caused many of the objections which have been hastily advanced to fall into insignificance. The German Battle Fleet would have been placed in a difficult situation, for they would have been forced by public opinion to take some action, and this would have had to have been carried out in the Baltic, in the face of a large fleet of submarines and of extensive and unknown minefields. . . .

The final verdict is now immaterial; but, in all fairness, everyone must agree that the conception was a bold one, which, if successful, offered such substantial advantages (advantages that put in the shade any that success at the Dardanelles might have brought about) that it ought to have received, at the time, the most careful and complete consideration. It should certainly not have been shelved, contemptuously, as impossible. It may well be acclaimed in future years as a sign of genius, and not of madness, on Lord Fisher's part.[38]

The first paragraph strikes me as of special importance. The critics of the Baltic Scheme have ignored the probability that the operation would have provoked a general fleet action that could well have seriously weakened the High Seas Fleet, even if the expedition itself had been cut to pieces at sea or on land.

It was not until 25 January 1915 that Fisher handed his Baltic

[37] James, *A Great Seaman*, p. 138, quoting from the Oliver MSS.
[38] Bacon, *Fisher*, ii. 190–1.

paper to the Prime Minister, in the form of an appendix, 'On the possibility of using our Command of the Sea to influence more drastically the Military Situation on the Continent', to a print entitled 'Memorandum by the First Sea Lord on the Position of the British Fleet and its Policy of Steady Pressure'. The latter was a critique of the Dardanelles operation, which was then under discussion. Asquith decided not to circulate this print to the War Council. 'Why he has suppressed it,' Fisher informed Bonar Law, 'is beyond my comprehension. Anyhow he is Prime Minister and there's the end of it.'[39] Fisher's later version was that the print had not been circulated 'in view of my acrimonious attitude against the Dardanelles operations then being incepted'.[40] There is probably some truth in this, as the Prime Minister was keen on getting on with an offensive operation that divided the soldiers, sailors, and politicians the least, and that was the Dardanelles campaign. Another probable reason for his frigid attitude was the mining policy that was an integral part of Fisher's project. The Cabinet were not yet prepared to offend the neutrals gratuitously.

The Baltic Scheme was by now completely overshadowed by the Dardanelles. It was not stone dead, however. An impromptu War Council meeting on 16 February 1915 decided to build special transports and motor lighters for landing 50,000 men, and Fisher continued to hope, right down to the War Council on 14 May 1915, that the scheme would be attempted that summer. It is, therefore, all the more incomprehensible why he hugged his paper to his bosom and refused to have the details of the operation discussed by the Admiralty War Staff and the General Staff and precise plans worked out.

He never wavered in his belief that the consequences of a Belgian-*cum*-Baltic operation would have had momentous results. '. . . had the British Expeditionary Force of 160,000 men been landed at Antwerp by the British Fleet in August, 1914 (instead of occupying a small sector in the midst of the French Army in France), the War would certainly have ended in 1915. This, in conjunction with the seizure of the Baltic by the British Fleet and the landing of a Russian Army on the Pomeranian Coast, would have smashed the Germans.'[41]

[39] Letter of 31 Jan. 1915; Blake, *The Unknown Prime Minister*, p. 237.
[40] Undated marginalia in a copy of the print; Lennoxlove MSS.
[41] Fisher, *Records*, pp. 229–30.

The Baltic Scheme never came to life, nor did any of the others. Oliver 'hated' all these projects—Heligoland, Borkum, the Baltic —nor was Jellicoe smitten with any of them. Another difficulty was that even greater confusion prevailed at the War Council when that body tried to agree on an offensive strategy. Fisher compared its meetings with a game of ninepins. Everyone had a plan—a ninepin, which in falling knocked over its neighbour. The most formidable obstacle of all to Admiralty amphibious schemes was the Army's deep reluctance to commit the first-class regular troops that would be needed. When Churchill brought the idea of seizing an advanced base before the War Council on 1 December (he offered it as the most effective way to parry any invasion attempt, since the movements of the German Fleet would be kept under constant observation), Kitchener would not promise troops for the operation. All the troops of good quality were needed on the Continent to contain as many enemy divisions as possible and prevent an overwhelming concentration against the Russians.

The military also killed off the promising Zeebrugge operation, a project that held the field from mid-November into January. It originated with the C.-in-C. in France, General Sir John French, after the German Army had occupied the Belgian coast. He pressed for a large-scale outflanking operation on that coast, with the support of the Belgian Army, to turn the German right flank in Flanders. The Admiralty, in search of an offensive strategy, succeeded in broadening the operation. The War Staff was deeply concerned over the development of important U-boat bases at Zeebrugge and Ostend (occupied by the Germans on 15 October), which posed a threat to cross-Channel communications and the safety of the transportation of troops to France. These ports were not demolished when evacuated, as the War Office had been confident of driving the Germans from the coast, in which event the ports would have served as important bases. A division of the 3rd Battle Squadron bombarded Zeebrugge on 23 November with poor results: the Germans quickly repaired the damage. The Admiralty shifted their sights. By the end of December they had succeeded in enlarging General French's plan to include the landing of an outflanking force at Zeebrugge in connexion with the Army's advance up the coast to the Dutch frontier. The Fleet would co-operate by guarding the left flank of the Army. The sinking of the *Formidable* added urgency to the objective of depriving the Germans of their Flanders U-boat bases. It was very nearly the one offensive operation on which Churchill, Fisher, Wilson, and Jellicoe could agree!

The War Council vetoed the scheme on 7 January, but at its meeting of 13 January Churchill argued so persuasively that it approved the naval preparations for the joint attack while postponing a final decision on the operation until the beginning of February. Kitchener had supported it until now, but his second thoughts doomed it. He lacked the extra guns and shells that the Army would require, and General Joffre, the Commander-in-Chief of the French Army, was for various reasons making difficulties. The Army encouraged the Admiralty to undertake the bombardment and blocking of Zeebrugge as an all-Navy project. Although the War Staff, Jellicoe, and especially Wilson were willing, Fisher would not consider this alternative. The results of the 23 November bombardment were not encouraging, and they risked the loss of old battleships. The plan finally foundered on Joffre's objection to transferring the British Army to the coastal end of the line, switching positions with the French and Belgian troops which occupied the 30 miles between the B.E.F. and the sea. The War Council of 28 January abandoned the joint operation. The upshot was that Zeebrugge and Ostend were left to develop into a serious threat to Allied communications. Large naval forces had to be maintained in the Straits of Dover, and the bloody Flanders campaign of 1917 (Third Ypres) might not have been launched, had there been no anxiety at the Admiralty about the enemy U-boats and destroyers at Zeebrugge.

To summarize the situation in January 1915: the Heligoland project was dead; the Belgian coast operation (the only one on which there was general naval agreement) was dead by the end of the month; Borkum and the Baltic Scheme were becoming ever more remote possibilities, because each had little more than the support of its chief sponsor. With the prospects of a naval offensive or amphibious operation in northern waters in the near future fading, Churchill became absorbed in the brilliant prospects which were unfolding in the Mediterranean.

IX

The Dardanelles Operation: Inception

(JANUARY 1915)

(*Map* 7)

So, through Churchill's excess of imagination, a layman's ignorance of artillery, and the fatal power of a young enthusiasm to convince older and slower brains, the tragedy of Gallipoli was born.

C. E. W. BEAN, *Official History of Australia in the War
of 1914–18. The Story of Anzac.*

It is my hope that the Australian people, towards whom I have always felt a solemn responsibility, will not rest content with so crude, so inaccurate, so incomplete and so prejudiced a judgment, but will study the facts for themselves.

CHURCHILL, *The World Crisis.*

I. GENESIS

THE best illustration of Churchill's strength and weakness as a war-time First Lord is the Dardanelles adventure, the most controversial incident in his entire official career.

Our story begins in 1906, when the Government had faced the possibility of war with Turkey over the Sinai boundary dispute. The C.I.D. had discussed ways of putting pressure on the Turks so as to bring them to terms or, failing that, to bring a war with them to a prompt conclusion. The discussions and papers[1] boiled down to this. The General Staff and the Admiralty were agreed that the military seizure of the Gallipoli Peninsula, with a view to the

---

[1] Minutes of the 92nd, 93rd, and 96th meetings of the C.I.D., 26 July, 13 Nov. 1906, 28 Feb. 1907, respectively; an Ottley (D.N.I.) paper, 'The Forcing of the Dardanelles (the Naval Aspects of the Question)', 8 Aug. 1906; C.I.D. Paper 92-B, a General Staff memorandum on 'The Possibility of a Joint Naval and Military Attack upon the Dardanelles', 20 Dec. 1906, and Ottley's remarks in an attached memorandum. All these sources are in the Lennoxlove MSS.

capture of the forts overlooking the Dardanelles, coupled with the passage of the Dardanelles by a British fleet, would be a 'death-blow' to the Sultan's power. Both Services were, however, fully alive to the formidable difficulties involved in a joint attack on the Dardanelles. The C.I.D.'s conclusion (28 February 1907) was that a Gallipoli landing 'would involve a great risk, and should not be undertaken if other means of bringing pressure to bear on Turkey were available'.

Neither the C.I.D., nor the generals, nor the admirals gave any consideration to a purely naval attack on the Straits—then or at any time down to 1914. The telling consideration for the Admiralty was the British naval tradition that the attack of warships on forts without military help rarely produced worthwhile results. (A. K. Wilson was the one important dissenter among the senior officers of this time.) This tradition included Nelson's dictum that 'any sailor who attacked a fort was a fool', and the attempt in 1807 by seven ships of the line under Admiral Sir John Duckworth to force the Straits. The squadron ran the gauntlet of the forts with little damage on the way up and cruised in the Sea of Marmora, but was mauled on its return through the Straits, the Sultan having in the interval strengthened its defences. The exploit was held thereafter as a warning and an object lesson. The tradition was fortified by Admiral Hornby's report in 1878 (he was Mediterranean C.-in-C.), by the objection of the Admiralty to the Salisbury Government's proposal to force the Dardanelles at the time of the Armenian massacres (November 1895), and by the Russo-Japanese War. In this war the Japanese Fleet bombarded Port Arthur's defences with little result and had, in the end, to land a large army.

Coming to 1914, the *Goeben* episode and its aftermath, the Turks' defiant rejection of the British demand that the crews be re-patriated, and Souchon's appointment as Commander-in-Chief of the Turkish Navy, pointed to an early Turkish entry into the war on the side of the Central Powers. From the first month of the war, consequently, Churchill had his eyes on the Dardanelles. Taking advantage of a Greek offer of naval and military assistance, the First Lord arranged with Kitchener on 31 August for the drafting of a joint plan for the surprise seizure of the Gallipoli Peninsula by a Greek army and the British Mediterranean squad-ron in the event of Allied hostilities against Turkey. If successful, it would make possible the entry of a British fleet into the Sea of Marmora. For various reasons nothing came of the proposal. Churchill introduced this episode at the Dardanelles Inquiry in 1916 as proof that he was 'perfectly aware that the right and obvious method of putting a British fleet in the Marmora was by an amphibious attack on the Gallipoli Peninsula'.[2]

On 31 October 1914, upon the expiration of an ultimatum to the Turks regarding the *Goeben* and other unneutral acts of the Turkish Government, Britain found herself at war with Turkey, although war was not formally declared by Britain and France until 5 November. On 3 November an Anglo-French squadron, on orders emanating from the Admiralty, carried out a 10-minute bombardment of the outer forts of the Dardanelles at a range of 13,000 yards. One fort was damaged. The object was to find out by a practical test 'what the effect of the ships' guns would be on the outer forts . . The result of that bombardment did to some extent encourage us to think the ships could injure the forts from their fire and injure them from ranges at which the forts could not reply.'[3] The cost of this premature attack far outweighed the slight advantages, since it put the Turks and their German military advisers on the alert. From that moment there was no possibility of surprise, and the Turks began to pay special attention to the defences of the Straits. This is what Admiral Sir Henry Jackson (who was employed on special duties on the Admiralty War Staff, 1914–15, and often attended the War Staff Group meetings) and Commodore Bartolomé (Churchill's Naval Secretary) had in mind when they told the Dardanelles Committee that the bombardment was a mistake. To Jellicoe it was an 'unforgivable error'; to Admiral Bacon, 'an act of sheer lunacy'. (Both were writing in the post-war period.)

The idea of a serious attack on the Dardanelles was discussed at the first meeting of the War Council, 25 November, in the course of discussions on measures for the defence of Egypt. Churchill

[2] The Commission of Inquiry into the Operations at the Dardanelles, set up in 1916, held 89 sittings in that year and 1917 and questioned numerous witnesses, whose testimony it heard. Its full *Proceedings* containing a verbatim report were not published, but these form the basis of the Commission's published reports: *Dardanelles Commission. First Report*, 12 Feb. 1917 (Command Paper 8490), *Supplement to First Report* (Command Paper 8502), and *Final Report*, 4 Dec. 1917 (Command Paper 371). The latter include only selected portions of the testimony. Evidence from this source is quoted as 'Dardanelles Commission'.

[3] Churchill's testimony; *Dardanelles Commission.*

suggested, with Fisher's 'hearty concurrence', a joint attack on the Gallipoli Peninsula as 'the ideal method' for defending Egypt, because a successful attack would mean control of the Dardanelles and the ability to dictate terms to Turkey. The proposal ran into a Kitchener *non possumus*: troops were not available. The immense authority and enormous prestige of this strong silent man of awesome presence, who was at once War Secretary and virtually his own Chief of Staff, and his well-known resentment of criticism, were such that, 'When he gave a decision,' Churchill told the Dardanelles Commissioners, 'it was invariably accepted as final. He was never, to my belief, overruled by the War Council or the Cabinet in any military matter, great or small. . . . Scarcely anyone ever ventured to argue with him in Council. . . . All-powerful, imperturbable, reserved, he dominated absolutely our counsels at this time.'[4]

At the turn of the year the Government was engaged in an inquiry into the best field of operations for the new armies (to say nothing of the reinforced fleets and vast quantities of *matériel* of all kinds) which would be ready in the spring. There was an urgent need to resolve sharply conflicting strategic alternatives. On one side were the 'Westerners', the leading generals, supported by the French Government and High Command, who maintained that the decisive area was France, that the path to victory lay over the corpses of German troops and through the line of enemy entrenchments, and that the withdrawal of troops for operations elsewhere might expose the Allies to crushing and possibly irretrievable defeat. This position was anathema to the 'Easterners', who included the admirals, Hankey, and most of the ministers who sat on the War Council. This group, seeing no possibility of a breakthrough in the mud, barbed wire, and trenches in France, wanted to find an alternative theatre of war for the new armies. For them the key to victory lay in an offensive somewhere in the Near East — a campaign that would knock out Turkey and coax Italy and the Balkan neutrals into the war on the Allied side. The discussion of alternative strategies did not relate to any immediate military operations, since troops and munitions would not be available until the spring. Asquith stood poised between the two schools in the War Council.

Two ugly situations in the East helped to galvanize the War

[4] *Dardanelles Commission.*

Council's thinking in January. One was the very serious plight of Serbia. The New Year opened with rumours of Austro-German plans to crush Serbia with overwhelming force in the spring. Bulgaria was the crux of the situation. Her attitude had been menacing to the Allied cause ever since the war broke out. 'Some successful military action in the Balkans was urgently needed to deter Bulgaria from joining the Central Powers, who would then overwhelm Serbia, and to influence Greece and Rumania', whose military help to Serbia the Allies had been unable to enlist.[5] Moreover, Bulgaria on the side of the Central Powers would mean the establishment of through communications with, and a consequently rejuvenated, Turkey. The problem was, then, to deter Bulgaria from entering the war, to save Serbia, and if possible to win the pro-Ally Balkan neutrals over to the Allied side. A resounding military success against Turkey might accomplish these vital objectives.

The other factor was the precariousness of the Russian situation, owing to the serious shortage of war *matériel* and to Turkish pressure in the Caucasus. The latter turned out to be the catalytic agent that put an end to the aimless discussions in the War Council and the Cabinet.

It all began dramatically on 2 January with an appeal from the Russian Commander-in-Chief, the Grand Duke Nicholas, for a 'demonstration' against Turkey, 'either naval or military', which would relieve the pressure on his forces in the Caucasus. Some action against Turkey seemed urgently required, both in response to the Grand Duke's request and to open an adequate and permanent supply line to Russia, as well as to save Serbia. On 3 January a Foreign Office telegram (actually drafted in the War Office after Kitchener had discussed the matter with Churchill) promised to help the Russians by making a demonstration against the Turks.

It is an ironic fact that the Turkish offensive was collapsing at this very time. On 4 January the Turkish forces were routed by the Russians at Sarikamish in Russian Armenia and forced to retreat. Other Russian successes in Armenia followed in the next ten days. The Grand Duke failed to inform his Allies of these

[5] A Cabinet paper prepared by Hankey for the Dardanelles Commission, 'The Dardanelles Inquiry. Notes for Evidence Explaining the Reasons for the Various Decisions Taken by the Government', 11 Aug. 1916; Asquith MSS.

events. The relaxation of the Turkish pressure so radically altered the situation that the proposed diversion entirely lost its immediate *raison d'être*.

The time and method of the demonstration had to be decided. Kitchener deemed that 'the only place that a demonstration might have some effect in stopping reinforcements going East [Adrianople to the Caucasus] would be the Dardanelles'. He insisted it would have to be a naval operation, since they would not be ready for anything involving large numbers of troops 'for some months'.

Churchill at first committed himself to nothing. Then, on the morning of 3 January, he received Fisher's 'Turkey plan' (actually, Hankey's Turkey plan with Fisher trimmings). It strongly recommended something considerably larger than a 'demonstration', specifically, a combined Greco-Bulgarian attack, with a Greek army to attack Gallipoli, the Bulgarians to go for Constantinople, and 'all Indian and 75,000 seasoned troops' from France (to be replaced by Territorials) sent out to Besika Bay, on Turkey's Asiatic coast, ten miles south of the entrance to the Dardanelles. Sound as strategy, the plan disregarded realities. Kitchener and Sir John French (to say nothing of the French High Command) would never have agreed to release the troops from the Western Front, Bulgaria and Greece were neutral and their intentions had not been declared, and, most importantly, Greece would never have allowed her arch-rival Bulgaria to attack Constantinople. To this point there was nothing in the plan that Churchill could regard as practicable. It was the last paragraph that caught his eye: 'Sturdee forces the Dardanelles at the same time with "Majestic" class and "Canopus" class [pre-dreadnoughts]! God bless him! [This represented quite a change, albeit evanescent, in Fisher's attitude towards Sturdee] But as the Great Napoleon said, "CELERITY"—without it, "FAILURE." '[6] In quoting this letter for the Dardanelles Commission, Fisher added: 'Instead of the principles of celerity and decision we had an interminable tragedy of delays . . .'

The significant thing about the plan was that it was the first time a responsible admiral had mentioned the forcing of the Straits by the Navy. Churchill seized on a part only of Fisher's scheme, ignoring his condition that the old battleships be supported by troops who would dominate the high land along the Gallipoli

[6] *Fear God and Dread Nought*, iii. 118.

shore of the Dardanelles. His imagination was fired. Later that day (3 January), with Fisher's concurrence he telegraphed Vice-Admiral Sackville H. Carden, whose small squadron lay off the Dardanelles: 'Do you think that it is a practicable operation to force the Dardanelles by the use of ships alone? It is assumed that older battleships would be employed . . . The importance of the results would justify severe loss.' Carden replied on 5 January: 'I do not think that the Dardanelles can be rushed, but they might be forced by extended operations with a large number of ships.'[7] He based this opinion (he told the Commission) 'on the superior gun power that I knew I should have at my command to the guns in the forts. I knew that the guns in the forts were not very modern; I was not aware of the extent to which the Germans had improved the question [*sic*] of movable armament on both sides of the Straits or of their very complete gun defences of the minefields.'[8]

Churchill replied on 6 January: 'High authorities here concur in your opinion. Forward detailed particulars showing what force would be required for extended operations. How do you think it should be employed, and what results could be gained?'[9] Churchill told the Commission that Fisher was not one of the 'high authorities' he had referred to. The Admiral 'expressed no adverse opinion at the time, but his view was a joint attack . . .' No, he meant only Oliver and Jackson, both of whom had expressed their opinions to him verbally. 'This coincidence in officers separated, and so differently circumstanced [as Carden, Jackson, and Oliver] impressed me very much . . .'[10] Actually, Jackson was not overly sanguine. His appreciation, written on 5 January but which Churchill saw on the 6th, *after* the dispatch of his second telegram to Carden, did not pronounce for or against the attack on the Dardanelles. It laid special emphasis on the 'unenviable position' of a fleet without secure communications, appeared to favour the support of ground forces to occupy Gallipoli and Constantinople, deprecated an attempt to rush the Dardanelles, and seemed to prefer a methodical step-by-step reduction of the forts in the Straits.

[7] *Dardanelles Commission.*
[8] *Ibid.*
[9] *Ibid.*
[10] *Ibid.*

Carden telegraphed his 'more detailed proposals' on 11 January. A. He would concentrate his fire on the entrance forts. When they had been reduced, he would: B. proceed to knock out the inner forts up to and including those at Kephez Point, eight miles inside the Straits. C. He would destroy the defences at the Narrows. D. Finally, he would clear a channel through the great minefield between Kephez and the Narrows, advance through the Narrows, and steam into the Sea of Marmora. Carden estimated the four phases would take about a month. His proposals were little more than a classification of the operations into four progressive phases, and, as one naval critic has said, they might have been 'applied to any enterprise anywhere from an attack on a Norman keep to a landing in Timbuctoo'.

The plan, if it can be so dignified, 'made a great impression on everyone who saw it,' Churchill told the Dardanelles Commission. 'It was in its details an entirely novel proposition.' The novelty, it transpired, lay in the abandonment of any attempt to rush the Dardanelles, and in the substitution of a scheme to attack the forts methodically and destroy them one by one. It is not clear just who were the 'everyone' who saw this plan. In *The World Crisis* Churchill cites the support of the 'four or five great naval authorities', including Fisher and Oliver.

Fisher was, to be sure, rather favourable at first. Indeed, he suggested on 12 January that if Percy Scott and the other gunnery experts could see no objections, the newly commissioned *Queen Elizabeth* might be sent to the Dardanelles to complete her gunnery exercises there, 'firing all her ammunition at the Dardanelles forts instead of uselessly into the sea at Gibraltar . . .'[11] The War Staff, it seems, indicated at this time that the newest of the dreadnoughts might play a decisive part with her eight 15-inch guns at ranges outside those of the forts. Churchill at once picked up the suggestion. 'We all felt ourselves in the presence of a new fact.' The First Lord had the mental image of the powerful *Queen Elizabeth* relentlessly pushing forward and blasting the Turkish defences to bits with tremendous salvoes of her big guns. His glowing account of the possibilities inherent in this 'new fact' converted Kitchener, who had not been impressed by Carden's 'detailed proposals'.

Churchill at once called for definite plans to be worked out for

[11] Fisher to Oliver, 12 Jan. 1915; *Dardanelles Commission.*

the naval operation, including the *Queen Elizabeth* in the available force. 'After long consultation at our daily War Group meeting', which suggests that the project had the support, or at least the acquiescence, of the War Staff Group, he brought it before the War Council on 13 January towards the end of a long and weary day. 'At this point,' Lord Hankey recalls, 'events took a dramatic turn, for Churchill suddenly revealed his well-kept secret of a naval attack on the Dardanelles! The idea caught on at once. The whole atmosphere changed. Fatigue was forgotten. The War Council turned eagerly from the dreary vista of a "slogging match" on the Western Front to brighter prospects, as they seemed, in the Mediterranean. The Navy, in whom everyone had implicit confidence and whose opportunities had so far been few and far between, was to come into the front line.'[12] Churchill offered Carden's telegrams of 5 and 11 January as evidence that an attack on the Dardanelles by ships alone was practicable.

This plan was based on the fact that the Dardanelles forts are armed mainly with old guns of only thirty-five calibres. These would be outranged by the guns of the ships, which would effect their object without coming into range. . . . The Admiralty were studying the question, and believed that a plan could be made for systematically reducing all the forts within a few weeks. Once the forts were reduced the minefields would be cleared, and the Fleet would proceed up to Constantinople and destroy the *Goeben*. They would have nothing to fear from field guns or rifles, which would be merely an inconvenience.[13]

Impressed by Churchill's enthusiasm for the plan and by Kitchener's endorsement, thinking nothing of Fisher's and A. K. Wilson's silence at the meeting, and realizing, as Kitchener made plain, that no troops were available, the War Council reached this provisional conclusion: 'The Admiralty should prepare for a naval expedition in February to bombard and take the Gallipoli Peninsula, with Constantinople as its objective.'[14] The decision has often been criticized as a monument to muddled thinking, that to say vaguely that Constantinople was the fleet's objective was nonsense. How could the Navy, unsupported by a large army, possibly 'take' the Peninsula, a very difficult area, and a city of a million people? Obviously, the Navy could do nothing of the kind.

[12] Hankey, *The Supreme Command, 1914–1918* (London, 1961, 2 vols.), i. 265–6.

[13] Hankey's notes of the meeting, as cited in the Cabinet paper, 'The Dardanelles Inquiry'; quoted by *Dardanelles Commission*.

[14] *Dardanelles Commission*.

In any case, Churchill had won the first round. Taking the War Council decision as virtual approval, the War Staff, assisted by Jackson, at once went to work on the necessary preparations for the naval operation, which was initially set for 15 February. Churchill quickly won the support of the French, who promised to put a squadron under Carden's command. He informed the Grand Duke Nicholas (19 January) of what was afoot and expressed the hope that at the right moment—after the destruction of the outer forts—the Russians would be prepared to co-operate by naval and military action at the Black Sea entrance to the Bosphorus.

Until now Fisher had acquiesced passively in Churchill's virtual usurpation of his functions. He did not have a very decided opinion against the operation and had even concurred on the 14th with a memorandum the First Lord sent to the Prime Minister which stated that the operation would require 'practically our whole available margin'. Thereafter he developed serious misgivings about the approval of the scheme in principle on the 13th, although Churchill told the Dardanelles Commission that Fisher's memorandum of 25 January was the first indication he had of the Admiral's misgivings. On the 19th we find Fisher pouring out his heart to Jellicoe: 'And now the Cabinet have decided on taking the Dardanelles solely with the Navy, using 15 battleships and 32 other vessels, and keeping out there three battle cruisers and a flotilla of destroyers—*all urgently required at the decisive theatre at home!* [See below, p. 231, for the actual number of big ships that were used.] There is only one way out, and that is to resign! But you say "*no*", which simply means I am a consenting party to what I absolutely disapprove. *I don't agree with one single step taken,* so it is fearfully against the grain that I remain on in deference to your wishes.' And, two days later: 'I just abominate the Dardanelles operation, unless a great change is made and it is settled to be made a military operation, with 200,000 men in conjunction with the Fleet.'[15]

By 25 January Fisher's restiveness spilled over into a memorandum for the Prime Minister, with a copy going to the First Lord. (Corbett and Hankey had lent a hand with it.) Three things bothered the Admiral: the fleet could be better employed elsewhere (the Baltic) than at the Dardanelles; the prospective

[15] *Fear God and Dread Nought,* iii. 133, 142.

weakening of the Grand Fleet; and technical objections to the Navy going it alone—he preferred a combined operation if there were going to be an operation at all. It was the second of these considerations, the margin of safety in Home waters, which formed the main point in the memorandum. 'So long as the German High Sea Fleet preserves its present great strength and splendid gunnery efficiency, so long is it imperative and indeed vital that no operation whatever should be undertaken by the British Fleet, calculated to impair its present superiority, which is none too great ... Even the older ships should not be risked, for they ... form our only reserve behind the Grand Fleet.'[16]

Churchill easily countered this argument. Heartily agreeing that Grand Fleet superiority must be maintained, he presented a wealth of detail to prove that the Grand Fleet was, and would continue to be, 'capable at any time of defeating the German High Sea Fleet in battle'.[17] His covering note to the memorandum assured Fisher there was 'no difference in principle between us. But when all your special claims are met, you must let the surplus be used for the general cause.'

Fisher did not think Churchill's reply met his case. Some time on the 27th he informed Asquith that he did not wish to attend the Council meeting the following day, as he did not agree with the First Lord and did not think it 'seemly' to indicate this at the meeting. The Dardanelles operation could 'only be justified on naval grounds by military co-operation, which would compensate for the loss in ships and irreplaceable officers and men. As purely naval operations they are unjustifiable, as they drain our naval margin—not too large ...' 'At any moment' the High Seas Fleet might come out to fight. 'I am very reluctant to leave the First Lord,' he concluded. 'I have a great personal affection and admiration for him, but I see no possibility of a union of ideas, and unity is essential in war, so I refrain from any desire of remaining as a stumbling block.'[18]

Asquith, who was worried by the growing friction between the two, took this particular 'almost daily' resignation threat seriously.

[16] 'Memorandum by the First Sea Lord on the Position of the British Fleet and its Policy of Steady Pressure', 25 Jan. 1915; *The World Crisis*, ii. 154–7.

[17] Churchill's memorandum of 26 Jan. 1915 for the Prime Minister (incorrectly given as 27 January in *The World Crisis* and in the *First Report*); *ibid.*, pp. 159–62.

[18] *Fear God and Dread Nought*, iii. 148.

He arranged a meeting *à trois* in his room on the morning of the 28th, before the War Council was to begin. After about three-quarters of an hour of talk, the Prime Minister made his decision. 'I am the arbitrator. I have heard Mr. Winston Churchill, and I have heard you and now I am going to give my decision. Zeebrugge will not be done; the Dardanelles will go on.' Whereupon he got up and walked off to the Council meeting, with Churchill and Fisher following.[19] Churchill understood Fisher to have accepted the naval attack, whereas Fisher did not regard Asquith's judgment as 'completely decisive', and thought time would be allowed for further thought.

Churchill opened the meeting by stating that preparations were in hand for starting the naval attack about the middle of February; Carden was confident it would be successful and did not anticipate real difficulties until the fleet moved to attack the Narrows. Fisher interjected that he had understood the question was not going to be raised that day. Asquith overruled him, whereupon he started to leave the room. His opposition was unmistakable. (He felt 'bloody-minded', he told the Dardanelles Commissioners.) Kitchener jumped to his feet and overtook the Admiral before he could make his exit. Assuming the unaccustomed role of conciliator, he pleaded with him. What did he have in mind? To resign, Fisher replied. 'I am never going back to that table.' The General 'turned on a lot of hot air' (as Fisher put it), pointing out he was the only objector at the War Council, that his duty was to continue in office, and so on. Fisher afterwards recalled that Kitchener was 'so earnest and even emotional that I should return that I said to myself after some delay: "Well, we can withdraw the ships at any moment, so long as the Military don't land," and I succumbed.'[20] He 'reluctantly' gave in and returned to his seat.

Kitchener warmly supported the naval attack. 'If successful, its effect would be equivalent to that of a successful campaign fought with the new armies. . . . if satisfactory progress were not made, the attack could be broken off.' (He had made the same point at the 13 January Council.) Balfour and Grey backed him up, the former with enthusiasm. 'It was difficult' for Balfour 'to imagine a more helpful operation.' A successful attack on the Dardanelles would cut the Turkish Army in two, give the Allies

[19] Fisher's testimony; *Dardanelles Commission*.
[20] Fisher, *Memories* (London, 1919), p. 59.

control of Constantinople, and enable Russia to resume her exports. Grey liked the operation because it would 'finally settle the attitude of Bulgaria and the whole of the Balkans'.

The meeting then adjourned for several hours. After lunch, Churchill corralled Fisher in the First Lord's room and persuaded him to undertake the operation. When the discussion was resumed at 6 p.m., the First Lord announced on behalf of the Board of Admiralty that they had decided to undertake the task with which the War Council had charged them, subject to the right to break off the operation. The Council gave the Admiralty the go-ahead. (This decision was not communicated to the whole Cabinet until a day or two before the launching of the operation on 19 February. The Cabinet quickly approved without any discussion.) Fisher was present and gave his tacit, 'lingering and reluctant consent to the Dardanelles bombardment as a great diplomatic and political necessity'. Lord Esher found him 'in low spirits' the next day. Fisher told him that 'for the first time in his life he was a pessimist'.[21]

There were two special reasons why he stayed on. He wanted to oversee the completion of the great shipbuilding programme he had initiated ('I knew that the moment I turned my back the thing would stop'); and, in his judgment, the chief professional advisers of the Government should not resign when their advice was disregarded unless they believed the operation would inevitably end disastrously. 'The attempt to force the Dardanelles as a purely naval operation would not have been disastrous so long as the ships employed could be withdrawn at any moment, and only such vessels were engaged, as in the beginning of the operations was in fact the case, as could be spared without detriment to the general service of the fleet.'[22] 'When I finally decided to go in,' he said later, 'I went the whole hog, *totus porcus.*' 'No one worked harder or more loyally' in its early stages (that is, until 18 March), Asquith told the Dardanelles Commission.

2. RATIONALE

Nearly everybody who played a part in the big decision believed that joint operations offered a greater chance of success than did a

---

[21] Journals, 29 Jan. 1915; *Esher,* iii. 212.
[22] *Dardanelles Commission.*

naval operation. Hankey and Fisher, in particular, felt very strongly on this. The former from the very first regarded the operation as a 'speculation', unless a sizeable army was present with the fleet to take the forts in reverse. 'I warned everybody about this, but it was like talking to a wall.'[23] 'The Dardanelles futile, without soldiers!' cried Fisher in a note to Lloyd George, and he never ceased to reiterate this basic principle. Richmond was almost violent on this point. 'Winston, very, very ignorant, believes he can capture the Dardanelles without troops . . .'[24] Admiral de Robeck told the Commission that 'everyone [of the senior naval officers in the Mediterranean Squadron, presumably] thought it was better to have a combined operation . . .'[25]

Now, Churchill was neither ignorant of the 1906–7 discussions nor of the experience of naval history, both of which strongly deprecated unsupported naval action against forts. He admits that 'the established opinion at the Admiralty was that the days when the British Fleet could force the Dardanelles without the aid of an army had ended in the 'seventies and 'eighties'.[26] He, too, wanted a joint attack. He told the Commons in November 1915, and later the Dardanelles Commission, that, had he known three months earlier that in May 1915 an army of 80,000–100,000 men would be available for the attack, the assault by the Navy alone would never have been ordered. Unhappily, a joint operation appeared to be out of the question in view of Kitchener's attitude. The Field-Marshal had estimated on 13 January that 150,000 men would be needed, but that he had few troops to spare. He was concerned with home defence, and he was also unwilling to pull any divisions from France, especially as General French wanted large reinforcements to enable him to undertake the offensive operations he was concerting with General Joffre. The Dardanelles Commission criticized the War Council for accepting Kitchener's statement hastily and on faith. The Council, they maintained, should have taken steps to satisfy themselves that that was the case. 'Had this been done we think that it would have been ascertained that sufficient troops would have been available for a joint naval and military operation at an earlier date than was

---

[23] Hankey to Esher, 25 Mar. 1915; Esher MSS.
[24] Diary, 9 Feb. 1915; *Portrait of an Admiral*, p. 140.
[25] *Dardanelles Commission.*
[26] *The World Crisis*, ii. 103.

supposed.'[27] Besides, even a small military force could at the outset have achieved what a large force could not achieve at a later date.

More than Kitchener's attitude is needed to account for the precipitate decision on 28 January to proceed with the naval operation. There was a sense of urgency in the air, and this explains the choice as between a naval attack and marking time until troops were available. Hankey's testimony makes this clear.

Q. But the question of whether it would have been better to wait a few weeks till the troops were ready to make the combined attack it was not thought necessary to discuss?—*A*. [Hankey] It was very difficult to wait. The circumstances were very, very pressing indeed; we were giving no display of any sort of interest in the Near East; our whole diplomacy was going to pieces from the fact that there was no display of force. That was because of the continual lack of success. The Russians were not doing well in the East, and there were all these rumours going round that the Russians were short of ammunition. We were displaying no interest at all. The Bulgarian attitude was getting every day more threatening, making the military position of Serbia, which was, of course, the linch pin of the whole thing, more and more critical. Roumania was cooling off. It was a terrible situation. It is very easy, looking back in this room, to discuss it after the event, but when I cast my mind back to that time and I think of the desperate situation, the desperate difficulty of helping Serbia, I do not see how there could have been delay.[28]

It was, moreover, the general understanding of the War Council and the naval experts that the naval attack could be broken off at any time without serious loss of prestige. That is, if the attack proved too difficult or too costly, it could be treated as a naval demonstration and abandoned. This comforting thought served to still much of the potential opposition to the operation.

A very important factor was Churchill himself. His enthusiasm swept the War Council into the undertaking. Lloyd George has written: When Churchill 'has a scheme agitating his powerful mind, as everyone who is acquainted with his method knows quite well, he is indefatigable in pressing it upon the acceptance of everyone who matters in the decision'.[29] The famed Churchillian impetuosity, eloquence, and doggedness carried the day.

[27] *Dardanelles Commission.*
[28] *Ibid.*
[29] *War Memoirs of David Lloyd George* (London, 1933–6, 6 vols.), i. 395. (The pagination in the American edition is different.)

He dazzled himself and everybody concerned with pictures of the tremendous military and political effects that would follow the breaching of the Straits and attacking Constantinople. More than self-mesmerism was involved. One propulsive consideration was the fleet of heavily armed old battleships, which were adequately protected for action at medium ranges. They were lying idle, since they were not fit to meet the enemy's dreadnoughts in the North Sea. Churchill did not doubt that the Navy could afford to take great risks with these pre-dreadnoughts. The chief source of his exuberant confidence was his belief that their 12-inch guns and the 15-inch guns of the *Queen Elizabeth* could silence the Turkish forts. Especially did he rely upon the latter's guns, with their high velocity and (when using reduced charges) high trajectory, to knock out the forts seriatim while outranging them. As this was happening, the ships would sweep open a passage through the minefields to and through the Narrows. The First Lord did not appreciate, nor did the War Staff, that super-dreadnoughts, although they probably could outrange all the fortress guns at nine or ten miles, could hardly expect to do much damage at this distance.

Profoundly impressed by the ease with which the high-angle fire of the German heavy howitzers had destroyed the powerful Antwerp, Liège, and Namur forts, Churchill was misled by a too sanguine view of what the big gun could accomplish at sea. If forts were powerless against these heavy land-guns, mainly of 5·9-inch and 8-inch calibre, it seemed a reasonable deduction that the Turkish forts, with the short range of their guns, could not possibly stand up to the 12-inch and 15-inch batteries of the battleships, the ships-versus-forts tradition notwithstanding.

The Admiralty War Staff was inclined to agree with Churchill. The results of the Belgian bombardments had impressed Oliver. The high-angle fire at Antwerp (which he had experienced in person), Liège, and Namur 'influenced me to some extent, and I will tell you how. The Dardanelles forts were big forts with a good deal of masonry work. They were fairly good targets, and there was something tangible to shoot at. I thought that a large shell with a high explosive would have had considerable effect on them.'[30]

The War Staff and the First Lord ignored or underestimated the

[30] *Dardanelles Commission.*

fundamental difference between controlling the German guns from forward positions, comparatively close to the target and camouflaged from the eyes of aeroplanes, and laying on indistinct targets as much as eight miles away with no means of accurately spotting the fall of shot. There were no observers on shore to direct and spot the fall of shot, and the experts overrated the effectiveness of seaplanes in spotting. These craft experienced difficulty in rising from the water in anything but a calm sea, and, in any event, they were unable on account of the weight of their floats to fly high enough to do their job properly.

Perhaps the most telling argument on the misleading analogy between the Belgian and Dardanelles forts was that made by Admiral Tudor, the Third Sea Lord, before the Commission. 'You cannot expect to get anything like the same degree of accuracy with high-angle fire from a long-range gun at extreme ranges that you can expect to get at a very moderate length [range] from howitzers—proper high-angle guns. Certainly, in firing at forts out there with the limited angle of elevation the guns were capable of, you could not expect to get anything like the results you get in the ordinary way from land-service howitzers. It must be remembered the maximum elevation our guns were capable of was about 15 degrees.'[31]

Disregarded by Churchill and the War Staff was the historical lesson that ships were at a great disadvantage in attacking forts. Mahan had pointed this out in his *Naval Strategy* (1911): 'Ships are unequally matched against forts. . . . A ship can no more stand up against a fort costing the same money than the fort could run a race with the ship.' Not often in history had success been achieved by ships engaging forts. (Rooke's seizure of Gibraltar in 1704, Vernon at Porto Bello in 1739, and Nelson at Copenhagen in 1801, are the more notable exceptions.) Admiral Dewar succinctly gives the reason for this situation: 'The fortress gunner can easily see the ship he is firing at and a great column of water marks the position of his shot, short or over. The fortress gun, on the other hand, merges into the landscape and at long ranges only betrays itself by an occasional flash. Observation of fire is also very difficult unless a forward observer can be used. The sailor has the further disadvantage that the whole of his ship is

---

[31] *Ibid.* Actually, the guns in the modern ships (represented at the Dardanelles by the *Queen Elizabeth*) were capable of 20 degrees of elevation.

vulnerable to attack, whereas only a direct hit puts his opponent out of action.'[32] To this one might add that gunfire from a fort is more accurate than that from a ship, since the shore platform is steadier and the range-finding facilities are more stable.

The damage done by Churchill's and the Staff's excessive faith in the supremacy of naval guns over forts is illustrated in Balfour's reaction:

No doubt it would be very desirable, if only it were possible, to have a land force—Greek or British—co-operating with the Fleet at Gallipoli. But I understand the Admiralty view to be that with our 12 and 15 in. guns all the Turkish heavy artillery could be silenced, and that, when silenced, such light field guns as the enemy possessed would be insufficient effectually to obstruct the passage of an armoured Fleet. If this be so (and it is a purely technical question) the co-operation of a military force is not absolutely necessary; and the Fleet may for this operation be regarded as self-sufficing.[33]

Other technical difficulties involved in a naval operation were not foreseen, such as the danger from mines, nor did the Admiralty give much thought to an incalculable factor, the amount of opposition to be expected from mobile guns and its effect upon sweeping. The Dardanelles Commission pointed out these difficulties *ex post facto*. 'The waters readily lent themselves to be defended by mines, and the mine-fields could be easily protected by gun fire. . . . The topography of the land on each side of the Straits was most favourable for concealed batteries of guns and howitzers . . .'[34] How, given these conditions, were the minesweeping trawlers going to clear the strongly defended minefield? It should not have required clairvoyance to foresee the deadly obstacle the mine would be in the Straits, particularly after the experience in Home waters in the early months of the war. How many at the Admiralty knew, or remembered, that the Japanese, in the Russian War, had lost nearly one-third of their battleships from one small minefield, that mines had been considerably improved since then, and that intelligence reports pointed to the Turkish mine defence of the Straits as being more efficient than the gun defence?

[32] K. G. B. Dewar, *The Navy from Within* (London, 1939), p. 190. The gunnery considerations are spelled out in Scott, *Fifty Years in the Royal Navy*, pp. 327–31. Churchill's version is in *The World Crisis*, ii. 103–8.

[33] Balfour's notes on Fisher's 25 January memorandum, 1 Feb. 1915; Balfour MSS.

[34] *Dardanelles Commission.*

Faulty British intelligence greatly underestimated the Turkish defences in the Straits. In general, the degree of Turkish resistance which would be encountered was not thoroughly explored, incalculable factor though it was. The naval authorities were lulled into believing that the enemy's resistance would not immediately be very effective by such factors as the successful operations of the light cruiser *Doris* on the Syrian coast late in December and early in January.[35]

Since Churchill, the War Staff, and Carden ignored or minimized the technical difficulties involved in a naval operation, it is not surprising that the War Council wore blinkers and gave absolutely no indication of any awareness of these obstacles.

And what if some ships did get through to the Sea of Marmora, how were they to be supplied with their communications exposed to attack, unless the forts were captured and the batteries destroyed, that is, unless the Peninsula was held? Indeed, nobody except Jackson seems to have had the hardihood, until after the operation was begun, to ask what the fleet was to do if it managed to reach Constantinople. Kitchener, Grey, and the War Council in general saw no problem. They anticipated that the arrival of the fleet at the capital would finish the Turks: there would be a revolution in Constantinople. This was little more than a matter of faith, yet it was accepted by Carden and his successor, De Robeck, without questioning. This estimate was based on that of N.I.D. (Hall was absolutely certain there would be a revolution),[36] and was fortified, no doubt, by wishful thinking. But an appearance off, or even bombardment of, Constantinople would not necessarily have resulted in a Turkish collapse. The Sultan's Government had made their plans to retire to, and rule from, the hinterland of Anatolia. If the Turks did not surrender within a week or two, the Allied fleet would have been forced to sail back through the Narrows, *unless the Peninsula were occupied*. 'There would certainly have been a "God Speed" party on either cliff to see

[35] Churchill to Oliver, 19 Oct. 1916; Oliver MSS.

[36] *Dardanelles Commission*. The D.N.I. embarked on an extraordinary side venture in February 'to buy the Turks out of the war' by paying up to £4,000,000 to achieve this. Clandestine negotiations reached the point where two of Hall's agents met with a Turkish delegate at Dedeagatch on 15–16 March. The talks failed because the British would not give assurances that Constantinople would remain in Turkish hands after the war. Captain G. R. G. Allen, 'A Ghost from Gallipoli', *Journal of the Royal United Service Institution*, May 1963. Cf. the somewhat different version in James, *The Eyes of the Navy*, pp. 61–4.

them off.' In short, without an army of occupation the fleet could have accomplished no lasting results.

Churchill made the plunge without having consulted the military experts. None of the artillery experts at the War Office was asked his opinion on the ships-versus-forts problem. Nor was the General Staff ever asked to express any opinion about the practicability of the naval attack or the applicability of the Namur–Liège experience to a naval bombardment in the Dardanelles. There was no joint staff planning, either. 'The two Staffs were in touch' is all Churchill could claim before the Dardanelles Commission. General Callwell, the D.M.O., is certain that had 'the three eminent naval experts who dealt with the project and who were more or less responsible for its being put into execution [Fisher, Jackson, Wilson] . . . met three representatives of the General Staff, Sir J. Wolfe-Murray, General Kiggell and myself, let us say, sitting round a table with no Cabinet Ministers present, I am certain that the report that we should have drawn up would have been dead against the whole thing'.[37]

Churchill had at best obtained the perfunctory support of his professional advisers. The First Lord, declared the Dardanelles Commissioners, 'was carried away by his sanguine temperament and his firm belief in the success of the undertaking which he advocated. Although none of his expert advisers absolutely expressed dissent, all the evidence laid before us leads us to the conclusion that Mr. Churchill had obtained their support to a less extent than he himself imagined.'[38]

This was the case. Let us begin with Fisher's opinion. From beginning to end he disliked the operation on technical grounds. 'I must reiterate,' he testified, 'that as a purely naval operation I think it was doomed to failure.'[39] He could not welcome a scheme which flew in the face both of Nelson's dictum and of his personal knowledge of the Dardanelles problem derived from his command of a battleship in the Mediterranean (1877–8) and his experiences at the bombardment of Alexandria (1882) and as Mediterranean C.-in-C. (1899–1902). He appreciated the formidable obstacles represented by Turkish mines and forts in the Narrows, and

[37] Callwell, *Experiences of a Dug-Out, 1914–1918* p. 92. Lieutenant-General Sir James Wolfe Murray was the C.I.G.S., and Major-General L. E. Kiggell, the Assistant C.I.G.S., at this time.

[38] *Dardanelles Commission.*

[39] *Ibid.*

believed that only a joint operation could promise success. Also, he was sincerely alarmed over the siphoning away of so much naval strength.

Fisher was not alone in feeling that the withdrawal of the old battleships would to a certain extent jeopardize British sea power —that in case of a major battle-fleet action in the North Sea, both sides would probably be so knocked about that the pre-dreadnoughts could well tip the balance. Jellicoe fully shared the First Sea Lord's apprehensions, as did the Junior Sea Lords. Churchill thought that a good many of these ships were practically useless and, if not used at the Dardanelles, would go on the scrap heap in 1915. That was definitely not the feeling of the Sea Lords and the C.-in-C., certainly not before Jutland seemed to prove that only modern capital ships counted in a fleet action.

Two factors will explain why Fisher's attitude did not carry decisive weight. First, and this is one of the tragedies of the affair, when arguing against the Dardanelles he generally pressed the Baltic Scheme, on which his heart was set and for which the armada of 600-odd vessels was, hopefully, being prepared. Fisher never disguised his priorities, as, for instance, in this exchange at the Commission's hearings. *Q.* 'Do I understand that your main objection to the Dardanelles Expedition was that it might interfere with your Baltic project?' *A.* 'Quite right. I was going to lose ships in the Dardanelles that I wanted to lose only in the Baltic, besides losing officers and men.'[40] This line of talk in January 1915 gave the Dardanelles advocates a beautiful chance to spread the word that the old Admiral's formal objections were based on his preference for an attack elsewhere, and not on any inherent unsoundness in the naval plan. Others, like the Prime Minister, who were open-minded on the subject, got the same impression from Fisher himself.

In the second place, Fisher, in the words of the Commission, 'did not at the time record any such strongly adverse opinions as these [his 'doomed to failure' remark quoted above], neither does he appear to have impressed others with the strength of his objections'.[41] Bartolomé never remembered 'a reasoned statement' by Fisher against the operation in War Staff Group meetings. The only argument he advanced against it was 'the usual naval one,

[40] *Dardanelles Commission.*
[41] *Ibid.*

that ships are never very successful against forts'.[42] Nor had he spoken out on the obstacles, technical or other, at the crucial War Councils of 13 and 28 January.

How are we to explain his silence at these meetings? 'Mr. Churchill knew my opinion. I did not think it would tend towards good relations between the First Lord and myself nor to the smooth working of the Board of Admiralty to raise objections to the War Council's discussions. My opinion being known to Mr. Churchill in what I regarded as the proper constitutional way, I preferred thereafter to remain silent.'[43] A variant of this factor is Fisher's loyalty to Churchill, the man who had brought him back from retirement in the face of strong opposition. There is another explanation. Fisher testified before the Commission that he considered neither himself, nor A. K. Wilson, nor Sir James Wolfe Murray as members of the War Council, but only as 'the experts who were there to open our mouths when told to' by the Cabinet Ministers. Wilson took the same position—that it was not his business to interfere, and that he should not express an opinion there unless asked to do so. The Commission condemned the excuse that the business of the experts was only to answer specific questions. The two Admirals 'must have been aware that the questions which the Council had to decide were of so technical a nature that none but expert opinion could be of any value . . . therefore, although they were not asked definitely to express their opinions, they should have done so'.[44]

Churchill's view was that he invariably spoke at the War Council in the name of the Admiralty, giving expression to the views agreed upon at the War Staff Group meetings. Fisher and Wilson 'had the right, the knowledge, and the power at any moment to correct me or dissent from what I said, and who were fully cognisant of their rights'.[45] The Commission, nonetheless, deemed that Churchill was not entirely blameless. Since he knew he only had the First Sea Lord's 'silent, but manifestly very reluctant, assent to the undertaking', and since the other experts were not enthusiastic, he should have asked Fisher and Wilson to speak their minds at the Council, so that the Council would be in

[42] *Dardanelles Commission.*
[43] *Ibid.*
[44] *Ibid.*
[45] *Ibid.*

possession of the arguments on both sides. At the least he should have presented their views. Instead he left the clear impression at the War Councils of 13 and 28 January that his view was the considered opinion of the Board of Admiralty as a whole, which was not the case. As Wilson told the Commission, at these Councils Churchill 'rather passed' over the unfavourable opinions of the Admiralty regarding an exclusively naval attack. 'He was very keen on his own views.'

Q. In what way did you think the First Lord on the 28th failed to represent the difficulties to the War Council?
A. In the first place, he kept on saying he could do it without the army; he only wanted the army to come in and reap the fruits, I think, was his expression; and I think he generally minimised the risks from mobile guns, and treated it as if the armoured ships were immune altogether from injury. I do not mean to say that he actually said they were immune, but he minimised the risk a great deal.[46]

Asquith, Grey, Balfour, Haldane, Crewe, and Lloyd George, all War Council members, agreed with Fisher and Wilson that it was the experts' duty to give opinions only when asked; it was not the practice to ask them to express their views. But they expected the experts to speak up if they disagreed seriously with the views of the Service ministers in the Council. They therefore assumed that if the experts did not dissent from the views of the Service ministers in the War Council, they assented or at least acquiesced. It was also 'certainly very strongly' Hankey's view that the experts' silence after their Chief had spoken was understood to mean acquiescence. Yet it is inconceivable that any member of the War Council could have been in doubt about Fisher's attitude after he had tried to leave the meeting on 28 January. No one thought of asking him to explain his opposition.[47]

The Commission was very critical on this point. The Council, above all the Chairman, Asquith, 'should have encouraged the experts present to give their opinion, and, indeed, should have insisted upon their doing so.... What actually happened was that the stress laid upon the unquestionable advantages which would accrue from success was so great that the disadvantages which

[46] *Ibid.*
[47] One possible explanation, an almost incredible one, is that not all members of the Council were aware of what was happening. Thus, Balfour, Haldane, and Asquith claimed in their Dardanelles testimony they had no recollection of the episode. Churchill had noticed it, though.

would arise in the not improbable case of failure were insufficiently considered.'[48]

It could be that the politicians on the War Council asked the experts no questions on the 28th because, in Churchill's words, they 'earnestly desired action in this sense, and were not inclined to excite criticism or opposition which would throw us all back again into futility and delay'.[49]

Some of the difficulty was also due to the faulty composition and procedure of the Council. None of the civilian members of the Council, excepting perhaps Churchill, had any expert naval knowledge—'a lot of ignorant people', Churchill called the non-Service ministers—and the experts did not have equal authority and responsibility with the ministers. Also, the Council carried on its affairs in an unbusinesslike way. For one thing, as Lord Crewe said, 'the political members of the Committee did too much of the talking and the expert members too little', a view in which Haldane concurred. Nothing, moreover, was examined with thoroughness; proceedings were so casual and discussions so superficial that it was possible to leave a meeting with no clear ideas as to any decisions having been reached at all.

Asquith himself must be held responsible for this state of affairs. He was hardly an ideal chairman of the War Council. Although he presided at the meetings with great dignity, patience, and judiciousness, he was not endowed with a knowledge of war or an energetic, probing mind. The 'anaemic Asquith', Lord Esher once called him. Admiral Oliver has left this impression of how Asquith conducted War Council meetings. 'A discussion would go on and Ministers would ask questions of Service representatives and argue with others, Asquith would listen and would very rarely ask a question; more often he said nothing and made notes. When he thought there had been talk enough he would look up and say, "So-and-so is decided." There was never anything said after that and nothing was put to the vote.'[50] This may have been, as Oliver says, a very efficient way to manage his 'talkative Ministers', but it certainly was no way to decide the higher strategy of a war.

As regards the Admiralty experts other than Fisher whom the First Lord had consulted, they had agreed to an attack on the

[48] Dardanelles Commission.
[49] Ibid.
[50] James, A Great Seaman, p. 147.

outer forts and to progressive operations up the Dardanelles to the extent that they were practicable; but their concurrence, in the judgment of the Commission, lacked 'any great cordiality or enthusiasm'.

Only Bartolomé thought there was 'a very good chance' of the purely naval attack succeeding in reducing the forts. Oliver would have much preferred to wait until a joint operation was possible and careful plans had been drawn up. He acquiesced in the naval attack because he believed that the plan of a gradual advance was feasible. He based this opinion on the conviction, after consulting with Admiralty gunnery experts, that 'the special circumstances of the Dardanelles forts, combined with the character of their guns and those of the bombarding fleet, gave a reasonable expectation that the forts would be destroyed seriatim'.[51] Anyhow, he felt there was nothing to lose. It was an 'experimental' attack, which they could give up at any time, although he thought that, before the operation could bog down, troops would be available to ensure success.

As for Jackson, he always claimed that he had never agreed or advised that the operation should be undertaken by ships alone. He had 'always stuck' to his memorandum of 5 January, 'that it would be a very mad thing to try and get the fleet into the Sea of Marmora without having the Gallipoli Peninsula held by our own troops or every gun on both sides of the Straits destroyed'.[52] Since Jackson did not have 'accountable responsibility', he was somewhat reticent about expressing his views. Whether the First Lord was fully aware of his true feelings, he should not have claimed that Jackson shared his optimism. The First Lord 'probably stretched to the extreme what I said', was Jackson's comment on Churchill's claim to having had his support with reference to Carden's telegram of 5 January.[53]

Sir Arthur Wilson insisted he had never recommended the naval operation. 'I never strongly resisted it, because it was not my business to do so, but so far as I did remark on it, I was against it.' He thought there were better operations nearer home in which the ships could be used. On purely naval grounds he had thought the operation would be a 'possible success', subject to two 'ifs': if the

---

[51] *Ibid.*, p. 146.
[52] *Dardanelles Commission.*
[53] *Ibid.*

minefield could be cleared and the mobile guns dealt with. This was at best a qualified approval of the scheme. But it was on *political* grounds, rather, that Wilson opposed the attack. He thought it unwise 'to stir the Turks up—that if Constantinople was really attacked it would unite the whole of Turkey against us strongly, whereas I thought it very likely that if they were left alone we should have nothing . . . but simply attacks on Egypt, which would not be serious'.[54]

To sum up, Churchill's naval advisers were not nearly as sanguine as their civilian chief, but they went along, thinking that a naval operation could not lead to disaster because it could be broken off at any time.

Churchill had no support from senior officers outside his immediate circle of advisers. It was obvious to Percy Scott, the outstanding gunnery expert in the Navy, that with all the advantages that favoured shore guns, warships alone could not neutralize them. When Churchill offered him the command of the fleet (13 January), he displayed no interest, knowing it was an 'impossible task'.[55]

Other naval gunnery experts were not consulted at all. Churchill assumed that Oliver would pick the brains of all who might be helpful. This was not the case. Oliver did not consult Captain Thomas Jackson, his D.O.D., who was known to be a gunnery expert. Nor, beyond seeking information on a few purely technical points, did he bother to consult the D.N.O., Rear-Admiral Morgan Singer, 'the general adviser of the Board on all ordnance matters', as he described himself. Had he been asked for an opinion on the feasibility of a naval operation, Singer testified, he would have opposed it, because 'with ships against forts and concealed guns on shore the operation is almost impossible without an extraordinary expenditure of ammunition, and even then the results are very doubtful'.[56] Nor did Oliver seek the opinion of Rear-Admiral Bacon, a onetime D.N.O. of distinction who was having considerable experience of bombardment as commander of the Heavy Howitzer Brigade, of the Royal Marine Artillery, with the B.E.F. in France. Oliver apparently believed that, owing to his own

[54] *Ibid.*
[55] Scott, *Fifty Years in the Royal Navy*, pp. 295–6. Churchill never mentioned this, nor any other unfavourable opinions, at War Council meetings.
[56] *Dardanelles Commission.*

considerable gunnery experience, he could judge the possibilities of naval gunnery as well as anybody.

Churchill never invited Jellicoe's opinion, probably because he was aware that the C.-in-C. had in letters to Fisher described the naval operation as most unsound. Jellicoe maintained that the fleet alone could not deal with the situation, since gunfire alone was not capable of destroying forts. And he felt as Fisher did about reducing the Grand Fleet's narrow margin in the decisive theatre.

Neither did Churchill consult the Junior Sea Lords or keep them informed at any stage of the genesis or execution of the operation. It was his decided opinion that to associate them directly with the daily conduct of operations

would hamper fatally the executive action . . . I do not believe there is a better way of managing the great military departments than by a civilian head and a great soldier or a great sailor, those two working together absolutely. As long as they work together everything goes well; you have powerful direction, absolute decision—the power to run risks and the power to make secret plans. When they separate you have to make a new combination. But I do not believe there is a better method that can possibly be devised; and to increase the number of people who have to be consulted is only to make the men who are responsible exhaust themselves, in persuading others, so that strength is absorbed in that process and very little is left for the careful work of preparation on which victory depends.[57]

In accordance with this philosophy, as well as with the Distribution of Admiralty Business of January 1914 (the last pre-war Distribution), under which the First Sea Lord was solely responsible to the First Lord for advice on 'all large questions of naval policy and maritime warfare', once the war began the Board as a whole was not permitted to concern itself with operations and strategy. The 'centre of naval war direction' became the War Staff

[57] *Ibid.* This was also Fisher's opinion. 'A junta is a bad thing for a war.' Besides, 'there was not time to get all these fellows together and to consult them. . . . I was on the most perfect terms of affection with them all, but I had not time to go and talk to each of them as to what we were going to do with Von Spee, or somebody else. . . . In peace we have constant Boards, and there is time to go and talk to them. . . . it was impossible [in war].' Again, the Junior Sea Lords were 'tremendously occupied with their business in providing the personnel and stores and other things for the Fleet. I think it would have been a very great pity to have taken them away from their proper duties . . .' *Ibid.* Battenberg, before him, also considered that war plans and war policy lay wholly in the domain of the First Sea Lord and First Lord. It must be emphasized that neither the First Lord nor the First Sea Lord was obliged to consult his colleagues on the Board unless he thought fit to do so.

Group, in which the influence of the First Lord and the First Sea Lord was paramount. The Junior Sea Lords were informed that it was not intended that they should take part in councils of war. Each member went on with his departmental duties, of course. They accepted the situation, only asking that the Secretary periodically circulate to them, 'confidentially for information', reports on operations. The request was never complied with, according to their Dardanelles testimony. This contradicted Churchill's statement that he had arranged from the beginning that they should keep themselves posted on operations by 'daily perusal of telegrams, etc.', so that they might form 'a reserve of naval opinion to which the First Lord or the First Sea Lord could at any time refer'.[58] The secretiveness of the C.O.S., Sturdee, 'who did not readily part with important papers' (Graham Greene), was a factor in this unsatisfactory situation.

Annoyed by the fact that they knew nothing at all of the Antwerp operation and the dispatch of the Naval Division until they saw it in the press, Lambert and Tudor made written representations to Battenberg on 12 October 1914. They asked for periodic meetings of the Board's naval members at which the First Sea Lord could keep them posted on the important matters, even if they had no right, according to the Order in Council of 14 January 1869, to insist on Board discussion of war policy.[59] Prince Louis talked the situation over with them, but without any result. Although Oliver, on becoming C.O.S., was readier to co-operate than Sturdee had been, little was done to correct the situation. To the end of the Churchill–Fisher period, the Junior Sea Lords claimed in their Dardanelles testimony, they were never informed of, let alone consulted on, what was going on. In effect, as Churchill put it, they 'fell, naturally and automatically, to some extent into the position of the old Navy Office. They supplied men, ships, and stores. They were not formally consulted in the main operations and movements.'[60] In a word, the Board as such no longer assumed any collective responsibility for the general conduct of affairs. In leaving the Junior Sea Lords out in the cold as regards the Dardanelles operation, the First Lord was acting on perfectly legal

[58] *Ibid.*

[59] Orders in Council are orders issued by the Sovereign (acting on the advice of the Government and when formally attended by at least three Privy Councillors) under prerogative or statutory powers.

[60] *Dardanelles Commission.*

and historical grounds. His wisdom in not tapping this large reservoir of professional experience is, of course, another matter.

No Board meetings were held on the subject and none of the Sea Lords was asked to express an opinion—not even Tudor, a former D.N.O. whose opinions on the possibilities of high-angle fire from ships against forts would have been worth soliciting, one would think. Once, in January 1915, Tudor had ventured to express his opinion to Churchill: 'I have heard some rumours about it. I am rather interested in the Dardanelles, because I spent my early life in the service in the vicinity of the Dardanelles, in the Gulf of Zaros, and if you want to take the Dardanelles, in my opinion it ought to be done with troops landing at Port Bakla and I have always wondered why the Greeks did not do that when they were fighting against the Turks [the First Balkan War, 1912].' *Churchill*: 'Well, do you not know why they did not, and why we do not?' *Tudor*: 'Well, I suppose we have not got the troops and they had not.' *Churchill*: 'Exactly.' *Tudor*: 'Well, you won't do it with ships alone.' *Churchill*: 'Oh yes, we will.' Tudor shrugged his shoulders and said: 'Well, if you are going to do it with ships it will be [a] very long and difficult business.' That remained his opinion. His intervention 'was not welcomed, and it had no effect.' He kept his counsel thereafter.[61]

The Second Sea Lord shared Tudor's doubts. Hamilton testified that he 'never thought a naval attack without military support would be of any use. . . . Because I did not believe, with the present power of ships against forts, that even if they got through they would ever be able to keep up communications with the fleet inside.' That is to say, they would have the history of Duckworth's attempt in 1807 over again. But Hamilton never got the opportunity to express this opinion to the First Lord formally. It was only in the course of 'informal conversations' that he conveyed the idea.[62]

So completely in the dark were the Junior Sea Lords that Tudor claimed that he knew of the impending naval operation 'only by

[61] *Ibid.*

[62] *Ibid.* Hamilton went so far as to assert that the First Lord 'never mentioned the opinion of the other Sea Lords, first because it was never asked formally, and the reason being that he knew quite well by casual conversation that we were all dead against him.' Hamilton to Jellicoe, 22 Nov. 1915; Jellicoe, 'A Reply to Criticism'. There is a very similar statement in Hamilton's diary, 16 Nov. 1915; Hamilton MSS.

rumour and not from any information from the remainder of the Board of Admiralty'.[63]

To sum up, Churchill had succeeded in obtaining no more than, in the words of the Dardanelles Commission, 'a certain amount of half-hearted and hesitating expert opinion' in favour of the naval operation. But he had dazzled—hypnotized almost—the politicians with his pictures of the great political and military results which would follow a successful naval attempt to force the Dardanelles. And always there was the comforting thought that, as was understood from the beginning, the naval attack could be broken off, if it did not go well.

[63] *Dardanelles Commission.*

X

The Dardanelles Operation: Execution

(FEBRUARY 1915–APRIL 1915)

(*Map* 7)

In an effort to satisfy the urgent needs of diplomacy, Britain's fleet was to attempt, without the aid of a single soldier, an enterprise which in the earlier days of the war both the Admiralty and the War Office had regarded as a military task. The operation would, moreover, be many times more difficult than in the early days of the war. The Germans had already had six months in which to improve the defences of the Straits, and the minefields were continually growing. The enterprise was perhaps still capable of accomplishment, if the Government were ready to face the inevitable loss of ships. . . . But there must be no indecision, no faltering, and no delay.

> BRIGADIER-GENERAL C. F. ASPINALL-OGLANDER,
> *Military Operations, Gallipoli.*

Not to persevere—that was the crime.

> CHURCHILL, *The World Crisis.*

I. THE NAVAL OPERATION: FIRST STAGES

FROM its mouth at Cape Helles in the Mediterranean to where it reaches the Sea of Marmora, above the town of Gallipoli, the Dardanelles is about 41 miles in extent. At their mouth a little over two miles wide, the Straits run in a north-easterly direction, broadening to their maximum width of between four and five miles in Eren Keui Bay, and gradually narrowing to a breadth of less than two miles at Kephez Point, 11 miles from the entrance. At the Narrows, between Chanak and Kilid Bahr, about 14 miles from the entrance, the Straits close to three-quarters of a mile and then broaden to an average width of four miles for the rest of their course. The Narrows end at Nagara Point, 18 miles from the entrance to the Straits.

The main forts of the outer defences, that is, at the entrance, were at Kum Kale, on the Asiatic shore, and Sedd el Bahr, at the tip of the Gallipoli Peninsula, with supporting forts, respectively, at Orkanie and Cape Helles. They mounted 27 guns of 3·4-inch to 11-inch calibre, although only four could fire over 11,000 yards. The first step in Carden's plan called for destroying the two forts on each entrance headland by naval gunfire. He would then tackle the intermediate defences, from inside the entrance up to the Narrows. They were mainly the 100 guns, none over 8·2-inches—mobile howitzers and guns mounted in batteries (Fort Dardanos was the principal fort of the intermediate defences)—and searchlights on Kephez Point on the Asiatic side and at the mouth of the Soghanli Dere on the opposite side. The main purpose of the intermediate defences was the protection of the minefield between Chanak, in the Narrows, and Kephez Bay, containing well over 300 mines moored in ten lines.

The objective of Carden's third step, the Narrows, was protected by the inner defences, a complex of eleven forts at the foot of the massive Kilid Bahr plateau on Gallipoli and on its steep sides and summit, and, on the Asiatic side, at Chanak. The defences included 88 guns, ranging up to six 14-inch Krupp guns, searchlights, and the northern portion of the minefield. The Narrows were favoured with a swift four-to-five knot current running towards the Aegean, a situation made to order for drifting mines. The guns of the forts covered the principal minefield, which was off Kephez Point; carefully concealed searchlights had been established to detect any night-time attempt to sweep the mines. At the narrowest point in the Narrows, moreover, the Straits turn to the north for four miles before resuming their north-easterly course to the Sea of Marmora. This situation was made to order for a raking fire from scores of guns at Nagara Point down towards the entrance of the Narrows. If Nagara Point could be passed, the only important obstacles the fleet need fear were mines and the *Goeben* in the Sea of Marmora. Also favouring the defenders were the steep and rough shores of the Dardanelles on both the European side—the Gallipoli Peninsula—and the Asiatic side, particularly the former.

It was the view of the German military adviser to the Turks, General Liman von Sanders, that the mines were the primary defence of the Dardanelles, and that the function of the guns in the forts was simply to protect the minefields from interference. The problem faced by the Allies, put succinctly, was this: The bristling arsenal of guns in the forts were difficult to destroy by long-range naval gunfire; this made it impossible for the fleet to sweep up the mines; until this was done, it was impossible to close the forts.

Carden's force consisted of the *Queen Elizabeth* (which had not joined when the action was commenced on 19 February), the battle cruiser *Inflexible*, the *Lord Nelson* and *Agamemnon* (last of the pre-dreadnoughts, mounting four 12-inch guns and ten 9·2-inch), ten older battleships (eight carried four 12-inch and twelve 6-inch guns, the other two, four 10-inch and fourteen 7·5-inch), four old French battleships, and a miscellany of lesser vessels of every description, including cruisers, destroyers, and mine-sweeping trawlers. The fleet base was Mudros Bay in Lemnos, 50 miles west of the mouth of the Dardanelles, which was put at Britain's disposal by the Greek Government a few days before the bombardment. The Greeks also permitted the Allies to use Imbros, Tenedos, and Mitylene.

The commander of the combined fleet, Carden, held the post by accident. The logical choice to command the fleet was Vice-Admiral Arthur H. Limpus, who had been head of the British Naval Mission in Turkey until it was withdrawn in September 1914, and was a fine officer who knew the Dardanelles and Turkish capabilities. He had left Constantinople when Turkey was still a neutral. Because the British Ambassador felt it would have been very irritating to the Turks to appoint the man who had worked so closely with them, the Admiralty had chosen Carden, then Superintendent of Malta Dockyard. This was 'a chivalry which surely outstripped common sense'. Churchill was under no illusions about Carden. 'As for Carden, he has never commanded a cruiser squadron, and I am not aware of anything that he has done which is in any way remarkable.'[1] Fisher had an even lower opinion of Carden. 'Who expected Carden to be in command of a big fleet! He was made Admiral Superintendent of Malta to shelve him!'[2] He would no doubt have removed him but for the sudden emergence of the Dardanelles operation. General Birdwood correctly sized up Carden, when he warned Kitchener early in March that the Admiral was 'very second-rate—no "go" in him, or ideas, or initiative'.[3]

[1] Churchill to Fisher, 23 Dec. 1914; Lennoxlove MSS.
[2] Fisher to Jellicoe, 16 Mar. 1915; *Fear God and Dread Nought*, iii. 166.
[3] Philip Magnus, *Kitchener: Portrait of an Imperialist* (London, 1958), p. 322.

Under Carden were Rear-Admirals de Robeck (Second-in-Command) and Wemyss (S.N.O. in charge of the Allied base at Mudros). Commodore Keyes served as Carden's Chief of Staff. Rear-Admiral Guépratte, the commander of the French ships at the Dardanelles until June 1915, was an improvement on Carden. He was a dashing leader, always eager to attack, though pompous and full of outward show.

*　　*　　*

And so the fleet would try to force the passage of the Dardanelles and reach Constantinople. Churchill had no intention of calling on the Army for large-scale aid; some small landing parties to complete the demolition of the forts and guns would suffice. Accordingly, he would not hear of sending out the naval infantry —the whole of the Royal Naval Division, as pressed early in February by Oliver and Richmond. All he would send out (6 February) were two battalions of Marines from the Royal Naval Division (2,000 men), to provide landing parties for destroying Turkish guns. They arrived at Lemnos on the 23rd. While the First Lord grimly held on to the bulk of the Naval Division, the need for important military help became more apparent with each passing day.

On 15 February Jackson emphatically stated in a memorandum that the naval bombardment was a sound military operation only if 'a strong military force is ready to assist in the operation, or, at least, follow it up immediately the forts are silenced'. Such a force was needed to occupy the Gallipoli Peninsula, since the pressure of strong Turkish forces there 'would not only greatly harass the [naval] operations, but would render the passage of the Straits impracticable by any but powerfully armed vessels, even though all the permanent defences had been silenced'.[4] At this time Richmond used similar arguments in an eloquent plea for a joint operation. 'The bombardment of the Dardanelles, even if all the Forts are destroyed, can be nothing but a local success, which without an army to carry it on can have no further effect.' Fisher and Hankey praised Richmond's paper, which expressed their ideas.[5] Fisher urged the First Lord (16 February) to press on

---

[4] *Dardanelles Commission.* Churchill read Jackson's memorandum to the War Council.
[5] Richmond's memorandum, 'Remarks on Present Strategy', 14 Feb. 1915; *Portrait of an Admiral*, p. 145.

Kitchener the need to send 'divisions' out to Lemnos immediately.

A more important development was Kitchener's promise at the Council meeting of 9 February: 'If the Navy required the assistance of the land forces at a later stage, that assistance would be forthcoming.'[6] Soon afterwards the 29th Division, which had been earmarked for Sir John French's command, became available. In addition, the repulse of the Turkish attack on the Suez Canal early in February and the report that the Turks were withdrawing their troops from Palestine towards Constantinople set free a sizeable part of the Egyptian garrison. Another factor was the failure of the diplomatic efforts late in January to enlist Greek and Serb military co-operation.

These expressions of opinion and the new factors led to an important decision on 16 February. An informal meeting of six of the ten members of the War Council (including Asquith, Kitchener, Fisher, and Churchill) decided to take advantage of the unexpected availability of troops by massing a considerable army on Lemnos, to be used if required. The precise functions of this force were left vague. Two battalions of the Royal Marines were, as just noted, already en route; the 29th Division, which had been intended for France, would leave within ten days; an Egyptian force would be sent if needed; and the Admiralty was 'to make arrangements to collect small craft, tugs, and lighters in the Levant'. In short, the enterprise was beginning to assume the form of a combined operation, although there was still general confidence, in the War Council and in Carden's squadron, that the fleet would force the Dardanelles and that the military would be needed only to complete the demolition of the forts and to knock out the concealed howitzers. What Churchill had in mind was that the Army (at least 50,000 men) should be poised 'either to seize the Gallipoli peninsula when it has been evacuated, or to occupy Constantinople, if a revolution takes place. We shd. never forgive ourselves if the naval operations succeeded and the fruits were lost through the army being absent.'[7]

Everything now depended on the results of the naval attack, which was set for 19 February. (By a curious coincidence, this was the anniversary of Duckworth's rushing of the Straits in 1807.) The long-range bombardment of the four outer forts, out of range

[6] *Dardanelles Commission.*
[7] Churchill to Kitchener, 18 Feb. 1915.

of the enemy's guns (but closing to 5,000 yards by the late afternoon) was opened just before 10 a.m. by the *Inflexible* and five battleships. The ships pulled back at dusk. The net result of the heavy and prolonged fire at short range was slight, as the fire was inaccurate and there were no direct hits on guns or mountings. Seventy per cent of the guns remained in a serviceable condition, Carden reported some time afterwards. He was not disappointed with the day's work, since, he claimed, these guns would not be usable for a considerable time: their magazines had all been blown up and the communications to their control position were probably all destroyed.[8]

Severe gales and low visibility prevented the resumption of the bombardment until the morning of 25 February. Firing mostly at close range, the fleet was able to silence the forts at each side of the entrance. Demolition parties of marines, landed on 26 February, 1 and 4 March to destroy the forts, were only partially successful before being driven off by the defenders, who, once the ship fire lifted, had sifted back into the forts. Nevertheless, it was judged that enough had been accomplished for the next phase of the operations to begin: the reduction of the intermediate defences, including the clearing of the great minefield. The new stage began on 1 March. That night the minesweepers swept the water below Kephez Point in preparation for the battleship attack on the Kephez forts the next day.

By the end of February the original idea of limiting the operation to a fleet operation and stopping if not successful had been weakened and a major joint operation was envisaged. One new factor was the growth of the idea (it was held by Grey and Kitchener, for instance) that for reasons of prestige it would be impossible to break off the operation if the Navy failed. Another was the growing doubt of the Generals that the Navy would succeed. General Sir William Birdwood, who had been sent out by Kitchener on 23 February to reconnoitre the situation, let his Chief know that, given the formidable character of the Turkish defences on Gallipoli, he did not think the Navy could do the job alone. This was also the opinion of the commander of the Egyptian garrison, General Maxwell, as he wrote Kitchener on 28 February. Lord Sydenham, the onetime Secretary of the C.I.D. and an ordnance expert of some repute, expressed the same idea. The

[8] Carden's testimony; *Dardanelles Commission.*

destruction of the outer forts would be nothing. 'A large military force is necessary, and unless and until it is ready it would have been best to let the outer forts wait.'[9] On 24 February Kitchener told the Council that he 'felt that if the Fleet would not get through the Straits unaided, the Army ought to see the business through'.[10]

Equally important, it was becoming apparent to Carden and his senior officers that a large-scale military operation would have to be launched to capture the Gallipoli Peninsula. The object would be to ensure the Straits being kept open for continuing operations in case the appearance of the squadron off Constantinople did not have the expected decisive result.

For a while, following the decision reached by the ministers on 16 February, there was a good prospect that troops would shortly attack as well as ships. Then, on 19 February, Kitchener withdrew his consent to the dispatch of the 29th Division. On the 26th he informed the War Council that he would make no final decision on the 29th Division until the situation on the Eastern Front had cleared. The Russians had suffered severe reverses, which opened up the possibility of the Germans being able to transfer troops to the West. Churchill's impassioned pleas at the Council meetings of 24 and 26 February for the instant dispatch of the division were fruitless. The First Lord was still optimistic about the Navy's ability to force the Straits without military help; he wanted troops within reach in the Levant for contingencies—'to reap the fruits [if the fleet got through] or to help the Navy through if we were checked, or conceivably it might at a certain stage have brought Greece in'.[11] He had some support in the Council, but it went along with Kitchener in the final decision on 26 February.

It was not until 10 March that Kitchener released the 29th, and it did not get away until 16–23 March. The holding back of the division for three weeks had momentous consequences, Churchill believes.

If this Division had gone as was decided on the 16th February and in the transports we had collected, we could have begun to embark it from the 22nd; it would have reached the Dardanelles about the same time as the Naval attack culminated and was expected to culminate

---

[9] Sydenham to Esher, 26 Feb. 1915; Esher MSS.
[10] *Dardanelles Commission.*
[11] Churchill's testimony; *ibid.*

for good or for ill, and at the same time as all the other troops reached that theatre. In that event if we had met with success the Army would have been able to reap the fruits. And confronted as we were with a check, the Army would have been strong enough in the opinion of Generals to begin an immediate attack upon the Gallipoli Peninsula. If you question Sir Ian Hamilton and General Birdwood, I believe they will say that the absence of the 29th Division on the 22nd or 23rd March was the decisive factor in leading them to postpone the military attack on the Peninsula until they had gone back to Alexandria, and repacked, and so on.[12]

The absence of the 29th was the 'decisive factor' because it was 'the vital *key* division, the sole regular division, whose movements and arrival governed everything'.[13]

Kitchener has not lacked defenders. Churchill's criticism that a single division could not have affected the result in the West, misses the point, according to General Maurice. The issue, Maurice insists, was not one involving a single division, but rather of a heavy and continuing drain on British resources that a fresh military enterprise might entail. Robertson has made the same point: 'To force the Dardanelles, dominate Constantinople, and open up the Bosphorus, was a task that might well call for the services of many divisions . . .'[14] This consideration was undoubtedly present in Kitchener's mind. He, moreover, hesitated to incur the liability of a new campaign at a time when he was under tremendous pressure from Sir John French and Joffre to reinforce the Western Front. They feared that the severe Russian setbacks just suffered in Poland and the Bukovina might release great masses of German troops for a fresh offensive in the West.

Whatever the justification for the three weeks of shilly-shallying on the 29th Division, this hard fact remains. Had Kitchener acted boldly at the end of February and bent every effort towards preparing a large and well-organized amphibious operation, the Peninsula probably could have been taken. There was only one Turkish division there at the time. It could have been quickly polished off, had an adequate military force been available

[12] *Ibid.*

[13] *The World Crisis*, ii. 214. The Dardanelles Commission were equally critical of the delay in the dispatch of the 29th.

[14] Major-General Sir Frederick Maurice, *British Strategy* (London, 1929), p. 101; Field-Marshal Sir William Robertson, *Soldiers and Statesmen, 1914–1918* (London, 1926, 2 vols.), i. 103.

quickly, before the Turks could reinforce their troops substantially. In this connexion, it seems a pity that the Russians vetoed (3 March) a Greek offer on 1 March to send three divisions to Gallipoli. Under no circumstances would they sanction a Greek army in Constantinople.

On 10 March Kitchener reported that the situation on the Eastern and Western Fronts was clear enough to enable him to release the 18,000 men of the 29th for co-operation with the Allied squadron. Also available, he informed the War Council, were the Australian and New Zealand (Anzac) Corps (34,100 men), the Naval Division (11,000), a French division (18,000), and a Russian army corps (47,600), making a total of 128,700 men. The actual total was 81,000, since no Russian military support was possible till the Allies had obtained access to Constantinople and controlled the Black Sea.

On 12 March General Sir Ian Hamilton, who had seen more active service than any British officer at that time, was appointed to command the troops being assembled at Lemnos. His written instructions, received from Kitchener on the 13th, were meagre and not entirely clear. (They struck one of the Dardanelles Commissioners as appearing 'like the utterances of a Delphic oracle'.) This much was plain: the scope of the military operations had not yet been decided, and Kitchener still hoped the Navy would be able to force the Straits without military help. He told Hamilton the day before that he hoped that the Navy would force the Straits without military help. 'He said,' Hamilton testified before the Commission, 'we soldiers were clearly to understand that we were string number 2. The sailors said they could force the Dardanelles on their own, and we were not to chip in unless the Admiral definitely chucked up the sponge.'[15]

Because of the lack of a sense of urgency—they were, after all, 'string number 2' and no major ground action was anticipated in the near future—the preparations for an eventual amphibious operation were inadequate, to say the least. Hamilton, when he left for the Aegean on the evening of the 13th, took out with him a 1912 handbook of the Turkish Army, a pre-war report on the Dardanelles defences, and an out-of-date map. This was all the information put at his disposal. And he had neither a staff nor a detailed plan.

[15] *Dardanelles Commission.*

The confusion was quickly compounded by the arrival of the troops at Mudros without their stores and equipment, which had been stowed on slower transports. The loading itself was chaotic, with guns separated from ammunition, primers separated from shells, etc. In such a logistic topsy-turvy, and with the dock and shore facilities at Lemnos inadequate for straightening out the mess, Hamilton had no choice but to send the early arrivals on Mudros to Alexandria, almost 700 miles away, and to re-route his other transports there. The reorganization of the whole force and its equipment occupied all hands for a month. This explains why the Army was unable promptly to land on Gallipoli, after the events of 18 March pointed to the definite need for an amphibious strategy.

The failure so to stow the ships in England that they could readily be discharged when they reached their destination was partly the fault of Graeme Thomson, the Director of Transports at the Admiralty. He was, in his own words, 'responsible for carrying everything by ship for the Army, Navy and other Departments of the Government—sea transport generally'. Churchill was, indirectly, not blameless in the matter. Graeme Thomson had been the civilian Assistant when Churchill appointed him Director in December 1914 over the arguments of Oliver and Graham Greene. 'He knew the City end of the work,' Oliver maintains, 'and all about taking up ships, etc., but nothing about war.' They wanted Vice-Admiral Sir Edmond Slade, a far abler man, appointed. 'Had he been D. of T., the transports for the Dardanelles would have been properly loaded and arrived in the proper order.'[16] Churchill was indirectly responsible in another way. He 'took a tremendous interest in transport matters,' says Graeme Thomson, 'and used to deal direct with me a very great deal'.[17] The Army must bear a share of the responsibility, since the War Office had accepted the Director's arrangements. As Graeme Thomson testified, 'When we get our indents from the War Office we propose which units and which stores should go into particular ships. If the War Office accept that, I am afraid the War Office must take the responsibility for any dislocation that ensues.'[18]

[16] Oliver MSS.

[17] *Dardanelles Commission.* Churchill admitted that he worked the naval transport with the Director, and not through the Fourth Sea Lord, though transport was under the latter.

[18] *Ibid.*

In extenuation of the Army's apparent blunder, I must re-emphasize that the troops left before there was any plan, let alone a decision, to attempt a landing in force in the Straits.

Whatever reservations the Generals may have had about the success of the naval operations—and Callwell, we know, was downright pessimistic on the eve of De Robeck's determined attack—public opinion was optimistic. *The Observer* predicted (28 February) that 'one of the memorable efforts of all history will be steadily carried to success . . .' The *Globe* chimed in (4 March): 'It is probably not rash to assume that Constantinople will be under the guns of the Allied Fleet within a comparatively short time.' The leading Service journal, the *Naval and Military Record*, was especially sanguine (3 March): 'The ship of war has proved superior to the fort . . . sufficient has been achieved to lead to the confident anticipation that at no very remote period the Dardanelles will be thrown open.' These are typical expressions of opinion. Here and there, as in the *Daily News* and *Manchester Guardian*, there were voices of warning that the forts could not be disposed of by the ships alone, and that they should not expect an easy or rapid success.

The War Council itself was so confident of the success of the naval operation that the principal business of its 10 March meeting was a discussion of the political and strategical questions likely to arise after the fall of Constantinople! Russia had been pressing to know where she stood with Britain and France in regard to Constantinople and the Straits. When Russia had put in a claim for both immediately after the Turkish entry into the war, the Government had asked their naval and military advisers if they had any objections on strategic grounds. They had none, although the Admiralty recommended that as an offset they should have an additional base in the eastern Mediterranean—specifically, the splendid Turkish port of Alexandretta, the probable terminus on the Mediterranean of the Baghdad Railway. Now, at the Council of 10 March, following the reiteration of the Russian claim on 4 March, Kitchener agreed with the naval view. 'With Russia in Constantinople, France in Syria, and Italy in Rhodes, our position in Egypt would be untenable if any other Power held Alexandretta.' Fisher stressed Alexandretta's special importance as an outlet for Persian and Mesopotamian oil, and Churchill saw in Alexandretta the site of an important naval base.

'If we succeeded in shattering German naval power we ought to be able to build a Mediterranean fleet against France and Russia.' The conclusion of the Council (which was approved by the Cabinet) was that Russia be informed that her proposals were agreed to, 'subject to the war being prosecuted to a victorious conclusion' and certain other conditions.[19]

The naval situation in the second week of March hardly justified the confidence of public opinion or the War Council. Churchill was wearing his rose-tinted spectacles when he wrote to Jellicoe on 9 March, 'Our affairs in the Dardanelles are prospering, though we have not yet cracked the nut.' His imagination leaped beyond Constantinople. 'Constantinople is only a means to an end, and that end is the marching against Austria of the five reunited Balkan States.'[20]

It had been comparatively easy to silence the outer forts by engaging them beyond their effective range. The ships had been in the open sea, well clear of minefields, and able to shoot from any angle without interference of any kind. It was another story once the squadron began to operate inside the narrow Straits against the intermediate defences. Churchill sums up the obstacles this way: 'The minefields blocked the passage of the Straits and kept the Fleet beyond their limits. The minefield batteries prevented the sweeping of the minefields. The forts [at the Narrows] protected the minefield batteries by keeping battleships at a distance with their long guns. The mobile howitzers [intermediate defences] kept the battleships on the move and increased the difficulty of overcoming the forts. So long as all four factors stood together, the defences constituted a formidable obstruction.'[21]

Carden's conduct of the operations inside the Straits was utterly lacking in vigour and determination. On 2 and 3 March, for instance, three battleships only, of the eighteen available, engaged the intermediate defences. Indeed, in the first three weeks never more than a quarter of the squadron was sent into action against the forts at a time. The bombardments were partial and desultory. And yet Carden was optimistic. On 2 March he

[19] Minutes of the 17th meeting of the War Council, 10 Mar. 1915; Asquith MSS. The Council took no decision on Alexandretta, since Asquith was opposed to the Admiralty-War Office desire for its acquisition, probably because of the fear of French complications.
[20] Jellicoe MSS.
[21] *The World Crisis*, ii. 256.

reported that, given fine weather, he hoped to be off Constantinople in about two weeks. There was joy at the Admiralty. Fisher, his forebodings momentarily submerged, proposed to take command of the next and vital stage of the operation, the attack on the Narrows. Thereafter difficulties and setbacks multiplied.

On 5 March, although the bombardment of the intermediate defences had not been decisive, Carden began the next phase, the reduction of the forts at the Narrows. Indirect long-range bombardments by the *Queen Elizabeth* (firing over the Peninsula from a position just south-west of Gaba Tepe), which were repeated on 5 and 6 March, produced no important results. 'The failure was due,' says Churchill, 'to the restriction on the expenditure of ammunition and to the inadequate aerial observation.' On the 7th and 8th direct attacks were resumed on the forts inside the Straits by the two 'Lord Nelsons' (while the four French battleships pounded the intermediate defences) and the *Queen Elizabeth* (8 March). Again the military results were unimportant. The minesweepers had achieved even less on the nights of 6, 7 March.

The naval attack had come to a virtual standstill. 'We are going to get through,' Keyes noted in his diary on 8 March, 'but it is a much bigger thing than the Admiralty or anyone out here realised . . .'[22] Opinion on the spot was more than ever in favour of military co-operation. Carden himself was no longer optimistic over the naval prospects. His interview with Birdwood off Tenedos in the *Swiftsure* left the General with a gloomy impression of British prospects. He telegraphed to Kitchener on 5 March that he was 'very doubtful if the Navy can force the passage unassisted'.[23] On 10 March Carden wired the Admiralty an appreciation of the situation that pointed to a stalemate. 'We are for the present checked by absence of efficient air reconnaissance, the necessity of clearing the minefield, and the presence of a large number of movable howitzers on both sides of the Straits, whose positions up to the present we have not been able to locate. Meanwhile, every effort will be made to clear the minefield by night, with two battleships in support. . . . Our experience shows that gunfire alone will not render forts innocuous . . .'[24] The Admiral had put his finger on the cardinal difficulty, one that most people on the spot

[22] Keyes, *Naval Memoirs*, i. 207–8.
[23] *Dardanelles Commission*.
[24] Keyes, *Naval Memoirs*, i. 209–10.

241

realized by this time, that even if there were efficient spotting, events had proved that long-range fire alone would never neutralize the forts. Ships must close to decisive range to demolish them. The problem was how to do this in the face of minefields protected by mobile batteries.

Keyes thought the Admiral exaggerated the danger of enemy gunfire. 'Against moving ships it was very inaccurate and not really dangerous.' Little damage had been suffered so far. 'I felt it was time to get on with the business, and that the minefields must be swept at all costs.'[25] He persuaded Carden to make a determined attack on the Kephez minefield. The plan was to send seven sweepers (the maximum number that could operate in the channel below Chanak) into the Dardanelles after dark, supported by the old battleship *Canopus*, the light cruiser *Amethyst*, and destroyers. Since the sweepers could make little progress against the strong current, the *Canopus* would go in first and knock out the searchlights just below the minefield; the sweepers would then steam through the minefield and, when above it, they were to sweep down with the current.

The plan foundered when tried on the night of 10 March. The *Canopus* attempted unsuccessfully to knock out the searchlights of the intermediate defences. Keyes bitterly remarked that 'for all the good we did towards dowsing the searchlights we might just as well have been firing at the moon'. The sweepers got above the minefield without loss and tried to sweep down with the strong current, but they were discovered by the searchlights and were subjected to a hot fire from the mainland batteries. They became 'so agitated that four out of the six—the seventh is a leader—did not get their kites down, and so swept the surface.'[26] One trawler was sunk by a mine; three enemy mines were exploded.

The operation was repeated the next night without a supporting battleship, so as to surprise the enemy. This time the trawlers retired as soon as they came under fire in the glaring rays of the searchlights.

The less said about that night the better [wrote Keyes]. To put it briefly, the sweepers turned tail and fled directly they were fired upon. I was furious and told the officers in charge that they had had their opportunity, there were many others only too keen to try. It did not

[25] *Ibid.*, p. 210.
[26] *Ibid.*, p. 212.

matter if we lost all seven sweepers, there were 28 more, and the mines had got to be swept up. How could they talk about being stopped by a heavy fire if they were not hit. The Admiralty were prepared for losses, but we had chucked our hand in and started squealing before we had any.[27]

On 12 March the French had an unsuccessful try against the minefield. An Admiralty telegram of 11 March, received by Carden the next day, showed that their Lordships were getting impatient over the seeming lack of determination behind the attacks. It had been drafted by Churchill and had the approval of Fisher and Oliver.

Caution and deliberate methods were emphasised in your original instructions . . . If, however, success cannot be obtained without loss of ships and men, results to be gained are important enough to justify such a loss. The whole operation may be decided and consequences of a decisive character upon the war may be produced by the turning of the corner of Chanak; and we suggest for your consideration, that a point has now been reached when it is necessary to choose favourable weather conditions to overwhelm forts of the Narrows at decisive range by bringing to bear upon them the fire of the largest possible number of guns, great and small. Under cover of this fire landing parties might destroy the guns of the forts, and sweeping operations to clear as much as possible of the minefield might also be carried out.[28]

Captain A. C. Dewar has tartly commented: 'It is one of those peculiarly objectionable messages, in which the man on the spot is not only urged to attack but told how to do it . . . In its easy and superficial reference to very difficult or impracticable tasks, it bears the unmistakable impress of the First Lord's hand.'

However that may be, Carden had no objections, and at noon on 13 March he wired his full concurrence with the Admiralty's view. The time had come for 'vigorous sustained action . . . In order to immediately follow up silencing of forts at Narrows with close range bombardment it is necessary to clear the minefield at Kephez. . . . A final attempt is to be made tonight; if it fails also it will be necessary to destroy fixed and mobile light guns defending minefield before continuing sweeping.'[29]

[27] *Ibid.* Churchill's telegram to Carden on 14 March made the same point: 'I do not understand why minesweepers should be interfered with by firing which causes no casualties.' *Ibid.*, p. 216. The harsh criticism of the sweepers by Churchill and especially by Keyes was quite unjustified, as we shall see below, pp. 263–5.

[28] *Dardanelles Commission.*

[29] Keyes, *Naval Memoirs*, i. 214.

The action that night (13–14 March) was undertaken by seven trawlers and five picket boats provided with explosive sweeps (on which see below, p. 351), supported by the old battleship *Cornwallis*, the *Amethyst*, and destroyers. It was a final and desperate attempt against the Kephez area—to obtain a clear channel up to the Narrows by knocking out the searchlights and sweeping unhampered, more or less, in darkness. The sweeper crews had been beefed up with an infusion of volunteers from the regular Navy, and with a commissioned officer in command of each trawler. There was the usual preliminary slow progress against the current and the passage through the illuminated area. A very heavy fire from the warships made little impression on the searchlights and the minefield batteries. The enemy was fully alerted. At the right time, when the sweepers were in the middle of the minefield, every searchlight was turned on and every gun opened fire. The trawlers held on to the turning point, a mile above Kephez Point, that is, above the minefield, then swung around. Only two were able to get out their sweeps, as a storm of shell from the Narrows and intermediate defences smashed kites, winches, and other essential gear. Four trawlers and one picket boat were put out of action. The crews had put on a better show, yet the sweeping results were nil.

It was at last appreciated that trawler minesweeping at night under heavy gunfire was a practically impossible operation. The covering ships simply could not knock out the searchlights or the minefield batteries. One alternative remained, Carden, De Robeck, and Keyes realized—to have a try by day. The general idea of the plan was, in De Robeck's words, to have 'a try in daylight hours by driving the Turks away from their guns, which would admit of the trawlers getting into the mine field and being able to sweep the passage'. De Robeck afterwards admitted that the idea of daylight operations had occurred to him and Carden 'in view of the Admiralty suggestion that it was time to press for a decision'.[30]

The plan of attack was issued on 15 March. The next day Carden resigned his command for reasons of health. He was a worrier, had had stomach upsets, and was in imminent danger of a nervous breakdown. He had imparted no vigour to the operations and a change was overdue.

[30] *Dardanelles Commission.*

On 17 March Churchill telegraphed De Robeck, appointing him Carden's successor. Although Wemyss, who commanded the base at Mudros, was S.N.O. at the Dardanelles, he was willing to forget that and to work under his junior, so that De Robeck might see through successfully the operation in which he had been playing a leading part. Churchill has described the tall, broadshouldered, handsome and charming De Robeck as 'a good sea officer and a fine disciplinarian', who 'bore an exceptionally high reputation in the service'. Birdwood called him 'a real fine fellow —worth a dozen of Carden'. Admiral Sir Sydney Fremantle ranked him with Jellicoe and Beatty as one of the three greatest sailors of World War I. This is a mite generous, although he did hold the first and third aces—a gift for leadership and for taking subordinates into his confidence. As late as 25 March, despite the disheartening experience on the 18th, Sir Ian Hamilton could write, 'All the Navy with one accord say he is *the* man for the job now on hand, and confidence in him has increased rather than lessened since they have seen him stand firm in the grip of nerve shattering misfortune.'[31]

On the eve of the operation, 17 March, a conference was held at Tenedos in the *Queen Elizabeth*: De Robeck, Keyes, Guépratte, Wemyss, Hamilton (who had arrived that day), and others. De Robeck was confident he could silence the big guns of the forts; what worried him was the enemy's mobile artillery—the howitzers and field guns firing from concealed positions, which made the clearing of the minefield 'something of a V.C. sort of job for the smaller craft'. Even if the fleet broke through into the Marmora, these movable guns would make it very unpleasant for the transports and store ships which followed. The Admiral, nonetheless, was confident he could force a passage without large-scale military help. At least he would have a 'real good try' first.

2. FAILURE

(See Map 7, inset)

On 18 March De Robeck tried the new plan of attack of having the battleships during the day simultaneously silence the forts at the Narrows and the batteries protecting the Kephez minefield, and then have the trawlers go in that night to clear a channel through the minefield. The following morning, if all had gone

[31] Hamilton to Asquith, 25 Mar. 1915; Asquith MSS.

well, the fleet would enter Sari Sighlar Bay and destroy the Narrows forts at short range. With the forts completely knocked out, the trawlers would proceed to sweep the minefield at the Narrows, and the way would lie open into the Marmora. This was, at any rate, the plan.

At 11.25 a.m. an outer squadron of the four most powerful British ships, *Queen Elizabeth*, *Inflexible*, and the two 'Lord Nelsons', went into action about six miles up the Straits. They bombarded the Narrows forts while the *Prince George* and *Triumph*, on either flank and slightly to the rear, engaged the intermediate-defence batteries. The squadron was beyond the range of the Chanak and Kilid Bahr forts, but was peppered by the mobile howitzers and field guns of the intermediate defences without serious damage. Shortly after noon, the guns of the intermediate forts having fallen silent, the inner squadron of four French battleships (with the *Majestic* and *Swiftsure* on either flank), which had followed a mile astern, closed the Narrows forts at 8,000 yards, and at the same time they pounded the intermediate defences with their secondary armaments. Towards 2 p.m. the Narrows forts were nearly silenced. The French squadron was now recalled, and a relief inner squadron of six old British battleships (including the *Irresistible*) moved up. As the French withdrew, the *Bouvet* suffered a heavy explosion at 1.54 and sank in a few minutes with the loss of 640, nearly her whole complement. It was thought that a shell had burst in her magazine. The relieving squadron advanced in pairs, each in turn, to a 10,000-yard range. The Narrows forts once more came to life; but the big guns were again practically silent by 4 p.m.

De Robeck now sent in the trawlers to clear the way for point-blank fire. They were unable to reach the Kephez minefield. When the mobile artillery of the intermediate defences poured a murderous fire on the sweepers, four trawlers turned and fled the Straits. The other two did not succeed even in getting their sweeps out; they, too, simply turned about.

Hard on the heels of the sweeper reverse, the *Inflexible* struck a mine at 4.11, took a serious list, and limped out of the Straits towards Tenedos. She was saved only by the fine seamanship of her Captain (R. F. Phillimore, well known in the Service as 'Fidgety Phil'). A few minutes later the *Irresistible* was also mined and drifted towards the Asiatic shore.

It was impossible for De Robeck to persist in the attack in the face of such losses, the fact that the intermediate forts were not yet controlled, and, above all, the uncertainty as to what had caused the losses. The attackers were in the dark as to what exactly had happened. They suspected that floating mines, sent down with the current, or torpedoes from shore tubes, had been responsible. It was not learned until much later that the real villain in the piece— 'it altered the whole course of history,' says Keyes—had been a little row of twenty moored mines a small Turkish steamer, the *Nousret*, had laid in Eren Keui Bay parallel to the shore in the early morning of 8 March. Minesweepers had swept the general area several times, and reported it clear. They worked on the assumption that if they found nothing in the central part of the channel, the sides would certainly be clear! Seaplanes had located nothing suspicious.

At 5 p.m. the Admiral decided to recall his ships from the Straits. At 6.05 the *Ocean*, while going to the aid of the *Irresistible*, ran into the *Nousret* minefield. Both battleships foundered during the night. And so ended the action of 18 March.

Over 600 officers and men were lost because of the mines (mainly from the *Bouvet*); only about 20 were killed or wounded by the Turkish guns. Of the sixteen big ships engaged, three battleships had been sunk, and three others, including a battle cruiser, were *hors de combat*: the *Inflexible*, which was put out of action for six weeks, and the French battleships *Gaulois* and *Suffren*, which were seriously damaged by gunfire. For this steep price in men and *matériel*, it was learned after the war, two 14-inch guns and two or three smaller ones in the forts were put out of action and a few other guns were disabled temporarily. Not a single gun protecting the minefield was damaged, and the main minefield was untouched. On the other hand (and here the warnings about the folly of ships engaging forts had proved groundless), the Turkish guns had done negligible damage, although the action lasted nearly seven hours, during which the ships were practically sitting ducks. The minefield, not the guns, had been the principal barrier, because some of the ships, at least, might have forced their way past the forts, which had been severely shaken.

It did not help that the operation was such a poorly planned one. For instance, a fair number of the best type of spotting aeroplanes and a number of fast sweepers would have offered a better prospect of success. Five inferior seaplanes had been used. These, carried by the *Ark Royal*, were early types, unable to get up much above 2,000 feet. The trawlers with their sweeps out had been able to make only about 3 knots against the current. Admiral of the Fleet Lord Cunningham, who as a young officer served at the Dardanelles, was never able to understand why the eight 'Beagle' class destroyers—'fully as efficient as fast minesweepers'—were not used. Their officers 'spent the afternoon playing bridge, listening to the bombardment, and intercepting wireless reports as to the progress of the action. It was exasperating, to say the least.'[32] Fully as exasperating to some observers at the time was the way secrecy had been disregarded. Hankey told General Haig (3 April) that the operation had been run 'like an American Cinema Show', meaning, said Haig, 'the wide advertisement which had been given to every step long before anything had actually been done'.[33]

Later in the war, Enver Pasha, the Turkish War Minister, was supposed to have said: 'If the English had only had the courage to rush more ships through the Dardanelles, they could have got to Constantinople; but their delay enabled us thoroughly to fortify the Peninsula and in six weeks' time we had taken down there over 200 Austrian Skoda guns.'[34] General Liman von Sanders and other enemy sources testified after the war that the defenders were demoralized, being desperately short of mines and shells.

If these reports, made long afterwards, were accurate, it is possible that the attack would have succeeded, had it been renewed within a few days (or perhaps even within a couple of weeks) and been aided by the troops on the spot, and especially if it had been combined with reorganized sweeping. 'That is the tragedy of Gallipoli,' sighs Philip Magnus, making use of the historian's prerogative of hindsight. Churchill has written in similar terms. The factor of Turkish morale, however—assuming it can be taken at face value—was not known to the attackers.[35] Moreover, and this remained the key consideration, the main forts

---

[32] Cunningham of Hyndhope, *A Sailor's Odyssey* (London, 1951), p. 65.

[33] Robert Blake (ed.), *The Private Papers of Douglas Haig* (London, 1952), p. 90.

[34] *The World Crisis*, ii. 264.

[35] But the Admiralty was aware of the Turkish ammunition shortage. See Churchill's telegram of 24 March to De Robeck, below, p. 256. The status of Turkish morale is a moot point. There is evidence that the repulse of the naval attack had actually strengthened the morale of the garrison.

had been severely damaged, *but not the minefield defences*. The failure on the 18th was owing to mines and not the Turkish guns (although the Turks thought their batteries had sunk the ships). The action pointed up once more the dilemma that 'the battleships could not force the Straits until the mine field had been cleared—the mine field could not be cleared until the concealed guns which defended them were destroyed—they could not be destroyed until the Peninsula was in our hands, hence we should have to seize it with the Army. Any main operations must therefore be postponed until such time as preparations for a combined attack could be made.'[36]

De Robeck was depressed over the results on the 18th. He spoke of 'disaster' and expected his immediate supersession. This mood vanished and he turned rather cheerful following meetings on the morning of the 19th with Wemyss and Keyes, although, as we shall see, their advice was contradictory. The buoyant Chief of Staff was 'coldly confident' after the action on the 18th that success was within their grasp. His optimism was founded on his impression when he had steamed into the Straits in a destroyer the night after the action looking for the *Irresistible* and *Ocean*. He had seen and heard nothing; the Turks seem to have shot their bolt. He 'had a most indelible impression that we were in the presence of a beaten foe. . . . it only remained for us to organise a proper sweeping force and devise some means of dealing with drifting mines to reap the fruits of our efforts.'[37] De Robeck and Keyes agreed on the immediate reorganization of the sweeper force. The latter also pointed out that the old battleships *Queen* and *Implacable*, due shortly, were better ships than the lost pair. The C.-in-C.'s first telegrams after the action (19, 20 March) revealed his intention of having 'another "go" ' at the Turks.

If ever the purely naval operations were going to be called off, this was the time, after the 18 March repulse. It had been the understanding from the start that this would be done if the Turkish resistance proved tough. Yet, despite Fisher's warning (he had said it before) that twelve battleships would be lost before the Navy alone could force the Dardanelles—the losses on the 18th were only the beginning—there was agreement at the

[36] Admiral of the Fleet Lord Wester Wemyss, *The Navy in the Dardanelles Campaign* (London, 1924), pp. 41-2.
[37] Keyes, *Naval Memoirs*, i. 245.

Admiralty, even on Fisher's part, that the naval operations must continue despite the losses.

The First Lord was not discouraged by the setback on the 18th. 'I regarded it as only the first of several days' fighting, though the loss in ships sunk or disabled was unpleasant. It never occurred to me for a moment that we should not go on, within the limits of what we had decided to risk, till we reached a decision one way or the other. I found Lord Fisher and Sir Arthur Wilson in the same mood. Both met me that morning (the 19th) with expressions of firm determination to fight it out.'[38] Churchill felt it necessary to reassure Fisher that the 18th was without significance. 'I doubt if all told we have 150 casualties. Remember, we cannot man the monitors and the new ships without laying up most of the old battleships. As long as the crews are saved, there is no cause for serious regret. You and A.K.W. [Wilson] were splendid yesterday [at the War Council] . . .'[39]

The War Council had on 19 March (its last meeting until 14 May) authorized the continuation of naval operations if De Robeck agreed. Churchill now telegraphed the Admiral (midnight, 19/20 March) in encouraging terms, adding that, in addition to the *Queen* and *Implacable*, en route, they had just sent out two more old battleships, the *London* and *Prince of Wales*. The French were sending out the *Henri IV* as replacement for the *Bouvet*. De Robeck replied (21 March): 'From experience gained on 18th, I consider that the forts at the Narrows, and the batteries guarding the minefields, can be dominated, after a few hours' engagement, sufficiently to enable minesweepers to clear Kephez minefield.'[40] He proposed to proceed as soon as the reorganized sweeping force was ready: destroyers were being fitted as sweepers, etc. Apparently he was not going to wait for military assistance, especially since Hamilton had told him on the 19th that he could not move until he had reorganized his army at Alexandria and Port Said.

The Generals did not share the Admiral's confidence that the fleet could get through alone. Indeed, the Army, which was not ready to undertake serious land operations yet, was rather annoyed with what it regarded as the premature attack of

[38] *Dardanelles Commission.*
[39] Churchill to Fisher, 20 Mar. 1915; Lennoxlove MSS.
[40] Keyes, *Naval Memoirs*, i. 255–6.

18 March. 'We had hoped,' wrote the D.M.O., 'that the fleet would not have been quite so definitely committed until we were in a position to land considerable bodies of men at various points to follow up any advantage gained.'[41]

Hamilton and Birdwood, after watching the bombardment, were now positive that the Navy could not do the job alone, 'and that if the Army is to participate its operations will not assume the subsidiary form anticipated. The Army's share will not be a case of landing parties for the destruction of forts, etc., but rather a case of a deliberate and progressive military operation carried out in force in order to make good the passage of the Navy.'[42] Kitchener, who was by now of the same mind, telegraphed Hamilton later that day that the passage of the Dardanelles had to be forced, even 'if large military operations on the Gallipoli Peninsula by the Army are necessary to clear the way . . .'[43] Hamilton, in the opinion of the Dardanelles Commission, was justified in regarding Kitchener's telegram as a 'peremptory instruction that he was to take the Peninsula'. But the Generals were agreed that the initiative for the change in strategy must come from the seamen.

Everything hinged on De Robeck, who as late as the 21st was 'prepared to go forward irrespective of the Army'. He had been having second thoughts, perhaps as a delayed reaction to Wemyss' advice to him on the 19th, which was to hold up 'any main operations . . . until such time as preparations for a combined attack could be made'. The Admiral exploded a bombshell on the morning of 22 March. The occasion was a conference of the Generals and Admirals on board the *Queen Elizabeth* at Mudros. 'The moment we sat down de Robeck told us *he was now quite clear he could not get through without the help of all my troops*.'[44] Hamilton had not been joyful about the prospect of sending up troopships, storeships, and colliers in the face of the mine danger, even if the

[41] Callwell to Fisher, 20 Mar. 1915; Lennoxlove MSS. Birdwood, C.-in-C., Anzac Corps, said the same thing later. 'From my experience it would not have been possible to have landed before the middle of April, and that being so, the Navy should not have gone in, in my opinion, in advance and given away the show before that time.' *Dardanelles Commission.*

[42] Hamilton to Kitchener, 19 March (received *after* the War Council of that morning); *Dardanelles Commission.*

[43] *Ibid.*

[44] Diary, 22 Mar. 1915; General Sir Ian Hamilton, *Gallipoli Diary* (London, 1920, 2 vols.), i. 41.

fleet had got through. He, therefore, needed no convincing by De Robeck on the 22nd. 'So there was no discussion. At once we turned our faces to the land scheme.' The decision was to discontinue the naval attack in favour of a joint operation as soon as the Army was ready to occupy the Peninsula. This, Hamilton said, could not be before 14 April.

What had happened to alter the Admiral's thinking? Keyes suggests that the responsibility for a second attack, in the light of the severe losses of the first one, was too much for his Chief. Here is how De Robeck himself explained to the Commission his complete change in plan.

De Robeck. I think it was obvious [from the Turkish resistance on the 18th] then that the Turk was not going to give in easily; he was going to fight the whole way; and what one had been led to suppose, namely, that if we issued with the Fleet or arrived at Constantinople with the Fleet, there would be a change of Turkish Government, went by the board. It appeared clear that we had to fight the whole way and if we went to Constantinople we should have to go there with troops as well as ships.

Q. Was it your opinion then that as regards the ships they could only possibly get into the Sea of Marmora by destroying the forts and guns completely?—*A.* Yes. If you are talking about the forts—those low down ones, yes, perhaps we could have destroyed them; but the guns they placed on the hills and the howitzers and so on, we could not have destroyed.

Q. Was it evident to you on March 23 that if you did get the Fleet through into the Sea of Marmora your lines of communication would not be clear?—*A.* Quite.

Q. And was that the dominating consideration which, after consultation with Sir Ian Hamilton, you settled?—*A.* Yes, I think it was obvious we had to fight the whole way and we could not expect to finish the whole operation in a week by appearing at Constantinople—there had to be a campaign in the Marmora.

Q. So it was obvious to you that you would first of all require the army to keep the lines of communication?—*A.* Yes. . . .

Q. Were those the two dominant considerations which weighed with you in coming to the conclusion which was then telegraphed?—*A.* Yes, that it was necessary to hold the Peninsula.[45]

Keyes, who had kept his counsel at the big conference, was 'sick as a she-bear robbed of her cubs that his pets: battleships, T.B.s

[45] *Dardanelles Commission.*

[torpedo boats], destroyers, submarines, etc., should have to wait for the Army'.[46] Later that day he tried to persuade his Chief that they should not give the Turks time to improve their defences. They should renew the naval attack without waiting for the Army. He held that the key to success lay in clearing the minefield, the 'only real obstacle', and he was confident this could be done once the reorganized, 'thoroughly belligerent minesweeping and netting force' was ready, which meant about 4 April. Volunteers from the *Ocean* and *Irresistible* were being prepared for service in the trawler sweepers (most of whose crews were permitted to return to England), eight destroyers were being fitted as sweepers, and other preparations were being rushed. Keyes never doubted, then or afterwards, 'that from the 4th April, 1915, onwards, the Fleet could have forced the Straits, and with losses trifling in comparison with those the Army suffered, could have entered the Marmora with sufficient force to destroy the Turco-German fleet. This operation could have cut the communications—which were sea-borne—of any Turkish armies either in Gallipoli or on the Asiatic side, and would have led immediately to a victory decisive upon the whole course of the War.'[47] All this sounds fine, only Keyes did not face up to the problem of how the naval guns could silence the protecting batteries at the Narrows. Certainly the results on the 18th gave no cause for optimism on the results of a second attack.

De Robeck preferred to make certain by waiting the extra days till the Army was ready to co-operate by seizing the Peninsula below the Narrows. His telegram to the Admiralty on 23 March ran:

At a meeting to-day with Generals Birdwood and Hamilton was informed by the latter that the Army will not be ready to commence military operations until the 14th April.

All guns of position guarding the Straits must be destroyed, in order to keep up our communications when the Fleet gets through the Sea of Marmora. These guns are numerous, and not more than a small proportion of them can be put out of action by gun-fire. . . . It does not appear to me practicable to land a sufficient force inside the Dardanelles to carry out this service. This view is shared by General Hamilton. On the other hand failure to destroy the guns may well

[46] Diary, 24 Mar. 1915; Hamilton, *Gallipoli Diary*, i. 50.
[47] Keyes, *Naval Memoirs*, i. 186.

nullify any success of the Fleet, by enabling the Straits to be closed up, after the ships have gone through, and there may not then be ships available to keep the Straits open, as losses may be heavy.

Until the Sea of Marmora is reached, the mine menace, which is much greater than we expected, will remain. This requires careful and thorough treatment, both in respect of mines and floating mines. Time will be required for this, but arrangements can be made by the time the Army will be ready.

A decisive operation about the middle of next month, appears to me better than to take great risks for what may well be only half measures. . . .

I think it will be necessary to take and occupy the Gallipoli Peninsula by land forces before it will be possible for first-rate ships, capable of dealing with the *Goeben*, to be certain of getting through, and for colliers and other vessels, upon which the usefulness of the big ships largely depends, to get through.[48]

This telegram, received at the Admiralty at 6.30 a.m. on the 23rd, was read by Churchill

with consternation. I feared the perils of the long delay; I feared still more the immense and incalculable extension of the enterprise involved in making a military attack on a large scale. The mere process of landing an army after giving the enemy at least three weeks' additional notice seemed to me a most terrible and formidable hazard. . . . Moreover, what justification was there for abandoning the naval plan on which hitherto all our reasoning and conclusions had been based? The loss of life in the naval operations had been very small. In the whole operation only one ship of importance (the *Inflexible*) had been damaged . . . As for the old battleships, they were doomed in any case to the scrap-heap. Every ship lost was being replaced. . . . Why turn and change at this fateful hour and impose upon the Army an ordeal of incalculable severity? An attack by the Army if it failed would commit us irrevocably in a way no naval attack could have done. The risk was greater; the stakes were far higher.[49]

As he told the Dardanelles Commission, 'I believed then, as I believe now, that we were separated by very little from complete success.' He lost no time in convening the War Staff Group and putting before it a draft telegram ordering De Robeck to renew the attack 'at the first favourable opportunity' and to 'persevere methodically but resolutely'. He should 'dominate the forts at the

[48] *Dardanelles Commission.*
[49] *The World Crisis*, ii. 233.

Narrows and sweep the minefield and then batter the forts at close range . . .' 'For the first time since the war began,' Churchill relates, 'high words were used around the octagonal table.' Everybody was against him except Bartolomé. Oliver, Fisher, Wilson, and Jackson would not support him. The last three had never shared the First Lord's enthusiasm for the naval campaign. De Robeck's telegram gave them the ammunition they needed to stand firm. 'Lord Fisher took the line,' Churchill has recorded, 'that hitherto he had been willing to carry the enterprise forward because it was supported and recommended by the Commander on the spot. But now that Admiral de Robeck and Sir Ian Hamilton had decided upon a joint operation, we were bound to accept their views.'[50]

Churchill discussed the matter with Balfour and Asquith and found them sympathetic. The Prime Minister noted that De Robeck 'seems to be in rather a funk' and 'the naval experts seem to be suffering from a fit of nerves'. He agreed with Kitchener and Churchill that 'the Navy ought to make another big push as soon as the weather clears. If they wait and wait until the Army is fully prepared they may fall into a spell of bad weather or find that submarines, Austrian or German, have arrived on the scene.'[51] Asquith did not pretend to understand the technical considerations. He only knew that the delay was 'very unfortunate. Visible progress and, still more, a theatrical coup in that quarter would have goaded all the laggard States into the arena.'[52] But neither he nor the First Lord would overrule the Board, especially since the Generals on the spot were of the same opinion as the Admirals. Churchill bowed to his professional advisers and De Robeck 'with regret and anxiety'—but not before he made an attempt to change De Robeck's mind. His long reasoned telegram of 24 March, agreed to with extreme reluctance by Fisher, did not mention that the War Staff Group had already decided the matter!

What has happened since the 21st to make you alter your intention of renewing the attack as soon as the weather is favourable? We have

[50] *The World Crisis*, ii. 234. Churchill claims he had Oliver's support: 'The Chief of Staff was quite ready to order the renewal of the attack . . .' *Ibid.* Oliver's testimony does not bear him out. He was prepared to go along with the amphibious operation, as recommended by De Robeck and Hamilton, who were 'fully conversant with the circumstances'. *Dardanelles Commission.*

[51] Diary, 23, 24 Mar. 1915; Asquith, *Memories and Reflections*, ii. 80–1.

[52] Diary, 5 Apr. 1915; *ibid.*, p. 86.

never contemplated a reckless rush over minefields and past undamaged primary guns. But the original Admiralty instructions and telegram No. 109 [to Carden, 15 March] prescribe a careful and deliberate method of advance, and I should like to know what are the reasons which, in your opinion, render this no longer possible, in spite of your new aircraft and improved methods of minesweeping. We know the forts are short of ammunition. It is probable that they have not got many mines. You should be able to feel your way while at the same time pressing hard.[53]

The First Lord's appeal had no effect on the C.-in-C., who on the 26th telegraphed the Admiralty: 'For the Fleet to attack the Narrows now would jeopardise the success of a better and bigger scheme and would, therefore, be a mistake.'[54] The next day he sent off to Churchill a full, clear, and forceful appreciation of the situation which in essence repeated the main points in his telegram of 23 March: (1) mines commanded by mobile field batteries could not be swept until infantry silenced the guns; (2) that forts could be destroyed by gunfire alone had been 'conclusively proved to be wrong'; (3) so long as the forts were intact, it would not be practicable to supply the fleet, even if it were able to bull its way into the Marmora. These considerations argued cogently for the occupation of the Gallipoli Peninsula. A combined operation would effect 'decisive and overwhelming results'.[55]

The arguments in this telegram were, writes Churchill, 'decisive. At the Admiralty they consolidated all the oppositions to action.' The First Lord with profound reluctance agreed to the Admiral's proposals (27 March). He laments that the Admiral was actuated by a 'sentimental' regard for his old battleships. They were 'sacred' to him. 'They had been the finest ships afloat in the days when he as a young officer had first set foot upon their decks. The discredit and even disgrace of casting away a ship was ingrained by years of mental training and outlook. The spectacle of this noble structure on which so many loyalties centred . . . foundering miserably beneath the waves, appeared as an event shocking and unnatural in its character.'[56] This accusation is unfair to De Robeck and makes little sense. The Admiral's decision was based

---

[53] *The World Crisis*, ii. 235–7.
[54] *Dardanelles Commission.*
[55] *The World Crisis*, ii. 244–7.
[56] *Ibid.*, p. 244.

on hard facts, not sentiment, and required considerable moral courage.

No definite decision was made by the Cabinet, nor by the War Council. Rather was it generally understood after about 23 March that a joint operation on a large scale directed towards the occupation of the Peninsula was the next move. The Dardanelles Commission summed up the political and strategic considerations that tipped the scales:

During this period negotiations took place for the intervention of Italy on the side of the Allies; and the course of these negotiations made it undesirable to discontinue operations after the failure of the naval attack. . . .

In addition, the failure to penetrate the German lines at the battle of Neuve Chapelle and in the Champagne (Perthes) had strengthened the view that a stalemate had set in in the West. The need for relieving the pressure in the Caucasus still existed. The urgency of opening up a line of communications, first to supply Russia with munitions and military stores, and secondly, to enable the Russian harvest of 1914 to be exported and thus reestablish the Russian exchanges, had not diminished. And undoubtedly the fear existed that to abandon the enterprise might have had a bad effect in Russia.

These considerations, together with the fact that the military difficulties had not been sufficiently realised, seem to have led to the decision to initiate the joint naval and military attack on the Gallipoli Peninsula.[57]

Churchill's heart must have ached when he wrote this epitaph on the Dardanelles adventure:

Henceforth the defences of the Dardanelles were to be reinforced by an insurmountable mental barrier. A wall of crystal, utterly immovable, began to tower up in the Narrows, and against this wall of inhibition no weapon could be employed. The 'No' principle had become established in men's minds, and nothing could ever eradicate it. . . . Instead [of renewing the attack upon the Narrows], they [the Fleet] waited for nine months the spectators of the sufferings, the immense losses and imperishable glories of the Army, always hoping that their hour of intervention would come, always hoping for their turn to run every risk and make every sacrifice, until in the end they had the sorrow and mortification of taking the remains of the Army off and steaming away under the cloak of darkness from the scene of irretrievable failure.[58]

[57] *Dardanelles Commission.*
[58] *The World Crisis*, ii. 252–3.

We can safely give the remainder of the Dardanelles operation cursory treatment in this and in a later chapter, since it now became an amphibious campaign with the role of the Navy confined to subsidiary operations—covering landings of the Army, supplying the Army, supporting it by fire, etc. 'The army thenceforth became the principal agent, and the control of events rested with the War Office and not the Admiralty' (Churchill).

The preparations for the joint operation were handled stupidly. Never since the Crimean War had a military expedition been dispatched in so haphazard a fashion. The element of surprise was forfeited from the beginning. Mudros harbour swarmed with ships, its shores were alive with people, and the Egyptian press was permitted to report Allied troop arrivals and their destination.

On 25 April, everything being ready at last and the weather having improved, the Army's 'glorious effort and tragic failure' began. The objective of the famous Battle of the Beaches was to secure the high ground overlooking the Narrows. Once the heights were occupied, the forts could be silenced and the fleet would then try again to get through. After severe fighting and heavy casualties, landings of 29,000 men were effected on the toe of the Peninsula at Cape Helles, and at Anzac (as it was hereafter to be called), just above Gabe Tepe, on the Aegean coast 13 miles north of Cape Helles. The operation was only a half-success, as it became apparent by 8 May that nothing further could be achieved without reinforcements.

A War Council was held on 14 May to assess the situation and decide whether it was worth while to persist with the operation on the Peninsula. Apart from the military prospects, three considerations weighed heavily: (1) Given the uncertainty of the Balkan States, especially Bulgaria, it was important to do nothing which would reflect weakness; (2) an abandonment of the Gallipoli venture would have a very bad effect upon British prestige in the East; (3) the campaign had so far, in the Russian view, relieved Turkish military pressure on Russia. The sense of the Council was that reinforcements be sent out for a fresh assault. But no final decision was reached. The political crisis then intervened.

3. POST-MORTEM

At the time and for years afterwards Churchill was the public scapegoat for the disastrous first phase of the campaign. He was almost universally held directly responsible for the failure because of his alleged interference in matters of tactics and strategy. Typical was the outburst of the *Morning Post* leader (23 April 1915), under the heading 'The Dardanelles Blunder': British 'constitutional theory has no place for a civilian Minister who usurps the functions of his Board, takes the wheel out of the sailor's hand, and launches ships upon a naval operation. . . . We have seen, at Antwerp, in the case of Cradock's squadron, and in this disaster of the Dardanelles, how a nation is punished which persists in allowing its politicians to conduct naval operations.' So bitter was the feeling against the (by then) ex-First Lord that a 'distinguished diarist' could write in a late stage of the campaign, 'If Winston were to put his foot near the Peninsula I believe he would be scragged alive.'[59] Wemyss charged that Churchill's name would be 'handed down to posterity as that of a man who undertook an operation of whose requirements he was entirely ignorant'. When the *First Report* was published, *The Times* made this observation (9 March 1917): 'He was at least consistent in his purpose when all the rest were vacillating. But it was the consistency of a dangerous enthusiast, who sought expert advice only where he could be sure of moulding it to his own opinion, and unconsciously deceived both himself and his colleagues about the real character of his technical support.' Post-war comments have, in general, been no less harsh, as, for example:

To use the naval plan to kindle 'tremendous hopes'; to let the doubters suppose that it could be broken off if it was not successful, and then, when it proved unsuccessful, to reinforce the 'tremendous hopes' by the 'dire necessity' of going on—this may have been the way to 'light up men's minds' and to 'wrest an army from France and Flanders' but it was not the way to procure a cool and objective examination of either the naval or the amphibious plan on its merits, or to secure the correct timing and sequence of the two operations, if both were accepted.[60]

[59] Cited in John North, *Gallipoli: the Fading Vision* (London, 1936), p. 54.
[60] J. A. Spender and Cyril Asquith, *Life of Henry Asquith, Lord Oxford and Asquith* (London, 1932, 2 vols.), ii. 162.

The charges have been exaggerated. There is no denying that Churchill was the prime mover in the Dardanelles adventure. The main responsibility for the conception and a large responsibility for the inauguration of the campaign and for its continuation beyond the point of no return rest with him. Jellicoe is undoubtedly right when he says, 'Churchill's insistent pressure is what prevented the "breaking off". Of that there can be no doubt.'[61]

In retrospect, historians have come to evaluate the Dardanelles conception as a magnificent one, indeed as the most brilliant strategic conception of the entire war. Wisdom after the event may even suggest that the principal Allied effort in 1915 should have been made at the Dardanelles and Gallipoli. If the Straits could have been forced and Constantinople taken, it would have given the Allies free access to Russia, rallied the Balkan states against Turkey and Austria, cut off supplies to the Turkish armies in Gallipoli and Asia Minor, forced the Turks to sue for peace, and rendered unnecessary the Salonika and Palestine campaigns. Such results might have shortened the war by one year and possibly two, have kept Czarist Russia afloat and the world safe from Communism. At a reunion of Gallipoli veterans in 1957, Lord Attlee, himself an army survivor of the campaign, paid this tribute to Churchill: Gallipoli 'was an immortal gamble that did not come off . . . Sir Winston had the one strategic idea in the war. He did not believe in throwing away masses of people to be massacred.'

As regards the actual plan of campaign and its execution, it is not true to say that Churchill overrode his expert advisers. Graham Greene, the Secretary of the Admiralty, has made it perfectly clear that important questions relating to the operations were discussed at War Staff Group meetings, and when decisions were reached, they were often embodied in minutes dictated by the First Lord and concurred in by the First Sea Lord. '. . . no order of any importance was issued without the approval, or concurrence, of both the First Lord and First Sea Lord, who were the principal members of the Board concerned, though sometimes orders had to be given without the prior sanction of either the First Lord or the First Sea Lord.'[62]

[61] Jellicoe Marginalia, *The World Crisis*, ii. 215.
[62] 'Dardanelles Operations', a memorandum prepared for the Dardanelles Commission, Aug. 1916; Graham Greene MSS.

This is not to say that Churchill bears no responsibility for the botching of a magnificent conception. In the first place, he overestimated the value of naval guns with flat trajectory against land defences. The Australian Official History puts the matter harshly: '. . . the fallacy of Churchill's theories as to naval gun fire has been proved by the blood of thousands . . .'[63] He recognized early one respect where he had gone wrong. He told a confidant that 'his calculations had in a measure been put out by the mobility of the Turkish guns, which enabled them to train readily on the ships which were confined in a narrow area'.[64] Yet, if we are to convict Churchill on this count, we must associate expert Admiralty opinion with him. It was, nevertheless, not so much the ineffective gunfire as the inefficient minesweeping that prevented the passage of the fleet, and for this Churchill's was not the primary responsibility.

In the second place, the naval operations, which served to warn the Turks, should never have been undertaken until an adequate army was available. The initial mistake was, then, to attack the forts alone, without waiting for the presence of an army that could occupy and hold the Gallipoli Peninsula. From this stemmed a succession of blunders. The lesson was not learned in time that combined operations was the only way of taking offensive action against a continental enemy. Although Churchill did all he could to get troops sent to the Dardanelles, this does not absolve him from the error of imagining that the fleet alone could deal with the situation, and from the blame of pushing through the attempt to force the Straits without troops. 'I wish to make it clear,' he wrote to the War Secretary, 'that the naval operations in the Dardanelles cannot be delayed for troop movements, as we must get into the Marmora as soon as possible in the normal course.'[65] The conception of a one-sided naval operation was due mainly to Churchill's impetuosity, even if Asquith and Kitchener were of the same mind as the First Lord. 'Winston was always in a hurry', Lord Attlee has written of Churchill in World War II. 'He didn't like to wait for the pot to boil, you know.' This appraisal equally fits the First Lord of 1914-15. Declared Richmond at the time,

[63] C. E. W. Bean, *The Official History of Australia in the War of 1914-18. The Story of Anzac* (Sydney, 1921-4, 2 vols.), i. 504.

[64] Diary, 22 Apr. 1915; *Lord Riddell's War Diary*, p. 80.

[65] Churchill to Kitchener, 4 Mar. 1915; *The World Crisis*, ii. 195-6.

'He should have done as Sir John Norris did [1740] when he was told to force the entrance to Ferrol without an army, and told the Council that it was impossible.'[66] (The attack upon Ferrol by the fleet alone was abandoned, but the Prime Minister vetoed Norris's proposal of a joint expedition.)

In the third place, he failed to present fully to the War Council the opinions of his professional advisers. A glaring instance was the War Council of 28 January.

In the fourth place, Churchill should have relied more on his professional advisers and on the War Staff, even though the latter was not a fully developed organization. Considered Staff appreciations were not asked for, except for two appreciations from Admiral Jackson on the 5th and 15th of January.

The planning and preparation of the operation were, of course, another matter. The co-operation between the Admiralty and the War Office was something less than whole-hearted and adequate, and was worsened by the 'triangular tug-of-war' between Churchill, Fisher, and Kitchener. There was no investigation of the feasibility of the operations by a joint naval and military staff before they were attempted. The planning was too much departmentalized. The War Council concentrated its attention on the political ends and paid insufficient attention to the naval and military means for achieving them. (The secondary status of the professional experts is a factor here.) It was inexcusable that they did not elicit the opinions of all the experts who attended the meetings. And they made no attempt to secure from the General Staff and the Admiralty War Staff what Lord Hankey calls 'a proper balance sheet, a profit and loss account of the commitments involved in the Dardanelles operations . . . Probably the real reasons were the general confidence in Kitchener and (especially in Kitchener's mind) the need for secrecy.'[67]

The more I study the campaign, the more I am disposed to agree with Admiral Wemyss: 'The blame for this tragedy [120,000 men were lost before it was over] cannot be laid at the door of any one individual, but must be attributed to system, the system that places the direction of naval and military operations solely in the hands of men devoid of the knowledge and experience necessary for the task, and immune, moreover, from the consequences of

[66] Diary, 28 Apr. 1915; *Portrait of an Admiral*, p. 156.
[67] Hankey, *The Supreme Command*, i. 324.

their actions . . .'[68] To this basic weakness I would add the absence of a special section of the War Staff (there was no Plans Division until 1917) to examine with care and in the light of expert technical considerations the feasibility of an operation and to hammer out its preliminary details. Rear-Admiral F. H. Mitchell's Committee, which examined the Dardanelles defences after the war, emphasized the need to subject any such operation to careful staff investigation. 'There is little doubt that, if the matter had received the close attention of a fully constituted Naval Staff, certain matters, such as . . . the difficulties of the sweepers would have been cleared up by trial.'[69]

On the technical naval side, the real obstacles were the minefields of the Narrows, against which the minesweeping was utterly inefficient, and their protecting batteries, which the naval guns never silenced. The minefields were the crux of the situation, since the old battleships could evidently be sunk by striking one mine. To sweep the minefields was a hazardous matter. It could be accomplished only if the minefield batteries could be dominated while the sweeping was going on. But it was not possible for the warships to knock them out. Long-range or indirect fire proved ineffective. To be effective, the ships would have had to close in on the coastal guns and pound away, and this was not possible until the mines were cleared. Thus was the vicious circle completed.

Keyes is unfair in putting so much of the blame on the trawlers' crews. He accuses them of 'not playing their part'. But the sweeping was manifestly impossible unless the searchlights were destroyed first. When they were not destroyed, it was fantastic to expect unarmed trawlers, held in the searchlights and under a hot fire at short range, to continue methodically sweeping a passage. This side of the coin deserves to be elaborated.

Unlike the regular naval personnel, who had served for years under discipline in their battleships, cruisers, destroyers and submarines, and had been trained for war, and war alone, the trawlermen had received

---

[68] Wemyss, *The Navy in the Dardanelles Campaign*, p. 283. Lord Ismay, Hankey's post-war successor as Secretary of the C.I.D., has explained how the matter would have been handled if the expedition had been proposed in 1941, instead of in 1915. See the suggestive passage in *The Memoirs of General the Lord Ismay* (London, 1960), pp. 163–4.

[69] 'Report of Dardanelles Committee, Admiralty' (1919), p. 51, cited in the Naval Staff Monograph, *The Naval Staff of the Admiralty*, pp. 70–1.

fio real training before being sent oversea, and were a rough-and-ready crowd fiercely independent and conservative in their outlook.

Some men are naturally brave. Some men feel fear and do not show it; but steadfastness under shell-fire is largely produced by discipline, training and experience. Except in very rare cases it is not a natural human characteristic, and no General wishing to win a battle would put untrained and untried troops in the forefront of the engagement and expect them to comport themselves like Napoleon's Old Guard at Waterloo.

Yet this was what these rugged fishermen were apparently expected to do in the Dardanelles—to sweep minefields at night under the blinding glare of searchlights and heavy gunfire at ranges of 3,000 yards and less.[70]

Keble Chatterton cuts to the heart of the matter: 'The fishermen had been asked to do the Navy's job, and had no more succeeded than if the Navy had been sent to catch fish off Iceland.' Not only were there too few trawler minesweepers, but they were totally unsuitable for the job. They were wooden ships, and, with their sweeps out, were too slow to make much headway against the strong current. Once lit up by the searchlights they became sitting ducks for the mine batteries at a range of about a mile. It was asking too much of these ex-fishermen who manned the trawlers, and who had little experience of facing heavy gunfire, to carry on 'in their helpless and practically motionless little ships'.

The real culprits were not these undisciplined, untrained Grimsby and Hull fishermen, who had been hurriedly recruited for a task beyond their abilities; nor the officer in charge, who was handicapped by having himself had no previous sweeping experience. The responsibility lies rather with the proper authorities at the Admiralty for failing to organize an efficient personnel for this crucial test and to supply the minesweepers the squadron required. The reorganization of the minesweepers' personnel by 26 March (they were now manned mostly by naval ranks and ratings), as well as the fitting of destroyers with improvised sweeps, came a little late in the day, after the basic change in strategy had been as good as made.

Although the reorganized sweeper force consisted of eighty vessels at the end of April (only twenty-one trawlers, all slow, had been available as late as 18 March), nearly half of which could sweep at 14 knots, it is by no means certain that this force

[70] Taffrail, *Swept Channels*, pp. 153-4.

would have achieved any more success in sweeping a channel through the formidable mine barrier between Kephez and Chanak so long as the minefield batteries were intact *and the sweeping system was unaltered*. The latter was impracticable under the conditions at the Dardanelles. The sweep used throughout the war consisted of a 2½-inch wire, whose depth was regulated by a heavy wooden kite, towed between two sweepers steaming about 500 yards apart. Generally, the momentum of the sweep-wire could, in the case of fast sweepers, cut the moorings of mines. But until serrated wire was introduced in 1916 slow sweepers like trawlers usually had to circle slowly round a mine and drag it out to sea or into shallow water, where they could sink it by gunfire. This was, and could only be, a slow and deliberate process. It was complicated enough in daylight. (In Home waters this was the only time it was performed.) At the Dardanelles it had to be carried out at night and under heavy fire.

One by-product of the Dardanelles was the strengthening of Admiralty opinion, at a time when Kitchener was still full of the dangers of invasion, that the enemy could not possibly land an army of 70,000 men on the British coast without first defeating the Royal Navy. After all, as A. K. Wilson pointed out, 'The opposition from the Turkish forces was probably much more formidable than an enemy would encounter on our coast', because the possible positions for landing in the Gallipoli Peninsula were very limited in number. In all other respects, however, the British had 'enormous advantages' at Gallipoli which the Germans would not have if they attempted invasion, such as: 'The [Gallipoli] coast was known to be clear of mines and there were no submarines by day or torpedo craft at night to be feared. Lighters were collected at Mudros and Tenedos in the immediate neighbourhood, and there was no possibility of their being interfered with while being towed to the points of landing until they actually came under the fire of the shore.'[71]

The naval phase of the Dardanelles campaign represented a disastrous episode in the careers of Churchill and Fisher. It led directly to their removal from the Admiralty and the inner war councils of the Government, so robbing the country of two men of genius from its small store of men of exceptional talent. To this sad story we must now direct our attention.

[71] Wilson's memorandum of 13 May 1915.

XI

The May Crisis

(MAY 1915)

I look upon it as a *sine qua non* that the First Lord and the First Sea Lord should be like Siamese twins, otherwise the business could not go on.

FISHER at the Dardanelles Inquiry, 11 October 1916.

The situation is curious—two very strong and clever men, one old, wily and of vast experience, one young, self-assertive, with a great self-satisfaction but unstable. They cannot work together, they cannot both run the show.

BEATTY to Lady Beatty, 4 December 1914.

I. PERSONAL FACTORS

THERE had been, as we have seen, various disagreements between Fisher and Churchill, minor (e.g., over mining policy and Fisher's uncontrollable urge to sack incompetents) and major (e.g., over Zeppelin matters). The breaking point for Fisher came in May, and the direct cause was, simply and purely, the Dardanelles campaign—the profound disagreement over the depletion of the Navy in Home waters to provide reinforcements for the Dardanelles. This is not the whole story.

There was a set of important underlying causes of the May crisis, beginning with the incompatibility in temperament and outlook of the two principals, which prevented them from working very long together in harmony. They had great personal admiration, respect, and even a certain fondness for each other, and were able to work for a time in perfect amity. 'I am attached to the old boy,' Churchill wrote to the Prime Minister just before the May crisis. And yet a break may have been inevitable from the first, for here were two autocrats—two men of strong personality, with brilliant intellects and active minds, each accustomed to being absolutely supreme in any work he undertook, and each intolerant of criticism or opposition. 'Neither of them intended to budge an inch, and the final stages of the controversy resembled the collision of two powerful but uncongenial chemicals.'

A second underlying cause of the ultimate clash between the two friends was their difference in habits. Admiral Bacon and Captain T. E. Crease, Fisher's Naval Assistant, have made much of this peculiar cause. Fisher invariably awoke between 4 and 5 a.m., had a cup of tea and plunged into work in bed, poring through telegrams and papers that had reached his office during the night, among them memoranda from the First Lord on all conceivable naval subjects. He did most of his best work that required concentration and clear thinking in these hours before breakfast. After breakfast he would go to his office, but when his mind was agitated, as through annoyance with Churchill, he would attend matins at Westminster Abbey before the War Staff Group meeting or other current work of the day, in order to restore his equanimity. He had pretty well had it by six or seven, when, usually after a final talk with the First Lord, he went home to dinner. He rarely returned to his office, and he ordinarily retired early, around 9 p.m.

Churchill kept very different hours. Up at 8, he stayed in bed till very late in the morning. 'He presented a most extraordinary spectacle, perched up in a huge bed, with the whole of the counterpane littered with dispatch boxes, red and all colours, and a stenographer sitting at the foot—Mr. Churchill himself with an enormous Corona Corona in his mouth, a glass of warm water on the table by his side and a writing-pad on his knee!'[1] He would usually start his day at the Admiralty at 10 a.m. The important hours for him were from about 10 p.m. until 1 a.m. After a post-luncheon nap, he would return to his office and work until dinner. Refreshed by good food and drink and by congenial society, he would go into high gear, 'starting the nightly strafe of memoranda, full of brilliant ideas that seldom could be taken seriously in the morning.'[2] He worked until one or two in the morning. It was during this period of the day that he prepared most of the important minutes and memoranda that he sent to Fisher.

The effect often was [writes Crease] that Lord Fisher, having as he thought settled up all outstanding matters with the First Lord before

---

[1] Rear-Admiral Sir Douglas Brownrigg, *Indiscretions of the Naval Censor* (London, 1920), p. 12.

[2] Crease to Admiral Sir Reginald Hall, 7 Nov. 1932; Crease MSS.

going home to dinner, and having gone to bed soon after dinner, was confronted only a few hours later, in the early hours of the next morning, with an entirely fresh set of memoranda, minutes, proposals, suggestions, etc. In April and May of 1915 these nearly always dealt with various phases of the Dardanelles projects, and there is no doubt that at this time the procedure had become very irksome to him, and got on his nerves, so that he often started the day incensed against the First Lord. . . .

Lord Fisher latterly also resented Mr. Churchill's habit of discussing matters, more especially with regard to the Dardanelles, with Sir A. K. Wilson and Sir Henry Jackson before speaking with him and of thus coming to him with preconceived ideas.

I am sure that these, and other similar minor matters, had collectively considerable influence on Lord Fisher's attitude at this time towards Mr. Churchill. Personal trifles often disturb the relations of men more than differences of opinion on grave issues.[3]

There was a third underlying factor of a personal nature, revolving about Churchill's conception of his duties. Some people might suppose, as Asquith did, that the First Lord represented the collective judgment of his colleagues, but as a matter of fact he was under no obligation to consult the other members of the Board unless he thought fit to do so. The First Lord's sole responsibility to the Government and Parliament for all the business of the Admiralty was indisputable. It went back to the Order in Council of 1869. Presented by Gladstone to the Privy Council for the express purpose of enabling his henchman Mr. Childers to reduce the Navy in the teeth of the Sea Lords' opposition, it gave the First Lord absolute power on the Board. (How much responsibility and power the Sea Lords had before 1869 is a matter of dispute.) It was laid down that 'the First Lord being responsible to Your Majesty and Parliament for all the business of the Admiralty, the other Members of the Board should act as his Assistants in the transaction of the duties', and they were all made responsible to him. This wording was modified in the Order in Council of 19 March 1872, when Goschen was First Lord. The reference to the other members of the Board as assistants to the First Lord was dropped, and the Order in Council ran simply: 'The First Lord to be responsible to Your Majesty and to Parliament for all the business of the Admiralty', the various members

[3] Crease MSS.

of the Board and the Financial Secretary being made responsible to the First Lord for such business as he might assign to them individually. The wording was repeated in the Order in Council of 10 August 1904, which was in force when the war broke out. Expounded Graham Greene,

The question of the constitution of the Board has formed the subject of enquiry by Parliamentary Committees and much discussion from time to time, but since 1888 [when Beresford resigned his position as Fourth Sea Lord and raised the question on account of his differences with the First Lord and the First Sea Lord] there has been no serious attempt made to dispute the position laid down in 1869 and 1872. . . . it has [since 1888] never been questioned that the decision of the First Lord is final as regards matters coming under the administration of the Board, whether these matters are dealt with Departmentally or at a formal meeting of the Board.[4]

Of course, how strictly a First Lord interpreted the Orders in Council depended to a great extent on his personality. Thus, McKenna during his tenure as First Lord (1908–11) did not find it difficult to harmonize his sole responsibility with non-interference in professional matters. It was different in Churchill's time, particularly after the war began. Churchill felt 'it would be quite impossible for any First Lord to accept the whole of this burden [sole responsibility] and at the same time be deprived of proposing steps which may be proved to be necessary and right'.[5] He therefore chose to exercise the right to criticize, to propose, and to suggest.

Churchill's regular intervention in purely expert affairs irked Fisher, who believed strongly that such matters ought to be left for the Sea Lords and the technical departments to deal with. Two months of the ways of this gifted amateur were almost enough for the Admiral.

Winston has so monopolized all initiative in the Admiralty and fires off such a multitude of purely departmental memos (*his power of work is absolutely amazing!*) that my colleagues are no longer '*superintending Lords*,' but only '*the First Lord's Registry*'! I told Winston this yesterday and he did not like it at all, but *it is true*! and the consequence is that the Sea Lords are atrophied and their departments run really by the Private Office, and I find it a Herculean task to get back to the right

[4] Graham Greene's memorandum for Balfour (the First Lord), 1 Dec. 1915; Graham Greene MSS.
[5] *Dardanelles Commission.*

269

procedure, and quite possibly I may have to clear out, and I've warned Winston of this.[6]

Above all was Fisher more and more irritated by the First Lord's methods in dealing with telegrams, and in issuing often in his own name the executive orders to the fleets, squadrons, and ships. Crease wrote from first-hand observation: 'The telegrams quoted in his Book [*The World Crisis*] were, generally speaking, the result of discussion at the "War Group" in the Admiralty, and usually, if the First Lord prepared the consequent telegram, he sent the draft for Lord Fisher's concurrence. On some occasions Lord Fisher objected to a proposed telegram. But on other occasions no draft was sent.'[7] Therein lay the difficulty. Churchill never failed to consult the First Sea Lord, but he often initiated orders to the Fleet, and *then* consulted him.[8] There was nothing unconstitutional or illegal in this practice, since the First Lord was, in the words of a former First Lord, Sir James Graham, the 'supreme and controlling authority' at the Admiralty. But it certainly had not been the traditional procedure. As Graham Greene put the matter, 'I think that very few First Lords would attempt to deal with the initiation of orders to the Fleet, they would probably prefer to indicate their views on a point of policy and ask the First Sea Lord to have those instructions put into the form of orders to the Fleet.'[9] Here we have the nub of the matter. The First Lord was transgressing not his rights, but the accepted practice that only the First Sea Lord had the right of initiative, and after that his proposal should be sent to the First Lord for approval.

The Junior Sea Lords supported Fisher with an unsolicited minute addressed to him and Churchill on 16 May 1915: '. . . the present method of directing the distribution of the Fleet, and the conduct of the war by which the orders for controlling movements and supplies appear to be largely taken out of the hands of the First Sea Lord is open to very grave objection.'[10] Churchill replied

[6] Fisher to Jellicoe, 20 Dec. 1914; *Fear God and Dread Nought*, iii. 99–100.

[7] Crease MSS.

[8] Graham Greene confirmed that this was Churchill's practice: *Dardanelles Commission*. Fisher admitted at the Inquiry that, barring one lapse (see *Fear God and Dread Nought*, iii. 210), the First Lord had consulted him before sending out orders to the Fleet which were not initialled by him, Fisher.

[9] *Dardanelles Commission*.

[10] *Fear God and Dread Nought*, iii. 235. The other minutes in this exchange, which follow, are in the Hamilton MSS.

(17 May): 'No order of the slightest consequence affecting the movements of the Fleet and its distribution has ever been issued except with the authority and agreement of the First Sea Lord.' The Sea Lords agreed (18 May), while pointing out that the statement did not fully meet their contention. 'In most cases action has been initiated by yourself and referred to the First Sea Lord for concurrence. What we maintain is that all such orders should be initiated by the First Sea Lord and referred to you for criticism and concurrence.' The difference between the two methods is obvious. The same minute asked for an assurance that all the Sea Lords should be consulted and kept informed on large points of policy.

As regards the latter point, Churchill accepted (19 May) their claim and proposed in future to review the war situation in weekly meetings of the naval members of the Board under his presidency. No action was ever taken, since he left office very soon afterwards. Concerning the major point, Churchill conceded it was 'better that the First Sea Lord should make proposals and the First Lord criticise them or concur. But no rule can be laid down. Certainly under the Patent the First Lord has unquestioned power not only of veto but of initiative.'[11]

This brings us back to the central issue. Fisher and his naval colleagues thought that the First Lord, his rights notwithstanding, should not initiate orders to the Fleet; that their initiation by the First Lord was contrary to the spirit, if not to the letter, of the Letters Patent; and that all operational orders should be initiated by the First Sea Lord and then go to the First Lord for approval.

Most of Churchill's telegrams, moreover, leave the impression (as through his marking them 'private') that it was the First Lord speaking and not the Board. 'They speak for themselves,' Crease observes, 'and any Naval Officer reading them will see the reason for Lord Fisher's irritation, which was not decreased because as a rule there was nothing definite to which exception could be taken! . . . I had ample evidence of the irritation so caused, by the sulphurous (to use Mr. Churchill's own expression!) comments of Lord Fisher as he read his daily copies.'[12]

[11] Royal Letters Patent are letters, signed by the sovereign, used to put into commission powers inherent in the Crown—the executive powers, in this case, assigned to the Lords Commissioners of the Admiralty when a new Board is formed. A Board Patent is, then, a Royal Letters Patent.

[12] Crease MSS.

The basic trouble was that Churchill had acquired the habit during peacetime of speaking and acting on behalf of the Board of Admiralty on his own responsibility, since his First Sea Lords had been of different calibre and temperament from Lord Fisher. Nor did the Junior Sea Lords have the ability or forcefulness to keep the First Lord straight. In his eagerness to get on with the work he did not attach much importance, either in this or in other matters, to the form so long as the substance was secured, and doubtless he believed he was the best interpreter of the Admiralty instructions and views even in operational matters. As is well known, he exhibited exactly the same tendency in World War II of collecting the operational strings into his own hands. Sir Oswyn Murray, a longtime Secretary of the Admiralty (1917–1936), may well have had Churchill in mind when he wrote: 'In regard to professional questions, the First Lord's duty is really to collect, to co-ordinate, to test and to give effect to, the best professional advice. It is not the mark of a "strong" First Lord to be always trying to lead his professional advisers. . . . On the other hand when the questions discussed are mainly of an administrative character, the "strong" First Lord will see that his own experience and knowledge of affairs are vigorously brought to bear upon them, before he arrives at a decision.'[13]

Long before the May crisis Fisher had reluctantly become convinced on personal grounds that he and the First Lord could no longer work together. He did not carry out his many threats to resign, because of his loyalty to and affection for Churchill, his gratitude to the First Lord for having brought him back to the Admiralty, and because of Jellicoe's reiterated advice. The C.-in-C. pressed him to hold on, as he felt that Fisher 'could probably check Mr. Churchill's dangerous assumption of executive authority better than anyone else'.[14]

It needed a catalytic agent to bring matters to a head.

2. THE CATALYTIC AGENT: THE DARDANELLES

Fisher had agreed with extreme reluctance on 28 January not to resign and to support the operation. But it meant, as time went on and as he had foreseen, a gradual draining of Britain's naval

[13] Murray, 'The Admiralty. VIII. The Modern Board of Admiralty and the Nature of Its Responsibility', *Mariner's Mirror*, Jan. 1939.

[14] Jellicoe, 'A Reply to Criticism'.

resources from the decisive theatre of war, particularly after the 18 March operation. The naval demands of the Dardanelles were jeopardizing the superiority of the Grand Fleet that was so essential to the successful prosecution of the war.

From the end of March (at which date sixteen battleships and twenty-four destroyers were at the Dardanelles, to say nothing of aircraft, net-layers, monitors, repair ships, light cruisers), Fisher was full of fears about the possible consequences of the drain. 'I consider that we have now descended to the bare minimum of superiority in Home Waters, and that to dispatch any more fighting ships of any kind to the Dardanelles operations would be to court serious losses at home.'[15] He returned to this theme regularly. Jellicoe and the Sea Lords were in absolute agreement with him. Fisher went so far as to attempt to impose restrictions on the use of the *Queen Elizabeth* (that she be not risked inside the Straits) and the two 'Lord Nelsons', and to begrudge every piece of *matériel* and every reinforcement sent to De Robeck. His harassment reached the point where Churchill cried out, 'Seriously, my friend, are you not a little unfair in trying to spite this operation by side winds and small points when you have accepted it in principle?'[16]

Two events late in March underscored for Fisher the danger of continuing to draw heavily on home resources for the Dardanelles operations. The first was the report that the High Seas Fleet had started to sally forth on the 29th, and had been, Fisher believed, frightened back into port by 'the outburst of wireless . . . that told them they were found out, so they scuttled home . . .'[17] The second event was the menacing German attitude towards Holland in the last week of March. They were, intelligence reports indicated, putting pressure on the Dutch to declare for or against them, and the General Staff was pressing for a violent solution. Churchill was as anxious as Fisher about the possibility of a German combined attack on Holland. Among the counter moves considered at Whitehall, in the event of German military action, were the landing of troops (from Sir John French's command mainly) at the Hook of Holland, and the establishment of a submarine-

---

[15] Fisher to Churchill, 31 Mar. 1915; *Fear God and Dread Nought*, iii. 179.

[16] Churchill to Fisher, 11 Apr. 1915; *ibid.*, p. 194.

[17] Fisher to Jellicoe, 2 Apr. 1915; *ibid.*, p. 184. This High Seas Fleet reconnaissance, for such it was, is noteworthy as being the first occasion when airships were able to co-operate tactically with a fleet.

destroyer base at Terschelling. Fisher alerted Jellicoe and Beatty to the probability of the High Seas Fleet being drawn out by the British moves. '*This may happen at any moment,*' Fisher warned Beatty (26 March). The Dutch scare lifted in the second week of April. Hankey thought that the Russian victories in the Carpathians and the 'apparently menacing attitude' of Italy had made it less likely that the Germans would move against Holland for the time being. It was agreed at the Admiralty that the question of Holland wanted watching.

Fisher lived in expectation of some cunning move by the new and seemingly more aggressive German Naval Command. Reports on 17 April that the High Seas Fleet had once more ventured out, but had suddenly bolted home upon hearing British wireless, made Fisher all the more certain that the enemy was up to something and only awaited a favourable opportunity. He pointed out five important objects which Germany would seek to achieve by a success at sea: (1) to cause the retention of the new British army at home; (2) to cause the withdrawal of warships from the Dardanelles; (3) to lessen the possibility of early Italian and Rumanian intervention on the Allied side; (4) to ease the serious food shortage with which Germany was (reportedly) about to be faced; (5) to prevent the great supplies of ammunition due for delivery from the United States. 'The above considerations might not unreasonably be held to justify a desperate move on Germany's part.'[18] These possibilities emphasized the need to keep the Grand Fleet at maximum strength.

As regards the Dardanelles, Fisher was not optimistic about the prospects of success in the projected joint operation, 'the very biggest "gamble" that any government ever acceded to!' First reports after the landings convinced him the campaign was going to be a very rough one. 'But that comes from Winston's folly, supported by Mr. Balfour, in trying to do it alone with the Navy, and hence giving two months' time to enemy instead of a surprise.'[19]

The Army was at a complete deadlock by 9 May. The heavy

[18] Fisher to Churchill, 23 Apr. 1915; *ibid.*, pp. 202–3. These exact points had been made in a letter from Hankey to the Admiral on 22 April; Asquith MSS.

[19] Fisher to Jellicoe, 27 Apr. 1915; Lennoxlove MSS. Jellicoe echoed him. 'Those d—d politicians who started the Navy on to a show that should have waited for the Army, and 2 months too soon.' Jellicoe to Hamilton, 29 Apr. 1915; Hamilton MSS.

losses it had suffered (nearly 20,000 casualties), and the realization that it could do nothing more without large reinforcements and replenishment of ammunition, which would require at least a month, instilled a strong desire in the Dardanelles fleet to renew the naval attack. De Robeck was infected to the point where he wired the Admiralty on 9 May indicating a lukewarm interest in renewing the naval offensive.

Weighing heavily with Churchill against a decisive naval operation were these arguments: army reinforcements were on the way, four battleships and four cruisers were to be taken from De Robeck for service with the Italians in the Adriatic, U-boats were reported in the Aegean, and the Navy had increased responsibilities now that troops were on the Peninsula. He was, however, 'extremely anxious for a limited operation'—an attempt to sweep the Kephez minefield under cover of the fleet, which would compel the forts to exhaust their ammunition. In discussing the matter with Fisher on the morning of 11 May, 'he had no idea,' he claims, 'of pressing for a decisive effort to force the Straits and penetrate the Marmora'. Fisher either misunderstood the scope of Churchill's proposal or, more likely, he was afraid that if it succeeded, it might lead to a renewed all-out naval effort. Later on the 11th he cogently recapitulated all the arguments against an attempt to 'rush the Narrows' before the army had effectively occupied the adjacent shores. Churchill assured the Admiral that evening that he would never receive from him 'any proposition to "rush" the Dardanelles'.

The First Lord abandoned, for the moment anyway, his idea of a limited operation. He would have been content to ask De Robeck to let the Admiralty know what he intended before he took any action, but Fisher wanted the Admiral 'on *no* account to take decisive action without our permission'. Churchill demurred to sending a telegram 'which might have the effect of paralysing necessary naval action as judged necessary by the responsible Admiral on the spot'. In the end this was the telegram that went out to De Robeck at 5.40 p.m. on the 13th: 'The French Minister has received a telegram from Admiral Guépratte that you are contemplating some decisive action in the Straits in support of the Army: you must let us know what you intend *before any decisive step is taken* and obtain Admiralty sanction beforehand.' This compromise, says Crease, did not satisfy Fisher entirely. The Sea

Lords, who had seen the telegram and the minutes, as well as Fisher's memorandum of 11 May, promptly sent a joint minute to Fisher, associating themselves with his views 'as regards using the fleet to force the Dardanelles by rushing the Narrows, also as regards any further depletion of our strength in Home waters'.[20]

His hand thus strengthened, Fisher was able to have the last word. At 8.40 that evening (13 May) an Admiralty telegram went off in direct reply to De Robeck's telegram of 9 May. 'We think the moment for an independent naval attempt to force the Narrows has passed, and will not arise again. . . . there can be no doubt that with time and patience the Kilid Bahr plateau will be taken. Your role is therefore to support the army in its costly but sure advance, and to reserve your strength to deal with the situation which will arise later when the army has succeeded with your aid in its task.'[21] This was destined to be the last telegram Churchill and Fisher ever sent together.

The sinking of the old battleship *Goliath*, with the loss of 570 lives, on the night of 12 May in the Dardanelles (torpedoed by a German-manned Turkish destroyer) prompted Fisher to insist on the recall of the *Queen Elizabeth*. He was no longer prepared to risk this new super-dreadnought at the Dardanelles in view of reports of impending U-boat activity in that area, and he was prepared to resign on this issue. The settlement he reached with Churchill on the afternoon of the 12th was that she would sail at once to join the Grand Fleet and be replaced immediately by the older battleships *Exmouth* and *Venerable* and the first two 14-inch gun monitors.

It was obvious at a conference held at the Admiralty that evening that Kitchener was unhappy over this 'desertion' of the Army. He 'pointed out that the withdrawal of . . . the principal naval unit engaged on the operations would have a very serious and depressing effect on the army engaged in Gallipoli, at the same time greatly exhilarating our enemy . . .'[22] An excited Fisher bounced up from the table and said that if the *Queen Elizabeth* were not ordered home at full speed that very night, he would leave the Admiralty right then and there! The First Lord stood by his agreement with Fisher—'somewhat reluctantly', it seemed to Callwell, who was present—and at 9.30 that evening a telegram

---

[20] The documents cited in this paragraph are in the Crease MSS.
[21] *The World Crisis*, ii. 348.
[22] Kitchener to Asquith, 13 May 1915; Magnus, *Kitchener*, p. 338.

went out to De Robeck ordering the *Queen Elizabeth* to be hustled home.

The meeting of the War Council on 14 May was one of 'almost unrelieved gloom' (Hankey). There was no reason for cheer. The *Queen Elizabeth* was being recalled, German submarines were in the eastern Mediterranean, the British attacks in France had failed, and *The Times* had that morning disclosed the shortage of shell. 'Intense anxiety and extreme bad temper,' writes Churchill, 'all suppressed under formal demeanour, characterized the discussion.' Kitchener made a bitter complaint about the *Queen Elizabeth*, whose unique qualities for that theatre, he admitted, had been a strong determinant in his decision to support the Dardanelles operations. He again practically accused the Navy of leaving the Army in the lurch when it was struggling for its life. Fisher, no longer silent, interjected that he had been against the operations from the beginning, as Kitchener and the Prime Minister well knew. Churchill tried to console his colleagues: there was no reason for despondency or alarm, the campaign had never depended on the *Queen Elizabeth*, etc.

The meeting had a very important result, even if no clear-cut decisions were taken. As Fisher interpreted the drift of the discussion, a further diversion of ships to the Dardanelles was foreshadowed. He could see that 'the great projects in Northern waters which I had in view in laying down the Armada of new vessels were at an end', and that he was faced 'by a progressive frustration of my main scheme of naval strategy. . . . If the huge commitment at the Dardanelles was to be continued, it was clearly better, in the very interest of the Dardanelles operations themselves . . . that they should be henceforth directed on the naval side by somebody who believed in them.'[23] When he returned to the Admiralty late in the morning, he told Crease what had happened and remarked that he did not think he could remain on much longer. Only one more straw was needed to break the old Admiral's back, and this was provided by Churchill late on the 14th.

At about 6.30 p.m. on the 14th Churchill spent about half an hour with Fisher in the latter's room.[24] He left with a cheery 'Well, good-night, Fisher. We have settled everything and you

[23] *Dardanelles Commission.*
[24] The story that follows of the events of the next twelve hours is taken from Crease's account in his papers.

must go home and have a good night's rest. Things will look brighter in the morning and we'll pull the thing through [i.e., the Dardanelles] together.' As soon as the First Lord left, the Admiral called in Crease and told him he 'need not pack up just yet', as the meeting had been satisfactory: they had reached what he considered a definite and final understanding regarding the naval reinforcements to be sent to the Dardanelles (it was Crease's recollection that he only mentioned six monitors and four 'Edgar' class cruisers fitted with bulges), and he concluded, in a jocular vein, 'But I suppose he'll soon be at me again.'

At about five the next morning (15 May), Fisher received four minutes from Churchill.[25] They called for reinforcements considerably in excess of what had apparently been agreed upon some ten hours earlier. Crease has pointed out that paragraph six in the crucial first minute, which called for sending two more 'E' class submarines (the newest class) to the Dardanelles, was a wholly new proposal which had not been discussed at all the night before. It 'concerned him [Fisher] deeply', as he held strong views that more submarines could not be spared from Home waters. 'This new proposal,' Crease continues, 'together with the enlargements that a few hours had produced in respect to 15-inch howitzers, 9·2-inch guns and the number of monitors, etc. (for the numbers of these set out in the minute greatly exceeded those in Lord Fisher's mind when Mr. Churchill left him in the evening) convinced Lord Fisher that there was no finality about any agreement reached with Mr. Churchill on the subject of Dardanelles reinforcements, and caused his immediate resignation when it reached him.' Fisher made the identical point himself in his letter to Churchill of 16 May, after he had submitted his resignation.[26]

Fisher probably read the First Lord's minutes between 5 and 6 o'clock. Although they were merely proposals and called for discussion of any controversial points, as the First Lord's covering note stated, they were for Fisher the last straw, as he realized that any concessions would only be followed by fresh demands. Before breakfast he had written and sent in his resignation (his *ninth* and

[25] They are given in *Fear God and Dread Nought*, iii. 222–6.
[26] *Fear God and Dread Nought*, iii. 231. Hankey's diary of 15 May corroborates that Churchill's order of 14 May 'for a mass of naval material for Dardanelles' was the last straw. *The Supreme Command*, i. 315.

last) to Churchill and Asquith, and set in motion plans for going to the Duke of Hamilton's home at Strathaven in Lanarkshire, 'so as to avoid all questionings'.

3. THE TITANS DEPART

On the morning of Saturday, 15 May, Fisher dramatically pulled down the shades in his office and walked over to the Treasury to break the news to Lloyd George. 'A combative grimness had taken the place of his usually genial greeting; the lower lip of his set mouth was thrust forward, and the droop at the corner was more marked than usual. His curiously Oriental features were more than ever those of a graven image in an Eastern temple, with a sinister frown.'[27] Lloyd George had no luck in persuading him to postpone his resignation till Monday, so that he could put his case before an emergency War Council. He refused to wait another hour. He was off for Scotland that night. Lloyd George saw Asquith at once. The Prime Minister's reaction was 'Fisher is always resigning. This is nothing new.' Convinced by Lloyd George that Fisher really meant it this time, the Prime Minister addressed a peremptory note to Fisher that morning ordering him in the King's name to remain at his post. This finally reached the Admiral in a room in the Charing Cross Hotel, and he went to see the Prime Minister that afternoon. Asquith could not shake his decision to resign, although he no longer spoke of leaving for Scotland at once. Nor could he be dissuaded by Churchill's appeal on the 15th. The Admiral in reply (16 May) poured out his heart: 'YOU ARE BENT ON FORCING THE DARDANELLES AND NOTHING WILL TURN YOU FROM IT—NOTHING. I know you so well! . . . *You will remain.* I SHALL GO. It is better so. Your splendid stand on my behalf with the King and the Prime Minister I can NEVER forget, when you took your political life in your hands and I really have worked very hard for you in return—*my utmost*—but here is a question beyond all personal obligations.'[28]

Except for a midday visit to the Admiralty on Monday, the 17th, to superintend the removal of his personal things, the Admiral does not appear to have visited his office after the morning

---

[27] Lloyd George, *War Memoirs*, i. 225–6.
[28] *Fear God and Dread Nought*, iii. 231.

of the 15th. Hidden away in the First Sea Lord's residence in Admiralty Arch, he kept in touch (through Crease) with the war situation, for a few days anyway: all important papers were brought to him, etc. Bacon has suggested that Fisher's reason for keeping away from the war room was his fear of Churchill's persuasiveness.[29]

On the 16th the pressure on him to remain at his post mounted —from McKenna, his good friend and former Chief; from the Prime Minister, who refused to accept the resignation until Fisher had presented to him his precise grounds; from Churchill, who claimed that the resignation would be exploited all over the world as an admission of failure at the Dardanelles, and 'might prove the deciding factor in the case of Italy, now trembling on the brink'; and from the Sea Lords, in a memorandum to Fisher and Churchill, in which they associated themselves with the former's insistence on not allowing the Dardanelles to 'jeopardize the crushing superiority of the Grand Fleet which is essential to the successful prosecution of the war', and his dissatisfaction with 'the present method of directing the distribution of the Fleet', under which the First Sea Lord had largely lost executive control of fleet movements. But, they added, all differences 'should be capable of adjustment by mutual discussion and concession'. Fisher regarded this as 'EXCEEDINGLY BAD ADVICE', apparently feeling (as did Jellicoe) that they, too, should have resigned, if only out of a loyalty to a colleague. All these pressures only strengthened his resolve to clear out the next day. On that day, the 17th, an important development changed everything.

The resignation of Britain's most respected and trusted admiral, coming on top of the revelation of a shortage of high-explosive shell, threatened to topple the Government. To stave off the Conservative attack on both counts, Asquith agreed to the formation of a Coalition Government. A talk with Grey at the Foreign Office on the 17th, coupled with a letter from Asquith later that morning, both urging him to do nothing and say nothing for a few days, entirely changed Fisher's outlook. He was now sure that the impending reconstruction of the Government, of which Asquith, and presumably Grey, too, had informed him, would mean that Churchill would not be in the Cabinet ('always circumventing' him). He was now ready, as he told Grey, to

[29] Bacon to Crease, 25 Oct. 1929; Kilverstone MSS.

remain with himself or McKenna (a few days later, it was McKenna or Bonar Law)—but *not* Balfour, 'as he was hand in glove with Mr. Churchill over the Dardanelles adventure'—as First Lord. The mistrust in which Churchill was held by the Conservative Party—the Dardanelles had deepened it—made it certain, in Fisher's thinking, that Churchill would have to go.

By the 18th it was common knowledge that the First Sea Lord had tendered his resignation. The press was united behind him. He was 'indispensable'. The *Globe's* page-one headline on the 18th read: 'LORD FISHER MUST NOT GO', and the story opened: '*Lord Fisher or Mr. Churchill? Expert or amateur?*' This was the line adopted by several newspapers. *The Times* (18 May) went one step further, proposing Fisher as First Lord, an appointment that 'would undoubtedly command great popular approval . . . The suggestion has been frequently made already in many quarters.' The same idea was advanced that day by the *Daily Telegraph*, the *Globe*, and, the following day, by H. C. Ferraby, the *Daily Express* Naval Correspondent. *The Army and Navy Gazette* (22 May) cited all the historical precedents of sailors at the head of the Admiralty in time of war—Wager, Anson, Keppel, St. Vincent, and Barham—all with happy results, as full justification for Fisher being appointed First Lord and with a seat in the Cabinet. Fisher naturally found the idea attractive. On the morning of the 18th he told Hankey that 'forty per cent to sixty per cent of his energy has to be devoted to managing his First Lord, and he wants this for the Germans; so he wants to be First Lord. I pointed out to him how troublesome all the deputations and other "blatherumskites" would be. "Oh! I know all about receiving deputations," he said, "the first rule is to put them in a draught." '[30]

The feeling of dismay over Fisher's leaving the Admiralty was general in the Fleet. Here is how Jellicoe analysed Fleet opinion: 'Lord Fisher had many enemies, more enemies than friends, in the service, but even his enemies have been saying that his presence at the Admiralty was essential, as he was the only person who could tackle the 1st Lord. . . . Winston Churchill is a public danger to the Empire . . .'[31] Beatty and Tyrwhitt were other senior officers who for the same reason dreaded Fisher's going.

Jellicoe pleaded with Fisher to stay. He had a special reason:

[30] Diary, 18 May 1915; Hankey, *The Supreme Command*, i. 316.
[31] Jellicoe to Hamilton, 19 May 1915; Hamilton MSS.

it was rumoured during the 17th that A. K. Wilson had been offered Fisher's post and had accepted. This was the case. Churchill had asked him on 16 May to take office as First Sea Lord. Although Wilson had agreed after hesitation, he never took over the duties, for he decided the next day to postpone a definite decision, and on 19 May he withdrew his acceptance upon learning that Churchill was not remaining as First Lord. He would serve under nobody else, since, as he informed Asquith (19 May), he had agreed to undertake the office of First Sea Lord under Churchill 'because it appeared to me to be the best means of maintaining continuity of policy', and the 'strain' of serving under a new First Lord 'would be far beyond my strength'.[32]

Jellicoe had the profoundest distrust of Wilson's strategic views and of his capacity to tackle the First Lord.

> Sir A. K. W. made the most ludicrous proposals early in the war [on Heligoland] and we all doubted his sanity. I despair when I think of the uses to which the Grand Fleet may now be put . . . I *know* that Sir A. K. W. is no match at all for a politician, even were his own views sound. The least appeal placed on the score of duty will cause him to agree to *anything*. He *never* asserted himself as 1st S.L. even with McKenna. He certainly won't with W. C. He will *never* consult with the other S.L.'s. All this I know from 2 years with him on the Board. I am really in despair, and I know quite well that every flag officer will be the same, *Bradford* more than anyone. Sir A. K. was never a strategist— a brilliant handler of fleets but nothing more. We all used to pray that war would never come while he commanded the Channel Fleet [1905–7].[33]

Fisher threw away the powerful trumps in his hand, Fleet and press support, with two foolish deeds, the first on 17 May. That afternoon Room 40 deciphered signals that pointed to a sortie of the High Seas Fleet after dark. Jellicoe and Beatty were alerted. Crease informed Fisher and told him it was his duty to take over,

---

[32] Asquith MSS.

[33] Jellicoe to Hamilton, 19 May 1915; Hamilton MSS. In the same vein, three days later: 'The flag officers afloat are even more distrustful of A. K. than of W. C. . . . I as well as the rest would view this [appointment] as a national disaster. . . . We don't think that any one in a sane condition *could* have pressed as he did for a bombardment of Heligoland. Beatty, who has just left here in *Lion*, was far more emphatic about this even than I am. There is only one opinion; though I have of course not asked for opinions, they have been pressed upon me with great emphasis.' *Ibid.* Fisher, to whom the C.-in-C. wrote in similar terms on 20 May, agreed (22 May). '*A. K. Wilson will wreck his country if First Sea Lord!*'

if only for this one job. The Admiral replied that he was not needed—that he had full confidence in Oliver, and that Wilson would give him all the support he needed. Bacon says that he stayed put in his house because he was firmly convinced that the High Seas Fleet had gone to sea only 'to test whether we had occult means of reading their cipher signals'. Hamilton rushed over to the War Room to act as First Sea Lord. Early the next morning it was learned that the German Fleet had ventured out only to cover minelaying operations in the Dogger Bank. It was back at its base before Jellicoe could possibly catch up with it.

Although the excitement quickly subsided, Fisher's inaction in this crisis made it practically impossible for any Government to keep him in office. Professionally, of course, he was dead in the wrong, since his place was at the Admiralty until his resignation was accepted. The Prime Minister was enraged by Fisher's 'desertion' of his post. 'Strictly speaking, he ought to be shot: in any case it is a crime which ought not to be condoned, and still less to be rewarded.'[34] Fisher's behaviour forfeited the sympathy of the King, who on the 15th had deplored Fisher's resignation. It was 'bound to have a deplorable, if not a disastrous, effect upon the public, not only at home, but abroad'.[35] This was no longer his attitude after the High Seas Fleet incident. He was shocked by the Admiral's abandonment of his post at such a crucial moment. Fisher likewise lost the support of the Sea Lords. They were disgusted with his 'running away from his responsibility at a time when things looked black for his country.' This could easily have had catastrophic results, had there been a major fleet action. The Second Sea Lord, who had had no experience in handling such matters, would have been put in a most difficult position. The Sea Lords now turned against Fisher, two days after they had entreated him to return to his post. They now regarded him as a danger.[36] Unwilling to act openly because they would be suspected of motives of self-interest, they enlisted the help of Hall, the D.N.I., who was in touch with members of the Government.

Before Hall could accomplish anything, Fisher had destroyed

[34] Asquith to Balfour, 20 May 1915; Balfour MSS.

[35] Journals, 15 May 1915; Esher, iii. 235.

[36] Jellicoe, too, came around to this position. 'Now that I know all the facts I feel that you and the other Sea Lords took the right course. Certainly . . . Lord Fisher was quite wrong in giving up all work without being relieved.' Jellicoe to Hamilton, 27 May 1915; Hamilton MSS.

himself. Completely confident that his position was secure, because he would be indispensable to the new Government, and believing that eight of the Conservative Cabinet ministers-designate were working on his behalf and against Churchill staying on, he proceeded on the morning of the 19th to dictate to the Prime Minister his own terms for returning. The document began with a trumpet blast: 'If the following six conditions are agreed to, I can guarantee the successful termination of the War and the total abolition of the submarine menace.' They 'must be published verbatim so that the Fleet may know my position'. The six conditions were:

(1) That Mr. Winston Churchill is not in the Cabinet to be always circumventing me, nor will I serve under Mr. Balfour. (2) That Sir A. K. Wilson leaves the Admiralty and the Committee of Imperial Defence and the War Council, as my time otherwise will be occupied in resisting the bombardment of Heligoland and other such wild projects. . . . (3) That there shall be an entire new Board of Admiralty. . . . *New measures* demand *new men*. (4) That I shall have complete professional charge of the war at sea, together with the absolute sole disposition of the Fleet and the appointment of all officers of all ranks whatsoever, and absolutely untrammelled sole command of all the sea forces whatsoever. (5) That the First Lord of the Admiralty should be absolutely restricted to policy and parliamentary procedure . . . (6) That I should have the sole absolute authority for all new construction and all dockyard work of whatever sort whatsoever, and complete control of the whole of the Civil establishments of the Navy.

Accompanying this 'Preamble' of six conditions was a memorandum headed: 'NEW MEASURES DEMAND NEW MEN!' Mainly, it listed the various personnel changes that were to be made. The new Sea Lords would be Admirals Bethell, Singer, and Inglefield; the post of C.O.S. was to be abolished, 'as First Sea Lord resumes his control as formerly'; Captain Howard Kelly would command the *Tiger*, *vice* Pelly; etc. Also it called for increasing the aircraft on the East Coast, immediately laying down all available mines, ordering home the two 'Lord Nelsons', breaking up the Naval Division, and other measures.[37]

Hankey, who saw Fisher's terms that morning, 'remonstrated, and told him his terms were impossible, and no self-respecting Minister would look at them'.[38] Nothing could stop the rampaging

[37] *Fear God and Dread Nought*, iii. 241–3.
[38] Diary, 19 May 1915; Hankey, *The Supreme Command*, i. 316.

Admiral, who proceeded to submit the document to the Prime Minister. It was a fatal blunder. He had, as his great admirer and onetime Chief, Selborne, remarked, 'made an ass of himself' in writing this 'quite indefensible letter' to the Prime Minister. 'What unimaginable folly of Fisher!'[39] Even Bacon admits that Fisher had gone too far in dictating to the Prime Minister, and he questions the value of the proposals themselves. 'The Board he proposed was a weak one, and he intended to part with everyone who would attempt to exercise any control over him—he saw himself as an uncontrolled autocrat. . . . At this time, his age and the strain of the last six months at the Admiralty had begun to warp his calm and clear judgment, and had made him more intolerant of opposition.'[40] His conditions reflected his exasperation over the fact that the Fleet was not making the most of its opportunities, and that only he could rectify that by taking over the supreme direction of the war at sea. But he had gone too far. His 'extraordinary ultimatum' savoured of 'megalomania' to Asquith. '. . . the whole of his conduct at this critical time convinced me that it had become impossible that he should remain responsible for the Admiralty.'[41] To the King he remarked that the document 'indicated signs of mental aberration'.

Still the Prime Minister did not accept Fisher's resignation. On the 21st he sent Spender, the Editor of the *Westminster Gazette* and long a Fisher supporter, over to see the Admiral and inform him that Churchill was leaving the Admiralty and would be succeeded by Balfour in the new Coalition Government. Fisher told Spender in 'emphatic and somewhat racy language' that he would only serve under Bonar Law or McKenna, that he was even less willing to serve under Balfour than under Churchill, since he held the former 'really more to blame' for the Dardanelles. He threatened to get up in the Lords 'and tell the facts'. It was, Spender recalls, 'one of the most painful hours in my life. All his pent-up bitterness and accumulated grievances against politicians came pouring out . . .'[42] Since Asquith had pretty much made up his mind that he wanted Balfour as First Lord, Fisher had to go, all other considerations apart. When he learned that Balfour was to become

---

[39] Selborne to Balfour, 19 May 1915; Balfour MSS.
[40] Bacon, *Fisher*, ii. 271–2.
[41] Asquith, *Memories and Reflections*, ii. 113.
[42] J. A. Spender, *Life, Journalism and Politics* (London, 1927, 2 vols.), ii. 71.

First Lord, he knew that it was all over. He could not work with him.

The next day, 22 May, was the fateful one. Crease, McKenna, and Hankey, Fisher's closest advisers in those critical days, were all emphatic that he should go away. The main consideration was that in his excited state there was no telling what foolish things he might say or write. Besides, it was quite settled that he would not be retained at the Admiralty. They expected that public opinion would before long effect his return to the Admiralty. At midday he agreed to leave London if he could get authority, since his resignation had not been accepted and, technically, he was still First Sea Lord. He left that afternoon for Glasgow. Asquith, though very angry with Fisher, sanctioned his departure, and this was wired to him at Crewe by Crease.

That evening Asquith finally accepted Fisher's resignation. It is extremely unlikely that Fisher's going to Scotland had any bearing on the decision, for he had before then destroyed all chances of remaining First Sea Lord. If there was a decisive factor, it was the prospective appointment of Balfour as First Lord. Fisher would either refuse to serve under him, or if he would, he could not work cordially with him. The King brought this consideration to Asquith's attention on the 22nd, after their midday conference: 'The King thinks it important that Lord Fisher's resignation should be accepted before the new First Lord is appointed: otherwise the first act of Mr. Balfour would be the getting rid of Lord F., which the latter would not fail to make use of in the Press and elsewhere.'[43]

Fisher's great career was over. His undiplomatic behaviour, to put it charitably, did credit neither to his shrewdness nor to his sense of duty. Never again was he directly concerned with the conduct of the war at sea. He lingered on, a 'helpless spectator', in Churchill's words. The country was deprived of his driving force and imaginative powers—and not only his.

Churchill's position had become shaky on the 17th, when he learned that a Coalition Government was to be formed and that one of the conditions of Asquith's pact with the Conservatives was Churchill's transfer to an inferior Cabinet office. The Opposition maintained that while a strong and famous man was First

[43] Stamfordham to Bonham Carter (Asquith's Private Secretary), 22 May 1915; Asquith MSS.

Sea Lord, some check was imposed on Churchill, whereas an ordinary sailor would be helpless. They would not tolerate a tame Board, subservient to his policies. Bonar Law, Lansdowne, and the other Conservative leaders insisted on this concession as part of the price for Conservative participation in a Coalition Cabinet. The King wanted Balfour as First Lord, as Churchill had become 'impossible'.[44] In the end, Asquith gave in to Tory pressure 'with the greatest reluctance', sacrificing Churchill to national unity.

Churchill waged a grim, uphill fight to remain at the Admiralty. One tactic was to tie himself to Fisher, whose star seemed to be in the ascendant. Churchill, surprisingly, was unaware that the Admiral had virtually burned his boats. (He did not learn of Fisher's 'astounding ultimatum' until long after the war.) On the evening of the 17th, through George Lambert, the Civil Lord, Churchill offered Fisher a seat in the Cabinet if he would stay on with himself as First Lord. The Admiral 'rejected the 30 pieces of silver to betray my country'. Lambert came again twice, and Macnamara, the Parliamentary Secretary, once, on this errand.[45] It is very unlikely that Asquith, to say nothing of the Opposition, would have sanctioned Churchill's plan, had it met with Fisher's approval.

On the 17th Churchill informed the Prime Minister that he would take no office in a reorganized Government except the War Office or the Admiralty, though he would be 'sorry to leave the Admiralty, where I have borne the brunt.' Failing either, he hoped for 'employment in the field'.[46] His hand was strengthened, so he thought, by A. K. Wilson's informing the Sea Lords and the Prime Minister on the 19th that he would serve under 'nobody else as First Lord'. 'This is the greatest compliment I have ever been paid.' Not even an impassioned plea from Clementine Churchill (20 May) that the Prime Minister should not 'waste this valuable war material', who had 'the supreme quality which I venture to say very few of your present or future Cabinet possess—the power, the imagination, the deadliness to fight Germany',

[44] Diary, 22 May 1915; Windsor MSS.

[45] Hankey was a witness to Lambert's mission on the 19th. 'In the evening Churchill offered Fisher any terms he liked, including a seat in the Cabinet, if he would stay with him at the Admiralty. The message was brought verbally by Lambert, the Civil Lord, while I was with Fisher at his house in the evening, but Fisher's reply was to tell Churchill to go to hell.' Diary, 19 May 1915; *The Supreme Command*, i. 316.

[46] Asquith MSS.; likewise the other correspondence quoted in this paragraph.

could dissuade Asquith. On the 20th he asked Churchill to take it as settled that he would not remain at the Admiralty. Churchill finally accepted Asquith's decision on 21 May. 'I shall not look back,' he promised. He would accept any office, 'the lowest if it is of use—in this time of war', and, if there were nothing for him in the new Government, 'some employment in the field'.

At first it was planned to put him in the Colonial Office. Asquith suddenly withdrew the offer—we do not know exactly why[47]—and he was relegated to the sinecure Duchy of Lancaster, a post ordinarily reserved for 'beginners in the Cabinet or for distinguished politicians who had reached the first stages of unmistakable decrepitude' (Lloyd George). Nor could the loss of income of about £3,000 a year have been very pleasant for him. For the next six months he was on the fringes of the central prosecution of the war.

Both afloat and ashore the Navy received the news of Churchill's retirement from Whitehall with a feeling of great relief. As Admiral Colville told the King, 'He was, we all consider, a danger to the Empire', and Beatty wrote to his wife, 'The Navy breathes freer now it is rid of the succubus Churchill'. Jellicoe was not sorry to see him go. He had for long 'thoroughly distrusted Mr. Churchill because he consistently arrogated to himself technical knowledge which, with all his brilliant qualities, I knew he did not possess'.[48] The *Morning Post, Daily Express, National Review,* and *Naval and Military Record,* among other journals, were also pleased at the resignation of this clever amateur who had interfered in technical matters and exercised autocratic authority over a fighting Service. J. L. Garvin prophesied better than he knew (*The Observer,* 23 May): 'He is young. He has iion-hearted courage. No number of enemies can fight down his ability and force. His hour of triumph will come.' This was one of the few kind valedictories in the press.

[47] There is only this clue in a note from Lord Emmott, Director of the War Trade Department (he had been Under-Secretary of State for the Colonies, 1911–14), to Asquith on 20 May—that if Harcourt had to leave the Colonial Office in the reconstruction of the Cabinet, 'I implore you, for the sake of the Dominions, not to put Churchill there. An office revolt might be the first result. That could be faced even if it took place; but the effect on the Dominions would be lamentable and possibly disastrous. He has neither the temperament nor manners to fit him for the post.' Asquith MSS.

[48] 1 June 1915, Windsor MSS.; 21 May, Beatty MSS.; Jellicoe, 'A Reply to Criticism'.

The brutality of the fall had stunned Churchill, and his leaving his beloved Admiralty was, in the words of his Private Secretary (Marsh), 'a horrible wound and mutilation . . . it's like Beethoven deaf', and the prospect of comparative inactivity was almost unbearable. The break with Fisher saddened him. 'My separation —quarrel there was not—from our august old friend is quite among the most painful things in my life. I have been looking through all the letters he wrote me and musing regretfully upon the vanished pleasures of his comradeship and society.'[49] Churchill's very dignified departure—there were neither accusations nor recriminations—won him a great deal of sympathy.

Once it was certain that he would not be retained, Churchill became keenly anxious about his successor. He recommended Balfour, confident that he would follow his Dardanelles policy. Asquith, too, wanted Balfour in the Coalition Government and had approached him as early as 17 May. Balfour was extremely reluctant to be responsible for 'any heavy administrative office, except the Admiralty', although he personally preferred to join the new Government without a portfolio, or to accept a non-administrative office like the Chancellorship of the Duchy of Lancaster. Selborne and others pressed him to go to the Admiralty, and he finally agreed.

The Coalition Government assumed office on 25 May with Balfour as First Lord. (The date of the new Board's patent was the 27th.) The appointment was well received in the Navy, both in the Admiralty itself and by sailors everywhere. As Jellicoe declared, 'Mr. Balfour is absolutely sound in his views.' The Conservative press accepted the appointment with satisfaction. His brilliance and his familiarity with defence problems marked him out as pre-eminently fitted for the post. The Liberal press was lukewarm, because it held him almost equally responsible with Churchill for the Dardanelles, but especially because his appointment meant the definite retirement of the professional seaman in whom the nation had the most confidence. The Conservative press, too (the *Morning Post* was the noteworthy exception), wanted Fisher to stay, and the disappointment was great when Balfour's appointment led to Fisher's definite retirement.

It had been pretty well decided by the 21st that Balfour would

[49] Churchill to Jellicoe, 1 June 1915; letter in possession of the Dowager Countess Jellicoe.

go to the Admiralty. His first problem was the choice of a First Sea Lord, an exceptionally difficult task after Fisher had held the post. Fisher himself received scant consideration. Balfour was afraid 'Jacky is really a little mad. He has been using, I hear, the most violent language about me, when I believe at one time he used to "butter me up to the skies". I am not sure that even if Asquith consented to his remaining at the Admiralty, he (Fisher) would consent to serve under me. There would be no use our attempting to work together unless he really was prepared to go cordially with me.'[50] Fisher's return was, so far as Asquith was concerned, an academic question. Quite apart from the obstacle of his recent antics, and the fact that it was pretty certain that Fisher would not serve under Balfour, he was now believed to lack the sustained administrative capacity that was needed at the Admiralty. Moreover, as Bonham Carter warned, were Fisher to return, 'his first interest would be head hunting'. Lastly, Fisher's presence would have meant that the Dardanelles would not be given a fair chance.

Jellicoe would have been the unanimous choice had there been a logical successor to him as C.-in-C. Of those who had had experience of high command, only Admiral Sir George Callaghan was a possible replacement, and he was not thought to be up to the task. Beatty, who was generally regarded as the best of the younger men, was believed to lack the necessary administrative capacity. Jackson was a strong possibility to succeed Fisher. 'He has been in the machine from the beginning of the war, his paper work is admirable, and he would have the confidence of the Admiralty and I think of the fleet. On the other hand, according to his own opinion, he is not at present really sufficiently acquainted with the North Sea position, as the nature of his work has not admitted of this.'[51]

Churchill tried to persuade Wilson to serve under Balfour, and Asquith, seemingly unaware that he would have been utterly unacceptable to the Fleet, seriously considered appointing him. He was strongly influenced by Bonham Carter's report that Wilson had 'the confidence of the Fleet [!] and the necessary prestige with the public'. Bonham Carter had a solution (which Hankey had suggested to him) to Wilson's objection on account of

[50] Balfour to Selborne, 20 May 1915; Balfour MSS.
[51] Bonham Carter's memorandum of 20 May 1915; Asquith MSS.

overwork: the appointment of Jackson to the post of an additional Sea Lord 'to relieve the 1st Sea Lord of administrative and paper work and so leave him free to devote his energies to the big issues. . . . If after a time he found the work too heavy, Sir H. Jackson, having then had the opportunity of learning the naval position in all its respects, could replace him, Wilson returning to his present post.'[52] Asquith liked this suggestion; but Wilson simply refused to be First Sea Lord. This came as a relief to Balfour, particularly after a strong letter from Selborne (with whom he was in constant touch at this time) on 20 May:

Wilson is a very bad administrator. I never did a better day's work in my life than when I removed him from the Admiralty, where he was an utter failure [as Third Sea Lord, 1897–1901], and a mischievous failure too, to command at sea, where he was really great. . . . They [senior naval officers] all say that he is a dangerous adviser now, that having been always obstinate, in his old age he refuses to recognise how much matters have changed in the last ten years, that nothing will induce him to admit that the submarine is a grave danger to all ships of war, and that he has been constantly urging that Jellicoe should be ordered to attack the forts of Heligoland with the Grand Fleet, which seems to me stark, staring madness.[53]

This left Jackson, who had the support of Hankey, Bonham Carter, and Churchill, for all of whom he was second choice. His name being almost unknown to the nation, the appointment elicited a lukewarm reception. It was, on the whole, well received in the Fleet. Colville opined that the Navy had in the new First Sea Lord 'a man who they trust and respect', and Wemyss rated it 'the best possible appointment under the circumstances'. Beatty, on the other hand, feared the worst: 'God knows what the result will be. I fear he is not man enough for the job.' Jellicoe's position was in between these extremes. He was 'quite sure that the Naval policy will now be sound', but wondered whether Jackson's health would stand the strain, whether he would not over-worry. 'He is rather apt to be worried by paper work.'[54]

On 5 June Churchill delivered a panegyric upon his stewardship

[52] *Ibid.*

[53] Balfour MSS.

[54] Colville to King George, 1 June 1915, Windsor MSS.; Wemyss' letter of 30 May 1915, Wester Wemyss, *Wester Wemyss*, p. 226; Beatty to Lady Beatty (anticipating Jackson's appointment), 22 May 1915, Beatty MSS.; Jellicoe to Hamilton, 27 May 1915, Hamilton MSS.

at the Admiralty in a brilliant speech to his constituents at Dundee. He was full of confidence as he declared that the terrible 'dangers of the beginning of the war are over and the seas have been swept clear; the submarine menace has been fixed within definite limits; the personal ascendancy of our men, the superior quality of our ships on the high seas have been established beyond doubt or question. . . . Everything is in perfect order. Nearly everything has been foreseen. On the whole surface of the seas of the world no hostile flag is flown.'

He also prepared a statement of his Admiralty administration for Cabinet consumption. It dealt with the naval position in the decisive theatre of the North Sea. His figures showed that there need be no anxiety about the result of a general action in Home waters. Taking the Grand Fleet and the Harwich Force together, the position was:

	G.B.	High Seas Fleet
Dreadnoughts	25	17
Battle Cruisers	9	5
Pre-dreadnoughts	10	10
Armoured cruisers	17	4
Modern light cruisers	30	16
Destroyers	96	88 to 110

These figures did not give 'any true idea' of the strength of the Fleet, since 'the weight of metal ship for ship and squadron for squadron in the line, apart from numbers, shows an enormous preponderance'. And before the end of 1915 the Fleet would receive these new ships: 7 dreadnoughts, 12 light cruisers, 65 destroyers, 62 submarines, 37 monitors, and 107 sloops and smaller anti-submarine vessels.[55] Five months later he prophesied: 'Time will vindicate my administration of the Admiralty, and assign me my due share in the vast series of preparations and operations which have secured us the complete command of the seas.'[56]

To attempt an estimate of the four years that Churchill, prior to World War II, regarded as 'the most memorable' of his official career—it was his work during the critical pre-war period that will give him a secure place in naval history. 'There is one thing

[55] Cabinet Paper, 'The Naval Situation at Home', 30 May 1915; *The World Crisis*, ii. 525–7. He could not have foreseen the serious delays that developed in the new construction programme.

[56] Churchill to Asquith, 11 Nov. 1915; Asquith MSS.

at least,' Kitchener assured him in the darkest hour of his fortunes, 'they can never take away from you. When the war began, you had the Fleet ready.' Churchill's wartime service is more difficult to evaluate, particularly since it is easy to be blinded by his skilful and resolute leadership of the country to victory in World War II. His impulsive and headstrong nature, and his flouting of precedent and conventional methods, certainly made him a difficult man to work with. His rather amateurish strategic ideas (though sometimes sound and even brilliant), his impatience to hit back at the enemy, and his extremely irritating methods, above all his habit of plunging into all the technical details of naval business with complete assurance, often hindered as much as it helped the war effort. As Graham Greene later remarked, 'If he had done less himself, things would certainly have gone more smoothly.' And, one might add, certain regrettable incidents might have been avoided.

At the same time the Royal Navy and the British nation will never forget the debt due to Churchill's invaluable traits: his great ability, magnificent courage, initiative, fiery enthusiasm, and willingness to accept responsibility. He had brought to the Admiralty the driving force which had been needed at the moment, and which was largely absent from the Admiralty throughout the rest of the war. I subscribe to Fisher's sincere tribute: 'I backed him up till I resigned. *I would do the same again!* He had courage and imagination! *He was a war man!*'[57] Curiously, Churchill had used very similar language about Fisher. When Keyes remarked (November 1915) that Churchill had 'nursed a viper' when he had recalled the old Admiral in 1914, Churchill rapped out, 'And I would do it again; he brought such fire and vigour into the production of ships.'[58]

Keyes's epitaph is a fitting close to this chapter. 'The Navy lost in the course of a few days the services of an Admiral who was one of its outstanding figures of the last hundred years—and the greatest producer of material in its history—and of an Administrator to whom it owed, in a great measure, its readiness for war in August, 1914.'[59] They were succeeded by men who were never able to fill their large shoes.

[57] Fisher to Lord Cromer, 11 Oct. 1916; *Fear God and Dread Nought*, iii. 375.
[58] Keyes, *Naval Memoirs*, i. 455–6.
[59] *Ibid.*, p. 343.

PART II

The Balfour–Jackson Period: The First Year
(May 1915 – May 1916)

XII

The New Board of Admiralty

Then came Mr. Balfour and Sir Henry Jackson: the philosopher wedded to the scientist. The outcome was from the start assured. Speed of action waited on cautious conviction. The temperament of super-intellectuals leads to inaction rather than action; the fiery energy that drove the Admiralty during the previous six months suddenly vanished, and was succeeded by a period of sound, but lethargic, administration.

ADMIRAL SIR REGINALD BACON, *Lord Fisher of Kilverstone*.

Balfour's principal value lies in the fact that he gives Jackson, Oliver, and the Commanders-in-Chief a free hand, and has been perfectly successful in protecting them from outside pressure.

A. H. POLLEN (the naval journalist) to Captain H. W. Richmond, 22 March 1916.

1. BALFOUR AND JACKSON

THE onetime Conservative Prime Minister (1902–5) and Leader of the Opposition (1905–12) was one of the most impressive men of his generation. His figure was tall and elegant, his face refined, and his voice distinguished. He was renowned for his personal charm, courtly manners, intellectual gifts (he was well versed in science, philosophy, and music), great moral and physical courage, political acumen, and mastery of the art of parliamentary debate. His brain was absolutely first rate—razor-sharp, penetrating, analytical. 'Balfour gave to politics the finest mind of his generation', in the opinion of the first Earl of Birkenhead, himself one of the great men of the day. Although Balfour did not possess an expert knowledge of naval affairs, he had a deep personal interest in all matters connected with defence, having been practically the founder of the C.I.D. and its first chairman. His patience, cheerfulness, and imperturbable calm had won him the reputation of being an easy man to work with.

These were formidable assets that the new First Lord brought with him to Whitehall, and they were productive of much that was good. This side of Balfour is well summed up by Graham Greene, the Secretary of the Admiralty. As an administrator,

he acquired an efficient grasp of the Administrative and Technical questions which came before the Board . . . To me, as Secretary of the Admiralty, he was accessible at all times, and never showed the slightest impatience or reluctance to discuss matters of business, however departmental . . . In his presence all men seemed rather small and inferior, and this placed him as First Lord in an unrivalled position for settling differences of opinion or deciding important questions. Naval officers knew that he would give what they had to say the closest consideration and would support loyally his official colleagues and advisers, and would never attempt to influence them to do what, as practical seamen, they might consider unwise.[1]

In other words, Balfour, unlike his predecessor, was happy with a more traditional interpretation of his duties, that of '*Primus inter pares*', as Goschen (First Lord, 1895–1900) had spoken of himself. He acted as the representative of the Cabinet and was content to supervise and co-ordinate the work of the Admiralty. 'All would acknowledge,' he wrote at the end of his tenure, 'that a First Lord who insisted on running the Admiralty without regard to naval opinion would be a serious danger.'[2]

'The effect of Balfour's personality at the Admiralty,' writes his official biographer, 'was exactly that which the Prime Minister had no doubt reckoned upon when he sent him there as Mr. Churchill's successor.' Serenity and union were restored to the Admiralty—*but at a high price*. Balfour was, let us face it, a lethargic man. His energy was desultory.; he lacked sustaining power. Lloyd George's verdict is a fair one: 'He lacked the physical energy and fertility of resource, and untiring industry for the administration of the Admiralty during the Great War . . . Clearly he was not the man to stimulate and organise the activity of the Navy in a crisis.'[3] Another count against him was his philosophic temperament, which made for a leisurely reflection on the big problems. This is what Lloyd George had in mind when he described Balfour as a 'dawdler', who would dawdle the nation into disaster. As early as the third week of the new Board, a visitor

[1] Graham Greene's memorandum, 'Earl Balfour as First Lord of the Admiralty', Feb. 1934; Graham Greene MSS.

[2] Blanche E. C. Dugdale, *Arthur James Balfour, First Earl Balfour* (London, 1936, 2 vols.), ii. 147.

[3] Lloyd George, *War Memoirs*, ii. 1017.

could note the very marked change in the atmosphere in the First Lord's room. 'In Winston's time one felt the whole machine pulsating. To-day a marked calm pervaded the First Lord's room.'[4]

Jackson was not a particularly happy choice, though perhaps the best possible one at the time. He had less sea experience as a flag officer than almost any admiral on the active list, his only command having been that of the Cruiser Squadron in the Mediterranean, 1908–10. He never went to sea again, uncertain health being, it seems, an important factor. Although he had studied war and strategy and had been head of the War College (1911–13) and Chief of the Admiralty War Staff (1913–14), his forte always was weapon development. He had the highest reputation as a scientific naval officer. Few previous naval officers had been able to add the magic letters 'F.R.S.' (Fellow of the Royal Society) to their names. He had done good work for the Navy in the development of the torpedo service and of wireless telegraphy.

Jackson was sensible and level-headed, but he lacked the three aces. He had little of his predecessor's leadership capacity, fertile imagination (except in scientific matters), and talent for using the brains and ideas of juniors, to say nothing of Fisher's energy. Temperamentally, he was the opposite of Fisher—reserved, morose, and not possessing much small talk. Personally, he was not the easiest man to get along with, his health no doubt affecting his temper. Jellicoe understood him well. 'I fear Jackson will only get irritable at all this bombardment of letters. I know him so well and told Balfour of this trait in his character.'[5] Jackson was a great gentleman, but when his health was bad, he could be uncivil even to his Chief, and the latter would naturally take offence. The Secretary and the C.O.S. had a plan to deal with such occasions. 'We used to give them time to cool down and then Graham Greene went and talked to Balfour and I talked to Jackson and we always managed to get them to make it up.'[6] It was not only Balfour with whom he had trouble. Jackson's tactlessness with the politicians, as in War Council meetings which he often attended, led to cool, and sometimes strained, relations between them and him.

---

[4] 11 June 1915; *Lord Riddell's War Diary*, p. 103.
[5] Jellicoe to Beatty, 26 June 1915; Beatty MSS.
[6] James, *A Great Seaman*, p. 149, quoting from the Oliver MSS.

The job, proving too much for his talents and his temperament, resulted in an acute case of pessimism. Thus, six months after Jackson had assumed office, the Second Sea Lord regretted to find that when one went to see him, 'He does nothing but groan and sigh and be miserably pessimistic. I fear he will not last long . . .'[7] Indeed, with a lethargic First Lord and a pessimistic First Sea Lord setting the tone, the atmosphere at the Admiralty was generally one of depression. Gone were the confidence and buoyancy of the Churchill–Fisher régime.

Jackson often complained that he had no time to think. This is not surprising, considering how he concerned himself with trivia. The rule that every paper and telegram, however insignificant, requiring a decision must be referred to the First Sea Lord and the Chief of the War Staff was strictly enforced. Whereas Fisher had not concerned himself with trivia, nothing was too small for his successor. As an illustration, we find the First Sea Lord in August 1916 writing to Admiral Bayly at Queenstown about a certain Lieutenant-Commander who was addicted to drink and who had run up an excessive wine bill in the wardroom. And here is an example of the kind of red tape and excessive centralization at the Admiralty that flourished in the Balfour–Jackson period and for which the First Sea Lord was primarily responsible. Admiral Colville, C.-in-C., the Orkneys and Shetlands, reported to Jackson on 'the growing paper work and red tape connected with the trawler patrols', a 'serious matter' on which he had already written to the Second and Fourth Sea Lords.

Instead of its being as it was an elastic organization (as when first started up here), now, if a trawler is moved from one Div^n to another, a W/T set shifted, from one trawler to another, etc., etc. (all for the efficiency of the patrols in *war time*), reams of correspondence turns up. I should have thought that an Admiral Com^{dg} on the spot was the person to do this, informing the Admiralty he had done so. I actually had my reasons in writing called for, as I had shifted the W/T from a very inefficient *trawler*!! to an efficient one without asking the Ad^{ty}!! though I of course reported it. A voluminous weekly return has to be sent in giving number of days trawlers are out, etc., etc. It is all to my mind such a mistake, reduces the efficiency of the patrols by keeping officers who should be out on patrol tied to an office stool, and generally gives the impression that, *although war time*, officers are not trusted to see

[7] Diary, 20 Nov. 1915; Hamilton MSS.

[that] their vessels under their orders are fully doing their work. Things must be in a bad way if this is the case. One would really imagine from some of the correspondence that a trawler was a battleship.[8]

Is it any wonder that we find Jackson constantly wailing about the paper work, for much of which he was himself responsible? 'The mass of paper work is overwhelming and gives me no time for thought...' 'Paper work here increases to an overwhelming extent and makes one's life almost a burden.' 'I've been worried to death with papers and committees since my return and see no relief from them.'[9]

The principal shortcoming of the new Board was that Balfour and Jackson made a poor combination. Lord Hankey sums up the situation pithily: 'The Admiralty jumped from one extreme to the other. In place of two men of driving power, initiative and resource, but occasionally lacking in judgment, there were now in charge two men of philosophic temperament and first-rate judgment, but less dynamic than their predecessors.'[10] This loss in driving power at the Admiralty was quickly manifest, as the authorities returned to their leisurely, almost peacetime, tempo. Declared a flag officer, 'The new Board strikes me as being an extraordinarily gentlemanly one, on which it must be a pleasure to serve—but one wonders if there ought not to be a touch of devilment introduced, just *one* underhand member to compete with those rascals over the water.'[11]

One particularly damaging result of this 'apathetic way of doing things', to quote Percy Scott, was to delay the fitting of director firing to the ships. The fitting had proceeded rapidly in the first ten months of the war, and, had the pace been maintained, the whole Fleet would have been equipped by the end of 1915.[12] Instead, at Jutland the C.-in-C. had only six ships completely fitted with director firing, that is, primary and secondary armament both. Other instances of the loss in 'push' will occur in the narrative.

Another shortcoming of the Board was its lack of harmony.

[8] 15 July 1915; Jackson MSS.

[9] Jackson to Jellicoe, 2 Sept. 1915, 10 Mar., 18 May 1916; Jellicoe MSS.

[10] Hankey, *The Supreme Command*, i. 335.

[11] Rear-Admiral Trevylyan Napier (commanding 2nd L.C.S.) to Hamilton, 6 June 1915; Hamilton MSS.

[12] Scott, *Fifty Years in the Royal Navy*, p. 292.

2. THE JUNIOR SEA LORDS

Jellicoe's hope that the new Navy high command would include officers with recent sea experience was not realized. Hamilton, Tudor, and Cecil Lambert remained on the Board—all second-rate men and without first-hand knowledge of the war at sea. This detracted from the authority and prestige of their position in the eyes of the Fleet. Oliver, undoubtedly a tower of strength, stayed as C.O.S., and A. K. Wilson remained, like some pre-historic figure, loosely attached to the C.O.S., receiving copies of Room 40 signals, consulted on important subjects, working on plans for minor operations, experimenting with new gear, etc. (He did not retire until August 1918.)

'Do at the Board all the business which possibly can be done at the Board. Churchill has almost killed it. You can give it fresh life.'[13] Balfour took Selborne's advice to heart. At the outbreak of the war, the Board as such, that is, as a collective body, had fallen into abeyance. Whereas there had been twenty-four Board meetings in 1913 and eight in 1914 up to the war, but only nine during the balance of 1914 and only three in 1915 up to the change of the Board on 27 May, there were fourteen subsequently through December 1915. Moreover, Balfour gave the Junior Sea Lords regular access to all the daily telegrams. And still they were unhappy. They were apprehensive, and with good reason, that the public held them equally responsible with the First Sea Lord and the First Lord for operations, though in fact they were no more consulted on this aspect of the naval war under Balfour than under Churchill.

Matters came to a head in November 1915, when Churchill, in defending his role in the Dardanelles campaign (House of Commons, 15 November), made clear on his own showing that he had assumed responsibility for naval dispositions, strategy, and tactics without reference to the Board. The public discussion that followed this revelation (much of it hostile to the former First Lord) prompted the Junior Sea Lords to send a collective minute to the First Lord on 22 November. It was a claim for the recognition of their right to share in the formation of Admiralty war policy, and was couched in moderate terms. 'We did not want to make it too bad tempered,' explained Hamilton, 'as Balfour is so

[13] Selborne to Balfour, 19 May 1915; Balfour MSS.

exceedingly considerate in every way that it seemed churlish to appear in any way to aim our remarks at him. Our complaint is with the system that allows such people as W.C. to ride roughshod over the Naval Lords.'[14]

'The conduct of the naval campaign and Parliamentary debates,' ran the minute, 'shows that the Sea Lords are not the accepted advisers of the First Lord on Naval War policy. They may not be and in many cases have not been informed of what that policy is until after it has been embarked upon, and even on technical matters within the scope of the Departments under their individual superintendence First Lord can and does consult subordinates to the exclusion of the superintending members of the Board.' By 'subordinates' they meant the Chief of the War Staff and the various heads of the Staff. Instead of acting in an advisory capacity, as the founders of the Staff had intended, 'when War broke out, the Sea Lords were excluded from and the Chief of Staff was included in the Councils for consideration and decision of Admiralty war policy. The Chief of Staff does not and cannot share responsibility for that policy. His functions have become mainly executive rather than advisory.'[15] The minute concluded with these observations:

The principle on which the Order in Council is based that the supremacy of the First Lord is complete and unassailable has been pushed too far, and has tended to imperil and at some future time may again tend to imperil national safety. . . . Our conviction [is] that had the naval members of the Board been regularly and collectively consulted on large questions of war policy during the progress of the present naval campaign, some at least of the events which the Empire does at this moment deplore so bitterly, would not have happened, and that until the authority and responsibility of the Sea Lords is enlarged and defined, there will be no adequate assurance that similar disasters will not recur in the future.[16]

[14] Hamilton to Jellicoe, 29 Nov. 1915; Jellicoe, 'A Reply to Criticism'.

[15] Privately, Hamilton expressed this point more forcibly. 'Now the C.O.S., instead of acting in that capacity to the First Sea Lord, is really the chief adviser of the 1st Lord. The 1st Lord is constantly closeted with the C.O.S. and different heads of the War Staff, to the absolute exclusion of the Sea Lords, who should be the real War Staff of the Navy. The result of consulting juniors, who are not giving responsible advice, is that they only give advice, or rather answers, to specific questions, and do not consider the whole question.' Diary, 23 Nov. 1915; Hamilton MSS.

[16] The Dardanelles Commission used this quoted material; the whole minute is in the Hamilton MSS.

When the Sea Lords told Jackson what they were doing, he insisted on backing them up with a minute to the First Lord, 25 November.

> I have had considerable experience of Admiralty work and ways during the last 20 years, and feel that a change in the position of the Sea Lords has slowly but surely taken place, tending to relegate them to administrators only, and weakening their positions as advisers and executive authorities, concurrently with a strengthening of the civilian authority and power. . . .[17]
>
> The Sea Lords intimate in their Minute that they are but seldom consulted by you as to the conduct of their departments, and not at all as to the conduct of the War; and that you probably obtain your information from their subordinates. As to the latter I frequently do the same in unimportant matters, as the time of the Board is valuable and should not be wasted in giving information about minor details. In important matters, I, however, consider they have every right to be heard . . .

Jackson did not think the time was 'opportune for attempting any dramatic changes in organization'; he would only suggest that 'a periodical conference might go far to clear the air, and keep us all in touch with one another'.[18] This from one whose dislike for conferences was well known.

Much of the impact of these minutes was neutralized by the Secretary's notes on the Junior Sea Lords' minute which he prepared for the First Lord. The more telling comments are worth producing *in extenso*:

> I think the present First Sea Lord will uphold the view that the First Sea Lord is wholly responsible for war plans and war policy, and he has the C.O.S. and the War Staff to help him.
>
> The Third and Fourth Sea Lords have never in my experience shared in the responsibility vested in the First Sea Lord, the Second Sea Lord invariably acting for him in his absence. . . .
>
> The First Lord is head of the Admiralty Office and has always had

---

[17] On this the Secretary commented: 'The gradual change referred to has taken place, but it is not due to the direct action of civilian First Lords as much as to the gradual transformation of an exclusively seaman's service into one largely depending upon civil experts of all kinds. The change has not been confined to the First Lord, but it has affected the First Sea Lord, whose position relatively to the others, has also grown in importance.' Graham Greene, 'Notes on the First Sea Lord's Minute'; Graham Greene MSS.

[18] Hamilton MSS.

the right to consult heads of Departments, apart from the Superintending [Sea] Lords. As a rule the Superintending Lord is informed by the Head of a Department of any important direction given by, or conversation with, the First Lord, but to assert that the First Lord is only to take his views and facts from the Superintending Lord would place him in an impossible position and the whole administration of the Admiralty would be impaired. I agree, however, that the late First Lord was too prone to ignore the claims of his proper advisers and colleagues to be consulted, and this is the main cause of the complaint against him.

The Naval Lords regard with some jealousy the position of the C.O.S., but it should be remembered that he is the direct subordinate of the First Sea Lord, and his authority to act begins and ends with the confidence reposed in him by the Superintending Lord. As Head of a Department the First Lord has also a claim to consult him directly. . . .

The Sea Lords' complaint, so far as it is not concerned with Mr. Churchill's peculiar methods of administration and other by-gones, is really levelled against the First Sea Lord rather than the First Lord.

The following seems to be the position which the First Lord should take up in regard to the Sea Lords' Memorandum:—

(a) That the First Lord recognises fully the First Sea Lord's responsibility for advising him on all large questions of war policy:

(b) That it is open to the First Sea Lord to consult the other Sea Lords on such matters, or particular aspects of them, whenever he may think it necessary, and there is no objection to the First Sea Lord arranging to hold periodical meetings of the Sea Lords for such a purpose:

(c) that in discussing any such questions between the First Lord and the First Sea Lord, the latter may recommend the presence of all or any of the other Sea Lords, as he may think fit, if matters of importance affecting their administrative spheres should be involved, or if they have important views which the First Sea Lord would like them to have the opportunity of expressing in person:

(d) that on all important questions within the spheres of the respective Members of the Board, Naval and Civil, the First Lord wishes to consult and to be consulted by them according to the regular practice and tradition of the Admiralty, but it should be made clear that with this usage has always co-existed the practice of the First Lord consulting the Heads of the Admiralty Departments personally. If the Members of the Board are to keep their position as advisers on policy and as executive authorities, and are not to be relegated to the position of purely Departmental administrators, this practice is essential.[19]

[19] 1 December 1915; Graham Greene MSS.

What was the result of this flurry of minutes? Hamilton informed Jellicoe on 29 November that he did not expect, nor did he think it would be in the national interest, 'to rake up controversy' by passing a new Order in Council; but he hoped the minutes would 'make Balfour see the advisability of working the present regulations so as to do away with the objections to them . . .' He was to be disappointed. Board meetings became more frequent and discussions at them fuller, so much so that Hamilton could grumble that 'we talk too much'. But that was all. The Junior Sea Lords were not consulted on strategic matters, nor was their responsibility enlarged or defined. In other words, the fundamental position was unchanged: the Junior Sea Lords continued to have no share in the direction of the war at sea.

The Balfour Board was, as regards personal relations, not an altogether happy one. Graham Greene had the respect of the Sea Lords, but not so the other civilians—Macnamara, the Financial Secretary, Hopwood, the Additional Civil Lord, and the Duke of Devonshire, who had succeeded George Lambert as Civil Lord in the May 1915 shake-up. The 'long harangues' of Hopwood and Macnamara at Board meetings had no excuse, in Hamilton's opinion, 'except the intense delight of those gentlemen at hearing their own voices'. Among themselves the Sea Lords had their problems. Jackson's irritability did not make him popular with his colleagues, although they respected his professional talents.

The most serious personal problem that plagued the Board was the attitude of the other Sea Lords and Jellicoe towards Lambert, the Fourth Sea Lord. Jackson did not trust him, and Hamilton and Jellicoe had no confidence in him. Invariably brusque in manner, stubborn, tough, espousing unpopular causes with sweeping statements ('his best *Daily Mail* manner', as Hamilton described it), he was a thorn in the flesh of his colleagues and the Grand Fleet alike. For instance, he was a great economizer, which never earned anybody popularity. 'His one idea,' complained the C.-in-C., 'seems to be to cut down expenses on the service that really matters, viz. the Grand Fleet. I suggest that he turn his efforts to the Admiralty!! I hear most of the clerks get considerably higher pay than in pre-war days. His own office must be most expensive with all the literary productions that emanate from it, which so far as we can see are largely superfluous.'[20] Especially did Lambert

[20] Jellicoe to Hamilton, 20 Jan. 1916; Hamilton MSS.

exasperate Jellicoe with his campaign early in 1916 to reduce the number of hospital ships in the Grand Fleet. His idea was that there would not be over 200 wounded in a great North Sea battle. Hamilton found his colleague's view on medical problems 'somewhat Spartan and peculiar. His opinion appears to be that caring for sick and wounded in war is very much overdone and that they had better be left to die.'[21] Actually, Lambert had a more important reason: the pressing need for mercantile tonnage.

Although 'the feeling against him [Lambert] in the Fleet is very strong,' wrote Jellicoe, 'and we should all rejoice at a change there',[22] Lambert was not relieved until the very end of 1916. Indeed, there was but one change in the Junior Sea Lords between the outbreak of the war and December 1916. In June 1916 Gough-Calthorpe relieved Hamilton as Second Sea Lord, with the latter taking over the Rosyth command from the energetic Lowry. At last some sea experience was brought to the Board.

[21] Diary, 22 Jan. 1916; *ibid.* See below, pp. 394–5, for a further reference to the hospital-ship imbroglio, which had Hamilton and Jackson lined up against Lambert and Tudor, with Balfour in the middle.

[22] 7 June 1916; Hamilton MSS. Another issue on which Lambert antagonized his colleagues was his contention in the spring of 1916 that the war could only be won by young men. In accordance with this idea, he would like to have removed all the admirals commanding at sea, from Jellicoe down, and to make Tyrwhitt C.-in-C. Hamilton found it difficult to take such nonsense seriously. 'I am afraid Lambert fraternizes too much with politicians and has got some of their silly, impracticable habits of thought.' Diary, 5 May 1916; *ibid.*

XIII

The Mediterranean:
Problems Old and New

(JUNE 1915–MAY 1916)

(Maps 2 and 7)

Abandoned at the moment when victory was still within our grasp, the campaign of the Dardanelles will remain through all ages to come an imperishable monument to the heroism of our race, to the courage and endurance of our soldiers and sailors, to the lack of vision and incapacity of our politicians.

WEMYSS: *The Navy in the Dardanelles Campaign.*

Now it is all over there is no doubt the right policy has been followed, as the troops could not have gone forward, in the military opinion . . . and it was 20 to 1 against [the Navy] getting past even Chanak.

DE ROBECK to Admiral Sir Henry Jackson, 24 December 1915.

1. THE DARDANELLES: LIQUIDATION

THE first big question that confronted the new Board was whether to back the continuation of the Dardanelles operation (or Gallipoli operation, as the essentially military phase came to be called). Balfour, who was still impressed with the tremendous strategical advantages that would flow from the successful outcome of the campaign, fully supported it. Jackson went along because the country was deeply committed. He would have preferred to use the Fleet in its traditional sphere of action, that is, against the enemy's main fleet and for the protection of trade.

The military attack was renewed on 6–7 August, when two new divisions were landed at Suvla Bay, just north of Anzac Beach, and the Anzac and Suvla Bay forces attempted to break out for a drive straight through the mountains to Kilid Bahr and the Narrows. But the heat, flies, and disease had exhausted the Army (this affected the Turks equally); British tactics were bad, staff work primitive, and the command at Suvla timid and confused (the senile and incompetent Stopford had never before commanded troops in war); and resources were once more inadequate. (Reinforcements were, throughout the campaign, invariably small and late.) Though the battle lasted until 29 August, the issue was decided by the 10th. The Turks succeeded in nailing the Allies down to their landing areas, and the campaign once more came to a standstill. Never again was the Army to attempt to push forward from its beachheads at Cape Helles and Anzac.

The failure of Suvla Bay had two results. It touched off a movement in governmental and Service quarters for the evacuation of the Peninsula, and it revived the idea of forcing the Dardanelles by naval action alone.

To evacuate or not to evacuate was the great problem that was heatedly debated at the Dardanelles and in Whitehall during the autumn of 1915. The evacuators were many and powerful: most of the Generals on the spot (but not including Hamilton or Birdwood, who firmly believed that the Army could do the job if reinforced sufficiently), the War Office (with Kitchener vacillating), and various members of the Cabinet and the War Committee.[1] The case for evacuation, summarized, was as follows: (1) The Anzac-Suvla position was not well adapted for defence against sustained attack. (2) Gallipoli was but a 'side-show', and

[1] The Dardanelles Committee had replaced the War Council on 7 June. It was supposed to limit its activities to the Dardanelles campaign. This proved impossible, and gradually it took on the attributes of a war committee, co-ordinating and supervising operations in all war theatres. Originally a fairly small Cabinet committee, it expanded to the unwieldy size of the old War Council. It held its last meeting on 30 October and was replaced on 2 November by the War Committee. As defined by the Prime Minister, the latter was 'an executive body; that is to say they give directions; they order operations'. Almost all questions of high policy were brought to it. As in the case of all its predecessors, its decisions still needed Cabinet approval. In practice, the Cabinet only very rarely reversed or revised the War Committee's decisions. It was, at the start, much smaller than the War Council or Dardanelles Committee. Only three were present at the first meeting on 3 November—Asquith, Balfour, and Kitchener. Thereafter 'the usual process of rapid growth set in', to quote Lord Hankey, who was its Secretary. Lloyd George (Minister of Munitions) and Grey joined at the second meeting, Bonar Law and McKenna soon afterwards, etc. The First Sea Lord and the C.I.G.S. always attended after the first meeting, although Hankey says it was never made clear whether as members or as 'expert assessors'. The growing size of the Committee was a great weakness. Two others were the 'system of dual responsibility' (see below) and the fact that, except for the Prime Minister, all the members were too busy with departmental as well as Parliamentary duties, hence lacked time for the proper fulfilment of Committee duties.

the military effort should be concentrated in France. (3) The large and regular wastage of personnel on the Peninsula. The Army needed large reinforcements if it was to resume the offensive. But men were not available. (4) The opening of direct German communications with Turkey, and the consequent likelihood of German artillery being sent to Gallipoli, threatened to make the Allied position untenable.

The third and fourth considerations are intimately connected with the story of Allied military operations elsewhere. Few troops could be spared for Gallipoli because, in the first place, the Loos-Champagne offensive on the Western Front (25 September–14 October) put a serious drain on Allied manpower: a quarter of a million French and British troops were lost. More importantly, troops for Gallipoli were unavailable because of the Salonika campaign. German victories on the Russian Front and the Allied stalemate at Suvla Bay had finally induced Bulgaria to join the Central Powers (6 September) and to prepare with them to invade Serbia. The French saw only one way to save the Serbs, namely, by sending a large army to the Greek port of Salonika. Since Serbia had no seacoast, Salonika was the one route by which Allied aid could reach her. The force available was not strong enough to have helped Serbia in time, but it was hoped that its presence in Salonika (the pro-Ally Greek Prime Minister, Venizelos, had given his permission) would encourage Greece to join the Allies. Allied troops began to land at Salonika on 3 October. Four days later the storm burst. Powerful Austro-German forces invaded hapless Serbia from the north—Belgrade fell on the 9th— and the Bulgarians invaded from the east (11 October). Britain and France declared war on Bulgaria on 15–16 October. The Allies could not reach the Serbs; their advance into Macedonia accomplished nothing, and they had to fall back on Salonika. Greece remained neutral. By mid-December the Serbian Army had been smashed.

Salonika was the French idea, and it had been forced on the British Government over the strenuous opposition of the military and naval experts. The General Staff held Salonika to be a futile dissipation of force. The Admiralty opposed Salonika because the Navy had not enough small vessels for the protection against submarines of an additional long line of communications, and were hard put to protect the line to the Gallipoli Peninsula. The

Cabinet had given in to French views to avoid a rupture in the Entente. This was not the first time, and certainly not the last, that British war strategy suffered from the irksome disability of being 'tied to the tails of the French'.

Salonika all but finished the Dardanelles. One British division and one French division were sent from the Dardanelles to Salonika in October; worse, the growing demands of Salonika made it practically impossible to send reinforcements to Gallipoli. By early January 1916, 150,000 Allied troops were tied up on the Salonika front, and, by the end of the war, over 600,000. This force did little fighting, while suffering enormous losses from malaria in the marshes of the Vardar and Struma, until late in 1918, when it was able to advance and defeat Bulgaria. 'They were,' says Oliver, 'a lasting liability on the Navy for communications and transport by sea.' Finally, Bulgaria's adhesion to the Central Powers made the Allied footing in Gallipoli untenable by opening up a direct overland route for German supplies to Turkey.

The cause of the evacuationists was immensely strengthened by General Sir Charles Monro's report. The Dardanelles Committee had sent him out to Gallipoli to report on the advisability on purely military grounds of evacuating the Peninsula, or whether another attempt should be made to capture it. 'General Monro was an officer of swift decision. He came, he saw, he capitulated.' Churchill's sarcasm was not misplaced. Monro was an arch Westerner for whom a hasty examination of the situation on the Peninsula was sufficient. He telegraphed Kitchener on 31 October recommending evacuation on military grounds, and then stayed on as Sir Ian Hamilton's replacement. 'The decision to supersede Sir Ian Hamilton shows more clearly than anything else which way the wind was blowing. So long as he remained in command there was little prospect of a withdrawal.'[2] For Keyes it was 'a black day', since Hamilton had the 'vision' to see the 'unlimited possibilities' in the new naval plan that he had hatched. Two days later (2 November) the exclusion from the newly formed War Committee of Churchill and Curzon, two of the leading opponents of evacuation, were further straws in the wind.

The anti-evacuationists had their backs to the wall. Evacuation was for them unthinkable. It would 'make the Dardanelles into the bloodiest tragedy of the world', because of the severe losses that

[2] Hankey, *The Supreme Command*, i. 430.

could be expected: no less than 50 per cent of the force, Hamilton informed Kitchener (12 October), though, privately, his figure was 35–45 per cent. Hamilton had powerful allies in the Cabinet: the Prime Minister, Churchill, Balfour, and Curzon.

Keyes and Wemyss used the same argument, partly, no doubt, as a matter of tactics. For them, however, and for those they were able to convert, the great argument against evacuation was the promise of success in a naval attack, that is, in a reversion to the initial strategy of the operation. The reorganized sweeping flotilla, the much improved air service, the presence of the monitors, and the exploits of the submarines, which had obtained a partial naval command of the Sea of Marmora—these factors had, they believed, completely altered the picture since 18 March. The submarine story is worth special mention.

The daring, skilful, almost incredible performance of a handful of British submarines in the Marmora in 1915 is a glorious page in the traditions of the Royal Navy. The ordeal of the 'E'-type boats was a frightening one. They faced a variety of hazards: guns, torpedoes, depth charges, mines, and steel-wire anti-submarine nets strung across the Narrows. They had no anti-mine gear, no metal blades that could shear off mine-mooring cables or nets. They would simply charge through the net. A peculiar hazard was the strong stratum of fresh water, about ten fathoms deep, that poured down from the Marmora and often threw the boats violently out of control. In all, seven British submarines were engaged in the Marmora during 1915, of which three were lost (two of them in the Marmora).

The Australian *AE-2* (Lieutenant-Commander H. H. G. D. Stoker) was the first submarine to force her way in—on 26 April. She was sunk in action with Turkish warships on 30 April. The exploits of Commanders E. C. Boyle (*E-14*) and M. E. Nasmith (*E-11*), each of whom earned a V.C. for his work in the Marmora, are especially remarkable. The daring D'Oyly-Hughes, Nasmith's First Lieutenant, also deserves mention. The first British boat to enter the Marmora, stay there a while, and come out again was *E-14*. Boyle started through the Dardanelles on the night of 26 April, got through despite minefields and gunfire—diving, surfacing, diving, weaving, running (to quote William Guy Carr's delightful *By Guess and by God*) 'as blind as kittens tied up in a sack', and leading 'the life of a weasel in a hen-yard with the whole neighbourhood out hunting it'. Boyle was recalled by wireless on 17 May. Two days later, *E-11* slipped through the Straits and bobbed up in the crowded Golden Horn, 25 May, the first enemy craft to enter those sacred precincts in 500 years. Nasmith sank a ship (keeping his periscope up long enough to take a snapshot through it of the ship going down), threw the capital into a state of panic, and came out of the Marmora on 6 June. On another occasion (altogether, he was in the Marmora for over three months, including one stay of 47 days), with few torpedoes left, Nasmith began to use a tricky manœuvre. He set the torpedoes to float at the end of their run if the target was missed, so that, if the sea was smooth enough, they could be recovered and, after the unscrewing of the firing pistol, a dangerous operation, reloaded into the tubes, guided by men working in the water. The first time, Nasmith extracted the pistol personally. Thereafter he allowed D'Oyly-Hughes to do it, as he was also very much at home in the water and Nasmith had complete confidence in his ability to do it without running any undue risk.

The last submarine in the Marmora, *E-2*, was recalled on 2 January 1916. The total British bag in 1915 was: 2 Turkish battleships, 1 destroyer, 5 gunboats, 9 transports, over 30 steamers, 7 ammunition- and store-ships, and 188 sailing vessels.[3] The submarines so harassed enemy shipping as to practically paralyse it by the autumn. The Turks were using the Marmora only for the most urgent supplies, usually by day, and troops bound for the front were forced to proceed by rail to Rodosto, then march three days inland, instead of the former simple journey by boat. But for the tragic incompetence of Stopford and the consequent failure of the Suvla operation, the submarines might have had a decisive effect on the campaign.

Not only were conditions more favourable for a naval attack, but De Robeck's fleet was restless with its passive role of bringing reinforcements, munitions, and supplies to the men in the trenches and evacuating the wounded. The diehards among the officers had been on the warpath since the Army's failure in August. They talked incessantly of making a final effort to force the Straits. Wemyss, Major W. W. Godfrey of the Royal Marines, De Robeck's War Staff Officer, and especially Keyes were the leading

---

[3] Lieutenant-Commander Kenneth Edwards, *We Dive at Dawn* (London, 1939), p. 182.

spirits. They were unaware, not that it would have mattered much, that Hankey had thrown a cold douche on unilateral action by the Navy in his report of 30 August, after a visit to the Dardanelles. He found that 'a few responsible naval officers' favoured a renewal of the 18 March attempt and had worked out an attractive plan for a surprise attack, but that 'the overwhelming majority of naval officers in the Eastern Mediterranean are utterly opposed to it', and they included the C.-in-C. himself. It would be 'a mistake for the Government to *order* an attack of this kind except in the last resort, or in any way to urge the Vice-Admiral to a course to which he is opposed'.[4]

On 23 September, Keyes submitted a proposal that resembled the 18 March plan, except that the attack would be simultaneous with the next military offensive on Gallipoli. De Robeck was not impressed. Nothing had happened since 18 March to remove his fear that they could not overcome the mine and torpedo risk. 'After our daily argument,' Keyes wrote to his wife (26 September), 'the Admiral concluded: "Well, Commodore, you and I will never agree . . ." I said: "Our forefathers would not have hesitated or stopped to count the cost." He replied, "You would do what old Duckworth did: go up and get stuck there, and have to fight your way out, losing heavily—having achieved nothing." I replied that I was not thinking of Duckworth but others of another calibre. It is hard to be patient.'[5]

Keyes submitted a fresh scheme to the Admiral on 18 October. It involved a complete change of strategy in that it discarded the gradualism that was central to all earlier plans. It also involved substantial naval reinforcements in the way of old battleships and 'special service ships'. The latter were 'dummy battleships'—old merchant steamers disguised as battleships which were to be prepared as mine-bumpers. (This would perhaps have consisted of shoring up bulkheads and filling the holds with flotation material such as empty oil drums.) The special service ships would be used 'to clear a passage through the minefields and mask the torpedo tubes, instead of employing sloops and destroyers to sweep'. The main idea was a headlong surprise rush through the Straits

---

[4] C.I.D. Paper No. G-19, 'The Dardanelles. Memorandum on the Situation', 30 Aug. 1915; Asquith MSS. There is a summary of the paper in Hankey, *The Supreme Command*, i. 406-7.

[5] Keyes, *Naval Memoirs*, i. 437-8.

at dawn. Preceded by the old battleship *Redoubtable* (late *Revenge*, of the pre-dreadnought 'Royal Sovereign' class), which had blisters on her side (that is, bulges for torpedo protection) and six or eight special service ships, a squadron of five or six old battleships, two cruisers, and destroyers was to steam straight through the mine-field and the Narrows, the destroyers providing a smoke-screen. The squadron was to keep going even though unswept mines and unsilenced guns remained, and once through it would engage the Narrows forts in reverse. Simultaneously, a squadron of ten of the better pre-dreadnoughts, with sloops and destroyers for sweeping, would pin down the Narrows forts with a heavy bombardment from below the Kephez minefield. A third squadron, composed of monitors, blistered cruisers, and the old battleship *Swiftsure*, would engage the Narrows forts from the western side of the Peninsula. The army on Gallipoli was to distract the enemy fire, no more. Keyes counted heavily on surprise, smoke-screens, and dummy battleships enabling a portion of the break-through squadron to reach the Marmora. There it would cut the single road on the neck of the Peninsula, the Bulair Isthmus, which supplied the Turkish divisions on Gallipoli. The submarines had already virtually cut the sea communications with Gallipoli.

How practicable was the plan? Of course, we shall never know, for it was never tried; but it does seem that it would have stood a better chance a few months earlier, before the German U-boats had begun to prowl in the Mediterranean. There were about a dozen there by the end of November, six of which were at Con-stantinople. De Robeck's battleships would have made excellent U-boat targets in the cramped limits of the Marmora. Corbett, nevertheless, called Keyes's a 'daring' conception that 'seemed at least the only way in which success could be snatched from the failure'. To Churchill the plan was 'remarkable for its audacity'.[6]

Wemyss liked the Keyes plan. Not so the C.-in-C. In conversa-tion and writing then and afterwards, Keyes gives the impression

---

[6] Corbett, *Naval Operations*, iii. 203; *The World Crisis*, ii. 493. Keyes, *Naval Memoirs*, i. 440–3, has the 18 October memorandum. *Dardanelles Commission* has it, too, with Keyes's interpolations. Corbett adds a few details of the plan as finally worked out. Keyes offered De Robeck an alternative to the surprise attack—'forcing a passage under cover of a heavy and deliberate bombardment from inside and outside the Straits'—but he indicated his strong preference. 'I have put the general outline of this scheme to the members of your Secret Committee, and I understand that they are all, with the possible exception of Captain Dent, in favour of a surprise attack.'

that he was the only senior officer with courage and imagination, and that De Robeck, Jackson, Kitchener, and Monro were all faint-hearted. This is quite inaccurate, not least of all as regards De Robeck. The Admiral was a fearless man who would flinch at nothing if he was convinced that it had a good chance of success and would help to win the war. Although he had no faith in the Keyes plan, he was willing to give his Chief of Staff a fair chance to state his case to the Lords of the Admiralty in person. It was a magnanimous gesture, although the Admiral prejudiced the plan in advance by writing to the First Sea Lord (20 October) that it would 'not lead to any result if we got through with a few ships. It most probably leads [sic] to a most colossal disaster!' The Turks would not capitulate if Constantinople were bombarded, nor abandon Gallipoli, because four or five ships managed to get through into the Marmora. 'They have several months supply on the peninsular [sic] and unless we can pass our colliers and supplies through the Straits, we cannot carry on an effective campaign in the Marmora. To do so we must take and destroy all the Turkish forts in the Straits, and it must be a combined operation with the Army. . . . If we can keep up a steady pressure and the Turks cannot get much ammunition through, we are getting nearer the end than by making mad and heroic efforts that cannot bring about a final result!'[7] This was the very argument, and a sound one, that the C.-in-C. had used on 23 March. And it was proper for him to make it now, as it was he, not Keyes, who had the responsibility for success or failure. It is interesting to speculate on what De Robeck would have done if Keyes had succeeded in persuading the Admiralty and the Cabinet to adopt his scheme. It is my guess that he would have resigned his command rather than carry out an operation which he believed would be disastrous. The contingency did not arise.

Keyes arrived in London on 28 October and during the next six days had interviews with Balfour, Oliver, and the Sea Lords. He did not help his cause by his undiplomatic extra-Admiralty campaign to win support. He was 'wild in his abuse of the Admiralty, calling the Board cowards [and] old women'.[8] Balfour gave Keyes sympathetic hearings and rather liked the plan the

[7] Jackson MSS.
[8] Diary, 25 Nov. 1915, on the authority of Lord Stamfordham, whom Keyes had seen during his stay in England; Hamilton MSS.

more he heard of it. But as he told Keyes, the decision would be greatly influenced by the attitude of Jackson and Oliver. It developed that the First Lord did not have the seamen with him, and he would not go against their advice. The C.O.S. and the Sea Lords, though non-committal before Keyes, actually were not at all excited over the scheme, and this was particularly true of Jackson, whose opinion mattered most. (Keyes had carried away the impression that 'Oliver at least was fairly disposed towards the scheme, but that Jackson 'was for it sometimes—sometimes not!') They estimated that twelve battleships would be lost, which was too high a price to pay. The Second Sea Lord referred to it as a 'wildcat scheme'.

Apart from the expected costs, and, if anything, more important, the First Sea Lord and the C.O.S. were lukewarm because the Navy's resources were so over-extended by the Salonika enterprise. There was even the distinct possibility in November of war with Greece, which had adopted a threatening attitude to the Salonika force. (Venizelos had resigned on 5 October, when the pro-German King Constantine insisted that Greece remain neutral.) Jackson was unhappy over the general prospect and not looking for fresh naval commitments.

The demands on our resources are beyond our capabilities. R. [Roger Keyes] wants 24 more trawlers, though we must send that number in addition for the Salonika route, and our Mediterranean transports which are and will be employed till the end of the year carrying ¼ million troops are almost unescorted in the Mediterranean, and we still have the Dardanelles to maintain as before. If Greece is nasty we shall have to coerce her . . . The situation can't get much worse . . . there are now 50,000 French and English troops in Southern Serbia . . . There are 100,000 more going there, and when landed these troops will require about 4,000 tons of stuff landing at Salonika per diem . . . Persia is also being coerced into war and we expect it daily and are weak everywhere there. The only bright spot is Baghdad, which we should capture soon and hold the main road into Persia from the West.

Excuse my growl, but you see I have plenty to occupy my thoughts.[9]

[9] Jackson to Jellicoe, 1 Nov. 1915; Jellicoe MSS. The Greek crisis was so grave that the Prime Minister put this problem to the Combined War Staffs: 'On the assumption that either Greece takes the offensive against the Allies or that we are called upon to put pressure upon her, the Joint Staffs are requested to advise the Cabinet what steps of a naval or military character we ought to take.' The paper submitted by the General Staff and the Admiralty War Staff on 1 November called for 'severe

The Greek situation did not improve. 'Greece is very shaky, and say they'll disarm any allied troops which may retreat from Serbia into Greece (i.e. if they can), so we must be ready to bring pressure immediately if necessary, and Fremantle may find himself off Athens or the Piraeus any day.'[10]

Jackson and the War Staff were only prepared to order a fresh attempt to force the Straits *à la* Keyes, *if the Army would do its share*. Now, Kitchener, who was enamoured of Keyes's plan, was ready to co-operate in a joint offensive. His idea was that as soon as there were ships in the Marmora, the Army (40,000 men) would seize and hold the Isthmus of Bulair, to supply the ships if the Turks on Gallipoli held out. Specifically, the Army would transport the necessary stores from the Gulf of Xeros into the Marmora. On the morning of 3 November the War Staff Group reached a 'provisional conclusion', which Balfour communicated to Kitchener that day in this very convincing note:

The scheme of rushing the Straits was not finally ruled out; but treated as a simple naval operation, altogether independent of a simultaneous and determined attack by the Army on the Turkish positions, its utility was regarded as at least doubtful. A fleet could not be self-supporting in the Marmora for more than three weeks at most; and the difficulty of getting out of the Marmora is probably greater than the difficulty of getting in. There is no doubt that in three weeks the Turkish transports (outside the shelter of the Bosphorus) could be practically annihilated, and that much damage could be caused to the railway, ammunition factories, etc., in the neighbourhood of Constantinople itself. These results alone however hardly justify the inevitable losses which a double journey through the Dardanelles would entail. A good deal more might be hoped for if the fleet in the Marmora could, by obtaining supplies, dominate that sea for a considerable period. But it is probably more difficult to get colliers and merchant ships safely through the Straits than vessels like destroyers, which are fast, or battleships, which are well protected. The scheme which you suggested this morning . . . seems impracticable. I do not speak of the military difficulties (which it is not our business in this Office to

pressure', such as the destruction of the Greek Fleet, the blocking of the Corinth Canal, the capture of Greek shipping in Allied and non-Allied ports, and the blockade of Greece. 'The Question of Coercive Action against Greece'; Lloyd George MSS.

[10] Jackson to Jellicoe, 11 Nov. 1915; Jellicoe MSS. An Anglo-French squadron in the Aegean, with Rear-Admiral Sydney Fremantle in command of the British ships, was prepared to take immediate offensive action if the Greeks tried to interfere with the Allied force at Salonika.

consider) . . . To land thousands of tons of coal in the Gulf of Xeros; to transport it, probably under shell fire, over the rough and roadless peninsula, is, we believe, impossible. But were this accomplished, our difficulties would be only beginning. The ships could only coal with the help of lighters . . . we could not take them up the Dardanelles . . . If we had them, it would not be easy to load them with coal, and during the operation they would always be open to submarine attack.[11]

The whole matter boiled down to this. The Admiralty would accept the Keyes plan for a surprise rush if the Army simultaneously made an advance to seize the Narrows forts. The Army was by then too exhausted to be able to do this (hence, Kitchener's Bulair proposal, which looked to be somewhat easier to execute)—certainly not without reinforcements, and this was impossible on account of Salonika and the clamour of the Westerners that Gallipoli was a side-show.

Keyes, who was still in London, only saw the rosy side of the picture. For him 4 November was a 'red-letter day . . . I felt sure that I had won my battle.' The Admiralty were ordering important reinforcements to the Dardanelles: four old battleships, four destroyers, twenty-four armed trawlers; the Admiralty and War Office appeared ready to collaborate in a joint attack on the Straits. The fly in the ointment was Kitchener, who had not yet accepted the Admiralty's version of a joint offensive. On the evening of the 4th the Field-Marshal left for the East to make a personal inspection of the situation.

Kitchener conferred with De Robeck and the Generals at Mudros, 10–11 November. (He inspected the Allied positions on the following days.) The Admiral told him that any attempt to force the Straits would be folly; he was prepared to evacuate Suvla and Anzac, but favoured retaining Helles, to help the Navy blockade the entrance to the Dardanelles. The Generals did not even raise the idea of a naval attack, with or without military support. Except for Birdwood, and with or without qualifications, they were ready for evacuation; even Birdwood's resistance to evacuation had greatly weakened, now that reinforcements seemed remote.

On 22 November, Kitchener cabled home his long-awaited (and reluctant) recommendation. A combination of factors had gone into it: De Robeck's attitude towards a naval attack, the requirements

[11] Asquith MSS.

of Salonika, the influence of Kitchener's adviser, Major-General Henry S. Horne, who was a Westerner *par excellence*, and Kitchener's preoccupation with Egyptian security. The cable stated that, as German assistance for the Turks on the Peninsula was now 'practically available', the British positions there could not be maintained and 'evacuation seems inevitable'. Suvla and Anzac should be evacuated at once, and Helles retained for the present. 'This would prevent the Turks from establishing a submarine base in the Straits [which would facilitate attacks on Allied shipping in the Mediterranean]; and would also facilitate the task of withdrawal from the two northern beaches.'[12]

Keyes's last words to Kitchener, just before the Field-Marshal departed for London, were: 'I am not beaten yet, Sir, and I am not going to be.' They shook hands on it. 'A very pertinacious young man!' Kitchener remarked to Birdwood.[13] Keyes would have felt even more miserable had he known the contents of the Prime Minister's telegram that day to Kitchener. The War Committee, on the strength of Kitchener's views, and also of a General Staff paper of 22 November, had unanimously recommended to the Cabinet (23 November) that the entire Peninsula be evacuated, including Helles. (Both the General Staff and Admiralty War Staff had urged that Helles be kept.) The naval advantages of holding Helles were 'not commensurate with the military disadvantages involved'.[14]

One might have thought that the unanimous recommendation of the War Committee, two of whose members, the Prime Minister and the First Lord, had been among the staunchest of anti-evacuationists,[15] would have ended the Hamlet-like debate, that the Cabinet would have confirmed the decision, and that orders would have gone out promptly for the evacuation of the whole Peninsula. Not so—the Government wasted precious weeks in making up their mind. Hankey cites as an important reason for the 'exasperating delays' the dual system of responsibility referred to

[12] *Dardanelles Commission.*

[13] Diary, 23 Nov. 1915; Keyes, *Naval Memoirs*, i. 470.

[14] *Dardanelles Commission.*

[15] As recently as 19 November, Balfour had written a Cabinet paper urging that they cling to Gallipoli, to avoid the heavy manpower and prestige losses that would accompany evacuation. He was all for not deserting, 'in the sight of East and West, an important strategic position, which had been gloriously captured, is gloriously held, and may, perhaps, never be dangerously threatened.' 'Gallipoli'; Lloyd George MSS.

above. 'The Cabinet must needs have its say. At this point indeed the disadvantages of dual control in the Supreme Command made itself felt as never before or after.' The Cabinet 'was unwilling to trust implicitly the strong War Committee it had itself created. Ministers who were left out must needs assert themselves. Decisions taken in the smaller body which was far better equipped with information and expert advice, had to be fought out again in the larger. On matters of major policy debate among the nine must needs be repeated among the twenty-one.'[16]

Curzon led the anti-evacuationists, Bonar Law the evacuation-ists, in a sorely divided Cabinet. Debate was heated, and a mountain of memoranda kept the fire stoked. Hankey, directed by the Prime Minister to declare his views, contributed a paper (28 November) that spoke out against evacuation: it would leave Turkey free to concentrate all her forces against Russia and Britain in the Near East, there was danger of a separate peace by Russia, and so on. They should send to Gallipoli the four divisions at Salonika—they were about to be set free by the Government's decision to put an end to that campaign—'to save the position on the Gallipoli peninsula, and, if possible, to take the offensive'.[17] The idea had some appeal for Jackson and Oliver, who were willing to have another try at the Dardanelles if the four divisions were sent to reinforce the troops on Gallipoli. Jackson's feelings about evacuation were ambivalent. He rather preferred 'another good attempt' by the Army and Navy, but if the soldiers would not play up, he saw an important advantage in evacuation. A large proportion of De Robeck's fleet could be sent home, which would ease the serious manning problem 'immensely'.[18] The Cabinet grasped at the Salonika straw. On 2 December they decided to examine the question of how swiftly an offensive could be launched from Suvla with the British divisions at Salonika. How soon could they be transported to Mudros? the Admiralty asked Wemyss. (He had relieved De Robeck on 25 November, when the C.-in-C., suffering badly from insomnia, had sailed home for a rest.) Wemyss hustled Keyes over to Salonika on the 5th to make the arrangements.

---

[16] Hankey, *The Supreme Command*, ii. 459, 464.

[17] Brigadier-General C. F. Aspinall-Oglander, *History of the Great War. Military Operations. Gallipoli* (London, 1929–32, 2 vols.), ii. 431.

[18] Jackson to Jellicoe, 21 Nov. 1915; Jellicoe MSS.

It was the French who gave the *coup de grâce* to this eleventh-hour scheme. They had reluctantly given in, at the strained Calais conference on 4 December, to the British insistence on withdrawal from Salonika. The very next day, at a conference of Allied Generals and Staffs at Chantilly, the French reopened the whole question. They were determined to hang on at Salonika, and they had the Russians and Italians with them. Isolated, Britain accepted the French position to preserve a measure of Allied unity.

Chantilly scotched the idea of reinforcing Suvla. The evacuationists in the Cabinet now had the upper hand, and on 7 December the Cabinet once and for all decided on evacuation, with Helles to be held for the present to avoid the admission of complete failure. 'From this moment,' Churchill dryly comments, 'the perplexities of the British Government came to an end. Henceforward they remained steadfast in pusillanimous resolve.'

Meanwhile, since De Robeck's departure the energetic and tenacious Wemyss, with Keyes's close collaboration, had been waging a tremendous last-ditch fight, firing off a series of telegrams to the Admiralty, attempting to convert Monro, etc. 'I consider that a combined attack by Navy and Army would have every prospect of achieving decisive results,' Wemyss telegraphed the Admiralty (28 November). A violent gale, heavy rains, bitter cold, and a blizzard, 26–28 November, severely damaged or destroyed the piers and a number of small vessels, and resulted in thousands of casualties through sickness, frostbite, and drownings (in the flooded trenches). Wemyss used this spate of terrible weather to show that Turkish army morale had been shaken, and how unwise it would be at that time of year to count on the prolonged period of good weather needed for evacuation.

Wemyss was fairly optimistic as late as 7 December because of Kitchener's reconversion, the contemplated withdrawal from Salonika, and the reports of growing Turkish demoralization on account of the storm and other events. Then this telegram arrived late on the 7th: 'In view of unanimous opinion his Majesty's Government have decided to shorten the front by evacuating Anzac and Suvla.' 'The blow was bitter,' was Wemyss' reaction, 'and all the more so since the heights to which our expectations had been raised had been great. I had no illusions about "shortening the front" . . . evacuation of Suvla and Anzac could only herald that of Helles, must inevitably lead to retirement from the Peninsula and an inglorious termination of the campaign.'[19]

Wemyss was not yet beaten. After breakfast on the 8th he shot off a telegram to the Admiralty, stating that the Navy was

prepared to force the Straits and control them for an indefinite period; cutting off all Turkish supplies which now find their way to the Peninsula either by sea from the Marmora or across the Dardanelles from Asiatic to European shore. The only line of communications left would be the road along the Isthmus of Bulair, which can be controlled almost entirely from the Sea of Marmora and the Gulf of Xeros. What is offered the Army, therefore, is the practical, complete severance of all Turkish lines of communication, accompanied by the destruction of the large supply depôts on the shore of the Dardanelles. In the first instance I strongly advocated that the naval attack should synchronize with an army offensive, but that is not a necessity and if the Army will be prepared to attack in the event of a favourable opportunity presenting itself, nothing more need be required of them. The Navy here is prepared to undertake this operation with every assurance of success.[20]

Other telegrams, to Balfour and Jackson, followed, breathing complete confidence in success, given the chance. They were fruitless. The Admiralty would not hear of the Navy attempting single-handedly to force the Narrows, and they would not question the decision of the Government to evacuate Suvla and Anzac, 'in view of the individual and combined appreciation of the responsible Generals and the great strain thrown on naval and military resources by the operations in Greece'.[21] On 12 December, Wemyss telegraphed the Admiralty, accepting the Government's decision 'with the greatest regret and misgiving'. Not quite, for three days later he made one last desperate attempt to breathe life into the naval attack. He first urged the military seizure of Achi Baba, without which the Helles zone was exposed to artillery fire from the Asiatic shore and from the north of Achi Baba, and so

[19] Wemyss, *The Navy and the Dardanelles Campaign*, p. 224.
[20] *Dardanelles Commission*.
[21] *Ibid*. This telegram followed a Board meeting on the 10th, at which Balfour had regretfully announced that no effort would be made to force the Dardanelles with ships, since the bulk of naval opinion, including that of the Sea Lords, was against it. On this Admiral Hamilton commented in his diary: 'We [the Junior Sea Lords] have not been formally asked, nor have we been given the materials on which to give a considered opinion. Nevertheless I have no doubt he is correct in his intelligent anticipation of what our opinions would be.' 15 Dec. 1915; Hamilton MSS.

would be untenable. Given the occupation of Achi Baba, the naval attack on the Narrows would be successful.

The Forts can't stop us. By direct and indirect fire they would soon be silenced. The torpedo tubes are the worst menace, but with the nets devised by Captain —— [?] and with the element of surprise that would be given to the attack, I think the dangers would be tremendously diminished, and . . . we should not lose more than 3 ships. Surely such a loss would be justifiable under the circumstances. God knows I am not bloodthirsty and should hate to throw away life uselessly as much as anybody, but in this case the stake played for would amply justify it. . . .

There remains the question of mines. Such mines as are still there can be calculated to have lost a great deal of their efficiency, and many have broken adrift. The sweeping will be greatly increased in efficiency, and protection of ships by means of wire hausers towed with a kite would help to render this danger much less. The rushing through of an advanced Squadron has been principally arranged for to prevent any floating mines being liberated above the Narrows and new minefields laid. . . .

Immediate action or complete evacuation seems to me to be the only two logical alternatives left.[22]

It was to be the latter. The Generals were unanimously of the opinion that the capture of Achi Baba was beyond their resources. Besides, retention of a foothold on the Peninsula at Helles continued the dispersion of effort, and 'concentration' was the new slogan of the General Staff. On 23 December the War Committee, on the advice of General Monro, the General Staff, and the new C.I.G.S., Sir William Robertson, decided to evacuate Cape Helles. The Cabinet confirmed the decision on the 27th, with Balfour, who was furiously against it, apparently standing alone.

The evacuation of the Peninsula posed problems of a terrifying magnitude. 83,000 men had to be secretly withdrawn from Suvla and Anzac in a night-time operation, and 35,000 more from Helles,[23] to say nothing of hundreds of guns, thousands of vehicles and animals, and vast quantities of stores. All this was to be accomplished in the season of winter gales, under the enemy's eyes (the coast was believed to be under enemy submarine surveillance,

---

[22] Wemyss to Jackson, 15 Dec. 1915; Jackson MSS.

[23] There had been a reduction in the 134,000 men on the Peninsula at the end of November (of whom 10,000 were French) in the preliminary stage of evacuation which had begun before receipt of evacuation orders.

and the Turkish trenches were nowhere over 300 yards away from the Allied trenches—in some places, only five yards), on open beaches within effective range of enemy guns, and in confined waters that invited submarine attack.

In the annals of war no evacuation on this scale had ever been attempted. The prospect was frightening and the tension before and during the evacuation was great. The General Staff estimated losses of 50,000 men, and Wemyss shuddered over the 'horrible' possibilities, should the 'slightest hitch occur. One wretched stupid Private might well cause a disaster!'[24] This did not prevent him from carrying out his share of the operation calmly and efficiently. The evacuation of the Suvla–Anzac bridgehead began on 8 December and was completed on the night of the 19th/20th. The following night a fierce gale swept the Peninsula! The Helles evacuation took place in the first week of January and was completed during the night of the 8th/9th, despite a rising gale. The evacuation was effected so skilfully that the Turks were entirely ignorant of what was going on. Not one life was lost in the entire operation, and most of the impedimenta was brought off. Faultless staff work, perfect discipline, excellent inter-Service co-operation, and good luck in the shape of a spell of perfect weather account for the remarkable achievement.

Gallipoli ended, then, with 'the melancholy success of a brilliantly executed evacuation', which half persuaded the British people that the Allies had won the campaign. But, of course, as was said of Dunkirk a quarter of a century later, wars are not won by evacuations. Nobody knew this better than the Admiralty. When the Government proposed to give De Robeck a baronetcy and Keyes the K.C.B. for their services in the campaign, the Second Sea Lord, who was consulted, recommended against it. He did not think a baronetcy should be given for a failure, 'however brilliant'. He would suggest only a K.C.M.G. and a Military C.B. for the Admiral and the Commodore, respectively. In the event, De Robeck and Keyes had to rest content for the time with a K.C.B. and a C.M.G., respectively. Wemyss sailed for home on 24 December, to be appointed K.C.B. for his Dardanelles service, and C.-in-C., East Indies.

De Robeck put his house in order upon returning to his command (22 December). 'I have told Keyes in a heart to heart talk

[24] Wemyss to Jackson, 15 Dec. 1915; Jackson MSS.

that if he remains, he must do so as C.O.S., and not as "leader of the Opposition". . . . The soldiers call him the "lunatic sailor".'[25] Well, the 'lunatic sailor' to his dying day never doubted for a moment that the Navy should and could have forced the Straits. 'If we had merely steamed steadily through at a moderate speed in line ahead, with the anti-mine devices we had developed, quite sufficient ships would have got through into the Marmora to achieve our object . . . even twelve obsolete battleships [the Sea Lords' estimate] would not have been too high a price to pay for all that could have been accomplished.'[26] I doubt that many students of naval history will accept this conclusion. In evaluating Keyes's proposals we have to bear in mind that the judgment of this gallant officer was often overruled by his fiery temperament, and that he never looked much further than the launching of the operation.

The Cabinet, the Generals, and De Robeck made the right decision. An all-important point is: What could have been achieved if a few ships did get past the guns, mines, and torpedoes guarding the Narrows? How could they have been supplied, and what chance would they have had of making the return voyage? Even if the forts were silenced, the Turks could have brought heavy mobile guns to the southern bank and, firing at point-blank range, could have done great damage to ships passing through the Straits. De Robeck was right in believing that the Turks would not capitulate if Constantinople were bombarded (stiffened by their German advisers, the Government would surely have cleared out of the capital), or abandon Gallipoli, because four or five ships got through the Dardanelles. From the beginning every scheme

[25] De Robeck to Jackson, 24 Dec. 1915; *ibid.* Keyes's anguish of heart is mirrored in a letter of that time. De Robeck's 'fear of having to do *anything* in the Straits ever since the 18th March would be rather pathetic if it was not so distressing and had not had such a ghastly effect on our whole policy and been mainly responsible for the miserable fiasco out here. W.C. [Churchill] will never forgive him. . . . At least R.W.'s [Wemyss's] telegrams show that the fleet out here did not share his (de R's) opinion and that there was still a fair fighting spirit in it when we were defeated by the politicians, *that* K. [Kitchener], and those two stupid, shortsighted *little* Generals Linden [Lynden-] Bell [Monro's C.O.S.] and Monro. I think those craven hearted Admirals at the Admiralty must be given a share in the wretched business. Their acquiescence in a joint operation was very half hearted and they seized on K's weakness to shift the responsibility on to the War Office and shirk making a bold decision and forcing the Government to make the Army play up.' Keyes to his wife, 31 Dec., 1915; Keyes MSS.
[26] Keyes, *Naval Memoirs*, i. 523.

fundamentally depended on naval guns silencing the forts, but this was not possible in 1915 for the reasons noted below.

The military results of the whole Dardanelles–Gallipoli operation were severe blows to the Allied cause. British casualties totalled 205,000 (115,000 killed, wounded, or missing, and 90,000 evacuated sick), and the French casualties, 47,000. The Turks not only remained in the war, but for a time, thanks to the 20 divisions that were set free, they became more active. Thus, Turkish reinforcements helped in preventing the relief of Kut (Mesopotamia), where a beleaguered British army of 10,000 was starved into surrender in April 1916. Bulgaria joined the Central Powers. The Royal Navy suffered a blow to its prestige and a jolt to its pride.

But the great loss in prestige that had been predicted all along if the operation had to be ended turned out to be grossly exaggerated. And it would be a mistake to regard the campaign as a complete failure. The Official Military History arrives at this fair conclusion:

> Yet, though the campaign failed in its main object, it was not an unredeemed failure, and the work on the peninsula in 1915 contributed largely to the eventual winning of the war. It was in great part due to the attack on the Straits that the Germans cancelled their heavy offensive in the West which they had planned for the spring of 1915, that Italy entered the war, that Greece remained neutral, and that Bulgaria held aloof till the results of the campaign seemed clear. The threat to Constantinople protected the Suez Canal and relieved the Russians from Turkish pressure in the Caucasus. Finally, it was the heavy fighting in Gallipoli that destroyed the flower of the Turkish army[27] and prepared the way for Lord Allenby's victory in Palestine. These were solid advantages, even though they bear no comparison to the rich reward that awaited the capture of the Turkish capital.[28]

On the strategic side, the bombardment of forts was unquestionably under a cloud after the unsuccessful efforts at the Dardanelles, and this was to influence Grand Fleet strategy thereafter. More importantly, the disastrous experiences at Gallipoli discredited amphibious operations. This was the big 'lesson' of Gallipoli.

It is important to appreciate that naval support of an opposed

[27] The official Turkish estimate of their casualties was 251,000; some Turkish authorities put it as high as 350,000.
[28] Aspinall-Oglander, *Military Operations. Gallipoli*, ii. 486.

landing (in April and August), and of a land battle under trench-warfare conditions, which is what the operations settled down to, are quite distinct problems. Naval artillery support did not prove effective in *either* situation. Admiral Sir T. H. Binney, who had served on one of the bombarding ships, has pinpointed the naval reasons for the Army's failures on the Peninsula.

It [25 April] was an unhappy day for the bombarding ships, with a feeling of frustration that their tremendous power could not be made effective, a feeling that they had let the Army down. . . .

Is it small wonder that most of us came away from Gallipoli with the fixed idea that naval gunfire was of little avail in the support of a landing and that for any successful landing surprise was essential? . . . But what was wrong with the naval gun-fire on V Beach [at Cape Helles, 25 April], and for that matter on all the other beaches that were defended? . . . unsuitable ammunition and flat trajectories. . . . [and] only one ship was technically equipped for bombarding purposes, i.e., only one ship was fitted with a director.

Again, in the early days in Gallipoli ships were equipped only with anti-ship ammunition. This defect was later made good . . .

The flat trajectory was more serious, for at 2,000 yards nothing which we could do would destroy a trench, and it was galling to see successive rounds missing just short or skimming over the top of the skyline. Our technical equipment was not good enough to enable us to lay miles off the coast and lob shells without risk of hitting our own troops. . . . After the war there were many opportunities of discussing the support of a landing by naval artillery at the various Staff Colleges. Everyone was agreed that [what] was required was howitzer fire from ships, gunboats or barges.

After the troops had cleared the beachheads our bombarding efforts were for the most part equally disappointing. . . . our fire was chiefly directed on gun positions (very easy to silence, but very difficult to hit) and by indirect fire on supposed concentrations some distance in rear. What would we not have given for aircraft spotting, for Artillery officers to help us in the ships, for Forward Observation officers, or for any system of signalling which took less than half an hour to get through.[29]

E. Ashmead-Bartlett, who represented the London press throughout the Dardanelles campaign, testified on the crucial flat-trajectory problem as it applied to the second facet—a land battle under trench-warfare conditions.

[29] Binney, 'Gallipoli and Normandy', *Journal of the Royal United Service Institution*, Feb. 1945.

. . . the expectations formed of the Fleet's guns dismally failed to be realised . . . Nothing has been more disappointing than the effect of these high-velocity, low-trajectory shells, both twelve and six inch, on the enemy's trenches and field works. The Turks have proved themselves to be past-masters in digging themselves in. Time and again our troops have been held up in their attacks by suddenly finding themselves up against deep trenches, the existence of which had not previously been suspected, hidden as they are amidst the shrub and bracken. . . . direct shell fire from the ships do them practically no harm except by a lucky chance. For a high explosive shell of this sort must have something to burst against and if there is no parapet, these shells merely burst in front, making huge holes in the ground whilst the fragments fly right over harmlessly.[30]

There seems to have been an improvement in naval artillery support throughout the summer by the provision of more howitzers, better communications, and more air spotting, and by the autumn the Navy had begun to develop confidence in what it could do. But the limitations of ships' guns were not yet overcome. The germs of the desiderata listed by Binney were, however, planted on the Peninsula in 1915. They took nearly a generation to sink in, then resulted in the brilliantly successful heavy-gun support of the combined operations of 1942–4 in World War II.

For the moment the old problem of whether to use the national power to strengthen the armies of Continental Allies in the main theatre or to weaken the enemy by combined operations that made the fullest use of the British command of the sea was answered in favour of the former. The recipe for victory in 1916–18 was to be a combination of military operations on the Western Front and the exercise of economic pressure by the Navy.

It was not only at the Dardanelles; the year 1915 closed darkly elsewhere in the Mediterranean.

2. THE ADRIATIC AND THE MEDITERRANEAN

From the naval point of view this was a very secondary theatre of operations, and a peculiarly frustrating one. Let us first examine the situation in the Adriatic.

The Navy's commitment in the Adriatic was forced on the Government by political considerations: it was part of Italy's price for entering the war. (She declared war on Austria on 24 May.)

[30] *Dardanelles Commission.*

In accordance with the Anglo-French-Italian Naval Convention of 10 May 1915, four British light cruisers and a division of four old British battleships, together with certain light French units, reinforced the Italian Fleet in the Adriatic.

Italy's Adriatic forces were divided into two commands. The northern fleet, at Venice, whose backbone was three old battleships, had the task of keeping under observation the Austrian Fleet at Pola, Austria's one first-class naval base. The main Italian force was in the south, based on Taranto (dreadnoughts) and Brindisi (light craft and old battleships). Its commander, H.R.H. the Duke of the Abruzzi, was young, vigorous, charming, and a fine officer, popular with the officers and men of the whole Fleet. He initiated and directed all operations in the southern Adriatic, although he did not always have a free hand, since naval strategy was made in Rome. With the Duke at Taranto were the British pre-dreadnoughts. The latter constituted a separate division under Rear-Admiral Cecil F. Thursby, a pretty good sea officer of the old school who held no particular aces. Richmond, who served as Liaison Officer to the Italian Navy, sized him up not inaccurately: 'Don't think Thursby has many ideas . . . Rather a paint & uniform type, split yarns & that sort of thing.'[31]

The Duke had three main objectives. (1) To keep the fleet ready to meet the Austrian Fleet. This involved keeping battle-ready, and, to have early notice of enemy fleet movements, watching the Adriatic, north of Brindisi, with submarines, shore lookout stations, and occasional sweeps with light cruisers and torpedo craft. (2) To protect the Italian coast against raids by the use of mines, small submarines, armoured trains, and light-cruiser and destroyer squadrons. (3) To establish an effective watch in the Straits of Otranto to deny passage to the Austrian and German submarines. For the blockade the Duke had a supplemental force of patrol vessels at Brindisi commanded by an admiral and consisting of Italian light cruisers, destroyers, and armed merchant cruisers, and British light cruisers.

The blockade of the Straits of Otranto was ineffective from the start. The Admiralty had in May urged upon the Italians the establishment there of a patrol of trawlers and fishing-boats with nets, and had offered them fifty trawlers and some anti-submarine nets for the purpose. Although the Italians accepted, the vessels

---

[31] Diary, 29 May 1915; *Portrait of an Admiral*, p. 161.

were not dispatched, probably owing to the difficulty the Italians experienced in finding the crews and guns. By August 1915 it was clear that the Straits were a sieve. German submarines were evading the patrols of light craft, leaving the Adriatic at will, preying on Allied trade and transport routes in the Mediterranean, and returning up the Adriatic to Cattaro, their base. (They went to Pola only when in need of major repairs.) When the enemy transferred four new U-boats to the Mediterranean late in August, obviously preparatory to an intensified campaign, the Admiralty felt compelled to act. In September they dispatched sixty drifters with their full crews to Taranto (eighteen of them were sent to De Robeck in October). By the end of the month they had established their base at Brindisi and were laying an indicator-net barrier across the Straits.[32] The drifters were armed with British and Italian guns in October–November, and were reinforced in December by 40 more from England. The drifters worked across the Straits supported by the patrol vessels at Brindisi.

The net-drifter patrol was not a success. Submarines slipped through on the surface at night, or between the gaps in the nets, or on occasion by diving below the nets. The width (45–70 miles) and depth (300–500 fathoms) of the Straits made it difficult to block the passage of the enemy submarines. This was not all.

Much bad weather was experienced by the drifters during these winter months [1915–16]. Losses of nets [really expenditure, as they were meant to be expended] were heavy, some being carried away by submarine craft becoming entangled in them [that is, sometimes without the indicator buoys being activated], others, at times entire fleets, being slipped in order to give chase to an enemy submarine. . . . Difficulties were experienced by the drifters in keeping their assigned stations, owing to their inexperience of the currents in the Adriatic and the fact that many lights had been extinguished. Engagements with enemy craft were of frequent occurrence, though the drifters seem to have achieved little success in such encounters, largely, no doubt, owing to their small armament, the large German submarines mounting one or two 22 pdr. guns against the 3 pdr. or 57 or 47 mm. gun carried by the drifters.[33]

It was not until 13 May 1916 that the nets achieved their first

---

[32] On indicator nets, see below, pp.351–2.
[33] Naval Staff Monograph, *The Mediterranean, 1914–1915*, p. 206. A 'fleet' of nets was the whole string of sections towed by one drifter.

success, when the Austrian *U-6* fouled the nets of two drifters, came to the surface, and was sunk by their gunfire.

The Italian naval inactivity in the Adriatic put an extra burden on the patrol. Repeatedly, through the winter of 1915–16, the Austrians took the initiative with their inferior force. 'Every place of any importance upon the Italian Adriatic coast has been made to feel the presence of the Austrian ships or aircraft,' the British Naval Attaché in Rome, Captain William Boyle, reported on 28 September 1915. The Italians rarely succeeded in bringing the raiders to action. What is more, in the first four months of war the Austrians, at a cost of only two submarines and a few aeroplanes, inflicted these losses on the Italian Fleet: two cruisers, a destroyer, two torpedo boats, three submarines, and two dirigibles (in addition to damaging the British light cruiser *Dublin* by torpedo). 'In four months,' wrote the Attaché, 'the Austrian fleet has established a moral ascendancy in the Adriatic, and has played the part of the weaker force with conspicuous success. Not only has it succeeded in weakening the Italian fleet, but it has immobilised a force very considerably superior to itself.'[34] At one point, indeed, the Italian heavy ships were forbidden to leave harbour.

Richmond was so concerned about the Italian addiction for the defensive that he suggested to Jackson (21 June 1915) that 'strong representations' be made. This the Admiralty would not do. Richmond felt that the Italians could do much more 'if only they'd appreciate that they have a flotilla war on their hands & give up giving all their attention to the tactics of the big ships, calibration, & preparation for the "bataille classique." Let them hunt the Austrian Fleet with S.M.s & dirigibles constantly.... Worry their coast with small ships, strengthen the blockade to prevent supply-ships getting in ...'[35] His diary for the summer of 1915 is peppered with such remarks as 'This confounded defensive idea needs knocking out of their heads' (25 June) and 'These folk deserve to lose, for by Heaven they do nothing towards trying to win.... infantile, timorous strategy ...' (1 August).[36] By the middle of August, Richmond could take it no longer. 'Sick at heart of the whole thing,' he wrote to the Admiralty, seeking a command. They approved his return to England early in September, and a

[34] *Ibid.*, p. 203.
[35] Diary, 20 June 1915; *Portrait of an Admiral*, p. 174.
[36] *Ibid.*, pp. 176, 184–5.

month later gave him the command of an old battleship in the 3rd Battle Squadron.

Thursby picked up the refrain in his letters to the First Sea Lord. 'There is nothing going on here. The Italian Admiralty's latest orders to the C. in C. are that the cruisers are to go out as little as possible for the present' (2 September). 'If they would only take Cattaro, it would do more good than anything to reduce the submarines and would be the best thing they could do for us' (1 December).[37] But the Italians showed no serious interest in any scheme that involved a combined military and naval operation.

There was plenty of action during the Allied evacuation of the Serbian forces from Albania, December 1915–February 1916. Once the evacuation was completed, the Austrian cruiser raids ceased. Both sides were now quiescent, and there was merely the routine work of naval war: mine-laying, mine-sweeping, etc. Reported a bored Thursby, 'Except for the submarine warfare there is nothing to do here except keep the ships efficient and the men fit' (29 April 1916).[38] In the spring he urged without success that they should occupy some of the islands off the Dalmatian coast, so that they could keep a fixed patrol in the Adriatic above Brindisi.

As regards the Mediterranean proper, the Anglo-French Naval Convention of 6 August 1914 had put the general direction of naval operations there, including the protection of commerce, in the hands of the French. This had been modified when Turkey entered the war and the Dardanelles campaign was launched. Britain, with the assistance of a French squadron, now had charge of the eastern Mediterranean. These arrangements were over-hauled in June 1915. Excepting British waters (the vicinity of Gibraltar, Malta, and the Egyptian coast, and the British Dardanelles zone) and Italian waters, the French Mediterranean C.-in-C. had the responsibility for all the Mediterranean.

The great naval problem of the Allies in the Mediterranean was how to secure their sea communications against submarine attack. Allied merchantmen and the huge fleet of transports, supply ships, colliers, etc. needed to maintain the 400,000 British troops in Egypt and about Salonika, to say nothing of the 200,000

[37] Jackson MSS.
[38] *Ibid.*

French troops at Salonika and the troops on Gallipoli until the evacuation, provided attractive submarine targets.

In September 1915 the Germans opened their intensive submarine campaign in the inland sea (following the temporary decrease in the effectiveness of their campaign in northern parts). At that date there were fourteen German submarines in the Mediterranean: five large boats, U-boats proper (a sixth joined them in November), and two small ones (one' UB' and one 'UC'), working from Cattaro; five small ones were working from Constantinople, and two others had joined the Austrian Fleet at Pola. (The small boats had been shipped overland in sections in the spring and reassembled at Pola.) There were, in addition, seven Austrian boats at Pola.

The trouble-makers were the U-boats, four of which had slipped past the Gibraltar Patrol in late August–early September. The Patrol was too weak to prevent this traffic. A light cruiser, ten torpedo boats, and two armed boarding steamers, reinforced by nine trawlers and two sloops in the autumn, were all that Vice-Admiral Frederic E. Brock and his successor (27 October 1915), Rear-Admiral Bernard Currey, had to work with. At first the Admiralty had hopes of being able to seal the Straits of Gibraltar to enemy submarines by sending out sufficient small craft. But few could be sent, as they were too badly needed elsewhere. The Admiralty had, moreover, come to realize by November 1915 that sealing was at best too difficult and uncertain a task. Ordinarily, the U-boats passed through the Straits at night without any bother, approaching the Narrows on the surface and proceeding through them submerged. In 1915–17 there was practically nothing to stop them. It was not until 1918 that the Navy had enough trawlers and other patrol craft in the Straits to make the U-boats more cautious. But even then they had no particular difficulty.

The U-boats were responsible for five sinkings, all off the coast of Crete, in the first three weeks of September. The first serious submarine raid on Allied Mediterranean communications was an organized two-week spree, 28 September–11 October, which resulted in 19 sinkings. Altogether, during the autumn of 1915 in the Mediterranean, 54 British and 38 Allied and neutral ships were destroyed by half a dozen submarines. The Admiralty were alarmed. 'S.M.s in the Mediterranean are as bad if not worse than they have been in the North Sea. We are writing a paper on the subject for the War Council [War Committee], and it will open their eyes as to the effect of their military strategy on naval resources.'[39]

Another lull followed the November sinkings, particularly from the beginning of the New Year. Realizing this was but a respite, an Allied naval conference met in Paris on 2–3 December to work out more effective shipping protection and anti-submarine measures in the Mediterranean. The decisions reached were: (1) to divide the Mediterranean into eighteen patrol zones, of which four each were assigned to the British (Straits of Gibraltar, Malta–south coast of Sicily, Dardanelles–Aegean, Egyptian coast) and Italian fleets, and ten to the French. These roving patrols formed part of the contraband control service as well as operating against enemy submarines. (2) The French Mediterranean C.-in-C. would continue to be responsible for arranging the secret transport routes, and the commander in each zone, for the security of traffic in his zone. (3) As soon as possible, they would provide all merchant ships, especially troop transports and supply ships, with a gun crew and at least one gun.

To render the patrol of British zones effective, the Admiralty took steps to build up the strength of the patrols, which were based on Gibraltar, Malta, and Egypt, to a total of 11 yachts (nine of them armed), 30 sloops, 4 destroyers, and 96 trawlers (half of them armed).

The new patrol arrangements came into force on 1 January 1916. They did not work well. It proved very difficult to ensure that the responsibility for shipping leaving a zone was handed over to another Navy at the right time and place. The French and Italians were never able to visualize anything beyond their own particular locality. The different languages, customs, and methods also helped to make the December arrangements ineffective.

The end of the Gallipoli campaign made possible a slight redistribution of patrol zones at the Malta Conference, 9 March 1916. The whole of the route from Malta to Egypt now became a British zone. That is, Britain took over responsibility for the Aegean and the routes from Malta and Salonika to Egypt. The Conference gave consideration to extending the convoy system

[39] Jackson to Jellicoe, 11 Nov. 1915; Jellicoe MSS.

(one or two destroyers were being used to convoy large troop transports). But there were not enough destroyers available, it was felt, and the decision was to continue the patrol system, somewhat strengthened.

The Malta Conference did not solve anything. The system of secret routes and patrols was still not working too well; and the Otranto and Gibraltar anti-submarine patrols and net barrages were still not particularly effective. In the first five months of 1916 only one German submarine was accounted for in the Mediterranean (she was blown up by her own mines), and sinkings of shipping were rising. The January–March lull, when 13 British and 9 Allied and neutral ships were lost, was followed by a loss of 16 ships in April and 37 in May, with Italian shipping suffering most heavily. In the middle of March, as the situation started to worsen, the British began to divert Australian and Far Eastern shipping from the Suez Canal–Mediterranean route to the safer, if longer, route around the Cape of Good Hope. The only encouraging development in the first half of 1916 in warding off the U-boat pest was the defensive armament which the Admiralty were providing merchant ships carrying war stores and troops to and in the Mediterranean.

The U-boats got good results in the Mediterranean because, *inter alia*, they sent the best boats there, and under the command of the most experienced officers; operating conditions were unusually favourable: steamer routes were easy to find, and weather and visibility conditions were vastly better than in the North Sea; and counter-offensive measures were extremely inadequate. We must attribute a large share of the responsibility for the latter factor to the poor inter-Allied naval co-operation.

Part of the difficulty pre-dated the war, when the English and French had never, jointly and systematically, worked out the most effective use to which they could put their naval resources in the Mediterranean (or elsewhere). The British Government and the Admiralty, for good political reasons, had no desire for precise naval commitments.[40] They paid the price once war broke out. Italian entry into the war immensely complicated the task of effecting a reasonable degree of Allied naval collaboration, including the possible establishment of a unified command. The villain was the parochial mind. This was a symptom of the disease

[40] See *From the Dreadnought to Scapa Flow*, i. 306–8.

called national prestige, which would not permit a power to subordinate its fleet under a unified command not controlled by its own navy. It was obvious that either of the major Allied fleets in the Mediterranean was fully capable of dealing with the Austrians. The Italians alone had, in the summer of 1915 (Austrian figures in parentheses), 6 dreadnoughts (4), 8 pre-dreadnoughts and smaller battleships (9), 15 cruisers (9), 67 destroyers and torpedo boats (60), and 21 submarines (7 without the German boats).[41] But the difficulties of securing the co-operation of the French and Italian forces made it impossible to effect any redistribution. Each continued to be employed as a separate unit under its own independent command, the French fleet acting as a supporting fleet to the Italian. This was a sheer waste of strength, as Thursby and others often pointed out. Besides, there were not enough cruisers and destroyers to serve two fleets. Had the two combined under a single command, without doubt many of the old battleships could have been paid off or been used elsewhere, and the small craft released for the more pressing submarine problem. Well might Richmond cry out, 'What a damnable thing national conceit is!' Something more than national prestige was involved—there was bad blood between the two Navies. It was, Thursby noted, 'rather marked' at Brindisi.

British officers were friendly with their French and Italian opposites. However, the professional ineptness and jealousies displayed by the French and Italian Fleets were never-ending sources of British irritation and ineffective Allied naval co-operation. There is nothing new in this, of course. It happens between allies in all wars. Oliver found the Italians 'quite useless from a naval point of view. . . . They were jealous because our cruisers were more alert in sailing, when there was news of Austrian ships coming south, than theirs. They deliberately kept intelligence from our R.A. [Rear-Admiral Thursby] to enable their ships to get away before ours, and on occasions when enemy ships were sighted, they failed to support us.' Limpus, Admiral Superinten-dent at Malta, was almost as contemptuous. 'Our Mediterranean experience of them is that they are careful as to the probable weather before they commit themselves to going to sea.' Then there is Richmond's caustic rating: 'They had better sell their

[41] Naval Staff Monograph, *The Mediterranean, 1914–1945*, p. 143.

Fleet & take up their organs & monkeys again, for, by Heaven, that seems more their profession than sea-fighting.'[42]

The British opinion of the French Mediterranean Fleet was no more flattering. Limpus's patronizing evaluation is a classic of its kind:

Gallant, spirited and charming as our French Allies are, they are 25 years behind us in hard, practical, dogged sea patrol work. They will never learn in a year how to do it. We must therefore do the business part, that is Malta to Egypt and Egypt to Salonika, *ourselves*, while all the time humouring their susceptibilities, make our own patrol schemes and work them ourselves, carefully 'suggesting' what we are doing to the Commander-in-Chief so that he is under the impression that while, in accordance with the original convention, the British exercise command in the North, the French provide the general command in the Mediterranean and delegate this little side-show, here to us and there to the Italians, and so forth. But all the time with smoothness and with constant deference.

The blunt point is that we have the *men* (officers) who can do patrol work, and though we may be, and are, pressed to find a real sufficiency of fast sea-keeping craft, yet we *can* manage the areas allotted to us and they can *not* for want of both the craft and the alert, seabitten men to handle them.

But it is very important while we do it, to say smooth, nice things to them, to keep them in good humour with themselves and with us, in fact to play the extremely difficult game of working efficiently and loyally and with full friendliness nominally under the people who have not yet acquired the capacity to do it themselves. . . .

As to the Italians they are *children* at the game of the sea compared to the French.[43]

Thursby's opinion was no different. 'Our people are friendly with both, but prefer working with the French, who are gallant and good seamen but cannot stick it at sea for long. The Italians lack initiative, avoid responsibility and are not accustomed to Fleet work.'[44] Jackson, too, found both Fleets trying. 'The French small craft are weak and unreliable and want dash, and compare unfavourably with ours. The Italians are a hindrance and not a help, and think they can do anything without practice.'[45] On

[42] Oliver MSS.; Limpus to Jackson, n.d. (Mar. 1916), Jackson MSS.; diary, 18 Aug. 1915, *Portrait of an Admiral*, p. 192.

[43] Limpus to Jackson, 2 Feb., 1916; Jackson MSS.

[44] Thursby to Jackson, 12 May 1916; *ibid*.

[45] Jackson to Jellicoe, 11 Nov. 1915; Jellicoe MSS. The Italian Fleet, moaned Jackson (Mar. 1916), was 'as much use as a row of lifebuoys'.

another occasion, with reference to the submarine menace, the First Sea Lord unburdened himself. 'Ushant and the Western Mediterranean are the worst and they are in the French sphere of operations. The French prefer knowing the positions of S.M.s to hunting and destroying them, and are really very little assistance to us in the matter, but very touchy and grabbing and continually asking for conferences. They want all the command and honour and expect us to do the work. It is a case of "Save us from our Allies" all over the world.'[46]

Although Allied co-operation was wretchedly poor, even had it been good, the probability is that the sinkings would have gone on much as before, for there was no effective antidote to the U-boats short of convoy. The Allied Admirals were always howling for destroyers and wasting them on patrols, when a few of these craft together with trawlers and drifters would have been quite adequate for convoy escorts. The whole doctrine of trade defence, and not only in the Mediterranean, was wrong at this period.

The greatest source of annoyance to the Admiralty was the continuing drain of naval strength from Home waters to the Mediterranean. This would have been unnecessary, had there been effective Allied co-operation in that sea, and would have been bearable if the Allies were getting results. There had been a redistribution of naval force in the eastern Mediterranean after the evacuation of Gallipoli. De Robeck, Vice-Admiral, Eastern Mediterranean, and the main British squadron were in the Aegean, watching the Dardanelles, supporting the army at Salonika, protecting the occupied Greek islands, and maintaining the anti-submarine patrols in the Aegean and the blockade of Bulgaria. There were, in addition, the Gibraltar, Malta, and Mediterranean coast of Egypt submarine patrols, and the ships with the Italian Fleet.

Mediterranean needs and, even more, Allied pressures, unreasonable though they were, brought a regular flow of reinforcements, mainly of small craft, to those waters. On 1 June 1916 the Admiralty were maintaining in the Mediterranean an armada of 489 vessels, including 9 battleships, 17 cruisers, 17 sloops, 14 monitors, 38 destroyers, 18 torpedo boats, 16 submarines, 100 yachts and trawlers, 129 net drifters, and 47 minesweepers. This

[46] Jackson to Jellicoe, 12 Apr. 1916; *ibid.*

prodigious and largely unnecessary force had two bad consequences: it involved a 'ceaseless procession' (as Fisher put it) from England of colliers and 'upkeep' vessels, which made a serious dent in the mercantile tonnage available to feed Britain and keep her supplied with essential raw materials; and it deprived the Royal Navy of craft badly needed in Home waters.

'Everyone is screaming for destroyers,' grumbled the First Sea Lord, 'especially the French, and I have to harden my heart to all such requests, but they are very annoying.'[47] Jellicoe's dispatches during 1915–16 are laced with dirges over the dissipation of strength, above all in small craft, to the Mediterranean. Thus, 'I really can't see that the Italians have any claim whatever on our light cruisers [the four in the Adriatic]. They are our life blood absolutely.'[48] The Grand Fleet was short of these craft, he remonstrated with Jackson; he had a great preponderance of armoured cruisers, but they were very slow, and he needed the light cruisers to compensate for the destroyer shortage as compared to the enemy. With reference to the impending detachment of the light cruiser *Lowestoft*, Jellicoe protested, forgetting the source of his oil: 'I can't imagine that any vital interests are at stake in the Mediterranean. The safety of the Empire is at stake in Home Waters.'[49] 'Charity begins at home' was his slogan. Jackson sympathized completely with the C.-in-C., but political considerations again and again forced his hand, as now, when he was unable to prevent the *Lowestoft* from sailing for the Mediterranean. He was furious at the politicians for their weakness and for other reasons. They were like the soldiers of the opinion 'that the Navy is a common carrier and maid of all work to be used by anyone who wants anything done. My mistrust and dislike of politicals increases daily, the more I see of them . . . They seem to be doing their best to lose the war!'[50]

The concentration of battleship strength in the Mediterranean struck the Admiralty, the C.-in-C., Hankey, Richmond, and others as downright stupid. By the end of 1915 there was a staggering total of about forty Allied battleships there to oppose a dozen of the enemy. At Taranto alone, thirteen English and Italian ships of the line were riding at anchor. Twice in the summer of

[47] Jackson to Jellicoe, 21 Nov. 1915; *ibid.*
[48] Jellicoe to Jackson, 5 Sept. 1915; Jackson MSS.
[49] Jellicoe to Jackson, 30 Dec. 1915; *ibid.*
[50] Jackson to Jellicoe, 21 Nov. 1915; Jellicoe MSS.

1915 Richmond proposed a redistribution of battleship strength in the Mediterranean. He would have the Adriatic squadron recalled to Home waters ('The waste of these ships, strategically and financially, is utterly unjustifiable'), and replaced by the French, whose Mediterranean Fleet, now based on Malta, was doing little. This was a pious hope, as Richmond knew, since there was no chance that the French would contribute any more ships, let alone battleships, to the Adriatic unless they remained under their command. It was equally unrealistic for him to expect that the French would, as he recommended, throw their large submarines, which were 'no earthly use where they were', into the Italian command, to be used for searching out the Dalmatian channels. (The limited radius of Italian submarines was a drawback for this work.) 'Considering that M. Cambon [the French Ambassador in London] has been complaining that the British army with its 700,000 men does not cover a wide enough front . . . I think we have fair grounds to ask the French to take a little more of their share in the naval campaign in the Adriatic.'[51]

Jellicoe deemed it 'extraordinary' that they could not persuade the French 'to do their part', and Jackson quite agreed.

If they won't do anything there [Jellicoe complained], surely they can be asked to bring their ships near the Channel and so relieve your mind of enemy raids in that locality. . . .

If we can't persuade either France or Japan to take any share in the naval part of the war, our diplomacy must be rather weak. Japan owes us a great deal and I should hope might be *made* to tackle trade questions in Pacific.

I suggest that the Admiralty should say once and for all that our first duty is to our own country and that we cannot spare ships to a greater extent than at present to do work which our allies are perfectly capable of doing for themselves.

I feel very much for you at being obliged to carry out arrangements with which you do not agree.[52]

The Navy held the Government responsible for this state of affairs. We will examine elsewhere other factors which explain the growing hostility, and at times contempt, of the sailors for the politicians, who, in the eyes of the admirals, seemed ready to concede anything to Britain's Allies rather than offend them.

[51] Richmond to Jackson, 21 June 1915; Jackson MSS.
[52] Jellicoe to Jackson, 8 Nov. 1915; *ibid.*

XIV

Again the U-Boats, Minelayers, and Surface Raiders

(FEBRUARY 1915–MAY 1916)

This [submarine] menace is beyond question the most serious problem we have to face from the Naval point of view, and, unless the matter is grasped very firmly, is one that certainly will grow and develop to such an extent that it will bid fair to weaken and destroy us more than any other.

BEATTY to Balfour, 3 July 1915.

We could, I believe, bring the Germans to their knees in 3 months by the blockade if the Government would face the protests of neutral countries and take a firm stand and risk a war with the United States, Norway, and Sweden.

JELLICOE early in 1916.

1. THE NEW *GUERRE DE COURSE*

THE sixteen-month period that followed the Dogger Bank action was, in Home waters, essentially the story of submarine and anti-submarine, of minelaying and minesweeping. Fleet operations were subsidiary to the *guerre de course* (commerce warfare) and the British counter-measures.

There could be no objection to the use of the submarine against Allied warships, though many Englishmen, including naval officers, regarded the U-boats as underhand weapons and not quite proper. The real objection was to their use as commerce-destroyers. This was based on the fact that submarines often found it impossible to conform to international law when they acted in that capacity. Before destroying an enemy merchant (or passenger) ship, a belligerent warship must, according to recognized practice, ascertain its identity and make adequate provisions for the safety of crew and passengers. It was impossible for the U-boat, a small, cramped vessel, to take on board the personnel of a large ship.

342

The best it could do, if it destroyed the ship, was to give passengers and crew a chance to take to the lifeboats and to brave the perils of the ocean. Even this best was impossible, the Germans contended, when the British began to arm their merchant ships, for the U-boats were vulnerable craft. Accordingly, they found it necessary, more and more, to torpedo enemy merchantmen without warning. This violation of international law was justified with the argument' that armed merchant ships forfeited their immunity from attack.

In pre-war days the Germans had not thought seriously of a submarine war against commerce. They had neither made experiments nor carried out exercises to gain experience in this form of warfare. During the first six months of the war, Germany made no attempt to use the submarine to the utmost limit of its potentiality. The U-boats' functions were mainly reconnaissance and attacks on warships. The first British merchant ship to be attacked by a U-boat was the steamer *Glitra* on 20 October 1914. She was brought-to off the Norwegian coast and sunk by a boarding party, which opened her sea-cocks (after one of the officers had torn the Red Ensign to pieces and spat upon it). No lives were lost, as the ship's company were given ample time to lower their boats and make their escape. Sinkings continued on a minor scale. Down to February 1915 the German naval authorities professed to act, and on the whole succeeded in acting, with restraint. Unrestricted attacks on merchant ships, that is, without warning or attempt to save life, were only sporadic and not part of a policy. Merchant shipping losses in the first period (through January 1915) were not large: submarines sank a total of ten British merchant ships, only 7 per cent of the 273,000 tons of British shipping lost.[1]

German forbearance was temporary. Gradually, as the senior naval officers came to realize what the submarines were capable of, pressures mounted from within the Navy, abetted by the press, for a regular submarine campaign against Allied shipping without warning, on the ground that it was impossible to carry out

---

[1] In numbers of ships, the U-boats had accounted for 13 per cent of British losses. The breakdown of losses for the first six months shows: by surface craft: 51 ships, 215,000 tons; by mines: 14 ships, 37,000 tons; by submarines: 10 ships, 20,000 tons. In the same period the Germans lost 7 U-boats of the original 28 (24 overseas boats, 4 restricted to coast defence), or three or four more than the new boats built in these months.

commerce warfare on the surface with much success. The German Naval Staff was won over in January 1915; on 1 February the Chancellor, Bethmann Hollweg, did a *volte-face* (he had been wary about any gross violation of the accepted usages of naval warfare that would provoke neutrals into joining the enemy); and finally, on 4 February, the Emperor approved. On that day, on the pretext that Britain had violated international law by abolishing the distinction between conditional and absolute contraband, etc., Germany made her notorious proclamation of a war area—that the waters around Great Britain and Ireland were a 'war zone' in which, from 18 February, all merchant ships would be sunk, 'without it always being possible to avoid danger to the crews and passengers'. Neutral merchantmen in the war zone were warned that they would be exposed to grave risks. 'The declaration by its wording claimed for Germany the right to dispense with the customary preliminaries of visit and search before taking action against merchant vessels, and, in fact, to adopt a procedure hitherto limited to savage races making no pretence at civilisation as understood in Europe.'[2]

The surface raiders had all been accounted for by April 1915, and the submarines were now relied on to continue the *guerre de course*. In comparison with the objective of cutting Britain's sea communications and starving her out, the means were ridiculously small. The total number of boats available when the campaign started was 22, and these could work only in three relays. On 29 March the Flanders Flotilla (small coastal 'UB' and minelaying 'UC' boats) was created as a unit separate from the High Seas Fleet U-boats, with the mission of harrying the East Coast and English Channel traffic. During the period 18 February through April, British losses through U-boat attack totalled 39 merchant ships of 105,000 tons. This was nearly four-fifths of the tonnage sunk by the *Emden* and *Karlsruhe* during approximately the same period of time. That the Germans intended to use their submarines ruthlessly was proven on 7 May, when the great British liner *Lusitania*, unescorted and unarmed, was sunk by *U-20* without

[2] Naval Staff Monograph, *Home Waters. From February to July 1915*, p. 29. Actually, the limits of the authority of the U-boat commanders were not defined until later in the month. With considerable hesitation, Bethmann Hollweg agreed to the commanders being freed from all restrictions, subject to their using the utmost caution before sinking ships flying the American or Italian flag. The Emperor approved the compromise.

warning and with a loss of 1,198 lives, including 128 American. Strong American protests left the Germans unmoved.

Fisher's pre-war prediction had come to pass.[3] The U-boat had emerged as a commerce-destroyer which would not hesitate to sink ships without warning and without measures for the safety of crew and passengers. Yet the Admiralty had received with calm the German announcement of the intended operations against merchant shipping, doubting that the enemy had the means to do any serious damage. No appreciation of the situation appears to have been demanded from the C.O.S., nor by him from N.I.D.[4] The sinkings through May were of such bearable proportions that Churchill could later boast that 'the failure of the German submarine campaign was patent to the whole world'.[5]

Thereafter, however, the sinkings increased at a disturbing rate, reaching their 1915 (and pre-1917) high in August, when 42 British merchant ships of 135,000 tons were lost owing to enemy submarines. Including losses to mines, the figures were 49 ships of 149,000 tons. This figure represents an average size of 3,000 tons, which for those days was not far off the average size of the ocean-going ship. Especially hard hit was the Western Approaches, that is, the track followed by shipping entering the English Channel or Irish Sea from the Atlantic or Bay of Biscay. (The term 'South-Western Approaches' is sometimes used when the routes north of Ireland to the Clyde and Irish Sea are not concerned.)

Then came a sudden check to the campaign. The temporary and partial success of defensive measures was one reason. Of much greater consequence was the torpedoing of the British liner *Arabic* off Ireland by *U-24* on 19 August with the loss of some 40 lives, including three American. A sharp protest from Washington resulted in the German abandonment of unrestricted U-boat warfare (30 August). In future submarine commanders were not to sink passenger steamers, not even those of enemy nationality, without giving warning and saving the passengers and crew. This restriction, which involved the U-boats in the dangerous procedure of surfacing and stopping, together with the order of 18 September,

---

[3] See *From the Dreadnought to Scapa Flow*, i. 363.

[4] Naval Staff Monograph, *Home Waters. From February to July, 1915*, p. 53.

[5] *The World Crisis*, ii. 292. This passage should be contrasted with the poor success of the anti-submarine measures *per se*, as will be brought out below.

withdrawing the boats from the English Channel and the Western Approaches, where American shipping was concentrated, had the effect of virtually suspending the U-boat campaign in western waters for the remainder of the year. The sinking of the liner *Urbino* on 24 September was the last action of the 1915 campaign in the Western Approaches, except for a sporadic raid by one U-boat in December. Submarine operations in the North Sea had petered out by 1 October. At the same time, in the latter months of 1915, the Germans shifted their U-boat operations to the Mediterranean, where there was less chance of arousing the United States or other important neutrals. Also, the 'UC' Flanders boats became more active, 'spawning death' with their minelaying activity.

The year 1915 ended without either side gaining a decisive advantage. For the whole year 855,000 tons of British merchant shipping had been lost through enemy action: 748,000 by U-boats, 77,000 by mines, and 29,000 by cruisers and other surface craft. Compare these figures with the five months of 1914: 241,000 tons were lost, of which cruisers, etc. accounted for 203,000, mines 35,000, and submarines, not quite 3,000. New construction in the United Kingdom and the overseas dominions and colonies since the start of the war (1,306,000 tons) more than replaced the shipping losses. On the other hand, submarine casualties in 1915 were only 20, or 25 since the war started, whereas 61 units were added in the same period (that is, to the end of 1915). Germany began the year 1916 with 58 submarines.

The conduct of U-boat operations, which had been a much disputed question since the autumn of 1914 between the Naval Command and the political leadership (Bethmann Hollweg, the Chancellor, and Jagow, the Foreign Minister) flared up again in the first months of 1916. The cardinal question now, as always, was whether U-boats operating under restrictions imposed by the Government because of political considerations could be really effective. The endless wrangles between the two sides (a parallel to the bitter controversy between the British admirals and Government over blockade policy, on which see below, pp. 375–6) resulted in a vacillating policy. On 30 December 1915 the leaders of the Army and Navy reached complete agreement that 'there are no military reasons against the resumption of the submarine campaign', and that 'a submarine campaign conducted without any restrictions will, by the end of 1916, injure Great Britain to such an extent that she will be inclined for peace'. Admiral von Holtzendorff, the Chief of the Naval Staff, went even further, informing the Chancellor on 7 January 1916: 'If after the winter season, that is to say under suitable weather conditions, the economic war by submarines be begun again with every means available and without restrictions which from the outset must cripple its effectiveness, a definite prospect may be held out that, judged by previous experience, British resistance will be broken in six months at the outside.'[6] Tirpitz agreed. January was filled with lively exchanges of opinion between the Admirals (supported by the Generals) and the politicians. The Chancellor would not shed his misgivings—an unrestricted campaign would bring America and other wavering neutrals over to the side of Germany's enemies. Agreement was reached on a restricted campaign, to be started on 29 February.

The campaign was presaged by a German announcement on 11 February that 'enemy merchantmen carrying guns are not entitled to be regarded as peaceful merchantmen', because on nineteen occasions vessels so armed had (allegedly) fired on U-boats before they themselves had been attacked. Under the influence of the reaction in the United States, Holtzendorff added the limitation that enemy *passenger* steamers were to be spared as before even when armed. In their final form (13 March) the instructions for the U-boats read: '1. *Enemy merchant ships, encountered in the War Zone, are to be destroyed without more ado.* 2. Enemy merchant ships, encountered outside the War Zone, may only be destroyed without more ado when they are *armed*. 3. Enemy *passenger steamers* may not be attacked either inside or outside the War Zone by a submerged submarine, no matter whether they are armed or not.'[7] In other words, unrestricted warfare was postponed, but the U-boat campaign against Allied commerce was 'sharpened'.

The new German policy was launched with the torpedoing of

---

[6] The German Official History on the submarine warfare against commerce, by Rear-Admiral Arno Spindler, *Der Krieg zur See, 1914–1918. Der Handelskrieg mit U-Booten* (Berlin, 1932–41, 4 vols.), iii. 72–4.

[7] *Ibid.*, p. 103. Tirpitz had resigned the day before out of antipathy to the personality of Bethmann Hollweg, fury over the latter's soft-pedal submarine policy, and, the decisive factor, his (Tirpitz's) exclusion from all the important conferences on naval policy since the first of the year.

the first merchant ship of the 1916 campaign on 4 March. In April, 37 British ships of 126,000 tons were sunk by submarine, and six more by mines, for a total loss of 141,000 tons, the highest loss of tonnage since August 1915.

As had happened with the *Arabic*, the zeal of the U-boat commanders forced a modification of German policy. The culprit this time was one of the Flanders boats, *UB-29*, which on 24 March torpedoed without warning the unarmed French steamer *Sussex* on her usual trip from Dieppe to Folkestone. Many of her 380 passengers, including several Americans, were killed or injured, although the ship remained afloat. The incident roused great indignation in the United States. An ultimatum from Washington, presented on 20 April, gave Berlin the choice between a rupture in diplomatic relations and 'an abandonment of its present methods of submarine warfare against passenger and freight-carrying vessels'. Bending before this threat, the German Government had the Chief of the Naval Staff issue orders (24 April) to the High Seas Fleet and the Flanders Flotilla that 'until further orders, submarines may only act against commerce in accordance with prize regulations'. That is, submarines were not to destroy ships without examination of papers and proper steps for the safety of their crews, 'unless the ships attempt to escape or offer resistance'. Admiral Scheer, the new C.-in-C. of the High Seas Fleet, was bitterly disappointed. Believing that commerce war waged in accordance with prize law could not succeed and would only expose the submarines to excessive risk, he recalled all the High Seas Fleet submarines from the trade routes by wireless on 25 April, and informed the Naval Staff that the U-boat campaign against commerce was now discontinued. The Admiral commanding the Flanders Flotilla took similar action. This practically meant the abandonment of the second campaign in the War Zone round Great Britain. (The minelaying submarines and those in the Mediterranean were not affected.) The total loss of British mercantile tonnage through enemy action in May (all areas) was 20 ships of 64,000 tons, which dwindled further to 16 ships of 36,000 tons in June. The total British merchant-shipping loss for the first five months of 1916 (all areas), from submarines, mines, and cruisers, amounted to 131 ships of 442,000 tons. The Germans lost few U-boats in this period (seven) and these were more than offset by the thirty-four new boats which were completed.

2. ANTIDOTES TO THE U-BOAT

What was the Royal Navy doing all this time? Pre-war opinion, generally speaking, did not look upon submarines as a serious menace, whether to warships or merchant ships.[8] There was unanimity of naval opinion that the best, and quite sufficient, protection for all classes of ships, merchant as well as naval, was speed and zigzagging. The result was that there had been little progress in the development of anti-submarine weapons, tactics, and strategy, and progress in the first year or so of the war was slow. Thus, the pre-war committee at the Admiralty which dealt with the submarine problem was actually disbanded when hostilities broke out, and it was not until 8 December 1914 that the Admiralty formed the Submarine Attack Committee (S.A.C.), five officers and a staff, for 'investigation and preparing the best means of offensive attack of submarines'. (In September 1915 S.A.C. became the Submarine Committee.) Until the formation of the Board of Invention and Research in July 1915, S.A.C.'s responsibility included the consideration of all proposals and ideas on the subject emanating from inside and outside the Navy, the designing of apparatus, and the superintending of the manufacture and fitting of all anti-submarine appliances. Some of the ideas and suggestions received bordered on the comical, like the one to train sea-gulls to perch on submarine periscopes so as to make them more visible, and the proposal to arm specially chosen strong swimmers with sharp-pointed hammers with which to pierce the hull of a U-boat! Some of the ideas actually tried in the first days of the war were just as fantastic, as Commander Kenneth Edwards confirms from first-hand knowledge. 'The first anti-submarine patrol off Portland Harbour, for instance, was carried out by picket-boats (small steam-boats). Their anti-submarine armament consisted of a blacksmith's hammer and a canvas bag. The idea was that the hammer should be used to smash the periscope of a submarine, and the canvas bag to "blind" a submarine by being tied over the top of its periscope, but whether the periscope was to be tied up in the bag before being battered by the hammer or, for the sake of decency, afterwards, was never quite clear.'[9] The blinded U-boat was then supposed to surface,

---

[8] See *From the Dreadnought to Scapa Flow*, i. 330–5.
[9] Edwards, *We Dive at Dawn*, p. 369.

whereupon it could be destroyed by gunfire. It seems that the officers and men of the early anti-submarine patrols did not know that a periscope could be quickly lowered or that a submarine was equipped with two periscopes and only used one at a time.

The more serious anti-submarine devices, weapons, and operational resources evolved were many and varied.

Detection of U-boats by acoustic means seemed the most promising device. The hydrophone was originated by Professor William Bragg, of Cambridge, and Commander C. P. Ryan—a microphone that detected the beat of a submarine propeller at some distance. There were two main types: one was fixed on the sea-bottom and connected with shore stations, and the other was for use by hunting flotillas at sea. Trials began early in 1915. Although the device had emerged from the experimental stage by the autumn of 1915, and various shore hydrophone stations were established in 1916, it was not developed as a sea-service instrument until early in 1917—or beyond the terminal point of this volume.

The principal anti-submarine weapons were depth charges, 'modified sweeps', explosive paravanes, nets, and the guns of the defensively armed merchantmen.

Depth charges, or bombs containing high explosives which were set to explode at a predetermined depth under water, were invented early in the war. By the end of 1915 two standard designs had been settled on. Type 'D', a thousand of which were ordered in August 1915, contained 300 lb. of TNT or Amatol and was for issue to fast and heavy ships. Type 'D*', which began to be produced later in 1915, contained 120 lb. of high explosive and was for small or slow ships. A hydrostatic pistol with 40- and 80-feet settings fired the charges in both types. Distribution of the Type 'D' to the Fleet began early in January 1916, but until June 1917 the limited supply restricted the allowance of depth charges to two per anti-submarine vessel. The weapon had one serious defect: it inflicted little material damage unless exploded within a few feet of its target. Indeed, the depth charge did not achieve its first success until 22 March 1916, when the Q-ship (on which see below) *Farnborough* sank *U-68* off the coast of Kerry, Ireland. Despite its limitations, the depth charge was to become the most potent weapon of the anti-submarine forces.

The pre-war Submarine Committee had developed the 'single sweep', which consisted of an 80-lb. explosive charge towed by a plain (unserrated) wire sweep. It was the original mine sweep between two ships (the 'A' sweep, on which see above, p. 71) with the charge added. Probably in this optimistic idea of catching a submarine it was hoped that the sweep wire would render round the submarine when caught, so that it came into the bight of the sweep, where it would meet the 80-lb. charge. The 'modified sweep', an early wartime improvement, consisted of a long tow of nine 80-lb. charges. The towing wire was led through a sheave on a minesweeping kite, which gave it the required depth, and the farther end of the wire, beyond the last charge and of the same length as the charge wire, was brought back on deck. On fouling a submarine, the charges were fired electrically by a key pressed when contact with the submarine was shown by the tilting of a beam to which the two ends of the sweep wire were attached. Sweeps were extensively introduced at the beginning of the war into destroyers and other anti-submarine craft. Suitable for low-speed patrol work only, they achieved but one success.

The more effective explosive paravane or 'high speed anti-submarine sweep', which was introduced in the latter part of 1915, had practically superseded existing sweeps by the end of 1916. Originally fitted to destroyers, it was eventually extended to smaller craft of high speed, and was the one weapon available for seeking out and destroying submarines at destroyer speeds. Its advantage over the modified sweep, in addition to higher speed, was that, with a paravane well out and deep down on each quarter, it swept through a greater amount of water both in area and in depth. The functions of the depth charge and the high-speed sweep were, in a sense, complementary. The former was for use against a submarine the position of which was comparatively accurately known, while the latter dealt with a submerged submarine about whose position there was doubt. The high-speed sweep carried up to 400-lb. of high explosive, capable of being towed at a 200-feet depth.

Another weapon was the indicator net, which had been developed by the end of 1914. This was a light steel wire net, sections of which were lightly stopped to a jackstay buoyed with bottle-glass floats and kept extended by being towed at low speed by a drifter—or in suitable waters by being attached to mooring buoys. If a submarine fouled a net, it broke away that section from the jackstay and in so doing released a buoy which emitted a carbide flare and was thereafter towed along the surface by the submarine. The armed patrol vessels close to the net would then close in and attack. When the use of net cutters by the U-boats and some troublesome shortcomings of the indicator buoys somewhat nullified the utility of the indicator net *per se*, the most effective use for these nets was found to be in conjunction with electro-contact mines ('E.C. mine nets'). These net mines were small ones hung on the nets, spaced out both vertically and laterally and armed with plunger horns, some of which should be pressed in when a submarine charged a net, thus closing switches and exploding the mines. But the electric current firing the detonators was provided by a battery in the drifter (or in a buoy in the case of moored nets), so that the net could be laid without danger. The whole apparatus was quite safe until the wires were joined up to the battery.

Although the nets accounted for very few submarines, they had an important influence on German policy. The gloomy report of *U-32*, which escaped after being caught in the Dover Straits drifter net barrage (established in January 1915) on 6 April, resulted in a decision by the German Navy Command (10 April 1915) that the High Seas Fleet submarines were not to proceed to western waters by way of the English Channel. This meant they had to go an additional 700 miles to reach the Irish Sea, or 1,400 miles (an extra seven days) there and back. (The Flanders minelaying submarines and a few of the High Seas Fleet boats did continue to use the Channel.) The order was in effect until December 1916. The Admiralty does not seem at the time to have appreciated this success of the indicator-net barrage.

Because the semi-mobile Dover net barrage did not immediately prove very effective as a deterrent to the U-boats, it was decided on 23 February 1915 to erect a more solid and permanent obstruction in their path. A nearly 20-mile boom of heavy harbour-defence nets would be constructed across the entire breadth of the Straits to close the Narrows between Folkestone and Cape Gris Nez, with a 'gate' at each end. It was hoped to complete the project in four months.

It was a fine attempt [according to the Admiral in command at Dover], but the strong gales and heavy seas played 'old Harry' with the heavy floats and large hawsers: above all, the strain on the chain cables, due to the strong tides pressing against the floats and nets, was enormous, and produced unforeseen erosion in the bolts of the shackles as the sea lifted and lowered the whole structure. I have seen a 3-inch bolt of a shackle that had been chawed half through in a single gale. It would be difficult for anyone, who had not watched the behaviour of the boom in heavy weather, to picture the strains and erosion to which the component parts of the structure were submitted.[10]

The insurmountable difficulties, to say nothing of the heavy cost of maintenance, caused the Admiralty to abandon the un-completed boom (little more than half had been constructed) as impracticable in May 1915, and to remove the sections of the boom to the outer waters of the Firth of Forth.

In April–May 1916 a barrage of moored mine nets was laid off the Belgian coast, between Nieuport and the Scheldt, and supported by lines of deep mines. The object of this Belgian coast barrage was to restrict the movements of the minelaying sub-marines of the Flanders Flotilla at Zeebrugge and Ostend by confining their ingress and egress to one small channel off West Capelle on the Dutch coast. The barrage increased the difficulties of the Flanders U-boats, but the mines were apparently ineffective, and no submarine seems to have been actually destroyed by it. Admiral Bacon, however, attributed to the barrage the cessation of submarine activity against merchant ships between April and September 1916. Its apparent success led to the construction of a similar barrier across the Straits in the autumn of 1916 that did little to restrict the freedom of the U-boats.

Fleet anchorages were protected by booms of heavy nets intended to stop a U-boat attack. Post-war trials showed that a submarine with net cutters, which all the German boats had, could go through without trouble. But they could not know the British were not improving their nets, nor what other devilments in the way of mines they had in store for them. Consequently, only one or two U-boats made the attempt, notably *UB-116*, manned entirely by officer volunteers, which, a few days before the Armistice (28 October 1918), decided to have a last shot at Scapa.

[10] Admiral Sir Reginald Bacon, *From 1900 Onward* (London, 1940), p. 255. Vice-Admiral Bacon had succeeded Rear-Admiral Horace Hood at Dover on 13 April 1915. Bacon ('Porky' Bacon to the Service) was one of the best brains of his time, as everyone recognized. He had been chosen to start the submarine service in 1903, and afterwards became the first Captain of the *Dreadnought*. Unfortunately, he had not the gift for drawing loyal service from his officers and men—he did not feel that he needed any help from anyone else—and was not at all a popular figure.

She tore and passed straight through the nets of the Hoxa boom defence without any difficulty and was nearly in the Flow before she was blown up in one of the loop minefields which were the inner defence. These were lines of mines, each surrounded by an electrical indicating loop. When the observer noticed the tell-tale needle of a loop deflected and saw that there was no surface ship there, he pressed the button and the line of mines went up. This was, incidentally, the only time during the war that a shore control-station destroyed a U-boat.

In 1915 and 1916 the U-boats generally attacked merchantmen on the surface, bringing their victims to by gunfire or signal and then sinking them by torpedo or bombs. In this way they utilized their superior surface speed, were able to overhaul the ordinary cargo ships from any direction, and expended their few torpedoes with optimum results. The Admiralty believed that an armed merchant ship would have a chance of resistance and escape from a U-boat surface attack, since she had a higher and steadier gun platform and better chances of observation than the submarine, though the silhouette of a U-boat offered a small target for the often poorly trained gun crews. (The Navy during the war provided over 11,000 men for gun crews, the balance being made up from the crews of the ships themselves.) And whereas the merchant ship could afford to be hit several times, the submarine could run no risks. One hit might sink her or make it impossible for her to dive. Since fully half of the shipping losses from U-boats early in 1915 were due to the U-boat's gun, it was obvious that much of the submarine's offensive power would be removed if her gun attack could be defeated and she were forced to operate submerged. Once a U-boat dived, she lost speed and was forced to depend wholly upon her battery power and upon her strictly limited supply of torpedoes.

Before the war the Admiralty had instituted the arming of merchantmen on a limited scale, for the wartime defence of merchant ships against enemy armed merchantmen acting as commerce raiders. On the outbreak of the war thirty-nine large ships had been so fitted (two 4·7-inch guns) and this number was gradually added to as guns became available. Owing, however, to the large number of guns required in the early period for the armament of merchant cruisers and auxiliaries, progress in the arming of merchant ships was slow. It was not until the inauguration of the first U-boat campaign in February 1915 that the policy of arming such ships was again seriously taken up. Even then the limited supply of suitable guns made for rather slow progress before the latter part of 1916; only 766 ships had been armed by December 1915 and some 1,100 by mid-April of 1916 (excluding those sunk from any cause). The Admiralty ideal from the autumn of 1915 was the arming of every merchant ship. The results speak for themselves:

1 JAN. 1916 TO 25 JAN. 1917[11]

Defensively armed ships attacked	310
of which escaped	236
Sunk by torpedo without warning	62
Sunk by gun-fire from submarine	12
Unarmed ships attacked	302
of which escaped	67
Sunk by torpedo without warning	30
Sunk by gun-fire, bombs, etc.	205

Operational resources in the anti-submarine campaign included decoy ships, the Auxiliary Patrol, destroyers, submarine versus submarine, and aircraft.

'Special service vessels', or 'Q-ships', as they came to be called in the latter part of 1916, after the Admiralty gave them all 'Q' numbers (in press parlance, 'mystery ships'), are a trick as old as naval history—that of a wolf in sheep's clothing. The original idea for their use in the war has been variously attributed to Admiral Sir Hedworth Meux, C.-in-C., Portsmouth, Captain Herbert Richmond, and a clever captain, Alfred Ellison, S.N.O. at Lowestoft. Beginning in November 1914, the Admiralty prepared a number of these submarine-decoy ships. Their first success did not come until 24 July 1915. They were usually small tramp steamers and were manned with selected volunteers, under the command of R.N. officers who sported merchant-service type beards. They were armed with concealed guns (12-pdrs. and 6-pdrs. in the earlier and more successful ships, but some of the

[11] Technical History Section, Admiralty, Monograph TH 13 (1919), *Defensive Arming of Merchant Ships*, p. 19. The gross tonnage of a ship and the size of her complement determined the number and calibre of guns. Such guns as the 12-pdr. 12 cwt. were quite effective in keeping the earlier U-boats off. But more execution could be done with a larger gun if a U-boat risked a fight on the surface, and, accordingly, heavier gun-power, up to 6-inch, was introduced in British merchant vessels in the latter part of the war.

355

later ones had the heavier 4-inch and 4·7-inch) and were equipped
with depth charges for the *coup de grâce*, if needed, and later with
torpedo tubes. The Q-ship cruised on the trade routes as a peaceful, harmless-looking merchantman, 'a live trap baited with
human flesh to catch unsuspecting prey'. The whole idea was to
entice a U-boat to surface and close in for a kill by gunfire or/and
bombs because the Q-ship was too small to be worth a torpedo,
whereupon the Q-ship would open up at point-blank range.

Over 180 ships were fitted out, although about 30 was the
maximum that ever operated at one time. Their achievements
have been over-romanticized and exaggerated by a number of
writers. The 'watching and waiting was a long and tedious affair',
writes Gordon Campbell, and the total Q-ship bag was but 11
U-boats.[12] The 11 represent over seven per cent of the 145 known
U-boat destructions by British action in the war. But whereas up
until March 1917 the Q-ships had sunk seven submarines at a cost
of four of their number, thereafter they sank only four more, with
a totally disproportionate loss of 27 Q-ships. They had but one kill
after *U-88* on 17 September 1917, and that came on 9 November
1918. On this last occasion the Q-ship *Privet* helped to sink *U-34*,
but she was acting as an anti-submarine vessel, not as a Q-ship.
Towards the end of the war Q-ships were employed mainly as
convoy escorts.

One reason for the diminishing returns was that the secret was
out by 1917; another, that the U-boats had become wary because
of the armed merchantmen; and, finally, with the unrestricted
U-boat campaign of 1917–18, the submarines made no effort to
close ships they encountered. They would dispatch a torpedo and
ask questions afterwards. 'Unfortunately,' as Commander F.
Barley has observed, 'optimism continued to triumph over
experience as it has so often in our island story and until the war
ended Q Ships continued to be sent to sea with the disastrous
results recounted.'[13]

---

[12] Admiral Campbell claims that about 60 more were 'probably damaged to a
greater or smaller extent, with the result that they would be put *hors de combat* for some
time, and the nerves of the men would probably be shaken.' Rear-Admiral Gordon
Campbell, *My Mystery Ships* (London, 1928), p. 290. Commander Campbell (as he
was then) was the most successful and daring captain, his exploits earning him the
V.C. and promotion to captain in 1917.

[13] Barley, 'How We Can Learn from History', *Journal of the Royal Naval Scientific
Service*, Nov. 1957.

Another anti-U-boat measure whose effectiveness has been exaggerated was the Auxiliary Patrol, which was instituted in the first month of the war. It was composed at first of armed yachts, trawlers, and motor boats, with officers drawn from the R.N.V.R. The standard unit consisted of a yacht, four trawlers, and four motor boats. Units were sent to Scapa, Rosyth, and other places where they were most needed. By the end of 1914 there were about 750 craft. By November 1918, 3,100 Auxiliary Patrol craft of every description had been commissioned. In December 1914 the Patrol was organized into twenty-three patrol areas forming, supposedly, a continuous protective belt around the coasts of the British Isles. The duties of the Auxiliary Patrol were to carry out patrols of coasts and harbours. It was never the great success in protecting trade against submarines that it was acclaimed to be at the time. Captain Creswell goes so far as to say that 'except for those working with indicator nets I don't think they did much except enhearten us by being busy. The protective belt they were said to have formed was mostly a myth.'[14] Though their coastal patrols had little effect, vessels of the Auxiliary Patrol did prove moderately useful in combination with the larger anti-submarine vessels when the U-boat warfare intensified, and occasionally they made a kill.

From the start of their regular campaign against shipping the U-boats worked mainly in the areas of densest traffic: the approaches to the principal south-western landfalls (the Fastnet and the Scilly Islands) and the English Channel. For the protection of the trade through these waters the Admiralty depended on the 'offensive patrolling' of the routes by the Auxiliary Patrol Flotillas. This involved hunting the U-boat on the sight of one or on the report of an incident. The Local Defence Flotillas, though not a standing patrol, participated in the hunting—follow-up operations on reported incidents. Unfortunately, there was so much water to be covered that the chances of these forces of sloops, trawlers and other small craft (with some destroyers) intercepting the elusive submarine were hardly more than accidental. The situation worsened in 1916. The original plan of dispersal of shipping away from the usual routes in waters where the presence of enemy warships or mines was suspected had been the rule through 1915. It was founded on the hope that thereby

[14] Captain Creswell's letter to the author, 24 Oct. 1962. Newbolt's opinion (*Naval Operations*, iv. 356) is just as strong.

submarines would find fewer victims. Under the new plan in March 1916 (systematized on 1 July 1916), the Admiralty diverted shipping into well-defined 'approach routes' (changed at intervals) through the dangerous waters near the United Kingdom, on the theory that this would make it easier for the patrols to protect shipping. But the mere presence of patrolling vessels indicated the trade routes to the U-boat commander. He would stay clear of a patrol and, once it had passed, would wait for the shipping that was sure to come by.

Patrolling was, right into 1917, singularly ineffective, no matter how numerous the patrol craft became. 'It was extremely rare,' as Lieutenant-Commander D. W. Waters puts the matter, 'for patrols to be in the right place at the right time in the right force to repel an attack on a merchant ship, still less to find the enemy before he attacked.' Yet the complaint was only that patrolling was not as efficient as it should be. A man of Richmond's keen intelligence and knowledge of war could say as late as 1916 that 'Strategically, our pundits at the Admiralty have not yet realised that the way to protect trade is to cruise constantly in certain areas through which the trade passes.'[15]

Another aspect of the anti-submarine campaign, and a concomitant to the reliance on patrolling, was the building of a myriad of small ships—the comparatively fast 'mosquito fleet' of sloops, patrol or 'P' boats (small destroyers without torpedo tubes) and motor launches, and the trawlers and drifters of Admiralty design, more suitable for this work than their fishing prototypes. Balfour intensified the efforts of the Churchill Board of Admiralty in this area. The new First Lord believed that there were only two methods of dealing with U-boats: trapping them with nets or similar appliances, or employing against them an enormous number of small craft. The latter especially appealed to him, and soon after taking office he gave a large order for 36 sloops, etc., which light-craft programme was supplemented later in the year.

The new Board swiftly concluded that the destroyer, with its gun-power and sea-keeping ability, was the ideal offensive weapon against enemy submarines. The Churchill Board had ordered 93 destroyers and 9 destroyer leaders (large destroyers) during the war; the Balfour régime ordered 34 and 4 more, respectively,

[15] Diary, 28 Feb. 1916; *Portrat iof an Admiral*, p. 202.

through January 1916. More were not ordered because they took much longer to build than sloops and such craft, and because, by late 1915, those destroyers under construction were in arrears. Instead, the Admiralty attempted to persuade Jellicoe to detach some of his 70 to 80 destroyers for submarine-hunting, either in the North Sea, under the C.-in-C. himself, or in the Western Approaches, under Admiral Bayly. Jellicoe let out a cry of anguish when the proposal reached him. Were this done, he expostulated, 'The Fleet is at once immobilised. We cannot go to sea without them unless the Government is prepared to face heavy losses from S.M.s enroute south and still heavier losses from T.B.D.s when we meet the H.S.F.'[16] The Admiralty appreciated the force of the C.-in-C.'s argument, and instead detached four destroyers from Devonport for anti-submarine work under Bayly. Whenever Jellicoe did use his destroyers for anti-submarine operations at a distance from Scapa, as he was forced to often, he worried lest he have to proceed to sea without a full destroyer screen. Of course the lack of destroyers for U-boat work was due to more than fleet needs. There was a constant call on these craft for duty in the Mediterranean and for escort work during movements of single ships or squadrons between bases, and, most important, there were mounting construction delays.

Used for hunting down U-boats, the destroyers proved to be a disappointment, as the C.-in-C. had to confess in a memorandum on the efficacy of anti-U-boat measures. 'The destroyer is, of course, very efficient defensively as a screen to individual ships, or to a large number of ships, but, except in more or less confined waters, is not an efficient offensive weapon, because she must, with her present means of offence, actually get into contact with a submarine, or very nearly into contact, which is a difficult matter if the submarine has plenty of sea room.'[17]

Up to 1917, U-boats beyond the English Channel were practically immune to submarine attack, since the limited range of the boats in the British submarine patrols in the early part of the war (mostly of the 'C' class) confined them to coastal waters. Submarines, all the same, had some luck against the U-boats, accounting for a few with torpedoes.

Trade defence against U-boats also took the form of defensive

[16] Jellicoe to Jackson, 6 Sept. 1915; Jackson MSS.
[17] Jellicoe to Balfour, 29 Oct. 1916; Jellicoe MSS.

mining of harbours and off the coasts of the British Isles, and the mining of Heligoland Bight (on which see the next section); the frequent, though ineffective, bombing by aircraft of the U-boat bases on the Flanders coast (Zeebrugge, Ostend) and assembly yards (Bruges); and air patrols of U-boat transit areas. The emphasis in the latter was upon non-rigid airships (the S.S. or Submarine Scout airships), which were capable of more extensive operations in favourable weather than aeroplanes and seaplanes, whose limited endurance confined them to inshore work.

Beatty and Bayly independently proposed in the summer of 1915 that the submarine menace be dealt with by blocking the U-boat exits. They were unable to suggest any hopeful plan for accomplishing this. To the Admiralty it was plain that nothing short of large-scale combined naval and military operations had any chance. To have made such a proposal to the Army in 1915–16 would have been a sheer waste of time.

One of the more effective steps in the anti-submarine offensive was the creation of a new organization for the Western Approaches in July 1915. The first U-boat campaign in Home waters was meeting with success against shipping, while continuing to pose a threat to the Fleet in the North Sea. On 8 May and 19–20 June 1915, respectively, there were U-boat attacks, fortunately unsuccessful, on the 3rd Battle Squadron (one battleship just managed to elude a torpedo) and the 3rd Cruiser Squadron (one cruiser was hit). 'Submarinitis' (Tyrwhitt's term) was becoming a common complaint among the sailors, including Jellicoe and Beatty. 'We are all sharpening our wits on the submarine question,' Jellicoe wrote, 'as we *must* reduce their numbers rapidly before they become too serious a menace to the Fleet.'[18] The battle cruisers did their sharpening through a contest announced by Beatty on 10 May for the best anti-submarine papers. His officers submitted over sixty. Beatty judged that none of the suggestions in them could be selected 'as specially suitable for immediate adoption', though many were worth trying. One idea in the second prize-winner (by Secretary Frank Spickernell and Commander Plunkett), that trawlers in the North Sea should tow behind them submerged submarines, instead of a trawl, was tried out and found to be effective. The merit of the scheme was that it increased the submarine's range of vision, via the telephone from

[18] Jellicoe to Balfour, 29 June 1915; Balfour MSS.

ANTIDOTES TO THE U-BOAT

the trawler (arranged by means of a cable along the towing wire), while at the same time enabling submarines to work among British fishing craft without the latter being alarmed by sighting a periscope. When it became known in November 1915 that the Germans were aware of the ruse, it was abandoned.

It was against this background that Jellicoe suggested that 'great results might be achieved' if some capable officer were appointed who would have 'nothing else to do beyond directing the efforts of patrols on to any S.M. that is located'. He suggested Bayly for the appointment. 'He is wasted at Greenwich. He is full of energy and if anyone could get the machine to work quickly and effectively, it would be Admiral Bayly.'[19] He elaborated his idea in a letter to the First Sea Lord.

. . . it should be the sole business of one officer and staff to watch submarines that are located, and to get all available craft on to them on their probable course. There is much valuable information daily at the Admiralty on the subject. A close study of this information enables one to judge of the course and speed of certain submarines and to predict the times they will pass through certain areas. There are also innumerable daily reports of submarines sighted by our own or neutral vessels.

In my view, we should concentrate our patrols ready to meet them. Most of the information which I receive reaches me under present conditions too late to be of use to local patrols, and, moreover, I am not in charge of local patrols on the East Coast, so have no authority over them and can do nothing in the direction of general control. But a central head *could* do it and, I contend, successfully. . . . The War Staff have no time to do it, therefore I say appoint Sir Lewis Bayly, whose energy is unbounded. . . . My proposal is to place an officer in *supreme charge* of operations of a certain mobile force purely for submarine hunting. . . . A central organisation is urgently required. *At present no one really acts at once.* If the different patrols don't act, and act *in concert,* at once, it is too late. I am quite aware that there are large numbers of flag officers dotted round the coast, but many of them are, unfortunately, the wrong sort of flag officer and are lethargic. De Horsey is one example. Because we have some of the wrong sort, surely that is no reason why we should not get a really useful officer at the head. When we get the fast small craft going, the need of a head for our anti-submarine vessels will be greater than ever. There will not be cohesion between adjacent patrols unless someone is at the head.[20]

[19] Jellicoe to Balfour, 18 June 1915; *ibid.*
[20] Jellicoe to Jackson, 24 June 1915; Jackson MSS.

Beatty made the same suggestion in an equally forcible letter that may have deliberately exaggerated the U-boat threat. 'The gravity of this [submarine] menace has now increased to such an extent that new measures and more drastic action are imperative. . . . We have, in fact, to realise that, at present, the German Navy indisputably commands the North Sea. . . . I recommend that all the forces for hunting submarines be under the direction of one man [Bayly].' He envisaged a mobile anti-submarine striking force of at least 120 vessels: about 40 destroyers or torpedo boats, 6 yachts, 60 trawlers or drifters, and 14 submarines, to which should be added 6 or more airships, 20 or more aeroplanes, and a number of motor boats. He had one novel and far-sighted suggestion. 'German prisoners state that a British submarine has been destroyed by bomb from an aeroplane. Our own aeroplanes are used occasionally for reconnaissance, very rarely for attack. They have never yet successfully attacked a submarine, because they have so seldom tried. I suggest that, for submarine work, reconnaissance be entirely subordinated to attack and that aircraft be used in considerable numbers to concentrate for offensive action on every occasion that a favourable opportunity occurs.' He concluded: 'If the problem is not grappled now in the right way and by the right men, we may be faced in the near future with a naval disaster.'[21]

The eloquent arguments of the two principal flag officers at sea were productive of a half-victory only. On 12 July, to the Navy's surprise, the Admiralty appointed Bayly Admiral Commanding the Western Approaches (altered to C.-in-C. of the Western Approaches in May 1916), with headquarters at Queenstown. His task was to cope with the U-boat offensive in this most critical area, through which ships arrived from America with munitions of war, guns, machinery, etc. Bayly landed at Queenstown on 25 July, succeeding Vice-Admiral Sir Charles Coke, but with

[21] Beatty to Admiralty, 25 June 1915; Beatty MSS. A letter to Balfour on 3 July (*ibid.*) cleared up a misunderstanding. He was not concerned only with the menace as it affected the Grand Fleet. He 'fully realised that the menace to the Grand Fleet is only a portion, indeed a small part, of the danger that threatens the successful prosecution of the war. But the antidote to a part is the antidote to the whole. Offensive action against the danger is assuredly more efficacious than all the defensive measures in the world. . . . We must become offensive in our methods. We must have concentrated effort. We must have undivided control under one man who must be the *right* man.'

a greatly enlarged command and resources. All the western Auxiliary Patrol areas (with their craft) were put under Bayly's command. It covered all the western approaches to the British Isles, including the Irish coasts, Irish Sea, St. George's Channel, Bristol Channel, and the entrance to the English Channel.

Bayly accepted this difficult appointment with some 450 ships at his disposal. As the new light craft began to arrive, many were sent to Queenstown. The trawlers worked off the coasts, hunting for submarines or escorting ships; the drifters worked nets off places which it was important to keep clear; submarines (one at sea at a time) operated off the south-west coast of Ireland; and squadrons of about eight sloops patrolled specified areas on the trade route past the south of Ireland, or escorted valuable ships. The auxiliary patrols in the Western Approaches were not particularly effective during the climax of the first submarine campaign (August 1915). The U-boats could encounter all the targets they wanted outside the patrol areas and naturally found it more comfortable there. The patrols had even less luck in the second campaign (spring, 1916)—the U-boats then almost always operated beyond their reach. Bayly's trawlers could provide no protection more than 40 miles from shore, and the sloops no more than 80.

As usual, Bayly was a no-nonsense commander. 'In the handling of squadrons, individual ships, men, and even crises, Admiral Bayly's methods were direct, by the shortest route: his orders unequivocal, with an economy in words and clarity of thought that never failed to impress. Almost his first act at Queenstown was to issue a signal that all social calls were to be regarded as having been made and returned.'[22] At the same time, and again to the Navy's surprise, Bayly, a widower, was gradually humanized at Queenstown, thanks to a charming niece who kept house for him and served as his hostess.

To summarize the results of anti-submarine operations through May 1916: the Germans suffered 32 losses. Twelve of these can be put down to inexperience—being rammed (6), blown up on their own mines (2), torpedoed by a U-boat (1), and stranding (3). There were also two sinkings by trawler gunfire which were due to the submarines mistaking them for fishing trawlers. These

---

[22] E. Keble Chatterton, *Danger Zone: the Story of the Queenstown Command* (London, 1934), pp. 68-9.

figures hardly represent a brilliant success for 22 months of effort.[23]

The results of the offensive to the spring of 1916 were not, in the opinion of the Admiralty, unsatisfactory. Of course they did not know the true figures, and believed they had accounted for more U-boats. To be sure, Balfour was unhappy over the depredations of the U-boats, and at a 'confidential' press conference on 27 April 1916, he stated that the submarine and mine attack on merchant shipping was 'the most serious thing of all'. And yet he left his hearers with the impression that the Admiralty thought they had the U-boat menace well in hand. He asserted that, at a 'reasonable and conservative estimate', they had destroyed a submarine a week so far in the year, which he seemed to think was a fine achievement (actually, only five U-boats were lost in the first four months of 1916, and seven through May), that anti-submarine measures, like the provision of small craft, were being pressed, and that they were about as well off in merchant shipping as when the war broke out.[24] This statement was misleading.

The shipping situation was more serious, potentially at any rate, by early 1916 than figures of tonnage sunk might indicate. In the first place, under war conditions (in particular, the reduced supply of labour at the ports owing to enlistments, and sailing delays and the closure of ports through the mere threat created by U-boats, and the consequent unpredictable arrival of bunches of ships, the result of sailing large numbers of ships independently) the

[23] The German submarine losses during the war, chronologically arranged and with the cause cited in each instance, are in R. H. Gibson and Maurice Prendergast, *The German Submarine War, 1914–1918* (London, 1931, 2nd ed.), pp. 370–6. Spindler, *Der Handelskrieg mit U-Booten*, has the same figures with a few variations in the date and cause of loss. For the 18 U-boat losses not included above, the breakdown by cause is: mines: 5; Q-ships: 4; H.M. submarines: 3 (two of them by a submarine working with a decoy ship—a trawler towing a submarine); mine nets: 1; modified sweep, detection by indicator nets: 1; bombs (type unspecified), detection by indicator nets: 1; bombs (type unspecified), after fouling anchor cable: 1; cause unknown: 2. The contemporary Admiralty figure of 'known' losses was exactly right: 32 through May 1916. 'Reported Destruction of Submarines. Summary of Cases (from August 1914 until 31 December 1916)', an Admiralty document of March 1917; Admiralty Library.

[24] 'Report of Proceedings at Conference . . .'; Admiralty MSS. As regards the last statement the figures through the first quarter of 1916 show: 1,334,000 tons of merchant shipping lost and 1,399,000 tons of new ships actually brought on to the register in the United Kingdom and the Empire. (Fayle, *Seaborne Trade*, iii. 467, has a useful table of shipbuilding output.) Curzon made the same point as Balfour in the Lords on 3 May: the number of merchant ships lost in the war was almost exactly balanced by the new ships added to the merchant service during the war.

congestion of the ports had assumed serious proportions by early 1915. The resulting long delays in loading and discharge reduced the annual carrying power of the ships concerned by as much as 20 per cent. It was, says Fayle, 'one of the main factors, perhaps the chief factor, in producing shortage of tonnage'. Lesser factors in the drop in the delivery rate of merchant shipping (that is, the tonnage that the ships available could deliver over a given time), included the withdrawal of specialized mercantile types of ships for military purposes, and the unavoidable employment of less economic vessels in consequence for mercantile purposes.

In the second place, there was the prospect of a large tonnage deficiency in the trade of the United Kingdom itself. Commercial shipbuilding in the United Kingdom (except for oil tankers and frozen-meat ships) had declined seriously towards the end of 1915. Fayle gives the total output for the last quarter of 1915 as a mere 93,000 tons, 'little more than was required to make good the war losses of a single month'. Due to the comparatively satisfactory output of the first quarter, the total for 1915 was 651,000 tons, but this was only one-third of the 1913 figure. And the nearly half a million tons of shipping lost in the first six months of 1916 was two and a half times the shipbuilding output in the United Kingdom for that period.

The Admiralty had only the roughest ideas about the shipping situation, and many of these were quite unrelated to the facts. The reason for this was simply that the crucial facts were not known. The Admiralty just did not keep the requisite statistics. It is easy to censure them for this omission until one appreciates that, under the philosophy of war which had shaped naval thought for the past forty years, shipping statistics were unnecessary. Under the philosophy of defending the sea routes used by shipping, it was not essential to know what ships or how many went where and when. 'Look after the routes and the ships will look after themselves' was the dogma. Accordingly, nobody in the Admiralty (or elsewhere) kept the statistics necessary to know what ships were doing. For this reason the Admiralty (the decision-takers, at any rate) appear to have been ignorant of the alarming and continuing drop in the delivery rate of merchant shipping. This, essentially though not entirely the port congestion factor, together with the drop in merchant-ship building, presaged a critical situation long before matters were brought to a head by the German decision of early

1917 to loose their submarines without restraint against Allied and neutral shipping. Further factors were the taking up of more and more merchant ships for military store ships and transports, and the closing of the Mediterranean (March 1916) to ships destined for ports east of 100° E., which necessitated the immense haul around the Cape to the Far East and Australia. All these factors were, in the first half of 1916, more important than were figures of U-boat depredations.

The end of the second U-boat campaign only increased the complacency of the Admiralty. They do not seem to have given proper weight to the protests of the United States, which, more than the British devices and methods, had forced changes in German policy that had curbed the U-boats. What would happen if Germany defied the neutrals once and for all, and with a much greater fleet of submarines than was available during the first two campaigns? That there could be no permanence in the truce proclaimed by the enemy on 24 April should have been patent. Yet there was no sense of urgency at the Admiralty.

On the whole [a careful analysis of U-boat operations in the war concludes], little headway was made in combating the menace of the submarines [as of the spring of 1916]. True, a respite had been granted to the Allies during the summer, but it also deferred the development of an effective reply. The Allies at that time could not have fully known the reasons underlying the slackening-off of the attack. The wish was father to an erroneous conclusion. It was both convenient and consoling to presume that counter-measures were at last proving effective. For that complacent optimism a bitter price had, a year later, to be paid. For the turning-point in the whole sea war was near at hand. The event was about to occur [Battle of Jutland] which led Germany to relegate her battle-squadrons to a secondary position, and to stake her whole future upon the Submarine Arm.[25]

There was some question about the ability of the Board to deal with a campaign on an unparalleled scale. Hankey, a shrewd judge of ability, sized up the prospect this way: 'I don't believe the present Board are equal to tackling it.'[26]

The real difficulty cuts much more deeply. There was, at the Admiralty and afloat, altogether too much talk about 'offensive action' against U-boats and far too little thought given to what

[25] Gibson and Prendergast, *The German Submarine War, 1914–1918*, p. 95.
[26] Hankey to Esher, 5 Feb. 1916; Esher MSS.

was meant by 'offensive action'. What was, in effect, meant was trying to mine and bomb the U-boats in their bases, and, above all, to hunt them to destruction at sea. None of these measures was successful. The dogma 'Seek out and destroy the enemy' governed all activities and precluded rational action. While the main difficulty with hunting tactics at this time was the lack of efficient submarine detectors of submerged submarines, the strategy of hunting was fundamentally unsound; it left the initiative to the elusive enemy. As a consequence, hunting became a succession of futile follow-up operations after U-boats had achieved successful attacks in a diversity of places, for the one place where a U-boat (in practice) most probably would not be found was in the area in which it was being hunted, namely, the scene of its most recently reported activities. The so-called hunting of submarines was a waste of effort and of resources except very infrequently when luck intervened and a U-boat captain made a mess of things. Indicator nets used in narrow waters were an attempt to overcome the problem of under-water detection of submarines, but they had severe limitations and were often disappointing.

In the event, it was 'defensive measures' such as the arming and routing of merchantmen which proved much more successful in curbing the U-boats' successes, but what, eventually and decisively, defeated them was the so-called 'defensive' measure of convoy. This was because it concentrated the main anti-submarine effort where it was most likely to be effectual. It was impossible for a U-boat to attack a ship in convoy without risking being itself attacked beforehand; and if, despite this, it succeeded in firing a torpedo, it usually betrayed its position and exposed itself to immediate counter-attack. Why the Admiralty did not adopt the convoy system until the spring of 1917 is a tale reserved for the final volume of this saga.

3. MINELAYERS AND SURFACE RAIDERS

'Submarinitis' had its complement in the 'minitis' from which a number of admirals suffered. From June 1915 enemy minelaying took the shape of small minefields laid from specially built submarine minelayers (the 'UC' boats). Previously, the losses of ships by mines, though large, were not alarming. The submarine minelayer altered this, for the methods of dealing with a large concentrated field were unsuitable for small groups of mines laid promiscuously, and a considerable increase in British minesweeping work was rendered necessary.

The losses of British merchant shipping by mines steadily increased. The British tonnage total for the first five months of 1916 was 38 ships of 95,000 tons. February was the worst month of the war (except for July 1917): 14 ships of 36,000 tons. Mines began to take their toll of warships, too, in the first months of 1916. They accounted for the old battleships *King Edward VII* (6 January, 30 miles from the Pentland Firth) and *Russell* (27 April, off Malta), the light cruiser *Arethusa* (11 February, in the North Sea), and the cruiser *Hampshire*, with Lord Kitchener on board (5 June, off the Orkneys).

It was constantly present in Jellicoe's mind that they ran the grave danger of having the exits of the Grand Fleet mined prior to an offensive move by the enemy, and of suffering heavy damage by minefields laid across their probable route as they sped south. For these reasons he had constantly urged two policies. One was the imperative need to keep the area to the south-eastward of the Pentland Firth well patrolled, so that the approaches to Scapa Flow and the entrance to the Moray Firth might be protected. When, sometime early in 1915, the Admiralty decided that the submarine risk to cruiser patrols was too great, Jellicoe substituted armed boarding steamers, supplemented by a night-time destroyer patrol from the entrance to the Pentland Firth to the south-eastward. The weakness of this system was shown on 8 August 1915, when the German armed auxiliary *Meteor*, disguised as a merchant ship, sank an armed boarding steamer and laid a large minefield in the entrance to the Moray Firth. (She was scuttled by her crew the next day on the approach of three British cruisers.)

Since there were always one or more capital ships carrying out gunnery exercises or refitting at Invergordon, clear channels in the Moray Firth were essential for the efficiency of the Grand Fleet. The *Meteor's* effort added to the safety of the Firth, as Jellicoe had the greater portion of the minefield left down, only having side channels cleared. The Moray Firth position was henceforth too uncertain for the U-boats to risk re-entry. This does not explain why the Germans never systematically mined the actual main fleet entry channels to Scapa Flow. Admiral Sir Lionel Preston has always found this 'surprising'.

Since the war began, Jellicoe had been trying to persuade the Admiralty to lay mines close in to the German coast in the Bight, to hamper the operations of both enemy surface ships and submarines. The policy of mining the enemy's own waters had been in abeyance since January 1915 (when the Amrum Bank was mined), except for two minefields laid in May 1915, one north of Borkum Riff, the other near the field at Amrum Bank. Following the audacious and successful enterprise of the *Meteor*, Jellicoe intensified his efforts for additional mining of the Bight, in order to render dangerous the exit of enemy minelayers, as well as submarines, from their bases. The submarine menace rendered impracticable one way of doing this, the establishment of a fairly close blockade of the Bight. That left no alternative but to mine the Bight extensively and as soon as possible, from the Schleswig-Holstein coast to the Ems. 'This policy has been consistently advocated ever since the menace of the submarine showed the difficulty of keeping cruisers in considerable numbers in the North Sea, and I am more than ever convinced that it is absolutely essential to the satisfactory conduct of the war.' To render sweeping operations very risky for the Germans, there should be continual sweeps by light cruisers and destroyers down to the area of the minefields. In any case, as he had argued before, the minefields would give ample warning of any serious German operation, since it would be preceded by extensive sweeping operations. Concurrently with an aggressive mining policy, as a further safeguard against minelaying operations, it was essential, in spite of risks from submarines, to have a cruiser squadron with six or eight destroyers constantly in the North Sea.[27]

His efforts bore fruit as regards offensive mining. By the close of 1915 a fairly complete line of mines had been laid across the Bight, and this was occasionally reinforced in 1916. It was not, however, the '*complete* policy of mining the whole Bight' that the C.-in-C. advocated. The success of the policy was handicapped by the insufficiency of mines and the poor quality of those in use. 'Unfortunately,' remarked the C.-in-C., 'our mines seem to be possessed with the peculiar quality of going off when no one is touching them, and of drifting from their moorings almost as fast as they are laid. The latter point, of course, is of no consequence in the minefield laid in a fleet action, but it does mean that as fast

[27] Jellicoe to Admiralty, 14 Aug. 1915; Admiralty MSS.

as our mines are manufactured they are used to replace those which drift away from such minefields as the Dover minefield.'[28] An efficient mine was not available in quantity until the autumn of 1917.

The mining of the *King Edward VII*, the shortage of minesweepers with the Grand Fleet, and the great difficulties faced by the sweepers in northern waters owing to the frequent rough seas, reawakened Jellicoe's fears. 'It will be pure suicide taking the Fleet out without sweeping and I have nothing with which to sweep.'[29] He submitted two recommendations (11 January 1916) as 'the least that can overcome the mining menace and ensure freedom for the fleet under all conditions': an immediate increase in his minesweeping sloops from nine to twenty-four, and the fitting out and attachment to the Grand Fleet of four mine-bumping vessels, with two more going to Beatty. Without the extra sloops he could not guarantee that the fleet would reach southern waters without incurring risks of very heavy loss. The mine-bumpers (to precede the fleet in line abreast) were the only remedy for the weather conditions that often prevented sweeping operations. (We must remember that the Grand Fleet had not yet been equipped with paravanes.)

The Admiralty proposed to send Jellicoe thirteen more trawlers instead of the extra sloops. These were the new Admiralty trawlers, which were more powerful than the fishing trawlers that had failed at the Dardanelles. Though the trawlers could sweep efficiently, their sweeping speed was much less than the sloops', so more of them would have been needed if they were to cover the same ground in the same time. Thirteen more trawlers would, consequently, have hardly been enough. Moreover, there were not enough sloops to go around because France and Italy had been clamouring for them in the Mediterranean, where the submarine peril was greater than in northern waters. The Admiralty balked at the construction of mine-bumping vessels. They could not keep ahead of the fleet (the mine-bumper gear would reduce their speed), and, anyhow, there were more urgent construction needs. (None was ever built. The idea was neither popular nor practical, and the introduction of the paravane killed it completely.) The C.-in-C. was not satisfied, suggesting as regards the sloops that

[28] Jellicoe to Beatty, 7 Aug. 1915; Beatty MSS.
[29] Jellicoe to Jackson, 21 Jan. 1916; Jackson MSS.

' "charity begins at home", and that we should not run what, in my opinion, is a serious risk of so weakening the Grand Fleet as to make it possible for us to lose the command of the sea in home waters for the sake of satisfying our Allies. The danger [of mines] is very real and the disaster may occur in a few minutes without warning. It only requires the fleet to be inadvertently taken over one minefield for a reversal to take place in the relative strength of the British and German fleets. The existence of the Empire is at once in the most immediate and grave danger.'[30]

The First Lord agreed that the mine peril was 'really formidable' and that it was 'extraordinarily difficult' to deal with the mine-layers. 'I do not suppose that we have anywhere so strong a force of patrol vessels as that under your command; and yet apparently they have been able to get round the Orkneys and lay mines to the west of your position without being detected. We have suffered much in the same way at the southern end of the North Sea, and in the English Channel.'[31] But nothing was done immediately to meet the C.-in-C.'s wishes.

There was a revival of commerce warfare by surface raiders in the winter of 1916. The new German policy discarded the use of liners converted to auxiliary cruisers as being too heavy coal consumers and therefore dependent on a complicated supply system. The Germans now used ordinary steamers of moderate size and speed (which would not arouse suspicion on the trade routes), and of small coal consumption and large stowage.

First of the new raiders set loose on the same cruising ground as early in the war, the Atlantic between West Africa and Brazil, was the two-masted steamer *Moewe* (4,500 tons, 14 knots, four 5·9-inch, one 4·1-inch, two torpedo tubes, 500 mines, the laying of which was her first and principal task). She left the Elbe on 29 December 1915, disguised as an ordinary Swedish merchant ship, which disguise she changed several times with sheet-iron panelling and paint. (It was on the minefield that she laid west of the Orkneys on the night of 2 January that the *King Edward VII* sank a few days later.) She returned home on 4 March, after an Atlantic cruise of just over two months and a bag of 11 British merchant ships of 57,000 tons.

The *Greif* (4,963 tons, 13 knots, four 5·9-inch, two torpedo

[30] Jellicoe to Balfour, 25 Jan. 1916; Jellicoe MSS.
[31] Balfour to Jellicoe, 17 Jan. 1916; Balfour MSS.

tubes), disguised as a Norwegian steamer, left Germany on 27 February 1916. The Admiralty, in receipt of information that a raider had left Germany, arranged to intercept her by auxiliary cruisers of the Northern Patrol and cruisers and destroyers dispatched from Scapa and Rosyth. The armed merchant cruiser *Alcantara* met the *Greif* about 70 miles north-east of the Shetlands on 29 February. In a fierce action at point-blank range the *Alcantara* had virtually knocked out the raider, when she sank, apparently having been hit by a torpedo. The armed merchant cruiser *Andes* and the light cruiser *Comus* came up to deliver the *coup de grâce* to the *Greif*.

And so ended this brief resurrection of surface raiding. As in the first months of the war, the raiders managed to dislocate traffic, but did not inflict serious losses. Like their predecessors, they were severely handicapped by the lack of overseas bases.

4. THE BRITISH BLOCKADE

Pre-war British naval thought and war plans placed a high value on the effects of economic pressure on Germany.[32] This was now put to the test. German commerce carried in German ships practically ceased in the first days of the war, but supplies continued to reach Germany through neutral shipping and neighbouring neutral countries. It was obvious that the German economy would be dealt a serious and perhaps even a fatal blow, if Britain could control neutral shipping.

The means of control, sometimes called a 'long-distance blockade' (the Government always referred to the economic pressure on Germany as 'blockade' or a 'policy of blockade'), was quite different from the close blockade of the sailing-ship era. Mines, submarines, and modern coastal artillery had rendered this traditional type of blockade impracticable or impossible.

The naval aspect of the blockade, as it had evolved by November 1914, consisted mainly in intercepting neutral shipping en route to Dutch and Scandinavian ports. There were two routes by which goods might enter Germany by way of the northern neutrals: through the Straits of Dover or round the north of Scotland. A large minefield laid early in the war in the Straits compelled all vessels to pass through the Downs. (This is the passage—strictly speaking, the anchorage—between the Goodwin Sands and the

[32] See *From the Dreadnought to Scapa Flow*, i. 377–83.

coast of Kent.) There, at anchor, every ship that passed through the English Channel to or from Dutch or Scandinavian ports could be examined. In the case of the northern route, this procedure was out of the question. It was 450 miles from the north of Scotland to Iceland, and another 160 to Greenland. Once past this line, ships could make for the Norwegian coast and proceed to their destination inside territorial waters. The primary duty of the Northern Patrol was to watch the 610-mile line. (An important secondary effect was the interception of raiders when they got going.) The cruisers of the Patrol operated at a considerable distance from their bases, intercepting scores of vessels every week (the monthly average, March 1915–December 1916, was 286, exclusive of fishing and coastal vessels, which averaged 150 a month), and often remaining at sea for over a month. The vulnerability of the Patrol to U-boat attack and the almost incessant winter gales of wind and snow added to their hardships. In December 1914 the eight old armoured cruisers of the Patrol ('Edgars', built in 1893–4) were replaced by twenty-four armed merchant cruisers, which were faster and more seaworthy, with a greater radius of action. De Chair remained in command until March 1916, constantly increasing the efficiency of the blockade. In that month he became Naval Adviser to the newly appointed Minister of Blockade and was succeeded by Vice-Admiral Reginald Tupper.

The Declaration of London (1909) had divided goods into three rigid categories: *absolute contraband* (articles of an exclusively military character, e.g., guns and explosives), subject to seizure under all conditions; *conditional contraband* (goods susceptible of both military and non-military uses, e.g., fuel, clothing, foodstuffs), subject to seizure only if destined for the armed forces or a government department of the enemy state; and a *free list* (articles which could never be considered contraband, e.g., raw cotton, oil, rubber), which was always to be immune.

Upon entering the war, Britain, which had never ratified the Declaration, announced she would adhere to its terms subject to certain amendments in the contraband list. She then proceeded, beginning with the contraband lists issued on 21 September and 29 October 1914, to enlarge the lists of absolute and conditional contraband by adding many of the commodities defined by the Declaration as free. By the end of 1914, as the stalemate of trench warfare set in and the belief grew in Britain that the war would be a prolonged affair, the Government began to realize how important and even decisive the cumulative effects of the blockade could be. In the course of 1915, accordingly, the difference between absolute and conditional contraband was, in practice, wiped out. Simultaneously (particularly under the Order in Council of 11 March 1915, which was announced as a reprisal for the first unrestricted U-boat campaign), the doctrine of continuous voyage was extended until it applied to all goods bound ultimately for Germany. That is, all neutral goods having an ultimate enemy destination were liable to capture, even if the vessel were bound for a neutral port. The blockade of Germany included, by the end of 1916, various other measures, such as agreements for the rationing of imports of neutrals in contact with Germany, combined with purchase schemes with these neutrals which assured the British a certain proportion of their exported foodstuffs.

The neutrals (above all, the United States), who were piling up enormous profits in this phase of the war, complained persistently and vociferously over the interference with their trade by the stretching of international law and the British methods of conducting the blockade. To take one example, they resented the liberties Britain was taking with the traditional right of visit and search. The time-honoured procedure consisted in stopping and visiting a neutral merchantman to search for contraband, and either releasing the ship if none were found, or sending her to a prize court for legal action if contraband were found. Early in the war the British came to regard this as no longer practicable, because of the U-boat danger and the size of modern vessels. The Northern Patrol therefore sent many neutrals into the contraband control base at Kirkwall for a thorough examination, either conducting them thither or putting armed guards (as distinct from prize crews) on board to ensure that the masters followed instructions. (When seizure of cargo could not be justified, it was often purchased, to keep it from reaching Germany.) This procedure caused long delays and economic losses to neutral shippers. It was, therefore, at first resented by neutrals, as was the fact that ships were sometimes sunk while being taken in for examination. (After the war, Britain paid full value, plus 5 per cent accrued interest, for the losses so incurred.)

The effect of the economic pressure on Germany steadily increased, though the blockade would have achieved much more, had the Government enforced it more rigorously. But fearful of embittering neutral opinion and driving the neutrals, especially the United States, into Germany's arms, they often released neutral ships containing meat, wheat, wool, etc., that the Navy had, sometimes at considerable risk, sent into port for examination.

The Navy had little patience with what it regarded as the old-maidish fears of the politicians, and the whole issue aggravated the none too harmonious relations between the Service and the politicians. On a short visit to the Admiralty in mid-December 1915 Jellicoe tried for two hours to convince the First Lord and Lord Robert Cecil (Parliamentary Under-Secretary for Foreign Affairs) not to fear the neutrals, but to stiffen the blockade by really blocking imports into Germany. He failed. 'The truth is (don't breathe it),' he disgustedly wrote to Beatty, 'that Russia has less than 1,000,000 *armed* infantry. They say hostile action by Sweden would finish them. *We* and the French fear the Dutch, although I argued they would never go to war with us because of their trade. They also say that we and Russia are still absolutely dependent on the U.S.A. for munitions!!! All I could get was the concession that *when* Russia was in a better state we might reconsider the question. . . . The French politicians, they say, are worse than ours. Is that possible?'[33] Jackson, too, wished to see a blockade policy with teeth. 'I don't know what the Government are going to do yet [about Sweden], but I fancy they will declare a blockade, which of course we can't make effective in the Baltic, but, as I say, this war will make history and we need not be too particular about precedents.'[34]

Jellicoe's last remark above highlights the antipathy of the naval officers for the politicians, in this instance for the (alleged) pusillanimity of their blockade policy. Richmond vented his bitter feelings in his diary: 'We have a poor lot of diplomatists. . . . They release 90 per cent of the ships that our cruisers stop, and while they annoy neutrals by half-measures, they do not take whole

[33] 22 Dec. 1915; Beatty MSS. He wrote 'letter after letter on the blockade questions, but the F.O. seems quite imbecile. They are afraid of their own shadows and imagine every neutral is anxious to go to war with us and can do us harm. I don't believe it and I never shall till I see the declaration of war.' Jellicoe to Fisher, 20 Jan. 1916; *Fear God and Dread Nought*, iii. 291.

[34] Jackson to Jellicoe, 25 Jan. 1916; Jellicoe MSS.

measures to destroy the enemy's means of living. For twopence, if it would save them trouble, they will abandon our rights at sea again.'[35]

The appointment of Lord Robert Cecil on 23 February 1916 to head the new Ministry of Blockade marked the beginning of a stiffening of the blockade. A scholarly study of the Allied blockade summarizes in this way the effects of the economic pressure by the end of 1916:

> Just what effect the blockade had on the German army is difficult to say, but, so far as the Allied military leaders were aware at the end of 1916, German soldiers were well equipped. Ammunition and guns continued to be supplied in spite of severe shortages of manganese. In the process of steel making, substitutes for this steel-hardening material had been found, and the same was true in many other industries. By the end of 1916 leather and wool for shoes and clothing were scarce, and prices were high, but again substitutes were used. It is certain, however, that the brunt of the burden occasioned by the Allied blockade was borne by the civilian population, who were expected to sacrifice everything for the military needs of the state. . . . During 1916 shortages of milk and meat became more and more acute as forage supplies dwindled and almost disappeared; time after time the rations allowed the people were reduced. And even then there was not enough food available to give everyone the amount indicated on the meat, bread, and milk cards. . . . It was inevitable that disorders should result. Indeed the shortages were so great that neither the rationing system, nor the harvests, which each year of the war were a greater disappointment, nor the supplies received from the border neutrals seemed to have any appreciable effect on the deficiency. . . . Thus although economic pressure is of necessity rather slow in showing definite results, it was here that the Central Powers first revealed signs of collapse.[36]

Tirpitz had foreseen the result of the British blockade when he wrote in March 1915 that gradually it must affect the whole life

[35] 24 Nov. 1915; *Portrait of an Admiral*, p. 198. Richmond afterwards blamed the prolongation of the war into 1917 and 1918 on the fact that economic pressure, owing to neutral pressures, had not taken effect sooner. 'That loss of human life, that expenditure of wealth, and the exacerbation of national feelings were the price which was paid in order that individuals in neutral countries should enjoy their profits.' Richmond, *Statesmen and Sea Power* (London, 1946), p. 286.

[36] Marion C. Siney, *The Allied Blockade of Germany, 1914–1916* (Ann Arbor, Michigan, 1957), pp. 256–7. Fayle (*Seaborne Trade*, ii. 164–5) emphasizes the very serious effects of the fertiliser shortage, owing to the cutting off of imported fertilisers, on harvest yields as early as 1915.

of the German nation, and General Ludendorff, writing of the situation at the end of 1916, dolefully observed: 'If the war lasted our defeat seemed inevitable. Economically we were in a highly unfavourable position for a war of exhaustion. . . . Questions of the supply of foodstuffs caused great anxiety . . .'[37] But British admirals, although aware that a tight blockade would seriously weaken the enemy, economically, were impatient with this strategy of slow strangulation *per se*, and did not think it could play a decisive role in bringing Germany to her knees. For them the principal advantage of a strict blockade was that it might well force the Germans to try to raise the blockade by seeking a general fleet action. In any case, the Navy regarded reliance on a strategy of blockade as a poor substitute for the glory to be won by battle.

The 'anaemic' blockade policy was one of the counts against the Admiralty in the agitation that swept the country early in 1916. That this policy was *imposed* on the Admiralty by the Foreign Office and the Government, despite strong and repeated Admiralty protests, was not generally known outside the Service.

[37] Erich Ludendorff, *My War Memories, 1914–1918* (London, n.d. [1919], 2 vols.), i. 307.

XV

Unrest in the Country and the Fleet

(DECEMBER 1915–MARCH 1916)

Note this: no amount of Cabinet or War Council instructions are of the slightest use if those who have to carry them out are totally wanting in '*push*' and '*initiative*'! *There must be ginger at the top if you want ginger at the bottom!*
FISHER to Hankey, 2 March 1916.

I dare say you are an awkward subordinate! but I should like to see you First Lord of the Admiralty. So you would be, in any nation but ours. Fortunate, indeed, is the country, and opulent in high capacity, that is able to dispense with Lord Fisher in a gigantic war. I wish I could think that embarrassment of riches was the cause.
THE EARL OF ROSEBERY to Fisher, 30 March 1916.

I. CAUSES OF DISQUIETUDE

THE Navy was particularly silent in the latter half of 1915. There was no battle. Little or nothing was heard of its work. Yet in the first six months of Balfour's administration public confidence in the 'mighty, silent, ever watchful' Navy was very high. There was a general appreciation, by the press at any rate, that sea power was the dominating influence of the war, although it was of the armies that most was heard. On the first anniversary of the war, and again on Trafalgar Day, the press reminded the nation of the priceless service which its 'incomparable' Navy was rendering. The *Daily Telegraph* caught the mood of the country when it wrote (3 August): 'After the enemy had escaped from his clutches in 1782, Rodney remarked, " 'Tis provoking, but never mind it; their fate is only delayed a short time, for have it they must and shall." Admiral Jellicoe, and the officers associated with him, might make to-day the same declaration. But in the meantime, the victory lies with them; though the enemy has refused battle, the results of battle—the right to use the seas—are ours.' Taunting the German Navy was a favourite sport, as, for instance, the *Saturday Review* (21 August): 'Naval power does not in any real sense belong to a fleet which has dared two flying trips to the East Coast, sent an occasional vessel upon a hurried promenade within easy reach of port, and is reduced to striking under water . . . Germany alone among the nations which have talked of their ships has refused the ordeal by battle.' A *Punch* cartoon (29 December), under the legend 'Sweeping the North Sea', shows a boatload of admirals—the boat itself is tied at a German naval base—peering out to sea. Says the chorus of admirals: 'Still no sign of the British skulkers!'

This mood of trust and confidence faded during the winter of 1915–16. It was replaced by a mounting discontent with the Navy, or, strictly speaking, with the Admiralty. There had been no such press agitation since the Navy Scare of 1909. Six causes of the unrest stand out.

(1) *The 'make-believe blockade'*. Whereas a few organs of opinion like the Radical *New Statesman* and the *Nation* congratulated the Government for recognizing the limits of the use of sea power in dealing with neutrals, the overwhelming majority of newspapers and periodicals, as well as a City of London meeting on 14 February 1916, criticized the Government for not letting the Navy have a free hand in conducting the blockade. More specifically, they held the Board of Trade and especially the Foreign Office responsible for the restrictions on the Navy, and they blamed the Admiralty for too great subservience to these departments. It was senseless, so ran the argument, for England to play the game according to the accustomed rules when the Germans had made war so unutterably cruel. Asserted the *Globe* (1 January 1916): 'A boxer may desire to fight according to Queensberry rules, but if he finds himself assailed by a garotter with a knuckleduster he had better lay hold of a horseshoe "for luck", and use it without scruple. . . . Let the incomparable Navy which dominates the seas be given leave to tighten the strangle-hold it has put upon Germany, and crush the life out of our perfidious foe.' The Foreign Office attached excessive importance to the susceptibilities of neutrals, it was charged. The *Saturday Review* (29 January) explained that 'a belligerent cannot consent to be paralysed in its mightiest arm in order that the plenty of peace added to the

profits of war may be enjoyed by those who are happily out of the fighting. . . . Our errors do not lie in the direction of severity. They have lain . . . in the direction of an over-nice respect for documents.' Or, as the *Morning Post* viewed the matter (19 January), the Government 'have been conducting this war as if it were a General Election which could be won by fine phrases and by putting their adversaries in the wrong. If they had read a little history they would have known that invariably in the judgment of mankind that nation is right which is victorious, and that nation is wrong which is defeated.'

The Admiralty were in the awkward position of being blamed for a situation that was not of their making. The Second Sea Lord summed up their position:

There is trouble brewing now as regards the blockade; people are disposed to blame the Admiralty for the very inadequate results of it. This is not quite fair, as it is not properly an Admiralty responsibility to decide our policy, nor are we properly equipped to deal with the touchy feelings of neutrals and the requirements of our allies. We have however rather given ourselves away by creating a trade division at the Admiralty [August 1914] which can only tender advice to the F.O. [Foreign Office], as coming from the Board, and that only from one point of view which does not comprise the effect on neutrals and allies of what they propose should be done. In other words, we have, thanks to Winston's pushfulness, assumed a responsibility that we are not competent to carry through, and we thus expose ourselves to being made the whipping boy for the Government, a post they are always ready to foist on anyone and preferably the Admiralty, as the Lords are as a rule too patriotic to expose them.[1]

(2) *The successes of the Moewe.* The discovery that a German raider was again at work among merchant shipping gave an unpleasant shock to complacent faith in British control of the sea. It would have been more realistic to have accepted the fact that command of the seas never entailed the absolute ability to prevent all enemy operations. No blockade could be so complete but that, on a dark night, fog and judicious disguise might enable a blockade runner to break through successfully.

(3) *The Hindenburg affair* was another rude reminder that the Germans had surprises up their sleeves. For some curious reason the German authorities permitted the launching of the battle

---

[1] Diary, 14 Feb. 1916; Hamilton MSS.

cruiser *Hindenburg* on 1 August 1915 to be revealed, and this set off speculation in Britain about this newest of German capital ships. In late January 1916 rumours that the new ship carried 17-inch guns, the heaviest naval guns yet seen, were given credence in the *Manchester Guardian* and other newspapers. The journalist who had started the rumour based his conjecture on the finding of some shell fragments in Dunkirk fired from a naval gun which seemed to fit 'a weapon of that enormous calibre.

There were those Englishmen who already had the vision of a squadron of German 'Hindenburgs', carrying guns outranging those of the 'Queen Elizabeths', soon bursting forth from the Kiel Canal. (Germany never mounted anything larger than a 15-inch gun in her capital ships.) This particular danger was swiftly dissipated, after Balfour had reassured the country (House of Commons, 26 January) that there was no evidence, nor was it plausible, that the enemy had a 17-inch gun. The press, nevertheless, continued to speculate that the German Navy was up to something bold and imaginative.

(4) *British men-of-war were no longer much in evidence.* The general public did not understand the nature of maritime war any better in 1916 than it had in 1914. They wanted a battle, a *big* one, preferably. There had been no Heligoland Bight or Dogger Bank action to show that British command of the North Sea was more than a name, whereas enemy destroyers were active not far from the British coast, and German mines were causing numerous losses. The sinking of the sloop *Arabis* on 11 February 1916 by a torpedo attack from six destroyers, which exploit the German wireless trumpeted, made a painful impression in Britain.

(5) *The Zeppelin raids.* The bombing of the Midlands on 31 January 1916 (the first raid on England since 13 October 1915) and subsequent raids that culminated in a series on a wide range of targets from the southern counties to Edinburgh and Leith, 31 March–5 April, did not sit well with the nation. There was disappointment that these depredations had not encountered the 'swarm of hornets' of which Churchill had spoken some months back. The Admiralty still had responsibility for home air defence. But on 16 February the responsibility for the defence of London against German air raids passed to the War Office, and for the rest of the country a few days later. The R.N.A.S. was thereafter only responsible for enemy aircraft attempting to reach Great Britain.

(6) *The delays in naval construction*, owing principally to the Army's insatiable demands for manpower. Although the country as a whole was not aware of this situation until the Commons debates of 7, 8 March 1916, it was an open secret in governmental and shipbuilding circles. Rear-Admiral Sir Charles Ottley, the onetime Secretary of the C.I.D. and now a director of Armstrong, Whitworth (the armament manufacturers and shipbuilders), and Sir Philip Watts, the former D.N.C. and now adviser on naval construction to the Board, both complained to Hankey early in the year of the slackness in naval construction. They, and others, attributed the delays to the lack of push at the Admiralty.

The cumulative causes for dissatisfaction with the Admiralty's conduct of the naval war led to, and were summarized in, a seventh grievance. There was undeniably the feeling that more energy, initiative, farsightedness, and inventiveness were needed at the Admiralty. The Navy had been acting on the defensive mainly, 'content to defeat the various devices of the enemy', like the U-boat warfare. 'There is a growing tendency on the part of those in authority to "wait and see". That is not warfare' (*Naval and Military Record*, 9 February 1916). In Hankey's words, 'there was not much drive or punch' at the Admiralty.

Altogether, then, the public was not very pleased with the Admiralty. In the first months of 1916 the forces of discontent turned to Fisher as their mouthpiece and national saviour.

2. FISHER, JELLICOE, AND THE ADMIRALTY

We last saw the Admiral at Euston Station on 22 May 1915, when he boarded a train for his self-imposed Scottish exile. He had proceeded to Strathaven, in Lanarkshire, the home of an old friend and former midshipman of his, the Duke of Hamilton. He loved the great luxury with which he was surrounded and the rustic setting of moors, streams, grouse, and trout. The understanding sympathy of the Hamiltons helped him to recover his equilibrium. At first he appeared resigned to being cut off from the war effort. By the end of the second week he was profoundly regretting his mistake in leaving London and growing restless with his enforced idleness. On 5 June he suggested to Balfour that he would be ready to take Jackson's place if he went as C.-in-C., Mediterranean, as Jackson had assured him (31 May) was his 'chief desire'. Fisher also had in mind the possibility that Jackson would have to retire because of a chronic ailment which plagued him. Balfour gave him no encouragement.

In the following year and a half of campaigning to get back into the centre of the war effort, Fisher never doubted his own mental or physical capacity to carry on. Yet, as time went on, there was increasing doubt in higher circles about his fitness. Captain Crease, the Admiral's Naval Assistant at various times (including Fisher's first year at the B.I.R.), did not think Fisher 'ever recovered either his mental or physical balance', following the May crisis.[2]

Balfour soon found a position for which the old Admiral's talents seemed ideally suited. He prevailed on him to accept (5 July) the chairmanship of the newly established Board of Invention and Research, whose task was defined as 'responsibility for organizing and encouraging scientific effort in relation to the requirements of the Naval Service'. The B.I.R. was run by a Central Committee, consisting of Fisher and three distinguished scientists, assisted by a panel of consultants. The actual work of the Board's various sections, each staffed with technical experts, was concerned with original research, problems set by the Admiralty, and the investigation of proposals put forward by inventors and other members of the general public. In time, however, it concentrated on exploring solutions of the submarine problem. It did its most successful work in the development of anti-submarine listening devices.

Fisher entered his duties with his usual zest. 'The war is going to be won by many inventions', and the appointment 'promises to be a very big affair, as apparently I shall be able to direct big policies'. He must have derived amusement from some of the weird suggestions that came across his desk, like the one from a charwoman, who, distraught over a foul odour, suggested that it might be bottled up and used against the Germans!

He was not happy in his new role for long. The post was a purely advisory one and offered little scope for his energy and his genius, particularly as B.I.R. findings carried little weight and were apt to be pigeon-holed. His personal contribution in the first months, a proposal (complete with design) on 5 August for a 'submarine dreadnought' firing a 12-inch gun, was politely

[2] Crease to Admiral Sir Reginald Bacon, 7 Nov. 1932; Crease MSS.

considered, referred, and delayed. He was willing to come back to the Admiralty for six months as Third Sea Lord to carry it out, then retire to private life. It was then that Balfour told him, 'If once you put your foot inside the Admiralty, where should we all be?'[3] More frustrating still for the Admiral was his belief that the war was going badly 'for want of resolute direction'. 'This war won't end 'till we get rid of the jelly-fishes!'—among whom he included Balfour.

Four months of managing a 'chemist's shop' were quite enough for Fisher's restless spirit. On 28 October he asked the Prime Minister to make better use of his abilities, as he was 'doing nothing at all'. When, a week later, Asquith reorganized the Dardanelles Committee, rumour had it that Fisher was attempting to get a seat on the new War Committee. Whatever slim chance he had was snuffed out by a campaign to prevent such a 'disaster' mounted by the Second Sea Lord, who enlisted the support of the Chief Liberal Whip (J. W. Gulland) and Jellicoe. 'It would,' Jellicoe felt, 'be a fatal step. I don't agree with you as to all his sins, as I think without his energy re new construction we should now be in a shocking state, but I am fully aware of his totally wrong strategical notions [Fisher's Baltic Scheme?] and so are others to whom I should write.'[4]

Fisher's confidence that he might be recalled, whether to the Admiralty or the War Committee, was increased by the reception of his speech in the Lords on 16 November, the first of but two speeches he ever made before that body. The circumstances were as follows. Churchill, restless with his 'well-paid inactivity' as Chancellor of the Duchy of Lancaster, and disappointed that he had not been included in the War Committee, had resigned his

[3] Sydney Hall, Commodore (S), seems to have been the co-sponsor of the design. Eventually, in February 1916, the Admiralty placed an order for one boat with Vickers, although Fisher wanted at least six to be built at once. It was commissioned in April 1918 (*M-1*), and two others followed in 1919–20. The 'M' boats (officially described as 'monitor submarines') mounted one 12-inch gun, which could only fire its 850-lb. shell right ahead. The design was, technically, a success. In her trials *M-1* was stable and easy to control; she was able to do 15 knots on the surface and 10 knots submerged, and to dive in 90 seconds. The recoil of the gun did not sink the boat, as had been freely predicted. *M-1* never got a chance to prove her value in the war; but the design failed to justify itself operationally in post-war exercises. The fundamental error was, as Lieutenant-Commander Kemp sums up the matter, that of 'trying to use a submarine for purposes which a surface vessel was better qualified to carry out'. P. K. Kemp, *H.M. Submarines* (London, 1952), p. 98.

[4] Diary, 3 Nov., Jellicoe to Hamilton, 9 Nov. 1915; Hamilton MSS.

ministerial post on 11 November. Just prior to leaving for the Western Front, as a major of the Oxfordshire Yeomanry (he was promoted to lieutenant-colonel in December and took over the command of the 6th Royal Scots Fusiliers), he attempted to vindicate his record as wartime First Lord in an eloquent and powerful *apologia* before a sympathetic Commons (15 November). As regards the Dardanelles, he claimed that he 'did not receive from the First Sea Lord either the clear guidance before the event or the firm support after which I was entitled to expect'.

Fisher felt constrained to answer this remark in the Lords. Only about twenty peers were present, as nobody knew that a rejoinder to Churchill was to be forthcoming. Standing with his legs wide apart, as if he were on a rolling warship, and unfolding a large sheet of manuscript, the Admiral read his statement in a loud, commanding, quarter-deck sort of voice. It was possibly the briefest maiden speech ever delivered in either House—114 words, of which the most pungent were: 'I have been sixty-one years in the service of my country, and I leave my record in the hands of my countrymen. . . . It is unfitting to make personal explanations affecting national interests when my country is in the midst of a great war.' Almost before the cheers had died away, he had stuffed the manuscript into his jacket pocket, swung round on his heels, thrown a genial nod to the peers, and, smiling broadly, stridden out of the House. He had scored quite as effectively as Churchill by declining to make a speech. Never did he have a better press. The comment of the *Daily News* (17 November) was typical: Fisher 'firmly declined to be drawn into an unseemly personal wrangle. This is not the least of the great services Lord Fisher has done for the country.'

Nothing happened, and the beginning of the new year found the Admiral depressed once more. 'It is very hard,' he wrote on 2 January, 'when one feels at one's zenith to be locked out!' Realist that he was, he saw his only chance in a change of Government—a very improbable event, he believed. He assumed the functions of a gadfly in the early months of 1916, becoming at the same time the principal medium for the expression of the national unrest. Jellicoe collaborated with him.

The C.-in-C. had been drifting into bad relations with the Admiralty in the latter part of 1915 on account of blockade policy and the diversion of naval strength to the Mediterranean, even though he knew that the Admiralty were not entirely to blame. New sources of strained relations appeared at the turn of the year. They were summarized in an important letter to Fisher on 18 January 1916. The C.-in-C. informed him that the 18-inch battle cruiser *Furious* was 'hopelessly delayed'; 'destroyers that should have been delivered in October have not yet arrived'; similarly with regard to submarines due between June and December 1915. 'I should put the average delay at 3–9 months for all classes of ships. I don't know whether real efforts are being made to get the ships completed. All I know is that for several months I have not been allowed to send ships to Home yards to refit, on the plea that I am delaying new construction by doing so. . . . This is all for your private eye, but it is very disheartening at times.'[5] Here was the raw material for the campaign Fisher was about to mount against the Admiralty.

When Asquith asked Fisher (22 January) for his opinion as to the 'feasibility and probability' of Germany having 17-inch guns mounted in her battleships, the Admiral was unable to give an authoritative opinion,[6] but he took advantage of the request to raise these 'causes of disquietude' in two letters (24, 25 January): (1) They were lagging behind in destroyer construction. 'If the Germans have, as feasible, devoted their undepleted shipyards and their husbanded building resources in acquiring a big destroyer superiority over the number and quality of those possible to be with the Grand Fleet, then the issue of a fight between the two Fleets, till now assured to us, might be seriously imperilled.' (2) The *Furious*, which was supposed to be ready in the spring and which had been started in 1915 to provide against the possible eventuality of the Germans mounting a bigger naval gun than the British, was so delayed as not likely to be completed during the war. (3) The further provision of 18-inch guns which he had arranged for before he left the Admiralty had been suspended on his leaving. He had pressed Balfour to proceed with them, but no orders had been given.[7]

Fisher's 'violent attack' on the Board (or so the Second Sea Lord

[5] *Fear God and Dread Nought*, iii. 290–1.

[6] He wrote to Jellicoe soon afterwards that the 17-inch gun was in the *Hindenburg* and other ships, and on 3 February he told Asquith that it was 'feasible and probable' that such guns could be mounted, and were being mounted, in German ships, and that the answer should be a *20-inch* gun. *Ibid.*, p. 297.

[7] *Ibid.*, pp. 292–3.

regarded it) led to a careful examination of his charges by the First and Third Sea Lords. On the question of the Germans mounting a heavier calibre of gun in their battleships, Tudor had 'no hesitation in saying that the large majority of Naval Officers would agree that for Battleships of the existing displacements the limit lies with either the 13·5″ or 15″ gun, and that anything larger would reduce the fighting value of the ship'. His most telling point was 'the value attached by some people to guns of abnormal ranges is extremely doubtful from a practical point of view. It is seldom clear enough to use these ranges; it is next to impossible to spot at them; the number of hits obtained is excessively small; and the number of guns available for hitting is necessarily reduced.' His personal view was that 'the Germans would gain nothing by mounting 17″ guns in their Battleships, and that even if they did introduce these guns we should lose by imitating them'. He had no trouble demolishing the 'evidence' found at Dunkirk which had been the cause of the revival of the rumour. The gun which fired into Dunkirk was a 38-cm. calibre weapon (i.e., 15-inch), and fragments of shell which proved this were at the Admiralty.

Turning to the 'alleged delay' in the completion of the *Furious*, Tudor made this point: the contractors had believed they could deliver the ship in 16 months from the receipt of the gun drawings. Since these were received by the firm in April 1915, on their own showing they could not complete the ship until August 1916. 'No power on earth could have made her available for use this Spring —nor was it ever contemplated.' That was not the whole story. When Tudor had learned that the *Courageous* and *Furious*, being built by the same firm, were interfering with each other, he 'took the common sense action to give preference to the *Courageous*, not only because she was ordered first, but because her guns and mountings were not experimental and would be available in time, being originally intended for Battleships under construction. I should be very much surprised if there existed any Naval Officer who would not prefer a Cruiser with four 15″ guns of a well-tried pattern to one with two 18″ guns of a calibre never yet fired.' As for further provision of 18-inch guns, more could not have been ordered without interfering with the output of other guns so urgently required for both Navy and Army. That left the matter of the destroyers.

The first seven months of 1914, that is, prior to the war, there were delivered 18 destroyers, which averaged 20·3 months in construction. Since the war began, they had had 45 delivered (not including flotilla leaders), of which the 18 ordered before the war averaged 20·6 months to build, and 27 ordered during the war averaged 12½ months. They now had 120 flotilla leaders and destroyers under construction, with sanction to build 24 more destroyers and a leader when the shipyards could absorb them. 'Therefore, either from the view of time of construction or that of numbers it seems hardly humanly possible to do anything more.'[8]

Jackson supplemented Tudor's remarks. On the calibre of the German heavy guns,

Any further increase in fighting power such as higher speed, more armour protection, or 18" guns of the same number, would entail still greater dimensions, and would in fact involve a new programme of Floating Docks and enlargement of existing ones where this is possible. The cost would be very great, and the policy is one to be avoided unless forced upon us. There is no evidence whatever that Germany is adopting such a policy. . . . In my opinion the number of heavy guns in a battleship should not be reduced below the present standard of 8. If 18" guns were adopted the number would have to be reduced to 4 unless the dimensions alluded to above were greatly increased.[9]

Concerning the destroyers, they were building and ordering all that the country could turn out. Yet he conceded there was a shortage.

The shortage is due to the military strategy adopted, which necessitates escort or protection for the enormous number of transports in waters dangerous to them on account of submarines. The areas of these dangerous waters have increased, the wear and tear of the Destroyers is now being felt after 18 months of war to a greater extent than it was previously, and this necessitates continuous repairs in all available shipyards. . . . The rate of completion is now unfortunately falling off owing to the call on labour of the Munitions Department and recruiting officers, with no corresponding increase in energy on the part of the workmen to increase their indifferent weekly output. This was not

[8] Tudor's memorandum, 29 Jan. 1916; Admiralty MSS.
[9] The Board had, the day before, considered the advisability of going in for 18-inch guns on the projected capital ships. They decided it would be a mistake to mount less than six guns in a ship, since it was very difficult to find, and to keep, the range with fewer guns, especially at long range; and six 18-inch guns could not be mounted on capital ships of existing displacements.

foreseen by the late First Sea Lord when he prepared his programme of construction and inserted arbitrary dates for the completion of the vessels, which even under the most favourable circumstances were impossible of fulfilment. At the same time it might be noted that although the number of Destroyers actually under the orders of the Commander in Chief may not have increased to the extent desired or expected, their quality (recently) has increased . . .[10]

The two memoranda were discussed and approved by the Board on 4 February.

This settled nothing. Fisher continued to pound away, as in a letter to the Prime Minister on 3 February, on the theme of the 17-inch gun and the distressing delay in the *Furious*, destroyers, etc. There was 'absolutely no forgiveness possible' for these delays, as there was 'no valid excuse'.[11] In correspondence with his friends, his battle cry was *'Get Balfour out!'*

Jellicoe, as well as Fisher—the two were in regular communication in these months—was on the warpath. He wrote officially and privately to the Admiralty a number of times during January and early February. His main criticism was of the increasing delays in the completion of repairs to his ships, especially in the private yards, and with the delay in new construction of submarines, light cruisers, and, above all, of destroyers, of which by the end of January he had received but two of the seventeen he had been promised by January. He reminded their Lordships that destroyers were absolutely essential for submarine hunting as well as for screening and for a fleet action. Also, the troubles connected with Yarrow boilers in the light cruisers was offsetting the new light cruisers that were 'slowly (but very slowly) dribbling in', and at a time when they knew that the Germans were increasing the number of their light cruisers; and much the same thing was occurring with destroyers: boiler troubles and other defects had reduced his destroyer strength at a greater rate than new deliveries had added them, while he knew that the Germans had added many new ones. His most pressing need other than destroyers was in minesweepers, which, too, were being seriously delayed. 'I presume,' he wrote to the First Lord, 'the cause of many of our difficulties comes under the head of "Labour Troubles". I submit that there should be no "Labour Troubles" in war. If there is

[10] Jackson's memorandum, 30 Jan. 1916; *ibid.*
[11] *Fear God and Dread Nought*, pp. 296–300.

"shortage" of labour may it not be due to the fact that the Munitions Department is taking away men who should be engaged on Naval work? If that is the case I suggest that the men should be got back, otherwise there may be much heartburning later on when we find we are behind the Germans in light craft.'[12]

The First Lord countered that Admiralty information did not suggest any large increase in German strength in light cruisers and destroyers, but he 'shared to the full' the C.-in-C.'s anxieties about the delays in new construction and the repair of ships, which he agreed were due to shortage of labour; 'but I do not think you must infer from this, either that there are fewer men engaged on Admiralty work than at the beginning of the war, or that these men are on the whole shirking their duties. . . . The actual work being done in the Yards (both public and private) is far in excess of anything which we experienced in pre-war conditions.'[13] It developed that the labour shortage was mostly in the engine works, not in the shipyards. Jackson, too, admitted that repairs were getting 'more difficult. Lloyd George has pushed himself into such a position that he controls all labour, acts first and considers afterwards, and protests take weeks to get remedied.'[14] The nub of the matter lay in Jellicoe's reaction to this line of argument: 'No one seems strong enough to prevent Lloyd George taking away all our men.'[15]

The pot was now about to boil over. On 1 February Hopwood, the Additional Civil Lord, saw Fisher as an emissary from Balfour. The seriousness of the whole business was brought home to Hopwood and to the Board by his discovery of the continual correspondence passing between Jellicoe and Fisher, and the latter's revelation that he proposed at an early date and as a public duty to reveal in the Lords the complaints, anxieties, and criticisms of the C.-in-C. Jellicoe's 'indiscretion' and 'disloyalty' shocked the Board. Only Hamilton, Jellicoe's best friend on the Board, took a charitable view of his actions and motives. 'There are no doubt faults on both sides. He is often very unreasonable and does not take a broad view of things. On the other hand, the Admiralty often ride rough shod over him and will not listen to his arguments.

[12] Jellicoe to Balfour, 19 Jan. 1916; Balfour MSS.
[13] Balfour to Jellicoe, 31 Jan. 1916; *ibid.*
[14] Jackson to Jellicoe, 25 Jan. 1916; Jellicoe MSS.
[15] Jellicoe to Beatty, 29 Jan. 1916; Beatty MSS.

I very much blame the 4SL [Lambert], whose head is somewhat swollen.'[16]

There appeared to be only two ways to head off the explosive situation inherent in a Fisher *exposé* in the Lords. The first was suggested by Fisher to Hopwood—that he be given a position that carried responsibility. He would not accept any consultative or advisory position. What he most wanted was to be joint First Sea Lord, with responsibility for programmes, ships, output, etc.; Jackson would be First Sea Lord for policy, and the position of Third Sea Lord would go into abeyance. Hopwood flatly told him this was impossible. 'Policy, strategy and quality, character and quantity of ships are so mixed and interdependent that two First Sea Lords with the proposed delimitation of functions could not live together for a day.' The other possibility, suggested by Hopwood to the First Lord, was to invite Jellicoe to air his grievances at a War Committee meeting. 'With the destruction of Jellicoe's grievances either by acceptance or rejection of his points the danger, in Fisher's intervention, is drawn. Without the Jellicoe correspondence Fisher's cause becomes purely personal to himself and his own disappointments, and all that is comparatively insignificant. . . . I am seriously impressed with the danger if Jellicoe is not taken vigorously and tactfully in hand.'[17] Actually, Fisher had been pressing Asquith to give the C.-in-C. a hearing before the War Committee.

At this very moment Beatty weighed in. He had just seen the C.-in-C. for the first time in five months, and had left him so perturbed and despondent about the delays in construction that he felt impelled to write to the Prime Minister privately (3 February). He restated and endorsed Jellicoe's views and added a point of his own: the equally serious delay in battle cruisers (*Renown* and *Repulse*), which 'are to the Grand Fleet what Zeppelins are to the High Sea Fleet.'[18]

[16] Diary, 1 Feb. 1916; Hamilton MSS.

[17] Hopwood to Balfour, 1, 2 Feb. 1916; Balfour MSS.

[18] Asquith MSS. Beatty grossly overestimated the German achievement in battle-cruiser construction. True, the British had completed but one battle cruiser since August 1914, the *Tiger*; yet the Germans had added only the *Derfflinger* and *Lützow*, and not *Hindenburg*, which Beatty asserted was ready. (She was completed in October 1917.) Nor did Germany complete 'at an early date', or ever, two more, 'Ersatz Victoria Luise' and 'Ersatz Freya'. It is hard, though, to quarrel with Beatty's dictum: 'Surely it must be wise to calculate on the probabilities when our information is practically nil.' He expected the situation before the end of the year to be: eight

When the War Committee invited Jellicoe to attend, Fisher decided to await the effect of the C.-in-C.'s visit. If the latter's representation proved of no avail, he would expose the situation in the Lords. Fisher summed up for Jellicoe (12 February) the reasons for his and the country's uneasiness:

The righteous public anxiety as to the looseness of the blockade, the terrible delays in Admiralty shipbuilding, the taking away by Lloyd George of skilled workmen from our shipyards and his getting control of Admiralty shipbuilding materials, and, finally, the effete administration and conduct of the War by the Admiralty, so beautifully expressed yesterday by an Admiralty messenger to Sir Philip Watts: *'Lor, Sir! We are quieter here now, Sir, than we was in peace!'* And, finally, the very grave public anxiety as to whether the hitherto assured supremacy of the British Grand Fleet may not have been jeopardized by 18 months unstinted German efforts to effect a great German naval surprise . . .[19]

Another résumé for Jellicoe two days later added other causes for 'grave anxiety' that concluded with 'the most serious of all': 'Apathy, lethargy, irresolution, and stupid dissemination of naval strength, and an utter absence of imagination and audacity in conceiving vital blows, war-ending blows, on the enemy! We wait till we are kicked. We don't even kick back again. We put on a tin plate so that it shan't hurt so much when kicked next time. All our measures are preventive—Zeppelin and otherwise. It's a losing game to be on the defensive.'[20]

Jellicoe had his day with the War Committee on 17 February. The Committee first disposed of the 18-inch-gun problem once and for all. They agreed with the Admiralty that it was 'unnecessary and undesirable' to lay down 18-inch ships to deal with the heavy enemy ships rumoured to be armed with guns larger than the 15-inch. There was no evidence to support this. The more urgent need was to press the construction of other classes—light cruisers, destroyers, minesweepers, etc.[21] Afterwards Jellicoe wrote to Beatty: 'I can't say there was much result but at any rate they have heard my views on the shortage of small craft which I put

German and ten British battle cruisers, and, overall, the German eight were equal to the British ten, largely because of superior speed. He included the *Renown* and *Repulse* in his reckoning, but not the 'Freak Ships', *Furious, Glorious, Courageous*, as they could not be expected to engage successfully much more heavily armoured and armed ships.

[19] *Fear God and Dread Nought*, iii. 306.
[20] *Ibid.*, pp. 308–10.
[21] War Committee Paper W.C. 26 (minutes of the meeting).

strongly.'[22] To Fisher, upset by three Cabinet Ministers present telling him Jellicoe gave the impression of being satisfied with the Admiralty administration, he explained that 'the question of whether I was satisfied with Admiralty administration was never raised or put to me. It could hardly be put to me in the presence of the 1st Lord and 1st Sea Lord!!... I am still seriously disturbed at the shortage of small craft, and the last return sent me is even worse than anything I saw before. . . . What is wanted is a very energetic and pushing person whose sole business is to see that the Navy comes first in the labour market, until our position in this respect is secure.'[23]

There was only one visible effect of the C.-in-C.'s strong statement on construction delays. On 11 February the War Committee had recognized the gravity of the destroyer situation and agreed to the appointment of a Cabinet committee to meet with the representatives of labour and try to solve the labour question. Now, on the 17th, the War Committee decided on a different tack—to attempt to arrange with the shipbuilders for the 'dilution' of labour (with female and other unskilled labour) on the same lines already adopted by Armstrong's.

Jellicoe had hardly returned to the fleet when he sent off a memorandum to the Prime Minister setting forth all the old grievances again, and in somewhat sharper language. This time the Board got their blood up. Hamilton could not understand what his object was, 'unless he wants to come to the Admiralty or to cover himself in case of his being held [to] blame should anything go wrong. Both are most unworthy motives and I am disgusted and bitterly disappointed that Jellicoe should have descended so low.'[24] Jackson hit back at the C.-in-C. (2 March). 'Your views are now known to all responsible, and you know the situation as far as new construction, etc. is concerned, and how anxious we are to hasten it. Don't you think it is time the matter was dropped, as if continued it may set an example to others, and we or you may have juniors setting forth the inadequacy of their ships and complaining of their tools, instead of trying to make the most of what they have got, in the spirit of the true seaman of old.'[25]

[22] 20 Feb. 1916; Beatty MSS.
[23] 22 Feb. 1916; *Fear God and Dread Nought*, iii. 317.
[24] Diary, 1 Mar. 1916; Hamilton MSS.
[25] Jellicoe MSS.

If this did not succeed in stopping the agitation, from that quarter at least, Jackson was prepared to administer a severe rebuke to the C.-in-C. which would show him that he must keep in his place and that their Lordships intended to be top dog. Jackson's stinger brought about a truce.

As regards my paper to the Prime Minister [Jellicoe explained], I sent it because the Secretary's notes of the meeting did not represent what I said or intended to say, and as I had drawn up the paper in case I was asked anything about the comparative strength and offensive policy, it seemed best that that should be a considered paper and not a mere rambling conversation which the War Council degenerated into. Further, the conclusions reached seemed to ignore the points on which I laid stress. Surely it is best to try and get the new construction pushed on. The main difficulty seems to be labour, which is due to labour having been diverted elsewhere. . . .

As regards 'doing the best with what we have', I take it we shall do that, but the seaman of old was never satisfied with what we had any more than we are, witness Nelson and the cruiser [i.e., frigate] question. It is merely history repeating itself, but for 'Cruisers' read 'Cruisers and destroyers'. Also we are faced with entirely new methods of warfare, and to meet those methods it is obvious that we also must adopt new tools, and if I don't ask for them I should be to blame. I only wish I could exchange half a dozen battleships for half their value in light cruisers and destroyers.[26]

Jackson thanked him for his remarks about his paper. 'You have backed us up. Unfortunately it is the one subject the Government won't tackle, though the general opinion is that labour will be as amenable as anybody else during the war. . . . Your remark about Nelson and cruisers is excellent, and I know, like him, you'll do the best with what you've got, and we'll do the best to help you, only the worldwide scope of the war puts demands on us we cannot meet fully.'[27]

Jellicoe thereafter held his peace. Only the hospital-ship question seriously marred his relations with the Board during the spring. On 29 January the Admiralty had informed the C.-in-C. that the serious mercantile shipping shortage necessitated the withdrawal of two of the four hospital ships attached to the Grand Fleet, the *China* and the *Soudan*. (The four ships could accommodate 1,568 wounded, which allowed for but a two-per-cent

[26] Jellicoe to Jackson, 5 Mar. 1916; Jackson MSS.
[27] 7 Mar. 1916; Jellicoe MSS.

wounded list, though the expected percentage before Jutland, based on guesswork, was five per cent of the personnel engaged.) Jellicoe fired off a protest (3 February) that no reduction in hospital ships was 'in the least degree possible'. He estimated that in the battle fleet and cruiser squadrons alone there could easily be 2,000 wounded 'to be provided for in ships which are able to reach the base', pointed out that shore hospital accommodations at the main North Sea bases were extremely limited or non-existent, and stressed 'the utmost importance of ridding the fighting ships of wounded at the earliest possible moment after an action, for the sake of the wounded themselves, for the sake of having the ship ready for action in the shortest possible time, and for the sake of the morale of the men'.[28] He fought a clever and successful delaying action against what the Second Sea Lord admitted was 'a very shortsighted and stupid policy'. Nothing had been done by the time of Jutland, when the Grand Fleet had five hospital ships available.

Meanwhile, in February and March, the naval agitation had taken an interesting turn.

3. THE CAMPAIGN FOR FISHER'S RETURN

The *Manchester Guardian* and *The Observer*, whose respective Editors, C. P. Scott and J. L. Garvin, were ardent admirers of Fisher, led the drive for the old warrior's return to a central position in the war effort. The *Manchester Guardian's* leader of 7 February 1916 is an excellent statement of the Fisherites' case: 'Nothing must be taken for granted in war, and least of all in naval war. We need for the direction of our naval policy every ounce of our energy, every counsel of experience, and, above all, every impulse of restless ingenuity and of the spirit of innovation in which the British genius excels. It is notorious that our full store of these qualities is not being drawn upon. . . . Lord Fisher's immense experience, energy, and driving power are not used in such a position [as B.I.R. Chairman], and the nation cannot afford to waste them.' All shades of opinion were represented in the Fisher camp, for example, the *Naval and Military Record, Pall Mall Gazette, Standard, Daily Chronicle,* and *Daily News.*

There was no agreement on what the Admiral's role should be.

[28] Admiralty MSS.

Many of his champions wanted him back as First Sea Lord, and some as 'dictator' of construction (Lloyd George thought he would be most useful in that capacity) or as a member of the War Committee. Most, however, talked about his appointment as First Lord. A favourite argument here was reference to the fact that in the most critical moments of British history great sailors had been First Lords, notably St. Vincent and Barham in the years immediately preceding Trafalgar. Some of Fisher's partisans, like the *Naval and Military Record*, wanted an admiral as First Lord, and he need not be Fisher. The assumption was that a sailor could look after the interests of the Navy better, in Cabinet and War Committee meetings, than could a civilian First Lord.

The call for Fisher's return aroused the old antipathies in the anti-Fisher camp, whose campaign was led by the *Morning Post*, *Daily Express*, and *National Review*. A. H. Pollen, the naval journalist, and two respected retired Admirals, Sir Gerard Noel and Sir Arthur Moore, were prominent in the movement. Fisher was too old, they said, and *younger*, not older men, were wanted at the Admiralty; his methods and policies had raised so much opposition and controversy that his return to power would be disastrous to the loyalty of the Service; and the Navy and the country had full confidence in Balfour and Jackson. By way of proving his unfitness for a responsible post at the Admiralty, the *Morning Post*, in two scathing leaders (10, 11 February) that made Fisher see red, criticized his major reforms of 1904–10 and condemned him for 'shirking responsibility' in May 1915. The King was among those who looked upon the pro-Fisher agitation as 'very serious and very lamentable'. Admiral Hamilton early in February enlisted the D.N.I.'s support in a personal campaign to keep Fisher out of the Admiralty. Hall went to work on the editors to make them see that the agitation was harmful and unpatriotic. But neither Jackson nor Balfour 'would move in the matter on the ground that they didn't care if they were ousted'![29]

Fisher was not sanguine about his prospects for any of the positions earmarked for him by his supporters. (He held the King to be the principal obstacle in his path.) If he did become First Lord, he planned to ask Jellicoe to be First Sea Lord and to have Madden succeed him as C.-in-C. He claimed to be 'dead set' against the agitation to bring him back. Providence must be

[29] Diary, 11 Feb. 1916; Hamilton MSS.

allowed 'to come along when so inclined!' In practice, he was not averse to his admirers pulling political strings, as when C. P. Scott introduced Lord Loreburn into the matter. The latter formed a small committee of peers who were dissatisfied with Balfour's administration of the Admiralty to promote Fisher's cause. The Fisherites went to such extremes as arranging (10 February) for an exhibition of the Admiral's portrait in a shop window in a prominent London thoroughfare (St. Martin's Lane). A placard invited the passerby to sign a petition inside asking that he should join the Cabinet. Such tactics did Fisher's cause no good, even if there was no indication that he was responsible.

A leader of the Fisher partisans was the Duchess of Hamilton. At 38 still quite a beauty, she was also a wonderful person—kind, gentle, understanding, and devoted to causes, usually of a humanitarian kind. Her special cause at this time was Fisher. She worked tirelessly, using to the full her very considerable charm and political and social connexions to effect his restoration, which, she was convinced, was imperative in the national interest. To her flat near St. James's Palace she invited influential men for tea and propaganda.

Both the campaign for Fisher's restoration and the agitation against the Admiralty came to a head on 7, 8 March. On 7 March, before a full House of Commons reminiscent of pre-war days, and with Fisher conspicuous in his favourite place in the Peers' Gallery over the clock, the First Lord made his statement on the navy estimates. He devoted its major portion to a congratulatory and persuasive review of the work the Navy had already accomplished. He belittled the *Moewe's* depredations, and he told the House that never had so many ships been built or built so fast; that practically the whole shipbuilding capacity of the country had been absorbed by Admiralty work, and that, with the single exception of armoured cruisers, their supremacy in every class of ship was far greater than at the beginning of the war, and even in this class of ship they had an enormous superiority. There were still deficiencies in certain kinds of ships, imposed by the labour shortage. 'But up to the limits which labour offers us we are doing all that can be done in the way of shipbuilding . . .' He made the fantastic claim (few in the House knew the truth) that never had there been 'the smallest difference of opinion between the Board of Admiralty and the Admirals in command . . .'

Then Lieutenant-Colonel Winston Churchill spoke. He was back from Flanders on special leave to enable him to participate in the debate. Unknown to most people, some of his best friends and Fisher's, who had deplored their rupture in May 1915 and its aggravation the following November, had been working to heal the breach since just before Christmas. They had not succeeded in bringing the two men together, but it was understood that they would, if they met, not refuse to shake hands. The evacuation of Gallipoli two weeks later removed the great obstacle. The problem that had caused all their differences no longer existed. In the back of Churchill's mind was the thought that, as he put it to a friend some months later, Fisher 'cannot be trusted, but he is a man of genius. He can only work for three or four hours, but he is full of ideas and his three or four hours are worth more than other people's full time.'[30]

Churchill, thinner and looking remarkably fit and alert, spoke emphatically and uncompromisingly. He moved freely, impelled, it seemed to one observer, by a 'resistless dynamic force within him'. He was expected to dampen the pro-Fisher campaign. Instead, his outburst was the culmination of the discontent in the country and in the Fleet itself. He insisted they ought to credit the Germans with not having wasted their time, and with having completed every ship which was begun before the war. He was therefore alarmed over the serious construction delays. The First Lord had spoken of 'the limit of labour'. Churchill asserted there was no limit of labour where the Navy was concerned, and as the Navy was their paramount interest, everything else must give way to it. 'There are no competing needs with paramount needs.' He expressed dissatisfaction with the 'purely negative' strategy, bluntly stating that his Board 'would certainly not have been content with an attitude of pure passivity' in 1916. As an illustration, he could not understand the lack of enterprise in dealing with the Zeppelin raiders. Why not destroy their sheds? he asked, and he drew the biggest cheers of the day by recalling that in the early weeks of the war British airmen had found their way to Cologne, Dusseldorf, and Cuxhaven.

Churchill's speech was intended to lead up to his final point, during which members could scarcely believe their ears. ('The effect,' reported *The Observer's* Political Correspondent, was 'one

[30] 2 July 1916; *Lord Riddell's War Diary*, p. 199.

of stupefaction and bewilderment.') 'There was a time when I did not think that I could have brought myself to say this, but I have been away for some months, and my mind is now clear. The times are crucial. The issues are momentous. . . . The existence of our country and of our cause depend upon the Fleet. We cannot afford to deprive ourselves or the Navy of the strongest and most vigorous forces that are available.' He then crystallized the rather widespread popular feeling into the remark that there was 'a lack of driving force and mental energy' in the present naval administration. And he wound up: '. . . I urge the First Lord of the Admiralty without delay to fortify himself, to vitalize and animate his Board of Admiralty by recalling Lord Fisher to his post as First Sea Lord.' With this Parthian shot, he concluded amid a prolonged storm of cheers and cries of dissent. When Fisher rose to go as soon as Churchill sat down, a number of Liberal Members broke the rules by cheering him.

Anti-Fisherite and pro-Admiralty opinion accepted Balfour's assurances at face value and branded Churchill's speech as injudicious, particularly in its appeal on behalf of Fisher. The charge was freely made that the sole explanation of Churchill's conduct was his desire to destroy the Ministry in order to get back to place and power. For the *Spectator* (11 March), 'To watch this fevered, this agonized struggle to regain the political fortune which the arch-gambler threw away by his own acts is to witness one of the great tragedies of life.' 'Surely Winston Churchill must be going off his head like his Father did?' was Admiral Colville's unkind blast.

At the other end of the spectrum, the Fisherites were, of course, strongly impressed by Churchill's speech. But even among those journals which had not committed themselves to Fisher's recall, and which were, on the whole, satisfied with Balfour's statement, there was cause for disquiet in Churchill's remarks. *The Times* and the *Daily Telegraph* were among them, the former declaring (8 March) that Churchill's speech 'will certainly command a good deal of attention, because it expressed very vividly the vague popular anxiety which has lately been prevalent about our general naval position'. Even the *National Review*, vehemently anti-Churchill as it usually was, was forced to admit (April) that his 'irruption, however ill-meant, was not an unmixed evil', as in drawing attention to the labour problem that had 'been allowed to drift on from month to month, like everything else under the Wait and See dispensation, and now presents disquieting features . . .'

That Churchill's speech had irritated Balfour, normally a hard man to provoke, was clear when he came into the crowded House the following afternoon. There was a cloud on his face instead of the customary smile, and when the House got into Committee on naval affairs, he stepped to the table with something like impatience. His sole purpose, he said, with hardness in his voice, was to reply to Churchill's speech, 'unfortunate, both in form and substance'. Balfour then delivered one of his best debating efforts, speaking for three-quarters of an hour with vehemence and pitiless wit, as he by turns amused, enlightened, and startled the House. He 'roasted his predecessor over a slow fire', according to one eye-witness. According to another, Churchill, who sat in gloomy isolation in one corner of the Opposition front bench, 'literally writhed under the lash'. In his reply afterwards he had the grace to describe Balfour as 'a master of Parliamentary sword-play, and of every dialectical art'.

This was Balfour's case. The misgivings suggested by Churchill, especially in regard to the maintenance of the rate of construction, were not justified, and ought not to have been sown broadcast by him if they were. There had been no slackness in pressing on the construction of ships, though it had not proceeded so rapidly as they desired. This was due to the labour shortage. All three solutions to the labour difficulty were being tried—the recall of skilled mechanics from the trenches, more overtime, and labour dilution. Under all three heads, 'every effort is being made, and has been made, by the Admiralty to bring about a better state of things,' he asserted with emphasis. Secondly, he made great play with the singular history of Churchill's relations with Fisher. Whether or not Churchill's past strictures on Fisher's co-operation were justified, they absolutely disqualified him as an advocate for imposing that co-operation on somebody else. Churchill had complained (15 November 1915) that he had never had the support from Fisher which he had had a right to expect. '. . . why does he suppose that Lord Fisher should behave differently to me . . .? Is it my merits? Am I more happily gifted in the way of working with people than my right hon. Friend?' Moreover, no one was better fitted to be First Sea Lord than Jackson, a 'great public servant' of outstanding character, ability, and experience. Why, then, should he get rid of him? The First Lord announced that he would regard himself as 'contemptible beyond the power of expression if I were to yield an inch to a demand of such a kind, made in such a way. The right hon. Gentleman was not fortunate enough to get the guidance and support of the First Sea Lord when he was in office. I have had a happier fate. I have received both guidance and support from the present First Sea Lord.'

Churchill hastened to reply. He was at a disadvantage, since he was never at his best in impromptu speeches. As a rule he prepared his speeches with care, writing them out. (He resembled his father in that respect.) 'His oratorical engines are driven by midnight oil,' as one writer put it. On this occasion he had to think fast on his feet and without preparation. His reply was lame and halting and little more than a brief and hurried restatement of his case.

After the debates of 7 and 8 March, the press agitation, whether pro-Fisher or anti-Admiralty, gradually subsided. One facet of the agitation lingered on in some Service quarters—the demand for a seaman as First Lord, with Cabinet rank and a seat in the War Committee. The *Naval and Military Record*, which took the lead, stated the problem succinctly (5 April): 'The truth is that in these days the Navy is represented practically nowhere. The Navy is not important in the Cabinet, as the other Allied fleets are represented in the Allied Cabinets; it is almost without voice in the two Houses of Parliament; and it is apparent that in the matter of the blockade, the expansion of our military forces, and the grievances under which officers and men suffer the Admiralty to-day exercises little influence.'

Only one seaman had the stature, the prestige, to follow the brilliant precedent of Barham *et al.*, and he was completely out of the running after 8 March. Churchill's speech of 7 March made it impossible for Balfour to offer Fisher anything, since it would have the appearance of succumbing to outside pressure. Lloyd George recognized that, in this sense, the speech had been a great error. 'He should have stopped after criticising the Administration.'

Two events on the 8th drove the last nails into Fisher's coffin. While Balfour was replying to Churchill in the Commons, a row of sandwichmen paraded Whitehall bearing appeals like 'Give us back Fisher' and 'Give us back the man that won the Falkland Islands Battle'. The last placard expressly stated: 'Lord Fisher knows nothing of this, he has not been consulted, the need of the nation is great, modes of expression are few.' Responsibility for the demonstration lay with a particularly foolish and over-enthusiastic admirer of Fisher, an engineer named Alfred James who had never even met the Admiral.[31] That evening, at one of the theatres they had a song whose chorus contained the line, 'Give us back our Jacky'. At this point a claque at one side of the gallery shouted 'No! No!' and was answered by a very noisy claque on the other side roaring out 'Yes! Yes! Yes!' These undignified incidents (rumour had it that Horatio Bottomley, Editor of *John Bull*, financed them) did nothing at all to help Fisher's cause. Verily, he suffered much at the hands of friends and admirers.

While the sandwichmen were demonstrating, Fisher was testifying at a War Committee meeting, to which he had been invited at Lloyd George's dogged insistence. They asked him to substantiate all the statements he had been making about the delays in construction. He began by handing the Committee a brief memorandum dealing with the necessity of accelerating all vessels in hand and starting new construction in every vacant slip and pushing it forward with speed. 'But all is of no use unless some suitable person is placed in dictatorial command of the whole building programme . . .' It was vital to bring back at once the fleet and its auxiliaries in the Mediterranean, and to leave the French and Italian Fleets in charge. 'I have not been wrong hitherto,' he concluded, 'and I am not wrong now in predicting a naval disaster unless drastic action is taken, and I repeat, never has the existence of the British Empire been so menaced as at the present juncture, because of the possible German naval surprises in store for us.'[32]

We have two quite different versions of the degree of Fisher's effectiveness. Hankey wrote to Fisher that his appearance had 'exactly the right effect of dotting the "i's" and crossing the "t's" of Jellicoe's evidence. I cannot overstate my own gratitude to you, not only for coming yesterday, but for the persistence with which you have by letters and personal interviews compelled the War

---

[31] Alfred James to Admiral Sir Reginald Bacon, 10 Oct. 1929; Lennoxlove MSS.
[32] *Fear God and Dread Nought*, iii. 321n.

Committee to probe these matters to the bottom.'[33] On the other hand, Arthur Pollen, an opponent of Fisher, heard that his appearance had been

the most dismal failure. His main point was that the dates of his programme of construction had not been kept. The Admiralty had no difficulty in showing that his dates were meaningless or dishonest. He had practically forced the builders to promise deliveries months before delivery was possible—a thing they were perfectly willing to do if all penalties for non-delivery were waived, as in fact they were. Before the thing was over, Fisher lost his temper hopelessly and tried to brush the Admiralty objections on one side. All the War Committee are, I hear, agreed upon his failure, and he will probably not be asked to attend again, so that the whole intrigue has really fizzled out this time . . .[34]

Asquith's reaction to Fisher's appearance before the Committee leaves no doubt that he had not fared well. C. P. Scott, who saw the Prime Minister at 10 Downing Street on the afternoon of the 8th, to recommend Fisher's recall in the interest of 'allaying anxiety in the country', made these observations soon afterwards: Asquith's

manner was pretty cold. . . . He was silent and grim. . . . [I] talked continuously . . . for five or ten minutes . . . Then at last he began to reply. Fisher had been there that morning at the War Council, and they had heard what he had to say. What did it amount to? His answer was a contemptuous ejaculation and gesture, casting thumb back over shoulder as though to get rid of dirt. Then he broke out on them both [Fisher and Churchill], rising in his seat and marching to and fro. As for Churchill's speech [of 7 March], it was a piece of the grossest effrontery. . . . Then he quieted a little. 'I admit,' he said, 'that he has valuable qualities. He is a constructor, very fertile and ingenious; he is not a strategist; he would be no use in command of a fleet.' I suggested that, besides being an inventor, he was also an executant— that he had an extraordinary power of getting things done, and quoted Churchill's enthusiastic testimony to that effect. 'Oh! yes,' A. replied, 'he has no doubt what Americans call "hustle" ' and then went on to say that there was nothing extraordinary about him in this, and that others could do and were doing quite as well.[35]

Lloyd George, though confessing that Fisher had not done well

[33] *Ibid.*, p. 322.
[34] Pollen to Richmond, 22 Mar. 1916; Richmond MSS.
[35] From Scott's private papers; J. L. Hammond, *C. P. Scott of the Manchester Guardian* (rev. ed., London, 1934), pp. 194–6.

at the War Committee, thought he should come back to the Admiralty, where his driving force and ability to get things done were lacking. 'If we were faced with a sudden emergency, I should feel if Fisher were at the Admiralty, that everything would be done that could be done.'[36] But Lloyd George stood alone in the War Committee.

Finding it 'maddening being in London—powerless and cast out—and yet never in such vigour in all my life!', Fisher retired late in March 1916 to the Hamilton country place at Balcombe in Sussex. He returned to London, after about ten days, in a mood of black pessimism. He could not be consoled by Churchill, Hankey, George Lambert, and others, who begged him not to lose heart and to remember, in Churchill's words (14 May), that 'destiny has not done with you yet'. He could not see the light on the horizon that they professed to see.

He continued to fire broadsides at the Government and the Admiralty, only he directed them to his friends, and he shifted his sights to the Mediterranean and the Zeppelin and U-boat problems, in which areas he found plentiful examples of the 'unbelievably inept' strategy with which the war was being conducted. It made no sense to him that over a half million men were in Egypt and Salonika, with the total force against them consisting of two Austrian divisions (on the Salonika front), and necessitating the tying up of millions of tons of mercantile shipping in the Mediterranean and the large naval resources needed to protect this shipping. The size of the force the Admiralty was still maintaining in the Mediterranean made him speechless— almost. He realized the potential gravity of the renewed German submarine offensive and saw that it posed the threat of starvation if the slackness at the Admiralty persisted. Fisher had referred to the Zeppelin menace several times at the height of the agitation early in 1916. He returned to the subject on 1 May with a long memorandum. The new Zeppelins, it stated, had a 600-mile radius, could navigate at an altitude of 15,000 feet, and had a speed of 70 m.p.h. 'The 11 [rigid] airships we are building can't touch them! . . . It is astounding how little is realized of the Zeppelin Menace, and how it militates against the action of the British Grand Fleet, and how it renders so easy the fast German battle cruisers bombarding the East Coast, and renders feasible

[36] 12 Mar. 1916; *Lord Riddell's War Diary*, p. 165.

a possible German Army Corps in the Thames estuary.'[37] Fisher's Zeppelin fears were shared in the Grand Fleet.

Jellicoe had for a long time been apprehensive over the German lead in airships. He saw what a great advantage the Zeppelins would be to the High Seas Fleet as scouts, as well as for aerial spotting, on the day of battle. They would be able to give the German C.-in-C. full information as to British dispositions, while the British C.-in-C. would be entirely ignorant of the German dispositions. 'Acting in conjunction with his submarines they will be a great thorn in our side.' (He did not foresee the spotty efficiency of the Zeppelins when used for strategic reconnaissance, owing to the North Sea weather and navigational inaccuracies.) Worse still, he was unable to propose any means of meeting this menace. His experience with the *Campania* (seaplane carrier) led him to believe that seaplane carriers were not an effective substitute for airships. 'There are not many occasions on which seaplanes working from the open sea can rise into the air. The only possibility, therefore, of using seaplanes for this purpose in a fleet action is with light machines which can rise from the deck of a seaplane carrier.' Little progress in this direction was made down to Jutland. Nor did the C.-in-C. find that seaplanes could serve as an antidote to the Zeppelins. They had insufficient lifting power to climb above the Zeppelins. Nor could the 'aerial guns' reach the Zeppelins.[38]

Beatty was, if anything, more impatient than his Chief over the airship-building delays. A letter of inquiry to the C.O.S. on 24 December 1915 had elicited this highly unsatisfactory reply:

[37] *Fear God and Dread Nought*, iii. 347–8. There is no indication for whom this paper was written. Fisher was not too far off. The latest Zeppelin type, represented by *L-30*, first of the 'big six-engine ships', was operational at the end of May. Her maximum trial speed was 62 m.p.h., and she was capable of an altitude of 17,400 feet (though she flew at about 13,000 feet in her raids over England). After Churchill left the Admiralty, his anti-airship policy (he made an exception for the blimps) was reversed. In July 1915 the Board decided to lay down the nucleus of a rigid airship fleet, long-range, fast airships capable of fleet reconnaissance work comparable to what the Zeppelins could do for the German Fleet. One was building (*R-9*), three others were now approved, and seven more were ordered in January 1916. The first of these rigids, *R-9*, was not completed until November 1916. Alterations proved necessary, and she was not finally delivered to the Naval Air Service until April 1917. Of non-rigid airships the Navy had in June 1916 thirty-nine in service (nearly all S.S. ships—the original blimps) and a further thirty-seven building (the improved Coastal and North Sea types of blimps, with a greater radius of action).

[38] Jellicoe to Admiralty, 29 July 1915; Admiralty MSS. In May 1916 there were 1,131 aircraft in the R.N.A.S., comprising 408 seaplanes and 723 aeroplanes.

. . . the value of Zeppelins has been well shown in the war as we rarely send ships to Heligoland Bight or even Submarines without their being seen by Zeppelins if the weather is fit for flying. It saves the Germans sending out cruisers and in fine weather they can do all that cruisers can in the matter of getting information, and also a bit more. The Zeppelins we are building will not be in time for this war as even if finished before the war ends our people will have to learn how to use them. Kite balloons are the next best expedient and the *Campania* is being fitted for them.[39]

Beatty became madder than ever in the spring of 1916 as the snail's pace in airship construction continued. 'We cannot go on as in the past, viz. . . . our Zeppelin construction, about which the Chief of the War Staff wrote me $3\frac{1}{2}$ months ago that they were building but that they would be no use *this war*!! How long do they take to build and how long does the War Staff think the war is going to last, presumably about another three months!!'[40]

*   *   *

One can draw four conclusions from the agitation of 1916. First, the discontent was a good deal more than that of a band of Fisherites eager to reinstall their hero in Whitehall. It affected in varying degrees all shades of opinion, including the Navy itself. Jellicoe, Beatty, and many of their officers were not at all satisfied with the higher control of the Navy, though few of them would have welcomed Fisher's return to the Admiralty, except perhaps as Controller.

In the second place, the Board did not come seriously to grips with the central problem, the construction delays and their major cause, the labour shortage, until aroused to action by the pinpricks of Jellicoe, Beatty, Fisher, and public opinion. Even then months passed before any real difference in building output was evident. The Admiralty also attempted in the spring to alleviate the Grand Fleet insufficiency of destroyers, minesweepers, and light cruisers by carefully re-examining the distribution of ships outside Home waters, above all in the Mediterranean. It was possible to bring home only a few old battleships from the Mediterranean. This was of no use to Jellicoe, whose needs lay in other directions.

In the third place, the best solution to the construction delays

---

[39] Oliver to Beatty, 29 Dec. 1915; Beatty MSS.
[40] Beatty to Jellicoe, 14 Apr. 1916; *ibid.*

was not adopted, and this was as much the Board's fault as it was Asquith's or the War Committee's. The Board were afraid to have Fisher back in any capacity, which seems a pity. We can be reasonably sure, knowing his record and his talents, that had he been brought back as Controller (I am sure he would have accepted this junior position), he would have smashed the construction bottlenecks, and perhaps even have succeeded in bringing back many of the small craft in the Mediterranean. There would have been enough small craft by the end of the year to have satisfied Grand Fleet requirements and to have ensured the introduction of the convoy system much earlier than it was. One important argument used by the Admiralty against convoy—the paucity of escorts—would not have existed. What is more, Fisher would have imparted some corrective to the self-satisfaction, complacency, and passivity of the Board. On the other hand, it is fair to raise the question of how long he would have lasted, since he would have come into the Admiralty like a whirlwind. And how effective would he have been in view of his declining physical, and perhaps mental, powers? Here I prefer Churchill's evaluation to Crease's.[41]

Finally, the public agitation probably had something to do with the partial changeover from a defensive to an offensive strategy in the spring of 1916. This theme brings us back to the story of the Grand Fleet in the sixteen months that followed the Dogger Bank action.

[41] See above, pp. 383, 398.

XVI

The Grand Fleet: Watchful Waiting

(FEBRUARY 1915–MAY 1916)

> What then would draw the German Fleet from its harbours with the intention of battle? The blockade had not provoked them; the passage of the Army did not tempt them . . . What was there that we could do which would force the German Navy to fight us at our own selected moment and on our own terms?
>
> CHURCHILL, *The World Crisis.*

> Nothing in 1915 or after except the hope of engaging a portion only of the Grand Fleet. See Scheer and Tirpitz books. Plans were constantly carried out to tempt them out with portions of the Grand Fleet as a bait.
>
> JELLICOE, on the above passage.

> To strengthen our naval forces by every conceivable means, to add every new vessel to the Grand Fleet and to remain in an attitude of inactive expectancy was the sum and substance of the naval policy advocated from this quarter [Jellicoe].
>
> CHURCHILL, *The World Crisis.*

> Far from 'inactive', every scheme to tempt the High Seas Fleet out was put into operation. The High Seas Fleet was our objective.
>
> JELLICOE, on the above passage.

I. THE INVASION PROBLEM

THIS perennial diversion popped up again. Upon leaving the Admiralty, Churchill had pointed to the experience of the first ten months of the war as having made it all the more certain that the enemy would not attempt to land an army of 70,000 or more. If they did, it was 'doomed to certain disaster'.

It is not a question only of evading the Fleet, but of launching 70,000 men or upwards on the following enterprise, viz., to cross 250 miles of sea in the face of a decisively superior hostile navy; to disembark the army on an open beach (for all the ports are mined or otherwise defended), with all the chances of weather and the certainty of attack at the latest within a few hours by submarines and destroyers; to land in the face of opposition, for all the coast defence is thoroughly organized; to accomplish this task and land all the necessary artillery . . . with all the stores, appliances, transport, and ammunition . . . within a period at the longest of 20 to 24 hours, after which they must with certainty be at acked from the sea by a decisively superior force, their escort defeated, their transports destroyed, and their communications irremediably severed; and then with what has been landed, and only that, to enter upon the conquest of Great Britain. That is the proposition, for the sake of which Germany is incidentally to risk the decisive battle with her Fleet.

It was, and I believe is, the universal conviction at the Admiralty that no sane Government will entertain it for a moment. . . .

The Admiralty have always stated that the War Office should be capable of dealing with a force of 70,000 men with light artillery, not because they think such a force would be sent or could be landed, but to make assurance doubly sure.[1]

The case against invasion was never better stated. It fell on deaf ears at the War Office, which uneasily continued to increase the already very considerable military forces in the country. In January 1916 the new C.I.G.S., Robertson, arranged a fresh examination of the invasion problem by a joint Service conference. It reached these conclusions: that Germany, if prepared to assume the risks involved, could secretly collect an invasion force of approximately 10 divisions (160,000 men), with a limited supply of artillery, ammunition, and transport; and that she might succeed in landing the whole of this force, most likely on the East Coast from south of the Wash to Dover. The last was based on the assumption that the Navy could not ensure 'the effective interruption' of the landing operations in less than 24 hours after the sighting of the enemy's transports from British shores.[2] The scale of attack was more than twice as formidable as the long-standing Admiralty estimate had deemed possible. In accordance with these findings, Lord French, C.-in-C., Home Forces, felt justified in

[1] Churchill's Cabinet paper, 'A Note on the General Situation', 1 June 1915; *The World Crisis*, ii. 388-9.

[2] The proceedings and conclusions are in 'Report of a Conference . . . Held to Consider the Possibilities of Attack on the United Kingdom', 7 Jan. 1916. The conclusions are summarized in Robertson, *Soldiers and Statesmen*, ii. 8-9.

putting home defence requirements at a 'Field Force' of 230,000 men, with another 220,000 men for anti-aircraft defence, the garrisons for 'defended ports', and other sedentary duties. The General Staff found it impossible, in view of the needs of the Western Front, to meet these demands fully, but considered that the troops available, though poorly trained and equipped, were enough to deal with any landings the Germans were likely to attempt.

Why did the Admiralty give their approval to the findings of the Conference, which were so opposed to their long-held position, and which suggested that the Admiralty were over-timid? There is no ready answer, unless it be that the Admiralty did not take invasion seriously enough to wish to oppose War Office views. I can find no real fear or expectation of invasion at the Admiralty after 1914. It was the feeling of insecurity on the part of the *generals* that was responsible for retaining at home in the latter part of the war up to three-quarters of a million infantry alone (officers and men) of the Regular Army and Territorial Force (summer, 1917),[3] most of whom could well have been spared for service abroad. The effect was that the army in France on more than one critical occasion, as in the Battle of the Somme and in March–April 1918, was shorter of men than it need have been.

The findings did stimulate a rethinking of invasion strategy by the Navy. Correspondence between the Admiralty and Jellicoe, January–March 1916, resulted in agreement on the action to be taken in the event of an attempted invasion. Both considered that an attempt at large-scale invasion was in 'the highest degree improbable'. For the Admiralty it was 'almost certain that an invasion with much less than 135,000 men [the Germans were believed to have the tonnage to bring over a force of at least that size] could in the present conditions only result in the Force having to surrender without effecting anything of major importance'. Jellicoe's opinion was that invasion was much more likely to be attempted during a period of settled summer weather and by entry into some of the East Coast rivers rather than by a beach

[3] A War Office publication, 'Statistics of the Military Effort of the British Empire during the Great War 1914–1920' (1922). This figure does not include the cavalry, engineers, etc., nor the 200,000 officers and men of the overseas contingents in Britain at that time. All told, the average strength of the forces at home in the summer of 1917 was about 1,700,000. The strength of the B.E.F. was approximately 3,000,000 at this time.

landing. The former would be faster because of the wharfage, and the latter involved the difficulties of landing artillery. One of the principal points of disagreement was the question as to whether the transports or the High Seas Fleet was to be the first object of attack by the Grand Fleet if the High Seas Fleet were at sea. Jellicoe wanted to go for the German Fleet, with only such vessels as he could spare from that operation attacking the enemy's transports. The position of the Admiralty (strongly influenced by A. K. Wilson's opinion) was that the transports must take precedence. They were willing to let the decision rest with the C.-in-C., on the understanding that a proportion of his force be detailed, as soon as news was received of an invasion attempt, to attack the transports and their covering force, in co-operation with the local flotillas.

Since Jellicoe would be responsible for the execution of any orders given for the destruction of an invading force afloat, the Admiralty left the framing of these orders to him. Ultimately, on 10 March, they approved Jellicoe's draft orders of 2 March for the Grand Fleet in the event of invasion. These laid down the general lines on which the fleet would work. The probable scene of an invasion, if attempted at all, would be to the southward of Flamborough Head. The 3rd Battle Squadron and 3rd Cruiser Squadron (both at Rosyth) would attack the covering force (comprising the old battleships, it was expected), in order to allow the local patrols and light craft generally, including the Harwich Force, to attack the transports and the ships carrying artillery. The Battle Cruiser Fleet would proceed south, and if it met the High Seas Fleet, as was quite probable, it would keep touch with it, falling back on the main fleet if necessary. It 'should not force an action with the High Sea Fleet until the Battlefleet is within supporting distance, and the Vice-Admiral Commanding, Battle-Cruiser Fleet, should be careful to avoid being drawn into a position where he can be cut off by the High Sea Fleet'. The dreadnought battle fleet would move southward, its main objective the High Seas Fleet, and its secondary objective, that of preventing interference with the work of the 3rd Battle Squadron and local vessels.[4] There the invasion problem slumbered for six months.

The main task of the Grand Fleet was not the protection of England against a German invasion—that was regarded as too

[4] The correspondence and memoranda are in the Admiralty MSS.

remote a possibility—but the destruction of the enemy's naval forces. And here there were obstacles of some magnitude.

2. OFFENSIVE STRATEGY

The strain and responsibilities of war had compensations in the activity of the first period. In contrast, the year and more that followed the Dogger Bank action were quite uneventful for the Grand Fleet. Naval strategy consisted in sweeps by Grand Fleet vessels in the northern portion of the North Sea, mining, and, latterly, seaplane operations by the Harwich Force, supported on some occasions by Grand Fleet squadrons, and the concentration of the fleet for operations against the High Seas Fleet when the Admiralty were aware it had put to sea. The situation was somewhat paradoxical. Britain did not possess absolute command of the sea, since U-boats and occasional disguised raiders were able to pierce it. At the same time, because the enemy was content to keep the vast bulk of his Fleet in its ports and harbours, Great Britain was exercising a command of the sea more absolute than had ever been exercised by any country. She was keeping Allied trade routes open and denying them to the enemy.

This was no reason for jubilation in the Grand Fleet, whose officers yearned for battle. Their spirits were not lifted by the regular press reminders that Nelson himself had been in the Mediterranean two years without battle. Nor, as mentioned, did they consider the slow economic strangulation of Germany as a substitute for battle. The British naval tradition, as understood by the Grand Fleet, demanded one or more great clashes at sea. Even Nelson, after all, had had his Trafalgar. Finally, there was an awareness that victory was needed to keep up fleet morale. The knowledge of the Army's campaigns and losses had a depressing effect, coupled as it was with the tiresome months of waiting, with little activity beyond the usual and monotonous work—occasional sweeps, periodic target practices and tactical exercises, and incessant coaling.

'We are not overworked!' lamented Tyrwhitt. 'In fact, at times I am very bored, as I don't see any prospect of doing business at present.' Walter Cowan 'chafes at the "do nothing" stage that we have got into'. Ralph Seymour found life so 'fearfully monotonous' that if he 'didn't get something to do soon I feel I shall probably burst or something'. And a half year later: 'Anything worse than the boredom of the past year it is difficult to imagine . . .'[5] Beatty, outwardly serene and cheerful, often found himself in a mood of despair that was not untypical of the general temper of the fleet.

I heard rumours of terrific casualties [on the Western Front] . . . I don't think, dear heart, you will ever realize the effect these terrible happenings have upon me. It seems to turn everything upside down in my mind and leave only the one desire to do something, to destroy, to inflict punishment upon the German head. And I feel we are so impotent, so incapable of doing anything for lack of opportunity, almost, that we are not doing our share and bearing our portion of the burden laid upon the nation. . . . It is foolish, no doubt, but can't you understand the feeling of hopeless inutility which comes over me from time to time, when we spend days doing nothing, when so many are doing so much? At times life is nothing but the desire to accomplish something, and the seeming impossibility of being able to do so is like a weight at the end of one's heart which makes me feel sick at heart, as if it had turned into lead.[6]

The weather in the North Sea was all too often bad, and in the winter months was positively abominable. Gales raged for weeks together, with snow, rain, mist, and fog common, and with the limit of visibility usually six miles, and often less. These terrible conditions bred frustration and boredom. 'The horrid Forth [wrote Beatty], like a great ditch full of thick fog which makes everything so cold. My great Barns of Cabins are like Vaults. I never get them warm. . . . There is no joy in life under such conditions. . . . It's a wonderful thing Hope. We live on it, month in and month out. It's all that's left, and I don't give up. My time *must* come.'[7]

Others, like Hankey and Richmond, were disgusted with the lack of offensive spirit in the Navy. 'The Navy has completely lost the spirit of the offensive!' snapped the former. 'I cannot find a trace of it in any Flag Officer except Bacon! We shall have a shock

[5] Tyrwhitt to his sister, Frances Tyrwhitt, 2 Oct. 1915, and to his wife, n.d. (*ca.* 12 Nov. 1915) and 10 Dec. 1915, Tyrwhitt MSS.; Seymour's letters of 9 July 1915 and 10 Feb. 1916, Lady Seymour, *Commander Ralph Seymour, R.N.* (Glasgow, 1926), p. 73.

[6] Beatty to Lady Beatty, 21 May 1915; Beatty MSS.

[7] Beatty to Lady Beatty, 22 Nov. 1915; Chalmers, *Beatty*, p. 207. Jellicoe was haunted by the fear that the High Seas Fleet might put to sea in the southern part of the North Sea at a time when foul weather would prevent his destroyer screen from keeping up with the battle fleet.

one of these days, I am certain.'[8] Richmond put the blame squarely on the Admiralty.

> We are content to sit like a tar-baby, taking the punches of the enemy & hoping that his fists will stick somewhere—feeble, wretched policy, but natural to people whose upbringing does not put them in contact with military thought. Sir H. Jackson is an electrician & engineer, Oliver is a navigator—& he is the best of the lot—T. Jackson [D.O.D.] is a mathematician, Sir F. Hamilton is a social success, Tudor is a gunnery expert, Lambert is nothing in particular; & upon my soul the only man who has any military education is the civilian, Balfour, as his predecessor Churchill was.[9]

There was no dearth of offensive projects submitted at the Admiralty and in the Grand Fleet, none of them, note, with the objective of seizing an inshore base by a *coup de main*. (The Borkum-type operation had had its day by early 1915, although we find Bayly pushing for the seizure of Borkum as late as August 1915.) On 4 March 1915, for example, Churchill proposed to the C.O.S. that, when the Dardanelles operation was concluded, a squadron of 'Queen Elizabeths' should be sent into the Baltic to contain the High Seas Fleet. Oliver did not like the idea. The 'limited space in the Baltic would much circumscribe the activities of large fast ships and give the advantage to Destroyers and Submarines'.[10]

Bombardment proposals were favoured in the Grand Fleet. At the end of 1914 Captain W. W. Fisher submitted an outline plan (in which Captain Dudley Pound had collaborated) of a raid in the Bight. The Channel Fleet, two destroyer flotillas and attached cruisers, six submarines, six oil tankers, and twelve trawlers carrying oil would be used, with a portion of the Grand Fleet as a supporting force. The oil tankers and oil trawlers would be driven ashore and set on fire. The main objects were to destroy the Heligoland dockyard and draw heavy ships from Cuxhaven or Wilhelmshaven to sea, to be dealt with. Burney (Second-in-Command, Grand Fleet) killed the scheme. 'The present, in my opinion, is not the time for raids such as this whilst the German Fleet is in being, and if the Enemy is induced or forced to fight as a result of such a raid it would mean fighting an action on his own

---

[8] Hankey to Richmond, 18 Feb. 1916; *Portrait of an Admiral*, p. 201.
[9] Diary, 28 Feb. 1916; *ibid.*, pp. 202–3.
[10] Admiralty MSS.

ground, which is most disadvantageous to us.'[11] A month later W. W. Fisher sent through a proposal to draw out and destroy the High Seas Fleet. This plan called for three separate attacks on the High Seas Fleet at Schillig Roads, where a good part of it usually lay, on a day when it was reasonably certain it would be there, and when high water occurred at early dawn: (1) bombardment by five battleships at 10,000 yards; (2) torpedo attack by sixteen destroyers; (3) ram, gun, and torpedo attack by five more battleships, 'and when the air has cleared a bit, every available Torpedo Boat or Destroyer that has a torpedo still to fire should close and do so'. He stressed the paramount importance of utilizing darkness to cover the approach of the squadron up to the moment of reaching the shallows at the river mouth. Burney this time was non-committal, and it was Jellicoe who gave the plan the *coup de grâce*. He did not like 'the fact that our vessels are pushed *in daylight* into an area which is held by a very much stronger force of destroyers, submarines and light-cruisers, and that their chances of a successful attack, consequently, will be small'.[12]

Beatty at this time suggested a bombardment of Heligoland by a squadron of four old battleships. 'In retiring they would very likely be sighted by aircraft and might form a useful bait to draw out the German Battle Cruisers. Our Battle Cruisers would be in attendance and the Battleships should be protected from harm by retiring at 12 knots with four submarines and a half-flotilla in company.' Jellicoe did not care for it, as it 'would in all probability lead our ships over mine fields, and pinprick bombardments are not likely to yield results comparable with the probable losses'.[13]

Late in 1915, Rear-Admiral Sydney Fremantle, Second-in-Command, 3rd Battle Squadron, submitted a proposal for a half-hour dawn bombardment of Heligoland by a division of old battleships from the 3rd Battle Squadron. The secondary object was to destroy or damage torpedo craft in the harbour. He hoped that this 'insult' to their coast would force the enemy out. This would give (1) British submarines an opportunity to attack enemy ships proceeding out of the Bight to drive off the British battleships;

[11] Fisher to Hugh Evan-Thomas, Rear-Admiral, 1st Battle Squadron (who thought it 'well worthy of consideration'), 30 Dec. 1914, and Burney to Jellicoe, 3 Jan. 1915; *ibid.*

[12] W. W. Fisher to Evan-Thomas, 22 Jan. 1915, Burney to Jellicoe, 31 Jan. 1915, Jellicoe to Admiralty, 23 Feb. 1915; *ibid.*

[13] Beatty to Jellicoe, 20 Jan. 1915, and Jellicoe's minute; *ibid.*

(2) an opportunity for the submarines (by day) or destroyers (by night) to attack such an enemy force on its return; (3) the chance for a battle-cruiser action (the Battle Cruiser Fleet was to be in the position 55° N., 5° E., to cover the squadron's withdrawal) under advantageous conditions. It seemed to Fremantle fully justifiable to permit the four battleships to incur submarine and mine risks in an operation subsidiary to a fleet action. Bradford, Vice-Admiral Commanding 3rd Battle Squadron, had no use for the project. The C.-in-C. concurred. 'The Rear-Admiral has underestimated the extent of the minefields in the vicinity of Heligoland and has overestimated the damage likely to be inflicted by the ships. All recent experience has confirmed the view held by most Naval Officers that direct fire from ships can effect very little against good fortifications.' (Shades of the Dardanelles and Gallipoli!) Therefore, the attack was most unlikely to bring about any movement of the German Fleet.[14]

It was perfectly evident during 1915 that Jellicoe was not going to use the Grand Fleet for a direct attack on the enemy's ships so long as they resolutely stayed entrenched behind their harbour defences. They were so strongly protected by nature and man that an attempt to force these defences would assuredly, as Jellicoe viewed the matter, involve losses out of all proportion to any success that might be achieved. It was equally clear that he would not endeavour to bring the German Fleet to action in the Bight. The submarine and mine danger was the principal deterrent. A factor of no small importance was the destroyer situation. A serious strategical effect of the U-boat activity was that some of the Grand Fleet destroyers were often detached for anti-submarine work in Home waters. The effect was to deprive the Grand Fleet of what the C.-in-C. considered an adequate number of destroyers for any offensive action that he might have contemplated. Since it was apparent that the High Seas Fleet, just as terrified of mines and submarines, would not subject itself to similar disadvantages by fighting in the northern area of the North Sea, it appeared that nothing could happen and that the war would end in a naval stalemate.

This prospect did not please Lord Fisher when he was in power. The C.-in-C.'s policy of keeping clear of the Bight was

[14] Fremantle to Bradford, 5 Nov. 1915, Bradford to Jellicoe, 10 Nov. 1915, Jellicoe to Bradford, 16 Nov. 1915; *ibid.*

sound and obviously correct [but] it is difficult to accept that under no conditions whatever should he be ordered to take the Fleet to a position where he can effectively support other operations which may be in progress there. The Admiralty, knowing the whole circumstances of the war from moment to moment, must be free at any instant to give orders for the movements of the Grand Fleet . . . the Admiralty will well weigh all the risks before he is sent to engage in an area which is necessarily not so secure as the remoter parts of the North Sea, and the responsibility will lie with them.[15]

Fisher had no concrete suggestions for an offensive policy other than the Baltic Scheme.

The new Board were in agreement with Jellicoe's refusal to be stampeded into any hazardous adventures. No risks must be run that would threaten the British command of the sea, and, trying as it was for the Fleet and the country, the policy of the Grand Fleet must be a waiting one. None the less, as in Fisher's time, there was a hankering for a more vigorous strategy. Jackson's and Balfour's correspondence with the C.-in-C. are scattered with such expressions as these: 'I wish you could entice them out from Heligoland to give you a chance. Have you any ideas for it? I wish I had.' 'Have you, by the way, recently given much thought to a possible naval offensive against Germany in the Baltic or elsewhere?'[16]

What the First Lord had in mind by the latter query was not a division of the Grand Fleet, but the possibility of using old battleships when they returned from the Mediterranean. Jellicoe replied that it was

a matter which is continually absorbing my attention, but I have long arrived at the conclusion that it would be suicidal to divide our main fleet with a view to sending ships into the Baltic. Recent information [from the Naval Attaché in Norway] goes to show that the passage of the Great Belt, which is the only possible route, is practically prohibited by the minefields which exist at the southern end. I do not include submarines under this heading as they can pass through the Sound. I am all in favour of strengthening our submarine force in the Baltic as soon as weather conditions admit.

No other naval offensive appears to me practicable unless and until

[15] Fisher's minute of 7 Apr. 1915 on a dispatch from Jellicoe to the Admiralty of 5 Apr.; Lennoxlove MSS.
[16] Jackson, 2 Sept. 1915, Jellicoe MSS.; Balfour, 17 Jan. 1916, Balfour MSS.

our objective, the High Sea Fleet, gives us the opportunity. . . . until the High Sea Fleet emerges from its defences I regret to say that I do not see that any offensive against it is possible. It may be weakened by mines and submarine attack when out for exercises, but beyond that no naval action against it seems practicable.

Some of the older ships might be used in conjunction with monitors to support a flank move by the Army on the Belgian coast, but it has rather seemed to me that we have spoiled our opportunity of such a movement by repeating the action which we took in the case of the Dardanelles, by bombarding the coast, with the result that the enemy has, as far as I am aware, erected very strong fortifications to prevent, or to retard, a landing on this coast.[17]

After the First Lord had raised the question of a Baltic offensive again, wondering why the C.-in-C. did not consider the employment of old battleships, Jellicoe elaborated. He had not considered it, he said,

because, unless our force together with the available Russian force is in some degree comparable to the High Sea Fleet, it would be annihilated by that Fleet without any serious loss on their part. To obtain any reasonable prospect of successful engagement, or of even doing any serious damage to the High Sea Fleet, we should be forced to send Dreadnoughts through to help Russia, and even then the Germans are between us and the Russians and could engage us in detail. The Kiel Canal is of immense strategic value in this respect, and was of course constructed for that purpose.

If we could get a considerable submarine force through, it might well be worth while to risk old battleships as a bait to draw the High Sea Fleet over the submarines, but I am inclined to think the same result might be better achieved in the North Sea, when the submarines and battleships are available. A feint on Borkum might do it. I am all against a serious attack on Borkum, but a feint against either that Island or Sylt, if undertaken for the purpose of giving submarines a target, might well give good results. Monitors might be even better than battleships, if Borkum were selected. Their slow speed, etc., is against

[17] Jellicoe to Balfour, 25 Jan. 1916; Balfour MSS. The C.-in-C. was probably referring in the last paragraph to the bombardment of Zeebrugge by monitors of the Dover Patrol on 23 August 1915. This, the first of Bacon's bombardments of the Belgian coast, met with little success, although Belgian reports at the time stated that two submarines, the first lock, and the submarine-building factory had been destroyed. In fact, no submarines were destroyed nor damage done to the locks, and only slight damage was inflicted on the submarine-building plant. The bombardment of Ostend harbour on 7 September 1915 revealed that already the defences (including by now an 11-inch battery) were too powerful—for Bacon's forces, at any rate.

their employment near Sylt. We should, however, have to prevent zeppelins finding out that it was but a feint and until we were capable of attacking zeppelins there would be difficulty in this matter.[18]

The War Committee meeting of 17 February 1916 (the one attended by Jellicoe) exhumed Fisher's Baltic Scheme, only to reinter it quickly. Whatever chance such a naval offensive may have had in Fisher's time, it had none now. The enhanced effectiveness of mines and submarines made the supplying of a fleet in the Baltic too difficult and dangerous, and because of the unavailability of troops and the increased range and power of heavy artillery, the same could be said of the plan to seize and hold a coastal island. Nor could much be said for other possible offensive schemes. Closing German ports with blockships was ruled out by the unavailability of the very large number of mercantile ships required for a successful blocking; closing the ports with mines would be ineffective unless the High Seas Fleet could be defeated, for until then a close British watch on the minefields to prevent their removal was not possible. The War Committee concluded that the only feasible strategy was to remain on the alert, while doing everything possible to goad the High Seas Fleet to venture into the open seas.[19]

An offensive scheme strongly favoured by Richmond, Corbett, and Hankey early in 1916 did not directly involve the Grand Fleet. They wanted amphibious diversions on the Syrian coast, including Alexandretta, to prevent Turkish reinforcements going to their armies in Armenia or Mesopotamia, where, respectively, the Russians were punishing the Turks and the British force at Kut under General Townshend was besieged. The Admiralty and the War Office would not sanction such an offensive, the former because it could not, the latter because it would not. Too much of the Navy's resources were absorbed by Salonika, and Jellicoe was offering the most strenuous objections to the diversion of naval force from the North Sea. The Army was even less interested in another joint operation so soon after Gallipoli, although a quarter of a million troops were practically demobilized in the Mediterranean, at Salonika and in Egypt. With Churchill and Fisher off stage, ideas of a mobile war had increasingly taken second place to the generals' alternative of concentrating every possible soldier

[18] Jellicoe to Balfour, 3 Feb. 1916; Jellicoe MSS.
[19] Corbett, *Naval Operations*, iii. 314.

on the Western Front. By the winter of 1915–16 the 'hardened Westerners' were in control. Corbett was utterly disheartened. 'I can give you no comfort. The soldier square-heads have got hold of the war solid & refuse to do anything except on the Western Front, damn it!'[20]

The proponents of offensive action received unexpected support from the public agitation over the Navy early in 1916 and from the new command of the German Fleet.

3. ACTION IN THE NORTH SEA

(Map 8)

One reason for the quickened tempo of the war at sea from February 1916 was Admiral Reinhard Scheer. This able officer with a gift for command and a quick mind, a vigorous personality and wide war experience (he had been commanding the 2nd Squadron of the High Seas Fleet), succeeded the mortally ill Pohl as C.-in-C. on 24 January 1916. Pohl had made five sorties during 1915, none of them extending beyond 120 miles from Heligoland, and all of them, by Pohl's own admission, ineffective. Scheer was determined to pursue a bolder strategy, although no more than his predecessors did he seriously plan for a stand-up, give-and-take fight to a finish with the British Fleet. Early in February his staff produced a document entitled 'Guiding Principles for Sea Warfare in the North Sea'. Its three central ideas were: (1) the existing proportion of strength ruled out the High Seas Fleet seeking decisive battle with the Grand Fleet. (2) 'Systematic and constant pressure' must be exerted on the British Fleet to force it to give up its waiting attitude and send out some of its forces against the German Fleet. This would offer the latter 'favourable possibilities of attack'. (3) The German pressure should take the form of submarine warfare against commerce, mine warfare, attacks on the British-Scandinavian trade, aerial warfare, and the active employment of the High Seas Fleet in sorties.[21]

Using this memorandum as a general guide, and the free hand the Emperor gave him in February, Scheer imparted a more offensive direction to the activities of the High Seas Fleet. His first

[20] Corbett to Richmond, n.d. (ca. 13 Mar. 1916); *Portrait of an Admiral*, p. 205.
[21] Naval Staff Monograph No. 31 (1926), *Home Waters—Part VI. From October 1915 to May 1916*, p. 148.

operation, intended to build up fleet morale, was a destroyer sweep in the area east of the Dogger Bank on 10 February. It netted the *Arabis*, a unit of the 10th Sloop Flotilla engaged in sweeping one of the war channels. The whole Grand Fleet and the Harwich Force rushed out; they had not proceeded very far before the enemy force returned to its base.

On 5–6 March, Scheer took the bulk of the High Seas Fleet out of the Bight for the first of its 'greater enterprises'. They proceeded to a position off the Texel, in the latitude of Lowestoft, which was unusually far for the main fleet. It was, indeed, the farthest south the German Fleet ever came in the war. The object of the cruise was a hoped-for meeting with and destruction of any British light forces sent out to chase away the Zeppelins that had been sent ahead to bomb England. The operation netted little: two smacks, which were sunk by U-boats that operated off Lowestoft. Again the combined forces of the Grand Fleet had been out, but there was no contact.

The British now staged an offensive operation of their own. An Admiralty-approved Tyrwhitt scheme for an air attack on the Zeppelin base at Hoyer (on the Schleswig coast opposite Sylt) was carried out on 25–26 March. The plan called for the Harwich Force to escort the seaplane carrier *Vindex* and her five planes to a position 40 miles north-west of Hoyer. The battle cruisers came down to about 45 miles west of Horns Reef to give Tyrwhitt close support. The *Vindex* got her planes away between 4.30 and 5.30 on the morning of the 25th. Tyrwhitt managed to extricate himself from this dangerous area after a hectic day and night of gales, snowstorms, collisions, a night encounter with enemy destroyers, and reports that the High Seas Fleet was on the move, and to retire on the battle cruisers (about 6 a.m., 26 March).

Beatty spent 27 hours cruising in German waters, in the vicinity of Horns Reef, hoping to bring the enemy battle cruisers to action, but prepared to fall back on the Grand Fleet (which had put to sea at dawn, 26 March), if they were closely supported by the battle-ships. Hipper and the battle cruisers, with two battle squadrons in support, were at sea during the night of the 25th–26th, but did not advance beyond Sylt, or get within 60 miles of Beatty. At about 6.30 a.m. on the 26th they were, says their own account, forced to retire because of the exceptionally rough weather. At about noon that day Beatty and Tyrwhitt turned back.

The Admiralty summed up the lessons of the operation: '. . . as an air raid it was not much good, except to show that there were no airship sheds at Hoyer. [Only two of the seaplanes returned.] It showed that the Germans are ready to come out when their own coasts are threatened, and it looks as if your best chance to get at them is to go for them, apparently on a minor scale, but really with the whole Fleet quite close by.'[22] The specific suggestions for offensive movements made to the C.-in-C. in the following weeks were that air raids, mining activities, or an attack on Sylt might be made the means of drawing out the High Seas Fleet for action—'instead of acting entirely on the defensive according to existing war standing orders, as very little seems to result . . .'[23]

Jellicoe's reaction to these suggestions was that 'air raids and mining activities cannot be used as a means of drawing the High Sea Fleet to sea, but must be treated as a definite minor operation'.[24] The same paper cited the reasons for this conclusion, but they are given more concisely in a letter to Beatty.

There is a feeling at the Admiralty which I think may lead to their trying to persuade me into what is called a 'more active policy'. I notice signs of it, and it shews itself in the air raids, heavily supported. I am being pressed to plan another, the idea being that it will bring the German fleet out. But the difficulty is this. The raid *must* take place at daylight, otherwise the force would be reported approaching and 5 seaplanes would certainly not succeed in achieving anything with a mass of Zeppelins and aeroplanes against them. If carried out at daylight [and] the German heavy ships do move, they won't be clear of the minefields and in a position where we could engage them before about 4 p.m. This is no time to start a fight in those waters. It also involves our hanging about for a whole day in a bad locality expending fuel especially for T.B.D.'s. You can't wait for the following day as by then the T.B.D.'s are out of fuel and the L.C.'s getting very short. If we could stir them up at dusk and catch them coming out next morning, matters would be different, but I can't see how to do that.

The real truth to my mind is that our policy should be to engage them *not* in a position close to their minefields and therefore close to their S.M., T.B.D., and aircraft bases, but to accept the position that we must wait until they give us a chance in a favourable position. Patience is the virtue we must exercise. I am still trying to devise a

[22] Jackson to Jellicoe, 29 Mar. 1916; Jellicoe MSS.
[23] Jackson to Jellicoe, 12 Apr. 1916; *ibid.*
[24] Memorandum to Admiralty, 12 Apr. 1916; Beatty MSS.

means of drawing them further out, but I am bound to say I don't think air raids will do it. What do you think?

At the same time an air raid as a minor operation, especially if combined with some minelaying, is all to the good. . . .

Personally I think the Zepp raids are pure revenge, and also reconnaissance of the southern part of North Sea. Those who opposed the building of Zeppelins in this country 3 years ago have a heavy responsibility now.[25]

Beatty's reply is of the greatest interest and importance.

You ask me what I think? Well, I think the German Fleet will come out *only* on its own initiative when the right time arrives.

Air Raids on our part will *not* bring them out. It may, and possibly will, bring out a portion which could be snapped at by the Supporting Force we choose to utilize to support the Air Raiding Force. If the force they push out is large, i.e. Battle Cruisers supported by Battle Squadrons (one or two) it would go no farther than is necessary to reconnoitre and expose the full strength of the Force that we had in support. And as soon as they had made clear what constituted our Force they would act accordingly. If we were greatly inferior they might be tempted to prosecute their investigations, and attack further afield, otherwise they will withdraw. It is on such occasions we might be able to inflict some damage, risking something to do it. But I am firmly convinced that under no circumstances could we ever by taking the initiative induce them to commit themselves to an action which in any way could be considered decisive.

I am not arguing against air raids. Anything that we can do to harass and annoy has great advantages. And there is always the possibility that they may be tempted to overstep themselves, go too far with an inferior force, etc., which could be punished severely before it got back; and such operations fairly frequently may produce something which will be worth the risks. They would also have the advantage of denying him (the Enemy) the initiative, and so prevent him from bringing off any of his Set Pieces. But it is certain that he will *not* come out in Grand Force when we set the tune, i.e. to fight the Great Battle we are all waiting for.

Your arguments re the Fuel question are unanswerable and measure the situation absolutely. We cannot amble about the North Sea for two or three days and at the end be in a condition in which we can produce our whole Force to fight to the finish the most decisive Battle of the War: to think it is possible is simply too foolish and tends towards losing the Battle before we begin.

[25] 11 Apr. 1916; *ibid.*

As I said, my contention is that when the Great Day comes it will be when the Enemy takes the initiative; and I think our principal business now is to investigate the North Sea with minesweepers so that we can have a clear and fairly accurate knowledge of what waters in it are safe, and what are not; so that when he does take the initiative we can judge fairly accurately in what waters we can engage him. I think we can be quite sure that it will not be north of Lat. 56°.

What I am disturbed at is your remark that 'there is a feeling at the Admiralty, etc. to persuade me into a more active policy—and being pressed to plan another'. This is truly deplorable.[26]

This letter should once and for all dispose of the legend that Beatty was more offensively minded than Jellicoe. They had their differences as regards battle tactics, but on general war strategy they saw eye to eye.

The second of Scheer's important sorties (the first having been on 5–6 March) was the tip-and-run raid on Lowestoft, 25 April. Exactly what he had in mind is not clear, though Corbett's opinion is that evasion was Scheer's 'governing idea'—that he only intended a sudden blow on the East Coast and speedy retirement before he found himself faced with superior force. The demonstration of the German Fleet off the British East Coast was to coincide with the rising planned by the German-supported Irish nationalists for Easter Sunday.

The High Seas Fleet left the Jade at midday on 24 April, with the battle cruisers under Rear-Admiral Boedicker, in the absence of the ailing Hipper. The Admiralty were aware of the departure of the High Seas Fleet, though in the dark as to its objectives until an intercepted German signal at 8.14 p.m. (24 April) disclosed the enemy's objective to be Yarmouth. At 3.50 p.m. (24 April) they directed the whole Grand Fleet to be at two hours' notice, and, at 7.05 p.m., to raise steam and proceed to sea.[27] By midnight the battle and battle cruiser squadrons were steaming south against a strong head sea. Soon afterwards a depleted Harwich Force of three light cruisers and eighteen destroyers was proceeding up the coast. (Twelve destroyers had been detached on 22 April for the barrage operations impending against the Flanders coast.)

At 1.30 a.m. (25 April) the four German battle cruisers of the 1st Scouting Group (a fifth, the *Seydlitz*, had struck a mine near the

[26] 14 Apr. 1916; Jellicoe MSS.
[27] The British telegrams and signals on the raid are in Naval Staff Monograph No. 32 (1927), *Lowestoft Raid, 24th–25th April, 1916*, pp. 47–67.

Norderney Gap and had been sent back to the Jade), screened by the 2nd Scouting Group (four light cruisers) and two destroyer flotillas and their cruiser leaders, had reached a position about 65 miles east of Lowestoft and had turned to the westward. Scheer and the battle fleet remained in support of the battle cruisers in the open waters west of Terschelling, about 70 miles from the British coast.

At about 3.50 a.m. Boedicker's screen sighted British warships on their port side. This was the Harwich Force. Counting four battle cruisers and six light cruisers to the northward, Tyrwhitt sent an urgent signal to Jellicoe and Beatty and turned and made to the southward at full speed, hoping to draw the Germans away from Lowestoft. They refused to be enticed, and at 4.10 the battle cruisers opened fire on Lowestoft. They quickly silenced the two 6-inch batteries at the entrance, started several fires on shore, and destroyed about 200 houses, although only a few people were killed. At 4.20 the ships ceased fire and headed north for Yarmouth, which they began to bombard at 4.42. But only for a few minutes. Upon hearing the sound of fire from the southward, Boedicker turned away and steamed at full speed to the support of the 2nd Scouting Group, which was in action with the Harwich Force at long range. After failing to entice the enemy to the south, Tyrwhitt had gradually turned round to the northward to keep in touch. He was in a ticklish position with battle cruisers ahead and six cruisers on his starboard bow. He was forced to turn about and scamper away at full speed, though not before his flagship, the light cruiser *Conquest*, was heavily damaged.

Here was a splendid German opportunity to cut off and destroy a much weaker force. We know what Beatty would have done at this juncture, had the roles been reversed. Boedicker was no Beatty, and the Heligoland Bight action offered him no inspiration. On the grounds that Tyrwhitt's superior speed rendered pursuit useless, more probably, though, because of uncertainty as to what British force there might be behind Tyrwhitt's screen, at 4.55 a.m. Boedicker turned to the eastward, left the coast, and was lost to sight. At 5.20 a.m., when his battle cruisers were only 50 miles off, Scheer turned and speedily made for home. His strategy was no bolder than Boedicker's tactics. The condition of the February memorandum had been met: he had drawn an important detachment of the Grand Fleet into waters favourable for action; but his movements in the Lowestoft raid were not framed on those lines. 'He did not wait even to glimpse the masts of Admiral Beatty's light cruisers on the horizon, much less the appearance of Admiral Beatty or the Commander-in-Chief. The German History bewails Admiral Scheer's lack of information [the small assistance rendered by the Zeppelins detailed to assist the fleet in reconnaissance], and pleads it as an excuse for his speedy retreat to the Bight. . . . These plaints, however, do not explain the fact that the German Commander-in-Chief made no attempt to scout for the approach of the British forces by the ordinary means of light cruisers.'[28]

With characteristic doggedness Tyrwhitt had turned to the north-eastward at 5.40 a.m. to regain touch. At 8.30 a.m. he located the enemy (Boedicker) by his smoke, but ten minutes later the Admiralty ordered him to return to his base.

Where was the Grand Fleet all this time? The main fleet had been on its way south, sorely handicapped by the heavy sea and the absence of its destroyers. The sea was too much for them and they had become dispersed—a complication the C.-in-C. had always dreaded. He came down with only three attached cruisers to screen the whole battle fleet! When at about 4.30 a.m. Tyrwhitt's report of the sighting of the enemy reached Jellicoe, he had only arrived at the latitude of Cromarty. The Battle Cruiser Fleet, equally handicapped by the rough sea, was then about 165 miles ahead, in the latitude of the Farne Islands and roughly 220 miles from Terschelling. At 8.05 a.m. the Admiralty passed on to the Grand Fleet the intelligence that at 6 a.m. the enemy battle fleet was about 30 miles west of the Texel and 50 miles from Terschelling. It was on its way home and there was no chance of intercepting it. The German battle cruisers were at this time only 62 miles from the Terschelling area, whereas Beatty was still 132 miles from it, and Jellicoe, over 300 miles. At 11.10 a.m. the Admiralty ordered them both to return. The signal did not reach Beatty. A few minutes earlier the German battle cruisers had passed about 50 miles ahead of him, and at 11.45, when they turned to the eastward for home, he was still 45 miles away. His closest support, the 5th Battle Squadron, was 115 miles off, and the main body of the battle fleet was another 80 miles away. 'There was nothing in sight, all hope of cutting off the enemy had

[28] *Ibid.*, p. 37.

vanished, and the battle cruisers turned back at half-past twelve. The 5th Battle Squadron and battlefleet came down to meet them, and by 2.30 p.m. the whole fleet was making its way disconsolately home.'[29]

The Admiralty and Jellicoe were disappointed in the submarines. Of the six ordered to lie off Yarmouth, only one got within torpedo range of the German battle cruisers; before it could fire, they turned away. The six submarines from Harwich had no better luck, though they had opportunities to attack the battle cruisers and light cruisers when they were making for home. The U-boats had met with little more success.

On the German side, the battle cruiser *Seydlitz* had been mined and two of the eleven co-operating U-boats had been lost (one was bombed by a drifter off Walcheren, the other was stranded off Harwich and captured); on the British side, two light cruisers had been damaged (one by gunfire, the other by a torpedo), and a submarine had been sunk (torpedoed by a U-boat).

The raid was hardly a brilliant exploit, whether from the point of view of strategy, tactics, or results.

It was now the British turn. At about 3 a.m. on 4 May two seaplane carriers, escorted by the 1st Light Cruiser Squadron from Rosyth (Commodore Alexander-Sinclair) and sixteen destroyers of the 1st Flotilla, appeared off Sylt and attempted a bombardment of the Zeppelin sheds at Tondern. The enterprise was similar to the Hoyer Raid, except that the bombing, which was the primary object of the latter, was a secondary one now. The main purpose was to entice the High Seas Fleet out by using the seaplane attack as bait and to force it to fight by barring the way back. The battle fleet had by dawn on the 4th moved south to a position off the Skagerrak, with the battle cruisers to the south. Minefields were laid across the enemy's most probable course, and seven submarines watched the Horns Reef end of the Bight. The air raid was a dismal failure. Sea conditions were bad, and only one of the eleven seaplanes was able to take off and drop bombs on its objective. This did not matter too much—the real question was whether the German Fleet would move out. This it gave no intention of doing—bad weather and uncertainty as to the situation prompted Scheer to hold back.

At 12.05 p.m. the Admiralty had signalled that the enemy

[29] *Ibid.*, p. 33.

appeared unaware that the British Fleet was at sea. Having been off the Heligoland Bight for six or seven hours, the C.-in-C. decided it was pointless to wait any longer. At 2 p.m. he altered course for home, with the Battle Cruiser Fleet on a parallel course to the southward. The fuel situation was a factor in this decision. 'No purpose would be served,' he wrote in his official report, 'by our forces returning to the vicinity of the Horn Reefs at daylight on May 5. In view of the possibility of a movement on the part of the enemy on the night of the 5th . . . I deemed it advisable to replenish as quickly as possible . . .'[30] The High Seas Fleet did come out just before 3 p.m., but the Grand Fleet had already retired. The Germans came as far north as Sylt, then turned round at 2.30 a.m., 5 May.

Beatty returned to Rosyth 'with a sad heart', as he had anticipated a successful venture. Apparently not aware that the C.-in-C. himself was responsible for the decision to return to their bases, Beatty wrote to him with strong feeling: '. . . everything promised well towards fulfilling our final objective at daylight the next day. I had husbanded my destroyers' fuel and they were well able to have had a good period of full speed the next day and get home at 15 knots if required. You can understand my disappointment when we were ordered to return to Base. Why cannot the Admiralty leave the situation to those on the spot? . . . if we had been in the vicinity of the Horn Reef at dawn we should have had a glorious time. To miss opportunities which are so few and far between is maddening.' He unburdened himself further to his wife: 'For the life of me I do not know what to do to bring about the desirable result. But something must be done. We simply cannot go on missing chances like this.'[31]

But it was the Lowestoft raid and a long conversation with Tyrwhitt on its disturbing aspects that quite unsettled Beatty. He relieved his feelings with a blistering letter to the C.-in-C. (18 May) intended for Admiralty consumption mainly. The bulk of the letter was a strong condemnation of the War Staff for its lack of a plan to co-ordinate the movements of the various units in an action, with the resulting lack of cohesion between different units.

---

[30] Jellicoe to Admiralty, 10 May 1916; Naval Staff Monograph, *Home Waters. From October 1915 to May 1916*, p. 205.

[31] Beatty to Jellicoe, 7 May 1916, Jellicoe MSS., and to his wife the same day, Beatty MSS.

The system of water-tight compartments has reached its climax. The Chief of the War Staff has priceless information given to him which he sits on until it is too late for the Sea Forces to take action with any possibility of achieving a decisive result. What it amounts to is that the War Staff has developed into a One Man Show. The man is not born yet who can run it by himself.

There is no general plan laid down on which movements of the various units are governed. Every case that occurs is considered at the time, and orders are then issued. It is the Wait and See policy carried into Naval Strategy!! It is perfectly ridiculous and must be changed, if we are to achieve any success.

The 24th April was an object lesson which makes me weep when I think of it. There was absolutely no reason why every unit should not have been on the move 3½ hours before it was!! Commodore T and Harwich Force did not actually leave Harwich until 11 o'clock p.m. He received many contradictory orders and when eventually pushed out was told to do his best!! He had no idea where I was, or when I might be expected or where I was going to. I had no idea of anything appertaining to the Harwich Force—neither their position, composition or disposition. In view of the fact that the force is composed of Light Cruisers, Destroyers and Submarines, this would appear to be most desirable.

It amounts to this, that we were without general principles and had no plan, no combination and no decision. The opportunities of inflicting damage were priceless; they were thrown away and may never occur again.

Commodore T could have brought off a torpedo attack, our Submarines could have been in the right place at daylight. The Battle Cruisers and indeed the whole of the Grand Fleet could have been 3½ hours further South. The possibilities arising out of these *facts* are incalculable. The raid would never have taken place or if it had the raiders would have been severely punished, which would have produced a feeling of security in the country that would have strengthened the confidence in our Sea Power and produced a moral effect of extreme value to the nation—instead of the feeling of insecurity that actually exists and the continual questioning of what is the Navy doing.

As it is, the result is not fair to the Nation, is not fair to the Navy, and is not fair to you. The above is the minimum of what might have occurred. It does not require a very great stretch of imagination to conceive that the possibilities were such as might have led to a result which would have gone far towards affecting the whole trend of the War in our favour.

I cannot put all this into a Service letter, but I urge upon you, my dear Commander-in-Chief, to stop this perfectly hopeless way of muddling on. One of these days we shall be found out. The hollow mockery of our methods will be exposed, the opportunities that we have missed will be revealed. What then? . . .

We must have cohesion and combination, with a complete knowledge of what every unit is doing, going to do and expected to do.

It sometimes appears to me that we have lost sight of the old principle that 'the Navy's frontier is the enemy's coastline'. In these days it is determined by the minefields protecting the coastline, and this has permitted a relaxation of the principle, which has developed into a policy of defence instead of offence, and we consequently collect on our coastline instead of going for him directly he shows himself outside his minefields. Thus it makes it possible for the enemy to bring off raids and retire undamaged and unpunished. . . .

I am quite sure you will agree with all I have said . . .[32]

Concerning Beatty's leading point, that the system of working from different bases 'in water-tight compartments' prevented the best use being made of possible opportunities, Jellicoe thought it best for the Admiralty to give the Harwich Force its orders, since any attempt by himself to do this must mean delay. It was left for the events of Jutland to cause the Admiralty to clarify their intentions with regard to the Harwich Force.

4. STRATEGICAL REDISTRIBUTION

The Lowestoft Raid had important strategical consequences for Britain, as it led to a fresh examination of the distribution of the fleet in the North Sea. This was an old problem, the crux of which was the distance of Scapa Flow from the southern portion of the North Sea. The Admiralty wanted to concentrate the Grand Fleet in the Forth, where the battle cruisers had been since the end of 1914, in order to cover the coast, give greater security against raids, and increase the chance of intercepting the enemy. There was nothing in the south, apart from the Harwich Force and local patrols, to oppose raids, bombardments, or a surprise sweep along the East Coast, and the battle fleet at Scapa was too far north to succeed in bringing the enemy to action. And if it did, there was the danger of the destroyers being left with barely enough fuel to get home.

The Admiralty raised the question again in February 1916,

[32] Tyrwhitt MSS.

since they believed that the German Fleet under its new C.-in-C. was likely to revert to the bombarding raids of 1914. For two months Jackson, Jellicoe, and Beatty corresponded, trying to work out a solution based on the principle that, from a purely strategical point of view, the whole fleet, including the battle cruisers, should be kept concentrated at one base. Jackson and Oliver saw little chance of a fleet action so long as the main fleet was based on Scapa. The C.-in-C., too, felt 'very keenly the disadvantages of being so far away, but unless one could turn the British Islands 16 points and bring the West coast to the East, I see no remedy'.

Rosyth's strategic advantage over Scapa appears to have been exaggerated. 'From a strategical point of view, the actual saving in time and distance was rather less than might be expected at first, for to a point in lat. 55° N., long. 5° E., a fleet sailing from the Forth saved only some 70 miles in distance (measuring from Pentland Skerries and May Island), a gain of about four hours at 17½ knots, and the greater facilities for leaving Scapa with a large fleet reduced this by an hour. (To pass May Island required 4 hr. 47 m., to pass Pentland Skerries 3 hr. 50 m.)'[33]

The principal drawback of the Forth was the lack of space. To have based the whole dreadnought battle fleet, as well as the Battle Cruiser Fleet, at Rosyth in 1916 would have led to serious congestion. The first ships required to leave a base in the Forth were the cruisers, light cruisers, and battle cruisers, and therefore these vessels should be berthed below (that is, to the east of) the Forth Bridge. It would, in the C.-in-C.'s view, be possible to berth the ten battle cruisers and perhaps seven cruisers below the bridge; but no more than 21 or 22 of the 29 dreadnoughts, together with four cruisers, eight light cruisers, and the flotillas, could be berthed above the bridge. Furthermore, none of the berths below the bridge could be used with safety until this outer anchorage was made secure against torpedo attack. (The anchorage above the bridge was well protected from all forms of attack by water.) Again the C.-in-C. enumerated Scapa's advantages, such as comparative freedom from minelaying, smaller liability to submarine attack, immunity from air raids, very much less fog except in the summer, and the immeasurably greater facilities for keeping the fleet efficient. On the other hand, a great disadvantage was the

---

[33] Naval Staff Monograph No. 33 (1927), *Home Waters—Part VII. From June 1916 to November 1916*, p. 20 and notes 3 and 4, as slightly edited by me.

difficulty of getting the destroyers south with the battleships, owing to the greater distance from the probable scene of action, and the probability of meeting bad weather on the way, and this difficulty alone, he said, would cause him to welcome most heartily any scheme by which the battle squadrons could be based farther south.

The C.-in-C. was unable to find a happy solution, much as he hated the thought that the enemy could move in the southern part of the North Sea without interference from the Grand Fleet. He vetoed Beatty's suggestion of 19 February (pressed again on 3 March) that the 5th Battle Squadron ('Queen Elizabeths'), fastest in the battle fleet, be moved to Rosyth as a replacement for the 3rd Battle Squadron and stiffener to the Battle Cruiser Fleet. (It was believed that the *Lützow* and *Hindenburg* were about to join Hipper. The former had, but the latter was not completed until October 1917.) 'The stronger I make Beatty, the greater is the temptation for him to get involved in an independent action.' And the fast squadron would lead to Beatty getting far afield from him, which could be disastrous. Also, and most important, the 'Queen Elizabeths' in the C.-in-C.'s battle plans were not intended to form part of the main line of battle. They were to be an independent squadron, to be used as the circumstances of a battle dictated.[34]

The Lowestoft Raid intervened before anything could be decided about the strategical disposition of the Grand Fleet. 'The expected blow had fallen,' writes Corbett; 'nothing had been near enough to prevent it or to retaliate; the chance of an action had been missed. It was now imperative that something must be done at once . . .' The Germans had not ventured farther south than Lowestoft; but this was far enough to give the Admiralty the jitters, particularly as they had knowledge that besides the Lowestoft bombarding force, the Germans had at the same time sent a force of light cruisers and destroyers to sweep down the Belgian coast in search of British patrols. These, fortunately, had been withdrawn to protect shipping in the Downs. Next time, encouraged by their 'success' on 25 April, the enemy might be

---

[34] The more important February–April 1916 correspondence on the base problem includes Jellicoe to Jackson, 5, 8, 9, 13 Mar. 1916; Jackson MSS. Naval Staff Monograph, *Home Waters. From June 1916 to November 1916*, pp. 248–51, has other key correspondence.

bold enough to attack not only towns on the East Coast, but Dover and the shipping in the Downs, in threatening proximity to the vital line of British communications in the Channel. 'The enemy have practically tested our weakness in southern waters and will probably act again in those waters shortly,' the Admiralty informed Jellicoe on 26 April. To meet this threat there was only the single light cruiser at Harwich to which the 5th Light Cruiser Squadron had been reduced. Two of its units had been damaged on 25 April, and a third, the *Arethusa*, had been lost in February. Until the damaged ships were repaired, the Admiralty had to call on Grand Fleet resources to safeguard southern waters. What did the C.-in-C. propose?

To this query of 26 April Jellicoe suggested that the 3rd Battle Squadron and the 3rd Cruiser Squadron at Rosyth, with the *Dreadnought* when refitted, be based in the Swin (the northern passage of the Thames estuary), or at Sheerness or Dover, and that the Rosyth submarines be shifted to Yarmouth. The 3rd Battle Squadron of 'King Edward VII' class battleships (now seven, as the *King Edward VII* herself had been sunk) was the Cinderella of the Grand Fleet. The sailors knew it as the 'Wobbly Eight' because of the difficulty in steering the ships in bad weather or in shallow waters. It 'makes the men laugh when alluded to' was Richmond's wry reference to his own squadron. Jellicoe was, nevertheless, confident that it would be a 'sufficiently strong covering force to encounter enemy battle cruisers at present strength'. With minor alterations the Admiralty accepted these proposals and chose Sheerness for the base, with the Swin as the war anchorage. On 29 April the two squadrons sailed for Sheerness. It was now an independent command under Admiral Bradford. At about this time the Admiralty moved some of the monitors to the more undefended East Coast ports.

Without of course spelling out the new dispositions, Balfour used them in an effort to reassure the populations of Lowestoft and Yarmouth. His letter to their distressed Mayors, which was published on 10 May, intimated that a portion of the Grand Fleet would be employed in the south as a shield against enemy raids. It concluded with the admonition that 'another raid on the coast of Norfolk (never a safe operation) will be henceforth far more perilous to the aggressors than it has been in the past, and if our enemy be wise is therefore less likely'. When the Mayor of

Scarborough telegraphed to Balfour asking whether his remarks applied to Yorkshire, his answer was: 'General conclusion set forth in my letter is applicable to east coast.'

The First Lord's guarantees backfired. One group of critics attacked them on the ground that circumstances might enable the enemy to bring off another raid, which would afford occasion for German ridicule. 'The prudent cat,' moralized the *Globe* (10 May), 'does not indulge in vociferation when she is watching the rat-hole. She restrains herself until the quarry is actually under her claws.' Others challenged the wisdom of tying the naval forces to a defensive role. *The Times* (11 May) found this not a little disquieting. 'The First Lord appears to adumbrate a reversal of that policy of offensive defence which has been followed by our fathers with success since King Edward III fought the Battle of Sluys in 1340, and Drake singed the beard of the King of Spain nearly 250 years later. "The frontiers of England are the coasts of the enemy." Only once did our rulers voluntarily adopt an attitude of passive resistance as an exchange for one of active, resolute opposition, and then the Hollander came up the Medway and destroyed the ships off Chatham [1667].'

The shift of the 3rd Battle Squadron to the Thames was only a temporary expedient. The big redistribution problem remained—the question of transferring the main-fleet base from Scapa to Rosyth. This depended, according to a terse summary by the C.-in-C., 'upon whether the advantages gained by (a) Shortening the distance for intercepting the enemy's fleet, (b) There being a far greater certainty of the flotillas being able to screen the battle-fleet south, and remain in company with it whilst waiting,[35] (c) The concentration of minesweepers, destroyers, trawlers, and other small craft, in one port, and searching one set of approaches, are greater than the disadvantages [at Rosyth] of (a) Greater facility for mining the fleet in, (b) More foggy weather, (c) The presence of neutral traffic. . . . There is no doubt whatever that strategically Rosyth has the greater advantages.'[36]

[35] The problem of the small fuel capacity of destroyers gave the C.-in-C. as much anxiety as any other. It meant 'in effect that the battle fleet cannot keep the sea for more than about 2½ days if the action is going to be fought in that time. Consequently, this means that it is still more difficult for me to delay the action, once in touch with the enemy, for the purpose of getting clear of his prepared area.' Jellicoe to Beatty, 7 Aug. 1915; Beatty MSS. And see above, p. 422.

[36] Memorandum of 11 May 1915; *ibid.*

The decision of a conference at Rosyth on 12 May, attended by Jackson, Jellicoe, and Beatty, with their Chiefs of Staff, was to develop the Firth of Forth into a primary base. Although there was no definite decision that the centre of gravity was to be permanently shifted to the southward, it was generally understood that the battle fleet would be moved to the Forth as soon as the anchorage below the bridge could be made safe against submarines. Top priority was to be given to the new outer defences of the Forth. They were completed in 1917, and in April 1918 the battle squadrons moved to the Forth, which was thereafter the main base for the whole Grand Fleet. (It was possible to moor all the big ships above the Forth Bridge, and, generally, the cruisers and destroyers below the bridge.) Even then squadrons and individual ships constantly used Scapa.

Within a week of the Rosyth Conference the Admiralty had evidence that something big was afoot on the other side of the North Sea.

XVII

The Eve of Jutland

(MAY 1916)

It must never be forgotten that the situation on every sea, even the most remote, is dominated and decided by the influence of Sir John Jellicoe's Fleet— lost to view amid the northern mists, preserved by patience and seamanship in all its strength and efficiency, silent, unsleeping, and, as yet, unchallenged.

CHURCHILL in the House of Commons, 15 February 1915.

. . . offensive action of some kind against us at sea was imperative if the German navy was to justify its existence in the eyes of the people. A disillusioned nation which had borne the heavy burden of creating it was groaning under the increasing severity of the blockade, and calling ominously for retaliation. On land hope was waning. The appalling sacrifices which had been made in the desperate effort to win the Verdun salient had so far been made in vain. For the first time the spirit of the people was sick, and in the fleet alone was their present hope of a restorative.

CORBETT, *Naval Operations*.

1. THE TWO FLEETS

THE mood of the Grand Fleet on the eve of Jutland was one of frustration and exasperation, and uncertainty about the enemy's plans and movements. These put a severe psychological strain on the fleet. Officers and men were haunted by the fear that the day of reckoning might never come. Rarely has a fleet so itched for action or had such confidence in the outcome. The intensive training helped to keep *esprit* high, as did the overwhelming preponderance in capital ships. There were now thirty-three dreadnoughts. Thirteen had been added since the war: the *Canada*, *Agincourt*, and *Erin*, requisitioned in August– September 1914 (the first, from Chile, the others from Turkey), but not available until 1915; the *Benbow* and *Marlborough*, of the 'Iron Duke' class, in November 1914; three 15-inch gunned 'super-dreadnoughts' of the 'Royal Sovereign' class, the *Royal Sovereign*, *Royal Oak*, and *Revenge*, between March and May 1916;

and a splendid fast division of five 'Queen Elizabeth' 'super-dreadnoughts', the *Queen Elizabeth, Warspite,* and *Barham,* in 1915, and the *Valiant* and *Malaya,* early in 1916. In addition, two 'Royal Sovereigns', the *Resolution* and *Ramillies,* were under construction (completed in December 1916 and September 1917, respectively). To the nine battle cruisers when the war started only one, the *Tiger,* had been added (October 1914); the *Repulse* and *Renown* were nearing completion. The Germans had added five dreadnoughts since the commencement of the war, the four 'Königs' and the *Bayern,* for a total of eighteen. Three 'Bayern' class ships were building, only one of which, the *Baden,* was completed (October 1916). To the five battle cruisers at the outset the *Derfflinger* and *Lützow* had been added in the first month or two. The seven had become six when the *Blücher,* a battle cruiser by courtesy, was lost in the Dogger Bank action. Only one battle cruiser, the *Hindenburg,* was building at the time of Jutland.

The combined Grand Fleet as it left Scapa Flow, Cromarty Firth, and Rosyth late on 30 May totalled 28 dreadnoughts, 9 battle cruisers, 26 light cruisers, 8 armoured cruisers, 5 destroyer leaders, 73 destroyers, a destroyer fitted as a minelayer (*Abdiel*), and a seaplane carrier (*Engadine*). Left behind were four capital ships and other units: the newly commissioned *Royal Sovereign,* and, in dockyard hands, the *Queen Elizabeth, Emperor of India, Australia* (battle cruiser), two cruisers, and seventeen destroyers.

The High Seas Fleet, when it sailed from the Jade and Elbe in the small hours of the 31st, consisted of 16 dreadnoughts, 6 predreadnought battleships, 5 battle cruisers, 11 light cruisers, and 61 destroyers. Two of the dreadnoughts were not fit for service: the *König Albert* was in the dockyard, and the *Bayern,* completed in March, was still carrying out trials and practices in the Baltic.

To sum up, the British Fleet had a 37:27 superiority in battleships and battle cruisers, or 37:21 in modern capital ships, and a 113:72 superiority in light craft. Jellicoe had other important advantages. The speeds of the two dreadnought fleets were roughly equal, the British 5th Battle Squadron apart—it formed a homogeneous squadron of four very powerful 'Queen Elizabeths' capable of 24 to 25 knots. But since Scheer was so foolish as to take a squadron (2nd) of pre-dreadnoughts with him (the 18-knot 'Deutschlands'), the British line actually had a speed advantage. The Grand Fleet Battle Orders gave the battle fleet a $1\frac{1}{2}$- to 2-knot superiority when the German 2nd Squadron was present. Jellicoe did not know the 2nd Squadron was out, and so, to the best of his knowledge, he had little or no advantage in speed. More pronounced, and of this Jellicoe was fully aware, was his superiority in gun-power. The battle fleet mounted 272 heavy guns against the German line's 200, an advantage greatly enhanced by a marked superiority in size. The British mounted 48 15-inch, 10 14-inch, 110 13·5-inch, and 104 12-inch, compared with the German 128 12-inch and 72 11-inch, representing nearly a $2\frac{1}{2}$ to one superiority in weight of broadside: 332,360 lbs. vs. 134,216 lbs.[1] The figures for the gun-power of the Battle Cruiser Fleet were almost as favourable: 32 13·5-inch and 40 12-inch vs. the German battle cruisers' 16 12-inch and 28 11-inch, or a broadside of 68,900 lbs. vs. 33,104 lbs.[1] The Grand Fleet was also superior in torpedo attack. Ship for ship the German capital ships and destroyers mounted more torpedo tubes than the British, but this was balanced by numbers. Of long-range torpedoes the British fleet carried 382 21-inch torpedo tubes, compared with the High Seas Fleet's 362 19·7-inch. (In a fleet action the 107 17·7-inch German torpedoes and the 75 British 18-inch would not count very much.)

Two deficiencies offset to an indeterminate degree the heavier calibre of the British capital ships. British armour-piercing shells for 12-inch guns and above were, in Dreyer's words, 'lamentably weak' when striking armour at oblique impact, compared with the German armour-piercing shells. This was not known prior to Jutland, nor was the grave liability of the ships' magazines to be ignited by flash from bursting shells, hence did not affect either side's plans or estimates of its capabilities. Jellicoe was in a sense further handicapped, and this he knew, by the incomplete state of the fitting of director firing gear. At the outbreak of the war only eight dreadnoughts were complete with directors for their main armaments. By the time of Jutland all the dreadnoughts and battle cruisers (excepting *Erin* and *Agincourt*) were fitted with main armament directors. The necessity of providing director equipment for the secondary armament of all capital ships was realized

[1] The figures discount the guns that could not be brought to bear on the broadside: British, twelve 12-inch; German, sixteen 12-inch and sixteen 11-inch. The British figures are from British official sources as published in *Brassey* and *Jane*, and the German from *Abmessungen und Gewichte der Schiffsartilleriemunition und ihrer Packgefässe* (Ministry of Marine, 1918).

late in 1914, and orders were given for its inclusion; but little had been done by 31 May 1916, owing to the very large demands for gear for the main armaments. No cruisers or destroyers had benefited by then.

The High Seas Fleet did not have a director firing system in the sense of Percy Scott's gyro-controlled firing system. The German capital ships were fitted with an electrical 'follow-the-pointer' system to ensure that all the turret guns followed the lateral movements of the gunnery officer's periscope in the conning-tower, and similarly the elevation of the guns was achieved by following a 'range pointer'. The chief thing, however, to note about German big-ship gunnery is that great importance was attached to accurate *initial* estimation of the enemy's range, and with their stereoscopic range finders the Germans achieved a higher accuracy in this respect than the British with their 'coincidence' range finders. The German capital ships possessed a further gunnery advantage in their heavier secondary armament, particularly in a night action: 5·9-inch guns as against the 4-inch in over half of the British ships. Only the *Tiger* and the latest dreadnoughts carried 6-inch. Undoubtedly the prime German advantages lay in the better protection against torpedo or mine attack (as through their more complete watertight subdivision below water) and the extent and thickness of their armour, as compared with contemporary British capital ships. The statistics on armour thickness for the latest battle cruisers and dreadnoughts are instructive (thickness in inches):[2]

	Main belt	Upper belt	Bow	Stern	Turret	Decks
Dreadnoughts						
'Royal Sovereigns'	13	6	4	4	13	1–4
'Königs'	14	10	6	6	14	2½–3
Battle Cruisers						
Tiger	9	6	4	4	9	1–3
Derfflinger	12	8	5	5	11	1–3

But we must remember that the comparatively thin armour on British capital ships was the price paid for a superior heavy armament, and was done as a calculated risk.

As regards the light cruisers, the British had in 1910 adopted an

---

[2] From the tables in Jellicoe, *The Grand Fleet*, pp. 310–13.

armament of all 6-inch, instead of mixed 6-inch and 4-inch, for the largest type, the 'Town' class. This made the 2nd and 3rd Light Cruiser Squadrons superior in armament to their German contemporaries, though not quite equal in speed. Only the newer, smaller type of British light cruisers, built primarily for fleet work, was faster than the corresponding German classes. The newest of these also had all 6-inch armament.

In the case of the destroyers, the German, being smaller than the British and carrying a heavier torpedo armament (they were called 'torpedo boats' and generally mounted six tubes), had much lighter gun armaments than their opponents. The British flotillas all mounted 4-inch guns, but only two-thirds of them had four torpedo tubes, the remainder two. (World War I destroyers of all navies carried one torpedo per tube—there were no spares.) It was some advantage that they were all oil-burning and had a greater radius of action than the German boats, though, as Jellicoe constantly emphasized, this was scarcely enough if operations should be prolonged.

The Germans had a clear superiority in airships, which should have permitted them, weather conditions being favourable, to obtain earlier and more definite information as to the Grand Fleet's whereabouts, strength, and movements.

Overall, the Grand Fleet had an overwhelming superiority *if the High Seas Fleet tried to stand up to it*, and this was fully accepted by Scheer, though he was no faint-heart.

*　　　*　　　*

The 1st Battle Squadron was under the Second-in-Command, Vice-Admiral Sir Cecil Burney, with his flag in the *Marlborough*. 'Burney is first-rate when in good health, which unfortunately is not always the case.'[3] Jellicoe's faith in Burney is difficult to fathom, as he had none of the qualities for commanding a great fleet. The officers of the Grand Fleet trembled at the thought of anything happening to Jellicoe and Burney having to take command. Writes Admiral James, 'If a submarine had sunk Jellicoe's flagship as she came out of Scapa, the Fleet and perhaps the fate of the country would have been in the hands of Burney—Jellicoe does not seem to have thought of that. [Jellicoe's Chief of Staff] told me that he tried to persuade Jellicoe to appoint a competent,

[3] Jellicoe to Jackson, 16 June 1915; Jackson MSS.

up-to-date Second-in-Command, and he always got the reply that Burney was a fine seaman. "Fine seaman" covered a multitude of shortcomings in those days.'[4] Incidentally, Colville was Jellicoe's choice to succeed him if anything happened to himself and Burney.

There had at least been some improvement in the command of the 2nd Battle Squadron. Jellicoe had become increasingly disenchanted with Warrender during 1915. 'Warrender gets awfully deaf at times and is inclined to be absent-minded, but on the other hand he has had unique experience in command and is excellent as a squadron admiral *in peace.* I am not always happy about him.'[5] He finally relieved him in December 1915, after his health had deteriorated further, with Vice-Admiral Sir Martyn Jerram. Jerram was a good all-round man, much respected, a fine seaman (in the best sense of that term!), but not an impressive personality and not gifted with the imagination, the creative powers, and the inspired leadership that distinguish eminent flag officers.

Vice-Admiral Sir Doveton Sturdee commanded the 4th Battle Squadron. He was capable of such a remark as this to a young Commander upon joining his staff, 'My motto is "Damn the staff!"' As he explained after the war, 'One of the disadvantages of the Staff system in the Navy is that there is too great a tendency of Senior Officers to consult their staff on vital questions instead of officers of riper experience holding responsible positions in the Fleet.'[6] On the other hand, he had had great sea experience and was undoubtedly an able squadron commander. Few officers of his generation had studied tactics more than he had.

Commanding the 5th Battle Squadron since August 1915 was Rear-Admiral Hugh Evan-Thomas, a lovable, straightforward, unassuming man, universally liked and admired by the officers and men of every ship and squadron he commanded—an efficient officer with a highly deserved reputation as a ship and squadron handler. He was a great personal friend and admirer of Jellicoe, with whom he had much in common.

The battle-cruiser-squadron commanders were three outstanding Rear-Admirals: Hood (3rd), de B. Brock (1st), and Pakenham (2nd), all of whom were discussed in Chapter I.

Of the cruiser-squadron commanders, only these need be

---

[4] Letter to the author, 31 Mar. 1962.
[5] Jellicoe to Jackson, 16 June 1915; Jackson MSS. Italics mine!
[6] Sturdee to Sir Henry Newbolt, Mar. 1924; Sturdee MSS.

mentioned by name: Commodores Alexander-Sinclair (1st L.C.S.) and Goodenough (2nd L.C.S.), and Rear-Admiral Sir Robert Arbuthnot, Bt. (1st C.S.). Arbuthnot, whom we have not met formally, merits a word. He was an exceptionally hard-working officer, endowed with great physical and moral courage and a splendid fighting instinct. 'He was a gallant soul,' in Lord Chatfield's judgment; 'at sea and in sport nothing daunted him.' At the same time he was without much imagination and the gift for the best form of leadership. He had the deserved reputation of a martinet—a stickler for the King's Regulations and Admiralty Instructions, and a driver of his men. Physical culture being his ruling passion (he was himself as hard as nails), he led his officers and men a pretty dance: there were constant physical drills and long marches, etc. They respected and feared him, and all too often disliked him. Jellicoe's estimate of him was a fair one: 'There is trouble in the 1st Cruiser Squadron. I put Burney on to investigate for the day. Arbuthnot is one of the finest fellows in the world, but somehow can't run a squadron. His ideals are too high and he can't leave people alone. He would be invaluable when there is fighting. I have the highest opinion of him.'[7]

The most noteworthy personnel development in the Battle Cruiser Fleet in 1915–16 was the augmentation of Beatty's staff with specialists of various sorts. Captain Rudolf Bentinck had become Beatty's C.O.S. in February 1915, with the job of running the logistics, meaning, says Lord Chatfield, 'everything except the fighting efficiency, which was to remain generally in my hands'. He was a very charming man and a good, sound all-round officer. 'Bentinck's personality inspired confidence. He was a man of fine physique with the features of a Roman patrician; a born aristocrat of the old school, yet always approachable; tactful but strong. In Beatty's own words, "He was a tower of strength" . . .'[8]

Considering how different they were in personality and temperament, Jellicoe and Beatty got along well. It was not often that they failed to see eye to eye. In Beatty's early wartime correspondence with his wife occur such references to the C.-in-C. as: 'He is splendid, Jellicoe, he always understands and gives consideration to one's views.' They were 'in perfect agreement . . . on every point which essentially affects me and my Command, and indeed

[7] Jellicoe to Jackson, 11 Sept. 1915; Jackson MSS.
[8] Chalmers, *Beatty*, p. 204.

I might say on all the principal features of the naval part of the War'. And to the C.-in-C., 'I know that on all the large questions we are of the same opinion.' When the C.-in-C. went on leave soon after the Dogger Bank action, Beatty urged him to take 'the greatest care of yourself. What we should do without you the Lord knows.'[9] On his part, Jellicoe found Beatty 'splendid'.

The devotion of the Grand Fleet to, and confidence in, the C.-in-C. grew as the weeks and months passed. Rear-Admiral Roger M. Bellairs, who was on his staff in the *Iron Duke*, has set down these impressions:

Lord Jellicoe worked with an amazing rapidity. When in harbour it was not his habit to sit at his ordinary large writing table, but at a tiny little affair in the middle of his cabin. To see him there reading despatches and memoranda, making pencil annotations and corrections, interrupted from time to time by the mass of matters and signals requiring immediate action, was to see a man who through years of training and control had brought the power of concentration to a fine art. Physical fitness was combined with this power of concentration. In the evenings in harbour he could be seen hard at the ball game, going at it with the terrific energy he put into everything he undertook. The exercise that he got out of a game of golf on the Flotta Links is well known, and certainly lives as one of the remembrances carried away by many who visited him in his flagship. This physical fitness combined with the mental and moral attributes he so abundantly possessed enabled him serenely to sustain his immense responsibilities—responsibilities always great but greater perhaps in the early stages of the War when so much was in the making.

Never did the writer see him out of temper or anything but cheerful, and infusing everyone with the joy of carrying out the work in hand. His calm outlook never deserted him. Care and responsibilities were when possible thrown off the last thing at night by the reading of thrillers of a particularly lurid description. Whenever he could he would thus indulge for a short time in this complete relaxation and change from the work and anxieties of the day.

2. THE RIVAL PLANS

The staff in the *Iron Duke* cudgelled their brains for a plan that would end the nerve-racking game of hide-and-seek and bring the High Seas Fleet into the warm embrace of the Grand Fleet.

[9] Beatty to Lady Beatty, 12, 21 Nov. 1914, 12 Aug. 1915, Beatty MSS.; Beatty to Jellicoe, n.d. (early Feb. 1915), Jellicoe MSS.

The Kaiser's Fleet was just as restless and confident. The staff in Scheer's flagship, the *Friedrich der Grosse*, burned midnight oil as they, too, tried to hatch a scheme that would produce an action in favourable circumstances.

In November 1914 Jellicoe had not thought it judicious to base his movements 'on so uncertain a factor as operations of seaplanes', nor did he consider aerial attack likely to bring out the High Seas Fleet. In the spring of 1916, nevertheless, the repetition of seaplane raids came to involve the co-operation of the whole Grand Fleet. It was now the C.-in-C.'s view that when air raids on the enemy coast took place, it was desirable that a supporting force, the battle cruisers, be within reach, with the battle fleet farther away but moving south. This strategy had not produced results. At the end of May Jellicoe prepared a juicy bait to lure Scheer out and to a position farther north than he had so far ventured. Two light cruiser squadrons were to proceed to the Skaw and then sweep down the Kattegat as far south as the Great Belt and the Sound. A battle squadron would be stationed in the Skaggerak in support, and to the north-west would be the main battle fleet and the Battle Cruiser Fleet in general support, ready to move south if a strong German force were reported at sea. Should the High Seas Fleet not venture far enough north to bring on an action, it would, at least, Jellicoe hoped, come out far enough to fall into a submarine-mine trap of three Harwich boats planted just south of Horns Reef (that is, in the northern exit from the Bight), two boats off the Dogger Bank, and the minefield which the *Abdiel* would lay south of Horns Reef. To prevent premature discovery of the trap, the seaplane carrier *Engadine*, escorted by a light cruiser squadron and destroyers, would be off Horns Reef on the look-out for Zeppelins.

This plan (an 'ostensibly daring plan', the German Official History sarcastically calls it) was scheduled for 2 June. Scheer forestalled it with the initial movements of a markedly similar plan. Its basic idea was to entice out the Grand Fleet as a target for his U-boats, which were to be stationed off the more important British naval bases, especially Rosyth. (The submarines were available for operations against the British Fleet after Scheer had recalled them from their commerce warfare duties on 25 April.) The U-boats had a twofold purpose: to equalize forces and to serve as reconnaissance for the High Seas Fleet. A bombardment of Sunderland by the 1st Scouting Group (accompanied by the 2nd S.G.) would cause Beatty to race out of the Forth to engage Hipper. The latter would lead the British force, or what was left after the U-boats had done their work, to the German battle fleet, which would be in a position 50 miles east of Flamborough Head. Scheer would polish off the Battle Cruiser Fleet before Jellicoe could arrive on the scene. This plan depended on extensive airship reconnaissance over the North Sea to ensure that Jellicoe was not engaged in a sweep down the North Sea when the plan was launched. The last thing Scheer wanted was a surprise meeting with superior British forces, particularly one far from the shelter of his bases.

The operation, which was originally planned for 17 May, was postponed to 23 May owing to the *Seydlitz* (mined on her way out for the Lowestoft operation) not being ready and to the development of condenser trouble in some of the dreadnoughts. On 17 May all the available U-boats put to sea, forming lines of observation between Norway and the Forth. On the 23rd they took up positions off the Grand Fleet bases. All airships were ordered to be ready by the 23rd. On that day 'inadequate repairs' to the *Seydlitz* caused a further postponement to the 29th. The *Seydlitz* was ready by then, but the easterly and northerly winds blowing in the Bight ruled out airship reconnaissance. The 30th was the last possible day for the operation, since the U-boats, with their limited endurance, had orders to leave their stations on the evening of 1 June. The weather remaining unsuitable for the Zeppelins, Scheer was forced on the 30th to substitute his alternative plan, which did not depend on them. Its main objective was the same as that of the first plan—to get the British to send out their forces, so exposing them to U-boat attack. This was to be achieved, not by a bombardment of the coast as in the first plan, but by the ostentatious appearance of the 1st and 2nd Scouting Groups in the Skagerrak. They were to proceed up the Danish coast as if intending to fall on the British cruisers and merchant ships so often reported in the Skagerrak. The plan also offered the prospect of engaging sections of the Grand Fleet in waters fairly close to the German bases, or, at any rate, in such a position that retreat before superior forces would be easy. Zeppelin co-operation was not essential for this operation, as the one exposed German flank could be guarded from surprise by cruisers and flotillas.

The executive signal for the operation to take place was made at 3.40 p.m., 30 May. At 1 a.m. on the 31st Hipper and the 1st and 2nd Scouting Groups and three flotillas left the Jade for the Skagerrak. His orders were to show himself off the Norwegian coast before dark on the 31st, so that the British would be sure to get wind that a detachment of the High Seas Fleet was at sea and would, Scheer hoped, send out a sizeable force. If Hipper met a superior British force, he was to try to draw it towards Scheer and the battle fleet. The battle fleet, the 4th Scouting Group, and the remainder of the flotillas put to sea at 2.30 a.m. on the 31st.

The Admiralty had had indications since 16–17 May, when they learned of the departure of nine U-boats from their bases, that some important operation was being planned. When no sinkings were reported on the succeeding days, although the boats were known to be in the northern part of the North Sea, their suspicions were intensified. They were certain that some considerable movement was in the offing when Room 40 detected on 30 May (reported to the Operations Division at 11.30 a.m.) that the High Seas Fleet had been ordered at 9.44 a.m. to assemble in the Jade Roads outside Wilhelmshaven by 7 p.m. At noon (30 May) the Admiralty warned Jellicoe that the High Seas Fleet might go to sea early the next morning. Shortly after 5 p.m. it became known that the High Seas Fleet had received an important operation signal (that of 3.40 p.m.). Although it could not be deciphered entirely, leaving Scheer's object still obscure, further delay could be dangerous. Whereupon, at 5.40 p.m., two hours after the German signal had been made, the Admiralty informed Jellicoe that the 'Germans intend some operations commencing to-morrow', and ordered a concentration of the Grand Fleet (Scapa and Cromarty forces) eastward of the Long Forties (about 100 miles east of Aberdeen), 'ready for eventualities'. By 11 p.m. the Grand Fleet and the Battle Cruiser Fleet were at sea, making for a rendezvous, chosen by the C.-in-C., about 240 miles from Scapa Flow and 90 miles west of the entrance to the Skagerrak.

What would Jellicoe's tactics be if he succeeded in catching up with the High Seas Fleet? Seven weeks before, he had spelled out the fundamentals of Grand Fleet strategy and tactics. There is nothing new in the document, but it does sum up the C.-in-C.'s thinking almost on the eve of Jutland.

The first axiom appears to me to be that it is the business of the Grand Fleet to nullify any hostile action on the part of the High Sea Fleet; secondly, to cover all surface vessels that are employed, either in protecting our own trade, or in stopping trade with the enemy; thirdly, to stop invasion, or landing raids, in so far as the strategical position of the Grand Fleet permits of this. [Beatty's copy has a marginal query against the last clause.]

So long as the High Sea Fleet is confined to its harbours, the whole of these desiderata are obtained, and although, of course, the total destruction of the High Sea Fleet gives a greater sense of security, it is not, in my opinion, wise to risk unduly the heavy ships of the Grand Fleet in an attempt to hasten the end of the High Sea Fleet, particularly if the risks come, not from the High Sea Fleet itself, but from such attributes as mines and submarines.

There is no doubt that, provided there is a chance of destroying some of the enemy's heavy ships, it is right and proper to run risks with our own heavy ships, but unless the chances are reasonably great, I do not think that such risks should be run, seeing that any real disaster to our heavy ships lays the country open to invasion, and also gives the enemy the opportunity of passing commerce destroyers out of the North Sea.[10]

Jellicoe would, then, not take unjustifiable risks to win a spectacular victory, a second Trafalgar. The superiority of the Grand Fleet over the High Seas Fleet must be maintained. These were the considerations uppermost in the C.-in-C.'s mind as his mighty armada headed into the black darkness of the North Sea for its rendezvous with the Battle Cruiser Fleet.

What were the feelings of the fleet as it left Scapa? The officers and men, from the C.-in-C. down to the humblest stoker, were confident, perhaps a trifle *over*-confident, of the outcome of an engagement. Only one difficulty was foreseen. As expressed in the recipe for jugged hare in Mrs. Glasse's famous cookbook, 'First catch your hare.' There was no excitement. After all, only the C.-in-C. and a few others knew of the tremendous possibilities. 'Just another b—— useless sweep,' murmured one of the officers in the *Iron Duke*.

---

[10] Jellicoe's memorandum for the Admiralty, 12 Apr. 1916, with a copy going to Beatty and possibly other flag officers in the Grand Fleet; Beatty MSS. The initial chapter of the next volume will discuss in some detail the Grand Fleet Battle Orders in force at the time of Jutland.

INDEX

All officers and titled people are indexed under the highest rank and title attained. All ships are British except where otherwise noted.

Abbreviations:

A.M.C.: Armed merchant cruiser
B.: Pre-dreadnought battleship
B.C.: Battle cruiser
Cr.: Armoured cruiser
D.: Dreadnought

L.C.: Light cruiser
M.L.: Minelayer
S.C.: Seaplane carrier
S.M.: Submarine
S.S.: Steamship

Z.: Zeppelin

449

Oxford and Asquith, 1st Earl of (Herbert
Henry Asquith, 1852–1928): 48, 180,
185, 384, 391; on Churchill, 8; and
invasion question, 61; failing confidence in Navy, 82; refuses Churchill's
resignation, 84; description of Fisher
and A. K. Wilson, 88; and Fisher's
restoration, 89–90, 279; reaction to
Scarborough Raid, 147; refuses
Fisher's resignation, 151; strategic
views, 177, 196, 202; and initiation of
Dardanelles operations, 208, 209–10,
211, 219, 221, 222, 277; and Dardanelles naval operations, 233, 255, 261;
and Fisher's resignation, 279, 280, 283,
284–6, 290; and Churchill's resignation, 287–8; wants Balfour as First
Lord, 289; considers A. K. Wilson as
First Sea Lord, 290–1; defines War
Committee, 309 n.; and Gallipoli, 312,
320; and Greek crisis, 317 n.; concern
over German 17-inch guns, 386; on
Fisher's War Committee appearance,
403

Pakenham, Adm. Sir William Christopher
(1861–1933): attributes, 13; in Scarborough Raid, 134; admiration for
Beatty, 170; relieves Moore, 171;
commanding 2nd B.C.S., 441
Patrol (L.C.): in Scarborough Raid, 137
Patrol Flotillas: 5
Pelly, Adm. Sir Henry Bertram (1867–
1942): in Dogger Bank Action, 160,
169, 171; defends himself, 169 n.;
Fisher plans to relieve him, 284
Phaeton (L.C.): brings down L-7, 46
Phillimore, Adm. Sir Richard Fortescue
(1864–1940): in Dardanelles operations, 246
Pohl, Adm. Hugo von (1855–1916): 45 n.,
173; succeeds Ingenohl as C.-in-C.,
165–6; attributes, 166; his sorties in
1915, 420; resigns, 420
Pollen, Arthur Joseph Hungerford (1866–
1937): opposes Fisher's return, 396;
on Fisher's War Committee appearance, 403
Pound, Adm. of the Fleet Sir Alfred
Dudley Pickman Rogers (1877–1943):
and proposal to draw German Fleet
out, 414
Preston, Adm Sir Lionel George (1875–
): commanding Grand Fleet
Minesweeping Flotilla, 71; on role of
minesweepers, 73 n.; on German
mining, 368
Princess Royal (B.C.): 16, 44, 119, 152; in
Dogger Bank Action, 157, 159–60,
162 n., 164, 168, 169

Privet (Q-ship): sinks U-34, 356
Public Opinion, British: and Goeben's
escape, 41; expectation of battle, 47,
49; taunts Germans, 49, 378–9; the
press and public impatience, 49–50;
on Heligoland Bight Action, 54; on
sinking of 'Cressys', 59; critical of
Churchill, 83; and guerre de course, 103–
104; on Battle of Coronel, 117; on
Scarborough Raid, 142, 147–9; on
Dogger Bank Action, 166–7, 171; and
naval situation after six months, 174–5;
optimistic on forcing Dardanelles, 239;
uneasiness in 1915–16 winter, 379–82;
and campaign for Fisher's return,
395–401; results of agitation, 406–7

Queen Elizabeth (D.): 152, 215 n., 414,
432, 437; in Dardanelles operations,
206, 207, 214, 231, 241, 245, 246; 273;
recalled, 276–7

R-9 (airship): 405 n.
Ramsay, Adm. Sir Bertram Home (1883–
1945): uneasy over defensive strategy,
82
Redoubtable (B): in Keyes's plan to force
Dardanelles, 315
Renown (B.C.): 392 n., 439; construction,
94–5; criticisms of, 96; strengthened
after Jutland, 96; raison d'être, 97; construction delayed, 391
Repulse (B.C.): 392 n., 437; construction,
94–5; criticisms of, 96; strengthened
after Jutland, 96; raison d'être, 97;
construction delayed, 391
Richmond, Adm. Sir Herbert William
(1871–1946): on Hood, 9; on passive
German naval strategy, 46; offensive
ideas, 50, 82; and German mining
policy, 72; favours aggressive mining
policy, 79; criticizes Churchill's Antwerp policy, 85; on Sturdee as C.O.S.,
92, 116; on Oliver as C.O.S., 92 n.;
estimate of Sturdee at Falklands, 124–
125; on Grand Fleet strategy, 176;
opposes Ameland project, 182; con-
demns Borkum scheme, 189; and
Dardanelles operations, 212, 232, 261–
262; on Thursby, 330; on Italian
Fleet, 332, 337–8; leaves Italy, 332–3;
on blockade policy, 375–6; on prestige
factor in Mediterranean, 337; on
superfluity of battleships in Mediterranean, 340–1; wants French to do
more, 341; and Q-ships, 355; on trade
protection through patrolling, 358; on
Balfour Board, 414; favours amphibious diversions, 419; on 3rd Battle
Squadron, 433

MAP I

SCAPA FLOW

HOME WATERS

THE MEDITERRANEAN SEA
AND SURROUNDING COUNTRIES
WITH THE CHASE OF THE GOEBEN AUGUST 1914

Gloucester ——— Goeben ———
Dublin —·—·— Breslau —··—··—
Battle Cruisers --------
1ˢᵗ Cruiser Squadron ···············

Where tracks of two or more ships coincide, only the track of the leading ship is shown

MAP 2

MAP 3

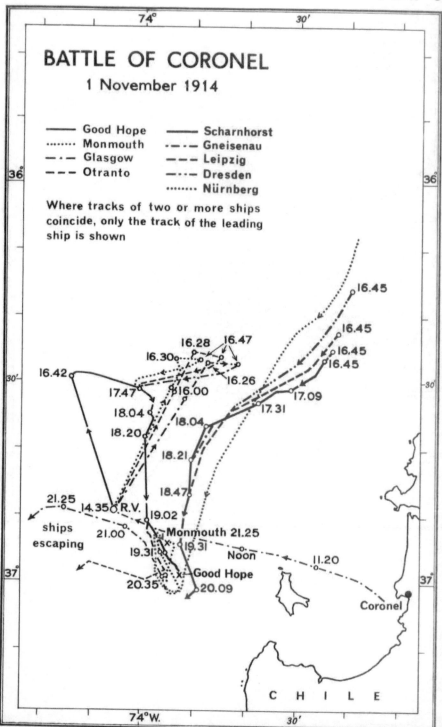

BATTLE OF CORONEL
1 November 1914

——— Good Hope   ——— Scharnhorst
········· Monmouth   —·—· Gneisenau
—·—· Glasgow   ——— Leipzig
——— Otranto   —··—· Dresden
           ········· Nürnberg

Where tracks of two or more ships
coincide, only the track of the leading
ship is shown

16.45

16.28   16.47
16.30   16.45
16.26   16.45
16.42   16.45
17.47   16.00
18.04   17.09
18.20   18.04   17.31
18.21
18.47
21.25   14.35 R.V.   19.02
ships   21.00   Monmouth 21.25
escaping   19.31   19.31
        Noon   11.20
20.35   Good Hope
20.09

Coronel

C H I L E

74°W.   30'

74°   30'

36   36
30'   30'
37°   37°

MAP 4

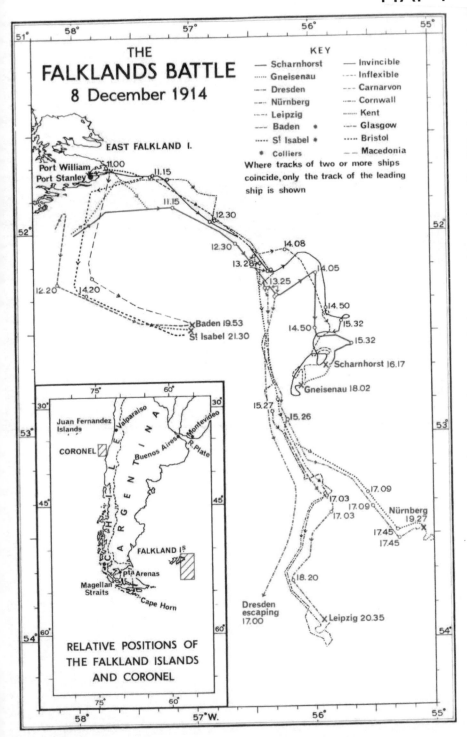

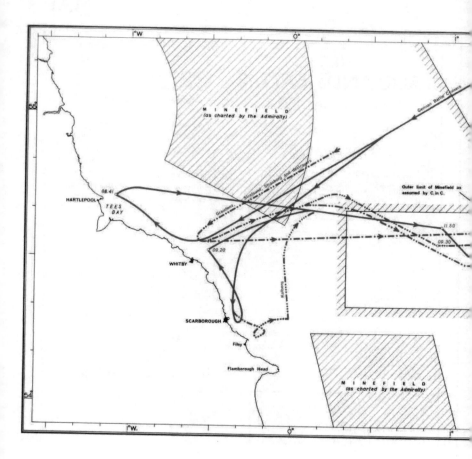

MAP 5

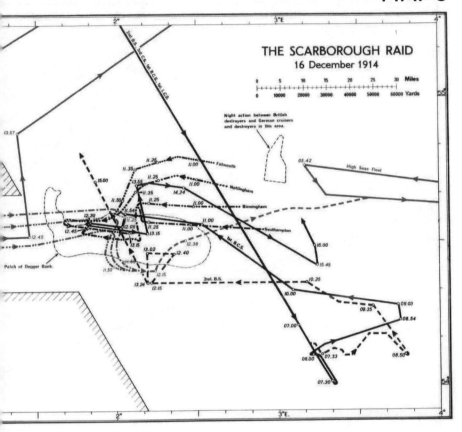

THE SCARBOROUGH RAID
16 December 1914

Night action between British
destroyers and German cruisers
and destroyers in this area.

High Seas Fleet

Patch of Dogger Bank.

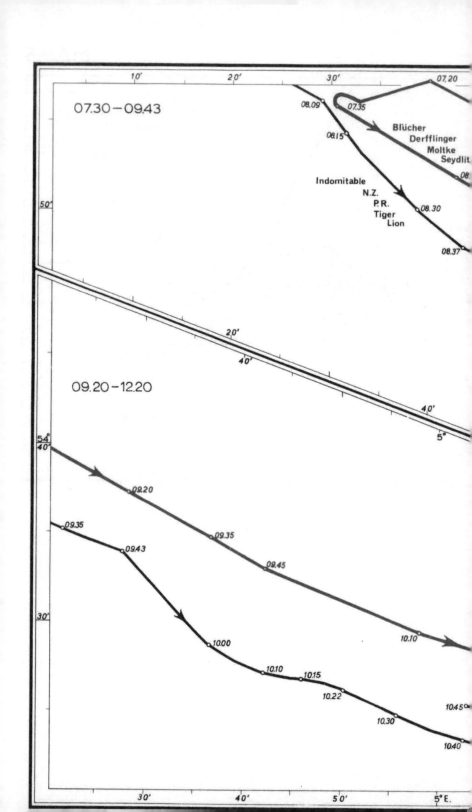

MAP 6

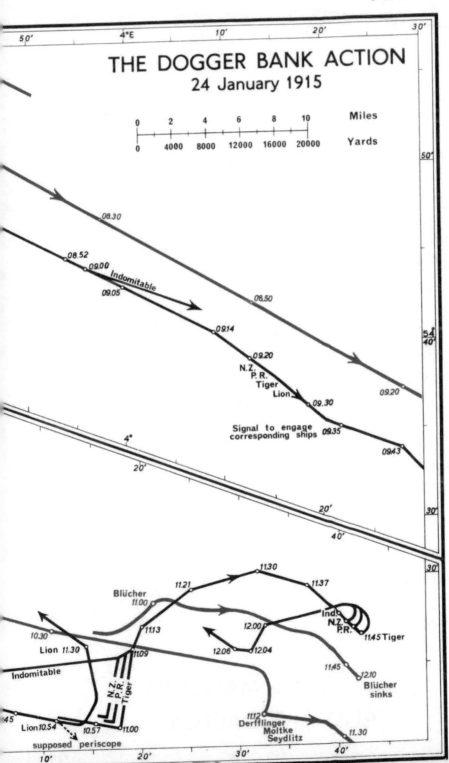

THE DOGGER BANK ACTION
24 January 1915

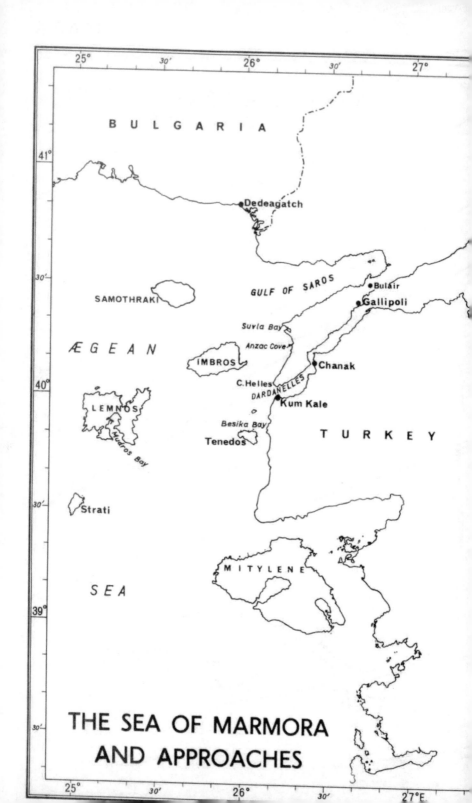

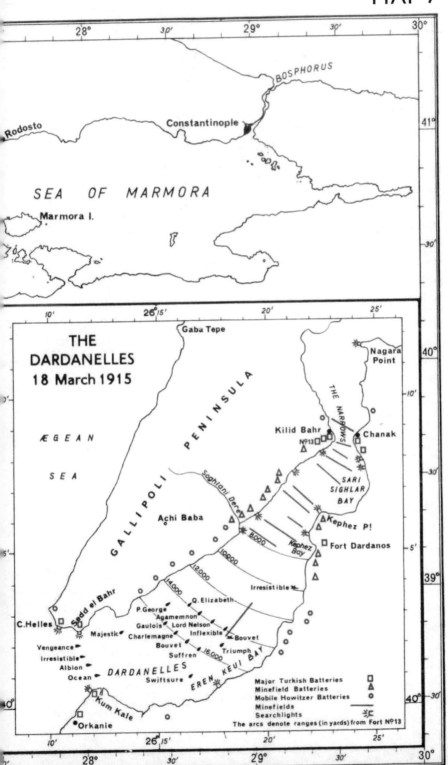

MAP 7

THE
DARDANELLES
18 March 1915

Major Turkish Batteries
Minefield Batteries
Mobile Howitzer Batteries
Minefields
Searchlights
The arcs denote ranges (in yards) from Fort Nº13

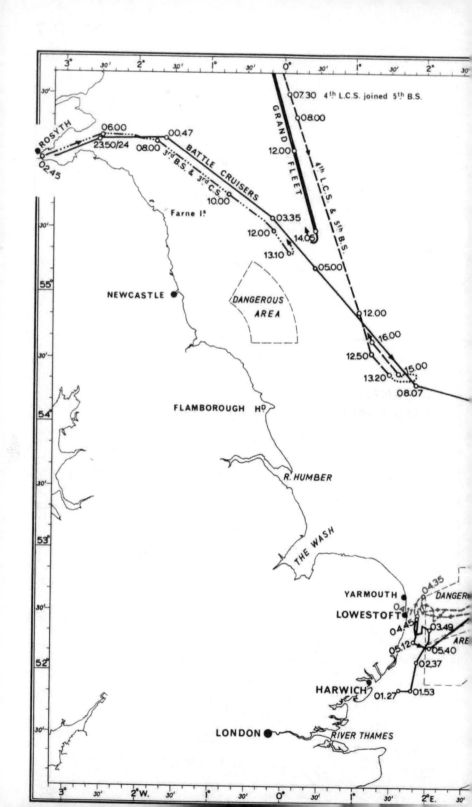

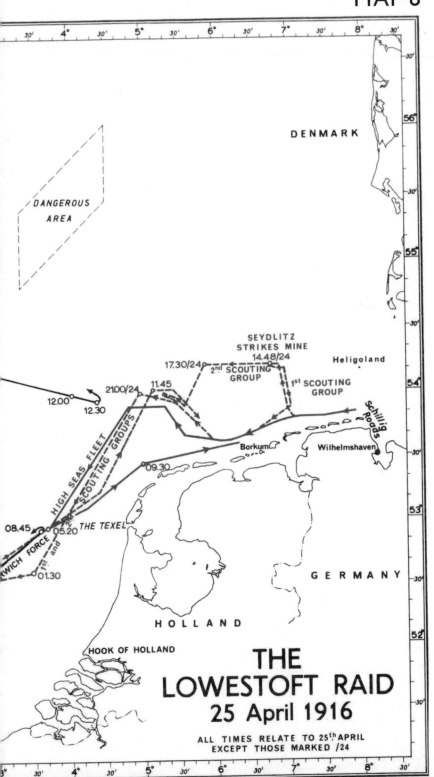

MAP 8

THE
LOWESTOFT RAID
25 April 1916

ALL TIMES RELATE TO 25th APRIL
EXCEPT THOSE MARKED /24